INDEX TO BRITISH
LITERARY BIBLIOGRAPHY

VI

"BRITISH LITERARY BIBLIOGRAPHY AND TEXTUAL CRITICISM 1890–1969

AN INDEX"

T. H. HOWARD-HILL

CLARENDON PRESS   OXFORD
1980

Oxford University Press, Walton Street, Oxford OX2 6DP
OXFORD LONDON GLASGOW
NEW YORK TORONTO MELBOURNE WELLINGTON
KUALA LUMPUR SINGAPORE JAKARTA HONG KONG TOKYO
DELHI BOMBAY CALCUTTA MADRAS KARACHI
NAIROBI DAR ES SALAAM CAPE TOWN

Published in the United States
by *Oxford University Press,*
New York

© *T. H. Howard-Hill 1980*

British Library Cataloguing in Publication Data
Howard-Hill, Trevor Howard
   British literary bibliography and textual criticism,
   1890–1969, an index.—(Index to British literary bibliography; 6).
   1. Publishers and publishing—Great Britain—Bibliography
   2. English literature—Criticism, Textual—Bibliography   3. English
   literature—Bibliography
   I. Title   II. Series
   016.0705'73'0941   Z324   79-40836

ISBN 0–19–818180–9

Text set in 8/9 pt Photon Baskerville, printed and bound
in Great Britain at The Pitman Press, Bath

PREFACE

Because this volume not merely indexes the two volumes of *British Bibliography and Textual Criticism* but provides, by the incorporation of the indexes of the preceding two volumes, an interim index to the whole series, it requires its own preface. Many of the subject headings and dates in the index were drawn from the items in the bibliography. On the other hand a surprisingly large number were not, and when commonly-available sources of information did not provide appropriate details, I had to draw upon the resources of a variety of public, university and national libraries—too many comfortably to list here. However, in light of the exceptional demands I made upon the national libraries of Ireland, Scotland and Wales, the British Library, and the Bodleian Library, Oxford, I may particularize them without offence to the other libraries. Nevertheless, I appreciate the help of all my correspondents in libraries on both sides of the Atlantic.

For support during the preparation of copy for the index I am grateful to Dr. Joel A. Myerson (Chairman, Xerox committee) and Dr. George L. Geckle (Chairman) of the Department of English, University of South Carolina, where the index was compiled. Lastly, words are inadequate to acknowledge the valuable assistance rendered with habitual cheerfulness by my Research Assistant, Miss Josie Shumake, during the past three years.

T.H.H.

Oxford
March, 1979

CONTENTS

INTRODUCTION

British Literary Bibliography and Textual Criticism, 1890–1969, an index unites in two sequences the indexes of the three separate bibliographies so far published in the series *Index to British Literary Bibliography*. Publication of five volumes of the series spans ten years and the composition of the series is somewhat perplexing to anyone who has not a firm mental grasp of the unavoidably repetitive terminology of the constituent titles. On that account it is desirable to establish at the outset what works are indexed in the present volume.

The first volume of the series, the *Bibliography of British Literary Bibliographies* (contracted as *BBLB*) was published in 1969, and a substantial supplement was included in the second volume of the series in 1971. During the preparation of later volumes in the series I gathered so many more items that the publisher was willing, *BBLB* being out-of-print, to issue a revised and enlarged second edition; it will be published shortly. Accordingly, index references to volume 1 here refer to the revised edition of *BBLB* which incorporates the 1971 Supplement and a significant amount of new material published through 1969. This second edition of *BBLB* has been completely reindexed to conform to the indexing conventions adopted in later volumes. (The second edition does, of course, contain its own index).

The second volume of the series, *Shakespearian Bibliography and Textual Criticism, a bibliography* (contracted as *SBTC*) was published in 1971. It too has been completely reindexed and the index incorporated here. *BBTC* contains a supplement to the Shakespeare volume, but the supplementary items are numbered and indexed as if they were printed originally in the second volume, *SBTC*.

The third volume in the series, intended to cover writings about British bibliography published before 1890, will not be published for many years. It falls outside the chronological coverage of the present index but, when revision of the series is completed at the end of the century, its index will be incorporated in the final index to the whole series, of which the present index is merely an interim part. However, volumes four and five—*British Bibliography and Textual Criticism, a bibliography (BBTC)*, published in 1979— supply most entries to the index. As the title of the series conveys, the *Index* was intended to occupy a prominent place in the overall scheme, affording a benefit to bibliographers which hitherto they had not known. Anyone who intends to use the bibliography frequently should, if he is wise, spend a little time to understand the organization of the index.

I. GENERAL ORGANIZATION. The index is divided into two main alphabetical sequences. (a) *Author and title index*: The first sequence lists the names of authors and compilers of the bibliographical books and papers and checklists recorded in the separate bibliographies of the series, with the names of editors of collections in which papers or checklists were printed, together with title entries for those few items like *CBEL* and *STC* often referred to by title. This index sequence gives the full names—when they have come to hand with relative ease in sources like *BNB*—of contributors who may be listed in *BBTC* with a shorter form of name, 'Pollard, Arthur W.' for example, rather than 'Pollard, Arthur William'. When I am not sure of the identity of writers with similar designations (*e.g.* Morris, John; Morris, John M.) I have not conflated the index entries. On the other hand, usually no distinction is made between authors writing under the same name (*e.g.* Hart, Horace). A name which is present in the index only because the individual was the editor of a collection in which a bibliographical paper was printed (*e.g.* Immroth, John P.) is distinguished by parentheses surrounding the item reference in the index: parentheses also identify the secondary editorial contributions of such bibliographical writers as J. C. Maxwell, the editor of Greg's *Collected Papers* which are often cited in *BBTC*. (b) *Subject index*: Topics written about in the books and papers listed in the bibliographies are indexed in the second sequence—which is naturally of more interest to users of the bibliographies. The rest of this introduction will describe its characteristics. However, attention should be drawn to the identification of the volumes in which the items referred to in the two index sequences are printed. (c) *Volume references*: *BBTC* consists of 15,156 items and consequently contributes the greatest number of references to the index; those references are not specifically identified to the user, although he will notice that the direction line at the foot of each page informs him that items numbered higher than 8221 will be found in volume 5. Items printed in the second revised edition of *BBLB* are identified by '1:' printed before the sequence of item numbers referring to volume 1, and '2:' is used for the Shakespeare volume, *SBTC*. However, an exception to the practice just described may disconcert the unwary user. Volume 5 contains supplementary entries for *SBTC* which complete the record to 1969: the supplement will be incorporated in a revised edition of *SBTC* should one be called for. In the meantime Shakespearians should not be deprived of the additional material, much of which came to hand in out-of-the-way places during the compilation of *BBTC*. In the index, references to the supplementary Shakespeare items printed in volume 5 are given the prefix '2:' as if they were printed where, by rights, they should have been. Accordingly, a Shakespearian who is referred from the index to *SBTC* and does not locate the object of his inquiry should turn to the Shakespearian heading of volume 5. (There are Shakespeare references in the index which do indeed direct the reader to *BBTC* but they refer to items where the Shakespearian interest is usually subordinate).

II. SUBJECT HEADING SUBDIVIDERS. The application of the formal subject heading subdividers listed in the Table of abbreviations needs to be understood by the user for, although many (*e.g.* –*Bibs.*) are obvious, others are not so straightforward. Only after the function of the subdividers is understood can the overall structure of the subject index be appreciated. Since the principal object of the subject indexing was to provide for all logical approaches to the bibliographical materials, most headings with the formal subject subdividers can be reversed to supply main subject headings under which references otherwise scattered throughout the index can be listed together. The first formal heading subdivider offers a good illustration of the process:

(1) –*Bibliogr. descr.* The main headings which were subdivided by this

heading are displayed again under the main heading BIBLIOGRAPHICAL DESCRIPTION where also entries for items about bibliographical description in general are listed. Many of the heading subdividers discussed in the following notes are capable of being reversed (*e.g.* BIRMINGHAM–Ptg.; PRINTING–Birmingham), the references to items in the bibliographies being printed in both places, so as to provide alternative and direct access to the appropriate information. However, since not every heading subdivided in this manner is reversed, I should explain the exceptions.

(2) *–Bibs.* after subject and author headings precedes references to checklists, catalogues and bibliographies which were usually recorded in *BBLB*. However, entries with this subheading are not reversed; that function is served by the subject index of *BBLB* itself. Also, for the same reason, the checklists which are noted in connection with particular items in *BBTC* are not indexed as occurring in *BBTC* unless they occur *only* in that bibliography: they are listed, annotated and indexed in *BBLB*. (This practice involves bibliographies of manuscripts included in *BBTC*: see under *–Ms/s.*).

(3) *–Bksllng.* is used after place and personal names to record items which refer explicitly to bookselling and booksellers; an article about an author's dealings with booksellers (say, Dr. Johnson selling review copies, if that ever occurred), or variations in the prices of his first editions would lead to the use of this subheading. For places (but not for authors) the entries are reversed under BOOKSELLING, PROVINCIAL.

(4) *–Bkbndng* is similar in function to the preceding subheading and like it the entries for names of places are reversed under the main heading BOOKBINDING, PROVINCIAL. For authors the subheading draws attention to items about the binding of their work or their relations with bookbinders.

(5) *–Collns.* when modifying the name of a *library* distinguishes items about particular works owned by corporate libraries from items about the history or organization of the library. (For individual bookcollectors or authors the appropriate subject heading subdivider is *–Libr.*). However, *–Collns.* is used after names of individuals to identify material about collections of or about their works, and articles about bookcollecting in connection with individual authors or subjects. Hence an article about the Hyde collection of Johnsoniana is indexed as HYDE–Libr. and JOHNSON–Collns.

(6) *–Handwr.* identifies items about handwriting and the palaeographical study of an author's manuscripts and is not used with or in place of *–Mss.* when there is no palaeographical connection specified in the title of the particular item. Headings with this subdivider are not reversed.

(7) *–Illus.* may occur after headings for forms, genres and subjects to refer to material about the illustration of or illustrations in, for instance, songbooks, novels or sporting books, and such headings are reversed under the main heading, ILLUSTRATION OF. When used after the name of an author to list items about an author's dealings with illustrators or about the illustration of his works, the headings are not reversed. Authors like Blake and Thackeray who were themselves illustrators have also a special form of heading, –AS ILLUSTRATOR, which occurs after the main author sequence, to distinguish the appropriate aspects of their secondary bibliography. It is also worthwhile mentioning that individual illustrators' names in the index are further subdivided by

the titles of works in which they participated as illustrators as well as those of which they were the authors.

(8) –*Libr/s.* is used in the singular after the names of individuals to separate items which deal with their personal libraries, books borrowed by them from other libraries and any books at all which were in their possession: the heading is designedly capacious. On the other hand, the plural –*Librs.* is used after the names of places to announce references to items about libraries or collections of books associated with particular localities. Such headings are reversed under LIBRARIES, PROVINCIAL, the geographical subdivisions (by county) therefore bringing together references which otherwise would be scattered amongst the headings for circulating, parish and school libraries and the like which are also subdivided by place for most specific reference. However, libraries which have their locations identified (*e.g.* BLICKLING HALL, Norfolk) or contain the name of a locality (*e.g.* BIRMINGHAM LIBRARY) have cross-references from the regional subheading under LIBRARIES, PROVINCIAL; their item numbers are usually not incorporated in the references from place and –*Librs.* The large number of items referred to from headings for the British Museum and the main university libraries emphasizes the necessity of the expedient.

(9) –*Ms/s.* Although the singular is used occasionally after a title heading, more frequently –*Mss.* is used after the names of individuals and subjects. All subjects subdivided by –*Mss.* are listed under the main heading MANUSCRIPTS (see, for example, –Methodists; –Novels). Headings for authors are not reversed, although the user will find a list of bibliographies of authors' manuscripts under MANUSCRIPTS–Bibs. (I have already mentioned in the introduction to volume 4 that although checklists of manuscripts are included in *BBTC* they are indexed as if they occur only in the revised edition of *BBLB* where they are also, more appropriately, printed.

(10) –*Paper* after headings for localities refers the reader to items relating to paper, papermaking and papermakers associated with that place but indexed more specifically under the respective appropriate subject headings. Paper mills are entered under their names and again under the locality. However, often the location of a mill which lies between two villages, say, or just outside a town, is specified differently from one authority to another. Consequently, to mitigate the effects of any imprecision in noting the geography of paper manufacture, references to papermaking entered under specific localities are gathered together under PAPERMAKING, PROVINCIAL, but that heading is not divided by places as similar subject headings are, counties providing the smallest unit of subdivision. A reader will find under PAPERMAKING, PROVINCIAL–Kent all references to Kentish papermaking, particular mills, and paper without having to consult the names of specific places or mills. The provision of cross-references to individual papermakers associated with the localities ensures that no relevant information will be missed.

(11) –*Ptg.* introduces items which describe printing in a locality or the printing of a kind or subject of literature (*e.g.* chapbooks, novels, natural history)—when the headings are reversed under PRINTING OF—and also, with the names of authors, accounts of the printing of their works and their dealings with printers.

(12) –*Publ.* is used in similar fashion.

(13) –*Text* after the names of authors includes references to discussion of par-

ticular readings, problems of canon where bibliographical or textual evidence is significant, revision and other aspects of textual criticism where the interest is more than bibliographical.

(14) –*Type* is used with place names and after the names of authors to distinguish items which relate to type, typefounding and the typography (when distinct from printing) of authors' works.

III. SUBJECT INDEXING. The object of the subject index is to provide the most direct access possible to the items printed in the bibliographies which might satisfy the reader's enquiry. Consequently, as the list of heading subdividers discussed previously shows, items in the bibliographies are indexed as specifically and fully as can be. The index's fullness is intended to compensate for the consequences of printing a bibliographical item only in one place in the subject arrangement of the respective bibliography, even though it might deal with a number of equally-important subjects. The index includes four distinct kinds of primary subject headings: (a) names of individual authors, bookcollectors, and persons connected with the booktrade; (b) names of localities, ranging from country houses (seats) to the four nations; (c) genres or forms of literature and publication, like novels, ballads and chapbooks, and (d) subjects, and functions of the booktrade (binding, printing, etc.). Headings in categories b–d may be subdivided by all or some of the other headings, *e.g.* MANCHESTER–Ballads–Bksllng.; BALLADS–Wales–Publ.; PRINTING–Newspapers–Oxford; and many may be given secondary period subdivisions also. The subdivisions can be arranged after the main headings in a variety of orders. However, with a few exceptions subjects are subdivided only once. Therefore, an article on the printing of chapbooks in Dublin in 1740 will be recorded initially under the headings DUBLIN–Ptg., CHAPBOOKS–Dublin; CHAPBOOKS–Ptg., CHAPBOOKS–1701–1800. A user who seeks access to an article on the printing of chapbooks in the eighteenth century will find the items he needs by noticing the coincidence of the item number under the two subdivisions of the CHAPBOOKS heading, and reversal of the appropriate headings caters for more precise approaches. Exceptions are the headings BOOKS, IRELAND, SCOTLAND and WALES, where subdivision by periods and reversal of principal headings printed elsewhere in the index bring about a somewhat more elaborate arrangement. Another exception is the subject subdivider –*Bibs.* which may be added to any subject heading however minutely subdivided.

The structure of the index, the reader may be surprised to be informed, is therefore relatively simple. Simple-minded, indeed, might be a better expression, although the simplicity was strenuously sought and laboriously obtained. Nevertheless, on account of its simplicity, the index is exceedingly redundant in two ways. First, as the Dublin chapbook example above illustrates, a single bibliographical item may supply a plethora of headings to the subject index and may, indeed, be entered more than once under different subdivisions of a single primary heading: an article on Norwich publishing and bookselling will produce item numbers under NORWICH–Bksllng. and NORWICH–Publ. Second, after the bibliographies were indexed, many of the main headings were reversed in the manner already referred to. To use the earlier example, DUBLIN–Ptg. became PRINTING, PROVINCIAL–Dublin; CHAP-

BOOKS–Ptg. became PRINTING OF CHAPBOOKS, and the period divisions became the main subdivisions of the nonce-heading BOOKS, allowing entries under CHAPBOOKS–1701–1800 to be listed again at BOOKS–1701–1800–Chapbooks. Consequently, the enquirer will find the full display of item numbers under the exact main heading of his enquiry: if he is interested in Dublin he will find references to Dublin chapbooks and Dublin printing under DUBLIN; if he is interested in chapbooks he will find reference to Dublin chapbooks, printing of chapbooks, and possibly eighteenth-century chapbooks (because not all subjects are divided by period) under the CHAPBOOKS heading. He will not need to pursue his investigations of the index further, unless of course he is explicitly referred to another heading. Redundancy was built into the index to allow the user to consult it with the smallest possible pause for thought; the firstlings of his head should be the firstlings of his hand.

However, although alternative and equal access is supplied for subjects where the subdivisions denote no inevitable priority (as PRINTING–London; LONDON–Ptg.) by reversal and repetition of references, there are other headings which are not reversed, because they provide more specific subsets of references initially provided under more general main headings. For instance, item references after the subject divider –*Text* used with an author's name might include an article about the editing of his works; the main heading EDITING is divided by authors' names, where the item would be particularized, but the EDITING subdivisions are not reversed, the particular items having already been listed under –*Text*. In the same manner items about the collecting of books written by individual authors such as Barrie, which are not distinguished under the author heading, are listed under the author subdivisions of BOOKCOLLECTING and also not reversed. (Another such analytical heading where the subdivisions are not reversed is BOOKTRADE, LISTS OF PERSONS CONNECTED WITH).

IV. REFERENCES. Printers, publishers and other persons connected with the booktrade have the locality of their main period of business activity supplied in the headings for their names. The localities were drawn from the usual booktrade dictionaries and when such an individual was associated with more than one place of business, I generally selected the locality at which he worked longest, or a place outside London. LONDON is not used, a decision I regret now since its use in the headings for members of the booktrade would serve to distinguish them from other persons listed in the index. The use of localities in headings is useful to distinguish synonymous individuals and identify those with common names but it is chiefly useful to provide for cross-references both from the place of booktrade activity and also from the activity itself. Accordingly, there are cross-references in the index from, for example, MANATON–Ptg. to the BOAR'S HEAD PRESS, Manaton, est. 1931, from BELFAST–Ptg. to BLOW, James, Belfast, d.1579, and from the regional subdivisions of PRINTING, PRIVATE and PRINTING, PROVINCIAL respectively. Similar practices were adopted with BOOKBINDING, BOOKSELLING, PUBLISHING and TYPOGRAPHY. However, unless a tradesman had equal fame in a number of trades, he is listed only under a single occupation; for instance, James Abree whom Plomer's *Dictionary* describes as a printer and bookseller is referred to only from PRINTING, PROVINCIAL–Kent–Canterbury and not under the corresponding heading for bookselling. Sometimes by the distribution of cross-references to individual printers, etc. under headings like PRINTING, PROVINCIAL there were regional subheadings which did not occur in the main alphabetical sequence of subject headings. In such cases the cross-reference was repeated under the main regional heading. An example will make this clearer. A reader interested in bookbinding in Bath should have his attention drawn to the items in the bibliographies which relate to Cedric Chivers. Hence CHIVERS, Cedric, Bath, fl.1853–92 generates a cross-reference under BOOKBINDING, PROVINCIAL–Somerset–Bath, and because there were no entries under BATH–Bndng. the cross-reference was repeated there for the reader who is primarily interested in Bath.

Other cross-references are lavishly supplied. In particular, headings like COLOUR PRINTING which may be sought both under the adjectival or nominative part (although the noun more often gives the main entry) are all provided with cross-references. So too are aspects of main headings like BOOKS–Prices or BOOKBINDERS–Labels. I should mention that the technical vocabulary which provides the index headings derives from the language of the bibliographical items themselves; I have not attempted to impose a standard nomenclature on subjects of which the terminology has naturally varied during the eighty years of scholarship covered by the bibliographies. However, the cross-references go some way towards compensating for variety of terms. Similarly, the ambiguity of reference of such descriptive terms found in the literature for libraries as circulating, proprietary and subscription, or church and parish, cathedral and diocesan has led to repeated references to a single bibliographical item under the alternative headings, and some of the entries may in fact be incorrect. Nevertheless, as indexer I have had no other recourse than to accept the terminology of the literature and to endeavour to compensate for its occasional variety by cross-references.

All these expedients have produced an index which is redundant by design. The user must therefore have confidence that the information he seeks will be found at the point of natural, therefore first, access, and that so long as his enquiry is confined to the one topic he need not explore the index for further information beyond the extent to which cross-references provided in the index direct him. However, there are a couple of exceptional headings which should be especially noticed. (1) PROVINCIAL is used to modify the trade headings (BOOKBINDING, PRINTING, etc.) for the purpose of separating regional subdivisions from the other subheadings of the main subject heading. (The county designators ignore the recent local government reorganization. Changes in the boundaries of administrative areas are irrelevant to the historical literature of bibliography of the periods covered. Abbreviations for counties are based on those used in the *Bartholomew Gazetteer of Britain* (1977)). Items which deal with London printing, etc. are indexed under the regional headings only when the local connection is explicit in the title of the bibliographical item; other items which treat of the London booktrade—as most must do—but do not establish the connection in their titles are indexed only under the general subject headings. Nevertheless, LONDON is included under the PROVINCIAL headings for booktrade-related activities although, in order to restrict the bulk of the index, there are no cross-references from, say, BOOKSELLING,

PROVINCIAL–London to individual London booksellers. (2) BOOKS is used as a nonce-heading to provide access to bibliographical items by period. In the first instance forms or subjects like NOVELS or NATURAL HISTORY were sub-divided by periods in the index only when there were a large number of items which specifically mentioned the historical period dealt with. The occasional item which does mention a period, when the heading is not divided by periods, was indexed under BOOKS–period if it related to a subject or under PRINTING–period if it concerned a form of printing or publication like CHAPBOOKS. Finally, all headings in the index subdivided by periods were subsumed under BOOKS and the conventional period subdivisions.

Amongst the vast number of numerical references in the index there will inevitably be some that are incorrect, through transposition, misreading and the like. However, very often the reader will be able to correct misprints by using the redundancy of the index, although this expedient will not avail if the items were incorrectly indexed in the first place. When an index reference under a particular subject heading leads a reader to an inappropriate item in a bibliography, often he can detect the correct reference by comparing the item numbers listed under the heading he started from and another reversed form of the subject heading. For example, if a reference listed under FICTION–Wales or BIRMINGHAM–Newspapers is incorrect, the correct reference may be revealed by consulting WALES–Fiction or NEWSPAPERS, PROVINCIAL–Warwickshire–Birmingham.

The intention of the multiplication and re-ordering of index headings and subheadings, together with the lavish provision of references, I repeat, is to allow the reader to approach the index with reasonable confidence that he will find at once all material relating to the specific subject of his enquiry—whether it be a name of an individual or place, a process, a literary genre or form of publication or an activity connected in some way with books or the booktrade—or be directed to it by the cross-references. It is necessary finally only to notice a number of headings which list individual members of classes about which information may be found in the index: they include BIBLIOGRAPHERS AND EDITORS; BOOK, PARTS OF THE; ENGRAVERS; ILLUSTRATORS; MAPMAKERS; TYPOGRAPHERS and SOCIETIES of different kinds. Although other classes could perhaps be given similiar treatment, it is not convenient to list individual BOOKBINDERS, BOOKSELLERS, PRINTERS and PUBLISHERS under those main headings as to do so would bulk the index excessively. Users should also be warned that the lists under the headings mentioned above are introduced by 'e.g.' not 'i.e.'; whether an individual is listed under one or another heading (usually only a single heading) depends mainly on how the individual was described in the literature included in the bibliographies. There will of course be other individuals who in fact should be included in the lists.

CORRECTIONS TO
BRITISH BIBLIOGRAPHY AND
TEXTUAL CRITICISM
(VOLUMES IV AND V)

Numerous items were inserted during a late stage of composition and, because the compiler did not see revises of the page proofs many errors 'escaped in the printing'. The index was made from the compiler's corrected proofs. Users of *BBTC* should therefore make the following substantive corrections in their copies. Reference is by item number and the number of the line after the first. Headings are indicated by the number of the closest item and 'H'.

388.3	O. M. *delete points*
464.2	Waverly *read* Waverley
468.2	revelaions; *read* revelations;
514H	1890' *read* 1890.
542	**Poston, M. L.** *read* **Poston, Mervyn L.**
830.4	19: *read* 19:73–6
896a.2	Bambridge *read* Bainbridge
900	D. Knight's *read* Domville's
1013.3	12: *read* 12:45–6
1015.3	16:F '96. *read* 16:61–3 F '96; 17:67–9 Mr '96.
1056	**J.** *insert* and **W. M. Palmer.**
1095	**W.** *read* **William**
1114	*Insert* 1114–15 Cancelled.
1160a.2	*Read* & home counties branch Lib Assn) new ser 2:5–7 '66.
	Repr. from Kentish Gaz 11 Mr '66.
1165.2	? *delete*
1286a.2	115 *read* 115l.
1327.2	l. *read* 1l.
1389.2	S '50 *read* S '50;
1440a.2	l–vii *read* i–vii
1449.5	1893. *read* 1893. v,223p. 17cm.
1500	**Caruthers, S. W.** *read* **Carruthers, Samuel W.**
.2	'52. *add* [Sg.: Caruthers, S. W.]
1520	*Insert* 1520–1 Cancelled.
1533	field *read* Field
1540g	in *read* yn
1777	O'D *read* O'D.
1835	**MacLochlain.** *read* **MacLochlainn.**
1842a	every *read* ever
1958	**MrC.** *read* **McC.**
1961	**Frank.** *read* **Frederic.**
2071	**R.** *read* **Robert**
2264a.5	lv.illus. *read* 1v. illus.
2267.2	7no76:'97–106 *read* 7no76: 97–106

2412a.2	[Canterbury: p. 359–68] *relocate at end of entry*
2413	— *read* **Plomer, Henry R.**
2454.3	From *read from*
2698b.2	19pt *read* 19ptl
2761	rarieties. *read* rarities.
2836a.2	[12]p *read* [12]p.
	covertitle. *read* Covertitle.
2868	(N.Y.) *delete*
2970	Bibliography). *read* bibliography).
3302a	and ... library. *read* [and ... library].
3383	sibthorpe. *read* Sibthorpe.
3471.5	Wright, *read* Wight,
3632.3	A *read* A.
3642.3	forgeries. *read* forgeries].
3710.3	155–92.and *read* 155–92 and
3713.3	155–92.and *read* 155–92 and
3732	Ullman *read* Ulman
3737a.2	Tate: *read* Tate;
3745a	Some *read* ... Some
	29ptl *read* 29pt
3763a	1820, *read* 1820;
	Os *read* Oc
3844H	**20th cent.** *read* **fl.1957**
3860H	**fl.1805** *read* **fl.1802**
3876H	**1773** *read* **1772**
3883	Ball. *read* Ball,
3890H	**BAILEY,** *read* **BALLEY,**
3898H	**fl.1798–1819** *read* **1774–1849**
3964a	& *read* and
.2	1922–3 *read* 1922–4
	1922–3. 2v. *read* 1922–4. 3v. 15cm.
3964bc	The picture *read* —The Picture
3992H	**d.1833** *read* **1760?–1835**
4011g	EDINBURGH *read* EDINBURGH.
4089H	**20th cent.** *read* **est. 1921**
4094.2	(N.Y.) *delete*
4096H	**fl.1796** *read* **fl.1793**

4384H RALPH, 1892– *read* RALPH
NICHOLAS, 1892–1960
4418H CHARLES, *read* SIR CHARLES,
4421mH GRAIG *read* CRAIG
4421m.3 *Includes* ... mills.
4400.2 (Not seen) *delete*
4545a.5 machine *read* machine.–The
mould machine in Ameri-
ca.–Further papermachine
4637.2 Claredon *read* Clarendon
4650a *Notice order*
4720H J., 1863–1929 *read* JOSEPH,
1862–1928
4745 fl.1768 *read* 1727–1803
4786 FRANCOIS, *read* FRANÇOIS,
4861a Abel ... & A. *read* Abel Heywood,
Abel Heywood & son, Abel Heywood & son, ltd., 1832–1932.
[Manchester] A.
4896H fl.1772–5 *read* fl.1767–1830
4897H fl.1789–1818 *read* fl.1778–1830
4918H *Insert* JAMES, THOMAS,
fl.1710–38
4919H *substitute* JAY, LEONARD, 1888–
4947 –1813 *read* –1817
5027c and *read* und
5027d.2 facism. *read* facsim.
5027e (Ein *read* (Een
5027r.2 1no1:–14 *read* 1no1:3–14
.6 2no4[113 *read* 2no4:113
.10 '25; *read* '25.
5027t.2 3no2:123–4 *read* 3no2:34–5 Je
5034aH 1894 *read* 1894–
5075a Shaaaber, *read* Shaaber,
.2 Pennsylavania *read* Pennsylvania
5092H est. 1845 *read* est. 1848
5120a Moran, James. *read* ——
5135 Hanns *read* Hans
5161H ext. *read* est.
5164 Hore]. *read* Hone].
5172 *Notice order*
5175 — *read* Nixon, Howard M.
5176 Nixon, Howard M. *read* —
5193a Antique *read* Halifax Antiqu
5214a (Notes *read* (Note
5301.2 (N.Y.) *delete*
5375H 1894– *read* 1894–1979
5377a '02 *read* '02.
5406 ser3pt2 ... *read* ser 3pt2 ...
5445H GEOFFREY, *read* GEOFFREY
5455H J., ... fl.1834–71 *read* John, ...
fl.1810–79
5456H 19th cent. *read* fl.1823
5467 ser4n15 ... *read* ser4 15 ...
5478 A., *read* A,
5479 A., *read* A,
5558 ports 24 cm. *read* ports. 24cm.
5564p – H *Notice order*

5564q *Notice order*
5564q.3 '57. *read* '57. illus., facsims.
6 mill[South Hytton, *read* mill
[South Hylton,
5644.3 19–4 *read* 1–4
5706H fl.1778–1800 *read* 1740–1807
5714a Für *read* für
5714e Papiermuhlen. *read* Papier-
mühlen.
5819 Hanns *read* Hans
5870.11 Ybk *read* Yrbk
5878H TUER *notice order*
5894 Hanns *read* Hans
5931 Costessy, *read* Costessey,
5972H 1741–98 *read* 1702–59
read — James Whatman, father and
son. London, Methuen, 1957.
(Repr. New York, Garland, 1979).
170p. 23cm.
5986H fl.1773 *read* fl.1774–92
5991H EDMUNDS, *read* EDMUND
6055 Duff. *read* Duff,
6139 Century]. *read* century].
6210a Kitburn. *read* Kilburn.
6312.3 illus., *read* illus.
6379.2 ser3no2 *read* Ser3no2)
6454 Roth, Cecil. *read* ——
6499 F. *read* Frank
6529.3 Reed *read* Reed *ib.*
6650 Tansell, *read* Tanselle,
6865 (N.Y.) *delete*
6871 L. S. *read* L. A.
7134.2 eee3s28. *read* Je '28.
7165.3 ser3:37–50 *read* ser3 26no1:37–50
7215.2 retaliation]. *read* retaliator].
7247.2 6pt4444: *read* 6pt4:
7423 (N.Y.) *delete*
7462 Hanns *read* Hans
7647.2 B. *read* B.;
7660 'y12. *read* '12.
7688 loyal *read* Loyal
7796 Poston, M. *read* Poston, Mervyn

VOLUME V (AUTHORS)

8344 friendship]. *read* freindship].
8464.3 falseone, *read* false one.
8946 (N.Y.) *delete*
9193 McCarthy. *read* McCarthy,
9294 Øsler, *read* Øsler.
9382.3 (Not seen) *delete*
9393a.3 i.e *read* i.e.
9884.2 J *read* J.
10813 Elegy *read* Elegy.
10814 Gray's *read* Gray's.
11088H fl.1671 *read* fl.1669–82
11579.2 D. *read* D '58.
11765 (N.Y.) *delete*
11978H 1884–1959 *read* d.1749

12229	Tannenbaum *read* Tannenbaum,
p. 374	SHAKESPEARE.3 971) *read* 1971)
277a	:1no]12: *read* [1no]12:
13810	**Arthur.** *read* **Arthur**
13401.2	the critic]. *read* The critic].

14054	Caledonius *read* Caledonius.
14062	**Brown, David D.** *read* ——
14203.4	cont.- *read* cont.
14227.2	'02, *read* '02;

Other corrections of bibliographical form or typographical convention may be made in the following lines. (Many spacing faults are ignored). — 14, 146.3, 252.3, 410.10, 593.3, 657.2, 785.2, 857a.3, 866a.3, 898.2, 1100d.3, 1101, 1101H, 1158g.2, 1170.4, 1180a.3, 1306a, 1306a.4, 1476a.2, 1501, 1541H, 1610.2, 1621.5, 1624.4, 1743.4, 2150, 2234.3, 2443a.5, 2635.2, 2721, 3156a.3–4, 3205.7, 3558.4, 3577H, 3636.2, 3727.2, 3765a.4, 3783.3, 3785.12, 3850H, 4011g, 4082a, 4161H, 4365H, 4419H, 4494, 4530H, 4538H, 4571m, 4737H, 4755H, 4785H, 4827H, 4898H, 4908H, 4940g.2, 4943.2, 4999.4, 5034aH, 5058H, 5069.2, 5073H, 5108f.4, 5183H, 5330H, 5432H, 5525, 5690.2, 5714d, 5716H, 5717H, 5719.3, 5753.3, 6488.12, 6646, 6654.4, 7359a.2, 7426.4, 7644.9, 10; VOLUME V (AUTHORS): 8373H, 8385H, 8443H, 8463.4, 8466.5, 9250H, 9467H, 9514, 9635H, 9781.5, 9864H, 10245.2, 10286.3, 10342.3, 10948, 11508.2, 11540, 11557, 12227, 372a.5, 1978a.2.

TABLE OF ABBREVIATIONS

The use of the following abbreviations, their application to the entries of the *Bibliography*, is discussed in the Introduction.

1: *Bibliography of British Literary Bibliographies* (rev. ed. 1980)
2: *Shakespearian Bibliography and Textual Criticism* (1971)
Aber. Aberdeen
A.D. anno Domini
archbp. archbishop
Ayr. Ayrshire

b. born
B.C. before Christ
Beds. Bedfordshire
Berks. Berkshire
Bibliogr. descr. bibliographical description (*Intro.*, p. x)
Bibs. bibliographies (*Intro.*, p. xi)
Bksllng Bookselling (*Intro.*, p. xi)
Bndng bookbinding (*Intro.*, p. xi)
bp bishop
Brecon. Brecknockshire
Bucks. Buckinghamshire

c. *cira* (about)
Caith. Caithness-shire
Cambs. Cambridgeshire
card. cardinal
Cards. Cardiganshire
Carms. Carmarthenshire
Carnarvs. Carnarvonshire
cent. century
Ches. Cheshire
co. county
Collns. collections (*Intro.*, p. xi)
Cornw. Cornwall
Cumb. Cumberland

d. died
Denbigh Denbighshire
Derbys. Derbyshire
Devon. Devonshire
Dumf. Dumfriesshire

est. established

Fifes. Fifeshire
fl. floruit (flourished)
Forfars. Forfarshire

Glam. Glamorganshire
Glos. Gloucestershire

Handwr. Handwriting (*Intro.*, p. xi)

Hants. Hampshire
Herefs. Herefordshire
Herts. Hertfordshire
Hunts. Huntingdonshire

Illus. illustration (*Intro.*, p. xi)
Inver. Inverness-shire
I.O.W. Isle of Wight

Lanark. Lanarkshire
Lancs. Lancashire
ld. lord
Leics. Leicestershire
Libr/s. library/ies (*Intro.*, p. xii)
Lincs. Lincolnshire

Merion. Merionethshire
Midloth. Midlothian
Mons. Monmouthshire
Ms/s. manuscript/s (*Intro.*, p. xii)

Norf. Norfork
Northants. Northamptonshire
Notts. Nottinghamshire
Nthmb. Northumberland
N.Z. New Zealand

Oxon. Oxfordshire

Paper papermaking (*Intro.*, p. xii)
Perth. Perthshire
Ptg. printing (*Intro.*, p. xii)
Publ. publication (*Intro.*, p. xii)

Renfrew. Renfrewshire
Roxb. Roxburghshire

Shrop. Shropshire
Som. Somerset
Staffs. Staffordshire
Suff. Suffolk

Text text (*Intro.*, p. xii)
Type. typefounding (*Intro.*, p. xiii)

Warws. Warwickshire
Westm. Westmorland
Wilts. Wiltshire
Worcs. Worcestershire

Yorks. Yorkshire

INDEX TO BRITISH LITERARY BIBLIOGRAPHY

VI

British literary bibliography
and
textual criticism 1890–1969
an index

INDEX OF AUTHORS, EDITORS, COMPILERS, AND TITLES

Compiled by Josie S. Shumake, M.A.

Alston, Robin Carfrae. 1:(1582) 1730 (1731) 2203–4 (2276a) (2282) (2283a) (2286c); 236 869 3609

Altamura, Antonio. 1:4513k

Altenberg, Bengt. 1:4012c

Altholz, Josef L. 1:657j 2261g; 7925

Altick, Richard Daniel. 1:8 657; 804 3465 6539 7911–12 8900 14426

Altman, George J. 2:1224

Alton, R.E. 11151

Altro, *pseud.* 8190

Amano, Keitarō. 1:21689g (4114r) (4217a) (4513e) (4707b)

Ambleside. Dove cottage *see* Dove cottage, Ambleside.

Ament, William S. 987

American art association, New York. 1:395 401 401d 1744 2866h–i 3074 3074h 3076c 3077 3082 3586; 2:289

American bible society 1:1495 1500

American bibliographic service. 1:44 47

American book collector. 1:113

American bookseller. 1:114

American collector. 1:115

American historical association. 1:21–2

American institute of graphic arts. Chicago chapter. Exhibition committee. 1:1350m

American library association. 2:40; 148

American notes (Bkmns J). 467 507 9642 11244 13608

American philosophical society. 1:1760n; 2456

American printer & lithographer. 1:116

American stationer and office manager. 1:117

American writer in England. 1:846

Amery, George Douglas. 1:5213–a; 6015

Ames foundation *see* Harvard university. Ames foundation.

Ames, Joseph. 6060

Amherst, William Amhurst Tyssen-, 1st baron Amherst of Hackney. 1:385

Amnéus, Daniel A. 2:1523

Amori di libro. 1:2570a

Amory, Hugh. 1:3307; 3380a 10525

Amy, Ernest Francis. 9419a

And, Metin. 2:119

Anderle, Othmar F. 1:4975b

Anders, H. 1:1424; 6723b

Anderson, A. 1:2098

Anderson, Alan. 1:3501; 10860

Anderson, Alexander. 1675

Anderson, Andrew H. 3364

Anderson, Arthur J. 1:4453

Anderson, Chester C. 11612

Anderson, D.M. 2:1460

Anderson, Donald K. 10575

Anderson, G.A. 11819 11824

Anderson, G.L. 10694

Anderson, Gregg. 7084

Anderson, Howard. 11994

Anderson, J.L. 2672

Anderson, J. Maitland. 1677a

Anderson James. 1:1724b

Anderson, James Seton-. 4435a 4720 6010 8044 9758 13075

Anderson, John. 1:1026–8 2677

Anderson, John Parker. 1:855 2365 2582h 2898a 3247 4220 4541–2 4598 4663 4718 4907 5212

Anderson, Paul Bunyan. 8228 9903 10528

Anderson, Peter John. 1:711 984–5 1001 1425d 1930 1930g 1935a 1961 3856 4054–6 4102–4 4712f; 1568 1643 1648–50 1658 1660–3 1682 3486 5991d 6505 6832 7003 7542 7545 7714 9353 10570 11526 11706 11997 12996 13488

Anderson, R.C. 8167–9

Anderson, Robert Bowie. 1:2211 2214d

Anderson, William James. 3381 8053 8087

Anderson auction co., New York. 1:384 388–9 1740

Anderson galleries, New York. 1:393–4 396 398 400–1d 518 665 3066b 3070f 3082 4649 4806 5101; 2:203

Andersson, Nils G. 7087

Anderton, Basil. 1:926 2458; 1321 4025–6 4030 7022

Anderton, Henry Philip John Ince-. 1181 2934 3838 3848–9 4897 5309 6937a 7647 8545 14248

Andhra university. 2:(952)

Andrade, E.N. daC. 1:(2520n)

Andrew, R.V. 1:2851

Andrews, C.S. 1:3774

Andrews, Charles Edward. 1:2532

Andrews, Charles M. 8092 13565

Andrews, Clarence A. 13070

Andrews, Cyril B. 2922

Andrews, Fanny. 1157

Andrews, H.C. 2879 3741 4407 7967

Andrews, H.K. 9165–6

Andrews, J.T. 9181

Andrews, John Harwood. 1:1818

Andrews, Natalie T. 1:2935g

Andrews, W. 7826

Andrews, William L. 4774 5384

Andronicus, *pseud.* 750

Angeli, Helen R. 13098

Anglica; Untersuchungen ... Alois Brandl. 11075a

Anglistische Forschungen. 1:2087

Angus, I. 1:4373

Angus, Norman S. 882 925

Angus, William Craibe. 1:2631–2; 748 9068 9078

Anikst, A.A. 1:4813a

Atkins, Stuart. 8230
Atkins, W.M. 3165a
Atkinson, Ann (Curnow). 1:3402
Atkinson, Daniel Hopkin. 2469
Atkinson, Dorothy F. 1:4753a
Atkinson, W.A. 7239
Atto, Clayton. 5698
Attwater, Donald. 1:3434w
Attwood, J.S. 1099
Atwater, V.G.B. 1:860a
Aubin, Robert Arnold. 1:2003a 2005 3011a
Auchmuty, J.J. 14538
Auckland. University. 2:1680; 4401
Auction sales (Bibliographer). 2582 2685–6
Auden, George A. (2629)
Auden. J.E. 2858
Augustan reprint society. 7450
Aularian series. 8521
Auld, Thomas. 6508 10810
Ault, Patricia. 9661
Ault, T. Norman. 1:1991–2; 6402 11059
    12829–30 12841 12945
Aurner, Nellie Slayton. 1:1282; 4261
Aus der Welt des Bibliothekars. 2448a 7615b
Austin, Gabriel. 3380a
Austin, Roland. 1:895–6 896d 1388b 1787
    1850 5086; 709 1117a–20 1129 1301 3966
    4835 5495 5573 6275 7725 7844 7862 8102
    10001 13527
Austin, Warren B. 12557
Australiana (Amat Bk Coll). 70
Australia Capital territory. 1:643b
— National library, Canberra. 1:641–2
Australasian universities languages and
    literature association. Congress, 9th.
    Proceedings. 13998
Austria. Nationalbibliothek, Vienna. 2:225
Auty, R.A. 14583
Averill, Esther C. 9044
Avis, Frederick Compton. 1284 1287 1289
    1619 3539 3541 3571 4193 4587 5158 5227
    5452–3 6132 6144 6147 6624 6639 6642–3
    6684 6689 6691 6693
Axon, Ernest. 1:3404 (3414) 5130b
Axon, Geoffrey R. 1:910; 1175 3820 5153
Axon, William Edward Armytage. 1:910a
    1386 1760e 1873a 2822 3019 3366 (3414)
    4350 4402g 4881 (5151); 550 705 941 1023
    1164a 1186 1203 1384 1449a 2509 2633
    2685 3613 3623 4248 4414 5491 5603 5713
    6814 6831 6996 6999 8033 8171 8258 8818
    9515 9517 9954 9956–7 9981 10540 11380
    12470 12674 13014 13257 13524 13882
Ayeahr, *pseud*. 3703 7384 10458 12297
Ayers, Eric. 6633
Ayers, Robert W. 1:4245 4422; 12439 12780
Aylward, J.D. 657 950 7259a

Ayres, F.H. 1:3697
Ayres, Harry Morgan. 9305 9316

B. 11921 13644
B., A. 1:1047
B., A.C. 1:4897a; 13934
B., A.W. 13166
B., B. 1:2519b
B., C. 14313
B., C.C. 2:650; 3578 3581 3671 4522 5094b
    5905 6271 6945 6996 9794 10001 10540
    10783 11007 12297 12313 12521 12545
    14496
B., C.W. 6446
B., E. 13209
B., E.G. 4407 4723 6356 7746 7872 10839
    12948
B., E.S. 3588
B., F. 7384
B., G.F.R. 2405 4640 6996 12999 13075
B., G.L. 8675
B., H.J. 8161
B., I.C. *see* Blackwood, Isabella C.
B., J. 1770
B., J.P. 7824
B., K.P. 1:698
B., L.R. 1:2449a
B., M.S. 1:3573; 10938
B., P. 2259
B., P.B.G. 1:1536k; 6974
B., R. 1077 2780 5046 7825 11963 13480
    13976
B-r, R. 2420 13638
B., R.A. 7732
B., R.L. 13644
B., R.O. 3858
B., R.P. 1:3711
B., R.S. 1:2323g; 709 1221 2954 4180 7250
    7427 7471 7647 7733 7746 7888 8545 9253
B., T.M. *see* Blagg, Thomas Matthews.
B., W. 7873 12645 12802 13176 14024
B., W.C. 2:711; 886 888 2407 3627 3632
    5296 5603 6724 9948 9987 10815 13049
    14156 14560
B., W.E. 6930
B., W.L. 3990
Babb, J. Staines. 10732
Babb, James T. 1:2869 4094g; 8490 9654–5
    11108–9
Babcock, Robert Weston. 2:1712; 7218 12627
    12828
Babcock, Robert Whitbeck. 1:2088–9a;
    2:219–20 230 1201 1274 1672
Babcock, Weston. 2:1489
Babington, Percy Lancelot. 1:4628 4859;
    13261 13306

Babler, Otto Frantisek. 1:4527c; 2:71 1586; 508 2257 3918 3925 4189 4720 6177 6356 13534

Babson institute, Babson park, Mass. Library. 1:4337 4339a

Background to print (Print in Brit). 3868 6125 6134

Backhouse, Janet. 3394

Backus, Edythe N. 1:1835; 9163

Baddeley, St.Clair. 2831

Baddeley, Vincent. 14423

Bader, Arno L. 12169

Badminton library. 1:2197

Baender, Paul. 413

Baer, Elizabeth. 3118

Bagguley, John R. 9171

Bagley, Helen Antoinette. 1:4568

Bagnall, B. 8026

Bagster, Robert. 3876

Baildon, William Paley. 1:1970; 6697

Bailey, D.S. 3354b

Bailey, Elmer James. 1:4196

Bailey, H. 2164

Bailey, J.B. 2012

Bailey, John Eglington. 1:3366–7; 2470

Bailey, Johnson. 2408

Bailey, Richard W. 1:2286e

Bailey, Shirley Jean. 1:4376

Baille-Hamilton-Arden, George, 11th earl of Haddington *see* Arden, George Baillie-Hamilton-, 11th earl of Haddington.

Bain, G.W. 1:927k; 1108

Bain, Iain S. 3982 5234 5260a 5563 5640

Bain, James Stoddart. 3879

Baine, Rodney M. 6775 9928 12752 13599

Baird, Donald. 1:1659

Baird, John D. 9725

Baird, Matthew. 9933

Bakeless, John Edwin. 1:4121 4126; 2:750

Baker, Alfred. 1:4425i; 5421a 5422–3

Baker, C.H. Collins. 1:4239–40; 4492 5851 12399

Baker, Carlos. 7865 10905

Baker, Donald C. 3364a

Baker, Doris. 1:2306b

Baker, Ernest E. 2:171 1285

Baker, Frank. 1:5069; 14293

Baker, H. Kendra. 7062

Baker, John M. 13054

Baker, John Milton. 1:4527p

Baker, Robert E. 967

Baker, Ronald. 8907

Baker, T. H. 6910

Baker-Smith, Dominic *see* Smith, Dominic Baker-.

Balch, Ruth. 1:4882

Bald, M.A. 1589

Bald, Robert Cecil. 1:3718 5174; 2:366 461 598 1508 1897 1907; 213 289 3529 5020 7146 7165 8455 8534 8915 8918–9 10250 10267 11881 12265 12269 12285 14368

Balderston, Katherine Canby. 1:3464d; 10744 10751

Baldi, Sergio. 10851

Baldock, G. Yarrow. 1:4404p; 1233 2420 10645

Baldwin, Edward Chauncey. 1:1549

Baldwin, P.S. 3365

Baldwin, R.C. 1:5087–8

Baldwin, Stanley Everett. 1:3927w

Baldwin, Thomas Whitfield. 2:228 614 1352 1825; 4897i 9575

Balfour, Graham. 13644

Balfour, M.C. 2859

Balfour, M.L.G. 13664

Balfour, Robert Edmond. 1:3137

Ball, A.W. 1:480

Ball, Alice Delany. 10363

Ball, F. Elrington. 2832 10648

Ball, Henry William. 3883

Ball, Margaret. 1:4600

Ballantyne, Hanson & co., Edinburgh. 1:1248c; 3886

Ballantyne, John W. 7557

Ballard, Ellis Ames. 1:3952 3954

Ballinger, sir John. 1:953 1507; 2:272; 14 1451 1471 1519 1526 1528 2723 3881 10717

Ballman, Adele B. 11673

Balniel, ld. *see* Lindsay, James Ludovic, 26th earl of Crawford.

Balston, Thomas. 1:1245f 1746–a 4138–b (4139) 4240 4563i 4693; 2327 3771 3891 4105 4762 5143–5 5576 5973–5 6610 7295 7297 7425–6 12405

Balston, William. 5972

Baltimore. Enoch Pratt free library. 1:2825

— Peabody institute *see* Peabody institute, Baltimore.

Bancks, Gerard W. 11908

Bandy, W.T. 1:808; 9225 9542

Banerji, Hiran K. 1:3300d

Bangor. University college of North Wales *see* Wales. University. University college of North Wales, Bangor.

Bangs and co. ltd., New York. 1:382 571

Bankart, Reginald. 7882

Banks, Charlotte. 1:2644h

Banks, Theodore Howard. 1:3011; 9950

Bannard, Henry E. 5273

Bannister, H.M. 13161

Baptie, David. 1:1827k

Baptist union of Great Britain and Ireland. 1:2254

Baugh, Albert Croll. 1:2780b; 2:533

Baughman, Roland. 1:4483a 5134; 784 8208a 14429

Baum, Paull Franklin. 1:2016 4544k; 12625 13088 13091–2 13830

Baumgartner, Leona. 1:3737

Baumgartner, Paul R. 6035

Baxter, Cyril. 3868–9 5043 6634 7926

Baxter, Frank Condie. 1:4028c

Baxter, James Houston. 1:346 750 998; 4723

Baxter, James P. 12564

Baxter, R.W. 4543

Baxter, Wynne Edwin. 1:4221 4228; 2:650; 12307 12310–11 12313 12323

Bay, Jens Christian. 2344 8123 8127 10100 11270 13921 14385

Bayfield, Matthew Albert. 2:841–2 843b 1158 1286–7 1882 1884

Bayford, E.G. 8899 11985

Bayler, Harold. 3789

Bayley, A.R. 1230 4897c 5074 7717–18 9179 10403 11007 13292 13638

Bayley, D.J. 1:4419

Baylor university, Waco, Texas. Library. 1:2577

Bayne, Thomas. 2:650; 7344 7826 8264 9020–1 9618 9706 10341 10403 12304 12313 12645 13166 13176–7 13527 14314 14475 14496

Bayne, William. 8923

Baynes, Norman Hepburn. 1:2658

Bazeley, William. 1:893 2775

Beach, Joseph Warren. 1:2356; 8321

Beach, Sylvia. 1:3879ah

Beachcroft, T.O. 1:3

Beadle, Clayton. 3714 3718

Beale, Joseph Henry. 1:2210 2214d

Beard, Charles R. 1:1464b

Beard, D.R. 1:941

Beards, Richard D. 1:4012a

Beardshaw, H.J. 1021

Beare, Robert L. 10435

Beaton, David. 1:989

Beattie, William. 1:466–7 1421a–2 4030d; 1610 1728 4370–1 4371a–2 11123

Beatty, C.J.P. 10941

Beatty, H.M. 1:3422; 10658–9

Beatty, Hamilton. 1:5178

Beatty, Joseph M. 1:2001 2794

Beaty, Frederick L. 12778

Beaujon, Paul, pseud. of Beatrice Lamberton-Becker Warde. 1:(3434u); 2:747; 5301

Beaumont, Comyns. 2:1905

Beaumont, Cyril William. 1:1261; 3967

Beaurline, Lester A. (213) (227) (390–1) 13696–7

Beavan, John. 11126

Beaven, A.B. 4418

Beaver, Hugh. 7420

Beazeley, M. 2620

Beck, F.G.M. 1401

Becker, Frank C. 13555

Becker, Ph.A. 1:2388n

Becker, Werner. 1:(4334a–c)

Beckwith, Frank. 2437 3031 3394a 11008

Beckwith, Frank S. 1:4442a

Beddingham, Philip C. 6310

Beddows, Harry T. 2425 8646

Bede, mother M. 1:3968; 11796

Bedford. Bunyan meeting library and museum see Bunyan meeting library and museum, Bedford.

— College of education. Library. 1:1573g

— Public library. 1:2613

Bedfordshire historical record society. 1:872–a

Bee, Alison K. see Howard, Alison K. (Bee).

Beebe, Maurice. 1:2741 2856 3223d 3512 3800a–b 3874 3879a 4012 5157

Beeching, Henry Charles. 2698b 9794

Beer, Gillian. 12252

Beer, J.B. 400 1280

Beese, Margaret. 13428

Beetenson, W.C. 10814

Begley, Walter. 1:1686d

Belden, Mary Megie. 1:3336

Belfast. Public libraries. 1:4503 4505

Belfast library and society for promoting knowledge. 1:1026–8 1030f

Beinecke, Edwin John. 13662

Beinecke, Walter. 8423

Belcher, William F. 7793

Beljame, Alexandre. 3453a

Bell, C.C. 8273

Bell, Edward. 3974

Bell, Eric Sinclair. 7323

Bell, F.P. 8026

Bell, H.E. 3690

Bell, H.W. 10291 11063

Bell, sir Harold Idris. 1:3335; 785 7223 8338 9158 10612 10719 10784 12647 13131 14014 14091 14507

Bell, Inglis F. 1:1659

Bell, James. 1:456

Bell, Mackenzie. 1:(4541)

Bell, W. Edmund. 1664a

Bell, Whitfield J. 8212

Beller, Elmer A. 3644

Bellet, H. Hale. 7952

Bellinger, Rossiter R. 11684

Bellows, Elizabeth E. 1:2439m

Bemrose, sir Henry H. 3989

Bence-Jones, A.B. see Jones, A.B. Bence-.

Bendall, Wilfrid E. 1:4823q

Bender, J. Terry. 1:3436 4177

Bendickson, Lodewyk. 500

Benedikz, B.S. 1:4760f
Benedikz, Phyllis Mary. 1:1781a
Benger, F.B. 2090 4623 6004
Bengis, Nathan L. 1:3184; 10299 10302
  10305 10309 10311–12
Benham, Allen Rogers. 1:410a 778
Benjamin, L.S. see Melville, Lewis, pseud.
Benkovitz, Miriam Jeanette. 1:3315; 10530–1
Bennet, Norman. 2:696
Bennett, A.L. 1:4169a
Bennett, Charles H. 14196
Bennett, Edward. 1:2917
Bennett, E.P. Leigh-. 6001
Bennett, Henry Stanley. 1:589 771 771d
  1419–20 5128; 2:118; 391 568 3454 3458
  3470 3478–9 3695 4296 4308 4315 8064
Bennett, J.A.W. 4344 4347 11087 14230
Bennett, James R. 1:1723c
Bennett, JoAnn Waite. 10623
Bennett, Josephine Waters. 1:813 4116c;
  2:(438) (788) 1981; 10993a 11584 12125
  12949 13571
Bennett, Josiah Q. 3382a
Bennett, N.E. 1:1030e
Bennett, Paul A. 4994 6114 (6299) 6301
  (6486–7) (6680–1) (6709) 6710 (13272)
Bennett, R.E. 8503 9683 10232 10239 12543
Bennett, Ralph. 4347
Bennett, Richard. 1:423
Bennett, S. (391)
Bennett, W. Leslie. 7026
Bennett, Whitman. 343–4 11236
Bennett, William. 1418 1432 3929 4191
Bensly, Edward. 1:3501a; 2:650; 964 2425
  2723 2780 2828 2953 3599 3723 5197 5569
  6288 6742 7667 7715 7717–18 7868 8315
  8681 8966 8996 9122–3 9126–8 9132 9135
  10829 10840 11384–5 11549 11970 12325
  12467 13579 13801 13884
Benson, A.C. 33
Benson, Carolyn. 13631
Bensusan, Geoffrey. 5454
Bensusan, S.L. 4627
Bentham, George. 1:3324
Bentley, C.F. 4421
Bentley, Gerald Eades. 1:1610; 2:443;
  8612–14 8619 8622 8631 8635–6 (9743)
Bentley, Gerald Eades, jr. 1:2485 3330;
  8625a
Bentley, H.H. 3998
Bentley, Norma E. 9148
Bentley, Phyllis. 8783
Bentley, Richard. 1:1264p; 2611 3995
Bentley, Wilder. 12524
Benton, Josiah Henry. 1:1251n 1516; 3915
  3932 3947
Bentz, Hans Willi. 1:3259
Berens, Lewis H. 1:5131

Berg, Virginia. 1:1891
Berg collection see New York. Public library.
  Berg collection.
Bergeron, David M. 11085
Bergholz, H. 9901
Bergman, Ted. 1:3185d; 10310
Bergonzi, Bernard. 14281
Bergquist, G. William. 1:1592
Berkowitz, David Sandler. 1:15 413
Berman, Ronald. 2:142
Bernard, Erwin. 7509
Bernbaum, Ernest. 1:627
Berol, Alfred C. 4505 9332 12672
Berry, George L. 2416
Berry, Lloyd Eason. 1:1989 3332; 4364–5
  10561 14134
Berry, Oscar. 5997
Berry, William Turner. 1:1147 1150h 1158–9
  1187 1204 1208–9 1266q; 1237 1367 3843
  4190 6090 6321 6615 6623 6628 6654 6716
  6720 7255
Bertie, Charles H. 9192
Bertram, Paul Benjamin. 2:1916
Bertrams ltd., Edinburgh. 4011g
Best, Maud Storr. 1:983
Best, Richard Irvine. 1:1016–17 4815j
Besterman, Theodore Deodatus Nathaniel.
  1:35 88 411–12 817 2457 3261 4072 4090;
  508 698d 4064 4155 9056 13324
Bethlehem, Pa. Lehigh university see Lehigh
  university, Bethlehem, Pa.
Betjeman, sir John. 6596
Bettany, G.T. 4822
Beveridge, Erskine. 1:997
Beverley, Stanley. 890a 891a
Bevington, M.M. 400
Bhattacharya, S. 11858
Biadene, Galeazzo. 2:133
Bibas, H. 12945
Bibby, Harold Cyril. 1:3779c
Biblio, pseud. 1:1037; 1786 2690
Bibliographer. 1:120
Bibliographica. 1:121; 281 814 817 2097 2104
  6152
Bibliographica Celtica. 1:1181
Bibliographia: studies in book history and book
  structure. 1:667 670 2415 4603
Bibliographical aids to research (Bull Inst Hist
  Res). 1719
Bibliographical and auction notes (TLS). 2136
  11440 13376
Bibliographical crossword. 293
Bibliographical miscellanies. 6264
Bibliographical notes (Baker Street J). 10295–7
  10299 10304 10306–7
— (Dublin Mag). 1:1652p; 2:653; 3077 8236
  9859 9894 11448 11964–5 12624 13583
  13746 13850 14073

Bibliographical notes (Irish Bk). 1838–9 1841 1945
  1989 3280 4811 5231–2 7552 9964 10730
  12182 13854–8 14597–8
— *(J Botany).* 6947
— *(TLS).* 2:736 1211; 637 848 1080 2328
  2925 2942 2956 3026 4088 4983 5291 6861
  6866 7606 7648–9 7752 7755 8254 8836
  8868 9056 9315 10080 10085 10096
  10110 10629 10873 10934 11423 11430
  11434 11985 12238 12367 12502 12614
  13197 13476 13481 13621 14033 14476
  14610
— *(Welsh Bib Soc J).* 1:962s; 929 1460 1463–7
  1488 1541 1548 1550 4127 4897g 5989
  6516 6555 7006 7261 11535 12106
  14017
Bibliographical notes and news (London Merc).
  455–7 460 2750 7959 8261 10743
Bibliographical notes and queries. 1:121a
*Bibliographical notes on works concerning the algae
  (J Soc Bib Nat Hist).* 6968
Bibliographical society, Cambridge *see* Cambridge bibliographical society.
Bibliographical society, Edinburgh *see* Edinburgh bibliographical society.
Bibliographical society, Glasgow *see* Glasgow bibliographical society.
Bibliographical society, London. 1:86–7 346k
  445 453 508 512 521–4 551 1281 1368
  1414–a 1426 1550 1602–3 1608 1685 1745f
  1747h–i 1832 1876 1994 2067 2612 (2816a)
  2831–2 3668 3994 4200–1 4585f 5139;
  2:892; 325 1056 1275–6 1356 2154 2897
  3409 3411 3414 3417 3422 3434 3444 3462
  5199 5744 5761 6042 6056 6060 6284 6575
  6583 8455 9867 10670 11887 12710 14435
  14562
— *Library.* 1:104
— *Illustrated monographs.* 1053 1353 1355
  2051a 6661 6670 7588
— *News sheet.* 335
— *Transactions.* 1:122
— — *Supplement.* 2:1443
Bibliographical society, Oxford *see* Oxford bibliographical society.
Bibliographical society of America. 1:88 90–1
  447 463 483
— *Papers.* 1:123
Bibliographical society of Chicago. 102
Bibliographical society of Ireland. 1:162;
  4568 14059
— *Publications.* 1:124
Bibliographical society of Lancashire. 103
  6456
Bibliographical society of the University of Virginia *see* Virginia. University. Bibliographical society.
— *Papers* see *Studies in Bibliography.*

Bibliographical supplements to British book news.
  1:3
Bibliographic index. 1:42
*Bibliographic notes on works concerning the algae
  (J Soc Bib Nat Hist).* 8158
Bibliographies of Guy's men. 1:2461 2595 3744
  3788 4000 4712
Bibliographies of Irish authors. 1:4361 4377
Bibliographies of modern authors. 1:680 682 685
  2389 2426 2437 2460 2463 2531 2545 2784
  2862 2968 2998 3166 (3249) 3314 3363
  3479 3583 3652–3 3746 3830 4013 4132
  4209 4274 4319 4331 4430z 4433 4474
  4576 4711 4759 4778 4940 (4977) 5200
Bibliographies of modern authors (London Merc).
  13607
Bibliographies of modern Welsh authors. 1:2967b
  2971b 3272g 3273n 3750k 4097h
Bibliographies of 1916 and the Irish revolution.
  1:2746 2791 2813 3312 3533 4092f 4109
  4365 4404
Bibliographies of younger reputations. 1:2859
Bibliography (TLS). 7481 11454 11899 12013
  12038 12243 13003 13217
Bibliography and sales (TLS). 2997 6767 8129
  8737 11772 12132
Bibliography in Britain. 1:83
Bibliography of modern authors. 1:3338q
*Bibliography: papers read at a Clark library
  seminar.* 238
Bibliolatry (Bkmns J). 2746
Bibliomanes (Bk Coll). 3183 14209
Bibliophile, A, *pseud.* 1993 2070
Bibliotheca annua. 1:617a
Bibliotheca antiquakeriana. 1:2269
Bibliotheca bibliographica Britannica. 1:15
Bibliotheca bibliographica incunabula. 1:413
Bibliotheca Lindesiana. 1:337 1460 1534 1870
  2045–6
Bibliotheck. 1:41 124
Bibliothèque de la Revue de littérature comparée.
  1:4829c
Bibliothèque nationale, Paris *see* France. Bibliothèque nationale, Paris.
Bićanić, Sonia. 14124
Bickle, Catherine H.W. 1:2240qc
Bickley, A.C. 2460–3
Biddulph, H. 6929
Biella, Arnold. 1:1640
Biemer, Günter. 1:4334c
Bien, Peter. 1:3414e
Biggane, Cecil. 1:4157
Bigger, F.C. 1:2459r
Bigger, Francis Joseph. 1:2434 2673 3138
  4990; 1753 1845 1863 2697 5009 10401
  12472–3 14173
Bigham, Clive C., 2d viscount Mersey.
  1:1389d; 5568

Bigmore, Edward Clements. 1:1139zy
Bilderbeck, J.D. 1:440
Bill, E. Geoffrey W. 3366 6888
Billing, Herbert S. 10622
Billings, Harold W. 13413
Bindings from Oxford libraries (Bod Lib Rec). 5061
Bindoff, Stanley Thomas. 1:4325e
Binfield, Ralph. 14444
Bingley, Barbara. 4033
Binns, Norman Evan. 1:1231; 264
Binyon, Robert Lawrence. 1:2473b; 8577 8584
Biographica et bibliographica (Nat Lib Wales J). 3018 3334 3346 4636 4942 5368 8263 9853 10625 11532 12221 12673 14002 14338
Biographics of eminent English booksellers (Morriss's Trade J). 4435 4470 4897a 5481
Birch, Brian. 11345–6
Birch, J.G. 4255–6 9254
Bird, A.J. 13648
Bird, E.S. 9828
Bird, Tom. 7709
Birkbeck, J.A. 6105 10780
Birkenough, Edwyn. 8059
Birley, Pauline. 1:4793
Birley, sir Robert. 1:880 1613; 3197–8 3235a 3332 5393
Birmingham. Central school of arts and crafts. School of printing. 1:1266a; 1435 3919 3921 3924 3926 3929 3983 4191 4310
— Public libraries. 1:479 946–a 1252b 3846–7; 2:237
— — Reference dept. 1:2032
— — Shakespeare memorial library. 2:177 238 301 330
— University. Library 1:1255 3385–6
— — Shakespeare institute. 1:3523
Birmingham, William. 1:3511
Birney, Earle. 1:4077c
Birrell, Augustine. 2741 3512–3 8939
Birrell, T.A. 10386 10388
Birrell and Garnett, ltd., London. 1:1201 1851
Birss, John Howard. 996 11832 12716 12986 13732
Bischoff, D. Anthony. 1:3703b
Bishop, Alison. 7254
Bishop, Leila R.M. 1:811
Bishop, Morchard. 9559 9662 13965
Bishop, Philippa. 1:2418
Bishop, W.C. 6923
Bishop, William John. 1:2225 4348
Bishop, William Warner. 1:536 537 539; 652
Bishop Lonsdale college of education, Derby. Library. 1:1573e
Bissell, E.E. 10799 12884 13822 14433

Bissett, John. 1:4563
Biswanger, Raymond Adam. 1:3222; 10410
Bizet, George. 1:2919
Black, A. and C., ltd. 499
Black, Duncan. 9322
Black, Frank Gees. 1:1693
Black, George Fraser. 1:922y 967 4108; 9028 9032
Black, Gerard. 1580
Black, Hester Mary. 1:(2310) (4270) 4356 (4432) 4782 4867 5206; 1694a 1836 2238 3297 13852
Black, Matthew Wilson. 1:2523j; 2:879–80 1656
Black, Michael H. 6889 6892
Black, Robert Denin Collison. 1:2172
Black, Robert K. 7311
Black, William George. 13800
Black art. 1:126
Blackburn, F. 2:362
Blackburn, Thomas H. 8658
Blackie, Agnes A.C. 4057
Blackie, Walter W. 4055–6
Blackstock, C.M. 1:811g
Blackwell, sir Basil Henry. 5633 5638
Blackwood, George W. 13180
Blackwood, Isabella C. 4062a
Blades, Rowland Hill. 4239
Blades, William. 1:560 1266p; 2398–9 2401 2496 3699 4161 4262 6261 6264 6329
Blagden, Cyprian Claude. 1:1139h; 878 1070 1714 3488–9 3570 3572 3680 3991 4183 5100 5524–5 5753 5758–60 5763–4 5767–8 5925 6117 6126 6736 6762 6790 7690
Blagg, Thomas Matthews. 1:932
Blair, C.H. 1565
Blair, Frederick G. 4890
Blair, Oswald Hunter. 3723 4522 8218
Blake, A.E. 4383
Blake, Caesar Robert. 1:4515b
Blake, John B. 7568
Blake, Martin J. 1:1055q
Blake, Norman Francis. 1:1285p; 4332–3 4337–41 4345–a 4346 4348 4350
Blake, Robert N.W. 1:(3149)
Blakey, Dorothy. 1:1368; 5195–6 5199 5201
Blakiston, H.E.D. 5733 8801
Blakiston, Jack M.G. 1:2845; 3312 3382b 14246
Blanchard, Frederic T. 1:3300c
Blanchard, Rae. 1:4771–4; 7773 13598
Blanck, Jacob. 1:(5076g)
Bland, David Farrant. 1:1735; 6214–17
Bland, Desmond Sparling. 1:1544 1594 1598 2197f
Bland, R.K. 981
Blandford, G.F. 4016
Blanford, H.F. 8132

Bridge, D. 5193a
Bridge, W.E. 1158g
Bridgeport, Conn. Sacred heart university *see* Sacred heart university, Bridgeport, Conn.
Bridgett, T.A. 12491
Bridwell, Margaret M. 1:2935g
Bridwell library *see* Dallas. Southern Methodist university. Perkins school of theology. Bridwell library.
Briggs, Asa. 1:1923 4553f; 1420
Briggs, Grace M. 1:934
Briggs, Ronald C.H. 1:1354 2824 4303–4; 5925
Briggs, W.G. 12127
Briggs, William D. 11544
Brigham, Clarence Saunders. 1:1893 2986
Bright, Allan H. 14212
Brightfield, Myron F. 1:1921 2920
Brighton. Public libraries. 1:430 444d 480 1479
Brigstocke, G.R. 3971
Brimmell, R.A. 10303
Brink, Andrew. 10451
Brink, Helen. 10451
Brinkley, R. Florence. 9540–1 9543
Brinnin, John Malcolm. 1:4934d
Brinton, Howard H. (8092)
Briquet album. 3805
Briscoe, John d'Auby. 10692
Briscoe, John Potter. 1:928; 1092 1314 1329 4114 8654
Brissenden, A.T. 4563
Brissenden, R.F. 1:4707s
Bristol. College of technology. School of printing. 3946
— Public libraries. 1:421 543 610 896p 1152 1484 1494 1855 2333a 2776 4207 4741
Britain in pictures. 6107
British academy. 1:1270g; 2:118
— *Annual Shakespeare lecture.* 2:735 792 857–8 866 872 874 891
British and foreign bible society. Library. 1:1471 1500
British book centre, New York. 2:121
British books. 1:191
British books in print. 1:1184e
British Columbia. University. Library. 1:4246
British drama league, London. Library. 1:1589b–c
British library *see* British museum
British library of political and economic science, London. 1:107
British magazine. 1:643
British medical association. 1:2226
British museum. 1:507 1149f 1154 (1462) 1474 1520 1573f 1760k 2033k 3568 4496 5192; 2:207; 1286a 2214 3205 3222 3379 3437 3452 7404 7457 7620 7623

— Dept. of manuscripts. 1:1650c; 7231
— Dept of printed books. 1:102 431 491 1283 1448 1795m 1848 2587a 2613a 2636 2679 2690a 2781d 2835 2985 3073 3098 3955; 2:173 239; 5839a
— — Thomason collection. 1:1972
— Map room. 1:1770
British paper and board makers' association. Technical section. 3781
British printer. 1:144
British records association. 1:1326
British union-catalogue of early music. 1:1837
Brittain, Frederick. 1:2276f 4475–6
Brittain, Robert E. 1:4699; 13458–9
Britten, James. 1:(4992); 6947
Britton, Charles J. 1:2154d 4329
Britton, John. 1200
Britton, Margaret C. 1:3150d
Broad, Charles Lewis. 1:4630
Broad, V.M. 1:4630
Broadbent, Henry. 10830
Broadhurst, Peter L. 1:2644h
Brocklebank, M.P. 2829
Brockway, Duncan. 1:3484; 10792
Brockwell, Maurice W. 4642 10698 14259
Brodribb, A. Gerald N. 1:2156y
Brodribb, C.W. 1:3501a; 12332
Brodribb-Irving, sir John Henry *see* Irving, sir John Henry Brodribb-.
Broke, John Henry Peyto Verney, baron Willoughby de *see* Verney, John Henry Peyto, baron Willoughby de Broke.
Bromby, E.H. 5863
Bromhill, Kentley. 10117–8 10123–4
Bromley, James. 9171 13613 14309
Bromley. Public library. 1:901
Bromwich, John. 6418
Bronson, Bertrand Harris. 1:4523; 2:1093 1238; 6135 9042 13043–4
Bronson, Walter Cochrane. 1:2844
Brontë, Charlotte. 5675
Brontë society. 1:2534–5
— Museum and library, Haworth. 1:2538
— — Bonnell collection. 1:2540
Brook, G.L. 6544
Brooke, C.N.L. 1:2551g 3699p
Brooke, Charles Frederick Tucker. 2:54 541 897 1083 1355–6 1362 1870; 6400 12140 12144 12147 12496 14222
Brooke, John. 1:4320p
Brooke, Leslie Ernest John. 1:1857
Brooking, Cecil. 7771
Brooklyn. Public library. 1:2576 3033 3319 3457 3832 4858 4885 4905
Brooks, Aurelia Emma *see* Harlan, Aurelia Emma (Brooks).
Brooks, Charles Stephen. 2:715
Brooks, Cleanth J. 11232 12755

Cambridge, David George. 1:1841b

Cambridge antiquarian society. 4185

Cambridge bibliographical society. 1:4166; 13636

— *Transactions.* 1:147 1951

Cambridge bibliography of English literature see also *New Cambridge bibliography of English literature.* 1:28 349–50 490 627 654 1139h; 2:37 75a 835–6

Cambridge history of English literature. 2:37 75a 835–6; 6069

Cambridge manuals of science and literature. 256

Cambridge university press. 1:1245a 1278 1497; 4161 4165–6 4176

Camden, C. Carroll. 1:(3849k); 6752–3 (11508)

Cameron, James. 1:1272 1586 4697

Cameron, James Reese. 1:4112h

Cameron, Kenneth Neill. 1:4657

Cameron, Kenneth Walter. 1:3656; 2:1613–14; 3000 12367

Cameron, Mary S. 10304

Cameron, Pamela (Brand). 1:549 580

Cameron, William James. 1:579–80 614–17 643b 1997 3207 5020; 170 897a 4402 4872 5025 8005–6 8021 8024 10382 10804 12766 12870

Caming, Marion. 1:404

Camp, G.C. 2:1714

Campbell, A. Albert. 1:1127 1946 3392m 3459p 4006t 4047f 4263b; 1770–2 1952 1973–5 6466

Campbell, Evans. 7402

Campbell, Hilbert H. 8234

Campbell, James. 14005

Campbell, James Dykes. 1:2582i 2826x; 5246 9171 9508 11805–6 14489

Campbell, Lily B. 619 628 635

Campbell, Nancie. 1:2637

Campbell, Olwen W. 2:739

Campbell, Stella C. 2:739

Campbell, Theophila C. 4182a

Campi Phlegræ. 1:3562

Canberra. National library of Australia *see* Australia. National library. Canberra.

Candy, Hugh Charles Herbert. 1:4234; 8857–8 9605 9756 10867 12327–8 12333 12343 12350 12360–1 12365

Canney, Margaret Bérengère Campbell. 1:359 4389 4585

Cannon, Arthur James S. 1:2184

Cannon, Garland Hampton. 1:3862

Cannon, I.C. 6146

Cannons, H.G.T. 1:1139c

Cant, Monica. 1:1638

Cant, Ronald Gordon. 1:1000

Cantrell, Paul L. 2:1735 1810

Canzler, David G. 11073

Cape Town, S.A. University. School of librarianship. 1:3531 4067 4513

Capell, H.W. 4954

Caplan, Albert. 1:4602

Caplan, H.G. 2:245d

Caplan, Harry. 1:2062d

Capper, J.B. 7752

Caracciolo, Peter. 10392

Carberry, Eugene. 1:3149v

Carbondale. Southern Illinois university *see* Illinois. Southern Illinois university, Carbondale.

Card, Robert A. 1:2185

Cardew, F. 6958

Cardiff. Public libraries. 1:953 1475 1485 2125; 2:191 208

Caretti, Laura. 1:3261

Cargill, O. 2:(438) (788)

Carhart, Margaret Sprague. 1:2378

Carl H. Pforzheimer library, N.Y. 1:4657

Carlisle. Public libraries. 1086

Carlow, George Lionel S. Dawson-Damer, viscount *see* Damer, George Lionel S. Dawson-, viscount Carlow.

Carlson, Carl Lennart. 1:1902a; 4214 7763

Carlson, Leland H. 1:3428

Carlson, Marvin. 1:1651 4635

Carlson, Norman E. 14472

Carlton, William J. 1:2280; 2964 3677 4432 6358 6751 7062 8172–8 8770–1 10138 10168 12714 12898

Carlton, William Newnham Chattin. 1:4230d 4652a; 2834 9035 10831 11285 12339 14182

Caryle's house memorial trust. 1:2706r–s; 9276–7

Carnall, G.D. 1:2671d

Carnegie institute of technology, Pittsburgh *see* Pittsburgh. Carnegie institute of technology.

Carnegie university. Library school. Library. 1:1553

Carnie, Robert Hay. 1:41 1006 2944; 1623–4 1627 1629 1676 1735–6 9791

Carnon, R.J.F. 1:2045; 885 7061 13689

Caro, A.E. 1:2485x

Carpenter, Andrew Isdell-. 8399

Carpenter, Charles C. 1:4625

Carpenter, Edward. 1:2713–14

Carpenter, Frederic Ives. 1:4752; 7105

Carpenter, George Rice. 1:4770k

Carpenter, James. 1:3477d

Carpenter, Kenneth E. 1004

Carrick, John Charles. 4427

Carr, Charles T. 1:1726a

Carr, Gerard. 1808

Carr, sr. Lucile *see* Carr, sr. Mary Callista.

Carr, sr. Mary Callista. 1:3099 3103

Carré, Jean-Marie. 1:821b
Carrington, Noel. 6788
Carroll, Diana J. 1:643b
Carroll, F. 1822 1925 4119
Carruthers, Samuel William. 1:2042; 1500 8042
Carruthers, William. 1:2038 2042
Carson, Alice Morgan. 9363
Carson, W.G.B. 3116
Carswell, John. 13140 13243
Carter, A.C.R. 2:1398; 484 2835
Carter, Alan. 1:4376a
Carter, Albert Howard. 1:1611; 2:1487 1978a
Carter, Arthur J. 5732
Carter, F.C. 11240
Carter, Frederick. 11933
Carter, G.E.L. 2:1031
Carter, Harry Graham. 1:1192 1195-7 1200 1207 1217 1374 3283g 4290; 846 1371 3784 4198 4479 4659-60 4922 5359 5361 5366 5364 5930 6371 6375 6414 6577 6627 6629 6718 10089 11911 12725
Carter, Hugh Sevier. 1:3660d
Carter, John Waynflete. 1:1162 1714 1720 1746a 2566a-ae 2569 2883-4 3716 3718 3724 3728 3824 4291p-r 5133a (5141) 5149; 76 92a 149 164 261-2 295 353 365 514 572 893 989 991 2098-9 2101-2 2104 2118-21 2125 2130 2135-8 2141 2171 2246 2311 2323 2327 2350 2353-4 2356 2358-9 2365-6 2369 2372 2374 2379 2388 2392-4 3001 3150 3285 3998 4001a 4725-7 4766 5214a 5218a 6286-7 6528 6940 7265-6 7270 7274 (7298-9) 7303 (7425) (7600) 8390 8481-2 8489 8536 8549 8610 8671 8832-4 8836 8841-2 8844-5 8850 8853 8853a 8866-7 8871 8881 9205 10140 10175 10398 10426 10428 10843 11122 11157 11161-3 11168 11178 11186 11190 11195-6 11202-4 11206 11209-10 11212 11216 11222-4 11227 11245 11795 12012 12037 12080 12239 12241 12289 12568 12592 12884 13254-5 13321 13368 13399 13520 13657 13659 13693 13877 13925 13959-61 14126 14205 14387 14396-7 14402 14410-11 14415 14420-1 14428 14434 14443 14445-6 14449 14453 14455 14578
Carter, Kenneth. 1:3603
Carter, Margaret J. 1:1601a
Carter, Pierson Cathrick. 2:531
Carter, W.T. 2665
Carter, Will. 5497 5499 8582
Carter, William. 1818 6310
Carteret book club. 6464
Cartledge, J.H. 3136
Carty, Charles F. 1:3032a

Caruthers, S.W. see Carruthers, Samuel William.
Carver, Patrick L. 891
Cary, Elisabeth Luther. 1:(3801) 4541b 4542b
Cary, Richard. 1:4783c
Casaide, Séamus úa see ÓCasaide, Séamus.
Case, Arthur Ellicott. 1:1994 4441; 12822-3 13754
Case, Ritt. 9520
Casey, Maie. 1:2886
Cash, C.G. 1:968
Cashmore, Herbert Maurice. 1:946-a; 508 1155 1417 2882 3813 3934 4624 4720 7967 9601
Caskey, John Homer. 1:4263m; 7741 12550
Caslon, H.W. and company. 4186
Caslon, R. 4199
Cason, Clarence E. 8386
Cassedy, James, see also ÓCasaide, Séamus. 1:732 1014 1018 1121 1132 1175 2897 3426 4083 4378-9; 1764
Cassell and co., pubs., London. 1:1280n
Casson, Leslie F. 2:573; 3261 3298
Catalogue of English books. 1:556
Catchpole, P.A. 4163
Cate, Chester March. 495 9142
Cattaui, Georges. 1:3257g 3260
Cattle, Frederic. 13887
Cauthen, Irby B. 2:1457 12603
Cavanaugh, sr. Jean Carmel. 3383
Cavazza, E. 1:(4962)
Cave, L.F. 4215
Cave, Roderick. 1:1235 1287f 1329n 1347r 1399y; 4111 4384 4753 4951 5596 5654-5 6390
Cave, Thomas. 3916 3924
Cavenagh, F.A. 1479
Cawley, R.R. 8835
Caxton club, Chicago. 1:3321; 2038 4007 4328 5168 5388 10100
Cecil, Evelyn. 1:2186
Cecil, Robert Arthur James Gascoyne-, 5th marquis of Salisbury. 3329 3384
Celer et audax, pseud. 1312 7655
Census of fifteenth century books. 1:447
Century of the English book trade. 3411
Chadwick, Esther Alice. 1:3405-6
Chadwick, Hubert S. 3223
Chadwick, Owen. 3132
Chadwick, T.L. 6701
Chalk, Edwin S. 7765 8190
Chalklin, Christopher William. 1158
Chaloner, W.H. 12900
Chambers, Charles Edward Stewart. 1:719b (1285x) 2754-5 (2756) 4037; 748
Chambers, David. 1:1240g; 2380 4464 4754 5701

Chambers, sir Edmund Kerchever. 2:60 90 858 863 867 1563 1768 1802; 4952 7129 12738
Chambers, George. 2557
Chambers, L.H. 4122 7660
Chambers, L.R. 8805
Chambers, Raymond Wilson. 2:1019 1886 1902; 556
Chambers, Robert. 4355
Chambers, William. 4356–7
Chambers, W. and R. ltd. 10824
Champenois, J.J. 7710 7718
Champneys, Norma Hull (Hodgson), lady Dalrymple *see* Russell, Norma Hull (Hodgson).
Chancellor, E. Beresford. 6471
Chandler, Edmund. 12668
Chandler, George. 1:4537; 4043 13076
Chandler, John E. 5096 5098
Chandler, Lloyd Horwitz. 1:3950; 11750
Chandler, William K. 12825 12911
Chanter, H. Prosser. 2780 3723 6704 7880
Chanticleer. 1:1332
Chap-book. 6327
Chapin, Howard M. 1:1305m; 4539–40
Chapin library *see* Williams college, Williamstown, Mass. Chapin library.
Chapman, Guy. 1:2415; 8479–80 8455
Chapman, Raymond. 2:1842
Chapman, Robert William. 1:364 1309–10 (2364) 2366a–8 3842b 3843–4 4485 4987; 2:882; 112 120–1 129 349 377 383 488 498–9 733 2151 2285 2305–6 2312 2358 2360 3445 3594 3596 3601 3641 3725 3744 6150–2 6280 6293 6334 6351 6517 8244 8311 8235 8238–9 8332–3 8336–7 8339–40 8343 8372 8555 8676–7 8680 8686 8695 8810 9399 9713 10752 10761 11387 11390–1 11393–8 11405 11413–14 11418–19 11425 11435 11442 11445–6 11450–3 11455–7 11459 11466 12035 12111 12338 12787 12790 12909 12965 13211 13220–1 13382 13393 14027 14094 14096–101 14105–6 14109 14115 14117 14180 14301 14511 14607 14610 14612
Chappell, Edwin. 1:4412–13; 12713 12715 12717
Chappell, Fred A. 1:5055
Chapple, John Arthur Victor. 9458 9460 11501 12870 13135
Chare, Penrhyn. 2:1398
Charles, Amy M. 11793
Charles, B.G. 3104 12636–7
Charles university, Prague *see* Prague. Charles university.
Charlton, H.B. 2:1481–2; 7883
Chancellor, E. Beresford. 7890

Charney, Maurice. 1:3702
Charteris, Evan Edward. 1:3479d
Chartist centenary committee, Newport. 1:3365
Charles Dickens library. 9997a
Chatto and Windus, ltd. 13802
Chaundy, Leslie. 1:2390 2526 3490; 8267
Chawner, George. 1:432
Chaytor, Henry J. 384
Checklist bibliographies of modern authors. 1:3364 3665 3690 5152
Checklists of twentieth-century authors. 1:685c
Cheney, Christopher Robert. 1:1286; 1347b 4366–7 4777
Chernaik, Judith. 13370
Cherry, T.A.F. 3330
Chesson, Wilfrid Hugh. 1:3916
Chester, Allan Griffith. 8100 8407 9449 11561
Chesterfield. Library and museum committee. 1:4786m
Chesterton, Gilbert Keith. 1:3356 3630 5005 5025d
Chetham society. 1:1778 1792
Chevron, *pseud.* 6268
Chew, Beverly C. 1:396 2661 5006; 2524 5139 5221
Chew, S.P. 9216
Chew, Samuel Cleggett. 1:2675 2682a; 7236 7436 9182
Chewning, Harris. 9427
Cheyney, Frances. 1:3255c 3257f
Chicago. Bibliographical society *see* Bibliographical society of Chicago.
— Caxton club *see* Caxton club, Chicago.
— De Paul university *see* De Paul university, Chicago.
— Newberry library *see* Newberry library, Chicago.
— Public library. 1:3269; 2:44
— University. Library. 1:1610
Chichester papers. 1:3437c
Child, Harold. 4795
Child, John. 6145 5700
Childs, James Bennett. 1:489
Chippindall, W.H. 7495
Chisholm, Hugh. 1:4194
Chiswick. Polytechnical college. School of art. 3923
Chiswick press. 4380
Chivers, C. 4383
Chope, R. Pearce. 5235 7639 12783
Christ, Jay Finley. 1:3185
Christensen, Francis. 14522
Christensen, Glenn J. 10962
Christian, Mildred G. 1:2541d; 8781
Christie, George. 1:3223
Christie, Ian R. 1:21
Christie, John. 13491

Christie, Manson and Woods, ltd., London. 2:181

Christie, Richard Copley. 175

Christie-Miller, Sydney Richardson *see* Miller, Sydney Richardson Christie-.

Christophers, Richard Albert. 1:2300b

Christophersen, Hans Oskar. 1:4069

Christy, Bayard H. 6917

Christy, Robert Miller. 1:4820q

Chrystal, George. 2064

Chubb, Thomas. 1:1762 (1770) 1786–7 1798 1802 1809

Church, A.H. (2023a)

Church, C.M. 2568a 2569

Church, Elihu Dwight. 1:387

Church, Elizabeth. 3889

Church, R. 7977

Churchill, George B. 1:1331; 10340

Churchill, Irving L. 12744 13371 13374

Churchill, William Algernon. 3797

Church of England. Central council for the care of churches. Committee to investigate the number and condition of parochial libraries belonging to the Church of England. 2446

Churchman, Philip H. 1:2679e 4601

Chwalewik, Witold. 2:1249

Civis, *pseud.* 979

Clair, Colin. 1:1366; 868 (3475) 4011 5900 6124 6142 6620 6890 8147

Clancy, Joseph P. 1:2355

Clancy, Thomas H. 1:2262 2266a

Clapp, Clifford B. 1:1490

Clapp, John Mantle. 7280

Clapp, Sarah L.C. 5318 6557–8

Clapperton, Robert Henderson. 3754 3757 3785

Claremont, Calif. Honnold library for the Associated colleges *see* Honnold library for the Associated colleges, Claremont, Calif.

Clarence, Reginald, *pseud.* 1:1588

Clareson, Thomas D. 1:3774

Clariores e tenebris, *pseud.* 2780

Clark, Alexander Frederick Bruce. 1:809

Clark, Andrew. 2592a

Clark, Arthur Melville. 1:3658; 11075

Clark, Cecily. 4308

Clark, Charles. 1:1336; 2:807–8; 1143

Clark, Cumberland. 273a

Clark, Ethel B. 11683

Clark, Evert Mordecai. 6885 6887b

Clark, John Willis. 1:4616f; 2402 2412a 2532a

Clark, Leonard. 1:3003–4 5211

Clark, Lilian G. 1:481

Clark, Lucy. 1:80; 6682

Clark, R. 13678–9

Clark, Ronald William. 1:(3549j)

Clark, Ruth. 1:3560

Clark, T. Hannam-. 1121

Clark, sir Wilfrid Edward LeGros. 1:3916n (4944)

Clark, William Andrews. 1:341 574 664 (1314) 1349 (2932) 3068–9 5102

Clark, William Andrews, memorial library *see* California. University. University at Los Angeles. William Andrews Clark memorial library.

Clark, William Smith. 1:2519; 8733–4 13414

Clarke, Archibald L. 1204 11971

Clarke, Cecil. 2:648; 1144 1397 3545 3582 5142 7660 7872 7875 11110 14314

Clarke, D.A. 1:1305

Clarke, Derek A. 1:80

Clarke, Desmond J. 1:1016h; 1823–4 1826 1830 1923 1986 1989

Clarke, sir Ernest. 6727 9395–6 10556 12907

Clarke, Frederick. 1:(2901)

Clarke, Harold George. 1:1259d 1259f; 3963 3965a

Clarke, Ignatius Frederick. 1:1669

Clarke, John S. 13486

Clarke, M.L. 12880

Clarke, Olive E. 1:1186c

Clarke, Stella Marjorie. 1:2386f

Clarke, Thomas Edward S. 1:(2624)

Clarke, William James. 1:930; 1342 1344 11734 11738 11764

Clarkson, Paul S. 11630 11634

Clary, William Webb. 1346–7

Clavel, Robert. 1:618–21

Clay, Charles. 14102

Clay, William M. 6853

Clayton, Cuthbert A. 1754

Clayton, E.G. 7655

Clayton, Herbert B. 4738 5446 6349 6838 7830 7848 7872 8239 13129 13974

Clayton, Thomas S. 2:1256 1917–18

Clear, Gwendoline Frances. 5692

Cleaver, A.H. 1:3081

Clegg, Samuel. 2647 2654

Clemens, Cyril. 14427

Clement-Janin. 4628

Clements, A.L. 1:4976f

Clements, Henry J.B. 2117 2139 2142 2639 2650 2666 2689 2857 2864 2866 2934 3721 13532 14215

Clements, Jeff. 1:2495; 8652 13062

Clements, Philip C. 678

Clements library *see* Michigan. University. William L. Clements library.

Clendening, London. 2:72

Cleveland. Medical library. 1:2195
— Public library. 1:4295
— Rowfant club *see* Rowfant club, Cleveland.
Cleverdon, Douglas. 1:3434u; 5218a 9488 14011–a
Clifford, James Lowry. 1:3834–5 4425a; 3380a 12789 13253 (13762) 13780
Cline, C.L. 1:4203; 10940 12253 13989
Clinton, W. Willis. 3794
Clitheroe, Barbara M. 1:2711
Clodd, Alan. 14257b 14258a
Clogstown, C.C. 3778
Closs, A. 13965
Clough, Eric A. 1:593
Clouston, W.A. 6809 13452
Clow, R. Austen. 1238
Clowes, Alice A. 1:3966; 5027
Clowes, William Beaufoy. 4392
Clowes, William Laird. 6507
Club of odd volumes, Boston. 3432 4247 4281 4287 5804 8574
Clubb, Merrel D. 11643–6
Clulow, George. 2593 10722
Clulow, Peter. 9167
Clyde, William McCallum. 3501 3503 3556 9772
Coates, Adrian. 3238
Coates, J.A.H. 2:1432
Coates, Willson Havelock. 1:1903
Cobden-Sanderson, Thomas James *see* Sanderson, Thomas James Cobden-.
Coburn, Kathleen. 9553
Cochrane, James Aikman. 5796 14128
Cochrane, Peter. 5792
Cochrane, Robert. 1702
Cock, F. William. 1062 1154–5 1159 2092 3723 4180 5050 6356 8056 8061
Cockalorum. 1:1334
Cockerell, Douglas. 4393
Cockerell, sir Sydney Carlyle. 1:1347x 1350 1353; 65 400 3093 4946 4964–6 4975 4986 6488 7977 10953
Cockle, H.D. 1:2231
Cockle, Maurice James Draffen. 1:2231
Codling, sir William R. 5013
Codlock, Roger. 8514
Coe, Charles Norton. 1:5175a
Coffin, Charles M. 10234
Coffin, Edward Francis. 1:2709; 9284
Coffin, Louis. 1:3637
Coggeshall, Edwin Walter. 1:3066b
Coghill, Nevill Henry K. 2:1625 1831
Cohen, Denis. 92a
Cohen, Edward H. 1:3704
Cohen, Henry, baron Cohen. 1:4674b
Cohen, Jane R. 4455
Cohen, Joseph. 12641–2 13077
Cohen, Morton N. 9338

Cohen, Ralph. 1:4960k
Cohn, Alan Mayer. 1:3875–8 3887; 11616
Cohn, Albert Mayer. 1:2930–1 2934 3991; 6937 10026–7 11605
Cohn, Ruby. 1:2413y–14
Colbeck, Norman. 1:5034; 5226a
Colburn, William E. 1:5; 5910–11
Colby, Elbridge. 1:3683–a; 194 7012 11111 13382
Colby, Robert A. 1:4366h
Colby, Vineta. 1:4366h; 12615
Colby college, Waterville, Me. Library. 1:148 3575 3588 3590–2
Colby library quarterly. 1:148
Coldicott, H. Rowlands S. 12784
Cole, Arthur. 330
Cole, George Douglas Howard. 1:2820a
Cole, George Watson. 1:66 88 387 514–15; 2:184 405 527; 113–14 118 178 190–1 315 317 496 606 609 2283 2286 6148 6278 7113 12053–6 14253–4
Cole, H. 10276
Cole, Richard C. 8719
Colebrook, Frank. 4959
Colebrook, Leonard. 1:5188
Coleman, A.M. 1705 9711
Coleman, Arthur Prudden. 1:834–6
Coleman, Carroll D. 4518
Coleman, Donald Cuthbert. 3758–9 3761a 3762 3765
Coleman, Earle E. 6339
Coleman, Edward Davidson. 1:1589f 1596 2199
Coleman, Everard Home. 706 750 1016 1167 1193 1195 1354 1452 2405 2407 2557 2560 2581 2605 3579 3703–4 3786 3860 4099 4644–5 4804 5133 5267 5409 5881 5897 5905 6267 6505 6656 6723–4 7000 7484 7655 7701–2 7825 8191 8218 9173 9613 10723 10736 11707 12315 12536 12800 13679 14241 14296
Coleman, J.J. 1:924
Coleman, James. 1:1055q 1095 1128 4095 4824m 5095; 12606 12891
Coleman, Marion Moore. 1:834–6
Coleman, S.A. 3772
Colenutt, Fabian. 13303
Coleridge, Ernest Hartley. 1:2678 2828y
Coles, William Allan. 1:4259 (4875); 11690 12462
Colgate, Henry A. 1:4806
Colgrave, Bertram. 8494
Collamore, H.B. 992 11157
Collections (Texas Q). 3285
Collectors and collections (Manuscripts). 8477a
Collector's piece (Bk Coll). 924 8853a
College of St. Mark and St. John, London. Library. 1:2033

Copinger, Walter Arthur. 1:415–17g 824
1936; 304 307 546 13014
Coral, Lenore. 5432
Corbet, A. Steven. 6980 8558
Cordasco, Francesco G.M. 1:628–a 1267
1690 1727 2620 2846 3029 3298 3420 3461
3896–8 3900a (4492) 4517 4706 4715–17
4722 4788 5037 5214; 2:80; 4091c 5192
8116 9467 10584 11631–5 11637–8 11641
13040 13498–501 13503–4 14336
Cordeaux, Edward Harold. 1:933–a 937b
Corder, Jim W. 2:(249)
Cordier, Jean. 1:4116a
Cordingley, James. 3965c
Corey, T.C.S. 9171
Corfield, W. 11732
Corkey, E. 8869
Corley, Nora T. 1:2104
Cornelius, Roberta D. 7140
Cornell, Louis L. 1:3959; 11785
Cornell university. Library. 1:5172 5174 5176
— Studies in English. 2:1720; 5541
Cornett, J.P. 1109 5564p
Cornfield, Violet May. 1256
Corns, Albert Reginald. 1:913 2074–5; 1185
Cornu, D. 13744
Corrigan, Andrew J. 6115
Corson, James Clarkson. 1:1544b 1938a
4595x–6 4690a; 8744 10889–90 11103
13219 13234 13236
Corsten, Severin. 5653
Cortissoz, Royal. 1:3063
Correspondence (London Merc). 5051 6703 7890
8026 8327 8497 8832 9186 9487 9757
10277 10349 10500 10919 10947 11824
12166 12190 13064 13303 13560 13607
14012 14088 14265 14579
Cosin's library, Durham see Durham. University. Library.
Coslet, Walter A. 6886
Costa, Richard Haner. 1:(4077d) 5053x
Cotterell, S.J.A. 8076
Cotterell, Samuel. 1:2249–a
Cotton, Albert Louis. 4963
Cottrell, G.W. 6919
Cotton, John. 1:1322g
Couchman, Gordon W. 10466–7
Coulson, E.G. 2:1324
Council for psychical investigation see London. University. Council for psychical investigation.
Couper, Sydney C. 1573 1577
Couper, William James. 1:1005d 1367 1394
1932–3 1934x 5154; 1574 1577 1585 1599
1654 1665a 1673 1688–90 1692 1733–4
2722 3835 4690 4712 4723 5191 5582–3
5912 5955–9 6744 9466 11386
Courthorpe, William John. 3617a 5239

Courtney, Charles J. 1:944h
Courtney, F. 3224
Courtney, W.L. 1:3445 4004
Courtney, William Prideaux. 1:1307 3838;
838 2672 4558 6769 7344 8653 10818
11385 14314
Courtney-Lewis, Helen see Lewis, Helen Courtney-.
Coustillas, Pierre. 1:3442 3451; 10707–11
Coventry. Public libraries. 1:2866f 3248f
Covington, W.H. 13167
Cowan, Charles F. 8160
Cowan, Patricia Mary. 1:3968a
Cowan, Robert Ernest. 1:341 574 664 1349
3069 5102
Cowan, Samuel. 4420a
Cowan, William. 1:442 1340 1343 1506
1512–13 1817 4061; 1553 4522 5991d 6835
6899
Cowen, David L. 1:2221a; 1713 1714a
Cowie, Alfred T. 11599
Cowgill, Logan O. 12768
Cowley, E. 5114
Cowley, John Duncan. 1:2212–13; 134 209
244 7475–6 13227
Cowling, Geoffrey Charles. 1:1801; 7514
Cowling, George Herbert. 2:1122
Cowper, B.H. 1:1345a
Cox, Edward Godfrey. 1:861
Cox, Edwin Marion. 1:3657; 599 2711 8856
8858 11043 11058 12801
Cox, Euan Hillhouse Methuen. 1:343 2526
Cox, Harold. 5095a 5096
Cox, J. Randolph. 1:2598a 3816a
Cox, Leslie Reginald. 1:4714n
Cox, Nigel S.M. (168)
Coxhead, Eileen Elizabeth. 1:3528
Coykendall, Frederick. 1:2528 4480; 6525
10902–3 11836 11863 11982 11984–5
Crabbe, George. 9738
Crabhorn, Edwin. 4282
Cragsley, pseud. 1570
Craig, Alec. 3506 11932
Craig, C. Leslie. 5084
Craig, Gordon. 2:209
Craig, Hardin. 1:490 2239–40; 2:438 442
926 939 1279 1313 1315 (1438) 1467;
(3976) 4915 7185
Craig, Mary Elizabeth. 1:1935; 1600
Craig, Maurice. 14583
Craig, Maurice James. 1:4838; 1820 1825
1843
Craig, Robert, and sons. 1:4421m
Craigie, Dorothy (Glover). 1:1720
Craigie, James. 1:3790–2; 11323–4
Craigie, William A. 12312 13073
Craik, George L. 14490
Craik, T.W. 14141

Cranbrook, John David Gathorne-Hardy, earl of *see* Hardy, John David Gathorne-, earl of Cranbrook.

Crane, Joan. 1:486

Crane, Ronald Salmon. 1:49 1885; 905 10745 10753

Crane, Walter. 4425

Cranfield, Geoffrey Alan. 1:1904–5; 7800

Cranston, M. 12015

Cranstoun, James. 1:4588

Craster, sir H.H. Edmund. 2745 2936 3185 4416 8038 11794 14307

Craven, Alan E. 2:615

Crawford, Charles. 8256

Crawford, James Ludovic Lindsay, 26th earl *see* Lindsay, James Ludovic, 26th earl of Crawford.

Crawford, Jane. 2:1258

Crawford, Joseph H. 1:1723m

Crawford, O.G.S. 7497

Crawford, Walter B. 14551

Crawford, William R. 1:2780a

Crawford library, Royal observatory, Edinburgh *see* Edinburgh. Royal observatory. Crawford library.

Cree, John. 1:2792b; 2579

Creed, John W. 7700

Creed, W.T. 1:3381y

Creighton, C. 2:1971

Creighton, Louise (von Glehn). 1:2918b 3670

Cremeans, Charles Davis. 1:2149

Cremer, R.W. Ketton-. 10853 11493 11866

Cresswell, Beatrix. 1097

Cressy, Serenus. 1:(2380q)

Cret, Paul Philipe. 2:286

Crighton, Marjorie Phyllis. 1:2217

Crinò, Anna Maria. 10393

Crippen, Thomas George. 1:2271 3550q; 13487

Cripps, A.R. 2:1209

Cripps, Matthew. 1:3940d; 11729

Crittenden, Walter Marion. 1:4595k

Crockett, W.S. 13181

Croessman, Harley K. 1:3876

Croft, Peter J. 11151

Croft, sir William. 1:1264 (1273); 4130 4136

Crofts, E. Whitfield. 2497–8 6944

Cron, B.S. 3239 5570

Crone, Gerald Rae. 1:1769; 3802 7510 8214

Crone, John Smyth. 1:1115 1121x 1122c 1705m 2076 2244e 2320b 2399t 2459r 2553r 2658s 3024 3329m 3628s 3920m 4089 4274b 4824k; 29–30 39 42 54 1766 1769 1773 1775 1777 1846 1848 1858 1861–2 1867 1887–8 1955 2667 2683–4 2691 2699–703 2712–15 2726–7 2733–4 2764 2800 2958 4013 4125 5059 5110 5664 5980 6423 6466 6913 7074 7869 8984

10748 12807 14173

Cronin, Grover. 11325

Cronin, Margaret. 13884

Crook, Arthur. 5218a

Crook, Ronald Eric. 1:4462

Crooke, W. 8203

Crooks, F. 2425

Cropper, Percy J. 1:1538; 1328

Crosby, Barbara (Stevens). 1:4975c

Cross, Edward R. 4571k

Cross, Tom Peete. 1:6

Cross, Wilbur Lucius. 1:3300 4790–2; 10497

Crosse, Gordon. 2:742

Crossey, J.M.D. 1850

Crossland, Charles. 1:949k

Crossle, Philip. 1:1065

Crotch, Walter John Blyth. 4264–7 4271

Crouch, Charles Hall. 1217 4407 7717

Crous, Ernst. 551

Crow, John. 1:77 4526; 281 8752 10725 11525 13048

Crowley, Francis J. 917

Crowell, Norton B. 1:2369

Crowther, W. 2533 5667

Croydon. Public libraries. 1:1805

Cruickshank, A.H. 12199

Crum, Margaret C. 1:1986p; 7622 8233 10265 10576 11061 11918 13686 14369

Crump, Charles George. 1:3366g

Crump, G.B. 1:4012a

Crump, Galbraith M. 13590–1

Crundell, H.W. 2:886 1271 1902

Crupi, C.W. 1:4219a

Cruse, Amy. 3442 3450

Cruse, D.A. 14173

Crutchley, Ernest Addenbrooke. 261–2 4167 (4168) 5215a 5218a

Cruttwell, R.W. 2:1221

Cubbon, A.M. 1:1796

Cubbon, William. 1:923 2560; 1296

Cullen, Sara. 1:1044a

Culler, A. Dwight. 9249

Culley, Ann. 1:4317n

Culliford, Stanley George. 2:1732 1734

Culprin, A.E. 2101

Cumber, Frank. 1:2270p; 5183

Cuming, Agnes. 2:727; 3490–1 11399

Cuming, G.J. 683

Cummings, Alexander. 6315–16

Cummings, W.H. 6275 9990 14024

Cummins, Geraldine. 1:(4734)

Cunard, Nancy. 1:1344–a; 4897e

Cundall, Joseph. 4027

Cuningham, Henry. 2:1064 1081 1120 1167–8 1178 1398 1441 1484 1506 1581–2 1611–12 1615 1707 1713 1786 1788 1971

Cunliffe, Rolf, baron Cunliffe. 1:538

Cunningham, Daniel John Chapman. 1:3549n
Cunningham, Gilbert Farm. 1:831–a
Cunningham, Robert Newton. 1:4311–12
Cunnington, R.H. 2:1429
Cunnington, Susan. 4253
Curious, *pseud.* 14177
Curle, James. 13196
Curle, Richard Henry Parnell. 1:919 2855m 2866h (2941) 2941b–c 5053a; 506 3314 5515 8137–8
Curnow, Ann *see* Atkinson, Ann (Curnow).
Currie, Barton Wood. 991 2319
Currier, Margaret. 1:1254
Curry, F. 7266 7663
Curry, John T. 2:650; 879 2580 9268 13525
Curry, Kenneth. 1:1903a 4740 4743; 13540 13543
Cursiter, James Walls. 1:1005
Curtis, F.J. 7352
Curtis, James. 10737
Curtis, Lewis Perry. 13617 13619–20 13622
Curtis, Mark H. 1:1347d; 4944
Curtis, Myra. 8865
Curtiss, Lionel. 1264
Curvey, Mary F. 1:4516m
Curwen, John Flavel. 1:1779 (1808)
Curwen, Harold. 4479 6203
Curwen, John Spenser. 3582
Curwen press. 1:1294–5
Cushing, William. 1:1435
Cuthbertson, David. 2692
Cutler, Bradley Dwyane. 1:684 2398; 10056
Cutler, C.V. 1:3753
Cutter, Eric. 1:3416g
Cutter, W.P. 2:1705
Cuttle, W.L. 6942
Cutts, John P. 2:1944; 8861 9602 11917 12049 12688
Cyril, *pseud.* 12465
Czeke, Marianne. 2:56
Czerwinski, Roman. 809
Czigány, Magda M. 1:826g

D. 2070 7384 14330
D., A. 6745 9144
D., A.M. 4096
D., C. 6996 13014
D., C.E. 3712
D., C.L. 2:1163; 12816
D., E. 7001
D., H.G. 2259
D., H.W. 933 1218 8260
D., K. 2:1061a
D., K.W. 1:2493
D., L.G. 3813
D., P. 11158

D., R. 8239
D., R.E. 14263
D., T.C. 14107
D., T.F. 943 7578 9499 10835
Dąbrowska, Jana. 2:140
Dack, Charles. 1:2807
Daghlian, Philip B. 9221
Dahl, Folke. 1:1874 1876–7; 852 7684
Daiches, David. 1:2
Dain, Neville E. 2:369
Daish, Alfred Newman. 6048
Dakin, S.B. 6098a
Dale, Cragsley. 1693
Dale, Donald A. 1:5123; 12721 13347 14349 14351
Dale, P.T. 14215
Dale, T.C. 5435 5532
Dallas. Southern Methodist university. 6893
— — Perkins school of theology. Bridwell library. 1:1497d
Dallas, James. 11007 11705
Dalliba, William Swift. 10307
Dalton, Jack P. 11613 11937
Dalziel and co., ptrs., London. 1:1298q; 4491
Dam, Bastiaan Adriaanus P. van. 2:832 861 1157 1177 1439 1546 1582 1673 1711 1751–2; 6064 10871–2 11074 11540 11557 12150–1
Damer, George Lionel S. Dawson-, viscount Carlow. 1:1289
Damon, Samuel Foster. 8574
Dance, D. 3225
Danchin, Pierre. 1:4953; 7905 13786
Dandy, J.E. 6964
Dane, Clemence, *pseud.* 1:3713
Daniel, Charles Henry Olive. 1:2525
Daniel, P.A. 2:645; 11797
Daniel, Robert W. 14523
Daniels, Earl. 10433 11329
Danielson, Henry. 1:680 846 (847) 2427 (2428) 2546 (2547) 2911 (2912) 2999 (3000) 3190 (3191) 3446 (3447) 3581 3584 3830 4031 (4032) 4070 4096 4099 (4100) 4153 (4154) 4205 (4206) 4214 (4215) 4268 4430z (4431) 4855 (4860) 5008 (5008a); 4514a
Danielsson, Bror. 1:3613h
Danks, Kenneth B. 2:430 435 439–40 675 922 1225 1229 1522 1549 1655 1756; 4916
Daoust, Edward C. 1:3076c
Dapp, Kathryn Gilbert. 1:3903
Darbishire, Helen. 616 12356–8 12386 12428 13323
Dargan, Dermot J. 1806
Darley, Lionel Seabrook. 4143
Darlington, Ida. 1:1795
Darlow, G.S. 1106a
Darlow, Thomas Herbert. 1:1471 1500

Dart, Thurston. 12520

Dartle, R. 10025

Darton, Frederick J. Harvey. 1:3080; 1263 2299 5276 7015 7057 10053

Darwin, Bernard. 1:(2189t); 5558

Darwin, K. 12076–7

Daube, D. 1:3156

Davenport, Cyril James Humphrey. 1:1259e 1270m 1315k 2934d 4038i 4884g; 1190 1192 2018 2022 2025a 2026 2031 2039–40 2044 2055 2058 2061 2065–6 2068–70 2072 2078 2297 4007 5081–2 5166–9 5385 5388 5623 6191 7362 7385 9391

Davenport, William H. 13326

Davey, Samuel. 11626

Davey, W.O. 2148

David, Richard W. 2:1245

David Nichol Smith memorial seminar, Canberra. 1:4707s

Davidson, Chalmers H. 2:1324

Davidson, G.W.H. 3263

Davidson, Gustav. 8872

Davidson, W.A.G. Doyle-. 10537

Davies, A.M.E. 1:5113

Davies, Alun Eirug. 1514

Davies, Andrew McF. 9880 9979a

Davies, David W. 9162

Davies, E.C. 1376

Davies, Godfrey. 1:17 605 4467; 2:311; 385 617 9909 12553 13752

Davies, Gwenllian M. 4802 4826

Davies, H.M. 2093

Davies, H.M.P. 3331

Davies, Hugh Williams. 3629 5053a 6671

Davies, Hugh W. 3629 5053a 6671

Davies, J. Conway. 3055

Davies, J. Michael. 4803

Davis, John H. 1:1347 1461 2269 2270c; 1450 1455 1472 2668 3547 14339

Davies, M.B. 1:4050g

Davies, Marie Thérèse Jones-. 1:2996a

Davies, Sarah H. 10614–17

Davies, William. 1:700a

Davies, William David. 1:3156

Davies, William Henry. 4925 4942 9857

Davies, sir William Llewelyn. 1:697 703; 2:652p; 1386 1468 1473–6 1481 1551 5696 8263 11124 12886 14152

Davies, William Twiston. 1:2383–4; 13861

Davis, A.G. 1:1817q; 8140

Davis, Arthur Kyle. 1:2344; 8285 8308

Davis, Bernard E.C. 13561

Davis, Bertram R. 9546 11849 13535

Davis, C. Rexford. 1:2821b; 9491–2

Davis, Dorothy R. 1:1572a

Davis, E. Jeffries. 590

Davis, George W. 10041

Davis, Harold H. 898

Davis, Henry W.C. (3436)

Davis, Herbert. 11927

Davis, Herbert John. 1:77 1192 1374 4833 (5128); 81 88 281 (3536) 4100 5228 6371 6375 7783 11579 13730 13740 13750 13762 13774

Davis, Howell Ll. 14291

Davis, James Richard Ainsworth. 1:3779a

Davis, Kenneth W. 1:4714s

Davis, Mary Gould. 1:1276t

Davis, Mary Louise. 1:2390m

Davis, R.G. 13507

Davis, Richard Beale. 1:4581; 3174 13148–9 13151 13153–5 (13543)

Davis, Robert Murray. 1:3313x; 10533 14257 14257b–c 14258

Davis, Robin John. 1:2414e

Davis, Rose Mary. 1:3211

Davis, sir Rupert Hart-. 92a 10669

Davis, W. Eugene. 1:4560a

Davison, J.A. 400 14447 14478

Davison, Peter H. 11082 12298

Davy, A.J. 4516

Davys, Mary. 1:1695

Dawson, Carl. 1:4402i

Dawson, Charles E. 3961

Dawson, Giles Edwin. 2:69 226 298 474 580 655 682 743 748 764 788 893 936 940 1039 1618; 386 (649–50) (3086) 5865 6249 (6411) (6562) 7172 (7998) (8518) (10637) (11711)

Dawson, Lawrence R. 1:5111r

Dawson, N.F. 1:3530

Dawson, Warren Royal. 1:3779b 4991; 8136

Dawson-Damer, George Lionel S., viscount Carlow see Damer, George Lionel S. Dawson-, viscount Carlow.

Dawson, William, bksllrs., London. 1:2230g

Dawson's book shop, Los Angeles. 1:3098c

Day, A.E. 1:4458; 13240

Day, Cyrus Lawrence. 1:2067 3220 4487a; 5431 8014 8185–6

Day, Kenneth. 1:1360d; 5078 (6646)

Day, Robert Adams. 1:1695 1700

Day, W. 2:516

Deakin, Andrew. 1:1829–30

Dean, Raymond. 907 2303 2307

Dean-Smith, Margaret see Smith, Margaret Dean-.

Dean, Winton. 2:123

Deane, A.C. 4490

Dearden, James S. 1:4557 5147; 1150a 13122–5 13127–8

Dearing, Vinton Adams. 399 408 411 419 8428 10385 12842 12853–4 12861 12866 14161

De Beer, Esmond S. 1:2009 3276d 4006g; 949 8839 10355 10360 11904

De Beer, Gavin R. 11905 14605
De Bernard, G. 6996
De Baun, Vincent C. 7915
De Bhaldraithe, Tomas. 1:3781
De Castro, J. Paul. 1241 6101 7727 10489
10494 10505
De Coverly, E.L. 5591
Dedmond, Francis B. 1:850
Deed, S.G. 1:362
Deedes, Cecil. 1057 6269 6275 6911 6925
Deeley, Ann. 6778
Dees, R.R. 13167
De Groot, Alfred Thomas. 1:2266d
De Groot, Hendrik. 2:1170-2
De Halsalle, Henry. 2320
Deily, Robert H. 1:652-3
De L., J. 7719 8779
Delafield, John Ross. 9948
Delafons, John. 10894
De la Mare, Judith. 1:5115
Delattre, Floris. 1:4332c 5157y
Del Court, W. 12325
De libris; bibliofile breve. 4370
Delisle, Leopold. 10195
Dembleby, J. Malham-. 8794
Deming, Robert H. 1:3879
De Morgan, Augustus. 7 102
Denbighshire. County library. 1:963 3861
Deneke, Otto. 1:2984
Dennis, G.R. 1:5076b; 3984 13712
Dennis, Leah. 12748
Denonn, Lester E. 1:4559gb–ge
Denson, Alan. 1:2311–12 2500g–h 2855d
2887d 3426d 4377a 4424d
Dent, Alan. 2:1220g
Dent, Hugh Railton. 4533 4535
Dent, Joseph Mallaby. 4532 4535 11239
Dent, Joseph M. and sons. 10559
Dent, Robert K. 1:1251
Dent, Robert W. 2:373
Denton, E.K. Willing-. 8696
De Paul university, Chicago. 1:3676
Deposited collections (Nat Lib Wales J). 3037
3055
De Quehen, A.H. 9151
Derby. Bishop Lonsdale college of education
see Bishop Lonsdale college of education,
Derby.
Derby, Edward Henry Stanley, 15th earl *see*
Stanley, Edward Henry, 15th earl of
Derby.
Derby and district college of art. 1094
De Ricci, Seymour Montefiore Roberto
Rosso. 1:340 346k 385 517–18 1281 1449a
4653; 2121 2313–14 2723 2897 6275 13311
13324
Derry, W. 1:4395c
Derry and sons, Nottingham. 4536

De Sausmarez, Maurice *see* Sausmarez,
Maurice de.
De Sélincourt, Ernest. 11656 14501–2 14506
14508 14529
Dessain, Stephen. 12569
De Ternant, Andrew. 2864 2882 7577 9768
Detmold, C. Charles. 2:553
Detroit. Wayne state university *see* Wayne
state university, Detroit.
Deutsch, Otto Erich. 1:4294; 7610 12519
13502
Deutschberger, Paul. 2:1904
Deutsche Shakespeare-Gesellschaft. 2:3 17
— Bibliothek. 2:33 35 81–2 98
— *Jahrbuch* see *Shakespeare Jahrbuch.*
— *Mitteilungen.* 2:78a
Deutsche Shakespeare-Gesellschaft West. 2:3a
De Vane, William Clyde. 1:2581; 8890
Devanter, Willis van *see* Van Devanter, Willis.
Devereux, E. James. 1:826–a; 937–40
Devereux, James A. 8068
Deval, Laurie. 12885
De Villamil, Richard. 12574
De Vinne, Theodore Low. 1:394; 2:1285;
4967 6364
Devon. County record office. 1:2772
Devon and Exeter medico-chirurgical society.
1:2224
Dew, G.J. 6275
De Waal, Ronald Burt. 1:3179y–z
Dewar, R. 9036
D'Ewes, sir Simonds. 1:1903
Dewey, Nicholas. 1:1599d
Dewischeit, Curt. 2:391
Dexter, Walter. 1:3083i 3095; 10054 10068
10076–7 10090–1 10124–6
Dey, Edward Merton. 2:1061 1765; 10939
Dibdin, Edward Rimbault. 1:3027–8; 5094b
9965 9990 10626
Dibdin club, New York. 3485
Dibelius, Otto Franz Wilhelm. 1:3066d
3073i
Dick, C.H. 13648
Dick, Hugh G. 5376 7198 12758 14067
Dick, J. 9014
Dickens, A.G. 12660
Dickens' birthplace museum, Portsmouth.
1:3055 3065 3070g
Dickens fellowship. 1:3054 3104
Dickey, Franklin. 9601
Dickie, William M. 2846
Dickins, Bruce. 1:1173 3918 5092–3; 1065
3300 4824 5985 6436 6536 7973 13361
Dickinson, Asa Don. 7336
Dickinson, C.E. Gildersome. 2405
Dickinson, J.C. 3697
Dickinson, M.G. 1102e
Dickinson, Philip George M. 1:1790d

Dickinson, W. Croft. 3447

Dickons, J. Norton. 1:949

Dickson, Alexander John. 1:822a

Dickson, Frederick Stoever. 1:4911; 10490 13980

Dickson, Robert. 1:713

Dickson, Sarah Augusta. 1:1531 2289; 12072 13103–4

Dickson, William Kirk. 1:442; 1642 1720d 1726–7 11250

Dictionary of printers and booksellers ... 1557–1640. 3422

Dictionary of the booksellers and printers ... 1641 to 1667. 3417

Dictionary of the printers and booksellers ... 1668 to 1725. 3434 3641

Dictionary of the printers and booksellers ... 1726 to 1775. 3444 3641

Diego, *pseud.* 10739

Diekhoff, John S. 12371 12387

Dieneman, W. 1:4969b

Digeon, A. 10498

Digesta anti-Shakespeareana. 2:79

Dilke, Charles W. 7817a 11651

Dillard, Henry Brown. 11170

Dillon, Arthur. 2:1786

Dimock, George E. 2:283

Dimsey, Sheila E. 4208

Dingwall, E.J. 9471

Dionisotti, Carlo. 10274

Directory of periodicals publishing articles in English. 1:14

Disher, M. Willson. 6236 7026

D'Israeli, Isaac. 4274 4259 4304

Ditchfield, P.H. 1041

Dix, Ernest Reginald McClintock. 1:734 740 (1011) 1013 1029 1031–6 1039–58 1063–4 1067–70 1072 1080–94 1096–9 1101–39 1174–6 1328 1427 1621p 1950 1952 1952b 2278 2620s 3334n 3466 3903m 4261 4990; 2:204 704; 900 1746–7 1750 1752 1755–6 1760–2 1766 1772 1774 1781 1783 1791–2 1796 1802 1849 1852 1853–5 1869–70 1872 1875–9 1882–5 1889 1894–6 1905–6 1908 1946–7 1958 1959a 1961 1976 1980 3444 3579 4184 4430 4548 4699–701 4703 4716 4808 4939 5041 5128 5308 5403 5447–9 5513 5685 6466 8985 9888 13733 14058

Dix, William S. 1:363f; 540

Dixon, G.S. 3019

Dixon, J. 12492

Dixon, James Main. 1:723

Dixon, Peter. 12878

Dixon, Ronald. 1354 6510 12926

Doane, Gilbert Harvey. 1:2654; 9203 9208 10347

Dobb, Clifford. 10269

Dobell, Bertram. 1:1183 4962; 8089 9171 10734 13424

Dobell, Bertram, ltd., London. 2:189

Dobell, Clifford. 1:4944a; 11140

Dobell, Percy John. 4554

Dobell, R.J. 6155 8993 9171

Dobie, Marryat Ross. 1:96; 1728 13216

Dobrée, Bonamy. 1:2; 2:810; 3453a 12836

Dobson, Alban Tabor Austin. 1:3152b 3153–d 3156; 10211

Dobson, C.S.A. 12073

Dobson, Henry Austin. 1:1402 1405 3674 (4468); 14 274 276–7 2525 2741 4435 5289a 5534 5800a 5997 4559b 10483 10488 10485 13165 14214

Dobson, William T. 3886

Dock, George. 11371

Docker, Alfred. 1:1305q; 4543

Dr. Williams's charity and library, London. 1:2272–a 2405b; 8429–30

Dodd, Mary C. 11092

Dodd, Mead and co., ltd., New York. 1:387 3940 3974 4436 4890; 2:463; 11728

Dodd and Livingston, ltd., New York. 1:4198

Dodds, Madeleine Hope. 1:2352a; 3741 3749 7154 9687 10724 13292

Dodge, R.E. Neil. 9266

Dodgson, Edward S. 1992 2593 3590 5780 6849 11110

Dodgson, John McNeal. 3286

Dodwell, C.R. 3240

Doig, Ronald P. 1:3485 3532 4400f; 1624 3226 3880 6120

Dollar, *pseud.* 8931

Dolléans, Édouard. 1:4385

Dolmen press, Dublin. 1:1311g

Dolphin, The. 1:151

Dolson, Guy B. 892

Domelen, John E. van *see* Van Domelen, John E.

Donaldson, Robert. 1:478; 1632 3332 4729 4843 7088 9813

Donkin, Bryan, co. ltd., Chesterfield. 4571k

Donnelly, Mabel Collins. 1:3449

Donner, Henry Wolfgang. 1:2419; 2:1514

Donovan, Alan B. 11341

Donovan, Dennis G. 1:2566a (2651a) 2996b (3659a) 4147j 4216a (4971b) (5052a); 9140a

Donovan, Thomas. 2:1063

Doran, Madeleine. 2:888 1353–4 1431 1434 1437; 8769

Dore, J.R. 6260 6803–6 6808 6813 6905 6908–9

Dormer, Ernest W. 10861

Dorricott, I. 1:1732

Dorsch, T.S. 2:1622

Dorset. County library. 1:3603

Dorset natural history and archæological society. 5102

Dorset worthies. 5102

Dorsten, Jan Adrianus van. 1;761 (1258); 866a 3953

Dottin, Georges. 1:730

Dottin, Paul Georges D. 1:2979 2982; 5537 5864

Douady, Jules. 1:3627

Double crown club, Oxford. 1:1337

Doubleday, William E. 1:2273a; (203)

Doudney, D.A. 1:1267

Dougan, Robert O. 1: 720 725 1335f 5205; 2:344a; 4767

Doughty, Dennis William. 1:1408c 5190; 1668 3301 5879

Doughty, George W. 12222

Doughty, Oswald. 13085 14430

Douglas, Isle of Man. Manx museum. 1:1796 2560

Douglas, A. 7890

Douglas, sir George. 1:1007

Douglas, John M. 1:3213 4252

Douglas, Noel. 11668

Douglas, Richard John Hardy. 1:2928

Douglas-Osborn, E.H. *see* Osborn, E.H. Douglas-.

Douglas, Robert B. 11110

Douglas, William. 9197 9990 12465

Dove, Jack. 1:374

Dove cottage, Ambleside. Local committee of management. 1:5767

Doves press, Hammersmith. 1:1312–13

Doveton, F.B. 6394

Dow, James M. 7490

Dowden, Edward. 8522 10819 13715

Dowden, bp. John. 1:1514; 1554 6899

Dowding, Geoffrey. 6719

Dowlin, Cornell Marsh. 9831

Dowling, John Nesbitt. 7660 7868

Dowling, Margaret. 5437 10289 11014

Dowling, V.H. 4120

Downey, Edmund. 1978 5859a

Downs, Brian W. 2:78 84

Downward, M.E. 1:2672

Doyle, Agnes Catherine. 1:2447

Doyle, Anthony Ian H. 1:472a–3 1453 1455 1781; 2:612; 1074 2179 3201–2 3133 3264 4098

Doyle, Paul A. 1:4008q 4359b 5041 5042c 5043; 13594 14257–a 14258a

Drake, Robert. 1:4571

Drake, S. 1:2777

Draper, Evelyn. 1:2168

Draper, John William. 1:2087 4165; 3519 6975 14422

Draper, Walter A. 11669

Dredge, John Ingle. 1:886 (2352) (2382) (2386) (2393) (2400) 2455–6 (2469) (2509) (2645) (2716–18) (2788) (2792) (2875) (2888) (3231–2) 3329t (3347) (3355) (3371) (3415) (3458) (3483) (3535) (3548) (3662) (3685–6) (3750) 3820n (3826) (3917) (3919–20) (3925) (4075) (4079) (4185) (4264) (4477) (4479) (4549) (4579–80) (4587) (4616) (4681) (4731) (4748) (4786) (4815) (4819) (4976) (4978) (4997) (5049) (5073) (5194)

Drew, Fraser Bragg. 1:4161; 12192–3

Drew, Helen L. 8967

Drew, Philip. 2:1535

Dreyfus, John Gustav. 1:1401b 1413; 3935–7 3941 5212 5598 5718a (6637) 6645 (6652)

Driberg, Thomas. 3049

Driver, sir Gordon R. 625 631

Dring, E.H. 8074

Drinkwater, John. 10788

Drummond, W.J.H. 12629

Drummond castle, Perth. Library. 1:335

Drury, George Thorn-. 1:600; 9682 10352 11585 12185 12759 14171

Dubeux, Albert. 2:62

Dublin. Feis Ceoil association *see* Feis Ceoil association, Dublin.

— Institute for advanced studies. 1:1017 4366f

— Milltown park college *see* Milltown park college, Dublin.

— National library of Ireland *see* Ireland. National library, Dublin.

— Representative church body. 1:1518

— St. Patrick's hospital. 1:4838

— University. Trinity college. Library. 1:425 2454 4834 4869 5104 5205

Dublin review. 1:1953

Dubno, Maria. 2:326

Dubois, Arthur Edwin. 1:3432

Duck, Leonard W. 1:3571b

Duckles, Vincent Harris. 1:1826; 7617a

Dudden, Frederick Holmes. 1:3301

Dudley, Eveline. 1:4520

Duerksen, Roland A. 13364

Duff, Edward Gordon. 1:427 445 498 508 510 868 920a 952 1182 1280x 1281b 1534d; 109 112 826 834 1025 1103 1197 1215 1443–4 1561–2 1581–2 1937 2005 2010 2012a 2019 2502 2557 2581 2634 2669 2716 3410–12 3624 3626 4240 4245 4249 4619 4705 4902 5170 5461 5492 5703 5733 5872 5896 6055–9 6069 6456 6564a 6899 6971–2 7382 8036 8659 9129 9131 9878 11032

Duffy, B.J. 5978

Duffy, E.M.T. 1:4292

Duffy, James O.G. 13809

Dugan, C. Winston. 1:1068

Dugdale society. 1420 10396
Duke university, Durham, N.C.
— Divinity school. 1:5069
— Library. 1:1669a–b
— — *Library notes*. 1:174
Dulau and co., London. 1:5103
Dulles, Joseph Heatly. 1:4090g
Dulles, William Crothers. 1:1740
Duméril, Edith. 1:3629q
Dunbabain, R.L. 13445
Dunbar, Viola R. 1:3800
Duncan, Douglas. 1:1390; 5574
Duncan, Robert. 13176
Dundas, Henry Charles Clement, 7th viscount Melville. 11538
Dunedin, N.Z. Otago university *see* Otago university, Dunedin, N.Z.
Dunfermline. Public libraries. 1:2637
Dunham, Mary. 4653
Dunham, William H. 9255
Dunhered, *pseud.* 2070
Dunkin, Paul Shaner. 1:4621; 148 364 366 648 6244 8363 9370 10371 10600 11136 13252
Dunkin, F.H.W. 5733
Dunlap, A.R. 2:1509
Dunlap, Joseph Riggs. 4334 13276
Dunn, George. 1:453
Dunn, Waldo Henry. 1:2466
Dunne, Tom. 11152
Dunstan, W.R. 2:1484
Dunthorne, Robert Gordon. 1:1748; 7327
Dunton, John. 1259
Dupee, Frederick Wilcox. 1:(3797–8)
Dupré, Robert. 12511
Durham. Cathedral. Library.
— University. Armstrong college, Newcastle-upon-Tyne. 2:209
— — King's college, Newcastle-upon-Tyne. Library. 1:1455 1544 1581 2226
— — Library. 1:152 1780–1; 3276
Durham, N.C. Duke university *see* Duke university, Durham, N.C.
Durham, Phillip. 1001
Durham philobiblon. 1:152
Du Rietz, Rolf. 1:2878a; 743 955
Durkan, John. 1:4112k; 1628 1677 5106–7 10190
Durkan, Michael J. 1:5209a
Durling, Richard J. 1:3738; 1723
Durning-Lawrence, E. *see* Lawrence, E. Durning-.
Dust, Alvin I. 9834
Dustin, John E. 13787
Dustin, Thomas E. 9323
Duthie, George Ian. 2:1217 1327 1451–a 1724 1755
Dutton, Meiric K. 345 2085

Duțu, Alexandru. 1:3098d; 2:124
Duval, Elizabeth W. 1:4028
Duval, Hanson R. 1:3776
Duval, Kulgin D., bksllr., Edinburgh. 1:721 726 2638d (3539) (4092) (4314)
Duval, Kulgin Dalby. 1:(4092a)
Duveen, Denis I. 6739
Dwyer, J. Thomas. 1:2676d
Dyboski, Roman. 1:3085
Dyer, Isaac Watson. 1:2708
Dysinger, Robert E. 1:4868
Dyson, Anne Jane. 1:1597
Dyson, Gillian. 1:4611; 13233
Dyson, Henry. 1:2

E., A.C. 10148
E., A.R. 12580
E., B.B. 8076 8880
E., J. 8592
E., K.P.D. 6697
E., L.E. 1:3964 (3964d)
E., R. 2:554; 8132
E., S.Y. 2:1570
Eager, Alan Robert. 1:1020 (1818)
Eagle, F. 7209 7031
Eagle, Roderick L. 2:1040 1707 1975; 4848a 7339 10579 13429
Ealing. Public library. 1:3155 5059 5081
Eames, Marian. 1:4360b; 5321
Eames, Wilberforce. 1:384 1186b 2039; (606) 3485 14461
Early, Benjamin W. 13536
Eason, Charles. 1:1481d; 6858a 6867a
Eason, T.W. 1:4525c
Eason and son, Dublin. 4612
Early English text society. 4267
East Anglian printers' alliance. 1:888
Eastman, Arthur M. 2:763 766–7 783
Eastman, James Alfred. 10846
Easton, Judith M. 1:5051a
Easton, Malcolm. 1:3360c; 4710
Eaton, Peter. 1:2798; 13279 14165
Eaves, Thomas Cary Duncan. 1:2691; 4035 5044 5544–6 8999 9217 10507 10852 10854 13034 13038–9
Ebel, Julia G. 1:771a; 873
Ebeneezer Baylis booklets. 3922
Eberle, Gerald J. 9847 12274
Ebisch, Walther. 1:1184c; 2:65 70 76
Ebsworth, J.W. 4062
Eby, Cecil. 13789
Eccles, G.W. 1:491
Eccles, J.S. 10298
Eccles, Mark. 4153
Eckel, John C. 1:3060 3075 3079 3082; 2351 9152 10034
Eckert, Robert Paul. 1:4942–3; 5400 14013

Ellis, Bradbury Pearce. 2:933
Ellis, F.H.S. 6068
Ellis, F.S. 4964
Ellis, Frank H. 12916
Ellis, Frederick Startridge. 4621a–b 10457
12302
Ellis, James. 5998
Ellis, Stewart Marsh. 1:2314 2421 2465a 2841
2843 2849a 3795 3931 4025 4040 4660a
4521
Ellis-Fermor, Una M. *see* Fermor, Una M.
Ellis-.
Ellis and Elvey, co. ltd. 3701
Elliss, Wesley James. 1:962t
Ellwanger, George Herman. 1:2141c
Elmen, Paul. 8253 9529 10256 12769
Elmes, Rosalind M. 1:748; 1798 4405
Elmquist, Karl E. 13053
Elshie, *pseud.* 13175
Elsley, Ralph C. 9372 9593 11587
Elson, Charles. 1:2880
Elton, Charles Isaac. 1:381; 2266 7576
Elton, Mary Augusta. 2266 7576
Elton, Oliver. 1:2303 3186–7 4450d
Elton, William R. 2:6 155
Elwell, T.E. 11751
Elwin, Malcolm. 1:4495 4918; 512 9238
Emanuel, Hywel D. 3104 3134
Emanuel, Victor. 1:5172
Emblen, D.L. 1:4530d; 3398
Emerson, Oliver F. 11377
Emery, C.M. 2:(908) (1908)
Emery, H.G. 1:4527
Emery, Norman. 1:941 2444a
Emmerson, Joan Stuart. 1:2229
Emmison, Frederick George. 1:1782
Empson, Patience. 1:3419
Empson, William. 2:1831; 12443
Emslie, Macdonald. 11576 12724 12726
Enck, John J. 12638
Encyclopædia Britannica. 2:90 917 963
Endicott, N.J. 8852
England. Royal college of surgeons *see* Royal
college of surgeons of England.
England, George. 10735
England, H.W. 6982
English, David John. 1:822n
English, J.S. 1:4217d
English, William A. 1:5042a
English association, London. 1:45 650 (2680)
(2829) (3905) (4647a) 4850 (5168); 2:36 60
158
English bibliographical sources. 1:554 617a–22
641–5; 6376 6379–80 6382–3 6385–7
English bookbindings (Bk Coll). 2175–6 2184–6
2196 2201–2 2205 2211 2213 2216 2232
2236 2238a–b 2239a–b 2243a 2250 3819b
3819m 3890 3905 3970 4049 4106 4113

4388a 4537 4592 4620k 4638 4678–9 4751
4776 4819a 4850 4904–5 5060 5071 5086
5108 5112 5120k 5165 5173–6 5206 5208
5219 5261 5426h 5451 5489–90 5523 5572
5592 5616 5626 5670 5810k 5855
English bookman's library. 2044
English dialect society. 1:925
English fiction in transition. 1:154
English Goethe society. 1:822a
English language notes. 1:53
English libraries, 1800–1850. 2443
English library. 1071 1375 2281
English library before 1700. 2445
English literary autographs (Bk Coll). 8303 8495
8532 8609 8764 8785 8879 8959 8982 9100
9239 9291 9407 9457 9549 9634 9718 9920
9963 10153 10377 10675 10777 10857
10969 11147 11203 11477 11602 11693
12022 12530 12643 12856 12914 13094
13120 13281 13342 13586 13601 13633
13772 13833 13944 13992 14197 14298
14540 14576 14599
English literary history see ELH.
English literature, 1660–1800. 1:48–9
English literature in transition. 1:154 690
English masters of black-and-white. 4447
English scientific autographs (Bk Coll).
8369b 8732 9349a 11003 12001 12901
13453
Engravers to watch (Bkmns J). 3824 3878 3898
3901 3906 3964 4104 4140 4390 4419 4441
4595 4610 4675 4713 4715 4790 4838 4878
4884 5177 5316 5404 5565 5702 5800 5928
6011 7415–16
Ennis, Lambert. 9842
Eno, Sara W. 1:2861
Enquirer, *pseud.* 8667
Enright, B.J. 3153 3203 4474 11296
Enthoven, Gabrielle. 7966
Epstein, Edmund L. 11598
Epstein, Perle. 1:(4077d)
Erdman, David B. 1:2486 2836; 2:1877 1907;
8627–8 8633 8638 9554 9556
Erie county, N.Y. Buffalo and Erie county
public library. 1:554c 624e
Ernest, Edward. 1:3510c
Ernle, Rowland Edmund Prothero, baron
see Prothero, Rowland Edmund, baron
Ernle.
Ersites, T.H. 5001
Erskine, A.M. 3302a
Eschelbach, Claire John. 1:3777
Escott, Thomas Hay Sweet-. 1:(4981)
Esdaile, Arundell James Kennedy. 1:1 28 77
1462 1685 4195 4197 4199; 259–60 265
269 281 351–2 3434 4601 7275–6 11367
11392 12046
Esdaile, Katherine A. 6554 7412 11766

Esher, Oliver Sylvain Baliol Brett, 3d viscount *see* Brett, Oliver Sylvain Baliol, 3d viscount Esher.
Esler, J. 5387
Esplin, David Grant. 1:581; 12137
Esposito, M. 1:444a
Essays and studies in honor of Carleton Brown. 10785
Essays critical and historical dedicated to Lily B. Campbell. 10374 12854
Essays honoring Lawrence C. Wroth. 1:1765g 2240w; 3118 7628
Essays in dramatic literature. 3976
Essays mainly on the nineteenth century. 3994 8763 9479
Essex. Education committee. 1:1782
Essington. 10458
Este, *pseud.* 7700 11536
Etheridge, Ernest. 3964a 3964c
Estève, Edmond. 1:2679d
Etherington, J.R.M. 8547
Eton college. Library. 2:183a
Ettlinger, Amrei. 1:837
Euren, Albert D. 1305
European, *pseud.* 928
Evans, Albert Owen. 1:825 5091; 929 1469
Evans, Arthur William. 1:3840 5015e
Evans, Austin P. 1:770a
Evans, Benjamin Ifor, baron Evans of Hungershall. 3060 9533 10632 14519
Evans, Charles. 8500 13929
Evans, D. 1:1181
Evans, D.D. 4809
Evans, D. Wyn. 13046
Evans, Dorothy F. (Atkinson) *see* Atkinson, Dorothy F.
Evans, Edward. 1743
Evans, F.D. 13209
Evans, F.H. 13712
Evans, Frank B. 1:777; 8739 13574 13577
Evans, George Eyre. 1:962–q; 1535–6 1538 2631 5562
Evans, Gwynne Blakemore. 1:3900; 2:371–2 765 1275 1277–8 1335 1402; 9340 10367 10383 10631 11639 11703–4 12392 12434
Evans, H.A. 2:1936; 10626 11542
Evans, Henry H. 3944
Evans, Henry Ridgely. 1:2241
Evans, Hywel Berwyn. 1:816–17
Evans, J.J. 1505a
Evans, Joan. 4545
Evans, John R. 1:2248
Evans, Lewis. 3705 4544
Evans, Luther H. 9336
Evans, N.E. 2:126
Evans, Olwen Caradoc. 1:1813
Evans, Robert Owen. 1:(3516); 12421
Evans, T.H. 1531

Evans, W. Cynon. 1:1732k
Evans, Willa McClung. 2:1974; 12047–8
Evenden, J. 8642
Everett, A.L. 2:1360
Everett, Charles Warren. 1:2448
Everitt, A.T. 10557
Ewbank, Inga-Stina (Ekeblad) *see* Ekeblad, Inga-Stina.
Ewen, Cecil Henry L'Estrange. 2:1034 1040
Ewen, Frederic. 1:625
Ewen, H. 1808
Ewing, Douglas C. 1:4260; 7324 8910 12463
Ewing, James Cameron. 1:2022 2631b 2633 2634a 2639; 2130 4107 9024 9038–40 9043 9045–6 9049 9052–3 9055 9057–60 9063–4 9066–7 9069–72 9074–6 9079–81 9084–90
Ewing, Majl. 1:1641–2; 811 8502
Ewing, S. Blaine. 10898
Exeter. Cathedral. Library. 1:2217
— Royal Albert memorial museum. Library. 1:2224
— University college of the south west of England. 1:2834
Exley, Arthur. 11898 14221
Expertiana (J Soc Archivists). 9011
Explicator, The. 1:1981a
Eyles, Joan M. 1:47140
Eyles, V.A. 221 8143
Eyre, Curzon. 4812 4814
Eyre, George Edward Briscoe. 1:569 697; 5736

F. 4013 4054 8198 14179
F., A.L. 3673
F., C. 1:4884f
F., D.B. 1:2101
F., F.J. *see* Furnivall, Frederick James.
F., G.S. 6855
F., H. 6356 6776 6896 8126
F., I. 3834
F., N.K. 1:1139w; 2215
F., R. 7596
F., R.E. 4905
F., R.O.L. 9758
F., S. 7667 9190
F., S.J.A. 2070 9990 10736 12943 14314
F., W.G.D. 8218
F., W.J. 8218
Faber, Geoffrey C. 1:3416c; 10648
Faber, R.S. 1105–6
Fabes, Gilbert Henry. 1:683 2832 3384 (3639) 4016 (4291) 4313; 2321 10621 13275
Fabian, Bernhard. 2:(1328); (4350a) 12160
Fæhn, Ingebjørg. 1:833p
Fairchild, A.H.R. 2:1289
Fairchild, Hoxie Neale. 2:1771
Fairchild, Salome Culter. 977

Fairley, B. 10280
Fairley, John A. 1:1541d 3289 3486; 3836
Fairley, Robin E.W. 10278
Falconer, A.F. 2:478; 12750
Falconer, Charles MacGregor. 1:4002–3
Falconer, J.A. 13193
Falkiner, W. 7384
Falkner, John Meade. 1107 2811
Fall, Christine. 1:4902 4904; 13967
Falla, P.S. 13368
Fama, *pseud.* 12732
Famous libraries (Bkworm). 2460–3
Famous publishing houses (Bkmn). 4062b
Fann, K.T. 1:2369g 5151p
Fanshawe, E. 10469
Fanstone, Ruth Isabel. 1:1559b
Faraday, E.R. 8326
Farjeon, Herbert. 2:754
Farley, Earl. 1:4635; 12982
Farmer, Bernard J. 1:2797 3638; 2361 3647
Farmer, David R. 1:1499 4582a; 11292–3
   11942
Farmer, Geoffrey A.J. 1:4403; 2:240
Farnham, Willard. 1:530a
Farnham, William Edward. 1:4587m
Farquhar, Samuel T. 6105
Farquharson, Arthur Spenser Loat. 1:3612
   5128p
Farr, D. Paul. 1:5044
Farr, Harry. 2:1941–2; 4374 5560
Farrand, Nancy. 1:3906a
Farrar, Clarissa Palmer. 1:770a
Farrar, Reginald. 1:3283
Farrer, James Anson. 3495 7333
Farrow, R.S. 2780
Farthing, J.C. 1294
Farrell, Frank J. 1309
Farrington, B. 13293
Fasciculus Ioanni Willis Clark dicatus. 1:2810
Faure, Jacqueline. 9352
Faverty, Frederic Everett. 1:2017a (2335)
   (2582a) (2817) (3320) (4845) (4886)
Fawcett, James Wilson. 1:2352a 4108d 4527a
   4595u; 1323 1595 2428 4571 7647 7895
   7898
Fawcett, T.C. 1:4682
Fawcett, Trevor. 1304 1308 3385 6384
Fawcus, Arnold. 1:2486a
Faxon, Frederick Winthrop. 1:1916f
Fay, H.C. 1:2760; 9373 9375
Feasey, Eveline Iris. 603
Feaster, John. 1:4317n
Federation of master printers … of Great
   Britain and Ireland. 1212 3863
Federer, Charles A. 2622 10589
Federman, Raymond. 1:2414ca
Fegan, Ethel S. 1:1219; 6463
Feilitzen, O. von. 7776

Feipel, Louis Nicholas. 1:3216; 10399
Feis Ceoil association, Dublin. 1:1828
Feisenberger, H.A. 12590
Fellowes, Edmund H. 2:1107 1109
Fellows, George. 6824
Fenn, G.M. 9985
Fenn, sir John. 2602
Fenn, Louie M. 1:4302m
Fenton, G.L. 8218
Fenton, William Arthur. 1064
Fèret, Charles James. 1016 2405 3704 8218
Ferguson, Alfred R. 11333
Ferguson, Donald. 8204
Ferguson, Frederic Sutherland. 1:4101;
   2:651; 325 646 967 1255 5646 5658–60
   6670 6672 12257
Ferguson, J. De Lancey. 9037 9041 9047
   9054 9767 11732–3 11766 13484
Ferguson, Joan Primrose S. 1:1934
Ferguson, John. 1:2100 2290 4595 4998; 180
   4687 8120
Ferguson, Mary C., lady. 1:3287 (4502)
Ferguson, Richard Saul. 1:1539–40; 6986–8
Ferguson, V.A. 1:4187
Ferguson, W. Craig. 2:1260 1295; 6685
Fergusson, James. 8721
Fermor, Una M. Ellis-. 2:85; 12146
Fern, Alan M. 1:1209; 4632 6720
Fernie, G. Elaine. 1:3968z
Ferrar, M. 6269
Ferrar, M.L. 14173
Festival of Britain, 1951. Scottish committee.
   1:720 725
Festschrift für Edgar Mertner. 2:1328; 4350a
Festschrift Ernst Kyriss. 2226 3958 8486
Fetter, Frank Whitson. 1:1939a; 1717–19
Feuillerat, Albert G. 2:909; 10910
Fiachra, Eilgeach, *pseud.* 12626
Field, E.M. (mrs. L.F. Field). 6995
Fielding, K.J. 10146 10149 10154 10158
Fields, J.E. 8975
Fifer, C.N. 8713
Fifeshire. County library. 1675
Fifoot, Erik Richard S. 1:4694
Figgins, James. 6565
Figgis, Darrell. 12335
Figgis, W.F. 4878a
Filby, P.W. 1:1725
Filipović, Rudolf. 2:125
Finch, Jeremiah S. 1:3982g 3983; 3034 8837
   8839 8842–3 8847–8 8855 11838–40 12791
Fincham, Henry W. 1:1524; 2395
Fincken, Christopher Roy. 1:777m
Findlay, James B. 1:2139
Findlay, L.M. 1:4856
Findlay, Robert R. 12092
Fine art society, London. 1:4893
Finerty, E.T. 831a 1139

Finkelpearl, Philip J. 5971
Finlayson, C.P. 1724 8924
Finlayson, James. 1:5036
Finney, Byron A. 1:3827k; 11370
Finney, Claude Lee. 1:3911; 11679
Finzi, John Charles. 1:5104f; 14324
Firebrace, C.W. 11737
Firkins, Ina Ten Eyck. 1:1638b–c
Firmin, Catharine K. 1:934a
First books of some English authors (*Bkmn*). 8886
    11653 11727 13082 13283 13639 13904
    13973
First edition club, Liverpool. 1:1229
First edition club, London. 1:132 681 1227
    1263 2684 3153 5201; 285 2086 2316
Firth, sir Charles Harding. 1:3316
Firth, John. 11621
Firth, Raymond William. 1:4112q
Fisch, Max H. 1:2195
Fisch, Ruth B. 1:2195
Fischer, Walther. 10450
Fisher, G. 5581
Fisher, J. 1:2119
Fisher, John Hurt. 1:36; 6027
Fisher, Margery (Turner). 1:(4976m)
Fisher, Sidney T. 2:233 241; 12792
Fishwick, Henry. 4791
Fiske, John Willard. 1:3203
Fitch, J.A. 1400
Fitzgerald, J. 2275a
Fitzgerald, James D. 2:411 414 417 840 1154
    1164
Fitzgerald, Maurice H. 11023 14559
Fitzgerald, Percy Hetherington. 1:2507 3050
    3061 3326y 3327; 2049 8672 9977 9991
    11373 11375 13172
FitzGibbon, Constantine. 1:4936t
Fitzhugh, Robert T. 9067
Fitzsimmons, W.J. 6270
Fitzwilliam museum *see* Cambridge. University. Fitzwilliam museum.
Fixler, Michael. 10464
Flack, G.E. 7647
Flaischlen, Cäsar. 1:2677g
Flamm, Dudley. 1:4906a
Flanagin, Isobel E. 1:2394
Flatter, Richard. 2:589 603 894 907 1250
    1452 1515 1548
Fleay, Frederick Gard. 1:1600
Flecker, James Elroy. 1:3330g
Fleeman, John David. 1:3849j 3850 3852
    3852c; 4010 11504 11507 11511–12
    11520–3 13522
Fleischmann, Wolfgang Bernard. 1:800a
Fleming, D. Hay. 1583
Fleming, John F. 2:305 331–2; 3380a
Fleming, Thomas P. 8760
Fleming, William H. 2:691–2

Fletcher, Edward Garland. 1:2938; 9893
    9896–7 14026 13251 14416
Fletcher, G.B.A. 1:3718 3720; 11163 11177
    12666
Fletcher, Harris Francis. 1:1728 4232 4241;
    11128 12368 12401 12406–8 12425 12444
Fletcher, Iain. 13069
Fletcher, Ian. 11372
Fletcher, Ifan Wyndham Kyrle. 1:1558 1590
    1980 2214m 2912d–e 4030t; 511 2324 2366
    6724a 7093–4 9854 11983
Fletcher, J.M.J. 2420 2423 2425 2791 2757a
    (2806a)
Fletcher, John Kyrle. 6561
Fletcher, John M. 3303–4
Fletcher, John R. 1:1853
Fletcher, John Walter J. 1:2414c 2414f
Fletcher, Joseph Francis. 1:4884b
Fletcher, T. Bainbrigge. 6982
Fletcher, W.G.D. 2780
Fletcher, William Younger. 1:(1447h); 2023a
    2027 2033–4 2037 2047 2274–5 2541 2547
    2603 2970
Fleuron, The. 1:155
Flew, G.S.M. 1:5053
Flood, William Henry Grattan. 1:1051 1834;
    1784 1874 1890 1897 5262 6785 11381
    13387
Florida. University. Library. 1:2733
Flory, Claude R. 13059
Flower, Barbara. (397)
Flower, Desmond John N. 1:1376–7 1708;
    92a 298 365 533 847 916 2385 3170 3523
    7599 7975 8796 10932 12833
Flower, Margaret Cameron Coss. 1:4767
Flower, Robin Ernest William. 2924 2984
    3913 7225 7988 8330 10278 10611 10994
    11159 12071 12286 12528 12669 13425
Flower, sir Walter Newman. 1:3565–(6)
    (3570); 4206
Floyd, Thomas Hope. 3287
Floyer, J.K. 2570a
Fluchère, Henri Auguste E. 1:4794a
Flynn, Vincent Joseph. 7355 13580
Foakes, R.A. 2:1386
Foat, F.E.K. 5690
Fogel, Adah Boraisha-. 2:95
Fogel, Ephim G. 2:1323 1877 1907; 7187
Fogle, Richard Harter. 1:657b
Föhl, Hildegard. 1:656
Folger Shakespeare library, Washington, D.C.
    2:5 286 294 299 323 366
Folio society, London. 1:13323a
Folkard, Henry Tennyson. 2:38
Folmsbee, Beulah. 7371
Fondren library *see* Rice university. Fondren library.
Fontaine Verwey, E. de la. 1:1353f

Fontaine Verwey, Herman de la. 867 3120–1 4999

Foot, Mirjam M.R. *see* Romme, Mirjam M.

Foote, Charles Benjamin. 1:382

Foras, *pseud.* 2:554; 4511 7743

Forbes-Leith, William *see* Leith, William Forbes-.

Ford, A.J. 5278

Ford, Brinsley. 1:3346

Ford, G. 4831

Ford, Herbert Lewis. 1:3863; 2:221

Ford, Hugh. 1:1344a; (4897e)

Ford, Newell F. 11687

Ford, P. 4830

Ford, Worthington Chauncey. 1:4330; 3432 12320

Ford, Wyn Kelson. 1:1826a

Fordham, Angela. 1:1770h

Fordham, sir Herbert George. 1:870 960 1025 1761 1776 1783 1788–90 2745 4360 4397; 1034–6 4185 5317a 7488–9 7499–500

Fordyce, C.J. 1:750; 11038

Forgotten processes (Inland Ptr). 3961

Forman, Harry Buxton. 1:659 2567 3904 (3906) 4188 4298 4648–9 5031; 4964 7849 8218 9175 9177 11654–5 11657 11676 11681 13285 13288 13291 14171

Forman, Maurice Buxton. 1:3906 4200–1; 7849 8218 8868

Forman, P. 670

Forman, W. Courthope. 14215

Forrer, L. 1:3273

Forrester, Felicitée Sheila. 1:2110d

Forse, Edward J.G. 3599 7062 7579 8016 13053

Forshaw, Charles F. 1:3347a; 3582 6997 8818 11110

Forster, Edward Morgan. 1:(3137)

Forster, Leonard. 10269 12979

Förster, Max. 2:427

Förster, Meta. 1:2578

Forsyth, Walter Greenwood. 1:5076

Forsythe, Robert S. 609 1705 7898–9 9191 11121

Fort, J.A. 2:1020 1483 1889

Fort, Joseph Barthélemy. 1:2668c

Fortes, Meyer. 1:(2553m)

Fortescue, George Knottesford. 1:102; 12 14 2632 5838–9 5839a 7940

Fort Worth, Tex. Texas Christian university *see* Texas Christian university, Fort Worth, Tex.

Foss, Hubert J. 7594 7598

Foster, Finley Melville Kendall. 1:776

Foster, Fred W. 1:2282g 2286s

Foster, I.J.C. 1:1186e

Foster, J.E. 5645

Foster, J.J. 10589

Foster, James. 1:1363

Foster, John C. 1:4990p; 8935

Foster, Joseph T. 2:302; 6234

Foster, Katherine. 8247

Foster, W.S. 1:5025–a

Foster, sir William. 9691 11702

Foulis, Douglas A. 4898

Foulis exhibition, Glasgow *see* Glasgow. Foulis exhibition.

Fountaine, A.C. 7296

Four talks for bibliophiles. 3236

Fowell, Frank. 3499

Fowler, Henry T. 6857

Fowler, J.E.H. 1:4366m

Fowler, J.H. 2885

Fowler, John Thomas. 2070 6190 6855 6923 7007

Fox, Adam. 1:4216t; 8521

Fox, Bernice. 8897

Fox, Charles Overbury. 14559

Fox, John C. 14185

Fox, Levi. 2:322 326

Foxcroft, Albert Broadbent. 1:532 3089

Foxcroft, Helen Charlotte. 1:2624; 8991

Foxon, David Fairweather. 1:74 554 617a–22 641–4 2989 3985 5139 5142; 157 158a 744 3492 4042 5367 6245 8245 8794 9472 9473a 9925 10514 11850 12649 12865 12871 12915–16 13600 14052 14431 14435 14440–1 14539

Foxwell, Herbert Somerton. 1:2162f (2523q) (3461w) (3500f) (3549a) (3670f) (4956c)

Foyles art gallery, London. 2203

Fozzard, P.R. 11933

Fraenkel, Josef. 1:1861

France. Bibliothèque nationale, Paris. 1:357 2912db 4150

— — Dept. des imprimés. 2:227

— Centre national de la recherche scientifique. 1:1592e

France, R. Sharpe-. 1163a 1164

Francillion, R.E. 9990

Francis, sir Frank Chalton. 2:300 338 (892); 52 80 93 (215) 284 289 300a 323 325 (563) 569 633 (646) (655) (735) (791) (1139h) (1760g) (2156) 3060 3154 3204 3527g 3645 3746 4101m 4417 4931 7859–60 7864 7867 12458

Francis, Jane. 1:362

Francis, John Collins. 2:273; 2070 3420 3719 4879 5094b 5243 5458 5708 5716 5929 6837 7702–3 7720 7723—4 7819 7826 7828 7831–3 7836–8 7845 7850–1 7856 12807

Francis, John O. 4062

Francis, T.R. 1:4958a–9; 9616 14049–50 14053

Francis, William W. 1:2215

Francis Bacon foundation, Pasadena, Calif.
1:2373
— Library. 1:545 611
Francis Thompson society. 1:4954b
Frank, Joseph. 1:1880 1998a
Frankau, Julia (Davis). 1:1414e 1414g; 7391
7406
Franklin, Burt. 1:4513d 4706
Franklin, Colin. 1:(1238); 5004 5378 6502
Franklin club of St. Louis. 1:3058
Frantz, Adolf Ingram. 1:822
Fraser, Dereck. 1345
Fraser, Galloway. 7872
Fraser, G.S. 1:(3228)
Fraser, George Milne. 1:1291k; 4468–a
4578–9 7002
Fraser, J. 5462
Fraser, Peter. 7692
Fraser, Russell A. 1:3550
Frauchiger, Senta. 1:3782m
Frazer, Lily, lady. 1:3361
Fréchet, René. 1:2506e
Fredeman, William Evan. 1:674 4296–7;
13095–6
Free library of Philadelphia see Philadelphia.
Free library.
Freedley, George. 11289
Freehafer, J. 13799
Freeman, Arthur. 1:2303g; 9944 10726 11803
13880 14271
Freeman, E.J. 1:3268
Freeman, Elsie T. 8477a
Freeman, Eugene. 1:(5089d)
Freeman, James C. 1:4190
Freeman, John. 1:(4268); 9487
Freeman, Richard Broke. 1:2956–7; 9824–5
Freeman, Rosemary. 1:1656
Freemantle, W.T. 1:950 3414q
Freer, Percy. 1:73; 266
ffrench, Albert. 1808 5830
French, Frances-Jane. 1:1653
French, Hannah D. 1615 1622 9769
French, J. Mitton. 1:1551; 7686 10238 11842
12372 12377 12379–80 12382 12384 12388
12395 12402 12411 12415 12422 12445
14469
French, Joseph N. 2:1241
French, Robert D. 13111
French, Walter Hoyt. 1:4089a
Frey, Ellen F. 14418
Freyer, Grattan. 14582
Freyer, Michael G. 1:3933d; 4568
Friday, pseud. of Henry C. Hutchins. 9898–9
9906–7 9910
Fridlender, I.V. 1:3095c 3100p
Fried, Harvey. 8773
Friederich, W.P. 1:654
Friedland, Louis S. 935

Friedlander, Arthur M. 9192
Friedman, Albert B. 7440 12753–4 13927
Friedman, Arthur. 1:3469a 3472; 10767
10771 10774 10777–8
Friedman, Lee M. 10201
Friedman, Melvin J. 1:2414b
Friedrich II, emperor of Germany,
1194–1250. 1:2193d
Friedrich, Paul. 2:1564
Friedsam library see St. Bonaventure
university, St. Bonaventure, N.Y. Friedsam
library.
Friend, Llerena. 13141
Friends of dr. Williams's library, London.
3087
Friends of the national libraries. 2234a 2247
Friends of the Trinity college, Dublin, library
see Dublin. University. Trinity college.
Library.
Friends of the University of Iowa libraries.
14366
Friends of the Wellesley college library.
1:5204b
Fries, Heinrich. 1:(4334a–c)
Frost, Edwin Collins. 2:1004
Frost, Maurice. 1:2112; 666 4116 4416a
7377–8 8543
Frost, W.A. 1:2519b 3794 4527; 4739
11327–8
Fry, E.A. 7490
Fry, Mary Isobel. 1:605 4467; 6779
Fry, Varian. 1:3254
Fry, W.G. 62
Fryckberg, Marjorie. 8164
Frye, Roland Mushat. 693
Fucilla, Joseph Guerin. 1:653 833; 2:76
Fukuhara, Rintaro. 1:3503; 10839
Fulford, R. 3368a
Fuller, George Washington. 1:1525; 2396
Fuller, Henry M. 8529
Fuller, John Frederick Charles. 1:2923p
Fullington, James F. 13372
Fullmer, June Z. 1:2974
Fulton, John Farquhar. 1:2514–16 2518 4077
(4186) 4459–61 4998; 7566 10288a 10674
12897 12899
Funke, O. 7354
Fung, S-K.S. 1:2499
Fungoso, pseud. 7435
Furber, Holden. 12075
Furlong, E.J. 8531
Furnald, Sara L. 7651
Furness, Horace Howard. 2:712
Furnivall, Frederick James. 2:390 400 1000
1150; 8885 9413
Fusillo, Robert J. 2:1299
Fussell, George Edwin. 1:860–a 862 2092–3
2097 4426 (5213a); 6728–32 6734–5 12136

Fussell, Kathleen Rosemary. 1:4426
Fussell, Paul. 11708
Fyfe, Florence Marjorie. 1:2193d
Fyfe, Janet. 1720
Fynmore, A.H.W. 1023 2258 6704 9077 9552 10127
Fynmore, R.J. 1024 2710 7490 7636
Fyrth, H. 6735

G. 497
G., pseud. see Armstrong, Terence Ian Fytton.
G., A. 3993 4702
G., A.B. 14370
G., A.D. 4181
G., A.W. 1022
G., D.J. 1:2944y
G., D.M. 9192
G., E.B. 2954
G., E.L. 6924
G., E.N. 13176
G., F. 10732 11374 13709
G., G. 12006
G., H.S., see Grazebrook, James Frederick.
G., J. 13330
G., J.M. 9474
G., J.W. 10287
G., L. 3597
G., M.N. 12536
G., N.S.H. 953
G., W.H. 10843
G., W.J. 7939
Gabel, John Butler. 9380
Gable, J. Harris. 1:4527b
Gabler, Anthony Jacob. 1:1886
Gabrielson, Arvid. 1:2202
Gadsden, W.J. 6821 7850 12594
Gaines, Barry. 12121
Gainsborough. Public library. 1:4217d
Galbreath, D.L. 2:650; 11736
Gale, Fred R. 7642
Gale, Norman. 1:(2808)
Galland, Joseph Stanislaus. 2:79
Gallatin, Albert Eugene. 1:2407–8 2430 2432 5076a
Gallaway, R.J. 4473
Galloway, David. 2:1095 1550
Gallup, Donald Clifford. 1:3255–7 3262 4510; 806 10431 10441–2
Gamble, William. 4793 6194
Gamble, William Burt. 1:1139y; 6256
Gamlin, Hilda. 10458
Gantillon, P.J.F. 10815
Ganz, Charles. 1:2899
Ganzel, Dewey. 4897cb
Gard, Roger. 11350
Gardiner, R.F. 7637
Gardner, Anthony. 2165 2198

Gardner, Frank Matthias. 1:1666 1670
Gardner, Frederick Leigh. 1:2241a
Gardner, dame Helen Louise. 1:(5128); 2:(964); (83) (3536) 10262 10271–2
Gardner, S. 6368
Gardner, W.H. 11151
Garland, Herbert. 1:2397; 115 125 601 4731 8037 8410 12084
Garnett, David. 5305
Garnett, Edward. 1:2866i 2868p
Garnett, F. Brooksbank. 7701
Garnett, Richard. 1:2596 2828 3478 (4220); 278 2550–1 3706 4225 9512 12601
Garnett, W.J. 10018
Garratt, K.B. 12094
Garrett, Christine. 8389
Garrett, John W.P. 2:(914)
Garrett, Kathleen Isabella. 1:590–1 5143–4 5146; 4452 7693
Garrison, Wendell P. 4014
Garrod, Heathcote William. 1:3399k; 934 2843 9609 11681
Garstin, John Ribton. 1:4502
Garvin, Katharine. 2:1772
Gasc, F.E.A. 7238
Gaselee, sir Stephen. 1:450–1; 204 557–8 5569 6075 6896 6930 10849 12709–10 12719 14191
Gaskell, John Philip Wellesley see Gaskell, Philip.
Gaskell, Philip. 1:1193 1256 1325 1327 1415 4166–7; 150 152 251–2 367 877 1694a 3135 3763 3940 3945 4696 4728 5307 5794 5945 6324 6335 6337 6614 6653 8667 12195 13965
Gaskin, J.C.A. 11259
Gaskin, L.J.P. 6980 8134
Gasquet, E.S. 953
Gasquet, F.A. 3415 8034–5
Gaston, Alfred J. 1:2153–b 2154c
Gate, E.M. 6847
Gates, Payson G. 11023 11274
Gathorne-Hardy, John David, earl of Cranbrook see Hardy, John David Gathorne-, earl of Cranbrook.
Gathorne-Hardy, Robert see Hardy, Robert Gathorne-.
Gatto, Louis C. 1:3196a
Gaute, J.H.H. 11224
Gaw, Allison. 2:859
Gawsworth, John, pseud. of Terence I.F. Armstrong. 1:686–7 (2302) (2322f) (2402) (2446) (2623) (2740) (2840) (2967a) (2997) (3235) (3427) (3745) 4052n 4215d (4346) (4359a) (4368) (4393) (4514) (4539) (4675) (4692) (4820); 2912a
Gawthorp, Walter E. 10042
Gay, Ernest L. 8398 10647

Gaylord, Harriet. 8867
Geach, Peter. 9339
Gecker, Sidney. 1:1665
Geddes, sir William Dugind. 1:(3855)
Geddie, William. 1:2034 (2387) (2436) (2814)
  (3168) (3217) (3240) (3633) (3636) (3689)
  (3756) (3760) (3789) (3828) (3922) (4062)
  (4263) (4589) (5196)
Geduld, Harry M. 5870 13280
Gee, John Archer. 1:4080; 3035 4151 9656–7
  12499
Geissendoerfer, J. Theodor. 1:3066
Gemmett, Robert J. 1:2414y 2418a; 8491–2
Gennadius, J. 7577
Gentleman's magazine. 1:643c
Gentry, Irene. 1:5054a
Geoffrey Keynes; tributes ... 1:3923n
Geographical society of Ireland. 1:1818
George, Irene. 1:3273r
George, J. 9942 12419
George, mrs. M.D. 7438
George, Robert Hudson. 3733
George Bell and son. 3972a
George Buchanan, Glasgow quatercentenary studies.
  1:2605
Georgetown university, Washington, D.C.
  Library. 1:540
Gerard, Ethel. 1409 1411 7491
Gerber, A. 1:826d; 6002
Gerber, Helmut E. 1:2450 3338–a 3348
  3380–1 3935 4265
Gerber, Richard. 1:1724
Gerevini, Silvano. 2:1683
Gerhardt, C. and co., New York. 1:4801
Gerish, William Blyth. 1:4351–2; 706–7 2405
  2420 3588 5287 6231 7393 8219 12594
  12783
German-Reed, T. *see* Read, T. German-.
Gerould, Gordon H. 10130
Gerould, James Thayer. 1:599 4482b; 11863
Gerrard, John Frederick. 1:1521
Gerrare, Wirt, *pseud.* 1:2190m
Gerrie, George. 5951
Gerring, Charles. 2045 3408
Gerritsen, Johan. 367a 422 3349 7212 8458
  9393a 11581 12018
Gerson, J.H.C. 14201
Gerstenberger, Donna Lorine. 1:14 4873
  5197b
Gertz, Elmer. 1:3611k
Gerwing, Howard. 1:4491j
Gettmann, Royal Alfred. 4002–3 6534
  12245–6 12481 12989
Gheerbrant, Bernard. 1:3883
Ghosh, J.C. 1:348; 11957
Giannantonio, Pompeo. 1:4545
Gibb, sir Alexander. 1:2637
Gibb, I.P. 1:3282w

Gibb, Jocelyn. 1:(4050)
Gibb, John S. 1:1329 1416; 4722 5952
Gibbings, Robert John. 1:1330;   4742
  4757
Gibbings, W.W. 3511
Gibbons, G.S. 2873 6446 7730 7734 7766
Gibbs, G.A. 8681
Gibbs, Henry Hucks, baron Aldenham.
  2:505; 4522 9685
Gibbs, J. 11047
Gibbs, J.M.W. 5271 10732
Gibbs, Warren E. 9527 14001
Gibson, Andrew. 1:4485w
Gibson, Frank A. 10133
Gibson, J.R. 3768
Gibson, M.A. 1380
Gibson, Reginald Walter. 1:2372–3 4284;
  701 8361 8367 12507–9
Gibson, Strickland. 1:77 937 2490–1 3369–70
  3965 5001; 2:524; 25 31 66 112 125 249
  281 528 554 620 625 631 1353 1356
  1360–1 1373 1380–1 2053 2065 2111 2149
  2199 2704–5 2708 2717 2737 3436 4010
  4498 4557 (5021) 5023–4 5290 5347 5355
  6079 6778 7258 7480 7563 7574 8648 9133
  12261 14384
Gibson, W.H. 1:2458
Gide, André. 1:(5097)
Giffard, N.D. 1:4618
Gifford, Florence M. 2259
Gilbert, E.W. 8213
Gilbert, Henry March. 1:897a (1845)
Gilbert, sir John Thomas. 1:740;   1747
  1826
Gilbert, Rose Mulholland, lady. 1:3429;
  (1747)
Gilbert, Stuart. 11590
Gilbert, Vedder M. 2:796
Gilbert, William. 2420
Gilbert White fellowship. 1:5079
Gilbertson, Richard. 11008
Gilberthorpe, Enid C. 1:1328p; 1442h
Gilburt, Joseph. 976 1695 2406
Gilchrist, Donald B. 11435
Giles, P. 2686
Giles, Phyllis M. 1621
Gill, Evan Robertson. 1:3435
Gill, W.W. 8282
Gillam, Stanley G. 3288 3370 3385a 5842
Gillespie, Sarah C. 5614
Gillett, Charles Ripley. 1:2051 2251; 3502
  10602
Gillis, William. 9097 10475 12699
Gillman, Charles. 2542
Gillman, Ianthe A.M.S. 2780
Gilloon, Robert Moffat. 1:2961p
Gillow, Joseph. 1:2255 2321
Gillum, W.J. 1:827b

Gilmour, John Scott Lennox. 1:2498 3660 3696 4008a 4500 4529; 4174–5 6953 6956 7328 7343 7914 13060

Gilpin, John. 6508

Gilson, D.J. 3349a 8350 8352–3

Gilson, E.P. 8344

Gilson, J.P. 2635 2642 9281

Gimbel, Richard. 1:3100; 10159 10161

Gimson, Basil L. 1:1794

Girvan, I. Waveney. 1:5117–18; 14345

Gittings, Robert William V. 2:(934) 1324; 10941

Gjelsness, Rudolph. 1:1529; 7241

Gladstone, Hugh S. 4031 7578–9 8195 12259 13041 14297

Gladstone, Joan M. 1:837

Gladstone, William Ewart. 10713 10718

Gladstone library see National liberal club, London.

Glaisher, James H. 5028

Glasgow. Foulis exhibition. 1:1324; 4691

— Kelvingrove galleries see Kelvingrove galleries, Glasgow.

— Mitchell library see Mitchell library, Glasgow.

— Public libraries. Mitchell library see Mitchell library, Glasgow.

— Royal philosophical society see Royal philosophical society of Glasgow.

— University.

— — David Murray lectures. 4417 12081

— — Hunterian museum. Library. 1:529 1326 2291 3793

— — Library. 1:717–19 1003 1362q 1460 1476–7 2100 2161 2604

— — Trinity college. Library. 1:1733

Glasgow bibliographical society. 1:1002; 4690–1 5582

— Records. 1:156

Glasgow university press. 4747

Glasheen, Adaline E. 13333

Glasheen, Francis J. 13333

Gleeson, L.P. 2955

Glen, Duncan. 1:4092c

Glenn, Keith. 13317

Glick, Claris. 2:1261

Glicksman, Harry. 12324

Gliddon, G.M. 11933

Glikbarg, Edith F. 1:100

Glikin, Gloria. 1:4516

Gloucester. Public library. 1:895a–b 896 1388b 4993

Glover, Arnold. 10812 11376

Glover, Dorothy see Craigie, Dorothy (Glover).

Glynn, T. 4748–9

Gnomon, pseud. 2557 5619

Gocking, W.E. 1:5161

Godfrey, John Thomas. 1:5085

Godfrey, Walter H. 2145

Godman, Stanley. 9331

Godshalk, William Leigh. 1:4688b; 9809–10 11001 12917 13436–7

Godwin, George Nelson. 1:897a (1845)

Goetsch, Paul. 1:1723 2030h 3442

Goff, Frederick R. 1:483; 3266 9865 11771 14140

Goff, Phyllis. 1:2489

Gogarty, Thomas. 1958a

Gohdes, Clarence. 1:848–9; 994 11670

Goldberg, Homer. 12628

Goldberg, Maxwell H. 11360

Golden, Samuel A. 3315–16

Golden cockerel press. 1:1332–4

Goldentree bibliographies. 1:490b 657a–b 4219a

Goldie, S. 1:4348

Golding, C. 7818

Golding, Louis Thorn. 1:3463e

Golding, S.R. 2:1893

Goldman, Arnold. 14128

Goldman, Arthur. 11609

Goldman, J.W. 1:2156

Goldring, Douglas. 1:3330f; 10559

Goldschmidt, Ernst Philip. 53 325 563 2155 2366 4170 14411

Goldstein, Leba M. 1:1467; 6794 12730

Goldstein, Malcolm. 2:1404

Goldstone, Adrian H. 1:4098

Gollancz, sir Israel. 2:211 550 (1157)–8 (1430); 11810 12495

Gollin, Richard M. 1:2819; 9483

Gomes, Celuta Moreira see Moreira Gomes, Celuta.

Gomme, Andor H. 2:807

Gomme, G.J.L. 10139

Gomme, Laurence. 1:4078; 11460 11979

Good, David. 2:1573c

Goodall, A.L. 1:3772; 7570

Goodbody, Olive C. 1:4407; 12692

Goodburn, George. 4557

Goode, James. 12345

Goodfellow, J.C. 1739

Goodman, C. 1:860

Goodspeed, George T. 894 8278–9 8403 8412–13 8921 10398 10606 10620 10895 11064 11122 11836 11877 12012 12677 13327 13495 13518 13694

Goodwin, Aileen M. 4460 4597

Goodwin, G.H. 8151

Gordan, John Dozier. 1:356 361 367a 368a 633a 2444b 3097 3450 4160 4634 4922 5175; 2:242; 3171 7270 7978 8032

Gordon, Cosmo. 1:437 443 2810; 2663 4692 6726 8853

Gordon, Cosmo Alexander. 1:779–80 2080–1; 10194

Great British libraries (TLS). 1530 1729 1941
  3166 3168 3184
Great Irish book collectors (Irish Bk Lover). 2699
  2701–3 2712 2714–15 2726 2733–4 2764
  2800
Grece, Claire. 13548
Green, Charles. 8818
Green, David Bonnell. 1:55; 3123 5372
  10975 11276–7 11698 14251
Green, Emanuel. 1:938
Green, F.G. 2480–1
Green, Gladys. 14119–20
Green, J. Barcham. 3755 3772
Green, John Albert. 1:905 2536 3018 3407
Green, Joseph J. 6852
Green, Patricia. 1:1378a; 5370
Green, Peter. 1:3488
Green, Richard. 1:2253 5065–7
Green, Roger Lancelyn. 1:1558a 1571 2731–2
  2734 3487 4004f–g 4005–6 4049 4164
  4260a; 9317 9324 9330 9333–4 9338 10798
  11897 11898–9 11901 12095 12464 12529
Green, Samuel G. 5519
Green, T.A. 1434–5
Green, Tom. 4608
Green-Armytage, R.N. *see* Armytage, R.N.
  Green-.
Greenberg, Herbert. 9218
Greenberg, Robert A. 13842
Greene, David H. 13848–9
Greene, Donald J. 1:3835 3845f 3849k;
  11496 11525
Greene, Henry Graham. 92a
Greene, Herbert W. 10869
Greene, Richard L. 11432
Greene, S.W. 6965
Greener, William Oliver. 1:2190m
Greenfield, Thelma N. 1:1601r; 2:(373) (962)
Greenhill, Harold. 13477
Greenough, Chester Noyes. 1:1551 2306
Greenshields, M. 1:2616
Greenslade, Rush. 1:4975
Greenwood, Frances Anderson. 1:2286k
Greenwood, G.B. 2439
Greenwood, sir Granville George. 2:534 846
  1010 1019–21 1024 1165 1883 1885 1887;
  9185
Greepe, Thomas. 1:2238
Greer, Louise. 1:2588
Greer, Clayton Alvis. 2:1342 1357 1361
  1366–7 1573 1652 1654
Greeves, J.R.H. 4085
Greg, sir Walter Wilson. 1:504 508 821a
  1407 1602–3 1608 2757 4133 4420a
  4527t–u; 2:147 178 183 399 401–2 404 417
  436 518 547 550 597–8 843 865–6 872 877
  887 889–90 903–4 1026 1155 1167–8 1190
  1199 1202 1217 1221 1241 1361 1435–6

  1440 1443 1447 1563c 1610 1675 1708
  1809 1821 1829 1882 1886; 46 82 106–7
  130 185–7 201–2 204–5 215 296 300a 325
  372 380–2 391 498 553 584–5 609 616
  1281 2566 3530 3533 3536 3563 3575 4008
  4146 4614 4663 5310 5740–1 5744 5749
  5755–7 5769 5871a 6056 6350–2 6354 6406
  6535 7090 7106–7 7117–18 7125 7130–1
  7141–2 7145–7 7156–7 7163 7179 7193–4
  7199 7207–8 7982a 8451 8453 8462 8916
  8943 9360 9420–1 9570 9572 9577 9861
  9934 9938 10565 10633–5 11015 11049
  11069–70 11075a 11548 11550 11553–4
  11558–9 11569 11801 11903 12108 12149
  12153 12198 12200 12223 12230 12268
  12537 12556 12657 12770 13058 13419
  13424 13592 14479
Gregg, John Richard. 1:5154s
Grego, Joseph. 1:3052; 9982
Gregor, Ian. 1:(2671d)
Gregory, A.D. 1:3858b
Gregory, K. 8504 11896 13612q
Greider, Theodore. 1:1635
Grieff, Louis K. 1:3350
Grenander, M.E. 1005
Greta. 13525
Grevel, H. (97)
Grew, A.M. 9307
Grey, Jill Elizabeth. 1:3311a
Grierson, sir Herbert John Clifford. 2:1105;
  8567 10218–19 10226 10247 12335–6
  12358 13289
Grierson, Mary. 1:4971m
Grierson, P. 1:4369t
Griffin, Charles and company, London. 4805
Griffin, Francis J. 1:2240p–q 4143; 6797
  6978 6981 8130 8135
Griffin, Gillett G. 8961
Griffin, J.M. 1:1837c
Griffin, Robert. 9171
Griffin, William H. 1:(2587)
Griffin, William J. 2:1658 1676
Griffith, Ben W. 13345–6 13350
Griffith, Dudley David. 1:2780
Griffith, John H. Sandham. 13292
Griffith, Reginald Harvey. 1:631 2683 3981
  4059 4440; 4471 7356 7668–9 7985 7987
  8264 10648 11835 12764 12808 12812–14
  12826 12835 12844 12855 12857 12913
  13756 13769
Griffiths, D.E. 1:4581m; 13157
Griffiths, E.F. 14065
Griffiths, G. Milwyn. 9603
Griffiths, J.M.I. 1:3857
Griggs, Earl Leslie. 1:669f 2813e 2824m;
  9530 9536 9550
Griggs, Irwin. 1:1922 1937 2552; 1709
Grigor, John. 5016 7851

Grime, R. 7260
Grimm, Verna Barstad. 1:1525; 2396
Grimsditch, H.B. 8479
Grinlinton, Margaret Shirley. 1:3953
Gritten, Archibald J. 1:900
Grobel, Monica. 11269
Grolier club, New York. 1:29 327–8 330–1
    359e 368 486 495–6 596 1200a 1621
    1660–1 1718 1735y 2101 2407 2431 2471–2
    2481 2508a 2781 3062–3 3805g 3197 3276
    3433 3591 3836 3950–1 4038 4222 4437–8
    4552–3 4651 4756 4802–3 4888 4913–14
    5010; 2:192; 128 300 538 2008a 2045 6266
    6573 6714 8693
Grolier society, Tokyo. 1:2474
Grönland, Erling. 1:(833p)
Groot, Hendrik de see De Groot, Hendrik.
Groschwitz, Gustave von. 1:1269g
Grose, Clyde Leclare. 1:18
Grose, M.W. (168)
Grose, Sidney Williams. 1:4229
Grosfils, Margaret Mary (Baker). 7693
Grosjean, Paul. 1:459
Gross, B.A. 666 4416a
Grove, G. 13889
Grove-White, B.E. see White, B.E. Grove-.
Growoll, Adolf. 1:(1186b) 4962b; 3484–5
Grubb, Gerald Giles. 10115 10119–20 10148
    10150 10155
Gruffydd, Geraint. 1502 1505 1540g
Grundy, Joan. 8862
Grundy, Lewis H. 903
Gruselier, Gregory. 7352
Grzegorczyk, Piotr. 1:2868m
Gualterus Dumlanensis, pseud. of H.W.
    Davies. 3629
Gückel, W. 1:2979e
Guddie, Erwin G. 5909a
Guegan, Bertrand. 3727
Guerinot, J.V. 1:4447
Guffey, George Robert. 1:(2936a) (2938m)
    2948a (3188a) 3650a (3867) (4275a) (4352h)
    (4488a) (4560) (4688c) (4710m) (4794p)
    4976g (5075n) (5183)
Guibert, J. 1:3280 4118 4218 4332 5150
Guides to the published work of art historians.
    1:2809m
Guido, John F. 4004
Guild, Edward C. 1:2018
Guild of women binders, London. 4812–16
    4818
Guiney, Louise Imogen. 7974
Guinness, H.S. 1899
Guitton, Jean Marie P. 1:4333
Gulick, Sidney Lewis. 1:4761; 13582 13587
Gullans, Charles B. 8356
Gulley, J.L.M. 4382
Gullible, Richard, pseud. 990 4360a 14450

Gullick, Norman. 1:3479d
Gulliford, H. 13191
Gulliver, Harold Strong. 1:4919
Gumbert, H.L. 1:1656a
Gumbley, Walter. 5579a
Gummer, Ellis Norman. 1:3034
Gumuchian, Kirkor. 7036
Gunn, W.A. 1:3365
Gunnell, Doris. 7870
Gun room library. 1:2190n
Günther, E. 1:2979e
Gunther, R.T. 2792 2874 8128 8318 10660
Guppy, Henry. 1:336 460; 2:543; 7 13 116
    126 2648 6275
Gurney, J.H. 12981
Gustafson, Margaret T. 1:4044
Gutenberg jahrbuch. 1:157
Guthke, Karl S. 9408 11989
Guthkelch, Adolph Charles Louis. 1:2307
    4281 (4841); 2:532; 728a 8224 13717
Guthrie, Douglas. 1:1943
Guthrie, James Joshua. 1:1380; 5396 5398
    6465 14012
Guthrie, William Keith Chambers. 1:2882h
Guttery, D.R. 3136 3155
Guttridge, G.H. 12887 14110
Guy, Robert. 7238 7818
Guyatt, E.J. 1:3629
Guy's hospital, London see London. Guy's
    hospital.
Gwynn, Aubrey. 8972
Gwynn, Frederick Landis. 1:4274a
Gwynne-Jones, A. see Jones, A. Gwynne-.
Gwyther, A. 6444

H. 6751
H., A. 4645 6047 10990
H., A.E. 2259
H., A.H. 1:1345a; 714
H., A.J. 1:5053q; 1181 4407 6177 6776 7751
    7899 8076 8175 12580 12948
H., A.M. 7774
H., A.P. 12474
H., B.S. 3739 7604
H., C. 13526
H., C.A. 2594
H., C.E. 6941 8431
H., C.J. 5298
H., C.W. 3957 7374
H., E.A.P. 3925
H., E.M. 6104
H., F. 13638
H., F.O. 1201
H., H.F.O. 1144
H., I.T. 2857
H., J. 1214
H., J.E. 5711a

H., J.H. 13911
H., J.R. 2:534a; 4607 7222 11732 11735–7
H., J.S. 2:1167
H., M. 3925 13975
H., M.J. 10644
H., N.W. 2:1506; 8328
H., O.N. 2:71; 2939 4905 7734 12503
H., O.O. 9268
H., S. 9278
H., T. 11981
H., V. 7647 10724
H., W.A. 12101
H., W.B. 1:3501a 3711; 1144 1238 2287 2710
   6172 6275 6830 6938 7872–3 8025 8108
   8553 8827 9176 9181 9777 9998 10292
   10716 13488
H., W.G. 8102
H., W.H. 7387
H., W.S.B. 1102 9264 12122
Haack, Peter R. 14071
Haas, Irvin. 1:1220–1 1289v; 4461
Haas, Lorenz. 6065
Haave, Herdis. 1:833p
Haber, Louis J. 1:387d
Haber, Tom Burns. 1:3730; 11173–4 11178
   11182 11187 11190–1 11204 11211 11225
Haberly, Loyd. 1:(1397); 4826
Hackett, James Dominick. 2940
Hackwood, Frederick William. 4893a
Haddington. Gray library. 1:575
Haddington, George Baillie-Hamilton-
   Arden, 11th earl of see Arden, George
   Baillie-Hamilton-, 11th earl of
   Haddington.
Haden, H.J. 1433
Hadfield, John. 1:358 2495; 10474
Haebler, Konrad. 128
Hagan, John. 14123
Hagedorn, Ralph. 1:2279g; 2258 4546
   6736–7 8877 72850
Hagemann, E.R. 1:3810
Hagen, Winston Henry. 1:393
Hagspian, John V. 10260
Hague, Richard. 3639
Hahn, Wiktor. 2:97
Haig, Robert Louis. 4475 5015 7780 7798
Haight, Anne Lyon. 10111
Haight, Gordon S. 10427 10429 11420
   12928–9
Haile, Martin, pseud of Marie Hallé. 1:(2321)
   4064
Hailey, E.M. 4467
Haines, C. Reginald. 2:1003 1014 1016 1028
   1788; 11547
Haines, J.W. 8814 13917 14013 14463
Haines, W. 1297 4856
Hair, P.E.H. 11710
Hale, C.P. 1202 2407 7384 9184

Hale, David G. 4400
Hale, George Ellery. 2836
Hale, J.R. 13061
Hale, W.G. 7002
Hales, G.T. 9497
Hales, John W. 1211a
Halévy, Elie. 1:(2448)
Haley, F.G. 7821 11110
Halfpenny, Eric. 3227
Halifax, Nova Scotia. Dalhousie university see
   Dalhousie university, Halifax, Nova Scotia.
Halkett, Samuel. 1:1437–9
Hall, A.E. 1:477
Hall, Alfred. 4228 4389 4827 5267 5520
Hall, Bernard G. 11044 14509
Hall, C.P. 1067
Hall, F.J. 8273
Hall, Fairfax. 1:1401g
Hall, Fred. 5131
Hall, Hubert. 1:916f
Hall, J. 12308
Hall, M. Foljambe. 5557
Hall, Norman A. 8870
Hall, P.E. 2229 3655–6 13945 13962–3
Hall, Ronald. 9970
Hall, Thomas. 1:2826a
Hall, Trevor Henry. 1:2140; 7482 12631
Hall, V. 2:(438) (788)
Halladay, Jean. 1:4558
Hallam, H.A.N. 3386
Hallen, A.W.C. 3787
Haller, William. 1:4737
Halliday, Frank Ernest. 2:86 127
Halliwell-Phillipps, James Orchard see
   Phillipps, James Orchard Halliwell-.
Halloran, William F. 8639
Halls, C.M.E. 1:3413c
Halpern, Sheldon. 1:4713
Halsband, Robert. 396 8316 12469 12875
   13793
Halstead, W.L. 9940 12177
Ham, Roswell G. 10351 10358 14172
Hamann, Edmund G. 4784
Hamel, Frank. 3498 7247 7410
Hamer, Douglas. 1:1464–b 4063; 1601 10472
   12003
Hamer, S.H. 3429
Hamill, Frances. 3461
Hamilton, Doris H. 5392
Hamilton, Eunice C. 1:3799
Hamilton, Frederick W. 6073
Hamilton, George Rostrevor. 1:3233
Hamilton, Harlan W. 1:2855h; 8716
Hamilton, Horace E. 14033–4
Hamilton, J.D. 13648
Hamilton, Marion H. 1:3205; 10380 10384
Hamilton, R. 1:4525c
Hamilton, S.G. 6827

Hamilton, Sinclair. 1:3712d
Hamilton, Walter. 1:1585; 5643
Hamilton, William Hamilton. 1:4156 4158
Hamlyn, Hilda M. 2435
Hamlyn, Martin G. 7257
Hammelmann, Hans A. 1:1412b 3374 3495–6 3623 5003–4; 4213 4786 5135 5819 5894 5916–17 6552 7462 7810a
Hammersmith. Public libraries. 1:1572
Hammerton, sir John Alexander. 1:2395y 3562c; 9997a
Hammond, Eleanor Prescott. 1:2781a; 9415–16
Hammond, Joseph W. 1816
Hampton, John. 12020
Hancock, Philip David. 1:970
Hancock, Thomas W. 12693
Hand, Charles R. 4680
Hand, Thomas W. 1441
Hand, W.D. 2259
Handleman, Celia. 2:1201
Handley-Taylor, Geoffrey see Taylor, Geoffrey Handley-.
Handy, A.M. 13896
Handover, Phyllis Margaret. 1:4291q 4501; 1285 3818 6163 6626 6636 6640–1 6646 6887 7801
Hands, Margaret S.G. 1:(1760g); 2435–6
Haney, John Louis. 1:2828 4893a; 9513 13907
Hanford, James Holly. 1:4219a; 808 874 3267 3317 8425 10551 12326 12330 12344 12426 13230
Hanham, Harold John. 1:22 1511c
Hanlin, Frank S. 11278
Hanna, Archibald. 1:2599; 8922
Hannay, David. 1:4718
Hannen, Henry. 1153 12595
Hansard, Thomas Curzon. 6385
Hanson, Laurence William. 1:1257 2169 2885; 2:303; 3561 3892 5502 7685 7767 8049 9475 9686 11768 13885 14478
Hanson, Thomas William. 2886 4615–18 14249
Haraszti, Zoltan. 526 610 737 2863 3857 (3947) 6864 6868 6932 7079 7601–2 7961 9306 9539 9627 9891 10704 10794 11305 11759–60 12351 12362 12525 12572 12834 13521 13741 13811 13863 14187 14389–91 14398 14572
Harbage, Alfred Bennett. 1:1606c 1607 1609 1614 1623 2961 3924; 7159 7161 7196 7205
Harben, H.A. 7484
Harberton, James Spenser, 6th viscount see Pomeroy, James Spenser, 6th viscount Harberton.
Harbord, R.E. 11781

Harbottle, Phillip James. 1:3283a–b
Harcourt, Lewis Vernon. 1:875–6
Hard, Frederic. 7081
Hardacre, Kenneth. 6143
Hardacre, Paul H. 1:2922; 11295
Hardcastle, C.D. 7375
Harden, H.A. 4096
Hardie, Martin. 1:1335k 1738 5076c; 4780 6192 13906
Hardie, William. 13952
Harding, Davis P. 6780
Harding, Jane DeBlois. 1:2347
Harding, W.N.H. 10415 10474
Harding, Walter N. 8189
Hardy, Charles Frederick. 2:1179
Hardy, John David Gathorne-, earl of Cranbrook. 1:2495
Hardy, Robert Gathorne-. 1:360 4876x–7a; 8968 11143 13159 13375 13866 13869–71 13873
Hardy, W.J. 2482
Hare, William Loftus. 4272
Hares, R.R. 2:99
Hargreaves, Cyril. 1:2616
Hargreaves, G.D. 8788
Hargreaves, Joan Margaret. 1:3668
Hargreaves, Phylis. 1:3514–15
Harington, J. 1:4010
Harkness, Bruce. 1:4242a; 227 12423
Harkness, Stanley Bates. 1:2670
Harlan, Aurelia Emma (Brooks). 1:2577–4087; 8875
Harlan, Robert D. 872 5795 5797 7811 8554
Harlech, William George A. Ormsby-Gore, 4th baron see Gore, William George A. Ormsby-, 4th baron Harlech.
Harley, John Brian. 1:3527; 7519 7530
Harling, Robert. 4741
Harlow, C.G. 12558
Harlow, Neal. 223
Harman, Marian. 1370
Harman, Richard Alexander. 1:1842
Harmon, Maurice. 1:739b
Harmatopegos, pseud. 8826
Harmsworth, sir Robert Leicester. 1:519 1489 1517
Harpenden. Rothamsted experimental station see Rothamsted experimental station, Harpenden.
Harper, Francis Perego. 1:1743; 11807
Harries, E.R. 1:2349
Harper, J.W. 14087
Harper, Kenneth E. 859
Harrap, George G. 13976
Harrier, Richard C. 14567b
Harries, E.R. 9856
Harris, Arget. 4109 8291
Harris, Bernard. 2440 2666

Harris, Brice. 14346–7
Harris, C.S. 900a
Harris, Edward B. 2:32 528 671–2; 3672
Harris, Elizabeth M. 1:1163; 6228
Harris, Francis T.C. 1:5154s
Harris, G. Edward. 1:4884
Harris, H.A. 1399
Harris, James Rendel. 1:745 (1384); 2:1707; 375 4112 8947
Harris, John. 1:2103d 3419
Harris, Mary Dormer. 5506
Harris, Seymour Edwin. 1:3923q
Harris, Wendell V. 1:1721–2 2910 5090; 5038a 9485b
Harris, William James. 1:770
Harris public library, Preston. 1:1573c 4949 4951
Harrison, Cecil R. 4840
Harrison, E. 10661
Harrison, Elizabeth Mary. 1:4118a
Harrison, Frank Mott. 1:1385a 2612–14; 5435k 5436 8951–5
Harrison, Frederic. 1:3613
Harrison, Frederick. 2347 2836a 3066 9279
Harrison, mrs. Frederick W. 1:4339
Harrison, George Bagshawe. 1:4422g 2:807 (875) 884 959; 47 3438 3446 13533
Harrison, H. Guy. 1:3176; 4840
Harrison, Harold. 1:1777
Harrison, James. 6393
Harrison, John. 6275
Harrison, John R. 12023 12028 12032
Harrison, Joseph LeRoy. 1:5076
Harrison, K.P. 2193
Harrison, Thomas P. 649
Harrison, William. 1:1777 1791; 7486–7
Harrison and sons, ltd., London. 4841
Harsin, Paul. 11912
Hart, Alfred. 2:428 1616; 7152
Hart, C.W. 11437
Hart, Clive. 11601
Hart, Dominic. 2:1231
Hart, E.F. 8002
Hart, Edward. 5293a
Hart, Francis Russell. 12039
Hart, H. Raven-. 1:2174
Hart, Horace. 1:68–9 1200; 2:516; 5332 5366 5720 5723 6195 6698
Hart, James D. 2:604; 13676
Hart, James Morgan. 1:4196
Hartelie, Olaf. 7626
Harthan, John Plant. 2168 2171 2222–3
Harting, Hugh. 1:5111d
Harting, James Edmund. 1:2192 3614; 1102
Hartley, Edward. 2:645
Hartley, Lodwick Charles. 1:2894–5 4789
Hartley, Miles E. 1438
Hartman, Herbert Weidler. 1:2824n

Hartman, Joan E. 13937
Hartnoll, Phyllis May. 2:123; 7026
Hartzog, Martha. 2242
Harvard library bulletin. 1:158
Harvard university. Ames foundation. 1:2210–11 2214d
— Graduate school of business administration. Baker library. Kress library of business and economics. 1:915a 2166–8 2170–1 4707
— Library. 1:110 158 1541 2019 2411 2432 2727 3642 3675; 4657
— — Houghton library. 1:3851 4520d
— — Widener collection. 1:338 2929 3067 4799
Harvard university library notes. 1:158
Harvey, David Dow. 1:3341
Harvey, John S. 7359
Harvey, Paul Dean A. 1:1807; 10170
Harvey, W.J. 10339
Harvey, William. 1:1540a; 4468a
Harvie-Brown, John Alexander *see* Brown, John Alexander Harvie-.
Hascall, Dudley L. 1:4217b
Hasker, Richard E. 2:1653; 5285
Haskell, Daniel Carl. 1:520
Haskell, Grace Clark. 1:4481
Haslam, D.D. 3074
Haslam, G.E. 1:1161 5145
Hasler, Charles. 6687 6690 6711
Hassall, W.O. 3084–5 3106–7 3268
Hastings. Brassey institute *see* Brassey institute, Hastings.
— Public library. 2:128
Hastings, William T. 2:236 578–9 881 1082 1641 1643; 11308
Haswell, Stephen. 13290
Hatch, Benton L. 1:3596
Hatfield, C.W. 1:2532b; 8792 8804a 10638
Hatton, Thomas. 1:1712 2074h 3078 3081 3091; 10095
Haupt, Hellmut Lehmann-. 1:1139e 1139i–j 2320c; 7434
Havard, William C. 1:4682h
Havens, Munson Aldrich. 1:1403f; 5802
Havens, P.S. 12363
Havens, Raymond Dexter. 1:1981e; 8015 11331 13531 13537–8
Haverfield, F. 4241
Haverford college. 1:541
Havering. Public libraries. 1:891
Havighurst, Alfred F. 1:679b
Haviland, Thomas P. 12389
Haward, Lawrence. 1:3013
Hawker, George. 4805a
Hawkes, Arthur John. 1:903 1266 4386; 2:882; 4050 12565
Hawkes, David. 14165

Hawkins, Aubrey. 7889
Hawkins, Desmond. 13447
Hawkins, E. 1:996
Haworth, Adrian Hardy. 1:3621p
Haworth, Peter. 2:1173 1595 1821
Hay, Denys. 14157
Hayashi, Tetsuro. 1:1468z
Haycraft, Howard. (7270)
Hayden, John O. 1:675
Haydock, James. 1:3444a–b
Hayek, F.A. 12288
Hayes, Gerald R. 10898 12542
Hayes, J. Gordon. 11412
Hayes, James. 926 1763 2489 10723
Hayes, Richard J. 3243 3387
Hayes, Thomas. 8101–a
Hayllar, F. 7878
Hayman, David. 11614
Hayne, Herbert G. 4415
Haynes, E.B. 10072
Haynes, Maria S. 1:4516h
Hayward, sir John. 2358
Hayward, John Davy. 1:594 1984–5 4836;
    2:308 1976; 4360 8786 9320 10248 10282
    10858 11294 14354
Hayward, John W. 13260
Hazard, Paul. 5281
Hazell, Ralph C. 4854
Hazeltine, H.D. 1:3923
Hazen, Allen Tracy. 1:1406 3842 3842d–3
    4823 5007; 2:751; 503 715 3681 3798 3927
    3943 4144 6237 6300 7647 8701 10850
    11426 11430 11433 11438 11449 11802
    12966 14192 (14200) 14202–4
Hazlitt, William Carew. 1:561 5719 1587;
    2:203; 442 515 2267–8 2271 2276 2280
    3667 9931
Head, Rachel E. 10723
Heal, sir Ambrose. 1:1575 2823–a; 2:1040;
    1262 1274 2428 3646 4434 4642 4832 4862
    4905 5196 5581 5691 6039 7248 7250 7508
    9601 10724
Healey, George Harris. 1:5176; 9908 9912
Healey, H.A. see Shane, T.N., pseud.
Heaney, Howell J. 1:80–1 3095a; 10128
    10132
Hearl, Trevor W. 1:2394a
Hearsey, Marguerite. 13136
Heartman, Charles F. 2898–9 7335
Heath, E. 12830
Heath, William Webster. 1:2510
Heawood, Edward. 1:1762a; 3728 3730–1
    3734 3743 3745 3793–5 3802 7501
Hebb, John. 5961 7703 9605 13972
Hebel, John William. 1:(3189); 5075 10317
Heckel, J.W. 1:3328
Heelis, J. Loraine. 13171
Heffner, Ray. 13567

H. E. Huntington library see Henry E. Hun-
    tington library and art gallery, San
    Marino, Calif.
Heilbronner, Walter L. 1:414
Heilman, Lee W. 8227
Heilman, Robert Bechtold. 1:1694e
Heilpern, Gisela. 1:5053f
Heinemann, F.H. 1:4969
Heinemann, William. 4858
Heintzelman, Arthur W. 4450
Held, George. 8030
Heley, Joan. 1:(3540)
Hellman, George S. 13653
Hellman, Milton A. 10430
Hellmann, G. 1:3429a
Helmer, Frederic Flager. 6659
Helsztyński, Stanisław. 2:140–1
Heltzel, Virgil Barney. 1:2035b 2148; 12947
Hely-Hutchinson, J.W. see Hutchinson, J.W.
    Hely-.
Hemlow, Joyce. 9001
Hemming, A. Francis. 6983–4
Hemming, H. Phipps. 2986
Hemming, R. 6268 7825
Hempill, A. 1062
Hempl, George. 11086
Hems, Henry. 1218 6745 7384 7818 7835
Hench, Atcheson L. 9425
Henchy, Patrick. 14059
Henderson, James. 1:1717
Henderson, James M. 1594
Henderson, Philip. 5003 8805–6
Henderson, Robert William. 1:2287; 8711
Henderson, S. 1:2741
Henderson, W.A. 2:394 700–1 1704; 6012
Hendrick, George. 1:14
Hendricks, Frederick. 2515 6265
Hendrickson, J. Raymond. 10859
Henkel, Arthur. 1:1656c
Henkel, F.W. 10557
Henkin, Leo J. 1:1713h
Henley, Elton F. 1:5165a–6
Henley, William Ernest. 1:3299
Hennessy, dame Una Pope-. 3998 10129
    10131
Henning, John. 1926 6434 13757
Henning, Standish. 2:1740; 3828 8477
Henry, Blanche. 12183
Henry, Anne W. 13829
Henry, Aurelia. 11541
Henry, Blanche. 6957 7348
Henry, Leigh. 1:2609
Henry, William H. 1:4179
Henry C. Folger. 2:283
Henry E. Huntington library and art gallery,
    San Marino, Calif. 1:159 514–15 1633d
    1663 1835 2216 2286 2690; 2:243; 6098a
    7150

Henshall, John M. 1:3347h 4185
Hepburn, Anthony G. 1:553 2639 3695a
Hepburn, J.W. 9102
Hepburn, James G. 1:1139l 2442 4022; 3477 8517
Hepworth, Philip. 1:1760m; 3182a 3350 3359 3388
Herbert, Arthur Sumner. 1:1500
Herbert, Robert. 1:1100 3673; 1957
Herbert, Thomas W. 14290
Herbert, William. 6060
Herbrüggen, Hubertus S. 4350a
Herbst, Hermann. 1:1139t; 2107
Hereford. Cathedral. Library. 1:471 481a; 3143 3249 3336 3404
Hereford, Philip. 10892
Herford, Charles Harold. 1:2887 5091v; 2:855 1483 1889; 11551 (11573)
Herne, Frank S. 1184 5406
Hernlund, Patricia. 5798–9
Herpich, Charles A. 2:647 650; 7872
Heron, Flodden W. 828 9307 9309 13656
Herr, Alan Fager. 1:2062
Herrick, Alan. 13259–60
Herrick, Robert F. 1:2276f
Herring, Jack W. 1:2591; 8909 8910a
Herring, Phillip F. 1:3879a; 11617
Hertfordshire local history council. 1:1856
Herz, N. 9178
Heseltine, George Coulehan. 1:2880h
Heseltine, Nigel. 1:2967b 2971b 3272g 3273n 3750k 4097h
Heslop, Richard Oliver. 1:925; 7344
Hespelt, E. Herman. 6992
Hessels, J.H. 4235
Hespelt, E. Herman. 6992
Hetherington, John Rowland. 1:2782–a; 2458 5927 6252 6936 7274 13000
Hetherington, Robert John. 6936
Heun, Hans Georg. 2:91
Heventhal, Charles. 1:2657; 9141
Hewins, G.S. 3741 4407
Hewish, John. 8809
Hewitt, Arthur R. 2857
Hewitt, J.A. 12562
Hewlett, Horace W. 2:333
Hewlett, Maurice Henry. 5053
Hewson, Michael. 1:82 10730
Heydet, Xavier. 1:4631a
Heyl, Edgar. 1:2141; 7483
Heywood, Abel. 6741
Heywood, C. 12220
Heywood, G.B. 4861a
Heyworth, Peter L. 3318 3394ab 9430 12443
H.G. Wells society, London. 1:5060
Hibbard, George R. 2:1370
Hibberd, Lloyd. 235 7617b

Hibernicus, *pseud.* 8865 9802 10849
Hibgame, Frederick T. 582 11963 12621
Hickman, T. 6009
Hickmott, Allerton C. 3244
Hicks, F.W.P. 518
Hicks, Muriel A. 8098
Hickson, S.A.E. 6667 8105
Higgins, Frederick R. 1808 (5820) 5830 6206 (6429)
Higgins, T.F. 13735
Higginson, Alexander Henry. 1:2182
Higginson, Fred Hall. 1:3499; 10807 11596
Higgs, Henry. 1:2165
Higham, Charles. 14312
Highfill, Philip H. 7934
Hilbish, Florence May Anna. 1:4707q
Hildyard, Margaret Clive. 1:4071
Hill, A.B. (3926)
Hill, Archibald A. 392
Hill, B. 9156
Hill, B. Rowland. 1:4624; 5970
Hill, Charles Jarvis. 1:3498
Hill, Harold, bksllrs., Newcastle. 1:1747g
Hill, James J. 11247 12644
Hill, Joseph. 1416
Hill, N.W. 8936 10862 13491
Hill, Peter Murray. 3651 4604 6540
Hill, R.H. 1:2215; 59 618 4251 9136 11127 11416 13307
Hill, T.W. 1:3066c 3094b; 7609
Hill, Trevor Howard Howard-. 1:582 585; 2:374 616 941 948 960 1863; 233 6713 8819 9746–7 9749
Hill, Walter Martin, bksllr., Chicago. 1:573c 3324f 3841ab 4804 4849e 5076e
Hill, Winifred C. 1:1706b
Hillebrand, Harold N. 1:4415q
Hilles, Frederick Whiley. 1:4512
Hillhouse, James Theodore. 1:1900h 4609; 8520 13215
Hillier, Richard L. 2:797
Hillman, E. Haviland. 4848
Hills, Gertrude. 10058 13654–5
Hills, Margaret Thorndike. 1:1495
Hilson, James Lindsay. 1:986–7 1009; 1740 3887
Hilton, Robert. 5333
Hinch, J. Dew. 1793
Hind, Arthur Mayer. 8594
Hindle, Brian. 1165
Hindle, Christopher John. 1:2490–1 3167; 621 8926 3975 7647 7752 8112 8648 9146 10258 10891 11096 13860
Hindley, Charles. 4210
Hinds, G.S. 6415
Hindu university, Benares. Dept. of English. 11858

Hinman, Charlton J.K. 2:581 583 585 590 592–3 599 606 610–11 624 945 949 1618–19 1730; 136 211 415
Hinton, Percival F. 1:4424 4583b; 7092 12449 12782 13062 13391 13853 14242
Hinton, V.H.F.A. 1:4310
Hints for collectors and marginalia (*Bkmns J*). 12604
Hippoclides, *pseud.* 6506
Hipwell, Daniel. 1744 2518 4418 4733 5250a 5929 11369 14284
Hirai, Masao. 1:3252
Hird, Lewis A. 1:3095d
Hirsch, Felix Edward. 1:3474
Hirsch, Lester. 10808
Hirsch, Rudolf. 1:80–1
Hirst, G.M. 13308
Hirst, W.A. 9287 11907
Hiscock, Walter George. 1:606–7; 717 722–3 2373 2941–2 3108 5841 6770 7605 9137 9311 9335 10353 10360 10463 10465 10564 12045
Historica, *pseud.* 6725
Historical society *see* Royal historical society.
History of the book trade in the north. 1:926k; 1087–8 1436
History of the book-trade in the north-east. 1086 1325 1425
Hitchcock, Elsie V. 12498
Hitchings, Sinclair H. 1:1191
Hittmair, Rudolf. 4273
Hjort, Greta. 2:1018k 1710
Hoare, J. 1:4401
Hobbes, J.L. 1:1854
Hobbs, John L. 4407
Hobhouse, Edmund. 2900
Hobsbaum, Philip. 11936
Hobson, Anthony Robert Alwyn. 1:1139v; 494 2180 2194 2239 2243 3269 3305 (3473) 4946 6225–6 7923 8484 8487
Hobson, Geoffrey Dudley. 1:113gs; 1606 2086 2093–4 2105 2122 2143 2154 2735 5105 5706
Hobson, J.S. 6808
Hobson, Kenneth. 2200
Hockett, Byrne. 8812
Hodges, John C. 1:2702; 9633
Hodges, M.L. 6353
Hodgart, M.J.C. 7787
Hodgkin, J. 1:2415
Hodgkin, John Eliot. 1:570; 5643 6265 7064 7656 8069 8108 8118 8479 10862 13022
Hodgson, G.B. 7826
Hodgson, H.J. 11946
Hodgson, J.E. 2:431; 8943
Hodgson, James. 5668
Hodgson, Norma Hull *see* Russell, Norma Hull (Hodgson).

Hodgson, Sidney. 195 3637 4602 5750 5752 5768a
Hodgson and co., ltd., London. 1:2866g 3588b 4228; 2:431; 4880
Hodnett, Edward. 1747h–i 7463
Hodson, L.J. 6701
Hodson, Leighton. 1:3463k
Hodson, V.C.P. 8192
Hoe, Robert. 1:388–9 572 629 1655; 2028
Hoeniger, F. David. 2:784; 6920 9946 14568
Hofer, Philip. 3473 3896–7 4657 6225 6303 7450
Hofman, Alois. 9235a
Hoffman, Charles G. 10573
Hoffman, Daniel G. 6761
Hogan, Charles Beecher. 1:4513h; 6931 8342 13118
Hogan, Francis Joseph. 1:403 672a 1709 2023
Hogan, J.F. 7636
Hogan, J.J. 2:1468
Hogg, William Dods. 1:3680
Hohlfeld, A.R. 1:821
Holbrook, John Pinckney. 1:2935; 4445–6 4480
Holden, Wilfred Herbert. 1264
Holder, Cecilia E. 1:3710a
Holdsworth, sir W. 1:5001
Holgate, Clifford W. 1134 1425
Hogrefe, Pearl. 871a
Holiday, J.P. 1:4507
Holland, David. 3186
Holland, Michael. 890
Holland, Norman N. 2:1534
Holland, Vyvyan Beresford. 1:1396w 5103
Hollings, Frank. 14092
Hollingsworth, Keith. 1:1717c
Hollister, Paul. 6523
Holloway, Owen E. 7893
Holman, Thomas B. 11658
Holme, C. Geoffrey. 1:1554 2285; 7019
Holmes, Beatrix. 6465
Holmes, F.M. 5478b
Holmes, sir Maurice Gerald. 1:2877–8 4631; 861 9673–4 13264
Holmes, Richard R. 2020 2558
Holmes, Ruth van Zuyle. 1:3211a
Holstein, Mark G. 2:754; 7338
Holt, Lee Elbert. 9159–60
Holt, Penelope. 5394 5561
Holtby, R.T. 3374
Höltgen, Karl J. 14247
Holworthy, Richard. 10214
Holyoake, George Jacob. 3546 5480 10412
Holzapfel, R.P. 1:4177a
Holzknecht, Karl Julius. 2:438 788
Homeland association. 1:1762
Honan, Park. 8906

Hone, Joseph Maunsell. 1:4269; 8525
Honeyman, R.B. 8870
Honigmann, Ernest Anselm Joachim. 2:950–1 961 1470 1689
Honnold library for the Associated colleges, Claremont, Calif. 1:934–a 2656
Honour, Frances M. 5034a
Honourable society of Lincoln's inn, London see Lincoln's inn, London.
Hood, F.C. 13243
Hook, Frank S. 2:244 609; 7181 9163–4 12687
Hook, Lucyle. 14358
Hooker, Edward Niles. 736 9953 11059
Hooker, Helene Maxwell. 10368
Hookham, George. 11549
Hooper, Edith S. 9830 11546
Hooper, James. 1:4326a; 749 2516 6505 7384 7826 8218
Hooper, Richard. 10722
Hooper, Walter. 1:4050; 11979
Hope, Alison. 1:5188t
Hope, Henry Gerald. 1871 7702 7822 9007 10736
Hope, J.E.S. 7842
Hopkins, Albert A. 1:2241; 10038–9 10043 10051 10059
Hopkins, Annette Brown. 1:3412–13; 10640
Hopkins, Frederick M. 9749 14399
Hopkins, Kenneth. 1:4454c
Hopkins, R.H. 11094
Hopkins, R. Thurston. 2746
Hopkins, Tighe. 831a
Hopkinson, Cecil. 1:2068–9 2190 3296 4961; 7615 8510 10478 12592
Hoppé, Alfred John. 1:2667; 9154
Hoppe, Harry Reno. 2:1522 1569 1716–18 1720 1740; 850 5186a 6003 6916 7170 8393
Hoppen, K. Theodore. 1838
Horden, John Robert Backhouse. 1:4478; 10601 12932–5 14247
Horder, Thomas J., baron Horder. 10531
Horn, Andrew H. 162
Horn-Monval, Madeleine see Monval, Madeleine Horn-.
Horn, Robert D. 1:2307; 8231
Hornbeak, Katherine Gee. 1:1760
Hornby, Charles H. St.John. 1:1242 1244; 3853 6465 6488
Horne, Alan John. 1:2523
Horne, Colin J. 2:248 768; 8709 11717
Horne, David Hamilton. 1:4406a
Horne, Herbert Percy. 2024 2074 2087
Horodisch, Abraham. 1:5104d; 14320 14322–3
Horrocks, Sidney. 1:903a–d 1233–4; 1198 3270 4764 6099 9547 10641

Horrox, Reginald. 2:462; 74a 10552 13466
Horrox, William Arthur. 1:2770
Horsefield, J.K. 744
Horst, Irvin B. 9687
Horton, C. 4897ca
Horton-Smith, L. Graham see Smith, L. Graham Horton-.
Hoskins, Edgar. 1:2038b; 2:1709
Hoskins, William George. 1:1767
Hosley, Richard. 1:1601c 2:(132) (156b) (658) (676) (1223) (1289) (1659) 1725–6 1729 1731 1736; (9939) (13152)
Hössle, Friedrich von. 5714
Hotson, Leslie. 2:1324; 3096 12129
Houdard, G.E. 14329
Houghton, Esther Rhoads. 1:1925a; 7927
Houghton, Walter Edwards. 1:1915 1927 2818r–9; 892 7923a 7928 12570
Houk, J. Kemp. 1:2373a
Houk, Raymond A. 2:1754; 12004
Houpt, Charles Theodore. 1:2316d
House, Arthur Humphry. 1:3703p; 10151 11144 11146
Housman, Laurence. 1:3712 3733; 11175
Houston, Guyla Ann Bond. 1:4028b
Houston, Neal B. 1:2133
Houtchens, Carolyn Washburn. 1:2017 (2470) (2701) (2706) (3016) (3626) (3761) (3971) (3992) (4271) (4597) (4736)
Houtchens, Lawrence Huston. 857 10116
Howard, Alison K. (Bee). 1:807
Howard, Edward G. 8217
Howard-Hill, Trevor Howard see Hill, Trevor Howard Howard-.
Howard, Leon. 12366
Howard, William J. 11517
Howarth, Patrick. 1:476of
Howarth, R. Guy. 2:(1596); 11061 11144 11368 12188 12713 13134 13415 14226
Howe, Ellic Paul. 1:1188 4291n 4707p; 1270–2 1275–7 4147 4828 4937 5092 5119 5211 5672 5700 6102 6162 6208 6451 6592 6604 6609 6619 6621 6675 7253 7903 7907
Howe, Olga. 6675
Howe, P. P. 7884 11017
Howell, A.C. 6044
Howell, John. 8639a
Howell, Wilbur S. 8533
Howgego, James. 1:1795
Howorth, Benjamin. 1169
Howorth, Henry H. 4223 4229
Howson, J. 3375
Howson, Roger. 7240
Hoy, Cyrus, 2:1915; 8463–4 8466–8 8471
Hoy, Peter. 1:810 4314b
Hrubý, Antonín. 403 406
Hubbard, Clifford L.B. 7089
Hubbard, Frank G. 2:1159 1174

Hubbard, Lucius Lee. 1:4828; 9887
Huber, R.A. 2:1913
Huberman, Edward. 13416
Hubler, Edward. 2:1438
Huchon, René Louis. 1:2901; 9727
Huck, Thomas William. 1225 1227 4688 7716–17
Huckabay, Calvin. 1:4244 4249d
Huddy, E.J. 1:1767g
Hudleston, C.R. 2258–9 4897f
Hudson, C.M. 8887
Hudson, Cecil. 7840
Hudson, Derek Rommel. 1:(4483); 1436 5361a–b 7922
Hudson, Elizabeth. 1:4733
Hudson, Frederick. 10935
Hudson, J.P. 11066
Hudson, Randolph. 1:1942
Hudson, Richard B. 12244 12247
Hudson, William Henry. 2:694
Hudson-Williams, A. see Williams, A. Hudson-.
Huff, William Howard. 1:4930–1
Hughes, Garfield H. 12727
Hughes, Helen Campbell. 12010 14504
Hughes, Hubert David. (1107) 2811 2822
Hughes, Leo. 1:3827
Hughes, Merritt Y. 12416 12443
Hughes, Randolph. 13814 13816 13818–19
Hughes, T. Cann. 1168 2670 7492 7671 10060 11068 11970 14505
Hughes, T. Rowland. 1258
Hughes, William John. 1:954
Hughey, Ruth. 7989 8358 10445 10892
Hughs, Charles. 10984
Hull. Marvell tercentenary celebration committee. 1:4144
— Public libraries. 1:5094
— University. 1:3360c
— University college. Religious activities committee. 1:1492
Hull, Charles Henry. 1:(3494a) 4417; 12760
Hull, Vernam. 13572
Hully, P.M. 1:4537g
Hulme, A. 2718
Hulme, E. Wyndham. 6349
Hulme, Hilda E. 2:927 1321
Humaniora; essays ... honoring Archer Taylor. 5376
Hummel, Ray Orvin. 1:2923; 8735 9434 9775 13523b
Humphreys, Arthur Lee. 1:325b 858 1542c; 455 457–8 707 728 1073 1227 1237 2517 2709 3633 4845–6 5029 5031 5074 5395 6349 6745 7344 (7512) 8219 8647 12052 12460 13527
Humphreys, Arthur R. 2:1296–7
Humphreys, Charles. 4897hh

Humphreys, Edward Morgan. 1476a 1496a
Humphreys, Jennett. 10722
Humphreys, Susan M. 11335
Humphries, Charles. 1:1414a 1831 3571; 7614 7625
Humphry, James. 1:1412 3326
Hunkin, J.W. 6955
Hunt, Christopher John. 1:373 926k; 168
Hunt, Rachel McMasters (Miller). 1:2126–9; 158
Hunt, Richard William. 1:(4450w); 3075 3109 8704 10580 12779 13862
Hunt botanical library, Pittsburgh see Pittsburgh. Carnegie institute of technology.
Hunt botanical library.
Hunter, A. O. 8478a
Hunter, Dard. 1:1139zb–zc; 3722 3724 3732 3801
Hunter, George K. 654
Hunter, J.V.B. Stewart. 1:4506
Hunter, sir Mark. 2:862 1150 1183
Hunter, Parks C. 13366
Hunter, R.J. 7552
Hunter, Richard A. 7570a 9139
Hunter, Sissie. 6701
Hunterian museum see Glasgow. University. Hunterian museum.
Huntingdonshire. County record office, Huntingdon. 1:1790d
Huntington library see Henry E. Huntington library and art gallery, San Marino, Calif;
Huntington library bulletin. 1:159
Huntington library quarterly. 1:159
Huntley, Frank L. 1:4218a
Husain, Itrat-. 10253
Husbands, H. Winifred. 1:2753
Hussey, Maurice. 720 10855–6
Hussey, Richard. 9690
Huston, Kenneth Garth. 1:3142
Hustvedt, Sigurd B. 716 12761
Hutcherson, Dudley. 2:423
Hutchings, R.S. 4200 6136 6630
Hutchins, Henry Clinton. 1:2980–1; 9886 9889 9898–9 9906–7 9910
Hutchins, Margaret. 1:3574
Hutchins, W.J. 1:822d
Hutchison, B. 1:763–5 815a 838a 847 848g 1323b 2315a 2385d 2519c 2852 3282p 3283k 3364a 3510d 3933 4040a 4094a 4098a 4217m 4464a 4483b 4530g 4567m 4676a 4897d
Hutchinson, Cecil G. 1:4455b
Hutchinson, F.E. 11045–6 14146
Hutchinson, George Evelyn. 1:5070
Hutchinson, H.R. 1:2187a
Hutchinson, J.W. Hely-. 1:1255; 2187

Hutchinson, Thomas. 1:3977 3979; 9514 11811 13177 14488 14490
Hutchinson, W.A. 8432 13480 14317
Hutchinson, W.M.L. 8677 9611
Huth, Henry. 1:390–2
Hutson, Harold H. 1:1485i; 6868a
Huth, Alfred Henry. 2:402 404 407; 177
Hutt, Allen. 6676
Huttar, Charles A. 14571
Hutton, Arthur Wollaston. 1:(5212); 11378
Hutton, Lawrence. 7379
Hutton, Muriel. 12083
Hutton, Stanley. 1124 14497
Hutton, William Holden. 1:4822b
Huxley, Leonard. 1:3779; 5680
Hyamson, Albert M. 1:2197x
Hyde, Donald Frizell. 1:3850–1; 3188 11467
Hyde, Douglas. 2728
Hyde, H. Montgomery. 3380a 11348
Hyde, Mary Morley (Crapo). 1:3850f; 92a 3188 11467 11469 11513
Hyde, Ralph. 1:1795n
Hyder, Clyde K. 1:4844y
Hyett, sir Francis Adams. 1:892–5 896d 2775; 704 1013 1015
Hynes, Sam. 1:3755h
Hyslop, R. 1:(4623)
Hytch, F.J. 1:3711; 4897c–ca 12632

I. 13168 14109 14174
Ichikawa, Sanki see Sanki, Ichikawa.
Idaho. University. Library. 1:4614
Ignoramus, pseud. 912 10425
Ilchester, Giles Stephen Holland Strangways, 6th earl of see Strangways, Giles Stephen Holland, 6th earl of Ilchester.
Illing, Robert. 3894
Illinois. Southern Illinois university, Carbondale. Library. 1:3887 4019 5053f
— University. Library. 1:1699 1728 4241; 2:228
Image, Selwyn. 4029
Immroth, John Philip. 2:(735); (46) 300a (341) (350) (3431) (3827) (6174) (6175) (6196) (6699) (7148) (10316)
Imrie, D.S.M. 1704
Incorporated society of authors, London. 6503
Index society, New York. 1:601
India. National library, Calcutta. 1:359a; 2:128a
Indiana. University. Humanities series. 5870
— — Lilly library. 1:368 3724 3731 4249a 5207
Indiana quarterly for bookmen. 1:160
Indiana university bookman. 1:160
Indiana university studies. 1:19

Ing, Catherine M. 1:28
Ingham, Ernest. 4740
Ingham, Patricia. 2:1471
Ingleby, A. 6844
Ingleby, Holcombe. 2:502 505; 3708
Inglis, Brian. 1827
Inglis, George S. 9011
Inglis, H.R.G. 1:1815
Inglis, John. 1:2628y
Ingpen, Roger Eric. 11409 13294
Ingram, A. 6910
Ingram, John Henry. 1:4120x; 6508 12138
Ingram, W.G. 7377 14289
Ingram, William. 2:343
Inland printer. 1:161
Inquirer, pseud. 6701
Inquisitor, pseud. 13386
Institute of chartered accountants in England and Wales. 1:2083
— Library. 1:2080–1
Institute of chartered accountants of Scotland, Edinburgh. Library. 1:2084
Institute of shorthand writers, London. Library. 1:2279i
Instituto Británico em Portugal, Lisbon. 2:129
Inter-American bibliographical and library association. 135
International association of antiquarian booksellers. 1:573
International conference on computational linguistics, New York. 2:948
International congress of bibliophiles. 2243 3473 6225–6
International congress of paper historians, 7th., Oxford. 1377 3783–4
International council of nurses. 1:4348
International Shakespeare conference, Stratford-upon-Avon. 2:949
Introductions to English literature. 1:2
Intze, Ottakar. 1:2681
Iowa. University. Humanistic studies. 2:1354
— Libraries. 1:5127b
Ireland. Geographical society see Geographical society of Ireland.
— Library association see Library association of Ireland.
— Music association see Music association of Ireland.
— National library, Dublin. 1:1016 1019 1828
Irish bibliographers. 29–30
Irish bibliographical pamphlets. 1:1013 1033 1045 1054 1097–8 1102 1109 1125
Irish book: 1:82 162
Irish book lover. 1:163 1010
Irvine, A.L. 4825
Irving, sir John Henry Brodribb-. 2:181

Irwin, Mary Leslie. 1:4983
Irwin, Raymond. 1:2118; 2443a 2451 2454
Irving, R.C. 13309
Isaac, Frank Swinton. 1:462 749 (1320); 843
6017 6575 6582–3 6588
Isaac, Peter Charles Gerald. 1:1274–6 1304–b
1306 1457; 1030–1 3831 4043 4045 4131
4133–4 4137–9 4513–14 6713a
Isaacs, A. Lionel. 3138
Isaacs, I.H. 577
Isaacs, J. 9628 9631
Isaacs, J.H. see also Temple Scott, pseud.
1:4719–20; 12051
Isham, sir Gyles. 13552
Isham, Ralph Heyward. 1:2508a
Isle of Man see Man, Isle of.
Ives, Samuel. 1:2230
Ivy, Geoffrey S. 2:1623

J., B. 1892
J., B.H. 13532
J., C. 1:3678; 7344
J., C.P. 5017 7009 9468 12166
J., C.S. 7636
J., D. 2:670 1007; 7115
J., H. 10720 11864
J., H.E.H. 14299
J., K. 1645
J., L.K. 7508
J., R.B. 13897
J., W. 1568
J., W.C. 901
J., W.H. 1368
Jack, professor. 5123
Jack, A.A. 1:650
Jack, E.G. 8221
Jack, Ian. 8910a 9562 9962
Jackson, Alfred. 1:4551; 2:730; 508 13101
Jackson, Allan S. 1:1636
Jackson, Berners A.W. 2:(235) (1913); (6133a)
Jackson, Bert W. 1:1358; 5073
Jackson, Dorothy Judd. 1:3782t–u; 11297
11299
Jackson, F.M. 14285
Jackson, George. 14288
Jackson, H.L. 5064
Jackson, Herbert. 7423
Jackson, Holbrook. 1:1297 1979 3322; 3360b
4563j; 321 4182 4275 4709 4982 4994 5350
5892 6077 6078 6098 6109 6114 6467 6469
8754 14555
Jackson, Macdonald P. 2:1369; 7189 12546
Jackson, R. Wyse. 1969 7775a
Jackson, Sara. 3139
Jackson, T.G. 2502
Jackson, W. 1:1540
Jackson, W.A. 3144

Jackson, W. Spencer. 1:4827
Jackson, Wilfrid S. 2:574
Jackson, William Alexander. 1:538d 542 577
2240w 3030 3263; 2:1229a; 232 297 325
622 656 659–60 667 897 2152 2169a 2927
3086 3097 3531 4036 5761–2 5914 6019
6039 6295 6302 6339 6343 6404 7628 8070
9692 10446 10875 13417 13877 14479
Jacob, E.F. 2901
Jacob, Gertrude. 1:4559g
Jacobi, Charles T. 2012 2290 3511 3580 3851
4379 4499 4503 4585 4630 4634 4756 4973
5302 5346 5409 5936 6255 6574 6702
12523
Jacobs, Joseph. 1:3740
Jacobs, Reginald. 4778 6846
Jacobson, D.L. 898a
Jacquot, Jean. 11090
Jaggard, W.J. 2:505
Jaggard, William. 1:906 1184 1345a–b; 2:34
55 67 71 187–8 361b 406 521 528 650 706
708 739 1003 1005 1016 1040 1043 1570
1639; 582 619 627 1144 1267 1414 1421
2070 2418 2682 3494 3584 3588 3692 3834
3865 3918 4909–13 5389 5600 5872 5883
5997 6199 6235 6275 6356 6510 6513 6560
6725 6870 6896 6902 6941 7001 7062 7076
7171 7239 7334 7344 7471 7636 8251–2
8431 8858 9253 10288 11261 12109 12943
12946 12948 13532
Jaggard and co. 3580
Jahn, Robert. 4362
Jakeman, Caroline E. 1:3841d
James, A.R. 11317
James, A.T.S. 2848
James, C.W. 2781 2887
James, D.F. 1424
James, H.E.H. 1:964; 1550
James, Harold E. 2:574a; 802–3 3245 3463
8268 10284 10618 10620 11920
James, J.G. Wallace-. 5897
James, J. Phillip Brutton. 6212
James, Montague Rhodes. 1:(426) 3706; 2765
2902 2938 3271 9867 12711 12657 13718
James, P. 10240
James, Philip B. 1:78 11399q–r 1554; 282
2095 2100 5402
James, T.E. 8118
James, T.L. 1549
James, W.P. 1:4575
James Ford Bell Lectures. 10314
Jameson, Margaret Ethel Storm. 1:4525
Jameson, Mary Ethel. 1:4555
Jameson, R. 11863
Jamieson, H.D. 3808a
Jamieson, James H. 1:996
Jane, Cecil. 2864
Janelle, Pierre. 1:4745

Jannattoni, Livio. 1:2570a
Janner, Oswald. 5601
Japan. Japan science council. Division of economics, commerce and business administration. 1:2168g
— Shakespeare association *see* Shakespeare association of Japan.
— Shakespeare society *see* Shakespeare society of Japan.
Jarratt, F. 925 2595 6696–7 7344
Jarvis, F.P. 11935
Jarvis, Rupert C. 1:3304; 3769 10508 10515 14459
Jasenas, Michael. 11784
Jaspert, W. Pincus. 6623 6628 6654
Jay, Frank. 4859 13488
Jay, Harriett. 1:2606
Jay, Leonard. 1:1252–b; 3919
Jayne, Sears Reynolds. 1:1760i 2838; 2441 3205
Jazayery, Mohammad Ali. 2:1461
Jeakes, Thomas J. 706; 3712 7826
Jebb, Reginald. 5579a
Jeffares, A. Norman. 1:(4826a)
Jefferson, D.W. 1:3966d; 2:(810)
Jeffreys, Alan Edward. 1:3282
Jeffreys, H.G. Gwyn. 6214
Jenkins, Clauston. 13797
Jenkins, David. 1523
Jenkins, David Clay. 1:1929
Jenkins, Frank. 6778a
Jenkins, Gladys. 1:2255a; 8082
Jenkins, Harold. 1:2787d; 2:1234 1247 1251 1906 1914; 4373 9437 12684
Jenkins, Herbert M. 10396
Jenkins, J.G. 1045 3779
Jenkins, Raymond. 13561 13567
Jenkins, Robert Thomas. 1:4416k
Jenkins, Rhys. 1098 3709–11 3713 3720 3735
Jenkinson, Francis John Henry. 1:453 877; 273 (545a) (829) 1048 1571 (4218a) (4572a) (6723)
Jenks, Edward. 11648–9
Jennett, Sean. 6123 6719
Jennings, Audrey. 11227
Jennings, Brendan. 6427
Jennings, O. 6658a
Jennings, P. 10820
Jensen, Bent Juel-. 1:3189–a 3230a 4427–9 4509–11 4687–9a; 687a 2382 4131 10320–8 10414 11233 13439–40 13442 13878 14274
Jensen, Gerald E. 10501 10503
Jenson, John R. 9296
Jeremy, Mary. 4305 4309
Jerman, B.R. 10208
Jerningham, Charles E. 7867a
Jerome, Joseph. 1:(4825a)
Jerrold, W.C. 1:4956

Jerrold, Walter. 1:3826a; 6057 9486 9516 9990
Jersey City, N.J. Public library. 2:45
Jervis, W.W. 1388
Jesperson, Otto. 2:1430
Jessel, Frank. 1961 3865 5425 9688
Jessop, Thomas Edmund. 1:2452 3758
Jews' college, London *see* London. University. Jews' college.
Jiriczek, Otto L. 8556
Jochum, Klaus Peter S. 1:5197v
Johannesburg. Public library. 1:1232
John Galsworthy, an appreciation. 1:3382
John M. Wing foundation *see* Newberry library, Chicago. John M. Wing foundation.
John Rylands library, Manchester. 1:326 336 429 458 460 498 1472–3 1481–2 4223; 2:193
John Rylands library bulletin. 1:164
Johnes, Herbert J. Lloyd-. 1299 3110 3334 4926
Johns, Francis A. 1:5003d–e; 14163–4
Johnson, Alfred Forbes. 1:97 755–8 1204–5 1208 (1287–8) 1745f (4291n); 74b 299 851 853 855 860 862–3 1273 1605 3111 3816 4192 4166a 4906 4918 4930 5211 6110 6114 6284 6301 6574a 6576 6578–80 6585 6589–90 6598 6603 6613 6615–16 6623 6625 6628 6647 6654 6669 6678 6715–17 6715a
Johnson, Alfred Lee. 4930
Johnson, Ann Cox-. 3189
Johnson, Arthur M. 423
Johnson, Charles P. 9972 9974
Johnson, D.W. 13160
Johnson, E.D.H. 5566
Johnson, Edgar. 1:4614b; 10143
Johnson, Francis Rarick. 1:2110 3524 3664d 4757; 3205 3696 6106 6409 10200 10203 10879 10997 10999
Johnson, Fred Bates. 9658
Johnson, Fridolf. 5306
Johnson, John De Monins. 5355 6097 6386
Johnson, Joseph. 1:4093
Johnson, L.G. 1:1939; 1715
Johnson, Lionel Pigot. 1:(3577) (3585)
Johnson, Margot. 3350a
Johnson, Merle. 1:(5076f–g); 346
Johnson, Priscilla. 4940
Johnson, Reginald Brimley. 1:2660 3311; 11263
Johnson, Robert Carl. 1:2351a (3401a) 3521a (3657a) (3969a) (4074d) (4082a) 4124a (4317b) (4325a) (4406aa)
Johnson, Robert E. 1:4516m
Johnson, Robert Underwood. 11659
Johnson, S.F. 2:1325

Josephson, Aksel Gustaf Salomon. 1:85; (102)
Joughin, George Louis. 1:3782
Journalist, *pseud.* 7632
Journal of librarianship. 1:165
Journal of the Printing historical society. 1:166
Journal of typographic research. 1:167
Joyce, Hewette Elwell. 1:2568a
Juchhoff, Rudolf. 1:410b 656
Judge, Cyril B. 3448
Judson, S. 1:5068a
Juel-Jensen, Bent *see* Jensen, Bent Juel-.
Jugaku, Bunsho. 1:2474; 8607
Jupp, Ralph Tennyson. 1:3070f
Jump, John D. 10566
Junor, John. 5088
Jusserand, J.J. 2537

K., A.M. 6733 8061
K., C. 6907 7700 10810
K., E. 2259
K., H.G.L. 13219
K., L.L. 7367 7495 8207 9347 10603 11647 12227 12663
K., M.J. 11761
K., W.R. 1552
Kable, William S. 1:2529g; 2:621 623
Kagarlitzkii, Julius I. 1:2858e
Kagitei, M.A. 3784
Kahl, William Frederick. 1:915a–b
Kahn, Sholom J. 2:1464
Kain, Richard M. 1:3871 3877; 11618
Kallich, Martin. 1:4817
Kalson, Albert E. 1:2806b 2:809
Kamm, Antony. 1:4976m
Kane, Peter E. 1:5075
Kane, Robert J. 9450
Kansai university, Osaka. Economic society. Materials section. 1:4114q
Kansas. University. Libraries. 1:139 3879 5206; 2:940; 226 239 742 4604 7816
Kaplan, H.G. 1:485d
Kaplan, Israel B. 8414
Karch, R. Randolph. 6608
Karslake, Frank. 1:334; 1054 1392 1415 2623 4525 4590 4815–16 5056 5375 5483 5979
Karslake, Madge. 4948
Karslake and company, bksllrs., London. 4815
Karlson, Marjorie. 11884.
Kaser, David. 11275 13231
Kastner, Leon Emile. 1:3193e; 10332
Katarskiĭ, Igor Maksimilianovich. 1:3100p
Katona, Anna. 1:2858f
Katz, Joseph. 1009
Katz, W.A. 7342a

Kaufman, Paul. 1:1760n; 1633 1669 1732 1741 2452 2456 2459 3289 3306 3376 3389–90 3395 3683 5773 8958 8963 13008 13529 13634
Kavanaugh, Edmund J. 6692
Kay, Arthur. 527
Kaye, Frederick Benjamin. 1:4115–16
Kazuo Araki *see* Araki, Kazuo.
Keane, Augustus Henry. 1:3901–2
Keane, Margaret. 3796
Keast, William R. 1:3196; 2:476; 11476 11478 11485 11494
Keatinge, Charles T. 4810
Keats-Shelley association of America. 1:54–5
Keats-Shelly journal. 1:54–5
Keats-Shelley memorial house, Rome. 1:676 2020–1
Kebabian, John S. 3359a
Kebbel, Thomas Edward. 1:(2898a)
Kebler, Leonard. 13647
Keefe, H.J. 4855
Keeler, Mary Freer. 1:17
Keeling, Denis F. 1:924d
Keen, Alan. 10914
Keighley, Marion. 1:951
Keir, David. 4398
Keith, Alexander. 2:673a; 3810
Keith, sir Arthur. 1:3916m
Keith, Sara. 1:1442g; 5237 6772
Kellaway, Charles W. 5070
Kellaway, W. 1:477
Kelleher, Denis. 1501 1817 3736 7256a
Keller, Dean H. 1:95
Kellett, E.E. 4777 7894
Kelley, Lauchlan Phil. 1:2571
Kelley, Maurice. 1:4236; 12367 12373–4 12397 12403 12409–11 12414–15 12435 12446 12450 12454
Kelley, Philip. 883–4
Kellner, Leon. 2:860
Kelly, Patrick. 1:4069d; 12031
Kelly, Paul V. 1543
Kelly, R.J. 1788 1880 1949 6422
Kelly, Thomas. 1307 2455
Kelly and co. 1201
Kelso, Ruth. 1:2146 2151
Kelvingrove galleries, Glasgow. 1:1002
Kemp, Ivor. 1:3734
Kemp, J.A. 1:2420
Kemp, John T. 7485
Kempel, Ben D. 5043 5543–6 13038–9
Kempling, William Bailey. 2:544 547; 8272 9955 11562 13913
Kempson, E.G.H. 3063–4
Kendall, Lyle H. 2:249; 11514 11902 12219 13879 13881 14451 14466–8
Kennedy, Arthur Garfield. 1:5 2201–2; 7353
Kennedy, Bruce. (10312)

Kennedy, C.M. 11707
Kennedy, Desmond. 1835 3808
Kennedy, James. 1:1437
Kennedy, M.J.O. 1:1341g; 4849
Kennedy, R.F. 9851
Kennedy, Roderick Stuart. 1:3638
Kennedy, Virginia Wadlow. 1:2825
Kenner, Hugh. 1:4052r
Kennethe, L.A. 10121–2
Kenny, Cyril E. 11996
Kenny, H.E. 605
Kenny, Shirley Strum. 13602 13604
Kent, Elizabeth E. 10759
Kent, Henry Watson. 1:331; 9967
Kent, Muriel. 7013
Kent, W. 8952
Kent state university. Library. 1:194
Kenton, Edna. 1:3805
Kentucky. University. Libraries. 1:2858
—— —— Margaret I. King library, Lexington.
    1:1543
Kenwood, Sydney H. 1:822g
Kenyon, sir Frederic George. 2:1888; 37
    10867 11652 12738
Kenyon, Lloyd Tyrell-, baron Kenyon.
    1:4251; 12459
Keogh, Andrew. 1:25 662 1254 2371 2451c
    (2465) (3010) (3504) (3580) (3942) (4798)
    (5025e); 8257
Keough, Lawrence C. 1:4626
Ker, C.S. 1:4076
Ker, Neil Ripley. 1371 1374 2438 2457 3043
    3088 3190–1 3390a 5908
Ker, William Peter. 10015
Kerby-Miller, Charles William see Miller,
    Charles William Kerby-.
Kerling, Nelly J.M. 4318
Kermode, John Frank. 2:1778
Kern, Jerome David. 1:400
Kern, John D. 1:1922 1937 2552; 1709
Kernohan, J.W. 4084
Kerpneck, Harvey. 12251
Kerr, Diana Rait. 1:2157
Kerr, Elizabeth M. 1:1694y
Kerr, Margaret M. 1:3648
Kerr, S.P. 119
Kerr, William Holmes. 10907
Kershaw, Alister. 1:2318a–19
Kershaw, S.W. 12655
Kerslake, John F. 11356
Kerslake, Thomas. 1:695
Kessary, Christopher. 2:71
Kessel, Marcel. 9201 9206–7 13316–17
    13323–4
Ketelbey, C.D.M. 5880
Kettle, Bernard. 7728
Kettlewell, J. 13064
Keynes, sir Geoffrey Langdon. 1:369 1382

2366 2368 2472 2479a–82 2486a 2488–c
2517 2530 2549–50 2562 2564 2566b 2939
3159–60 3162 3165 3275–8 3617–18 3628
3698 3923 3924s 4490–1 4582; 2:1939; 68
125 4039 5412 5416 5834 6210b 6279 8325
8565 8567 8569–70 8573 8587 8596–9
8601–2 8605 8616 8620 8623 8626 8629–30
8634 8640 8645 8770 8817–a 8830 8840
8849 9156 9715 10240 10251 10255 10262
10269 10460 10668 10670–1 11018 12029
13162 13866
Keynes, John Maynard, 1st baron Keynes.
    1:3358 4131; 12012 12576
Khan, M. Siddiq. 1:2704a
Kidd, James. 1:41 3425b
Kiddell, A.J.B. 1:2138
Kidman, Roy. 12982
Kidson, Frank. 1:1831 1833 3027a 3416b;
    5429 5932 7413 7584
Kiely, Benedict. 1:1723k
Kiener, Mary Aloysi. 1:4334
Kilgour, A.D. 1:3531
Kilgour, Frederick G. 1:3619f; 11002
Kilgour, Margaret. 9421
Killam, G.D. 1:1722c
Kilmarnock. Mackie Burnsiana library see
    Mackie Burnsiana library, Kilmarnock.
Kimber, Edward. 1:643c 644
Kimber, Sidney A. 3791 11713
Kimber, W.C. 7052
Kimmelman, Elaine. 9138 9229 11882
Kinard, Betty V. 7095 9325
Kind, John Louis. 1:5215
Kindilien, Carlin T. 1:2309; 8237
King, A.H. 2:1123
King, Alexander Hyatt. 1:1838 3568 4469;
    75 3246–7 3290 7611 7613 7618–20
    7623–4
King, Alfred J. 6267 8201 12536 13129
King, Arthur. 5944
King, C.M. (Key). 1:2247
King, Charles. 8932
King, Dorothy. 12460
King, E.M. 4829
King, Frederick Allen. 1:3801
King, Henry M. 1:2062d.
King, Hilda D. 1:2697b; 9250
King, Margaret I., library, Lexington see
    Kentucky. University. Margaret I. King
    library, Lexington.
King, R.W. 11023
King, Roma A. 8911
King, Shirley E.A. 1:(4968)
King, Thomas J. 2:617; 13420
King, William. 13736
Kingdon, John A. 4781–2
King's college school, Wimbledon see
    Wimbledon. King's college school.

Kingsford, Charles Lethbridge. 1:4404f; 10983
Kingsford, R.J.L. 6930
Kingsford, Walter B. 10412
Kingsland, William G. 14379
King's Lynn festival, 1967. 1:1236m
Kingston, Ont. Queen's university. Douglas library. 1:2600
Kinsey, J.M. 1:952c
Kinney, Arthur F. 10791
Kinsley, James. 9101–2 9112 14238
Kinsman, Robert S. 1:4696b; 13449–51
Kippenberg, August. 1:2975t
Kirby, Ethyn Morgan (Williams). 1:4466
Kirby, H.T. 1:3751; 9707 10760 10779
Kirby, John P. 1:1406; 5808
Kirk, Gerald A. 3307
Kirk, Rudolph. 3976
Kirk, S.J. 3631
Kirkby, C.V. 1:912
Kirkby, John. 10898
Kirkham, E. Bruce. 1:4028s; 11950
Kirkham, Michael. 1:3500
Kirkpatrick, Brownlee Jean. 1:3351 5158–9
Kirkpatrick, Thomas Percy Claude. 1:1947 2806m 3662g; 44 314 1779 1891 1907 4704 5514 8725 13737
Kirkus, Agnes Mary. 1:3419
Kirsch, Arthur C. 2:(132) (156b) (658) (676) (1223) (1289) (1659); (9939) (13152)
Kirschbaum, Leo. 1:1624; 2:434 895 1213 1442 1444 1446 1448 1485; 401 .3531 3562–3 7166–7 7179 7184 12155 14464
Kirsop, Wallace. 923
Kirwood, Albert Ernest Maldon. 1:3610; 4666 10986
Kitchin, C.H.B. 3272
Kitchin, George. 1:4047
Kite, J.E. 8807
Kite, V.J. 1:485 554b
Kitton, Frederick George. 1:3032 3051 3053–4; 9976 9978–80 9983–4 9986 13977
Kittredge, George Lyman. 6783
Kitts, J. James. 1110
Klein, David. 10577
Klemke, Elmer Daniel. 1:4270p
Kline, George Louis. 1:5089d
Klinefetter, Ralph A. 12062
Knapp, Lewis Mansfield. 4806 7795 13492–4 13508–9 13511 13514
Knapp, Mary Etta. 1:3399
Knapp, William Ireland. 1:2502
Knaster, Roland. 6723c 7249 7259
Knerr, Anthony. 1:3226; 10411
Knickerbocker, Kenneth L. 1:2582; 13815
Knickerbocker, William S. 2:1362
Knight, Charles. 3639a 4310
Knight, Douglas. 10763

Knight, Joseph. 1:(4542); 7819
Knight, Katherine. (3727)
Knight, William. 14490
Knott, Cargill Gilston. 1:(4321)
Knott, David H. 1296 7324a 9116g
Knott, Joan. 3399
Knotts, Walter E. 10653
Knowler. 5929
Knowles, David. 1:2568g 3699p
Knowles, Edwin B. 970 972
Knowles, Frederic Lawrence. 1:3938
Knowles, James. 1:1916
Knowles, John A. 2:1178
Knowles, Michael Clive see Knowles, David.
Knox, David J. 5681a
Knox, R. Buick. 1527
Knox, T.M. 1:2840t; 11038
Kocher, Paul H. 7160
Kohlmetz, George William. 1:4468
Kok, Abraham Seyne. 2:507
Kökeritz, Helge. 2:594 1246
Kolb, Gwin J. 5277 11486 11488 11491 11497 11505 11508 13010
Komarova, V.P. 2:131
König, Gertrud. 2:98
Konigsberg, I. 7359a
Konody, Paul George. 1:2914y; 4425
Kooistra, J. 1:4641–2
Köppel, Emil. 1:(2680g)
Korg, Jacob. 1:3440–3
Korninger, Siegfried. 2:(1368)
Korte, Donald M. 1:4717b
Kosok, Heinz. 1:1723 2030h 5040–a
Koszul, André H. 2:1067; 5876 13287
Kot, Stanisław. 959a
Kraft, James. 11349
Kramer, Dale. 10977 10982
Kraus, Hans Peter. 10314
Krayer, E. Hoffman-. 2257
Krebs, Heinrich. 1:4107a; 2:360; 1452 7352
Kreemers, Ralph. 1:4011
Kreig, W. (2448a) (7615b)
Krempel, Lore Sporhan-. 5714d–e
Kress library see Harvard university. Graduate school of business administration. Baker library. Kress library of business and economics.
Krishnamurti, Gutala. 1:4954b
Kronenberg, Maria Elizabeth. 1:1247f; 840 842 2903a 4768
Kronick, David A. 8155
Kropf, Hans. 1:2322c
Krueger, Robert. 681 9812 9850 10266
Kruyskamp, C. 1720
Krzyżanowski, Ludwik. 1:2872
Kubler, George Adolph. 5721 6355 6360
Kudzinowski, Czesław. (959a)
Kuethe, J. Louis. 12375

Vol. **1** = *Bibliographies*   **2** = *Shakespeare*   **4** = 1–8221   **5** = 8222–14616

Lennam, Trevor N.S. 7191
Lennep, W.B. van see Van Lennep, W.B.
Lennox, P.J. 1757
Leonhardt, Benno. 8443–7
Lenthicum, M. Channing. 613
Leroy, Gaylord C. 1:3773d
Leroy, Olivier. 1:2566
Leskien, Elfriede. 2181
Leslie, H.H. 7902
Leslie, John Henry. 1:2232–3; 7083 8010
Leslie, sir Shane. 2:567; 57 2904 12742
    13726 13738 13775
Leslie-Melville, Alexander Ronald see
    Melville, Alexander Ronald Leslie-.
Lester, John Ashby. 1:2964; 9841
Leston, D. 14477
Lethaby, W.R. 12701
Letts, Malcolm Henry Ikin. 1:4116b; 8826
    12123–4
Letwin, William. 1:2790b
Leuba, Walter. 1:4576c
Leudecke, Margaret Ann. 1:2582ac 2582b
Leuze, Otto. 6017a
Levidova, Inna Mikhailovna. 1:2532c 3303b
    3384p 4356a 4611b 4633p 4813a 5053w;
    2:131–a 143 149a
Levin, Richard. 420
Levin, Y.D. 2:131
Levine, Jane. 1:1736
Levine, Mortimer. 1:490a
Levinson, Harry A. 12224
Levis, Howard Coppuck. 1:1741–2
Levy, Charles S. 1:4689d; 13443
Levy, Goldie. 1:2817d
Levy, Matthias. 1:2279i
Levy, Maurice. 11993
Lewis, A. Henry. 1498
Lewis, A. Jenny see also Stratford, A. Jenny
    (Lewis). 14486
Lewis, Alfred Sydney. 1:3964; 1155 7596
    7714 7872
Lewis, Aneirin. 10455
Lewis, Charles Thomas Courtney. 1:1259b–c
    1259da–b 1270d 1356–7; 3960 3962 3963a
    3964b–bc 5027q 5045 6202
Lewis, Clarissa O. 1:4238; 12393
Lewis, Clive Staples. 2:877; 12352
Lewis, Frank R. 2987
Lewis, Gwyneth. 7513
Lewis, Helen Courtney-. 3960
Lewis, Idwal. 1:700h 709–b 908 1465i 1928u
    3536k; 4636 7972 9394
Lewis, Jenny see Lewis, A. Jenny.
Lewis, John S. 9761
Lewis, M. Gwyneth. 1:1813 1813b
Lewis, Oscar. 4282
Lewis, P.W. 1161b 3785a
Lewis, Penry. 11732

Lewis, R. 4654–5 6854
Lewis, Roy. 4950
Lewis, S.S. 2490
Lewis, T.H. 1511
Lewis, Walter. 4181
Lewis, Wilmarth Sheldon. 5019 14184 14186
    14188 14193–5 14200 (14203) 14204
Lewis Carroll centenary exhibition, London.
    1:2728–9
Lewy, C. 1:2530c
Lexington. Margaret I. King library see Ken-
    tucky. University. Margaret I. King library,
    Lexington.
Leyden, W. von. 12016a
Leyton. Public libraries. 1:890
Libbis, G. Hilder. 1:3783h; 11303
Library, The. 1:168
Library association, London. 1:165 593 838
    1020 1560 1669 1826a 1858 2030 2110d
    4462; 260 2455 2459 3376b 7045 7453
    8144 8153
— Arundell Esdaile memorial lectures. 2453 3310
— Eastern branch. 1:889
— Library. 1:106
— Library history group. 1:173
— Library manuals. 259–60 265 269
— Reference, special, and information sec-
    tion. North-western group. 1:1862
— University, college and research section.
    126
— — Scottish group. 1:41 125 281
Library association of Ireland. 1834
— Journal. 1:118
Library association record. 1:169
Library chronicle. 1:170
Library chronicle (University of Pennsylvania).
    1:171
Library chronicle of the University of Texas. 1:172
Library company, Philadelphia see
    Philadelphia. Library company.
Library history. 1:173
Library notes (Duke university). 1:174
Library notes (Kipling J). 11780
Library notes (Lib Chron Univ Pennsylvania).
    6878 7288 8365
Library notes (TLS). 634 2432
Library notes and news (Bull John Rylands Lib).
    2856 11404
Lichfield. City and county. 1:3836h
— Johnson house committee. 1:3841bb
Liddell, J.R. 2988
Liddell, Mark. 2:1530; 11642
Lidderdale, J.H. 11619
Liddon, Henry Parry. 1:(2273) (4471)
Lieberman, Ben. 5002
Liebert, Herman Wardwell. 1:359e 363g
    3845; 91 538 543 8717 10729 11462 11464
    11468 11489 14333

Liége. Université. Faculté philosophie. Bibliothèque. 11913

Lievsay, John Leon. 1:490b 832; 956 3147 3893 (13543)

Lightfoot, Clare. 1:1458

Lightwood, James Thomas. 1:2157p 3033a

Liljequist, Orval. 2:245

Lilley, George Peter. 1:4320

Lillie, W.W. 11909

Lilly library see Indiana. University, Library.

Limentani, Uberto. 1:3562

Limited editions club, N.Y. 1:151 1359; 2:754

Limouze, A. Sanford. 1:3416d; 7777

Linck, Charles E. 1:5042 5042b–c

Lincoln. Cathedral. Library. 1:456

— City libraries, museum and art gallery. 1:913 4900

Lincoln, David. 1:1238

Lincolnshire bibliographies. 1:2456

Lincoln's inn, pseud. 8404

Lincoln's inn, London. Library. 1:1970

Lindberg, Sten G. 2239a

Linder, Leslie Charles. 1:4450a; 5944 12884

Linderman library see Lehigh university, Bethlehem, Pa. Lucy Packer Linderman memorial library.

Lindimp, pseud. 13911

Lindley library see Royal horticultural society.

Lindsay, Charles L. 1:4058; 4644–5 7656 7658

Lindsay, David A.E., 27th earl of Crawford and Balcarres. 10461

Lindsay, David W. 11248

Lindsay, Jack. 4647 4649

Lindsay, James Ludovic, 26th earl of Crawford. 1:337 1460 1534 1870 2045–6; 2273 2865

Lindsay, Norman. 4647

Lindsay, Robert O. 10909

Lindstrand, Gordon. 1:2874; 9664 9666–a 9667

Line, Maurice Bernard. 1:838; 3771

Linen hall library, Belfast see Belfast library and society for promoting knowledge.

Lingel, Robert J. 1:4042

Linnell, C.L.S. 1:2492

Linton, Marion P. 1:1590e 1612 1760j; 1730 7097 7099 7188

Lillicrap, C.S. 12262 14295

Lisbon. Instituto Británico em Portugal see Instituto Británico em Portugal, Lisbon.

Lisney, Arthur Adrian. 1:2136

Lister, R.H. 1:493

Lister, R.J. 1:325

Lister, Raymond George. 1:1335 3480; 14604

Literary anniversary club of San Francisco. 1:4807

Literary property. 6503

Literature and science. 222

Little, Andrew George. 1:4404f (4971f)–g

Little, G.F. 1:2380 2704

Little, G.L. 14552

Littleboy, Anna L. 2766

Littledale, Harold. 2:1786

Littlehales, Henry. 1:3372

Litz, A. Walton. 1:3874 3879a; 11622

Litzinger, Boyd. 1:2582

Litzenberg, Karl. 12527

Liveing, Edmund G.D. 5941b

Liverpool. Cathedral. Radcliffe library. 1:372

— First edition club see First edition club, Liverpool.

— Medical institution. Library. 1:2230h

— Public libraries. 1:907

— University. Library. 1:468–9 499 1226

Livingston, Dorothy F. 1:2371

Livingston, Flora Virginia (Milner). 1:2727 3947–9 3991 4805 4853; 11739 11752 11754 13804

Livingston, Luther Samuel. 1:3940 3975–6 4198 4436 4890; 2:463; 2572 8886 10733 11653 11726–8 11809 11815 13082 13283 13639 13904 13973

Ljunggren, Evald. 2:1801

Lloyd, B.B. 1:3549n

Lloyd, Bertram. 609 10574

Lloyd, D. Myrddin. 1:701 707; 1499 1540 3112 6037 6435

Lloyd, D. Tecwyn. 1513 4614a

Lloyd, Hugh. 1:4411

Lloyd, J.D.K. 11224

Lloyd, James W. 5040

Lloyd, L.J. 2362 3205a

Lloyd, Llewelyn C. 1385 1386a 4943

Lloyd, William Supplee. 1:2978

Loades, D.M. 3507 7946 7951

Loane, George G. 3969 7996 8859 9364 9366–7 12816–17 12820

Löb, Ladislaus. 1:4458b

Lobban, J.H. 11054

Lock, R. Northwood. 6942

Lock, Walter. 1:3915

Locke, Harold. 1:2315 3181; 777

Locker-Lampson, Frederick see Lampson, Frederick Locker-.

Lockett, W.G. 13650

Lockhart, E.W. 1:441

Lodge, Oliver W.F. 11056

Lodge, S. 11920

Loeber, E.G. 3753

Loewenberg, Alfred. 1:1590b; 7728

Loewenfeld, K. 12143

Loewenstein, Fritz Erwin. 1:4633; 13269 13271

Lofthouse, Hilda. 3206

Loftie, W.J. 5915

Lofts, William Oliver Guillemont. 1:5005r

Logan, James Venable. 1:5160 5165

Logs, *pseud*. 1377

Lohf, Kenneth A. 1:2857

Lohrli, Anne. 10177 11893

Loiseau, Jean. 1:2889

Lomax, C.E. 7344

Lomax, Michael Trappes-. 4144a

Lombard, C.M. 1:812

London. Arts council *see* Arts council of Great Britain.

— Bibliographical society *see* Bibliographical society, London.

— British drama league *see* British drama league, London.

— British library of political and economic science *see* British library of political and economic science, London.

— Brompton oratory. 1:535

— Central school of arts and crafts. 4986 5159

— College of St. Mark and St. John *see* College of St. Mark and St. John, London.

— Congregational library. 1:2266k

— Corporation. Guildhall. Library *see* London. Guildhall library.

— Dr. Williams's library *see* Dr. Williams's charity and library, London.

— Fine art society *see* Fine art society, London.

— First edition club *see* First edition club, London.

— Guildhall library. 1:590–1 916 1429 1878–9 2145 2178 2281f 4279 4647

— Institute of shorthand writers *see* Institute of shorthand writers.

— Library association *see* Library association, London.

— Lincoln's inn *see* Lincoln's inn, London.

— Map collectors' circle *see* Map collectors' circle, London.

— Marylebone cricket club *see* Marylebone cricket club, London.

— North-western polytechnic. Dept. of ptg. 1271 4274 4304

— Polish library *see* Polish library, London.

— Press club *see* Press club, London.

— Printing historical society *see* Printing historical society, London.

— Public record office *see* Gt. Brit. Public record office.

— Royal college of physicians *see* Royal college of physicians, London.

— Royal college of veterinary surgeons *see*

Royal college of veterinary surgeons, London.

— Royal society *see* Royal society of London.

— St. Bride foundation institute *see* St. Bride foundation institute, London.

— St. Paul's cathedral. Library. 1:920

— Selden society *see* Selden society, London.

— Shakespeare association *see* Shakespeare association, London.

— Society of herbalists *see* Society of herbalists, London.

— Stationers' company *see* Stationers' company, London.

— Times bookshop *see* Times bookshop, London.

— University. 1:482

— — Council for psychical investigation. Research library. 1:2242–4

— — Goldsmiths' company's library of economic literature. 1:1535–6 2047

— — Imperial college of science and technology. 1:3779b

— — Institute of Germanic languages and literatures. 1:823

— — Institute of Latin American studies. 1:2289g

— — Jews' college. 1:921

— — King's college. 1:1496

— — — Library. 1:359 1618 3154 4389

— — London school of economics. 1:107

— — Queen Mary college. 1:4758

— — Regent's Park college. Angus library. 1:2253x

— — School of librarianship. 1:30–4 539b 544b 635 691 716g 777m 777x 801s 807 811 811g 811m 813f 822d–e 822m–n 822s 826g 843h 873x 881m–n 884x 897p 952c 1030e 1076 1172 1246 1262 1285 1298 1303 1305 1318 1323a 1338 1341g 1360 1362 1374s 1559b 1560 1578c 1601a 1652g 1754n 1767g 1775 1778d 1837c 1841b 1902c 1971t 2005e 2063c 2103b–c 2150 2223 2247 2240qc 2249c 2270a 2273b 2300b 2306b 2324 2351 2359 2374 2376 2379 2386f 2394 2395a 2404 2414e 2420 2435 2443–4 2468 2485x 2494 2499c 2671h 2672 2699 2711 2747–8 2751k 2763 2777 2786 2809 2886e 2891 2895p 2904 2914 2955 2995 3002 3141 3150d 3175 3179 3212 3218 3268 3282 3282w 3306 3318 3334 3349 3399a 3413c 3416g 3448t 3458d 3459e 3494 3530 3536 3540 3611 3629 3648 3668 3672 3695 3697 3699 3710d 3753 3784–5 3785d 3857 3858b 3906a 3923d 3928 3968a 3968z 4009a 4010 4051e 4060 4076 4118a 4142 4170 4187 4207a 4257 4292 4310 4319a 4320 4366m 4370 4401 4401d 4402gd 4417a 4419 4458 4462

London.   University.   School   of
librarianship—*cont.*
4507 4537g 4540a 4585 4611 4618 4636
4680h 4682 4685 4694 4696 4768–9 4787
4793 4824 4825d 4862 4866 4883 4955
4958 4962 4969b 4972 4979 5000 5025t
5045a 5051a 5053 5068a 5072 5110 5113
5115–a 5119 5158 5162 5190; 2:99; 4849
7441
— — University college. 1:3728; 12114
— — — Library. 1:2448c
— — Warburg institute. 1:833a
— Victoria and Albert museum, South Ken-
sington *see* Victoria and Albert museum,
South Kensington, London.
— Wellcome historical medical library *see*
Wellcome historical medical library, London
— William Morris society *see* William Morris
society.
— Wyclif society *see* Wyclif society, London.
London, William. 1:622
London and Middlesex archæological society.
5317
London magazine. 1:644
London publishing houses (*Bkmn*). 5094a 5122
5240 5676a
London. School of printing and graphic arts.
1256 1492 5013
London topographical society. 1:1795i; 7523
Loney, C.E. 1:4257
Long, B.S. 9678
Long, John H. 2:1572
Long, Philip. 1:4069b; 3899 12024 12027
Longaker, John Mark. 1:3178 3179a
Longman, Charles James. 1:2103; 5097–8
13024
Longman, W. 3430
Longueville, Thomas. 1:3139
Lonsdale, K. 1:2520n
Lonsdale, Roger. 8715 13467
Lonsdale library. 1:2196f
Looker, Samuel Joseph. 1:2500 2971 3820a;
2302 8406 9729 11358–9
Loomis, John T. 8452
Loomis, Richard. 13549
Lord, George DeF. 8020
Lord, H.M. 1:5110
Loring, Rosamund Bowditch. 6291 6303
Los Angeles. Public library. 1:4016g; 11922
Loserth, Johann. 1:5193
Loudan, Jack. 1:(4535)
Lough, John. 1657 12017
Lough, Muriel. 1657
Loughborough. Technical college. School of
librarianship. 6501
Lounsbury, Thomas R. 2:501 705
Louttit, W.E. 2259
Love, Walter D. 8981

Loveday, A.J. 1:1262
Loveday, John E.T. 13146
Lovelace, Edith, countess. 9197
Low, Anthony. 1:4218b
Low, D.M. 377 9202 10348
Low, James G. 1:1930g
Low, William. 1:1930g
Lowbridge, Peter. 1:3270h
Lowe, G. Burman. 3193 8248
Lowe, Gerald. 4836
Lowe, Robert Liddell. 8288
Lowe, Victor. 1:5087–8
Lower, Richard. 7570
Lowery, Margaret Ruth. 1:2475; 8589
Lowes, John Livingston. 9525
Lownes, Albert E. 6545 7550
Lowry, H.F. 1:2336f
Lowry, K.B. 9157 9774
Lowry, Margerie. 1:4077c
Lowsley, Job E. 3335
Lowther, Anthony W.G. 2205 2208 6307
10448 11065
Loyola university, Los Angeles. 1:4277 4283
Loys, mrs. Charles. 12883
Lubbock, S.G. 1:(3815)
Lucas, Edward Verrall. 1:2327; 5091
11812–13
Lucas, Frank Laurence. 1:5051; 14266
Lucas, George. 706
Lucas, J. Landfear. 3723
Lucas, Perceval. 7004 11732 12323
Lucas, R. Charles. 3098
Luce, A.A. 1:2452; 8530
Lucke, Jessie Ryon. 6154
Luckombe, Philip. 6376
Lucy, Margaret. 2:(34)
Lüdeke, H. 2:83
Ludovici, Sergio Samek *see* Samek Ludovici,
Samek.
Ludwig, Richard M. 1:3342; 10572
Luke, Hugh J. 9240
Luke, William B. 34 60
Lumbroso, Alberto Emanuele, barone.
1:2678g
Lumiansky, R.M. 8396
Lumsden, Harry. 1:3390
Lust, J. 1:3611
Luttrell society. 3204
Lutyens, Mary. 5245
Lutzki, M. 6450
Lyde, R.G. 1618 9321 11890
Lyell, James Patrick Ronaldson. 26 611 2363
4665 11322
Lyle, Guy R. 2915
Lyle, I.F. 12184
Lydenberg, Harry Miller. (561) 7641
Lynam, Edward W. 1:1179 1784; 1037 6424
6443 7505–6

Lynch, John Gilbert. 1:2429
Lynn, W.T. 6814 9705
Lynn, Mass. Public library. 2:46
Lyon, H.D. 2225 3291 12588
Lyon, Harvey T. 1:3560a; 10924
Lyons, J.J. 7077
Lyons, John O. 9098
Lysaght, Averil. 7456
Lyster, Thomas William. 1:3783
Lysart. 5905
Lytton, lord see Lytton, sir Noel Anthony Sacwen, 4th earl of Lytton.
Lytton, sir Noel Anthony Sacwen, 4th earl of Lytton. 9238

M. 1102 2611 7427 7727 8163 8175 9307 10648 12786 12948
M., A.R. 2866
M., A.R.L. 5197
M., A.T. 4522
M., B. 1214
M., D. 2605
M., F. 2560
M., E.B. 10620 10806
M., E.F. 4933
M., F. 14296
M., F.B. 6275
M., F.D. 8326
M., F.H.A. 1612 9900
M., G. 12212
M., H.A. St.J. 4779
M., H.C. 10485
M., H.E. 7825
M., J. 3712
M., J.A. 10803
M., J.F. 1267 4407 7746
M., J.G. 8938
M., L.M. 5428
M., R.A. 4794
M., S.D. 139
M., W. 1217
M., W.F. 2484
M., W.J. 9184
Maas, M. 12316
Maas, Paul. 2:890 1677; 397 8184 11570 12394
Mabbot, Thomas Ollive. 565 636 713 995 2829 6356 7748 8575 8585–7 9283 9397 9399–400 9607 10060 10449 10797 11154 11461 11672 12340 12347 12353–4 12376–7 12382 12384 12411 12415 13318–19 13530
Mac, pseud. 1:2519b
McAdam, Edward L. 1:3942; 387 8018 11433–4 14516
McAleer, E.C. 12535
McAleer, John J. 5845

MacAlister, sir I. 8737
Macalister, M.A.M. 7715
Macalister, R.A.S. 13648
Macalpine, Ida. 7570a 9139
McAnally, sir Henry. 1:346m; 6282 6298 8235
MacAodhagáin, Partholán. 12620
Macaree, David. 7278
Macarthur, D. 3124
McArthur, Herbert. 6721
MacArthur, William. 7352
McAtee, W.L. 12696
Macaulay, George Campbell. 2:1706 1766
Macaulay, James. 5247
McAvoy, William C. 1:84
McBurney, William Harlin. 1:1696 1699; 8405 11999
McCain, John W. 12359
McCance, Stouppe. 1:2065; 1770
McCann, Justin. 1:2380q
MacCarthy, Desmond. 1:3157
McCarthy, Justin. 1:4456
McCarthy, William H. 9193 9211 10750
MacCarvill, E. 1:5197
Mace, Herbert. 6798
McCheane, R. 11376
McChesney, Dora Greenwell. 2636
McClary, Ben H. 1010 5251a
McClelland, Aiken. 1:1039
MacClintock, William Darnall. 1:5027; 14237
McClure, Norman. 1:3609
MacColl, Alan. 10272
McColley, Grant. 10727
McCombs, Charles F. 1:2611a
McConica, James K. 3304
McCord, David. 14070
McCorkle, Julia Norton. 5152
McCormick, Jane. 1:5030e
McCracken, George. 14332
McCrossan, J.L. 1916
McCue, Daniel L. 13783
McCue, Lillian Bueno. 1:2703
McCusker, Honor. 698 4290 5488 6209 8388 10504
McCutcheon, George Barr. 1:3074 3586 (4917)
McCutcheon, Roger P. 4603 6784
MacDonagh, Frank. 1:2671
MacDonald, Annie S. 2067
MacDonald, D.B. 12764
McDonald, Donald. 1:2090
McDonald, Edward David. 1:3170 4014–15; 11919
McDonald, Gerald D. 11834
Macdonald, Hugh. 1:3201 3668 4584 4823; 2687 5811 7992 12187 14512
Macdonald, James Harold. 1:4747
Macdonald, James Ramsay. 6066 9709

MacLeod, Robert Duncan. 1:724b; 1617 1630

MacLeod, W. 1:4712f; 1642

MacLochlainn, Alf. 1:3011q; 1835 1842a 1860 1945 3875 4811 6443 12609

McLorn, M.E.R. 1:4768

Maclure, Alan F. 2785

MacLure, Millar. 1:2063

MacLysaght, Edward. 5164

McMahon, Morgan. 12101

McManaway, James Gilmer. 1:1625 4250; 2:22 132 156b 297 (331) 334 368 658 676 901 1212 1223 1289 1368 1570 1618 1659; (144) 222 (649–50) 2990a (3086) 3576 5470 (6411) 6457 (6562) 7171 7230 7689 7943 7995 (7998) (8518) 9803 9832 9939 10369 (10637) (11711) 12980 13152

MacManus, Michael Joseph. 1:1383 2308 2811 3663 4253 4273 4377 4864 4971; 54 1804 1956 2102 2908 3077 5417 6286 9894 11964–5 12485 12485 13758

McMaster, Helen. 14518

Macmath, William. 1:1460b; 1560 6781

MacMichael, J. Holden. 1214 1217 1221–2 1992 2070 3585 3860 3866 4406 4524 4749 4836 5273 5395 5872 5878 6513 6656 7586 7634 10736 13051

Macmillan, Alexander. 5123

Macmillan, B. 6527

Macmillan, George A. 5123 5699

McMillan, Nora F. 4145 8154

MacMillan, William Dougald. 1:1632 1633d; 7219 9451 11134 12091

Macmillan and co., London. 1:1363

MacMinn, Ney Lannes. 1:4217

McMullin, Brian J. 170

MacMurtrie, Douglas Crawford. 5339 6083 6103 6668

MacNaghten, Hugh. 2:1788

McNally, James. 8912

McNamee, Lawrence F. 1:10–11; 2:151

McNamee, William. 2282

McNaught, Duncan. 1:2635; 9023

McNeill, Bob. 5127d

McNeill, Charles. 1:747–8; 1797

McNeir, Waldo Forest. 1:4755; 2:(373) (962) 1472; 7175

Macomber, Henry P. 1:4338–9a; 12581 12585–6

MacPhail, Ian Murdoch MacLeod. 1:2100d

MacPhail, Ian Shaw. 1:546 1076 1316 4869–70; 163 368 6966 9709 13853

McPharlin, Paul. 985 2256–7 5420 5866 6356 6584 6707 7222 7887 7966 9682

McPherson, Brian. 1:3101

MacPherson, J.M. 1698

MacPike, Eugene Fairfield. 1:1576 3553–7; 104 10923 12575 12580

McQuiston, J.D. 7721

MacRae, John Findlay. 4186

Macray, W.D. 6262 6444 6996 7709 11365 11385 12536 13015

MacRitchie, David. 13186

MacRobert, T.M. 1:843h

McRoberts, David. 1:2041

MacShane, Frank. 1:3338a 3340

MacSweeney, J.J. 13292

McTear, J.S. 8191

McTernan, John C. 1965

Macwilliam, Alexander. 1898 1901

Macy, George. 2:754

Madan, Falconer. 1:935a–7 1299–302 1447 1871–2 2653 2724–5 2728–9 4109d–f 4471; 2:214 522–4 737 1011 1013 1398; 28 32 98 105 112 125 273 309 592 595 969 1351–2 1355 1357–8 1362–6 2729 4089 4493–6 4500 4502 4504 4572–3 4575 5331 5335 5338 5341 5343–5 5837 6313–14 6317 6420–1 6470 6900 7251 8595 9129 9133 9393 9753 10241 10604 11444 11974 12331 13110 13132–3

Madan, Francis Falconer. 1:2401 2764 4230 4242 4375

Madden, sir Frederic. 1:346k

Madden, John Lionel. 1:1927c 4680h 5209y

Madden, P.J. 1824 6439

Maddison, A.R. 2500

Maddison, Francis R. 1:3214; 2584

Maddison, R.E.W. 1:2517c; 3136 7948 8729–30

Madge, Francis Thomas. 1:503

Madge, Sidney J. 5012

Maffet, R.S., 1:1047 1066 1115 1240; 1770–2 1868 1962–3 1990 2691 4126 6466

Magaw, Barbara Louise. 1:4678; 13422

Magee, David Bickersteth. 1:5000q; 4589a 14473

Maggs, Bryan D. 2237

Maggs, Derek. 4357

Maggs bros., bksllrs., London. 1:351e 534–5 600c 863 1458 2440x 3845d 4234; 2:210 215; 2140 2209 2237 3036

Magoun, Francis P. 12337

Magrath, John R. 2:650; 2606 6845 8109 11997 12996

Magriel, Paul David. 1:2135

Mahl, Mary R. 13441

Mahony, Bertha. 1:(1749); (7443)

Mahoney, John L. 11498

Maidstone. College of art. 4330

Main, C.F. 10261 11577 13688 14558

Mainwaring, Marion. 1:2337; 8283

Mair, John. 11306–7

Maison, Margaret M. 1:1717d

Maitland, G.B. 5018

Maitland, William G.B. 11769 11775 11780

Maker, Harold J. 662 4996
Makower, Stanley Victor. 1:4527r 4583
Makers of public opinion (Public opinion). 3830b
3972a 5264 5526
Malawsky, Beryl York. 1:3253
Malcolm, C.A. 2679
Maldon. Plume library *see* Plume library, Maldon.
Malet, Harold. 838 6939
Mallaber, Kenneth A. 267
Mallock, Archibald. 1:2215
Mallowan, sir Max E.L. 1:5159d
Malone, David H. 1:654; 2:75a
Malone, J. 2:502
Malone society. *Collections.* 2:1914
Man, Felix H. 1:1754b; 6219a
Manceinion, *pseud.* 4489
Manchester. John Rylands library *see* John Rylands library, Manchester.
— Public libraries *see also* John Rylands library, Manchester. 1:661 910-11 2279h 5145
— — Moss side branch. 1:2536 3018 3407
— — Reference library. 1:1161 1233-4 3367
— University. *Publications. English series.* 3420
Mandahl, S.M. 7441
Mander, Gerald Poynton. 1:944; 1398 9569
Mander, Raymond. 1:2887j 4175c
Mander, Rosalie. 9704
Mangini, Nicola. 2:133
Mankin, Philip H. 12456
Manks, Dorothy S. 1:2821d
Manley, F.E. 4150
Manley, Francis. 6768
Manley, Frank. 14008
Manly, John Matthews. 1:688
Manly anniversary studies in language and literature. 9027 12819
Mann, B.K. 1:(3752) (3755) 3929
Mann, Irene. 14371-4
Mann, James G. 2928
Mann, Phyllis G. 9473
Manners, G.S. 9246
Manners, Walter E. 8108
Manning, H.C. 2:1182
Manning, Joseph. 7554
Mansbridge, F.R. 4164 6865
Mansfield, Milburg Francisco. 1:3936
Mansell, H.R. 7428
Mansergh, J.F. 748 4016 5255b 6231 6907
Manson, Margaret. 1:2320
Manson, T.F. 6510
Mantz, Ruth Elvish. 1:4118c
Manwaring, G.E. 2:1028; 2672 4251 7072 7347 12944 14554
Manx museum, Douglas *see* Douglas, Isle of Manx. Max museum.
Manzalaoui, M.A. 6138

Map collectors' circle, London. 1:1770 1770h 1772 1795n 1813 1818p-q 2879d 3347h
Map collectors' series. 3474 5239 6551 7521 7524-9 7531-7
Maples, A.K. 9187
Marcham, F. 4243 4266 8314 9933 11554 12594
Marcham, W. McB. 4243
Marchand, Leslie A. 3090 8782 9237 10405 11273 11699
Marchant, Francis P. 8997 10817
Marchbank, W. 13087
Marchetti, Ernest. 9188
Marchmont, Frederick, *pseud.* 1:2927
Marder, Louis. 2:4 103 105 111 134 152 492 622 804
Mares, Francis Hugh. 1:1601b
Margadant, Willem D. 3611 6253
Margaret I. King library, Lexington *see* Kentucky. University. Margaret I. King library, Lexington.
Margate. Public library. 1:900
Marginalia (Bkmns J). 2841 4263 5171 7071 8663 8778 9301 10040 10045 10279 10347 10423 10718 10754 11242-3 11743 12573 13807
Margoliouth, Herschel Maurice. 1:4145 4147; 8611 12186
Marilla, Esmond Linworth. 1:4996-a; 14148
Marillier, Harry Currie. 1:1846-7
Marion, Henri. 1:4068
Marion, sir Thomas. 7929
Marissel, André. 1:2414a
Markland, Murray F. 4326
Markland, Russell. 964
Marks, Carol L. *see also* Sicherman, Carol L. (Marks). 14080-1 14083
Marks, Jeannette Augustus. 1:1631; 7213
Marks, Percy J. 2:39
Marks, Ronald E. 12670
Marks, Seymour. 2:1033
Marks, Stephen Powys. 1:1795i; 7523
Marley, H. 8787
Marlow, Harriet. 928 6239 8488 9343-4 10682 11158 11192 13625 13701 13986
Marlow, Louis, *pseud. of* Louis Umfreville Wilkinson. 1:(4450y) (4451c) (4454) (4454g) (4455c) 4455y
Marriner, Ernest C. 1:1290; 4463
Marriot, Ernest. 2624
Marris, W. 1:1336; 4787
Marrot, Harold Vincent. 1:3383; 4129a 11984
Marschall, Wilhelm. 2:1183 1894
Marsden, Wilfred A. 125 2943 2957 4434 5589 7627 2123 12597 14405
Marsh, A.S. 1:3212

Marsh, sir Edward. 8327 9186 13303 13560 14088

Marsh, George L. 1:3905a 4508 4642b; 9027 10420 13006

Marshall, Arthur Calder-. 10378

Marshall, E. 10276

Marsh, R.C. 2:598

Marshall, Edward Henry. 1:2060 2:360; 371 888 925 2042 3578 6185 6910 6996 7384 8218 9875 10596 13470

Marshall, Francis Albert. 1:380; 11007

Marshall, G. 3578

Marshall, George O. 13938

Marshall, H.S. 1:2240p; 6949 6951 8130

Marshall, John. 3577 5915

Marshall, John J. 1:1122c 2244e; 1761 1771 1851 11028

Marshall, Julian. 8191 9694

Marshall, L. 2543

Marshall, R. 6704

Marshall, William H. 1:3246a; 9244-5 9247 10434

Marshallsay, D.M. 1:1246

Marsh's library, Dublin see Dublin. University. Marsh's library.

Marson, Clotilda. 8867

Marston, Edward. 2070 3620 3622 3623b 4509 4555 4600 4732 4735 4822a 4901 4935 5030 5076 5140-1 5187 5326 5535 5862 6510a

Marston, G.M. 7235

Marston, Robert B. 14211 14213

Marston, Thomas E. 671 674 9428

Martin, Benjamin Ellis. 1:(3972-3)

Martin, Burns. 1:4486; 2:436; 6786 12967 14144

Martin, C.G. 9665

Martin, E.J. 2098

Martin, Edward Alfred. 1:5080

Martin, G.W. 1112 1116

Martin, Jonathan. 5143

Martin, Leonard Cyril. 1:4995; 9755 9761 14149

Martin, Mary Forster. 11077 13682

Martin, R. 10839

Martin, Richard. 5143

Martin, Richard T. 13546

Martin, Robert B. 11723 12990-1

Martin, Stapleton. 1208 9258

Martin, W. 1:3755j

Martin, William. 7494

Martin, Willard Edgar. 1:2779

Martindell, Ernest Walter. 1:3944-6; 11756 11774

Martz, Edwine M. 10630

Martz, Louis L. 1:4721h; 10630 12512 13497

Maruzen co. ltd., Tokyo. 2:66

Marvell tercentenary celebration committee,

Hull see Hull. Marvell tercentenary celebration committee.

Mary, sr., of the Incarnation. 1:3143

Maryland. University. Dept. of English. 1:2858d

Marylebone cricket club, London. 1:2157

Mary Winifred, sr. 1:2855c

Marzials, F.T. 1:(4907)

Masengill, Jeanne Addison. 1:3302; 10510

Maser, F.E. 1:2871

Maslen, Keith Ian Desmond. 1:635 818 (1268-9) 1379 4446; 171 919 4102 5547 5579 6679 9913 9929 11118 12877

Mason, Alexander. 8822

Mason, C. 10395

Mason, John Henry. 3770 3775a 3844 5160-1 6567

Mason, Lawrence. 11714

Mason, Robert. 14128

Mason, Stuart, pseud. of C.S. Millard. 1:5097-100 5103 5105; 7344 7857-8 13064 14313-14 14316

Mason, Thomas. 6898 14252

Massé, Gertrude C.E. 1:2915

Masseck, Clinton Joseph. 1:3819

Massey, Dudley. 10606-7 11102 11109 12013 13032 13476 13625 13659

Massey, Irving. 13355 13367

Massingham, H.J. 2:840

Masson, Alfred. 7872

Masson, David. 1:3017

Masson, David I. 1:468-9 2191; 8993-4

Masterman, sir John C. 3368a

Masters, John E. 4761

Materials for the study of the old English drama. 2:1439; 11565 11574 11580

Mather, Frank Jewett. 4444

Matheson, Cyril. 1:966

Matthewman, S. 4867

Mathews, Albert. 1169 7663

Mathews, Alison M. 1:1902c

Mathews, Brander. 2029

Mathews, C. Elkin. 7344 8858 10990 11314 11714

Mathews, Edith E. 5163

Mathews, Edward Robert Norris. 1:421 896p; 1123

Mathews, Elkin. 10559 13846

Mathews, Elkin, bksllrs., Bishops Stortford. 1:2687 3840

Mathews, Ernest G. 1:842

Mathews, Godfrey W. 1:4536

Mathews, H.J. 7238

Mathews, Jackson. 92a

Mathias, W. Alun. 1:4578h; 13143

Matthews, Albert. 7663 12052 12958

Matthews, Arnold Gwynne. 1:2405

Matthews, Arthur D. 2:(908) (1908)

Matthews, Brander. 2:(719) (1640)
Matthews, D.A. 1:2904
Matthews, G.M. 13356
Matthews, J.H. 6827
Matthews, L.G. 9699
Matthews, W.R. 1:657
Matthews, William. 1:1511 1576d 2281; 2:420–1 425–6; 8392 12009 12090 12713 12718
Matz, Bertram Waldrom. 1:2706t 3032b 3056h 3965t; 9989 9993 10010 10019 10036
Matz, Winifred. 1:3033ab 4171e
Matzek, R. 1:3968b
Maud, Ralph. 1:4937; 12226
Maunsell, Andrew. 1:554
Maurer, Oscar. 6548 7916 12864
Maurice, A., and co. 748
Maurocordato, Alexandre. 1:673a
Mavrogordato, John. 2:882
Maxwell, Baldwin. 2:(1753)
Maxwell, Desmond Ernest Stewart. 1:5209
Maxwell, Herbert. 8076 10825 13015
Maxwell, sir Herbert Eustace. 1:992–3; 5687
Maxwell, Ian R. 10236
Maxwell, James Coutts. 1:(4527u) 5129–30 5163; 2:75a 147 807 1067 1094 1290 1319 1324 1415–16 1521 1656 1723 1831; (130) (186) (202) 205 (296) (391) 409 412 (3533) 6137 7142 (7199) 8916 9665 9760 (11015) (11075a) 11106 11342 11344 (11559) 11576 11704 (11801) 11931 12159 12179 (12198) (12200) 12429 (12556) (13058) 13363 13781 14074 14267 14567b
Maxwell, Leslie F. 1:2214
Maxwell, Sue. 12165
Maxwell, Vivian M. 1:1351w
Maxwell, W.G. Clark-. 2643
Maxwell, William. 1:1317; 10093 13262
Maxwell, William Harold. 1:2214
May, Frederick. 1:2390n 5187a; 954 11933
May, J. Lewis. 5038
May, Robert. 1964
May, S. William. 1171
May, William. 6013
Mayall, Arthur. 337
Maycock, A.L. 5087
Maycock, Willoughby. 4897c 7872
Mayer, Douglas W.F. 1:1711
Mayfield, John S. 13824–6 14437
Mayhew, A.L. 900a 962 13490
Mayhew, George Pershing. 1:4826b 4842d; 13776–7 13784 13788 13794 14596
Maynard, Katherine (O'Neill). 1:2030m
Mayo, Robert D. 1:1698; 7287 13224
Mayor, John E.B. 14162
Mayoux, Jean Jaques. 1:(2414f)
Mead, Herman Ralph. 1:2451 2608 2890

4043; 6031 8428 9441 9507 9698–9 9833 10134 10506 11067 11968 12930
Meadmore, William Smith. 4633
Medawar, sir Peter Brian. 1:(4944)
Medcraft, John. 1:1361; 3823 4110 4387 5286 5457 7024 7038
Medici society. 1:1294
Medley, D.J. 1:20
Medley, J.B. 9390
Medlicott, Mary. 1:2320bx 2920e
Mee, Arthur. 1532
Meeker, Richard K. 1:1701
Meeks, Leslie Howard. 1:3967
Megan, pseud. 6656
Megaw, Denis. 6599
Megaw, Robert N.E. 14575
Mégroz, Rodolphe Louis. 1:2868k 4540
Mehew, Ernest. 13674
Meister und Meisterwerke der Buchbinderkunst. 5594
Mejer, Wolfgang. 1:1139p; 2083
Melbourne. University. Queen's college library. 1:5068
— Victoria public library, museums and national gallery see Victoria, Australia. Public library, museums and art gallery, Melbourne.
Melhuish, W. Frognall. 6723a
Mellon, Paul. 1:486
Mellor, William. 4968
Mellown, Elgin W. 1:4314–16
Melo, Barbara. 2:(135)
Melville, viscount see Dundas, Henry Charles Clement, 7th viscount Melville.
Melville, Alexander Ronald Leslie-. 1:3310
Melville, Frederick John. 1:3664
Melville, Lewis, pseud. 1:2695 2820 4909 4912; 2062 7407–9 8564 10596
Melville, R.V. 8157
Men and matters (Bkmns J). 2294 9641 11237
Mendenhall, John C. 7284 8409a 9002
Mendenhall, Thomas C. 1:2289dc
Mengel, Robert M. 239 4091 8149
Menhinick, E.B. 11091
Menken, E. 14313
Mennie, D.M. 13212
Men of mark (Caxton Mag). 3988 4789 4839 4853 4903 5255 5688 5946
Men who make public opinion (Public Opinion). 5481a
Menzies, John and co., Edinburgh. 5179
Menzies, Walter B. 2141 2888 2991 9498 10610 11120
Mercer, Thomas Stanley. 1:3330h 4535; 11238 13074
Mercer, W.J. 1152
Mercer, William. 5178 11381
Merchant, W. Moelwyn. 2:1123m

Vol. 1 = Bibliographies   2 = Shakespeare   4 = 1–8221   5 = 8222–14616

Mercurius, *pseud.* 7658
Meric, A. 4863
Merivale, Herman. 1:(4907)
Meriwether, James B. 1:667g 2744a; 1002 9341
Merriam, Harold Guy. 5225–6 7886
Merrick, M.M. 4591
Merrill, George J. 6147a
Merritt, Edward Percival. 1:(1404) 1449 2039; 5804 5962 11383 14177–8
Merry, Dennis Harry. 1:933–a 937b
Merryweather, G. 3723
Merstham Georgian house. Library. 1:2483–4
Merton, Wilfred. 1126 6901
Mertz, Wendel. 2:726
Meserve, Walter J. 12797
Metcalfe, George. 8054
Metropolitan art association, N.Y. 1:4915
Metzdorf, Robert Frederic. 1:363; 3380a 7209 7455 11439 11479 11879 12995 13093 13542 13995
Metz, Rudolf. 1:3757f
Metzger, Bruce M. 6116
Meyer, H.H.B. 2:40
Meyer, Paul H. 11256
Meyer, Sam. 13576
Meynell, sir Francis Meredith Wilfrid. 1:1376–7 4213; 2:773a; 92a 328 3942 3946 5215a 5303–4 6107 6661a 6673
Meynell, Gerald T. 2290 6465 7636 13262
Meyerstein, Edward Harry William. 8326 8523 9401 9404–5 9546 9958 14039 14529 14534
Mez, John Richard. 2:88
Michel, Laurence. 9807
Michelmore, G. 2:1018
Michelmore, G., ltd., London. 2:277
Michell, A.L. 13360
Michels, John. 6924
Michigan. University. 10313
— — Dept. of English. 2:(871); 8162
— — Library. 1:2707
— — William L. Clements library. 1:2126
Micklewright, F.M. Amphlett. 793 5406a
Micklewright, George R. 1:4786m
Michot, Paulette. 3535
Middlemast, K. 1:3218
Middleton, Bernard C. 2230 2234 4823
Middleton, Joyce. 1:4051e
Middleton, R. Hunter. 4046
Milburn, C.H. 11770
Miles, *pseud.* 10824
Miles, Hamish. 5635
Miles, P.J. 1:544b
Milford, Robert Theodore. 1:1887 1889; 1078 1379 7676 7745 7748 7759 8273 8755 12467

Milic, Louis T. 1:2286d
Millar, A.H. 10732
Millar, David A. (8923)
Millar, Eric G. 2971 11353 11389 11763
Millar, Nola L. 1:5017y; 14232
Millard, Alice (Parsons). 1:1315 1351p 2476 4302c
Millard, Christopher Sclater *see also* Mason, Stuart, *pseud.* 1:3360; 14318
Miller, A.G. Schaw. 10094
Miller, Anita. 1:2444d
Miller, Aura. 2:1131–2; 820
Miller, Charles William Kerby-. 1:2331
Miller, Clarence H. 9700a
Miller, Clarence William. 1:536b 541 1342 2519a; 4860 5014 5284 6683 10462
Miller, Edwin Haviland. 1:2037 3522; 8055 10875 10880–1
Miller, Elizabeth V. 1:2850
Miller, Frances Schouler. 1:1633
Miller, Frank. 1:995
Miller, George M. 13024
Miller, Henry Knight. 1:1656e; 10520
Miller, J.F. 1:3634–5
Miller, Liam. 1:(2812) 3329; 4598–9 5231 12183
Miller, Sonia. 12418
Miller, Sydney Richardson Christie-. 1:347
Miller, Thomas. 1666
Miller, Thomas Yule. 1665
Miller, William. 1:3033b–d 3035–6 3066c 3083 3086 3313; 10002–3 10044 10051 10066 10083
Miller, William E. 684 1291 11119
Millett, Fred B. 1:688
Millhauser, Milton. 1:2755a
Milligan, Edward H. 1:1303 2098
Milligan, George. 1:1476–7; 6850
Millin, Samuel Shannon. 1:3194
Millman, William H. 2485
Mills, Richard L. 3099
Mills, Stuart. 1:1239
Milltown park college, Dublin. Library. 1:459
Milne, Alexander Taylor. 1:916g 2448c
Milne, Edward Arthur. 1:3816q
Milne, H.J.M. 12640
Milnes, J.G. 4574
Milne, James. 6524
Milroy, James. 11151
Milton studies in honor of Harris Francis Fletcher. 12440
Milwaukee. Public library. 2:245
Minchin, H.C. 1:(2587)
Mince, H.A. 8802
Mineka, Francis Edward. 1:1921a
Miner, Dorothy Eugenia. (13774–5) (14198)
Minet, William. 1:944h; 2850

Minet public library, Camberwell. 1:944h–i
Minnesota. University. 1:2485
Minns, sir Ellis Hovell. 1:426
Minoru, Toyada. 2:73 75
Minto, John. 203
Minto, William. 5210
Miriam, sr. 1:4184
Mirrlees, Hope. 9693
Miscellaneous antiquities. 5019
Mish, Charles Carroll. 1:1688 1699; 675 6617 7277 7290
Missouri. University. *Studies.* 2:1571
Mitchel, William. 566
Mitchell, Alexander. 1:685 3762; 11256 11258
Mitchell, Alison. 8247
Mitchell, sir Arthur. 1:968 975–7
Mitchell, C. & co. ltd. 1178
Mitchell, C. Ainsworth. 2060 11630
Mitchell, David. 5706a
Mitchell, Phillip Marshall. 1:803; 864
Mitchell, R.J. 11904
Mitchell, Stephen D. 9503
Mitchell, William Fraser. 1:2061; 1602
Mitchell, William Smith. 1:487 554a 1581; 1313 1620 1664 1720a 2162 2182 2195 2210 4677 4842 5297 5503 5895 8657
Mitchell library, Glasgow. 1:553 725 1002a 2639
Mitchner, R.W. 6026
Mitchenson, Joe. 1:2887j 4175c
Mithal, H.S.D. 14376
Mizener, Arthur. 11283
Mizuta, Hiroshi. 1:3669; 13479
MLA international bibliography. 1:43
Modder, Montague Frank. 1:2199a
Modern humanities research association. 1:40
Modern language association of America. 1:624 1609 2015 2017 2345; 2:880 1027; 405 7133
— Conference on Shakespeare research opportunities. 2:6
— *Publications.* 1:43
Modern philology. 1:57–60
Moffett, S.O. 11114
Mogg, William Rees-. 1:2625; 3308 3698a 8992
Molin, Nils. 2:93
Moller, Niels. 2:1611
Molyneux, Samuel. 1:370
Molyneux, William. 1:370; 1838
Monaghan, Frank. 4835a
Monat, O. 2:(135)
Moncrieff, Charles Kenneth Scott. 1:2962; 13648
Mongan, E. 1:2479
Monk, Samuel Holt. 1:3195; 13627

Monkman, Kenneth. 13635
Monoghan, T.J. 2:773; 11480
Monotype casters' and typefounders' society. 6621
Monotype recorder. 1:175
Monrad, Anna M. 1:1478
Monro, Harold. 6973
Monro, Thomas Kirkpatrick. 1:2563b; 8828
Montagné, Paul. 1:3509
Montague, John. 1:(2812)
Montague, M.F. Ashley-. 11876
Monteiro, George. 1:3960; 11343 11351 11788 14602
Montgomerie, William. 1:1468; 1635 6792 13235
Montgomery, Marshall. 2:848 1183
Monthly catalogue. 1:641
Monthly chronicle. 1:642
Montreal. McGill university *see* McGill university, Montreal.
Monumenta chartæ papyraceæ historiam illustrantia. 3764 3802
Monval, Madeleine Horn-. 1:1592e; 2:109
Moody, Theodore William. 1:2973
Moon, N.S. 3360
Moon, Z. 1:890
Moore, Anne Carroll. 5944
Moore, Cecil A. 4601a 8926
Moore, Doris L. 9238
Moore, Dorothy. 2:123
Moore, F. Frankfort. 1:2445
Moore, George Augustus. 2290
Moore, George Edward. 1:4270m–n
Moore, Harry T. 11933
Moore, John Robert. 1:2987; 154 5771 9902–3 9914 9916 9924 9926 10693
Moore, Samuel. 1:1281a; 3427
Moore, Thomas Sturge. 1:1319; 4626
Moorman, F.W. 11056
Moran, James. 1:1396t; 1288 3468 3870 4082 4201 4349 5120 5216–17 5258 5607 5617 5722 5906 5996 6033 6133 6166 6170 6327 6330 6332–3 6631 5120 14448 14456
Morant, Geoffrey McKay. 1:4404b
More books. 1:176
Moreira Gomes, Celuta. 2:104 135 144
Mores, Edward Rowe. 1:4290; 6114 6627 6573 6680
Moreton, R.L. 10544 13176
Moreux, Françoise. 1:3015
Morfill, W.R. 957
Morgan, Alice. 11006
Morgan, Appleton. 4662a
Morgan, Charles Langbridge. 5125
Morgan, Bayard Quincy. 1:819–21
Morgan, Charlotte Elizabeth. 1:1687
Morgan, Dewi. 3610
Morgan, E. Delmar. 8200

Mukherjee, Sujit K. 10885
Mulcahy, B. 1:4866
Mulhauser, Margaret. 1:2656
Mullens, William Herbert. 1:2114–16
Muller, James Arthur. 1:3395g
Müller-Schwefe, Gerhard see Schwefe, Gerhard Müller-.
Müllertz, Mogens. 2:472
Mullett, Charles F. 1:4425x
Mumby, Frank Arthur. 1:1184d; 3464 3480 3628 5127 5564a 5704
Mumey, Nolie. 258
Munby, Alan Noël Latimer. 1:1284 2326 4421; 2:1229a; 86 92a 2171–2 2163 2183 2370 2453 3068 3078 3091 3125–6 3144 3157 3175 3207–9 3228 3251 3292 3305 3337 3339 3361 3376a 3391 3400–1 3449 3455 3460 3653 4302 4376 4538 5999 6413 6543 7267 7975 8159 8262 9000 10442 12081 12582–4 12745 12831 13337
Mundy, Percy D. 5042 5642 5695 6211 6288 7435 8394 10765
Munford, W.A. 2443
Munro, Ion S. 3130
Munro, James. 5960
Munro, John. 2:1807
Munro, John M. 12482
Munsterberg, Margaret. 871 896a 4443 6022 6028 8280 8898 9065 9073 9629 11567 11572 12931 13033 13245 13402 13920 13924 14043 14133 14136 14147 14304
Munter, Robert LaVerne. 1:1951; 1844
Murdoch, Robert see also Lawrance, Robert Murdoch-. 1:1425 1931a–f; 1647 1739 5926 9015–19 9876 13174
Murdoch, Thomas. 1686a
Murdock, W.G. Blaikie. 1:3152 4844; 4459 9391a
Murgatroyd, Thomas. 1:3540m; 4848a 14291
Murphy, Gwendolen. 1:1550 2969 3001 4434 4816p 4941; 10349 14583
Murphy, James. 13489
Murphy, Mallie John. 2:1240
Murphy, Richard. 14583
Murray, Brian M. 1:1944
Murray, C. Clive. 5404
Murray, David. 1:744 1726 2604–5; 23 188 4691 4693 4695 8124
Murray, David Christie. 1:3666
Murray, Edward Croft. 11302
Murray, Francis Edwin. 1:3151; 99 10210
Murray, J. 2:505; 3588 6268 6938 9171
Murray, J.A.H. 12711
Murray, John. 1:2684; 5252b 5704 8702–3 9185 10810 13108 13158
Murray, Peter B. 9945 14076
Murray, Sylvia W. 1:4318
Murray, William M. 1:4317p; 12549

Murrey, Thomas Jefferson. 1:2141b
Murrie, Eleanore (Boswell) see also Boswell, Eleanor. 1:2066–7; 5431 8185–7
Mursia, Ugo. 1:2858h
Musgrove, Sidney. 2:1463; 9961 11079
Music association of Ireland. 1:3569
Muss-Arnolt, William see Arnolt, William Muss-.
Musson, A.E. 5093 5884
Mus urbanus, pseud. 2407
Muthuswami, B. 2:952
Mutter, R.P.C. 8964
Myops, pseud. 11812
Myrick, Kenneth Orne. 1:(4688b)
Myres, J.N.L. 1375 2445 11354–5
Myson, William. 1:1859

N. 3605 5197 8252
N., B.G. 6080
N., H.S. 3934
N., M. 8108
N., P.E. 13899
N., R. 4359a 4360
N., R.D.C. 7829
N., T. 7820
N., U.O. 6185
Naaké, John T. 957–8
Nadler, A. 3784
Nairn, A. 1:2379; 3537 5530
Namba, Toshio. 9110
Nangle, Benjamin Christie. 1:1901–2; 10758
Napieralski, Edmund. 1:1630c
Nash, George. 1:2912eb
Nash, John Henry. 1:1314h; 4586
Nash, Ray. 5510 7069
Nason, Arthur Huntington. 1:4677
Natal. University. Library. 1:583
Nathan, Norman. 2:607 1326; 12050
Nathanson, H. 1:2732; 9333
Nathanson, Leonard. 14375
Nationalbibliothek, Vienna see Austria. Nationalbibliothek, Vienna.
National book council see National book league.
National book league, London. 1:3 72 74 358 360 613 689 720 739i 1139v 1139zy 1189 1559 1569 1573d 1590 1648 1708 1714 1724b 1735 1754 1767 1984–5 2118 2157 2175 2179 3006 4213 4450a 4632; 2194 2351 3761
— Library. 1:105
National council of teachers of English. 1:39
National gallery of Scotland see Scotland. National gallery, Edinburgh.
National liberal club, London. Gladstone library. 1:2249b

National library of Australia *see* Australia. National library, Canberra.

National library of India *see* India. National library, Calcutta.

National library of Ireland *see* Ireland. National library, Dublin.

National library of New Zealand *see* New Zealand. National library, Wellington.

National library of Scotland *see* Scotland. National library, Edinburgh.

National library of Wales, Aberystwyth *see* Wales. National library, Aberystwyth.

National library of Wales journal. 1:177

National maritime museum, Greenwich. Library. 1:2289f

Naumburg, Carl T. 11776 11786

Naumburg, Edward. 1:3339; 9313 10571 14278

Naylor, Bernard. 1:2289g

Neale, Catherine M. 1:4354

Needham, Francis R.D. 2084 14185

Negley, Glenn Robert. 1:1669a–b

Neidig, William J. 2:408–10

Neighbour, Oliver Wray. 1:1840; 10477

Neill, Desmond G. 1:608 4395; 740 4947 8728 9346 9351 10529 12664

Neilson, George. 9770 10337

Neiman, Fraser. 1:2338; 8290

Nel mezzo, *pseud.* 374

Nelson, Alfred. 7945

Nelson, Axel. 13016

Nelson, Charles A. 2056

Nelson, Hector. 2504

Nelson, Lewis. 2:360b; 7331

Ne quid nimis, *pseud.* 6925 7938–9

Nesbitt, Charles F. 6879

Nethery, Wallace. 9826 11258 11853–4 11857 12026

Nettleton, George Henry. 1:4663f; 7279 10359 13397–9 13403

Neu, John. 1:2230

Neubauer, A. 957

Neuberg, Victor Edward Reuben Parvincio. 1:1537 1547; 4542 6994

Newmann, Walter. 2:135a

Nevada. University. Library. 1:2641

Nevill, Ralph Henry. 1:2285

Neville, Roy G. 8150 9792 9864 10194

Nevinson, Henry Woodd. 1:3579 4159d 4208 4473

Nevinson, J.L. 2:1548

Newark, N.J. Public library. 1:1226m

Newberry library, Chicago. 1:103 178 516 533 1483 1625 1656h 2148 2347–8 3881 4882

— John M. Wing foundation. 1:108–9

Newberry library bulletin. 1:178

New Cambridge bibliography of English literature.

1:376 657g 1139m 3104

Newcastle-upon-Tyne. Armstrong college *see* Durham. University. Armstrong college, Newcastle-upon-Tyne.

— Central reference library. 1325–7

— King's college *see* Durham. University. King's college, Newcastle-upon-Tyne.

— Public libraries. 1:926 1800; 2:87 183

— — Bewick collection. 1:2458

— Society of antiquaries *see* Society of antiquaries, Newcastle-upon-Tyne.

— — King's college. Library. 2195

— University. Library. 1:373 1548 1773 2121 2229 5209ac

— — Library. 3380

Newcastle imprint club. 6713a

New colophon. 1:179

Newcombe, Charles Frederick. 11 2649

Newcomer, Alphonse Gerald. 2:1080

Newdigate, Bernard Henry. 1:1242 (3189); 2:723b 1108; 730 2750 3822 3850 3852 3856 4087 4091 4115 4379 4391 4394 4458 4501 4584 4629 4706 4708 4731 4755 4759 4792 4864–6 4868 4908 4974 4976–7 4985 5175 5300 5399 5413 5419 5439 5511 5512 5579 5634 5636 5725 5805 5860 5918 5920 6277 6447 6479 6481 6570–1 6674 6702 10318 12475 13643

Newdigate, Charles Alfred. 1:1392–3; 841 4052

Newham, J.F. 967

New Haven. Southern Connecticut state college *see* Connecticut. Southern state college, New Haven.

Newman, Franklin B. 1:4723; 13506

New naturalist. 6958a

Newport. Public libraries, museum and art gallery. 1:(3272) 3365

Newport, R.I. Redwood library and athenæm *see* Redwood library and athenæum, Newport, R.I.

News and notes (Nat Lib Wales J). 2:653p; 564 1493 1497 1500 1540 3009 3029 3110 3112 3873 4796–8 4925–6 5696 7085 7548 7971–2 8666 9603 10550 11528 11530–1 12616 12636 12921

News and notes (TLS). 2:575; 3028 3032 4989 8546 10104 10955

New Shakespearana. 2:1

Newson, John. 6046m

New South Wales. Public library, Sydney. 1:485d 2876; 2:245d

Newstead abbey. Roe-Byron collection. 1:2689

Newth, J.D. 4053a

Newton, Alfred Edward. 1:402; 208 2284 2813 6286 7263

Notes on sales (TLS)—cont.
14066 14131–2 14272 14392 14480 14499 14510
Notes, queries and answers (Bkmn's J). 8225
Notes, queries, and answers (Welsh Bib Soc J). 11124
Notes, queries, and replies (Welsh Bib Soc J). 1473–5 1551 1892 12886 14152–3
Notopoulos, James A. 13329 13332
Nottingham. Mechanics institute. 1:2682
— Museum and art gallery, Nottingham castle. 2012a
— Public libraries. 1:928–9 5085
— University. Library. 1:4020
Novel-reader, *pseud.* 7301
Novello and co., London. 5314
Nowell, Charles. 1306–a
Nowell-Smith. Simon Harcourt *see* Smith, Simon Harcourt Nowell-.
Nowottny, Winifred M.T. 2:774 912 1242
Noyes, Alfred. 13819
Noyes, George R. 10338
Noyes, Gertrude Elizabeth. 1:1578 2147; 9502 14291
Noyes, Robert Gale. 1:1464f 1621x 1623a 1624f; 7153
Noyes, Russell. 14533 14549
Nungezer, Edwin. 11566
Nurmi, M.K. 1:2485
Nuttall, Derek. 1081
Nuttall, F.E. 11383
Nuttall, Geoffrey Fillingham. 1:2272 2405d (3356k); 3361a 8428a 8429 11495

O. 1193
O., E.M. 4181
O., W. 12805
Oakeshott, Walter F. 3176 12118–19 12952 12957
Oaten, Edward Farley. 1:333
Oates, John Claud Trewhard. 1:472 581c 881 1345 4794; 80 567 1068–9 1071–2 1613 2378 2382 2440 2445 3145 3229 3293 3352a 3353 3648 3652 3654 4899 5475 5477 6157 6308 11910 13630 13632 13636
O'Brien, Maurice Neill. 1:1589g–h
O'Broin, P. 12620
O'Callaghan, Phyllis. 1:4975a
ÓCasaide, Séamus. 1:75⁸ 1177 1465d 3426 4990; 1776 1785 1790 1794 1800 1806 1810–11 1859 1912 1942–4 1950–1 1953 1959–60 1968 1971–2 1977 1987–8 1991 2851 2917 2958 4351 4353 4669 5113 5577 6425 7078 7736 8011 8986 9726 10215 10927 12619 13734
O'Connell, Daniel. 1:459
O'Connell, J. Harlin. 2345

O'Connor, Daniel A. 1:2975g
O'Connor, Thomas Power. 5713a
ÓCuiv, Shán. 1:4366f
O'Dell, Sterg. 1:1685a
Odend'hal, Gabrielle. 1:4150
Odom, Keith. 3338
O'Donoghue, David James. 1:737 1828 2035 2705 3272t 4082j; 2:1164a; 1742 1778 1856 1886 2728 6466 10454 12472
O'Donoghue, F.M. 5434
O'Donovan, Anne. 284 9922
O'Dwyer, Edward John. 1:3031a; 9971
Oenslager, Donald. 1:2912f
O'Farrell, Thomas T. 1948 5533
Offor, R. 2945 6856
Offord, M.Y. 4335
O'Floinn, Sean. 1799 1981
Ogburn, Vincent H. 2:1568; 12740 12746–7
Ogden, Edmund. 1176 6099
Ogden, Henry V. 1:2105
Ogden, James. 1:3149d
Ogden, Margaret S. 1:2105
Ogilvie, James D. 1:717–19 982 1004; 1587–8 7942
Ogilvy, Murray. 8647
Ogle, Henry. 2607
ÓHaodha, Micheál. 1:3270f 5207b 7930
O'Hegarty, Patrick Sarsfield. 1:1073 1652g 2323 2700 2746 2791 2813 2842 2922h 3312 3533 3780 3880 4063h 4092f 4106 4109 4117 (4120) 4361 (4363–4) 4365 (4369m) 4404 (4432b) (4695) 4865 5202 5206; 2:231 653; 58 1812 1814 1819 1831 1918 1920 1924 2125 5205 8236 8895–6 9859 11448 11709 12237 12239–40 12485 12624 13079 13583 13746 13813 13850 14073 14279
O'Hehir, Brendan. 9951–2 11623
Ohio. University. Library. 1:537h
Ohly, Kurt. (2448a) (7615b)
Okeden, W.H. Parry. 2918
O'Kelley, Francis. 1:1454; 1821 1903–4 1913 5039 6238 14072
Okerlund, Gerda. 2:1317
Okita, Hajime. 1:3808
Old and rare books (Pub Wkly). 2346 14402
Oldenbuck, Aldobrand. 1702
Oldfather, W.A. 12385
Old Glasgow club. 1686a
Oldham, Ellen M. 9239a 9915
Oldham, James Basil. 1066 1369 2141 2162–3 2177 2217 2226 2382 2852 2946 2991 3051 3567 4422 5885
Oldham, Cecil B. 1:2068–9 4961; 2327 2443 3608 3799 7600 14478
Old Printer, An, *pseud.* of John F. Wilson. 5941a 5997–8
O'Leary, John Gerard. 1:26; 200 3113

Oliphant, E.H.C. 12539
Oliphant, Margaret Oliphant (Wilson). 4058
Oliva, Renato. 1:2414h
Oliver, *pseud.* 10737
Oliver, Edith. 7432 4435a
Oliver, Harold J. 12164
Oliver, Leslie Mahin. 960 4528 5977 10598–9 10877
Oliver, Peter. 1:5013
Olney, Clarke. 7892
O'Lochlainn, Colm. 1805 1808–9 1919 3092 4118 4399 5089 6426–7 6429–30 6432 6442 6988 12607–8 12610
Olson, Elder. 1:(4931)
Olybrius, *pseud.* 1:4895; 2257 8419 9613 13915
O'Mahony, Mathew J. 1:1652t
Omans, Stuart. 1:1619
O'Maonaigh, Cainneach. 6431
Omond, Thomas Stewart. 1:1999
O'Neill, Perry. 1:1533
O'Neill, George. 2:841
O'Neill, James J. 1:1589 1975
O'Neill, The. 1:4107a
O'Neill, Thomas P. 1829–30 1837 7256a
Ono, Barry. 14135
Opie, Peter. 11851
Oppel, Horst. 1:(1723) (2030h)
Oras, Ants. 12348
Orcutt, William Dana. 2:743a; 2088 5589a 6088
Ordish, T. Fairman. 2:498
Orel, Harold. 1:1716j; 7969
Ormond, Leonée. 1:3216a
Ormsby-Gore, William George A., 4th baron Harlech *see* Gore, William George A. Ormsby-, 4th baron Harlech.
O'Rourke, D.T. 1:1912
Orr, Alexandra Sutherland. 1:(2582i)
Orsini, G.N. Giordano-. 2:870; 948 11076 11078
Orson, S.W. 2:1060
Orton, Harold. 1:2
Osaka university of commerce. 1:4388
Osborn, E.H. Douglas-. 2:1272
Osborn, James Marshall. 1:3202; 3230–1 7082 10366 10654 11431 12113 12115 12614 13554 14082
Osborne, Charles Glidden. 1:4811
Osborne, Eric Allen. 1:1720 2375 3359 3690 3787 3816 4482 4482b; 2447 7323 8731 9820 9823 10055 10096–7 11316 11952 13914
Osborne, Lucy Eugenia. (128) 2125 6401 6665 11122
Osborne, Mary Tom. 1:1986
Osborne, Noel H. 1:3437c
Osbourne, John W. 9493 9495

Oscott. St. Mary's seminary *see* St. Mary's seminary, Oscott.
Osgood, Charles G. 13568
Osler, A. May. 12824
Osler, Alan. 9294
Osler, sir William. 1:2215; 8824 9124–5 9134
Osley, Arthur Sidney. 1:(3280d)
O'Súilleabháin, Pádraig. 1:2064
O'Sullivan, William. 3211 14305
Oswald, John Clyde. 6086
Oswald, fr., O.S.B. 7818
Otago university, Dunedin, N.Z. Library. 1:2009
Otrębski, Jan. (959a)
Ōtsuka, Takanobu. 2:920a
Ōtsuka, Kenji. 1:4302d
ÓTuathail, Eamonn. 2958
Our bibliographers (Friends' Hist Soc J). 15 17 20
Our portrait gallery (Brit Bkmkr). 3877 3969 3983 3987 4052 4086 4095 4142 4383 4397 4431 4529 4550 4646 4652 4674 4684 4718 4861 4953 5008 5121 5220 5401 5496 5549 5662 5681 5776 5966 6007 6049
Our public libraries (Bookplate Ann). 2525a
Ovenell, R.F. 3114
Overend, George Henry. 3716
Overton, Jacqueline M. 2:47; 7443
Overton, John. 1:1139zd; 3761
Owen, *pseud.* 7351
Owen, Bob. 1547 6754
Owen, Daniel E. 2:724
Owen, Douglas. 1222
Owen, Gail L. 1:2824d
Owen, Gwyneth E. 1:4406x
Owen, Hugh. 13971
Owen, J.H. 4763
Owen, J.P. 2613
Owen, Margaret. 1:4825d
Owen, Robert. 1:1928v
Owen, W.J.B. 2:1453; 5101 14541 14545 14547–8
Owen, William Thomas. 1:5112g
Owens, B.G. 10625 11528 11531 12673 12921 14002
Owl, *pseud.* 11362
Oxberry, John. 3981 4028 5669 10818
Oxford. Double crown club *see* Double crown club, Oxford.
— University. Bodleian library. 1:127 608 1760d 1836 1889 (3317) 4282 4686 (4746) 4944; 2:195 216 246 524; 2170 2248
— — Christ Church. Library. 1:606–7
— — Clarendon press *see also* Oxford university press. 1:1201a
— — Hertford college. Library. 1:506
— — *Lyell lectures.* 234 1281 3543
— — Magdalen college. Library. 1:527

Oxford. University. Oriel college. Library. 1:449
— — School of art. 4195
— — Wadham college. Library. 1:528
— — Worcester college. Library. 1:1605–6
Oxford, Arnold Whitaker. 1:2142–4
Oxford bibliographical society. 1:83 826a 1899 2896 3852 4069b 4119 4478; 1374 1636 3575 3819 3991 5359 5360 6627 11522 12024 12028
— Proceedings and papers. 1:181
— Publications. 1:181
Oxford historical society. 2479 2606 2843 4572–3
Oxford university press. 1:1189a 1200 1201a 1210; 5334 5342
Oyama, Toshikazu. 2:1685

P. 1:1137; 5989 14017
P., A.G. 3618b
P., C.H. 5074
P., D. 1967
P., D.O. 4851
P., F.J. 8218
P., G.H. 11810
P., H. 4516 6286 12474
P., H.B. 1151
P., J.C. 7823
P., O. 8044
P., R.W. 838
P., T.R. 6358
P., W. 6908
P., W.H. 4711
Pacchi, Arrigo. 1:3667
Pace, Claire. 1:(3260)
Pace, George B. 9424 9426 9429 9431
Pacey, Desmond. 8791
Packer, John William. 1:3562k; 3401a
Packer, Lona Mosk. 1:4541d; 13080
Pacy, Frank. 5629
Paddick, E.W. 6331
Padelford, Frederick Morgan. 1:3735–6; 8354 11230 13568
Paden, W.D. 1:4901; 13831 13930 13941 13949 13954 14355
Padwick, E.W. 271
Pafford, John Henry Pyle. 1:3923h; 2:620 1491 1862–3; 1428 2158 3607 8387 8390 8993 9817 10252 10583
Pafford, Ward. 9231
Pafort, Eloise. 1:1419 2279; 6029 8113
Page, A. 2724
Page, Eugene Richard. 1:2855
Page, Frederick. 1:4398; 8282 11264 11680
Page, H.R. 5777
Page, James Rathwell. 1:1522
Page, John T. 1:21; 1187 1312 2573 4556

4739 6275 6724 6938 7384 7828 8239 9987 9998 10412 10715 10823 12297 12323 13129
Page, W. 1:1784
Page, W.B.G. 1234 1440a
Paine, Clarence Sibley. 1:1620; 713
Painter, Anna M. 9048
Painter, George Duncan. 1:476; 156 3158 4322 4336
Paine, J. 1:5053q 5154p
Palacio, Jean de. 13358
Palfrey, Thomas. 10417
Palmer, Arnold. 2:954
Palmer, Cecil. 10037
Palmer, E. 10412
Palmer, Frank. 3499
Palmer, F.W. Morton. 3069
Palmer, George Herbert. 1:(3640) 3641–2 (3644)
Palmer, Helen H. 1:1597
Palmer, Henrietta Raymer. 1:772
Palmer, J.E.C. 1:2249c
Palmer, J. Foster. 2:710; 6827 8264 9884 12064
Palmer, Margaret. 1:1818p
Palmer, William Mortlock. 1056
Paltsits, Victor Hugo. 1:1480; 45 135 5485
Pane, Remigio Ugo. 1:841
Pargellis, Stanley. 1:20
Pangle, M.E. 12712
Pantazzi, Sybille. 1:3560b; 2227 5054 10925–6
Panter, George W. 13388
Pantzer, Katherine F. 688 694
Papali, George Francis. 1:1406s; 5869
Papantonio, Michael. 5137
Pape, Richard Otto. 2:1670–1
Paper maker. 1:182
Paper maker and British paper trade journal. 1:183
Paper publications society. 3764 3802
Paper trade journal. 1:184
Par, Alfonso. 2:64
Paradise, Nathaniel Burton. 1:4073; 7149
Parchevskaia, B.M. 1:2318m 4356a 5053w
Pardee, Avern. 1414
Pardee, Ruth. 1:2553m
Pardoe, Frank Ernest. 6499
Parenti, Marino. 1:827ac; 951
Paříková, M. 2:145
Paris. Bibliothèque nationale see France. Bibliothèque nationale, Paris.
Pariser, sir Maurice Philip. 14428 14447 14449
Parish, Charles. 2:237; 1420 11499
Parish, William A. 2:243; 7449
Park, Julian. 1:673; 8669
Park, Mary Cathryne. 643

Vol. 1 = Bibliographies   2 = Shakespeare   4 = 1–8221   5 = 8222–14616

Park, William. 1:367
Parke-Bernet galleries, New York. 1:402–4
  1712 2478 3095d 3954 3982 4808; 3067
Parker, Alan Dean. 1:3882
Parker, D.H. 702
Parker, Franklin. 1:5089
Parker, George. 7556
Parker, James. 10557
Parker, John. 1:2289e
Parker, R.J. 9884
Parker, R. Brian. 2:235; 6133a 10882–3
Park, W. 9103
Parker, W.M. 2:367; 11898 12038 13217
Parker, Walter Henry. 1:1666 1670
Parker, William Riley. 1:4235 4249; 146
  12369–70 12378 12390 12398 12440 12779
  13228 14145
Parkes, Kineton. 2050 3842
Parks, Aileen Wells. 1:4092g
Parks, Edd Winfield. 1:4092g; 2:1908
Parks, George B. 1:2391; 8209a 8312
Parks, Joseph. 14135
Parks, Stephen. 3685 4606 9115 9691
Parmentier, Alix. 1:5089f
Parr, Johnstone. 1:2108 3523
Parreaux, André. 1:2416; 8481a 8483
Parris, H. 1442
Parrish, Morris Longstreth. 1:1707 (2541)
  2722–3 2850 (3250) (3411) (3752) (3755)
  3929 (4496) 4921; 2113 7305 8351 8412
  8420 8796 9307 9618–20 10084 10087
  10105–7 10903 12985 13214 13658
Parrish, Stephen M. 1:1536t
Parrish, W.F. 9594
Parrott, Alice. 1:4753
Parrott, Thomas Marc. 1:2558; 2:545 898
  1192 1205 1438 1458 1644 1808; 7308
  9354 9356–8 9571
Parry, John Jay. 1:2345 2348c–d 4487;
  2:1278; 12974
Parry, Morris. 1:883d 1462a; 1075
Parry, Thomas. 9837
Parry, V.T.H. 1:(3785d)
Parson, J. 1227
Parsons, Coleman O. 1:4613; 4356b 10762
  13199–200 13239 13241
Parsons, Edward John S. 1:2048; 7507
  10666
Parsons, Howard. 2:1068–70 1231 1516
  1519–20 1679 1773 1775–6; 13040
Parsons, J. Denham. 2:650
Parsons, K.O. 1:3002
Parsons, Katherine de B. 14205
Parsons, Leila. 11033
Partington, E. 1:2671h; 2467
Partington, Wilfred George. 1:3192 4392
  5135 5138; 123 8794 10135 10805 12604
  12646 14183 14406 14417 14423

Partridge, Astley Cooper. 2:939 943 1943; 79
  9745
Partridge, Charles. 1:1559d; 3100 5929 8114
Partridge, Eric Honeywood. 1:1396 5026
  (5028) (5030); 5605
Partridge, Frances. 1:(3185ea)
Partridge, Robert. 3524
Pasadena, Calif. Francis Bacon foundation
  see Francis Bacon foundation, Pasadena,
  Calif.
Pascoe, Charles Eyre. 1212
Passey, J.M.D. 1:3458d
Passmore, John A. 1:2936
Paston, George. 5253–4
Paterson, Alex. 7826
Patmore, Derek. 1:4399 4592; 800
Paton, Henry M. 1607
Patricia, Mary. 1:3703
Patrick, pseud. 4524
Patrick, D. 9278
Patrick, David Lyall. 2:1674
Patrick, F.J. 2:313
Patrick, J. Max. 1:4284
Patrides, C.A. 11083
Patry, Madeleine. 1:4319a
Pattberg, Eugene P. 4194
Patterns of literary criticism. 298a
Patterson, Charles I. 11684
Patterson, Lyman R. 3542a 3544a
Patterson, Richard F. 11552
Pattison, Bruce. 7607
Patton, Cornelius Howard. 1:5173; 9531
Patton, Lewis. 1:4654d; 9528 13344
Patton, M.M. 1:2371
Paul, Charles Kegan. 1:1379p; 5377–8
Paul, Harry Gilbert. 1:3012
Paul, Henry Neill. 2:69 738 746 1193–4
Pawling, Sydney S. 4707
Payen, DeV. Payne-. 11830
Paylor, Wilfrid James. 1:4382; 12633
Payne, Alfred. 8183
Payne, Denis. 11878
Payne, Francis John. 2:1786; 2594 6945
  7364–6 12306 12309
Payne, John R. 1:1139x; 2244
Payne, L.M. 1:3619; 7567
Payne, Waveney R.N. 2:157 312 320 326;
  11855
Payne, William. 6926 14156
Payne, William L. 9908
Peabody institute, Baltimore. Library. 1:1725
Peach, Harry H. 9417
Peachey, George C. 1:4404p; 11701
Peacock, Edward. 1:4058; 886 6777
Peacock, Florence. 10645
Peacock, Markham. 14535
Pearce, E.C. 12656 12699
Pearce, Ernest Harold. 2694

Pearce, Ethel. 1:1633f; 7220
Pearce, T.M. 11923
Pearl, Morris Leonard. 1:2821
Pearsall, Derek A. 3309
Pearsall, Robert. 1:2589; 3794 6704
Pearsall, Ronald. 5238 7621
Pearson, Edmund Lester. 2295 2752
Pearson, Edwin. 6985
Pearson, F.S. 1:947
Pearson, Hesketh. 10686
Pearson, Howard S. 1:3215a; 1384 6746 7709 8118
Pearson, J. Sidney. 10738
Pearson, Karl. 8829
Pearson, T.S. 13651
Pearson, Terry P. 13690–1
Peavy, Charles Druery. 1:(2806) 4445
Peck, Louis Francis. 1:4051; 11985 11987 11990–2
Peck, Walter Edwin. 1:4642a; 13005 13295–6 13298
Peckham, H.H. 2352
Peckham, Morse. 1530 2377 2953; 997 7245 8375–6
Peddie, Robert Alexander. 1:65 410 424 434 436 663 1015 1139za 1143 1146 2100a; 196 548–9 1212 1222 2153 2407 2424 3486 3790 3863 3865–6 4013 4124 4246 4248 4252 5878 5955 6072 6084 6173 6198 6346–7 6568–9 6201 6833 7583
Pedley, Katherine Greenleaf. 14449a
Peers, E.A. 1:4601
Peery, William Wallace. 1:3297; 6410 7086 7171 9433 9545 9862 10479–82
Peet, William Henry. 1:1184 1184d; 337 750 839 1214 1230 1992 2070 3443 3449 3460 3464 3623 3628 3865 3887 4013 4359a 4360 4897c 5032 5273 5395a 5425 5781 5905 7716 8090 8218 10422 10733a 10736 11260 11819 12297 13159
Pegg, Michael A. 1:488; 12970
Peggram, Reed E. 12504
Peintres-graveurs contemporains (Gaz des Beaux Arts). 4628
Peirce, Butler. 193
Pelkam, R.A. 1419
Pemberton, W.B. 3012
Pendleton, J.W. 12360
Pengelly, R.S. 4863
Pennel, Charles A. 1:2413a (3345a) (4169b) (4677c); 10886
Pennell, Elizabeth (Robins). 1:2141d; 6188 6200 11030
Pennel, Joseph. 1:(3916); 6186 6188 6200 7386 9301 10026
Penniman, T.K. 1:4118h

Pennsylvania. University. Library. 1:171 603 1490 1665 2796 3671; 2:916
Penny, C.W. 10276
Penrose annual. 1:185
Penrose, Boies. 8216
Penwick, George. 10545
Penzer, Norman Mosley. 1:2650
Pepler, Hilary Douglas Clarke. 1:1391
Pepper, Robert D. 5902
Percy, bp. Thomas. 12756
Perkin, M.J. 1:2443
Perkin, M.R. 1:2891
Perkins, Walter Frank. 1:2094; 10698
Perkinson, Richard H. 8382 9846 14190
Perkins school of theology, Dallas. Bridewell library. 6893
Perles, Alfred. 1:(3227)
Perrett, Arthur J. 2:1807
Perrin, Michel P. 1:1630b
Perrin, Noel. 2:805; 3509
Perrin, William Gordon. 1:2234
Perring, Philip. 2:1562
Perrot, Francis. 12098
Perry, Marsden Jasiel. 1:401 1351
Perry, Warren. 11678
Perry, William. 1:1385; 641
Persecuted successors of Caxton (Morriss's Trade J). 4182b 4183
Pershing, James H. 1:4237; 3736 8278 12391 13694
Pertelote. 1:1333
Perth. Drummond castle see Drummond castle, Perth.
Peter, A. 1936
Peterborough museum society. Occasional papers. 9464
Peterborough natural history, scientific and archæological society. 1:2807
Peterhouse see Cambridge. University. Peterhouse.
Peters, Charlotte (Hodge). 1:4459–61 4998; 12899
Peters, J.F.H. 6498
Peters, John. 1:1413
Peterson, Annamarie. 1:5220
Peterson, Houston. 1:3265x
Peterson, Martin Severin. 1:3825
Peterson, Spiro. 9918 9921
Peterson, William M. 9452
Petersson, K. 2:650a
Petherbridge, M. 9391b
Petherick, E.A. 2:505; 8205
Petherick, John. 7658
Petre, Edwin Alfred Robert Rumball-. 1:1486 1493
Petrie, sir Charles Alexander. 1:4570
Petrie, James A. 3071
Pettegrove, J.P. 13312

Petti, Anthony G. 1:5000; 3322
Pettit, Henry J. 1:5216 5218–19; 14223
  14611 14613–15
Pettitt, Kenneth I. 8878
Petty, S.L. 2420 3712 4791 7872 8256 12460
Peyrouton, N.C. 10165
Pfander, H.G. 5406
Pforzheimer, A. 11758
Pforzheimer, Carl Howard. 1:577; 8278 8896
Pforzheimer library, N.Y. see Carl H.
  Pforzheimer library, N.Y.
Phelps, William L. 1:662; 8891
Phialas, Peter G. 2:1294
Philadelphia. Free library. 1:3094 3841c 4328
— Library company. 1:612
— Museum of art. 1:2479
— Rosenbach company see Rosenbach com-
  pany, Philadelphia.
Philbrick, Norman. 2:582
Philbrick, Thomas L. 1:1466; 6793
Philip, Alexander J. 5433
Philip, Ejnar. 4589 12533
Philip, Ian G. 2170 3014 3212 3902 5360
  5363 5796 11026–7
Philipson, J. 5518j
Phillip, John. 1208
Phillipps, James Orchard Halliwell-. 2:171
Phillipps, Joseph. 8404
Phillipps-Wolley, sir Clive see Wolley, sir
  Clive Wolley-.
Phillipps studies. 3125 3144 3175 3207 3292
Phillips, Arthur G.E. 1:2046; 2650
Phillips, Charles T.E. 3058
Phillips, Charles William. 1:461
Phillips, David Rhys. 1:1181 1280 3459; 326
  1456 1458–9 1463 1489 1541 5035 6555
  6557 7006 12106 12920 13046
Phillips, James W. 1833 1928 5223 6440
Phillips, Joe. 8218
Phillips, LeRoy. 1:3802–3
Phillips, R. 1:1298
Philpot, V.J. 1:3785
Philological quarterly. 1:48–9 52
Phin, John. 2:403
Phinn, C.P. 11052
Physick, John Frederick. 1:3437b
Pick, Robert. 1:823
Picker, Martin. 10937
Pickering, Charles L. 6493
Pickering, J.E.L. 7472
Pickering, R.Y. 8076 11862
Pickford, John. 1:3455c; 1016 1193 1378
  2562 4556 7384 7822 9005 9172 9685 9777
  10603 10801 10815–16 12297 12800 13173
  13176 13257 14241
Pickles, J.D. 1:376
Pierce, Dorothy. 1:3090
Pierce, Frederick E. 11099

Pierce, Gilbert Ashville. 1:3064
Pierce, William. 1:1364b 4128a; 5146 5149
Pierpont, Robert. 1:3711; 728 888 1229 1239
  2070 3552 3585 4021 4897c 5178 6513
  6838 6855–6 7351 7712 7863 7887 8681
  8818 9990 10001 10538 10815 10861 11382
  11730 11736 12167 12227 12675 13638
Pierpont Morgan library, N.Y. 1:1491 1562
  3848 4605; 300 2123a 3384 5597a
Pike, G. Holden. 4204a
Pillans, H. and J., and Wilson, ptrs., Edin-
  burgh. 1:1384g; 5418
Pillsbury, Stanley R. 5348
Pinchbeck, W.H. 2:650
Pineas, Rainer. 8391
Pingree, Jeanne. 1:3779d
Pinhorn, Malcolm. 1:5104g; 5694a 14328
Pink, H.L. 3145
Pinnock, C.L. 1:4979
Pinto, Vivian de Sola. 1:2 4020 4617 5123;
  11932 11937 14351 14357a
Piper, Alfred Cecil. 1:944x; 189 1132 1135–6
  1406–8 1410 4250 4526 4694 5962 7967
Pirie, N.W. 1:3549i–k
Pirie, Robert S. 8369a 10268–9 14311
Pissarro, Esther. 1:1319
Pissarro, Lucien. 1:1319; 4632
Pitcher, Seymour M. 12152
Pitman, Alfred. 5424
Pitt, S.A. 1:1002a
Pitt collection see Southampton. Public libraries.
Pittock, Joan. 14240
Pittsburgh. Carnegie institute of technology.
  Dept. of fine arts. 1:2127
— — Hunt botanical library. 1:2129
Plaat, F. 1:1139h
Plaistowe, Francis Gifford. 1:435
Plant, Arnold. 3525
Plant, Marjorie. 3453 3469 3480a
Plant, W.C. 2545
Plantnauer, Maurice. 8816
Plarr, Victor Gustave. 1:(3176); 11133
Platt, James. 902 7636 11731
Playfair, J.K.H. 1:3494
Pleadwell, F.L. 1266
Plincke, E.M. 1:4170
Plomer, Henry Robert. 1:506g 508 569 595a
  1401 1401d 1406p 1423 3624 (4430d); 824
  1073a 1160 1199 1205 1206a 1209–13 1224
  1243 1248 1758 1765 2409 2412–14 2574
  2608 3407 3409 3417 3423 3528 3433–5
  3441 3444 3551 3619 3630 3675 3811 4121
  4124 4152 4259 4412 4418 4531 4613
  4662ad 4664 4702 4807 5011 5132 5203
  5255b 5256 5323 5459 5463 5465 5505
  5657 5665 5711 5734 5826 5871 5893 6016
  6040–1 6056 6058–9 6062 6067 6071 6074
  6081 6084–5 6346 6461 6663 7657 7852

Plomer, Henry Robert—*cont.*
7941 7964 8081 8937–8 11013 11906 12689 12892 13423 13558–9 14560
Plooij, dr. 4112
Plowman, Max. 8572–3 8576 8579 8581 8583
Plucknett, Theodore F.T. 206
Plume library, Maldon. 1:362
Plunkett, Edward John Moreton Drax, 18th baron Dunsany. 1:2244e
Plymouth. Public library. 1:886b
Pocklington, Geoffrey Richard. 5689–90
Poel, William. 2:847–9 851–2 1148 1169
Pogson, K.M. 2782
Polak, Rose-Lida. 1:3448t
Poland, sir H.B. 838 10018
Polanyi, John. 1:4432c
Polhemus, George W. 8300
Polish library, London. 1:2870
Pollard, Alfred William. 1:427 493 507–8 521–4 775 1140 (1265) 1349 1401e 1444–5 1474 3397 4226 4430d; 2:184 207 383 385 397 404 407 410 414–15 837–40 844 848 857 873–5 1287 1311 1340–1 1351 1565 1650f 1708 1711 1882 1886; 6 8–10 14 33 35 38 106 108 110 (128) 147 181–2 192 197 199 204 207 279–80 310–13 318 320 498 505 548 552 575 593 596 598 600 604 614 748 830 1359 2044 2054 (2074) 2279 2288 2427 2599–600 2614–15 2651 2803 3405 3425 3516 3520 3533 3666 3668–9 4006 (4011) 4081 4117 4242 4266 4268 5739 6056 6060 6114 6148 6263 6272 6445 6464 6474 6478 6486 6488 6566 6666 6840–1 7121 7124 7234 7372 (7382) (7386a) 7390 7392 7411 7980–1 9412 9882 10491 11052 11076 11130–1 11975 12321 12596 12706 14213
Pollard, H.P. 7387
Pollard, H.T. 1167
Pollard, Henry Graham. 1:1139h 1186d 1186f 1201 1456 2569 3281 (4291a) 5133a (5141); 77 2207 2327 2447 3253 3462 3466 3493 3677–8 3740 3917 5058 5216a 5747–8 6092 6307 6532–3 6552 7070 7268 7298 8671 8868 9215 9739 10912 12997 13324 13916 14387 14411 14415 14420–1 14449
Pollard, Mary. 1:82 253 4407 4491a; 3339 4354 5232 10413 12692
Pollard, Matilda. 10724
Pollard, Robert. 1324
Pollard, Sidney. 5772a
Pollet, Maurice. 1:4698a
Pollin, Burton Ralph. 1:3461a 3462j
Polliot, Gilbert. 4632
Pollock, Frederick. 13246
Pollock, Pleasance. 6997
Pomery, James Spenser, 6th viscount Harberton. 10813

Pomfret, J.E. 5790
Ponsonby, Arthur William Harry, baron Ponsonby. 1:1575x
Poole, E. Phillips. 1:2544
Poole, M. Ellen. 7827
Poole, S. Lane-. 9171
Pope, F.J. 2616
Pope, Hugh. 6914–15
Pope, Myrtle Pihlman. 1:4952
Pope, Willard B. 11674
Pope and his contemporaries. 13762
Popham, A.E. 8590
Popkin, Richard H. 12955
Popović, Vladeta. 2:63
Popper, Monica. 1:4974a
Portal, sir William Wyndham. 5438 5441–2
Porteous, Catherine. 92a
Porteous, Crichton. 1:(3820a)
Porter, Charles P. 1054
Porter, Charlotte. 2:545
Porter, George William. 1:102
Porter, Mary. 4059 4061
Portrait of a bibliophile (Bk Coll). 1:5111m; 3268 3272 3284 3290 3321 3328 3342 3353a 3354a 9557 11295
Portretten van bibliophielen (Folium). 3120–1
Portsmouth. Dickens' birthplace museum *see* Dickens' birthplace museum, Portsmouth.
Portugal. Instituto Británico, Lisbon *see* Instituto Británico em Portugal, Lisbon.
Poston, Mervyn Lowe. 542 7796 11022 13222
Potter, Alfred Claghorn. 1:2411 2652; 2947 10648
Potter, Ambrose George. 1:3325; 10546–7
Potter, Esther. 1:2200; 7470
Potter, Greta Largo. 5921
Potter, George. 707 3671 5915 6856 8383–4 12323
Potter, George Reuben. 10246 10254
Potter, Lee H. 13798
Potter, Richard Montgomery Gilchrist. 1:2548
Potter, Robert A. 1:3225
Potter, W.A. 1:1903a; 1343–4
Pottinger, David T. 6600
Pottle, Frederick Albert. 1:2508 2508d 4443; 6357 7950 8678 8682–5 8689 8692 8698 8966 12845 13190 14553
Potts, L.J. 2:1183
Potts, R.A. 9777 10412 11814 12621 13014 14493–4
Potts, R.A.J. 1084 4021 7715 9619
Poulter, James. 3079–80 3146
Povey, Kenneth. 1:2896d 4970j; 159 1866 4285 6243 6246 6248 6341 6369 6378 9706 9709–10 9722
Powell, A.C. 10242
Powell, Anthony. 8319

Vol. **1** = *Bibliographies*   **2** = *Shakespeare*   **4** = 1–8221   **5** = 8222–14616

Powell, C.L. 9269
Powell, D. 1:2809–a
Powell, David. 9265
Powell, Everett G. 13837
Powell, F.R. 14119
Powell, Frederick York. 1:3941 4848
Powell, Lawrence Clark. 1:3224 3778 4016g
4017
Powell, Lawrence Fitzroy. 1:4408 4415; 2391
7739 8381 8681 8690 8699 9398 10802
11401 11405–6 11509 11922 11925
12694–5 12734 12736 12745
Powell, Roger. 2263
Powell, Walter. 1:946; 2:273b 362 544a
Powell, William Charles. 1:2326d
Power, sir D'Arcy. 1:2406; 1244 7559 8377–8
Power, Eibhlin. 1813
Power, P. 1789
Power, William R. 9501 11737
Powicke, sir Frederick Maurice. 1:(4971f)
Poynter, Frederick Noel Lawrence. 1:474
2219 2227 4119; 231 7564 7569
Prades, Juana de José. 1:3097e
Prague. Charles university. 2:149
— Municipal library. 2:145
— Městká lidová knihovna. 2:145
Prance, C.R. 12523
Prance, Claude Annett. 1:3397a–b 5082;
1278 2386 11856 11859 14016
Prasher, A. LaVonne. 11895
Prater, E.G. 1:3365d
Pratt, John M. 909
Pratt, Roland Davies. 1:1139k
Pratt, Willis Winslow. 1:2694–a; 9234
Praz, Mario. 1:1656a; 2:1532; 13808
Presbyterian historical society of England.
8042
Prescott, Joseph. 1:4515
Presidency college, Calcutta. 12117
Press club, London. Library. 1:1852 1888
Presser, Helmut. 4997
Prestage, Edgar. 5724
Preston. Harris public library see Harris
public library, Preston.
Preston, Kerrison. 1:2483–4 2489; 8610 8630
Preston, William C. 5236
Previté-Orton, C.W. 2810
Price, Allan M. 8061
Price, Cecil J.L. 1:1979p–q 4763; 7229 7971
13407–12 13468 13585
Price, Derek J. DeS. 12587
Price, F.G. Hilton. 5872
Price, George Rennie. 1:2996c; 2:1417;
12271–3 12275–7 12279–80 12282–4 14075
Price, Harry. 1:2242–4; 11724
Price, Hereward Thimbleby. 2:426 871 1046
1312 1316 1806 1811; 6178 6181 7155
8162

Price, J.H. 6968 8158
Price, John Edward. 1:3401b
Price, Lawrence Marsden. 1:743a 752–3;
2:56a 87a
Price, Mary Bell. 1:752–3
Price, Ursula E. 1:1775
Price, W.W. 73
Price, W. Arthur. 7548
Prideaux, Sarah Treverbian. 1:1139n–o 1739;
1564 2004 2010 2012a 2013–14 2016 2019
2057 2063 3812 5386 5450–1 7380
Prideaux, W.R.B. 1:1345a; 2609–10 2627
3674 8552 9752 9866 11539 11545 12941
Prideaux, William Francis. 1:2827 3323 3935
4543 4797 4805; 2:394 650; 99 104 179
338 870a 1226 2518 3577 4048 4470 5094b
5915 6193 6397 7002 7214 7717 7834 8270
8743 8818 9613 9794 9796–7 9800 9879
9990 10001 1025 10217 10403 10458 10484
10527 10539–40 10542 10547 10731 10736
10739 10816 10917a–8 11007 11053 11729
11808 11813 11818 12052 12521 12536
12594 12645 12807 13049 13081 13083
13383–4 13525 13640–1 13902 14175
14178 14313 14330 14495
Primrose, James Bartholomew. 1:1385; 4871
Prince, Thomas. 8966
Princeton university. Library. 1:311 363h
1707 2408 3958; 2:196; 541 792
Princeton studies in English. 14290
Princeton university library chronicle. 1:186
Pringle, G.S. 13650
Print. 1:187
Print council of America. 1:1269g 1754b
Printers of England (*Lib Asst*). 4523 5460 6005
Printers of note (*Inland Ptr*). 4249a
Printing and graphic arts. 1:188
Printing historical society, London. 4668
5672 5723
— *Journal.* 1:166; 6393
Printing trade relics, trophies, and curios (*Scott
Typogr J*). 6315
Printing up to date (*Caxton Mag*). 5333
Prinz, Johannes. 1:5121
Pritchard, Alan. 1:1162; 14470–1
Pritchard, Brian. 1:1841
Pritchard, George. 12561
Pritchard, J.E. 7493
Private libraries (*TLS*). 2981 2989–90 2992
2999 3002–3 3011–13 3014 3017 3021–4
3038 3045 6950 7022a 7068 7962 8077
8209–10 10933 11313 13742 14206
Private libraries association. 1:98 313 1235
1755 5188m; 2235 2393 5426 6310 7931
9971
Private libraries association quarterly. 1:189
Private library. 1:189
Private press books. 1:1235

Private printer & private press. 1:190
Proceedings of the Gibbon commemoration. 1:3421
Proctor, Mortimer Robinson. 1:1667–8
Proctor, Robert George Collier. 1:418–20
508 1265; 2400a 6056 7386a 13903
Proelss, Robert. 2:834; 280 4077
Progress guide to Anglo-Irish plays. 1:1652t
Prosser, R.B. 839 1195 1219 2017 2404
2416–17 3591 3721 5295 6234 6928 9270
Prothero, Rowland Edmund, baron Ernle.
1:4766
Proudfoot, George Richard. 2:22
Prouty, Charles Tyler. 1:(4425x); 2:(893)
1289 1365; (7170) 10637 (11682)
Prouty, Ruth. 10637
Providence, R.I. Brown university *see* Brown
university, Providence, R.I.
Provost, Foster. 1:4755
Pruvost, René. 932 6755 10870 10873
Pryce, G. 9299
*Publications of the Modern language association of
America.* 1:43
Public record office *see* Great Britain. Public
record office.
Publishers' circular and book sellers' record. 1:191
Publishers' devices (Bkmns J). 4583
Publishers of to-day (Pub Circ). 3830a 4204
4402 5094
Publishers' weekly. 1:192
Pullen, G.F. 1:2263; 3362
Purdom, Charles Benjamin. 1:(2390n)
Purdy, Richard Little. 1:3587 3598; 10424
10946 10949–50 10959 12236 13395 13404
14105
Purnell, C.J. 2422 2768 3016 6298
Purves, W. Laidlaw. 9877 9881 9883
Putnam, Bertha Haven. 1:2209; 7473 7477
Putnam, George Haven. 3406 3518
Putnam, Helen Cordelia. 1:4391
Pye, J. 2130
Pyle, Fitzroy. 2:1799; 635
Pyle, Hilary A. 1:4785
Pyles, Thomas. 2:1206

Q, A.N. 4662
Q. V., *pseud.* 10911
Quad, *pseud.* 12677
Quare, *pseud.* 12381
Quaritch, Bernard. 1:390 2648; 2012a 6822
13908a
Quaritch, Bernard, bksllrs., London. 1:381
3326f; 2079 2264 5486
Quarrell, W.H. 3694
Quarterly check-list of literary history. 1:44
Quarterly check list of renaissance studies. 1:47
Quayle, Eric. 1:2385e; 11035 13242–3

Queen's university, Kingston, Ont. *see*
Kingston, Ont. Queen's university.
Queries (Blake Newsl). 8639a
Quiller-Couch, sir Arthur Thomas. 4181
Quinby, Jane. 1:2127 2129 4450
Quinn, David Beers. 1:(3549); 1921 7953
Quinn, John. 1:665 5199
Quinn, Muriel S. 2131
Quintana, Ricardo. 1:2690
Quinton, C.L. 2:598; 890a 891a
Quinton, John. 1:924

R. 4844 6880 9119 9581 10047
R., D.M. 1454 7709 13457
R., E.H. 13075
R., F.H. 8102
R., G. 6777
R., G.O. 5005
R., G.W. 2673
R., H. 1055
R., J.F. 13084
R., J.H. 4154 6902
R., J.N.B. 1:2898
R., L.G. 2:362
R., L.M. 2:1005; 6838
R., M.U.H. 14297
R., P.N. 6234
R., S. 1282 9207
R., T. 1:2519b
R., T.B. 957
R., W. 1:5096
R., W.A. 4181
Rabb, Theodore K. 13145
Raben, Joseph. 13365
Rabinovitz, Rubin. 1:1724p (2323d) (4732a)
(5127)
Race, Sydney. 2:370; 9587–9 9591 9593–4
9596–700 10581–2 11286–7 11703–4
12129–30 12232–3 12775 14021
Rachow, Louis A. 2:335
Racin, John. 12956
Radcliffe, John. 886 888 3786 6265 6777
6996 8191 8201 10939 12943
Radcliffe, William. 1:2559
Radford, D. 1:2322
Radford, Emma Louisa, lady. 1100
Radford, Ursula. 1:2975; 4517
Radzinowicz, Leon. 1:4776f
Rae, Thomas. 1:1222 1235 1400; 5255c 5656
8718
Rae, W. Fraser. 5249–a 10655 11626
Ragan, Louise. 1:(2982)
Rainbird, George. 1:1754q; 6221
Raine, Kathleen. 92a
Rait, Robert S. 13183 13196
Rajan, Balachandra. 1:3256a; 12457
Raknem, Ingvald. 1:5058c

Raleigh, sir Walter. 14497
Ralph, Brenda Anne. 1:4009a
Ramage, David. 1:472a 547; 3214–15 3776
Ramello, Giovanni. 2:1189
Ramsden, Charles F.I. 1283 2188–90 2197
   2218 3254 4717 4891 5986
Ramsey, Gordon C. 1:2792a
Ramsey, Robert W. 2638 11547
Rand, Edward K. 12329
Rand, Frank Hugh. 1:3093
Randall, Dale B.J. 9297
Randall, David Anton. 1:2542 3181r 3181w
   (3597) 4606; 137 990 2327 2349 2389 3232
   6161 7309 8242 8786 8814–15 8817a 8870
   9485a 9653 9659a 10131 10294–7 10688–9
   10895 11206–7 11326 11765 11977 12170
   12751 12883 12988 13206 13671 13918
   13991 14263
Randall, John. 7384
Randolph, Mary Claire. 1:2007
Rānjī G. Shāhānī. 2:68
Ransom, Harry Hunt. 3526–7 3534 4921
   11252 12468
Ransom, Will. 1:29 1228 1230; 6475 6488
Rao, Balakrishna. 2:802; 13237
Rao, Kanatur Bhaskara. 1:3961
Raphael, Sandra. 1:1323a
Ratchford, Fannie Elizabeth. 1:4897 5136–7;
   12846 13805 13910 14407–9 14411 14413
   14419 14422
Ratcliffe, Edward C. 6935
Ratcliffe, F.W. 1:1545
Ratcliffe, Harland R. 10951
Ratcliffe, Thomas. 1:2519b; 706 4013 4739
   5031 6199 6824 6830 6989 7002
Rath, Erich von. 1:(410b)
Rattenbury, S.K. 1:5025t
Rattey, Clifford C. 1:484
Rattray, R.F. 13265
Rau, Arthur. 3353a
Raven, Anton Adolph. 2:1140
Raven-Hart, H. *see* Hart, H. Raven-.
Ravizé, A. 11260
Rawlings, Gertrude Burford. 6063
Rawson, Claude J. 12661–2
Ray, F.R. 9670 10339
Ray, George W. 1:2761a
Ray, Gordon Norton. 1:4921a 4924 5038;
   810a 2387 2392a 3159 4001 7322 14282
Ray society. 5515
Rayment, H. 13171
Raymond, William Odber. 1:2580; 14412
   14414
Rayner, Colin. 1:4882q; 13883
Raysor, Thomas Middleton. 2015 (2676)
   (2826) (3907a) (4646) (5162); 9522 14542
Rea, Robert R. 3832–3 7954 10673
Read, Bill. 1:4402h

Read, Conyers. 1:16
Read, Donald. 1178
Read, F.W. 7759 11629
Read, Newbury Frost. 1:3087; 10065
Read, Stanley E. 1:3676–7
Read, William Augustus. 1:401d
Reade, Aleyn Lyell. 3021 3872 4936–7
Reade, Brian. 11953
Reader, A, *pseud.* 10867
Reading. Public libraries. 1:873
— University. Library. 1:874
— — Museum of English rural life. 5709
Reading, Jack. 1:4882q; 13883
Recorder, *pseud.* 1:2031
Records of civilization. 1:770a
Redfern, L.M. 7865
Redgrave, Gilbert R. 1:521–4; 498 812 2277
   3548–9 3788 9174 9698–9 10459 14064
Redlich, Fritz. 3659
Redmill, C.E. 1:940x
Redmond, Philip. 13547
Redpath, mrs. Peter. 1:1960
Redstone, V.B. 5323
Redway, A.R. 13831
Redway, G.W. 2:1147
Redway, George. 887
Redwood library and athenæum, Newport,
   R.I. 2:197
Reed, Alfred. 1:3101
Reed, Arthur W. 2826 3554–5 5507–9
   11071–2 12497
Reed, Edward Bliss. 7597 8223
Reed, F.W. 6529
Reed, Isobel. 1:3101
Reed, John Curtis. 1:1369–70; 5222
Reed, Peter J. 1:2742
Reed, T. German-. 1:4026; 11748 11945
Reed, Talbot Baines. 1:1140 1266p: 3911
   5518 6563–4 6613
Reed, Thomas Allen. 5421
Rees, David Harding. 1:4928
Rees, Eiluned. 1:4408a; 1516 1546 12698
   12894
Rees, J. Rogers. 9519
Rees, Margaret Jean. 1:4540a
Rees, R.D. 1509
Rees, Thomas. 1200
Reese, Harold. 7993
Reese, William L. 1:(5089d)
Reeve, C.R. 12735
Reeves, Dorothea D. 1:1536v; 6976
Referee, *pseud.* 14424
Reference catalogue of current literature. 1:1184e
Register of books, 1728–1732. 1:642
Reichner, Herbert. 5637 13017
Reid, A.G. 2534
Reid, Alec. 1:2414j
Reid, Anthony. 1:5188m

Ringler, William. 1:1987 3482; 2:1466; 5472 9346 9584 12063 13430 13681

Ripley, S. Dillon. 1:2120

Ritchie, R.L. Graeme. 1:816

Ritchie, Ward. 1:672a 2023

Ritz, Jean Georges. 1:2529b 3703r; 11148 11244a

Riverside, Calif. University of California see California. University. University at Riverside.

Rives, Léone. 1:4497

Rivett, J.H. Carnac-. 11732

Rivière, Robert and son, London. 5552–3

Rivington, Charles Robert. 5726 5730–1 5733 5735–6 5738 5745 6047

Rivington, Septimus. 5554–5

Rivlin, Joseph Barry. 1:4140

Robb, James. 1:2102

Robb, N.A. 13319–20

Robbie, H.J.L. 10222 10224

Robbins, A.E. 5710

Robbins, Alfred F. 729 2420 3581 3585 3587 7633 7635–8 7640 7704 7839 9145 10486 13716

Robbins, Caroline. 3115

Robbins, G.A. 4383

Roberton, William. 1:3937

Roberts, Bryn F. 1:2349a

Roberts, Cecil M. 10559

Roberts, E.F.D. 12970

Roberts, Francis Warren. 1:4020d; 11926 11929 11937

Roberts, Gomer M. 1:5116g–h 5194f; 1484 1503–4 5832 5939 9394 11978 12893 14341–3

Roberts, John Hawley. 11671

Roberts, M.A.M. 8257

Roberts, Mark. 10271–2

Roberts, R. Ellis. 1:1330c; 4758

Roberts, R.F. 11588

Roberts, R. Julian. 1:1365c 3473; 678a 726 3233 5182

Roberts, Robert. 2:503–5; 6803 6808 6810 6814–15 6817 7818 11660 12297 12521 13169

Roberts, Stanley. 1:2877c

Roberts, sir Sydney Castle. 1:1277 2554 4425; 87 1061 3160 3310 4162 4171–2 4178 6158 9757 10280 11387 11402–3 11454

Roberts, Warren Everett. 1:4021

Roberts, William. 1:1292a 1447a 1873a; 2:525 1639; 579 832 848 881 948 1206 2012 2269 2292 2468 2486–7 2491–2 2520 2548 2554 2563–7 2575–7 2587 2650 2653 2659 2964 2993 3481 3603 3616 3631 3686 4248 4456 4510 4745 4749 4896 5090 5103 5186 5200–1 5236a 5691 5938 6407 6504 6655

7250 7283 7301 7346 7698 7711 7899 8199 8314 8357 8373 8742 8820 8939 9298 9510 9703 10712 10870 11010 11861 11943 11985 12007 12040 12319 12323 12492 12654 12904 13175 13388 13865 13886 13908 14177 14367 14380 14491

Robertson, Alexander Webster. 1:980–1

Robertson, sir Charles Grant. 1:5074

Robertson, Colin L. 1:588

Robertson, D.A. 9480

Robertson, D.S. 12412 12418

Robertson, Edward. 11284

Robertson, Jean. 1:1760a 2524a; 8747 8750–1 9368 13438

Robertson, John M. 1:2385

Robertson, Joseph. 1568

Robertson, M. 8804a

Robertson, W.S. 11675

Robin, pseud. 2425

Robinson, A.M. Lewin. 2:584 656; 5531 9555

Robinson, Anthony Lewin. 1:4094f

Robinson, Eric. 9562–3 9565

Robinson, Fred N. 6433 6441

Robinson, George W. 1:4464; 12903

Robinson, John. 7633 8496 10458

Robinson, W. Gordon. 3072

Robles, F.C. Sáinz de see Sáinz de Robles, F.C.

Robson, John M. 1:(657c) 4217b; (410) (6389a) (7936) (9293) 12293–5

Robson, P. 8997

Robson, W.W. 14015

Robson-Scott, William Douglas see Scott, William Douglas Robson-.

Roby, J.T. 10741

Rochdale. Public libraries, art gallery, and museum. 2:49

Roche, Thomas. 1:4317t; 2719 13578

Rochester, N.Y. University. Library. 1:3841

Rockhurst college, Kansas city. 1:4276

Rockingham. 6902

Rockley, Alicia Margaret (Amherst), lady. 1:2186

Rockwell, Ford A. 7963

Rockwell, K.A. 2:1243

Rodda, E.C. 11238

Roden, Robert F. 2588

Rodenberg, Julius. 1:1297g; 4482

Rodger, Alexander. 5942

Rodger, Elizabeth M. 1:1765 1778d

Rodgers, F. 1:4958

Rodgers, Tobias. 973a–b

Roe, F. Gordan. 4640

Roe, Herbert C. 9181 9183

Roe, J. 1093

Roellinger, Francis X. 9790

Routledge, George, ltd. 13108
Routledge, Thomas. 5564p
Row, Prescott. 12595
Rowan, D.F. 11471
Rowe, J. Hambley. 8008
Rowe, Kenneth T. 13427
Rowswell, Basil T. 2754
Rowell, George. 1:1647p
Rowfant club, Cleveland. 1:4468; 2308 2341
Rowlands, W. 1:1181
Rowntree, Mary Stickney. 1:2457m
Rowse, A. Leslie. 2:1324
Roxburghe club. 1:4747; 2187 3493 5568
5571
Roy, George Ross. 1:2641 2643–4; 1638 9108
9113 9116 12969
Roy, Ian. 3396a
Royal college of obstetricians and
gynæcologists. Library. 1:2225 2230i
Royal college of physicians, London. 1:3619
Royal college of surgeons of England. 1:586
3770
Royal college of veterinary surgeons, Lon-
don. Library. 1:2222–a
Royal Dublin society. 1:1074–5
Royal exconomic society, London. 13471
13479
Royal empire society. Imperial studies com-
mittee. 1:1706b
Royal geographical society. 1:1762a 1769
Royal historical society. 1:21–2 865 916f–g
2918 3421
Royal horticultural society. Lindley library.
1:2187a
Royal institute of international affairs.
1:4974a
Royal institution of chartered surveyors.
Surrey branch. 1:1816
Royal institution of Great Britain. Library.
1:2523 3282
Royal Irish academy. 1:(4357)–8
Royal philosophical society of Glasgow.
2:1154
Royal philosophical society of Scotland.
1:1726
Royal Scottish geographical society. 1:1813d
1815
Royal Shakespeare theatre, Stratford-upon-
Avon. Library. 2:234
Royal society of arts, London. Percy Smith
memorial lecture. 3942 3946
Royal society of London. 1:917m 3558–9
Roylance, Dale R. 6223
Royster, James F. 9949
Rozemond, Keetje. 5180
Rubens, Charles. 10073
Rubenstein, Jerome S. 14587
Rubinstein, Joseph. 14432

Rubinstein, Stanley Jack. 1:916d 7437
8667
Rudkin, O.D. 1:4749
Rudman, T. 3772
Rudolph, A.J. 2:505
Rudolph, Alexander. 1:3554
Rudrum, A.W. 14154
Ruff, William. 1:4608 4610; 8027 8281 13194
13201 13218
Ruhe, Edward L. 4477
Ruja, Harry. 1:4559h
Rule, John C. 1:4975c
Rumball-Petre, Edwin Alfred Robert see
Petre, Edwin Alfred Robert Rumball-.
Runnquist, Abe. 12214
Runyan, Harry J. 11166
Ruoff, James E. 9273
Ruppert y Ujaravi, Riccardo. 2:57
Rush, N. Orwin. 1:3589
Rushforth, Marjorie. 13876
Ruskin museum, Sheffield. 1:4553y
Russ, Elsie. 1393
Russell, ld. A.J.E. 7428 7891
Russell, A.W. 3397
Russell, Archibald G.B. 1:2471k–m
Russell, Constance. 6996 7384 12943
Russell, F.A. 11817 14177
Russell, G.H. 1:5156; 14484
Russell, June. 1:3672
Russell, Kenneth Fitzpatrick. 1:2220–1 2228
Russell, Norma Hull (Hodgson). 1:2896 4590
4662; 3991 9717 9723
Russell, Percy. 1:1794
Russell, Vera. 92a
Rust, Sydney J. 10098
Rutgers university. Library. 1:1875
Rutgers university library journal. 1:193
Rutherford, Andrew. 9235
Rutherford, W.G. 7109
Rutland, William R. 14423
Rutton, W.L. 12803
Ruybinx, Jacques. 1:5089b
Ruzicka, Rudoph. 4032
Ryals, Clyde deL. 13957 14327
Ryan, John Sprott. 1:3101
Ryan, Lawrence V. 1:3543; 10900–1
Ryan, Michael J. 1:1071 2685; 1873 6705
9194 13393 13397 13614
Ryan, Pat M. 1:4074b; 2:1657
Rybot, F.O. 7846
Rycroft, Harry. 1:4528
Ryder, Herta. 11608
Ryder, John Stanley. 4464 5260 6182 6370
6495
Rye, Reginald Arthur. 1:1535–6; 2131
Rye, Walter. 1:4564–5
Rylands, George. 92a
Rylands, W. Harry. 1182

Rylatt, J.H. 1:1259f; 3965b
Ryskamp, Charles. 1:2488c 2880d 2895q;
(792) 3380a 8624 8641 9716 9719 12874
13465

S. 2:840; 968 5953 7154 7234 7729 9780
10619 10657 12099 13030 13624 14266
S., A. 2415 2596 2617 11944 12002 12471
S., A.H.F. 2:1582
S., A.J. 2589
S., B.P. 7655
S., B.W. 9005
S., C. 1:3198; 7580
S., C.B.M. 5006
S., E. 5788 7238
S., F.G. 10276
S., F.P. 7504
S., G.S.C. 7427
S., G.W. 8724
S., J. 1737
S., J.B. 1:3455c; 580 2410
S., J.M. 7394
S., J.S. 12323 12566
S., N.S. 4238 5567 5676
S., R. 6232
S., R.F. 7421 7502 13456
S., S.M. 1177
S., S.P.E. 6925
S., W. 3860 6316 10817 13179
S., W.B. 1:5133; 2:650; 3486
S., W.P.D. 728 7844
S., W.S. 3627 3887 6838 7545 7711
Sabin, Frank T. 748 9975 13969
Sabin, Waldo. 4905 7729–30
Sachse, William. 1:594b
Sacks, Benjamin F. 1:4094d
Sackton, Alexander. 10440
Sackville, S.G.S. 14179
Saddlemyer, Ann. 1:5208; (4599) 12182
14597
Sadleir, Michael Thomas Harvey. 1:72 655
1706 1714–15 1938 1953e 2508h 2848
(3148) 3393–4 (3408) 3631 4086 4110
(4130) (4189) (4494) (4982) 4984–6 4989
5187–7; 325 767 791 1917 2081 2097 2121
2124 2138 2198 2317 2327 2333–4 2336
2351 2358 2368 2430 3162 3196 3994 3996
4005 4065 5049–52 5202 6161 6537 6942
7299 7302 7306 7310 7320 8341 8736–7
8767 10063 10206 11300 11986 12171
12243 12936 14089 14092 14102 14119
14476 14561–3
St. André, Nathaniel. 1:370
St. Andrews. University. Library. 1:475; 1678
— — Publications. 3559
St. Austell, pseud. 888–9

St. Bonaventure university, St. Bonaventure,
N.Y. Friedsam library. 1:4933
St. Bride foundation institute, London.
1:1141–2 1266q 1556
— Printing school. 5737
— Technical reference library. 1:424 1143
1146–7 1157 1203 1250
St. Dominic's press. 1:1391
St. Edmund's college, Ware. Old hall library.
1:502
St. John, Cynthia (Morgan). 1:5170
St. John, Judith. 1:1567
St. Leger, Kate. 6820
St. Louis. Franklin club see Franklin club of
St. Louis.
— Public library. 2:52
St. Marylebone. Public libraries. 1:2571 3182
4533
St. Mary's seminary, Oscott. 1:2263
St. Olaf college, Northfield, Minn. 1:1488
St. Pancras. Public libraries. 2:136
St. Paul's cathedral, London see London. St.
Paul's cathedral.
Saintsbury, George Edward Bateman. 1:2370
2440 3463
St. Swithin, pseud. 2:55 504; 1237 2070 6827
7825 8218 10403 10484 11862 12297
Sáinz de Robles, F.C. 2:365
Saito, Takeshi. 1:2499
Salaman, Malcolm C. 1:1738n
Sale, Helen S. 13448
Sale, Roger. 2:799
Sale, William Merritt. 1:1389 4519; 5541
13026–9 13031
Sale room (TLS). 2336 9308 14219
Sales (TLS). 492–3 3025 3036 3039 3046 3053
3056–7 3059 3061 6952 8078 8211 12505
Sales and bibliography (TLS). 2:295; 2147 2965
2970 2973 3020 8193 10092 10848 12241
12765 13700
Salisbury, Robert Arthur James Gascoyne-,
5th marquis of Salisbury see Cecil, Robert
Arthur James Gascoyne-, 5th marquis of
Salisbury.
Salmon, David. 2:414; 1543 4835 8108–9
9500–1 11529
Salmon, Vivian. 14264
Salmond, James B. 1678–9
Salomons, sir David Lionel Goldsmid-Stern.
1:1745
Salt, Henry S. 1:2391n 3817
Salter and Lees. 4582
Salter, J.W. 8132
Salter, S.J.A. 4016
Saltire society. Scottish tradition series. 1610
Salvin, Peter. 1:(2380q)
Salzman, L.F. 1413
Samaha, Edward E. 1:2915g 3640t (4976h)

Sambrook, A.J. 2:954; 13379
Samek Ludovici, Sergio. 1:2289db
Sampley, Arthur M. 12683
Sampson, Anthony. 2:770
Sampson, George. 1:(4281); 12312
Sampson, John. 1:499 2:1092; 8328 8563 8567-8
Sampson, Martin Wright. 1:5050
Sampson, R.A. 1:4321
Samuel, David. 1525
Samuel, Howard. 9361
Samuel, Wilfred S. 10209
Samuels, Jack H. 1:1718
Sanborn, M.R. 11732
Sandall, Thomas. 1187a
Sanderlin, George William. 1:2024
Sanders, B.C. 1:2589d
Sanders, Charles. 1:5046
Sanders, Charles Richard. 1:2711b 4818–k; 410 9289 9293 13683
Sanders, Chauncey Elwood. 10874-5
Sanders, Gerald DeWitt. 1:(3410) 4089a
Sanders, Lloyd Charles. 1:(4663)
Sanders, N.J. 1:3523
Sanders, Steven. 8904
Sanderson, James L. 8427 12559
Sanderson, John. 11749
Sanderson, Rupert. 10736
Sanderson, Thomas James Cobden-. 1:1314f–g 1315 1315e; 2:1090-1; 754 2001 2038 4583a 4586 4588a 4589a 5588 6488
Sandford, Christopher. 4379 4760 6114 6482 6487 6491
Sandison, Helen E. 10785-6
Sandoe, James. 1:4586
Sands, Donald B. 1:5; 4317 4323
Sanesi, Roberto. 1:4935
Sanford, John A. 13089
San Francisco. Literary anniversary club *see* Literary anniversary club of San Francisco.
— Public library. 1:4807
Sanger, Vincent. 1:2859
Sanki, Ichikawa. 2:73
San Marino, Calif. Henry E. Huntington library and art gallery *see* Henry E. Huntington library and art gallery, San Marino, Calif.
Santi, Aldo. 1:1656b
Sanville, Donald Walker. 1:3221; 10408
Sarason, Bertram D. 8976
Sargeaunt, John. 14179
Sargeaunt, W.D. 2:1158 1163 1165 1971
Sargent, George H. 347 462 467-8 507 4028 9643 10036 11244 11663 13299 13608
Sargent, Ralph M. 1:541; 9827
Sarkissian, Arshag Ohannes. 1:(3474)
Sasse, Konrad. 1:3564

Satchell, Thomas. 2:535
Sattler, Rolf-Joachim. 1:4974
Saul, George Brandon. 1:4 4780-1 5197u; 9681 13609 14584 14591-3
Sauls, Lynn. 11153 14084-5
Saunders, C.E. 1:1573e
Saunders, John W. 3468a (3476)
Saunders, W.H. 1:3055
Sausmarez, Maurice de. 1:4538
Savage, Derek. 2:1227
Savage, Ernest Albert. 89 2281 2418a 3424 12702
Savage, Henry. 1:4215b
Savage, Henry L. 2:316; 13018
Savage, J.E. 8459
Savage, Richard. 2:185
Savage, William. 6387
Saveson, J.E. 3256
Saver, Gordon C. 10795
Savin, Maynard. 13050
Sawin, H. Lewis. 1:4191
Sawyer, Charles J., bksllrs., London. 1:2465b
Sawyer, Charles James. 1:3084; 2299 10027 10053
Sawyer, F.C. 8152
Sawyer, F.G. 8141
Sawyer, John E.S. 1:3080 3084
Sawyer, Rollin A. 7478
Sayce, Richard A. 225 3230 6184
Sayer, Frank. 1303
Sayle, Charles Edward. 1:441 444 500-1 4224; 586 588 2590 2706 2794 2093 6006 6657-8 7467
Sayle, R.T.D. 1258a 2949
Scammon, F.J. 2:697
Scanlan, James P. 1:4217c
Scarlett, B. Florence. 6996
Scarlett, O.W. 1:4862
Scattergood, Bernard P. 6816 6828 10896
Schaar, Claes. 9808
Schad, Robert O. 2890 6098a
Schatzki, Walter. 7053 10864
Schatzki, Walter, bksllr., N.Y. 1:1557d
Schaubert, Else von. 2:1184
Schauer, Georg K. (6646)
Schear, Bernice Larson. 1:3365d
Schechter, Frank Isaac. 6664
Scheele, Margaret S. 6934
Schelling, Felix Emmanuel. 1:1601 3400; 2:287-8
Schelling anniversary papers. 2:724
Schenk, Wilhelm. 3101
Scheurweghs, Grace. 1:1729
Schick, George Baldwin. 4562 14239
Schiff, Gert. 1:3375
Schiffers, Norbert. 1:4334b
Schiller, Jerome P. 1:4513n
Schiller, Johannes Friedrich. 1:2972

Schilpp, Paul A. 1:(2530s) (4559gb–ge) (5087–8)
Schlauch, Margaret. 1:2345
Schleinitz, Otto von. 4968a
Schlengemann, E. 910 6287 8667 12837 14578
Schlieder, N. 3784
Schlochauer, Ernst J. 9436
Schloesser, F. 6742
Schlösser, Anselm. 1:819f
Schlueter, Paul. 1:2319
Schmid, Karl Friedrich. 1:2388q
Schmidt, Werner. 2:336–7
Schmidtchen, Paul W. 662
Schmitz, Robert Morrell. 2:757; 8557 12869 12872
Schmoller, Hans. 4661 5213 6163
Schmutzler, Karl E. 10987
Schnapper, Edith B. 1:1837
Schneider, Duane B. 1:4714
Schneider, Elisabeth. 1:1922 1937 2552; 1709
Schneider, G.A. 1:457
Schoek, Richard J. 13138
Schoell, Konrad. 1:2414i
Schoenbaum, Samuel. 1:1614–15; 8542 9604
Schoenwald, Richard L. 1395
Schofield, B. 3163 3257 10197 12578
Scholderer, Julius Victor. 1:366 464–5; 563–4 875 3294 6021 8041 8057 10597 11117 11995
Scholes, Percy Alfred. 1:2627–8 3621k; 1494
Scholes, Robert E. 1:3889; 2:790; 5529 11606 11615
Scholfield, A.F. 1:3815; 3060 12376
Schonberg, J. 9171
Schöne, Albrecht. 1:1656c
Schooling, J. Holt. 13106
Schorer, Mark. 1:4023; 11939
Schram, O.K. 5635
Schrire, D. 7521 7525
Schrickx, W. 9590
Schröer, M.M. Arnold. 2:1610d
Schücking, Levin Ludwig. 1:1184c; 2:65 70 76 1199 1288 1566 1880 1890
Schultheiss, Thomas. 1:2858g
Schultz, William E. 10649
Schultze, Rolf Siegmund. 1:1754 1754k; 1631 6218
Schulz, Ernst. 1:1757
Schulz, Herbert C. 1:372b; 545 6361 6388
Schulze, Fritz W. 14546
Schuman, Samuel. 1:1656d
Schwabe, Randolph. 1:4563i; 5576
Schwartz, Alan H. 1008
Schwartz, Elias. 8920
Schwartz, Harry Warren. 1:685c (2318) (2333) (2404) (2967) (3611j) (3775b) (3879i) (4359) (4581y); 2330 2339

Schwartz, Jacob. 1:345 2881
Schwarzschild, Monroe M. 4442
Schwefe, Gerhard Müller-. 1:12
Schweik, Robert C. 1:3838b; 10980–1
Schweitzer, Joan. 10180
Schwerdt, Charles Francis George Richard. 1:2197d
Schwoerer, Lois G. 1:2240a
Science fiction association. 1:1711
Scotland. Advocates' library see Scotland. National library, Edinburgh.
— Church of Scotland. General assembly. Committee on public worship and aids to devotion. 1:1733
— Institute of chartered accountants, Edinburgh see Institute of chartered accountants of Scotland, Edinburgh.
— National gallery, Edinburgh. 1:4604
— National library, Edinburgh. 1:367 712e 719a 1266m–n 1546 1940a 2130 3567; 2:247; 3258 4066 4073
— Royal college of physicians see Royal college of physicians, Scotland.
— Royal philosophical society see Royal philosophical society of Scotland.
— Scottish central library, Edinburgh. 1:244 1934
Scott, A.C. 14165
Scott, A.G. 1:475
Scott, Arthur L. 999
Scott, Clement. 1:4627
Scott, E. Kilburn. 3965 6210a
Scott, Edward J.L. 4224 4227 4230–1 4234 4236 4625 6014
Scott, G.K. 2439 6039 7301
Scott, George Ryley. 1:2138e
Scott, H.D. Colvill-. 9008
Scott, Inez. 2:1207
Scott, J.W. 7872
Scott, J.W. Robertson. 7908
Scott, James Edward. 1:3546–7; 10904
Scott, John. 1:2158–60 4148–9; 1555
Scott, Joseph W. 1:3728
Scott, Kenneth W. 1:2846 (4492); 2:80
Scott, M.I. 686
Scott, Mary Augusta. 1:827
Scott, Nathan Alexander. 1:2414d
Scott, Robert. 1593
Scott, sir S.H. 930
Scott, Temple, pseud. of J.H. Isaacs. 1:3448 3467 4299–300 (4827); 429 431–2 434–5 13711
Scott, W. 2:710–11; 728 1702 2666 2672 4125 5955 6235 6833 6969 7637 7858 9353 10218 10783 10862 10911 11383 12101 12958 13491 13638
Scott, W.R. 13473
Scott, W.S. 1:5083; 11109

Scott, Walter. 1:2556
Scott, William. 13512
Scott, William Douglas Robson-. 1:2289dd
Scottish chapbook. 1:724 (3286) (3541) (3921) (4105) (4113)
Scottish history society. 1:968
Scottish text society. 1:2034 3193e
Scottish typographical association, Glasgow. 5613–14
Scotus, *pseud.* 2:1639; 2070 4848
Scouten, Arthur H. 1:3827 4842; 2:296; 7788 13782 13790
Scribner, Lynnette L. 1:2120
Scribner book store, New York. 1:3181r
Scribner, publ., New York. 1:3381x 4805b
Scribner's, Charles, sons, ltd. 11175
Scripta mathematica studies. 1:2214s
Scroggs, E.S. 1:2789
Scruton, William. 2628
Scudder, Delton Lewis. 1:4884d
Scunthorpe. Public libraries. 2:137
Sealy, Douglas. 1:3900d
Searle, Alfred A. 1:3065 3070g
Searle, R. Townley. 1:3430–1; 3997
Seaton, Ethel. 10567
Secker, Martin. 339 5694a 5705 10559 11936
Secord, Arthur W. 9901 12074 13481
Secutor, *pseud.* 2289 10020
Sedley, Stephen. 4476
Seeber, Edward D. 9439
Seeberger, Alfred. 11799
Seeley, Frederick W. 5027p–q 5027s–t
Seeley, Service and co. ltd. 6530 13638
Seelye, John. 10442
Segar, Mary G. 1:4418; 12761–3 12765
Séguin, J.A.R. 1:3477a 4977d
Seitz, Don C. 1:5076d 5076f
Seitz, R.W. 10755–6
Selden, L. 10898
Selden society, London. 1:2197f
Select documents (Bull Inst Hist Res). 6092
Sellers, Harry. 1:77 827a 2946–7; 2:59; 281 629 947 2930 4434a 7991 9801 11005 13615
Selwood, E.H. 3052
Selwyn, D.G. 9754
Sen, Sailendra Kumar. 2:791; 12117
Sendall, sir Walter J. 1:2697
Senex, *pseud.* 2:744
Seng, Peter J. 2:1110
Senga, *pseud.* 10818
Senhouse, Roger. 3164
Senn, G.T. 12189
Sermones, *pseud.* 2769 3973 4553 4846a 4882 5095 5129 5162 5252c 5484 5604 5812 6052 6763 7010 9120 14382
Serif. 1:194

Serif bibliographies. 1:2414k
Seronsy, Cecil C. 6904 9804–5 9811–12
Seton, Walter W. 8506
Severne, Cecily. 3214a
Sewell, Brocard. 1:(3501); 1539 5579a 5580
Sewell, C.W.H. 9987
Sewter, A.C. 8625
Sexton, T.A.F. 1808
Seybolt, Paul S. 8548 13677
Seymour, M.C. 12126
Seymour, Mabel. 7751 10500
Seymour, W. Douglas. 9207
Seymour-Smith, Martin *see* Smith, Martin Seymour-.
Shaaber, Matthias A. 1:1873c 4990h; 2:745 880 899 1273 1293; 5075a 6292 7672 7675 7999 8266 8854 12270
Shaffer, Ellen. 4462
Shāhānī, Rānjī G. *see* Rānjī G. Shāhānī.
Shakespeare association, London. 2:211 550 725; 9789
Shakespeare association bulletin. 2:2 20
Shakespeare association of America. 2:2 5 20–1 156b
Shakespeare association of Japan. 2:66
Shakespeare in the southwest. 2:372a
Shakespeare jahrbuch. 2:3 17
Shakespeare jahrbuch (West) 2:3a
Shakespeare-Literatur in Bochum. 2:152
Shakespeare memorial association, Stratford-upon-Avon. 2:170
Shakespeare memorial library, Stratford-upon-Avon. 2:31 170
Shakespeare newsletter. 2:4
Shakespeare problems. 2:588 844 1071 1197 1217 1341 1886
Shakespeare quarterly. 2:2 5 18 21
Shakespeare reprints. 2:1145d
Shakespeare research and opportunities. 2:6 23
Shakespeare society of Japan. 2:7
Shakespeare society, New York. 2:1 551a
Shakespeare studies. 2:8 24; 9578
Shakespeare studies (Tokyo). 2:7
Shakespeare survey. 2:9 15–16 22
Shakespearean festival, Stratford, Ontario. 2:233 241
Shakespearean work in progress. 2:23
Shakespeare's birthplace trust, Stratford-upon-Avon. Library. 1:544; 2:185 212 223
Shakespeare's England. 3431
Shakspere studies. 2:1901
Shand, James. 6114 6591 13272
Shane, T.N., *pseud.* of H.A. Healey. 3861
Shanks, Edward. 7326a
Shannon, Edgar Finley. 1:4897b (4898); 13926 13933 13939
Shapin, Betty. 2:1218; 3528

Shapiro, Isaac Avi. 1:3523; 2:1490; 663 7947 8180 10229 10884 14226
Shapiro, Karl Jay. 1:2248m
Sharp, Evelyn. 1:4330g
Sharp, Henry Alexander. 1:1805
Sharp, Isaac. 15 17 20 10591
Sharp, J. Alfred. 1:2270d
Sharp, William. 1:(2582h) 4705
Sharpe, Richard Bowdler. 1:(5078)
Sharples, Edward. 9292
Sharps, John Geoffrey. 10643
Sharrock, Roger. 1:2617
Shattuck, Charles Harlen. 2:250; 12441
Shaver, Chester L. 12489
Shaw, A.E. 7350
Shaw, Alfred Capel. 2:177
Shaw, E.P. 10516
Shaw, George Bernard. 2:848; 13262
Shaw, George T. 1:905x; 1170 1173 7871
Shaw, Isabella. 1170
Shaw, John Mackay. 1:1573db–dc 2732–3; 4453 7060–1 9333 9778 11954
Shaw, Philip. 14155
Shaw, William. 1767
Shaw, William Arthur. 1:(2304) 2792b 2918 (3395) 4168 (4822); (2579)
Shaw and sons, London. 5641
Shawcross, J. 9518
Shawcross, John T. 7466 10273 10275 11915 12424 12431–3 12437–8 12442 12447–8 12452–3 12455
Shawyer, N.M. 1:634
Shaylor, Joseph. 2411 3426 3618a 3618c–d 3625a 3630a 3636 6938
Shearer, John E. 1:1814
Shearer, Thomas. 12743
Shearman, J. 6701
Shears, Holmlock. 2127
Shears, William Sydney. 5256–7
Sheavyn, Phoebe Anne (Beale). 3413 3418 3420 3476 3497 6512
Sheehy, Eugene Paul. 1:2857
Sheehy, Maurice. 1:4356d
Sheffer, Isaiah. 1:1596
Sheffield. Public libraries. 1:1149 1328p 1487 2715 3265; 1442h
— University. Library. 1:505
Sheldon, Esther K. 1:4673
Sheldon, Peter. 1:884x
Shelly, Henry C. 5878d
Shelley, I.G.M. 8945
Shelley, Philip Allison. 1:3661; 14564
Shepard, Leslie. 1:1385g 1557d 4525k; 5426
Shepard, William P. 381
Shepherd, Richard Herne. 1:2827 4887; 9509
Shepherd, T. 6838 7872
Shepherd, Thomas B. 5987
Sheppard, Douglas H. 11137

Sheppard, L.A. 3147 4303 4312 6862–3 6871 8066
Sheppard, Thomas. 1:1849 4714m
Shepperson, Archibald Bolling. 1:1710; 10512
Sherbo, Arthur. 1:1695h; 2:769 771–2 775 781 786; 11470 11472–5 11481 13462 13464
Sherborn, C. Davies. 1:2240p 4143 5078; 1707 3671 5643 7699 8130 12806
Sherburn, George. 2891 5873a 8226 12819 12830 12840 13771 14608
Shercliff, William Henry. 1:911
Sheren, Paul. 9741
Sheridan, Richard B. 8181
Sherill, L. 2:245
Sherman, Clarence E. 1:4152 4155
Sherren, Wilkinson. 1:3576
Sherrington, sir Charles Scott. 1:4674
Sherwin, Oscar. 12413
Sherzer, Jane. 2:707
Shideler, Mary (McDermott). 1:5111s
Shield, H.A. 2:1977; 4651
Shields, Alcuin. 6368
Shields, Katharine Gheen. 1:2395
Shine, H.C. 1:1924
Shine, Hill. 7807a
Shine, Wesley Hill P. 1:1924
Shipherd, H. Robinson. 7127
Shipley, John B. 1:3352 4485d; 741 7785–6 7789 9675 9927 10509 10512 10518 10585 12959–63 13035
Shipman, Carolyn. 1:572 629 1655; 9796
Shipman, Joseph C. 1:2196
Shipway, I.M. 1:2150
Shirai, A. 1:3462i
Shire, Helena M. 1621 1625
Shirley, George William. 1:994 1388; 1576 1578 1672 1674 5494
Shirley, Walter Waddington. 1:5193
Shober, Joyce Lee. 1:3777
Shore, T.W. 2411
Shorter, Alfred H. 1044 1083a–b 1100b–f 1101x 1104 1120a 1132a 1138 1156 1161a 1298a 1386a–b 1389–a 1412 1429a 1506 1626 1840 3749 3751 3764 3766–7 3773–6 3783–4 3807 4002a
Shorter, Clement. 1:3173 3804; 4125 7294 8662 8804 12122
Short-title catalogue ... 1475–1640. 1:521–4 532a
Short-title catalogue ... 1641–1700. 1:601–2
Showacre, Elizabeth. 3692
Shrewsbury school. Library. 3051
Shrimpton, R.A. 2:55
Shroeder, John W. 2:605 1757
Shugrue, Michael. 7802 7808
Shulman, David. 6872 7062

Shum, Frederick. 1:939; 1391
Shumaker, Eri Jay. 1:3710
Shuman, R. Baird. 12992
Shuttleworth, Bertram. 1:4028n 4669
Siberell, Lloyd Emerson. 1:4451 4455y
Sibley, Agnes Marie. 1:4443a
Sichel, Walter Sydney. 1:4569–70 4664
Sicherman, Carol L. (Marks) see also Marks, Carol L. 14086
Sideris, Joannis. 2:139
Sidgwick, Arthur. 1:4682g
Sidgwick, Eleanor M. 1:4682g
Sidgwick, Frank. 1:3373 5151a 5198; 322 12703 12707–8
Sidnell, M.J. 14594 14603
Sidwell, Joseph. 1:3946k
Siebert, Frederick Seaton. 3566 5746
Siegfried, Laurance B. 4132
Siegwart, Alfred. 8515
Sigma Tau, pseud. 13284
Signature. 1:195
Signet library see Society of writers to H.M. signet, Edinburgh. Library.
Signia, pseud. 4804
Sikes, Herschel M. 11023
Silkin, Jon. 1:4538
Sillard, P.A. 10813
Silo, pseud. 7001
Silver, Louis H. 1:2615; 8957 14224
Silver, Rollo G. 152 6168
Silvette, Herbert. 1:1617 3687–8
Silverstein, N. 11617 11624
Simeone, William E. 1:4527c
Simison, Barbara Damon. 2:1315
Simkins, Thomas M. 9232
Simmonds, James D. 1:4996a; 14151
Simmons, Charles Herbert. 1:4159
Simmons, Fanny E.L. 1:937
Simmons, Jack. 1:4742
Simmons, John Simon Gabriel. 1:252 937 1197 1210 3283g 4450q; 1371 (1377) (3784) 3802 4660 5356 5358 6722 9814
Simmons, Judith. 689
Simms, Rupert. 1:942; 1396
Simms, Samuel. 1:2244e
Simon, André L. 7065
Simon, Oliver. 1:99 1296; 4478–9 4483 4487 6203 (6577) 6607
Simon, S. 657
Simoni, Anna E.C. 1:1438–9; 6771
Simpkins, Diana M. 884
Simpson, Adrienne. 1:1841d
Simpson, Charles R. 2698
Simpson, Claude M. 1:1468b; 414 5431a
Simpson, Evelyn M. (Spearing). 1:3161; 10221 10223 10225 10235 10242 10244–5 10249 10876 11551–2 11563 11569 (11573)

Simpson, F.D. 7130
Simpson, H. Derwent. 2:1020
Simpson, Jean M. see Lefèvre, Jean M. (Simpson).
Simpson, Justin. 1312
Simpson, Louis Aston Marantz. 1:3682d
Simpson, Percy. 2:841 848 854 917 1158 1432 1881; 3564 3568 6398 6405 6414 7111 8460 9261 10237 10333 11537–8 11564 (11573) 11715 12267 12650–1 14403 14462 14497 14530
Simpson, Richard. 1:(2702)
Simpson, S.M. 1724 3542 12973 14158
Simpson, W. Alexander. 2089
Simpson, W. Douglas. 2920
Simpson, W. Sparrow. 1:920 4567x; 2530 6925
Simpson, William. 1683
Sims, George Frederick. 1:4380; 3682 5694 9659a 14163 14325
Sims, George Frederick, bksllrs., Hurst. 1:4454d
Sinclair, Kenneth V. 3324
Sinclair, T.A. 14004
Sinclair, William. 1:4263d; 7577 8440 10018 13191
Singer, Dorothea Waley. 1:2279e–f; 6738 8121–2
Singer, George C. 8881 14443
Singer, Hans Wolfgang. 6187
Singh, Bhupal. 1:1664
Singleton, Frank. 5856
Sinker, Robert. 1:492
Sinnhuber, A.M.W. 1:3334
Sinton, James. 1:1007–8 3645 4053; 11097 13373
Sirluck, Ernest. 3573 7944 12430
Sir Thomas Browne institute, Leiden. 866a
Sirr, Harry. 1:4690k; 12513–14
Sisson, Charles Jasper. 2:(89) 429 (774) 776 (912) 1071; 661 3538 4783 7132 8462 9932 10226
Sitwell, dame Edith. 12642
Sitwell, Sacheverell. 1:2119 2181; 3473 6226
Skallerup, Harry R. 1:2501
Skarshaug, mrs. Emory C. 1:2236; 7573
Skeat, Theodore Cressy. 1:1760k; 3142 9548 9560 10308
Skeat, Walter William. 1:4694a–b; 2:831 1530–1; 336 4246 9419
Skeel, Caroline A.J. 2817
Skelton, Raleigh Ashlin. 1:1770 2879d 3549; 7511–12 7515 7517–18 7520 7629 12598
Skelton, Robin. 1:5208; 1842 (4599) 14595 14598
Skerl, Margaret. 1:2914

Sketches of booksellers of the time of dr. Johnson
(*Pub Circ*). 4509 4555 4600 4732 4735
4822a 4901 4935 5030 5076 5187 5326
5535 5862

Sketchley, R.E.D. 1:1737; 7396–9

Skinner, Andrew S. 1:3010d

Skinner, Robert T. 4570

Skipper, Jean. 1:897p

Skipton. Public library. Petyt library. 1:371

Skues, F.W. MacKenzie-. 1:3951d

Slack, Robert C. 1:60; 10970

Slade, Bertha (Coolidge). 1:3234 4029 4039
4202; 127 10419

Slade, J.J. 1426

Slade, William Adams. 2:283–4

Slater, John Herbert. 1:658 2284 4800 4805c;
424–8 430 433 436–7 439–41 443–51 748
2264–5 2272 2278 3824 3878 3898 3901
3964 4104 4140 4390 4409 4419 4441 4595
4610 4675 4713 4715 4790 4838 4884 5177
5316 5404 5565 5702 5800 5928 6011 6825
7293 7415–16 12138 13978

Slater, Michael. 1:3036b

Slater, Montagu. 14087

Sledd, James H. 8409 11488 11491 11497
13010

Sleigh, Gordon F. 7781 12107

Slepian, Barry. 13791

Slicer, Thomas Roberts. 1:4648

Sloane, Clarence Edward. 1:4335

Sloane, Eugene Hulse. 1:3485e

Sloane, William. 1:1550a 1565; 7427

Slocum, John Jermain. 1:3885–a

Sluman, A.J. 7444

Slythe, R. Margaret. 1:2809m

Smail, Adams. 1687 1701

Smailes, T.A. 11940

Small, Miriam Rossiter. 1:4045

Small, Samuel Asa. 2:1448

Smalley, Donald. 14129

Smalley, George W. 5947

Smart, James P. 1:4554

Smart, Thomas Burnett. 1:2336

Smedley, Constance. 8402

Smedley, William T. 2:1028; 11800

Smiles, Samuel. 5250 5250b

Smidt, Kristian. 2:1469 1665 1688 1690

Smistrup, Torben. 4481

Smith, A. Hugh. 1:3869; 6318

Smith, Adelaide M. 1:633a

Smith, Alan. 14414

Smith, Alan Rae. 1:(3828a); 67a

Smith, Albert H. 1:13745; 4410 5292–4

Smith, Arthur Lionel. 1:4112

Smith, B.T.K. 8196

Smith, C.H. Gibbs-. 9238

Smith, C.S. 10276

Smith, C. Alphonso. 2:646

Smith, C. Ernest. 1:2808

Smith, Cecil. 2:198–9

Smith, Courtney Craig. 1:1996; 11088

Smith, D. 1:2232–3

Smith, David Baird. 1:529

Smith, David E. 1:2618; 8962

Smith, David Nichol. 1:2008 3838 4841;
2:728; 1608 5353 5357 11405 12110 14245

Smith, Dominic Baker-. 1:5002

Smith, Edgar Wadsworth. 1:3181u 3185c

Smith, Edward. 1414 1699 8219

Smith, mrs. Edward. 5687a

Smith, Elizabeth M. (5677) 5678

Smith, Elva S. 1:1553 1555

Smith, Francis Prescott. 9212

Smith, G. Barnett. 9505

Smith, George. 2090 2675 2770 4623 5116
5678

Smith, George Campbell. 1:2478

Smith, George Charles Moore. 1:505; 2639
7112 7114 7119–20 7122–3 7195 8009
10991–2 10996 12139 12622–3 12679–80
12973 12975a 13087 13875

Smith, Gerald A. 421 12179

Smith, Goldwin. 1:2365

Smith, Gordon Ross. 2:96 110

Smith, Grover. 11600

Smith, H.F.B. Brett-. 13316

Smith, H.G. 11846

Smith, H. Maynard. 2:650

Smith, H.S.A. 3340

Smith, Harry B. 9189 13301

Smith, Helen Ryland. 1:3399a

Smith, Herbert. 927

Smith, Herbert Francis Brett Brett-. 1:3271
4402gc; 10220 10985 11387

Smith, Isobel F. 1:2790w

Smith, J. de B. 13189

Smith, mrs. J.S. 1:4008

Smith, James. 5683

Smith, Janet Adam. 92a 13665

Smith, John. 3634 6379 6560

Smith, John Hazel. 2:1298 1598; 3116

Smith, Joseph. 1:2267–8; 2609

Smith, Kenneth. 1086

Smith, L. (2698a)

Smith, L. Graham Horton-. 2:71; 3749 7909
8379 12406

Smith, Lillian H. 1:1570

Smith, Lloyd Logan Pearsall. 1:(4877) 5185

Smith, Lucy Toulmin. 2:1003

Smith, M. Morton-. 1:1173a

Smith, M.S. 1:2621d

Smith, Margaret Dean-. 1:4430; 5432

Smith, Margaret S. 1:1760g; 2435

Smith, Martin Seymour-. 2:18; 2436

Smith, May. 1:4094e

Smith, Michael A. 5814

Smith, Minna S. 12785
Smith, Paul Jordan-. 1:687h (2520x) 2655–6 (3272f) (4097) (4978p) (5045) (5075k) (5091s); 2329
Smith, R.E.G. 1:1862; 4386
Smith, R.S. 1:4417a
Smith, Raymond. 3151
Smith, Reginald J. 339
Smith, Robert Dennis Hilton. 1:2736
Smith, Robert Metcalf. 1:652–3; 2:280 289 460 468–70 569–71 576–7 640 1219 1512; 13335
Smith, Roger. 1:3437
Smith, S. Goodsir. 1:(4092a)
Smith, Sarah Bixby. 1:2656
Smith, Simon Harcourt Nowell- *see also* Trevanion, Michael, *pseud.* 1:656 685 2529 2561 2607 3150 4530 4561 4568p: 64 124 129 369 870 2146 2366 2443 3359a 3543–4 3992 4205 4207 5052 5126 8499 8758 8762–3 8765–6 8787 9815 10087 10809 10843 10921 11019 11205 11280 11337–8 11352 11891–2 12242 12256 13063 13130 13544–5 13624 13836 13940 13943 13947 13964 13966 14060 14096 14105 14457–8
Smith, Sydney R. 1:2182
Smith, T.R. 2:362
Smith, Timothy d'Arch. 1:3193 4041 4048d 4533 4825–a 4936 5105; 13699 13846 14009 14566
Smith, W. Alexander. 1330 2493
Smith, W.C. 7614 7625
Smith, Walter E. 1:1469; 6802
Smith, Warren Hunting. 6283 7285 (14202) 14300
Smith, Wilbur J. 10182 11967
Smith, Wilbur Moorehead. 1:2250–a
Smith, William Charles. 1:1414–a 1831 3566–7d 3570–1; 5430 5933–5 6305
Smith, William Hanneford-. 3956
Smith, Wood. 9144
Smithers, Charles G. 4556 9685
Smoker, A, *pseud.* 8197
Smyth, Albert Leslie. 1:2945; 9793
Smyth, H. Gerald. 13981
Smyth, J. deLacy. 13727
Sneddon, David. 1:2634
Snell, Florence M. 11545
Snow, Vernon F. 3377 7459
Snyder, Alice D. 9526 9532 9538
Snyder, Franklyn Bliss. 9051
Snyder, Henry L. 4385 7814
Society for nautical research. 1:4412
Society for theatre research. 1:1590b 2912e
Society for the bibliography of natural history. *Journal.* 1:196
Society for the protection of ancient buildings. 3783

Society of antiquaries, Newcastle-upon-Tyne. 1:1800
Society of archivists. 516
Society of friends of St. George's chapel, Windsor castle. 5172
Society of herbalists. London. Library. 1:2180
Society of writers to H.M. signet, Edinburgh. Library. 1:428
Soden, Geoffrey Ingle. 1:3475
Soho bibliographies. 1:1327 2622 3172 3315 3351 3724 3807 3809 3885 4021 4532 4582 4694 5158–9 5204 5207 5209b
Solomons, Bethel. 13607
Solomons, David. 305
Solomons, Israel. 1230 7706 9347
Some British binderies (Bkbndr). 4355
Some British bookmakers (Brit Bkmkr). 4054
Some famous English bookshops (Lib World). 5053a
Some famous libraries (Biblioph). 2648
Some famous libraries (Bkworm). 2468
Some famous writers (Coventry Pub Libs Readers' Bull). 1:2396b 3192c 3585f 3946k 4157d 4628e 5057g
Some private presses (London Merc). 3850 4629
Some technical libraries (Bkworm). 2497–8 6944
Some uncollected authors (Bk Coll). 1:2353 2495 2498 2512 2522 2554 2561 2750 2795 2892 2939 2950 3150 3224 3281 3534 3621 3631 3660 3691 3696 4041 4380 4394 4427 4489 4500–1 4509 4531 4571 4583b 4590 4662 4687–8 5033 5082; 5134
Somerset. County library, Street. 1:3734
Somersetshire archæological and natural history society. 1:1802
Somerville, Edith Anna Œnone. 1:4679
Sommer, H. Oskar. 1:4683; 5311
Sommerland, M.J. 1636
Sondheim Moriz. 845
Sone, Tamotsu. 1:2587
Sonnenschein, E.A. 370
Sonnenschein, William Swan. 13897
Soper, H. Tapley-. 1102b 2255 2257–8 7242 7639 7645
Sopher, A. 1:1318
Sopher, R. 1:3175
Sorenson, Fred. 12946
Sorsby, Arnold. 7560–1
Sotheby and co., ltd., London. 1:334 399 538 600 1353 1443a 1489 1517 2477 3078 3092 3844 4811; 2907 13985
Sotheby, Wilkinson and Hodge, ltd., London. 1:380 383 386 391–2 570 632 2931 3944 4149; 2:179 182 276; 4817
Sotheran, H.C. 1021
Sotheran, Henry, bksllrs., London. 1:3068p 3980d

Sotonová, Vlastamila. 2:149
Soulsby, Basil H. 6518
Soutar, G. 7109
Southall, Raymond. 14569
Southampton. Public libraries. 1:370
— University. Library. 1:2098
Southam, B.C. 8345–8
Southam, Herbert. 1144 2425 6269
South Australia. Libraries board. 2:240 248
— State library. Research service. 1:623f
South Carolina. University. Dept. of English.
  1:2529g 2644
— — McKissick memorial library. 1:2644
Southern, Alfred Collingwood. 1:2256
Southern, R.W. 1:4450x
Southern Connecticut state college, New
  Haven see Connecticut. Southern Connec-
  ticut state college, New Haven.
Southern Illinois university, Carbondale see
  Illinois. Southern Illinois university,
  Carbondale.
Southern Methodist university, Dallas see
  Dallas. Southern Methodist university.
Southgate, J. 1:77; 281
Southton, J.Y. 10005
Southward, John. 1:1141–2; 6159 6312 6348
Southwark. Public libraries and Cuming
  museum. 1:344 3088; 2:50; 2841a
South-west Essex technical college. 1:1875a
Souvage, Jacques. 1:1659f
Sowerby, E. Millicent. 639–40 642 9843
Sowers, Roy V. 3165
Spackman, H.C. 13129
Spackman, M.L. 14265
Spalding, John Tricks. 1:857
Spalding and Hodge, London. 3737 5710
Spalding club. 1:980–1
Sparke, Archibald. 1:884 904 1850 2075
  2323g 2519b 3964; 2:55; 1027 1062 1102
  1143–4 1231 1703 2425–6 2723 2866 3632
  3723 3813 4642 4778 4897c 4897h 4905
  4924 5408 6844 6847–8 6851 6855 6948
  7222 7260 7414 7495 7596 7729 7731 7735
  7866 7872–4 7876 7880–1 8076 8249
  8553 8646 10047 10835 11817 11963
  12071 12099 12461 12632 13075 13480
  13980
Sparke, Winifred. 8026
Sparling, Henry Halliday. 1:1350; 4975 6785
Sparrow, John H.A. 1:2965 3716 3724 3924s
  4394; 400 724 8650 9609 9676 9695–7
  9730 9845 10227 10230 10247 10257 10259
  10262 10269 11012 11044 11158 11175
  12044 12648 13079 13247 13368 13918
Spaulding, Thomas M. 1:2235; 7572
Speaight, George V. 7021 7023 7033 7056
  9595
Spears, M.K. 1:4465

Special collections at Princeton (Princeton Univ Lib
  Chron). 5566
Special collections in the Reference library
  (Manchester R). 9547 10641
Specimens of early printing (Caxton Mag). 6566
Specht, Walter F. 6916a
Spector, Robert Donald. 1:4723a–b 11520
  11636 12490
Speer, Felix. 1:1920
Speer, Hal. 4567
Speight, E.E. 9414
Spelman, K.E. 13243
Spence, R.M. 2:360 394; 4522 13121 13454
  13905
Spence, Sydney Alfred. 1:2879
Spencer, Dorothy Mary. 1:1668c
Spencer, E.M. 1:4955
Spencer, H.D. 7046
Spencer, Hazelton. 2:213 217 363 758 1175
  1507 1583 1676; 7200–1 9573 9935
Spencer, Herbert. 4717
Spencer, Lois. 5843–4 9766
Spencer, Terence J.B. 2:(942); 94 13065
Spencer, Theodore. 1:1988
Spencer, Walter T. 5712 9171 9985
Spender, J.A. 1:(5032)
Spens, Janet. 2:1708
Sperling, John G. 1:2283
Spicer, A. Dykes. 3717
Spielberg, Peter. 1:3890; 11607
Spielmann, Marion Harry. 1:3510 4910
  4956; 2:528 530 550 651 716; 3632–3 6179
Spielmann, Percy Edwin. 1:1819; 2444 2448
  7582
Spiers, John. 10711
Spingarn, J.E. 2:698; 201 12064
Spink, Ian. 7621a
Spink, J.S. 1:1726b
Spinney, Gordon Harold. 1:1978; 12488
Spoerri, James Fuller. 1:3870 3881 3886;
  11597
Spokane. Public library. 1:1525; 2396
Spoor, John Alden. 1:3982
Sporhan-Krempel, Lore see Krempel, Lore
  Sporhan-.
Sprague, Arthur Colby. 2:224
Sprent, F.P. 1:1762
Spriet, Pierre. 1:2948b
Sprigge, S. Squire. 6503
Sprott, S.E. 11041
Spurrell, J. 1:2374
Squire, sir John Collings. 10559 11407
Squire, William Barclay. 1:1837; 10931
  12924
Staal, C. 9573
Stables, W. Gordon. 1:4876n
Stafford, T.J. 2:(372a)
Stafford, W.T. 1:3800a–b

Stevenson, J.H. 5104

Stevenson, Lionel. 1:1705 (2533) (2847) (3037) (3146) (3246) (3403) (3444) (3576) (3927) 4048 (4085) (4192) (4266) (4493) (4906) 4916 (4980)

Stevenson, Noragh. 1:1030f

Stevenson, P.R. 13223

Stevenson, W.H. 2:1017

Stewart, Andrew. 7759

Stewart, C.E. 5881

Stewart, Charles D. 2:1062

Stewart, James McGregor. 1:3956

Stewart, Jean. 1:(3260)

Stewart, Jessie G. 1:3613b

Stewart, Lawrence Delbert. 1:4589x

Stewart, Powell. 1:1892; 7687-8 12296

Stewart, R.W. 1:3149; 10207

Stewart, William. 1:714f 1387; 1579 1721 3604

Stickland, Irina. 13004

Stiles, Robert E. 11421

Stiles, V. 1:684

Stillert, Willy. 7448

Stillinger, Jack. 11692 11697 12290 12292 13575

Stillings, Frank S. 10936

Stillman, Donald G. 12383

Stillwell, Margaret Bingham. 1:463; 198 4971

Stilwell, John P. 14156

Stirling, Brents. 2:1405

Stirling, M.V. 1:2748; 895-6

Stirling, Matthew. 10282

Stisted, Georgiana M. 1:2647

Stoakley, R.J. 6036

Stock, Elliot. 8934

Stockholm. Royal library *see* Sweden. Royal library, Stockholm.

Stocks, E.V. 1:446

Stocks, J.E. 2641

Stockwell, LaTourette. 2:218; 43 1915

Stoddard, F.G. 12096 12796

Stoffel, C. 2:832; 6064 11074 11540

Stoke Newington. Public libraries. 1:2988 4225 5039

Stoke-on-Trent. Public libraries. 1:941 2444a

Stokes, E.E. 12532

Stokes, Francis Griffin. 10833 10844

Stokes, George Thomas. 1:2038a; 1934

Stokes, Henry P. 1:878t; 2:502; 1058

Stokes, Hugh. 9349

Stokes, Roy. 251a 265 269

Stokes, Walter E. 1:5089c

Stokes, sir William. 1:4816

Stoll, Elmer Edgar. 2:548

Stone, Bernard. 1:3227 4732

Stone, E. 12948

Stone, E.V. 13579

Stone, George Winchester. 2:1195

Stone, Janet. 5218a

Stone, Leonard. 3923

Stone, M.W. 1:1418 1563; 2:232; 7041 8603

Stone, P.M. 7300 10293 14260 14262

Stone, Reynolds. 4410 5213a 6310

Stone, W.G. Boswell-. 9613

Stone, Wilbur Macey. 1:3469 4880 5038a; 7016

Stone, William V. 1:3026b

Stonehill, Charles Archibald. 1:682 1442 (2963) 3169 (3177) (4210) 4396 (4945); 10495 11409 12737

Stonehouse, John Harrison. 1:3070; 5599-a 5778 10074 10078 14396

Stonham, Charles. 1:2115

Stopes, Charlotte (Carmichael). 1:1322p 1412e 3760a; 2:414 1015 1882; 581-2 589 2677 4662 4662b 5620 6808 6842 7979 9696 9782 9785

Storey, Graham. 1:3703p; 11146a

Storm, Colton. 2346 2352

Story, Patrick L. 11024

Stott, F. 1:539b

Stott, Raymond Toole. 1:2137 4175-6 4178-a; 10182

Stout, George Dumas. 7885 11665 11668

Stower, Caleb. 6380

Stoyle, F.W. 6381

Strachan, James. 3748 6884

Strachan, Lionel R.M. 1:3501a; 5197 6843 6896 6902 7344 8282 10344 10346 10425 13178 14520

Strang, William. 6187

Strange, E.H. 1:3083 3086; 10066 10086 10099

Strange, Edward F. 1:1979m; 7067 7957

Strangeways, Giles Stephen Holland Fox, 6th earl of Ilchester. 14198

Stranks, Charles James. 1:4878; 13868

Stratford, A. Jenny (Lewis) *see also* Lewis, A. Jenny. 1:2033k; 13684

Stratford, Ontario. Shakespearean festival *see* Shakespearean festival, Stratford, Ontario.

Stratford papers on Shakespeare. 2:235 1913

Stratford-upon-Avon. International Shakespeare conference *see* International Shakespeare conference, Stratford-upon-Avon.

— Royal Shakespeare theatre *see* Royal Shakespeare theatre, Stratford-upon-Avon.

— Shakespeare memorial association *see* Shakespeare memorial association, Stratford-upon-Avon.

— Shakespeare memorial library *see* Shakespeare memorial library, Stratford-upon-Avon.

Stratford-upon-Avon. Shakespeare's birthplace trust *see* Shakespeare's birthplace trust, Stratford-upon-Avon.

Strathmann, Ernest A. 2:1486; 915

Stratman, Carl Joseph. 1:1593 1594d 1595 1630 1630c 1649–50 1860 3208 3695a 4218aa 4960; 7101–3 7230a 7803 7945 10391 14053

Straus, Ralph. 1:1251 1293 1308 1396v 4578; 3912 4472 4559–60

Strauss, A.B. 11525

Streatfield, Richard A. 1:4423; 10929

Street, E.E. 7344

Street library *see* Somerset. County library, Street.

Streeter, Burnett Hillman. 2429

Streeter, Harold Wade. 1:1691k

Streissler, Erich. 1:3621w

Strena Anglica. 14546

Stretton, Gilbert B. 2506

Stříbrný, Zdeněk. 2:(149)

Strickland, Geoffrey. 11932

Strickland, W.G. 1893

Strong, H.A. 1:4107a

Stroup, Thomas B. 13020

Strouse, Norman H. 5598

Strout, Alan Lang. 1:1938a 1939b–41 3682a 4353a 4730; 4063–4 4067 4069–71 11103 11105 12036

Strunks, James B. 1003

Stuart, Dorothy M. 4327

Stuart, G. William. 2245 4520–1

Stuart, H. 11664

Stuart, H.B. 4581

Stuart, Vincent. 9781

Stubbings, Hilda U. 1:843b

Stubbings, S. 5551

Studi sugli apocrifi Shakespeariani. 2:1189

Studia bibliographica ... Fontaine Verwey. 9393a 11911

Studia di bibliografia e di storia in onore di Tammaro de Marinis. 2237a

Studies in art ... Greene. 13774–5 14198

Studies in bibliography. 1:79 197

Studies in English grammar ... Ōtsuka. 2:1685

Studies in English language ... Karl Brunner. 2:1368

Studies in English literature, 1500–1900. 1:56

Studies in honor of A.H.R. Fairchild. 7170 11682

Studies in honor of Hodges and Thaler. 13543

Studies in honor of T.W. Baldwin. 11128

Studies in Irish history. 1827

Studies in philology. 1:46

Studies in retrospect. 325 2155

Studies in social history. 3468a

Studies in the First folio. 2:550 725

Studies in Welsh book-land. 1483 2838 10899 12005

Studio, The. 1:1554; 7019

Stull, Joseph S. 11689

Stump, Walter Ray. 7233

Sturgeon, Mary C. 1:3296m

Sturman, Berta. 8461 9371 9947

Suckling, F.H. 1397

Suerbaum, S. (4350a)

Suerbaum, Ulrich. 2:(1328)

Suffolk institute of archæology. 1:2903

Suling, Karl-Heinz. 2:759

Sullivan, sir Edward. 1751 1768 1940

Sullivan, Frank. 1:4276–7 4283; 2:1510; 3804 8749 14139

Sullivan, Gertrude M. 2950

Sullivan, Howard A. 1:4349

Sullivan, J.J. 9432

Sullivan, John. 1:2787–a

Sullivan, Majie Padberg. 1:4276–7

Sultana, Donald. 9561

Summerfield, Geoffrey. 9462–3 9465

Summers, Alphonse Montague Joseph-Mary Augustus. 1:1368a 1622 1713 1720a 3755d; 2:752; 4547 5198 7153 7286 .8737–40 11943 11966 13003

Summers, Peter. 1:(2418)

Summers, W.H. 1043

Summerson, sir John N. 1:2103d (4417q); (6778a)

Sunderland antiquarian society. 1:(4623)

Super, Robert Henry. 1:2337a 2338b 2340g 3996; 8289 8922 8307 10586 11880 11883 11885–7

Surrey. 7875

Surrey lad, A, *pseud.* 9171

Surrey libraries group. 1:1859

Sutcliffe, Edmund Felix. 1:2266

Sutcliffe, G.W. 10683

Sutherland, A. Bruce. 1:3655–c

Sutherland, D.M. 1:1889

Sutherland, F.M. 1:2786

Sutherland, James Runcieman. 1:4550 (4707r); 2:760; 7761 10651 12830 12833 12849 14529

Sutro, Adolph. 1:1965

Sutro library, San Francisco *see* California. State library, Sacramento. Sutro branch, San Francisco.

Sutton, Albert. 1:902; 2:186

Sutton, Charles W. 1162 1168 1174 7841

Sutton, Enid. 1:2763

Sutton, H.B. 1:635

Sutton, Oliver J. 8219

Suzannet, comte Alain de. 1:3071 3092; 10062 10075 10136

Svaglic, Martin J. 12567

Swaen, A.E.H. 14554

Swan, Bradford F. 4541
Swan, Marshall W.S. 2:1940
Swann, Arthur. 13314
Swann, C. Kirke. 8145
Swann, Elsie. 1:4353
Swann, H. Kirke. 1:2116
Swann, John Hibbert. 1:661 2920d; 3687 10339
Swann, Thomas Burnett. 1:4734h
Swansea. Association of bookmen of Swansea and West Wales. 1:963e
— Public library. 1:963e 1181 4938 (5030f); 1545
Swanzy, T. Erskine. 13198
Swayze, Walter E. 1:5035 5164; 14250
Sweatman, F.J. 12879
Swedenberg, H.T. 10374
Sweet & Maxwell's complete law book catalogue. 1:2214
Sweet-Escott, Thomas Hay see Escott, Thomas Hay Sweet-.
Sweetser, Wesley D. 1:4096x 4098 4098c
Swem, Earl G. 1:1139d
Swenson, Paul B. 13996
Swindon. Public libraries. 1:3820
Swinyard, Laurence. 5315
Sydney. Australasian pioneer club see Australasian pioneer club, Sydney.
— New South Wales public library see New South Wales. Public library, Sydney.
Syers, Edgar. 7433
Sykes, Christopher. 92a
Sykes, E.G. 10026
Sykes, Henry Dugdale. 13381
Sykes, W.J. 12720
Sylvester, Richard S. 9348 12512
Sylvester, Walter. 706
Syme, S.A. 3576a
Symington, John Alexander. 1:530 2538; 2082
Symonds, Emily M. 5253–4
Symonds, John Addington. 1:(2923n)
Symons, Albert James Alroy. 1:1150e 1376–7 5201; 350–1 357–8 2114 2318 4671–2 6087 12476 13844 14393
Symons, Arthur William. 14 13810
Symons, L. Eleanor. 1:1578c
Synge, Patrick Millington. 1:2181
Szepsi Csombor literary circle, London. 1:826g
Szladits, Lola L. 1:375; 14603

T. 2739
T., A. 11810
T., A.H. 13532
T., C. 493
T., C.E. 2755

T., D. 1772
T., D.C. 10810
T., E.G. 1228 3487
T., F.J. 2411
T., G. 5774
T., G.H. 12536
T., H. 1:2629; 2619 6553
T., J.B. 13874
T., J.F. 6269
T., J.S.M. 8191
T., L.S. see Thompson, Lawrence S.
T., O.S. 9998
T., W. 5409
Table talk (Gent Mag). 1349
Tabor, C.J. 6813
Tagg, A.C. 1161
Tait, John G. 13207 13213
Takanobu Ōtsuka see Ōtsuka, Takanobu.
Takemi, Yamaguchi. 2:73
Talbot, James. 5815
Talbot, William. 1:851; 988 6520 8498 10416 11906
Tallon, Maura. 1:587; 1507 1510 1518 1540f 1544 1834 3325–6
Talmage, Irma. 1:1723g
Talon, Henri. 1:2674
Talnant, pseud. 4127
Tannenbaum, Dorothy Rosenveig. 1:2350 2413 2724 2759 3643 3650 3657 3659 4124 4151 4488 4677b 4971a; 2:20 1700 1815
Tannenbaum, Earl. 1:4019
Tannenbaum, Samuel Aaron. 1:2350 2412–13 2524 2758–9 2948 2996 3188 3345 3401 3520–1 3643 3650 3657 3659 3864–5 3969 4074 4082 4122–4 4137 4151 4169 4216 4317 4325 4406 4488 4677b 4684 4971a 5052;,2:20 572 731 885a 1019 1022 1024–8 1030 1032 1036–7 1065–6 1084 1106 1130 1188 1191 1196 1203 1208 1210 1214–15 1220 1399–1400 1425 1445 1500 1542 1597 1605 1617 1642 1700 1712 1769–71 1789 1815 1823–4 1840–1 1850–1 1860–1 1876 1891–2 1895–6 1901 1962 1973; 7138–40 7144–5 7151 8917 9362 9574 9576 9578–80 9744 10563 10565 11555 11559 12148 12200a 12229–30 12266 12993
Tanner, James T.F. 1:2414k
Tanner, Joseph Robson. 1:510 2280; 12704
Tanner, Lawrence E. 4324
Tanselle, George Thomas. 1:89; 164–6 169 172–4 335 1006–7 2240 6254 6344 6650 11620 12194
Taplin, Gardner B. 1:2570; 8877
Tapson, Frank. 1:98
Targ, William. 1:669 1565c; 2372 (5276) (9327)

Vol. 1 = Bibliographies   2 = Shakespeare   4 = 1–8221   5 = 8222–14616

Tarling, Alan. 5501
Tarr, John C. 4527 6605
Tate, Allen. 1:(3255c) (3557f) 4491i
Tate, W.E. 8744
Tate, W.R. 2407 13129
Tauchnitz, Bernhard, publisher, Leipzig. 847a
Taut, Kurt. 1:3564
Tave, Stuart M. 8442
Tawney, Richard Henry. 1:3563 5045 (5048)
Taylor, A.E. 1:2520; 12143
Taylor, Alexander B. 1:1816
Taylor, Alfred D. 1:2154
Taylor, Archer. 1:1437c; 6787
Taylor, Arnold C. 14497
Taylor, C.S. 7493
Taylor, Charlene M. 1:1699
Taylor, Charles H. 1:4655; 13349 13353
Taylor, Clyde Romer Hughes. 1:2840p 4047b
    5008b; 8874 12135
Taylor, Donald S. 9409
Taylor, Eric S. 14037
Taylor, Eva Germaine Rimington. 1:2188–9
    2214t; 8199
Taylor, Frank. 3040
Taylor, Frank J. 1:948
Taylor, G.A. 2:553
Taylor, Garland F. 13400
Taylor, Geoffrey Handley-. 1:1222 3693
    4048d 4162; 11129
Taylor, George Coffin. 2:1270; 9263
Taylor, Hasseltine Byrd. 1:2246
Taylor, Henry. 1076 7823
Taylor, I. 6696
Taylor, J.C.C. 13528
Taylor, John. 7381 8218 12659 13049
Taylor, John Russell. 6224 13948
Taylor, Kim. 3845
Taylor, Lawrence. 2080
Taylor, Marion A. 626
Taylor, Mary Eustace. 1:4213h
Taylor, Nancy E. 1:2995
Taylor, Norman. 1:885; 1090–1
Taylor, Olive. 5821
Taylor, Robert. 8790
Taylor, Robert H. 1:359e; 539 2371 3178
    3341 4000 14114 14116
Taylor, Samuel. 3215 3276
Taylor, Sue. 4752
Teagarden, Lucetta J. 1:4458c; 12896
Teall, Gardner. 11256 11666
Tearle, C. 11328
Tedder, Henry R. 1:4939; 14 6230
Tedlock, Ernest Warnock. 1:4017d; 11924
Teerinck, Herman. 1:4835 4839 4842; 13759
    13763–5 13768 13778
Tegg, W. 5929 12297
Telleen, John Martin. 1:4221c
Tempany, T.W. 3704

Tempest, H.G. 4120
Temple F-J. 1:(2319)
Temple, Phillips. 1:2975f
Temple, Ruth (Zabriskie). 1:678–9
Templeman, William Darby. 1:58 654 2582c
    3438 5217; 10695–9 14465
Templeton, Janet M. 1637
Tener, Robert H. 11288
Tenison, E.M. 1:3537
Tennant, sir Charles. 1:325ab
Tennyson, sir Charles Bruce Locker. 1:4900
    4902; 13952
Tennyson, G.B. 1:2712
Term catalogues, 1668–1709. 1:595
Terry, Altha E. 4160a
Terry, Astley. 13980
Terry, Charles Sanford. 719b–c 965–6
Terry, F.C. Birbeck. 3578 3704 10810
Teugh, Mark. 12501
Tevensham, Traviss Frederick. 4423
Tew, E.L.H. 10603 14286
Texas. University. 1:2572
— — Humanities research center. 1:365
    1499 2590 2640 3099 3103 3258 3398
    4020c 4458c 4582b 4735n 4751 5140;
    11939
— — John Henry Wrenn library. 1:339
— — Library. 1:172 2683 2694 3981 4654
    4837 4897 5137; 9224
Texas Christian university, Fort Worth,
    Texas. 2:249
Texas quarterly. Supplement. 14436
Thackeray, F.St.J. 2494
Theosophical society in England. 1:2457
Thiefes, P. 14025
Thimm, Carl Albert. 1:2176–7
Thin, James. 1700
Thinker's library. 3558
Thipps, R. 12807
Thirsk, James W. 1:5059
Thistleton, A.E. 9794 10740
Thom, Ian W. 12087
Thomas, Alan G. 1:3224 3228 5111m; 3127
    3342 7461 11482 11500
Thomas, Alfred. 1:1926; 11150 12671
Thomas, sir Ben Bowen. 1:1465h
Thomas, Beryl E. 1:2351
Thomas, C. Edgar. 1249 2707 3634–5 4719
    5275
Thomas, Charles. 1085
Thomas, D.S. 10523 14364
Thomas, sir D. Lleufer. 10456
Thomas, Donald. 3509a 6717 11625
Thomas, Edward see Thomas, Philip Edward.
Thomas, Ernest C. 13013
Thomas, F.H. Llewellyn. 3781
Thomas, sir Henry. 63 325 615 1257 2106
    2116–17 2128 2132 2933 2951 3800 3854

4269 4286 5468 5590 6010 7677–8 8110–11 8355 8950 9204 13144

Thomas, Lois Theisen. 1:4929

Thomas, Kenneth Bryn. 1:3168k

Thomas, M.M.A.A. 1:1338

Thomas, Mary Gwynneth Lloyd. 1:4419w

Thomas, Mary Olive. 2:1096

Thomas, N.M. 1:811m

Thomas, P.G. 8825 12737

Thomas, Peter William. 1:1881 2454g

Thomas, Philip Edward. 1:2503 3818 3819a

Thomas, R. 870a 11110 11870

Thomas, R.E. 1254

Thomas, R.N. 112

Thomas, R. George. 3216

Thomas, Ralph. 1:1184 2286j 3428a; 99 104 337 517 706 1214 3486 3577–8 3993 4375 4739 5667 6190 6267 6268 7387 7418 7591 8314 8544 8551 8559 8562 10191 11133

Thomas, Roger. 1:2405b; 3277 6777 7238 8430

Thomas, Sidney. 2:1721–2; 5684 7186 8165 9438

Thomas, Walter. 1:5214g

Thomas-Stanford, sir Charles see Stanford, sir Charles Thomas-.

Thompson, Alexander Hamilton. 1:887 3700

Thompson, D'Arcy W. 2:1158; 11442 13644

Thompson, E.H. 6269

Thompson, sir Edward Maunde. 1:5192; 2:1008–10 1012 1015 1019 1021 1023 1026 1881 1883–4 1886; 9783 11627 12538

Thompson, Elbert Nevius Sèbring. 1:4219

Thompson, Francis. 1:3651

Thompson, Harold William. 1:4101d

Thompson, James. 1:13

Thompson, James W. 10667

Thompson, John S. 6160

Thompson, John V. 2877

Thompson, Karl F. 8707 13628

Thompson, Lawrance. 2:755

Thompson, Lawrence S. 2259–61 3378 5354 6105 6108 6211 6560 6708 12580

Thompson, R. 2621

Thompson, Ralph. 9470

Thompson, Ruth D'Arcy. 1:4944b

Thompson, S.D. 2959

Thompson, Sylvanus Phillips. 1:2279d; 5644

Thompson, T.H. 8201

Thompson, W.D.J. Cargill. 3179 8408 8541

Thomson, Clara Linklater. 1:4518

Thomson, D. Croal. 4019

Thomson, Daphne W. 1:4513

Thomson, Frances Mary. 1:1419b 1548; 5518h 5518j

Thomson, Godfrey. 1:4748f

Thomson, Hugh W. 1:2082 2085

Thomson J. 10107

Thomson, James. 9031

Thomson, James B. 1:4927

Thomson, John. 1:4599; 3

Thomson, Joseph Charles. 1:3056 3978 4849 4891; 6149

Thomson, Myra. 1:822m

Thoresby society. 1:1812

Thorndike, Ashley H. 2:(719) 876 (1640)

Thorndike, Lynn. 13163

Thorn-Drury, George see Drury, George Thorn-.

Thorne, J.R. 3592

Thorne, S.E. 1:4568a; 13137

Thorne, W. Benson. 4077–9 4516 5536 7063

Thornton, James Cholmondeley. 4534

Thornton, John L. 1:2230i; 2433 7562 7565 7571 8144 8153 8661

Thornton, Richard H. 1:1428; 2:464 502; 1026 1565 1703 2032 3500 3589 3723 3787 4833 6269 6369 6846 7842 7847 11976 13169

Thornton, Weldon. 11603 11608

Thorp, John T. 1:2183a

Thorp, Joseph Peter. 1:1397a; 5639 6579a

Thorp, Margaret (Farrand). 1:3930; 11720

Thorp, Willard. 1:4556e; 10357 13117

Thorpe, Clarence D. 11681

Thorpe, F. 14135

Thorpe, H. 1:1807

Thorpe, James. 1:5124; (405) 407 414 529 3402 7210 7430 10764 12404 13338 14352–3

Thorpe, W.G. 8359

Thorson, James L. 1:2663; 9149

Thoyts, Emma Elizabeth. 3703

Thrall, Miriam Mulford H. 1:1918 2710 4111 4920

Three historical notes (Nature). 8726

Thring, G. Herbert. 339 3518 6503

Thurber, Gerrish. 5415

Thurley, R.L. 1:4787

Thurston, Herbert. 4413

Thwaite, Mary Florence. 1:1374c–d 1856; 5279 5282–3

Tibble, Anne. 9459–62 9465

Tibble, J.W. 9456 9465

Tibbutt, H.G. 1:2610; 8960

Tickell, Adeline Hill. 4596

Tickell, Richard Eustace. 1:4968

Tierney, James Henderson. 1691

Tilander, Gunnar. 3148

Tilley, Morris P. 12231

Tillier, Louis. 1:2444c

Tillinghast, William Hopkins. 1:1541

Tillotson, Arthur. 1:2942; 6403 11424 12112 12743 13553

Tillotson, Geoffrey. 1:3189; 96 6180 6403 8860 9262 11160 12652–3 14244

Tillotson, Kathleen Mary. 1:3102 (3189) 5210; 5628 9583 10174 10319
Tillyard, sir Eustace M.W. 2:1324; 7985 12334
Tilmouth, Michael. 1:1837a
Timai, *pseud.* 1603
The Times, London. 1:1850; 7764 7801
Times bookshop, London. 1:1236 1401b 3193 4304
Timko, Michael. 1:2819; 14283
Timmins, Samuel. 2:270
Timperley, Charles H. 4128a 4132 6382
Tindall, William York. 8761
Tingay, Lance O. 14118 14123
Tinker, Chauncey Brewster. 1:365 2336f 3837; 8606 14095 14103
Tinsley, William. 5858–9
Tisserant, Eugene. 131
Titchener, E.B. 1:5025–a
Titherley, A.W. 2:1737
Titzell, Josiah. 1:2077
Tobin, James Edward. 626 1643–4 4354b 4435 4826
Tobin, Terence A. 1:1637
Tocco, F. 1:4404f
Tod, Alexander Hay. 1:917
Todd, F.M. 14543
Todd, Ruthven. 1:2479a 4052q; 8604 8642–4
Todd, William Burton. 1:365 1908 1910 2621–2 2893 2954 2993 3303 3470–1 3684 4052 4084 4420 4444 4612 4762 4840 49578 4935 5125 5140–2 5148; 2:657; 153 164 393 742 1293 2238c 3459 4454 4560–1 5307 5820 6158 6311 6336 6338 6373 6375a 7051 7790–1 7797 7799 7804 7812 8317 8550 8670 8800 8974 8978 9615 9680 9702 9735 9821 9930 10162 10171 10181 10511 10514 10766 10769–70 10772–3 10775 11093 11113 11135 11155 11255 11257 11483–4 11487 11515 11988 12066–8 12100 12196 12768 12858 12865 13011 13045 13095 13226 13232 13238 13406 13507 13584 13767 13779 13832 13843 13951 14006 14046–8 14302–3 14337 14357 14436 14440–1 14452
To doctor R: essays. 1:4317r; 57 7168 12258
Toerien, Barend J. 1:5157t
Tokyo, Waseda university *see* Waseda university, Tokyo.
Tolfree, M.P.G. 1:5045a
Tolles, Frederick B. 14306
Tolley, A. Trevor. 1:4751f; 8323
Tolley, Cyril W. 1:584
Tolman, Frank L. 183
Tombo, Rudolf. 1:4107
Tomkinson, sir Geoffrey S. 6473
Tomlin, Eric W.F. 1:3252
Tomlinson, C. 7238

Tommasi, Anthony. 1:4012
Tompkins, A.D.R. 9720
Tompkins, D. 9654
Tompkinson, G.S. 1:1227
Tonkin, H. 1:3640u
Tonks, Henry. 2290
Tonson, Jacob. 5870
Tooley, Ronald Vere. 1:1747 1752 1766 2879d; 7524 7526 7529 7531–4
Toovey, C.J. 1:325ab
Torczon, Vern. 2:1259
Torfrida, *pseud.* 7634
Toronto. Public libraries. Osborne collection. 1:1567–8 1570
Torriano, Hugh Arthur *see* Marchmont, Frederick, *pseud.*
Toshikazu Oyama *see* Oyama, Toshikazu.
Tottenham, C.J. 6855
Tourneur, N. 2756
Tout, Mary (Johnstone). 1:4971f
Tovey, D.C. 12802 14023
Towle, Eleanor A. (Taylor). 1:4325m
Townsend, A. Cockburn. 1:2240r–s; 6982 8133 8142 8151
Townsend, Francis G. 8287 9481
Townsend, J. Benjamin. 7917 9839
Townsend, John. 13014
Townshend, R. Marsham. 6234
Townsend, Rebecca Dutton. 1:1254
Toyada Minoru *see* Minoru, Toyada.
Toynbee, Paget Jackson. 1:828–30; 942 945 4187 5807 10822 10824 10826–7 10832 10834 10836 10839 12905 14179
Tracy, Clarence. 1:4583b
Tracy, Walter. 6612 6618
Tranio, *pseud.* 371
Trapp, C.W. 13659
Travers, Michael. 6483
Tredrey, Frank D. 4068
Tree, Roland. 1:1765g 1772
Trefman, Simon. 12551
Tregaskis, James, bksllr., London. 1:3980; 730 2014a 2025a 8681
Tremaine, George. 12461
Trench, W.F. 2:1767; 12094
Trenery, Grace R. 1:1462d
Trent, William Peterfield. 1:2977; 2:1640
Treptow, Otto. 1:1399b; 5653
Trevanion, Michael, *pseud. of* Simon H. Nowell-Smith. 810 3025 3992 8757 11969 12781 13963 14443 14445
Trevor-Roper, Hugh Redwald *see* Roper, Hugh Redwald Trevor-.
Trewin, John C. 1:1648; 4829
Trinity college, Dublin *see* Dublin. University. Trinity college.
Troubridge, sir St.Vincent. 1:1634 1646–7; 7030

Walker, S.J. 7977
Walker, Thomas Alfred. 1:882
Walker, William. 4123
Wall, Barbara. 5579a
Wall, Thomas. 1929
Wallace, A.D. 1:(4515)
Wallace, Charles William. 2:1006
Wallace, John M. 1:1973
Wallace, Karl Richards. 1:2276
Wallace, Malcolm William. 1:3463d
Wallace, R. 3734a
Wallace, Robert M. 10505
Wallace, Walter Thomas. 1:395
Wallbridge, Earle F. 1:2077
Waller, A.R. 2:(37) (835–6); 3416 (3419) 9728
  12645
Waller, Frederick O. 2:962 1912; 11363
Waller, W.F. 10722 13706
Wallerstein, Ruth. 13086
Wallington hall, Northumberland. Library.
  1:373
Wallis, Alfred. 1:3620; 11007 12940
Wallis, J.P.R. 8580
Wallis, Lawrence W. 1:1345b; 4919 6125
  6134 6138–40
Wallis, Peter John. 1:2175a 2916 4814; 7551
  7553 8117 9764–5 12630 14168
Walmsley, D.M. 10436
Walmsley, R. 1179
Walpole, sir Hugh Seymour. 1:2860 3713
Walrond, H. 1:2103
Walsh, James E. 295a
Walsh, M.O'N. 1:762
Walsh, S. Padraig. 1:1656g
Walsh, Stevenson H. 10828
Walter, Frank K. 1:3858y 4425k
Walter, J.H. 2:1318; 10721
Walters, C. 13897
Walters, D. Eurof. 1:1463h
Walters, Edward. 5579a
Walters, Gwynfryn. 1:4408a; 1515 1546 3234
  12698
Walters, R. 9990
Walton, Francis R. 885
Walton, Hugh M. 2952
Walton, James Kirkwood. 2:22 1680 1684
  1686–7; 12116
Wankyn, C. 4407 7508 13615
Wann, Louis. 7135
Warburg institute see London. University.
  Warburg institute.
Warburton, Thomas. 961 990–1 2125 6286–7
  6289 6529 7217 7300 8403 8416 8418 8796
  10313 10432 10720 10988 11719 11920
  12012 12477–9 12678 13495 14262 14295
Ward, Addison. 1:627
Ward, sir Adolphus William. 1:(2900); 2:(37)
  (835–6); 3416 (3419)

Ward, Annette P. 2:58
Ward, B.M. 10635
Ward, C.A. 336 1193 4016 9014
Ward, C.S. 2:510
Ward, Charles E. 10189 10361–2
Ward, H. Gordon. 3640 7202
Ward, H. Snowden. 4246 9981
Ward, James. 1:928b–c 3456 5023–4; 14256
Ward, John. 2070
Ward, Paul L. 11860
Ward, Philip. 1:1401c; 3260 5717 5907
Ward, S.H. 1:5021
Ward, Sidney. 1:1245d; 3857a 4987
Ward, William S. 1:4402hb
Ward, William Smith. 1:1906
Warde, Beatrice (Lamberton-Becker) see also
  Beaujon, Paul, pseud. 1:1359; 4744 5218a
  5301 6586
Wardle, Arthur C. 4773
Wardrop, James. 1155 3102 5972a 6100
Ware. St.Edmund's college see St.Edmund's
  college, Ware.
Ware, Malcolm. 2:1253
Ware, Robert. 1:2454b
Wark, Robert R. 8617
Warner, Gilmore. 1:3721
Warmington, E.L. 10349
Warne, Frederick and co. ltd. 14297
Warner, George F. 11319–20
Warner, James H. 1:814–15
Warner, John. 1:3365; 7900
Warnke, Frank J. 11040
Warre, C.F. 1:3646
Warren, Arthur. 5982
Warren, C.F.S. 5296 7384 10896 13550
Warren, William. 9453
Warrilow, Georgina. 1:1193
Warsaw. Universytet. Biblioteka. 2:140
Warwickshire. County council. Records and
  museum committee. 1:1807 3214–15
Waseda university. Tokyo. Tsubouchi
  memorial theatre museum. 2:251
Washburn, Wilcomb E. 9868
Washington, D.C. Cathedral of St. Peter and
  St. Paul. Rare book library. 1:1498
— Folger Shakespeare library see Folger
  Shakespeare library, Washington, D.C.
— Georgetown university see Georgetown
  university, Washington, D.C.
Washington Square college book club see
  New York. University. Washington Square
  college. Book club.
Wason, George M. 7076
Wasserman, Earl R. 7994 10562
Waterhouse, Michael. 4826
Waterlow brothers and Layton, London.
  5948–9
Waters, Arthur W. 3621

Waters, David W. 1:2238
Waters, W. 5562
Waterson, David. 8945
Waterston, Robert. 1712
Watford. College of technology. 1:1162
Watkin, Hugh R. 1099a–b
Watkins, A.E. 1:2223
Watkins, David R. 12510
Watkins, Diana G. 1:4883
Watkins, Marie O. 2:52
Watkins, T.R. 2259
Watkinson, J. 6989
Watkinson, Raymond. 5005
Watney, Oliver Vernon. 1:337a
Watson, Andrew G. 1:550 4585f; 682 3343–4 3354 3363 3379 9869
Watson, B.G. 4545a 4571m 5564q
Watson, Barbara. 1:3141
Watson, Charles B. Boog. 1:1817
Watson, Eric R. 14331
Watson, Foster. 1:2277; 8106–7 14265
Watson, George Grimes. 1:7 350 376 657g 833a (1139m); 2:75a; (377) (391) 8656 9551
Watson, J. Seton-. 4189
Watson, James. 5960 6114 6383 10715
Watson, John. 2629
Watson, Melvin R. 1:1657
Watson, Sydney Felgate. 1:888; 1403
Watson, W.M. 1031
Watt, Alexander. 3700
Watt, Hugh. 1:2751
Watt, Hugh Boyd. 1:5077
Watt, Ian. 6549
Wattie, Margaret. 13078
Watts, C.T. 1:3492
Watts, G.H. 1:512
Watts, Theodore. 13895
Waugh, A.T. 2698a
Waugh, Alec. 5528
Waugh, Arthur. 4359 10095
Way, W. Irving. 2270
Way, T.R. 1:5076b
Wayne state university, Detroit. Library. 1:4349
Waynflete, George, pseud. 10283 13987 13993
Weale, William Henry James. 2002 2005 2007 2043 2080
Weare, G.E. 6742
Wearing, F.N. 7040
Weaver, Ann C. 931
Weaver, H.F. 8240 10023
Weaver, Warren. 1:2735; 9319 9326 9328 9337
Webb, A.P. 1:3582; 10942
Webb, Eugene. 1:2414g
Webb, Henry J. 1:2236a–7; 10202
Webb, Robert Kiefer. 1:4141

Webb, Sidney James, baron Passfield. 1:859
Webb, T.F. Albertoni. 9171
Webb, W.L. 1745 8914
Webb, William. 3952 4202
Webber, Winslow Lewis. 1:72
Weber, A. 10893
Weber, Carl Jefferson. 1:1352 3326 3504b 3575 3588–9 3592–5 3599–600 3604 3722 4036; 857a 4992 5893 7342 7460 8284 10553–4 10956–8 10960–1 10963–4 10966–7 10972 10978
Weber, Clara Carter. 1:3604
Weber, Hilmar H. 7679–80 7683
Webster, C.M. 1:4825y
Webster, Raymund. 1:2553
Wecter, Dixon. 14242
Wedderburn. A.D.O. 1:4556
Weed, Katherine Kirtley. 1:1890
Weed, Mary Eunice. 1:2707
Weedon, Margaret J.P. 1:3831 4843; 4938 7047 13795
Weekes, Ethel Lega-. 1099c 7471 13037
Weekley, A.S. 12128
Weekley, Montague. 4040 4044 4047
Weeks, Donald. 13068 13071–2
Weeks, William Self. 2:1187
Weihe, Kenneth G. 13114
Weil, Ernst. 1:1271 3617a; 849 854 2366 4770–1
Weiner, Albert B. 2:1253f–5
Weinreb, B. 3657
Weir, John L. 1:3783d; 734 1738 2960–1 2977 4785 5207 5988 8722 11804 12089 14459
Weiss, Harry Bischoff. 1:1542 1556a 1557 1557c 1982a 4274d; 4894 5882 6991 7017–18 7020 9712
Weiss, Roberto. 3354a
Weiss, W. 3784
Weitenkampf, Frank. 1:3095b 3675; 2:782; 502 5354 6210 10152 13990
Welby, Alfred. 7647 8016
Welby, Thomas Earl. 1:4861; 11876
Welch, Bernard Lewis. 1:4404b
Welch, Charles. 1:915 4647; 1192a 1194 1235–6 2478 2598 2657 5312 5317 12493–4
Welch, J. Cuthbert. 7701
Welford, Richard. 1:927 1873a; 1024 1320 4128 4686
Welland, D.S.R. 12642
Wellcome historical medical library, London. 1:474 2227 2530
Wellcome historical medical museum, London. 1:3822 4065
Wellesley, John. 658 6542 7581
Wellesley college. Library. 1:1990
Wellesley index to Victorian periodicals. 1:1927

White, Newport Benjamin. 1:456a 1518 2493 4831; 1801 1910–11 1966 10318 13395 13866 14131
White, Newport John Davis. 1935 1939 13714
White, Norman. 11151–2
White, R.B. 7792
White, Richard. 798
White, Robert. 3380 12297
White, Thomas. 10737
White, W.H. 6285
White, William. 1:2487 2521–2a 3158 3163 3718–b 3723 3725–7 3729 3872–3 3884 4018 4371 4390 4553y 4644–5a; 11164 11167 11169 1117–2 11175–6 11179–81 11183–5 11188–9 11193–4 11198–200 11202 11208 11213–15 11217 11219–21 11226 11228–9 11591 11604 14007 14010
White, William Augustus. 1:511 525
White, William Hale. 1:5166t; 14492
White line, pseud. 4019–24 6700
Whitebrook, John Cudworth. 1:2937 3230; 5898 10402
Whitehead, Thomas W. 1:3008
Whitehouse, A. 13819
Whiteley, Derek P. 10400
Whitesell, J. Edwin. 1:1981a
Whitewell, Robert J. 6723
Whitfield, A. Stanton. 1:2645a 3215a 3409; 8646
Whitford, Robert Calvin. 1:2794
Whiting, Brooke. 1:3225
Whiting, F. Brooke. 11262
Whiting, George W. 1:2762a; 9652 10356 10473 11556 14028
Whitley, Alvin. 11686 11972
Whitley, William Thomas. 1:2254; 8948
Whitlock, Baird W. 10270
Whitman, Malcolm Douglass. 1:2287
Whitmee, Dorothy E. 1:4696
Whitmore, J.B. 2:1776; 2419–20 5042 13024
Whitmore, Phyllis. 1:2494
Whitney, Henry Austin. 1:4233
Whitten, Wilfred. 5057
Whittingham, Alfred. 4378
Whitwell, Robert J. 6724
Whitworth, Adrian. 1:4758
Whyte, Frederick. 4858a
Whyte, John. 1:1931
Wiborg, Frank Bestow. 1:1139ya
Wickes, George. 1:3778e
Wicklen, S.I. 3951 4800 4927
Wicks, A.T. 1395a
Wicksteed, P.H. 14497
Widmann, Ruth L. 1:4317m
Wieder, Joachim. 7615b
Wigan. Public library. 1:353 903 1521; 2:38

Wight, Marjory. 3327
Wijnman, H.F. 5186b
Wikelund, Philip. 1:594a
Wilcock, A.B. 13888
Wilcox, John. 1:4515; 2:756
Wilcox, Stewart C. 11021
Wild, Margery Frances. 1:482
Wilde, A.D. 2:1158 1882
Wilders, John. 1:2664
Wiles, A.G.D. 8246
Wiles, Roy McKeen. 1:1532 1907 1911; 739 1133 1180 6943 7653 7810 7813 7815
Wiley, Autrey Nell. 1:4837; 9698 13755 13760–1
Wiley, Margaret Lee. 2:230
Wilkes, G.A. 9844 9849
Wilkie, James. 1603
Wilkins, William Glyde. 1:3057; 9994 9996–7 9999–10000 10007 10016
Wilkinson, Alice Margaret. 4329
Wilkinson, Cyril Hackett. 2827 3217 3368a 7096 8756 14348
Wilkinson, David Robert McIntyre. 1:2152
Wilkinson, Elizabeth M. 1:2609m
Wilkinson, J.T. 3081
Wilkinson, J.V.S. 3217–18
Wilkinson, Louis Umfreville see Marlow, Louis, pseud.
Wilks, John. 10192–3
Wilks, Samuel. 4822
Willans, Delia M. 7154
Willard, Helen D. 2:340
Willard, Oliver M. 644 4915
Willard, Rudolph. 6416 8104
Willcock, Gladys Doidge. 1:4472; 11231
Willcock, John. 6173
Willett, E.V. Anson. 10544
Willetts, Pamela J. 8998 10687
Willetts, R.F. 1:4956f
Willfort, Margarita. 1:3923q
William Andrews Clark memorial library see California. University. University at Los Angeles. William Andrews Clark memorial library.
William Blake, poet, printer, prophet. 8634
William Blake trust. 1:2486a
William L. Clements library see Michigan. University. William L. Clements library.
William Morris society, London. 1:1354 4303–4; 4334
William Morris society, Tokyo. 1:4302d
William Parks club, Richmond, Va. 1:1379c; 5374
William Sessions ltd., York. 5621
Williams, A. Hudson-. 1:5116a
Williams, A. Lukyn. 13455
Williams, Alun Llywelyn. 1:3820t

Williams, Aneurin. 1:699; 985 1231 1478 2829 4511 4642a 4897h 4924 5062 5330 5408 5556 5611 5827 5967 7419 7732 7737 7877 7881 9884 10047 10741 10840

Williams, Athro Ifor. 1480

Williams, Charles. 1:2563–a

Williams, Charles D. 1:4353b; 5371 7030–2 7035

Williams, D.D. 7376

Williams, David. 1:5112

Williams, E.I. 2783 11527

Williams, Edward. 4251

Williams, Eileen A. 1:3439

Williams, F.H.B. 1:3458e

Williams, Franklin Burleigh. 1:532a 551 555 2036 4250; 669 676–7 679–80 690 692 3041 3180 3296 3574 3693 3738 5847 6309 6562 7340 8254 8746

Williams, G.J. 1:4513u; 1512 11533

Williams, George Walton. 2:930 1454 1735 1738–9 1810; 4429 6372 9700b 9759 9762 13434

Williams, Glanmor. 5155

Williams, Gordon. 4047

Williams, H. Fulford. 2233

Williams, sir Harold Herbert. 1:3926 4830; 49 283 285 325 735 916 5099 11036–7 11716 13719–20 13723–5 13728–9 13731 13739–40 13747–8 13753 13770 13779

Williams, Howard B. 10306

Williams, Iolo Aneurin. 1:67 633 2002 2004 (2316) 2325 (2332) (2793) (2849) (3464) 4155 4267 (4660) (4665) 4760 (4779); 359 458 460 2300 2326 6286 7424 7431 7959 8012 8017 8261 8720 10745 11422 13917–18 14031 14294

Williams, Isaac J. 1:1745d; 1482

Williams, J.B., pseud. of J.G. Muddiman. 1:1873 1873b; 708 710 1187 1431 4160 4433 5848 7639 7659–60 7662 7664 9771 12759 14167

Williams, Joan. 1:4636

Williams, John Stuart. 1:4048b

Williams, Judith Blow. 1:2164

Williams, Marjorie. 12737

Williams, Owen. 1:963 3861

Williams, Philip. 2:921 1450 1459 1680 1827 1830

Williams, Ralph M. 10413

Williams, Sidney Herbert. 1:2721 2724–5 2734; 9300 9315

Williams, Stanley Thomas. 1:2940

Williams, T.W. 2630

Williams, W.J. 1:4908

Williams, William. 1:706 908 4587 5116 5195; 1485 1487 1490 1492–3 1495–6 3009 3018 3027 3029 4796–8 14153

Williams, William P. 1:2413a (3345a) (4169b) (4677c); 2:1627

Williams college, Williamstown, Mass. Chapin library. 1:2149 2669 4248

Williamson, Dereck. 270

Williamson, Edmund Schofield. 1:3050i 3051d

Williamson, Emma. S. 9992

Williamson, George. 4670 10231 10243 10264

Williamson, George Charles. 1:(3910); 1404 2291 7414 7599 8939

Williamson, George Millar. 1:4796

Williamson, H.S. 6595

Williamson, Hugh Albert Fordyce. 1:1189

Williamson, Hugh Ross. 2:1324

Willison, Ian R. 1:376 4370 4373

Williamson, Karina. 1296 13463

Williamson, Kenneth. 1296a

Willmett, H. James. 11837

Willoughby, Edwin Eliott. 1:5028b; 2:290–1 293 422 557–8 560–3 565 568 574b 749 777 925 1185 1618; 268 (649–50) 2978 3085 (3086) 4914 (6114) 6366 6399 6411 (6562) 6677 6681 6867 6874 (7998) 8366 8385 (8518) 9852 (10637) (11711)

Willoughby, Harold Rideout. 1:1483g–i; 6868a

Willoughby de Broke, John Henry Peyto Verney, baron see Verney, John Henry Peyto, baron Willoughby de Broke.

Wilmshurst, W.L. 9612

Wilmerding, Lucius. 1:404

Wilmot, B.C. 1:2600

Wilson, Angus Frank Johnstone. 3511

Wilson, C. Carus-. 7505

Wilson, Carroll Atwood. 1:2669 3591 3597; 14093 14111

Wilson, D.G. 9294

Wilson, sir Daniel. 5266

Wilson, Donald. 5133

Wilson, E.M. 7760

Wilson, Edward. 3393a

Wilson, Edwin G. 12299

Wilson, Elkin Calhoun. 1:2035a

Wilson, Frank Percy. 1:1758–a 2055 3616 (4324) 4690 4707r; 2:551 892 898 964; 83 325 650 6747 7759–60 8072–3 8753 9743 11568

Wilson, Frederick James Farlow. 6312

Wilson, George Francis. 1:2970 3747–9; 11240–1

Wilson, Gurney. 6917a

Wilson, Harold S. 11000

Wilson, James Grant. 1:(4911)

Wilson, James M. 2681 2784

Wilson, Jean C.S. 1:(3597)

Woodbridge, Homer Edwards. 1:4884a; 2:722
Woodbury, John P. 1:1744 (2933)
Woodfield, Denis Buchanan. 2219
Woodhead, Margaret L. 9968
Woodhouse, A.S.P. 1:2844a
Woodman, R.E.G. 10137
Woodress, James L. 1:1978i
Woodring, Carl Ray. 1:(3742) 3743 3984; 9558 11848
Woodruffe, Mary. 4017
Woods, Charles B. 10524
Woods, Frederick W. 1:2799–800; 9445–6
Woods, V.H. 2:341
Woodward, B.B. 3583
Woodward, Chester. 2:293a; 2343
Woodward, Daniel H. 1:2816; 1383 3698 9478 9835–6 10439 10608–9 12881
Woodward, Gertrude (Loop). 1:533 1483 1625
Woodward, Gwendolen L. 4990
Woodworth, Mary Katherine. 1:2597–8
Woof, R.S. 1:5179; 9564 14550
Woolf, Cecil. 1:2512 2774 2950 3171–2 3621 4531–3b 5033–5; 9441f 10284–6 13066
Woolf, Cecil, co., bkllrs., London. 1:4533a
Woolf, Henry B. 6417
Woolf, James Dudley. 1:3477g–h
Woolf, Leonard Sydney. 4887–9
Woolhope club. 3250
Woollan, J.C. 2578 4903 5122 5255 5946
Woollen, Henry. 2:362
Woolley, David. 9257
Woolmer, J. Howard, ltd., New York. 1:4077d
Woolven, G.B. 1:691
Worcester. Cathedral. Library. 1:437
Worcester, Mass. College of the holy cross. Dinand library. 1:4335
Worcestershire historical society. 1:947
Wordsworth, Christopher. 1:3210; 2806a 4232 14497
Wordsworth, Gordon G. 14497
Wordsworth, Jonathan. 1:5159m; 14487
Work of the private presses (Penrose Ann). 3851 4503 4585 4630 4634 4756 4973 5302
Working papers. 13960–1
Workman, D. Hansard. 13859
World bibliography of bibliographies. 1:35
World Jewish congress, London. British section. 1:1861
World's workers. 4204a
Worcestershire historical society. 7519
Wormald, Dorothy. 9330
Wormald, Francis. (1071) (1375) 2171 2445 3150 3819a 10928 13984
Worman, Ernest James. 3414 3550
Worrall, John 1:643a

Worrall, Walter. 2:1530
Worshipful company of stationers, London see Stationers' company, London.
Worthen, T. John. 11936
Worthington, Greville. 1:4603; 13208
Wotton, Mabel E. 14554
Woude, S. van der. (5186b) (9393a) (11911)
Wray, Edith. 1:1631a
Wreden, W.P. 2259
Wrenn, Harold B. 1:339
Wrenn, John Henry. 1:339
Wrentmore, Charlotte Q. 13116
Wright, Andrew. 9342
Wright, Andrew. 1:8; 9342
Wright, Andrew H. 1:2743–4
Wright, Austin. 1:59
Wright, B.A. 12420 12429 12443
Wright, B.P. 8201
Wright, C. Hagberg. 10280
Wright, Cyril Ernest. (1071) (1395) 2445 3163 3328 5299 5793 8621 10290 11107 12658 12699a 13541 14228
Wright, Elma. 8028
Wright, Eugene Patrick. 1:4735n
Wright, G.M. 1:2063c
Wright, G.W. 1267 2425 8175 8395 12467
Wright, H. Bunker. 1:4465; 12912
Wright, Harold J.L. 340
Wright, Herbert G. 13652
Wright, James Osborne. 1:572
Wright, John and sons, Bristol. 6038
Wright, Julia C.T. 12545 12547
Wright, Louis Booker. 2:310 319 323–5 342 345; 2392a 3181 3235 7216
Wright, Lyle H. 1:2286; 13589
Wright, Reginald W.M. 2077
Wright, S.G. 12181 12827
Wright, S.T.H. 1:244
Wright, Thomas. 1:2329 2474p 2649 2704g 2976 3785g 4396b 4402–a 4775
Wright, W. 5905 12297
Wright, W.S. 3182
Wright, William Aldis. 6819 6828–9 12315 12318
Wright, William Henry Kearley. 1:886b 3416; 1095 2592 10645
Wrigley, Elizabeth S. 1:545 611 2374f; 8369
Writers and their work. 1:3
Wroot, Herbert E. 2405
Wroth, Lawrence Counselman. 1:1190 1379c, (144) 5373–4 6094 6111–12
Wurtsbaugh, Jewel. 13564 13569–70
Wyclif society, London. 1:5193
Wyllie, John Cook. 6156 12021 13695
Wyman, C. William Henry. 1:1139zy
Wyman, William Henry. 2:30
Wyndham, George. 14326
Wyndham, Maud. 8738

INDEX OF SUBJECTS

Subject headings are sorted letter by letter to the first stop (a space is not treated as a stop) but prefixes like 'bp., archbp., sir, ld.' and county identifiers are ignored in sorting. British places precede the identical names of localities elsewhere. Headings between single quotation marks like 'BLUE PENCIL' are technical terms of which the meaning is discussed in the items referred to. Item numbers printed in **bold** face refer to the entries under the same subject heading in the main arrangement of the bibliography. Item numbers within parentheses are references, usually in *BBLB*.

ABOMINATIONS OF THE JESUITS EXPOSED, 1820. 1463
ABREE, James, Canterbury, 1691–1798. 1159 **3811**
ABRIDGEMENTS *see* STATUTES.
ACADEMIC DRAMA *see* DRAMA, ACADEMIC.
ACADEMY, THE. 7905
ACADEMY OF COMPLEMENTS, 1640. 577
ACCIDENCES *see* GRAMMARS.
ACCOUNT BOOKS. 6749 6778
ACCOUNTING. **6724–6**
— Bibs. 1:**2080–5**
— Collns. 6724a
ACCOUNT OF THE CONDUCT OF MARLBOROUGH, 1742. 11519
ACCOUNT OF THE PROGRESS OF THE GOSPEL. 5065
ACERBI, Guiseppe, 1773–1846. 955
ACHELLY, Thomas, fl.1568–95–Bibs. 1:**2303g**
ACHILL, co. Mayo. **1960**
— Bibs. 1:**1106**
— Ptg. 1960
— — Bibs. 1:1106 1240
ACHILLES TATIUS, c.500.
— *Clitophon and Leucippe.* 583
ACHILL PRESS, 1837–66–Bibs. 1:**1240**
ACKERMANN, Rudolph, 1764–1834. **3812–18** 6192–3
— Bibs. 1:**1240a** 1738–9
— Paper. 3817
ACKERS, Charles, 1702?–59. **3819**
— Bibs. 1:**1240c**
ACT FOR THE ENCOURAGEMENT OF LEARNING, 1710 see COPYRIGHT ACT, 1709.
ACTON, sir Harold Mario Mitchell, 1904–
— *This chaos.* 4897e
ACTON, John Emerich Edward Dalberg, 1st baron Acton, 1834–1902.
— Bibs. 1:**2304**
— Collns. 3117
— Libr. 3117
ACTS *see* COPYRIGHT ACTS; STATUTES.
ADAM, Robert, 1728–92–Libr. 2239a 2720–1
ADAM, Robert Borthwick, 1863–1940–Libr. 1:397–8 3681b 3835x 3839 3841; 11099 11432 11436 11460 11463 13111
ADAMS, Frederick Baldwin, 1910– –Libr. 1:192
ADAMS, George Matthew, 1878–1962–Libr. 1:3491a; 10701 10705–6 10796 11246
ADAMS, John, 1746–1817–Libr. 1:3110
ADAMS, John Couch, 1819–92–Libr. 1:329
ADAMS, Katharine (mrs. Edward Webb), 1862–1952. **3819a–b**

ADAMS, Orion, Manchester, 1717–97. 3820 4088
ADAMS, Robert, fl.1588. 7521
ADAMS, Roger, Manchester, 1661?–1741. **3820**
ADAMS, Sarah Fuller (Flower), 1805–48–Bibs. 1:**2305**
ADAMS, William J., fl.1841–54. **3821**
ADDISON, Charles Greenstreet, d.1866.
— *Catherine Hayes.* 13976
— *Damascus and Palmyra.* 13969 13975
ADDISON, Joseph, 1672–1719 *see also THE SPECTATOR.* **8223–34** 13602
— Bibs. 1:**2306–7**
— *The campaign.* 8231
— — Bibs. 1:**2307**
— *Cato.* 8230
— *The drummer.* 8227
— Handwr. 13601
— Latin poems. 8229
— *Letter from Italy.* 8228
— Libr. 8234
— Mss. 8233
— *Miscellaneous works.* 8224
— Publ. 8224 8229
— Text. 8223 8230
— *Works.* 8225–6
ADELAIDE, S.A. STATE LIBRARY *see* SOUTH AUSTRALIA. STATE LIBRARY, Adelaide.
ADELMAN, Seymour, 1906– –Libr. 1:4946; 14019
'AD IMPRIMENDUM SOLUM.' 3516–17 3521 3528 3533
ADLER, Elkan Nathan, 1861– –Libr. 3038
ADPAR, Cards.–Bibs. 1:1280
— Ptg.–Bibs. 1:1280
ADVENTURER, THE. 11401 11490 11510
ADVERTISEMENTS. 1782 1841 2350 2375 3635 3657–8 4003 4453 4785 5202 5277 5432 5870 6503 6529 6750 7035 7267 7528 7800 7813 7910 8117 8725 10361 11719 12445 12517 12813 13631 13773 13864 13918 14186 14608
— *Bibliogr. descr.* 149 153–4
ADVOCATES' LIBRARY, Edinburgh *see* SCOTLAND. NATIONAL LIBRARY, Edinburgh. ADVOCATES' LIBRARY.
Æ., *pseud. of* George William Russell, 1867–1935. **8235–7**
— Bibs. 1:**2308–12**
— Collns. 8237
— *Hero in man.* 8236
— Mss.–Bibs. 1:**2311**
ÆLFRIC GRAMMATICUS, fl.1006.
— Ptg. 6418
— *Testimony of antiquity.* 6418
ÆLIANUS, Claudius, 2d cent. 13727

ÆNEAS SILVIUS PICCOLOMINI (pope Pius II), 1405–64. 2530
AEROGRAPHY. 6228
— Bibs. 1:1163
ÆSCHYLUS, 525–456 B.C. 12880
ÆSOP, fl.570 B.C. 880 3896 4023 4331 5321 6020
— Bibs. 1:777e 1248k 2459 4360b
AESTHETICS–Bibs. 1:2087–9a
AGAS, Ralph, 1540?–1621. 7523
AGATE, James Evershed, 1877–1947–Bibs. 1:2313
AGENDA FORMAT see FORMAT–Agenda.
AGENTS LITERARY see also BROWN, A. Curtis, 1866–1945; BURGHES, Alexander Macleod, fl.1881–1912; JERDAN, William, 1782–1869; PATERSON, Thomas Vary, 1811–80; PINKER, James Brand, 1863–1922; WATT, Alexander Pollock, 1834–1914. 3477 4921
AGGAS, Edward, fl.1564–1601.
— Selections from Seneca. 889
AGREEMENTS, PUBLISHERS' see PUBLISHERS' AGREEMENTS.
AGRICULTURE see also GARDENING. 1847 6727–37
— Bibs. 1:2090–8
— Newspapers–Bibs. 1:2096
— Scotland. 6735
— 1475–1700. 6727–32
— 1701–1800. 6735
AGRIPPA VON NETTESHEIM, Henrich Cornelius, 1486?–1535. 2187
AIKIN, Anna Lætitia (mrs. Barbauld), 1743–1825 see BARBAULD, Anna Lætitia (Aikin), 1743–1825.
AIKIN, John, 1747–1822. 7000a
— Description of Manchester and district. 1176
AINGER, Alfred, 1837–1904. 3879
AINSWORTH, William Harrison, 1805–82. 747 752 831a 2322 8238–43
— Auriol. 8240
— Beatrice Tyldesley. 8243
— Bibs. 1:672 2314–15a
— Collns. 7322a
— Illus. 4447
— Jack Sheppard. 8238
— Libr. 10010
— Mss. 8243
— Nell Gwynn. 8242
AIRDRIE, Lanark.–Paper see CRAIG, Robert, est. 1820.
AITKEN, George Atherton, 1860–1917.
— Libr. 2658 2760
AKENHEAD, Robert, Newcastle-upon-Tyne, fl.1722–71. 1322
AKENSIDE, Mark, 1721–70. 8244–5
— Bibs. 1:2316–d

— Pleasures of imagination. 8244–5
ALABASTER, William, 1567–1640.
— Spirculum tubarum. 7073
ALBEMARLE–Bibs. 1:1721
ALBERT FRANCIS CHARLES AUGUSTUS EMMANUEL, prince-consort of England, 1819–61–Libr. 2216
ALBION PRESSES see PRESSES, ALBION.
ALCHEMY. 6738–9
—Bibs. 1:2100–d
— Collns. 6739
— Mss. 6738
ALCOCK, Deborah, fl.1866–1910–Bibs. 1:2317
ALCOTT, Louisa May, 1832–88. 978
ALCUIN PRESS, Chipping Camden, est. 1928. 3822
ALDENHAM, Henry Hucks Gibbs, 1st baron, 1819–1907 see GIBBS, Henry Hucks, 1st baron Aldenham, 1819–1907.
ALDINE EDITION OF BRITISH POETS. 5414
ALDINE PUBLICATIONS. 3974
ALDINE PUBLISHING COMPANY, 1888–1933. 3823
ALDINGTON, Richard, 1892–1962.
— Bibs. 1:2318–19
— Eaten heart. 4897e
— Last straws. 4897e
ALDISS, Brian Wilson, 1925– –Bibs. 1:2320
ALDRICH, Thomas Bailey, 1836–1907. 10139
ALEMAN, Mateo, 1547–1614? 11666
ALEXANDER, James, 4th earl of Caledon, 1846–98–Libr. 2:1976
Alexander, Samuel, 1859–1938–Bibs. 1:2320a
ALEXANDER, sir William, earl of Stirling, 1567?–1640. 461 8246–7
— Supplement to Sidney's Arcadia. 8246–7
ALEXANDER, William, York, 1768–1841. 5621 8099
ALEXANDER, archbp. William, 1824–1911–Bibs. 1:2320b
ALEXANDER GRAMMATICUS, fl.1460–1531. 574
ALEXANDER TURNBULL LIBRARY, Wellington, N.Z. see also TURNBULL, Alexander Horsburgh, 1868–1918–Libr.
— Collns. 1:578 585 1259g 1315e 1997 2840p 3479d 3953 4047b 5008b–c 5017y; 3032 6497 9773 11948 12135 12436 14232
ALEYN, Charles, fl.1638.
— History of Henry the seventh. 8248
ALFRED, King of the West-Saxons, 849–901. 8249
—Bibs. 1:2320bx
ALFRICK, Worcs.–Paper. 1429a

ALIENS *see* BOOK-TRADE–Aliens.
—, LISTS OF *see* BOOK TRADE, LISTS–Aliens.
ALKEN, Henry Thomas, 1785–1851. **3824** 6192
— Bibs. 1:1738 **2320c**
ALLAN, David, 1744–96. **3825–6**
ALLDE, Edward, fl.1583–1624. **3827–8**
— *Shakespeare's Romeo and Juliet.* 2:1740
ALLEN, Charles, Bristol, fl.1678. **3829**
ALLEN, David, Belfast, est. 1857. 3830
ALLEN, George, 1837–1907. **3830a–b** 5704 13107
ALLEN, Reginald, 1905– –Libr. 10685
ALLEN, Thomas, 1542–1632–Mss. 3088
ALLEN, card. William, 1532–94–Bibs. 1:**2321**
ALLEN AND UNWIN, est. 1914. 5704 5889
ALLENHOLME PRESS, Wylam, Nthmb., est. 1956. **3831**
ALLESTREE, Richard, 1619–81. **8250–3**
— Bndng. 2234a
— *Governance of the tongue.* 2234a
— *Whole duty of man.* 8250–3
ALLIN, RALPH, fl.1585. **8254**
— *Haven of hope.* 8254
ALLINGHAM, William, 1824–89. **8255**
— Bibs. 1:**2322–3**
— *Flower pieces.* 8255
— *Music master.* 7420a
ALLOTT, Robert, fl.1600. **8256**
— *England's Parnassus.* 8256
ALLOTT, Robert, fl.1625–35. 4374
ALL SAINTS' CHURCH, Hereford *see* HEREFORD. ALL SAINTS' CHURCH.
ALL THE YEAR ROUND. 10119–20 10150 10168–9 14107
— Bibs. 1:1716k 3061 3096
ALMACK, Edward, 1852–1917–Libr. 2073
ALMANACS AND PROGNOSTICATIONS. **6740–62** 7577
— Bibs. 1:899a 1189a **1425–30**
— Aberdeen. 1642 1654
— Cambridge. 1057
— Dublin. 1743 1882–3
— Ireland. 1743 1764 1796 1800 1882–3
— — Bibs. 1:1427
— Oxford. 1354 1378
— Scotland. 1568 1699
— Wales. 1480 1493 6754
— 1475–1640 1057 6741 6752–3 6758
— — Bibs. 1:1426–b
— 1641–1700. 6740–1 6746 6762
— 1701–1800. 4183a
— 1801–1900. 6742 7577 7827
—, LITERARY. 6743
—, NAUTICAL. 6744 6757

ALMON, John, 1737–1805. **3832–3**
— *Letters of Junius.* 11633
ALMS (EXETER BOOK)–Ptg. 6416
ALNWICK, Nthmb. **1314–16**
— Bible. 4514
— Bibs. 1:**926m**
— Bksllng. *see* GRAHAM, Alexander, fl.1746–86.
— Newspapers. 1316
— Ptg. 1314–16 4210
— — Bibs. 1:926m
ALNWICK MERCURY. 4514
ALONSO OF MADRID, fl.1578. 969
ALPHONSUS MADRILENSUS *see* ALONSO OF MADRID, fl.1578.
ALSOP, Bernard, fl.1626–41. **3834**
ALTEMUS, Henry, Philadelphia, fl.1902. 11220
ALTHORP LIBRARY *see* SPENCER, George John, 2d earl Spencer, 1758–1834– Libr.
ALTON, Hants.–Paper. 1132a
ALTSCHUL, Frank, 1887– –Libr. 1:4202; 12235–6 12244
AMBLESIDE, Westm. DOVES COTTAGE *see* DOVES COTTAGE, Ambleside.
AMBULATOR, THE. 7717
AMERICA–Bibs. 1:533c 674m 1694e
— Maps–Bibs. 1:1765g 1772
AMERICA, NORTH. 560
AMERICANA. 606 651 10913
— Collns. 2724 2836 2844 2906 3026 3036 3266 3359a 13236
AMERICAN ANTIQUARIAN SOCIETY. LIBRARY–Collns. 1:1466 1893
— — ISAIAH THOMAS COLLECTION. 6793
AMERICAN COPYRIGHT *see* COPYRIGHT, AMERICAN.
AMERICAN LITERATURE *see* FOREIGN BOOKS PUBLISHED IN ENGLISH– United States
AMES, Joseph, 1689–1759. 3475
— Libr. 2599
— *Typographical antiquities.* 6060 6120
AMHERST, William Amhurst Tyssen– , 1st baron Amherst of Hackney, 1835–1908–Libr. 1:385
AMHERST COLLEGE. LIBRARY–Collns. 1:5173; 14521
AMIS, Kingsley, 1922– –Bibs. 1:1724p (**2323d**)
AMORY, Harcourt, 1855–1925–Libr. 1:2727
AMORY, Thomas, 1691?–1788. **8257**
— *Life of John Buncle.* 8257
AMPERSANDS *see* TYPE–Individual sorts.
AMPHLETT, James, 1776–1860. **8258**
— *Newspaper press.* 8258

AMSTERDAM, Netherlands. 852 855 860
7506 7691
— Publ. 9886
ANAGRAMS. 518
ANALECTA HIBERNICA. 1911
ANALYTICAL BIBLIOGRAPHY see
BIBLIOGRAPHY, ANALYTICAL.
ANASTATIC PRINTING see PRINTING,
ANASTATIC.
ANATOMY–Bibs. 1:2221 2228
ANBUREY, Thomas, fl.1776–89.
— Travels through America. 8212
ANDERSEN, Hans Christian, 1805–75. 899
— Bibs. 1:802
ANDERSON, Agnes (Campbell), Glasgow,
1637?–1716. 1712 **3835–6**
ANDERSON, Andrew, Glasgow, d.1676.
4722 4746
ANDERSON, George, Glasgow, d.1647.
3837 4746
ANDERSON, John, 1815–1905. 29 1846
ANDERSON, Robert, 1750–1830.
— Smollett's Works. 13499
ANDERSON GALLERIES, New York. 478
2742
ANDERTON, Lawrence, 1575–1643–Bibs.
1:**2323g**
ANDERTON, Thomas, Manchester, fl.1762.
3838
ANDREWE, Lawrence, fl.1527. 6056 6081
ANDREWES, bp. Lancelot, 1555–1626. **8259**
— Bibs. 1:**2323k**
— XCVI sermons. 8259
ANDREWS, Elizabeth, fl.1663–4. **3839**
ANDREWS, John, b.1583? **8260**
— A subpoena. 8260
ANGELO, Domenico, 1717–1804 see
TREMAMONDO, Domenico Angelo
Malevolti, 1717–1804.
ANGELONI, Luigi, 1759–1843. 951
— Bibs. 1:**827ac**
— Esortazioni patrie–Bibs. 1:827ac
ANGLESEY. **1517**
— Bibs. 1:**961**
— Ptg. 1517
— Publ. 5697
ANGLESEY, Arthur Annesley, 1st earl of,
1614–86 see ANNESLEY, Arthur, 1st earl
of Anglesey, 1614–86.
ANGLIA, EAST see EAST ANGLIA.
ANGLING. 4776 **6763–8** 14211
— Bibs. 1:**2101–2**
— Collns. 4774 6763 6765–7
— Mss. 6768
ANGLO-AMERICAN EDITIONS see
EDITIONS, ANGLO-AMERICAN.
ANGLO-INDIAN LITERATURE–Bibs.
1:333 1664 1668c

ANGLO-IRISH LITERATURE. 792
— Bibs. 1:4 1652t 1719 2035
ANGLO-LATIN LITERATURE see also
FOREIGN BOOKS PUBLISHED IN
BRITAIN–Classical–Latin; SHAKES-
PEARE, William, 1564–1616–WORKS IN
LATIN. 3493 5574 **6925** 9417 9443 10715
10717 10815 12381 12451 12638–9 13469
13897 13945
— Bibs. 1:346 1443 1579–80 1607–8 1611b
1727–8 1983 1986g 3729 5193
ANGLO-LATIN POETRY see POETRY,
ANGLO-LATIN.
ANGLO-SAXON see PRINTING IN
ANGLO-SAXON.
ANGLO-SAXON REVIEW–Bibs. 1:1721
ANGUS. **1665–9**
— Librs. see also INSHEWAN. 1633
ANGUS, George, Newcastle-upon-Tyne,
fl.1783–1829. 3840
ANGUS, William, Newcastle-upon-Tyne,
fl.1789. **3840**
ANGUS, William Craibe, d.1899–Libr.
1:2632
ANGUS LIBRARY see LONDON.
UNIVERSITY. REGENT'S PARK
COLLEGE. ANGUS LIBRARY.
ANNA BULLEN, 1681?–Ms. 7204
ANNALS OF AGRICULTURE–Bibs. 1:5212–13
ANNALS OF THE FINE ARTS. 7892
ANNAN, Dumf.–Bibs. 1:995
ANNE, queen of Great Britain and Ireland,
1665–1714. 729 2918
ANNESLEY, Arthur, 1st earl of Anglesey,
1614–86. 9393
ANNOTATED COPIES. 1085 1258 11009
11094 11097 11145 11711 12079 12750
12785–6 12867 12870 12995 13653 13720
13731 14235
ANNOUNCEMENTS see PROPOSALS.
ANNUAL ANTHOLOGY. 11824
— Bibs. 1:1903b
ANNUAL REGISTER. 6375a 7774 7799 7809
8970–1 8976 8979 8973
ANNUAL REVIEW–Bibs. 1:4740
ANNUALS. 5909 13328
— Bibs. 1:1847a 1915a 1916f 1927b
— Bndng. 2119
— Illus. 7430
— 1801–1900. 6742 7430 7830 7879 7931
ANNUALS, THE. 7852
ANONYMA AND PSEUDONYMA. 2776
6769–72 8205
— Bibs. 1:577 **1435–42g**
ANSELM, St., 1033–109–Bibs. 1:**2324**
ANSTEY, Christopher, 1724–1805. **8261–2**
— Bibs. 1:**2325–6d**
— Election ball. 8262

Vol. 1 = Bibliographies   2 = Shakespeare   4 = 1–8221   5 = 8222–14616

ANSTEY, Christopher, 1724–1805. *Epistle to Bampfylde.* 8262
— — Bibs. 1:2326
— Mss.–Bibs. 1:2326d
ANSTEY, F., *pseud.* of Thomas Anstey Guthrie, 1856–1934–Bibs. 1:2327–8
ANTHOLOGIES *see also* MISCELLANIES, *and titles of individual anthologies.* 6775 8025 8029
— Bibs. 1:1443 1595 2035 4392
ANTI-JACOBIN, THE. 7767 7807a 7893
ANTIMETHODIST BOOKS–Bibs. 1:2253 2270d
ANTIQUARIAN BOOKSELLERS *see* BOOKSELLERS, ANTIQUARIAN.
ANTIQUARIAN BOOKSELLERS' ASSOCIATION. 245 2357
— LECTURES. 3157
ANTIQUARIAN BOOKSELLING *see* BOOKSELLING, ANTIQUARIAN.
ANTIQUARIAN PAPER *see* PAPER–Double atlas.
ANTIQUITIES OF IONIA, 1769–1840. 5699
ANTISHAKESPEARIANA *see also* BACONIANA; DE VERE, Edward, 17th earl of Oxford, 1550–1604. 2:79
ANTRIM. 1845–50
— Bibs. 1:1026–30f
— Librs. 1845
ANTWERP, Belgium. 868 1215 5186b 5477 14349 14351
— Ptg. *see* DOESBORCH, Jan van, fl.1508–40?; KEMPE, Adrian van Boukhout, fl.1536–7; MIERDMAN, Stephen, c.1510–46.
— MUSÉE PLANTIN MORETUS–Collns. 4969
ANWYLL, Lewis, d.1641–Libr. 2:652p
ANWYLL, Lewis, d.1776. 8263
APICULTURE *see* BEES.
APOLOGIA PRO CONFESSIONE, 1629. 636
APOLOGY FOR TALES OF TERROR, 1799 see SCOTT, Sir Walter, 1771–1832.
APOLLONIUS, Pergaeus. 7548
APPEAL FROM THE COUNTRY TO THE CITY, 1710. 4835b
APPEL, Rudolph, fl.1848–92. 3841
APPLEBEE'S WEEKLY JOURNAL. 7747 7808
APPLEBY, Westm.
— GRAMMAR SCHOOL. LIBRARY. 2999
APPLEDORE PRESS, 20th cent. 3842
APPLEGATH, Augustus, 1788–1871. 3843 6312 7903
APPRENTICES AND APPRENTICESHIP *see also* STATIONERS' COMPANY, LONDON–Apprentices.
— Bndng. 5700

— Ptg. 1275 3819 4662b 5092 5541 5614 5884 6129 6134 6671
APPRENTICES, LISTS OF *see* BOOK TRADE, LISTS–Apprentices.
APSLEY MILL, Hemel Hempstead. 1139 4544–5a
AQUATINTING. 6187 6192–4 6210 6214
AQUATINTS. 3473 5260–a 6192 6226 10699
— Bibs. 1:1739 1750–3
ARABESQUES *see* TYPE–Arabesques.
ARABIAN NIGHTS ENTERTAINMENTS. 870a 874
ARABIC *see* PRINTING IN ARABIC.
ARBROATH, Angus.
— Librs. 1633
ARBUTHNET, Alexander, Edinburgh, fl.1576–85. 1591
ARBUTHNOT, Forster Fitzgerald, 1833–1901–Bibs. 1:2329
ARBUTHNOT, John, 1667–1735. 8264–5
— Bibs. 1:2330–1
— *History of John Bull*–Bibs. 1:2330
— *Memoirs of Martinus Scriblerus.* 8264
— — Bibs. 1:2331
— *Of the laws of chance.* 8265
ARCH, Arthur, fl.1792–1838. 8099
ARCH, John, fl.1792–1838. 8099
ARCHER, Edward, fl.1656. 7207
ARCHER, Michael, fl.1634. 8266
— *Dream of bounden duty.* 8266
ARCHER, Thomas, fl.1603–34–Bibs. 1:1873c
ARCHER, William, 1856–1924.
— Bibs. 1:1597 2331m
— Publ. 4858a
ARCHERY. 6776
— Bibs. 1:2103
ARCHIMEDES, 287–12 B.C. 12793
ARCHITECTURE. 6777–8a
— Bibs. 1:2087 2103b–d 2106
— Collns. 3030
— Newspapers. 6778a
ARCTIC–Bibs. 1:2104
ARCTURUS. 11672
ARDEN, George Baillie-Hamilton-, 11th earl of Haddington, 1827–1917–Libr. 1:1470
ARDEN OF FEVERSHAM. 7128 7130 7140 7173 7182 7189
ARDEN SHAKESPEARE. 2:1444
ARENTS, George, 1875–1960–Libr. *see also* NEW YORK. PUBLIC LIBRARY. ARENTS COLLECTION. 1:2288; 7434
ARETINO, Pietro, 1492–1556. 6002
— Bibs. 1:826d
ARGENTINA *see* SHAKESPEARE, William, 1564–1616–WORKS IN ARGENTINA.
ARGENTINE, JOHN, d.1508–Libr. 3213 3303 3392

ARGYLE, Archibald Campbell, 8th earl of, 1598–1661 see CAMPBELL, Archibald, marquis of Argyle and 8th earl, 1598–1661.

ARGYLE, Archibald Campbell, 9th earl of, d.1685 see CAMPBELL, Archibald, 9th earl of Argyle, d.1685.

ARIA DI CAMERA, 1727. 1784

ARIOSTO, Ludovico, 1474–1533.

— *Orlando furioso.* 2:1811; 4663 12406

ARISTOPHANES, fl.444–380 B.C. 882

ARISTOTLE, 384–22 B.C. 883

ARITHMETIC. 7541 7549 7551

ARK PRESS, Totnes, fl.1957. **3844–5**

ARLEN, Michael, 1895–1956. **8267–8**

— *London venture.* 8267–8

ARMAGH. **1851**

— Bibs. 1:**1031–9**

— Ptg.–Bibs. 1:1031–5

ARMENIAN *see* PRINTING IN ARMENIAN.

ARMIN, Robert, d.1615.

— Ptg. 2:1450

— *Two maids of Moreclacke.* 2:1450

ARMINIAN NUNNERY, 1641. 5083

ARMORIAL BOOKSTAMPS *see* BOOKBINDINGS, ARMORIAL.

ARMS, ROYAL *see* ROYAL ARMS.

ARMSTEAD, Henry Hugh, 1828–1905. 7420a

ARMSTRONG, A. Joseph, 1873–1954. 14454

ARMSTRONG, Archibald, d.1672.

— *Banquet of jests.* 7466

ARMSTRONG, John, 1635–98.

— *Select and family prayers.* 3697

ARMSTRONG, John, d.1758. **8269**

— *History of the island of Minorca.* 8269

ARMSTRONG, John, 1709–79–Bibs. 1:**2332**

ARMSTRONG, Martin Donisthorpe, 1882– –Bibs. 1:**2333–a**

ARMSTRONG, Terence Ian Fytton, 1912– .

— Bibs. 1:1409.

— Libr. 2912a

ARMSTRONG BROWNING LIBRARY *see* BAYLOR UNIVERSITY, Waco, Texas. LIBRARY–Collns.

ARMY AND SHAKESPEARE–Bibs. 2:100

ARNALL, William, 1715?–41? **3846**

ARNOLD, Matthew, 1822–88. **8270–309** 14387

— *Alaric at Rome.* 8284 8289 14399

— Bibs. 1:652 **2334–44**

— Collns. 8281 8294

— *Death of Balder.* 8309

— *Empedocles on Etna.* 8278

— Handwr. 8303

— *Horatian echo.* 8272

— Letters. 8275–6 8285 8288 8293 8306 8308

— — Bibs. 1:2336b 2338a 2343–4

— Mss. 8291 8300–1 8305

— — Bibs. 1:2336f

— *New Rome.* 8305

— *Oxford lectures on poetry*–Bibs. 1:2337a

— *Poems.* 8286 8295 8297

— — Bibs. 1:2339

— *Poems of Wordsworth.* 8271

— Publ. 8292 8304 8307

— *The river.* 8291

— *St. Paul and protestantism.* 8287

— *Scholar gypsy.* 8273 8282

— *Selected poems.* 8298

— — Bibs. 1:2341

— *Sohrab and Rustum.* 8302

— *Strayed reveller.* 8270 8279 8301

— — Bibs. 1:2342

— *Terrace at Berne.* 8300

— Text. 8277 8282 8300

— *Thyrsis.* 8299

ARNOLD, Samuel, 1740–1802. 10936

ARNOLD, Thomas, 1795–1842. 8274

ARNOLD, William Harris, 1854–1923–Libr. 471 2293 2572 2796

ARNOULD, sir Joseph, 1814–86. 13913

ARRANGEMENT OF BIBLIOGRAPHIES *see* BIBLIOGRAPHICAL ARRANGEMENT.

ARROWSMITH, Isaac, Bristol, fl.1834–71. **3847**

ARROWSMITH, James William, Bristol, d.1913. 3847

ART *see also* ILLUSTRATED BOOKS; ILLUSTRATORS.

— Bibs. 1:**2105–6**

ARTANE, co. Dublin. **1942**

— Ptg. 1942

ARTHUR, legendary king of Britain, fl.520. **8310**

— Bibs. 1:**2345–9a**

— Collns. 8310

ARTICLES DEVISED BY THE KING, 1536. 671

ARTIST, THE. 7818

ARTISTS. 3429

ART NOUVEAU. 6224

ART OF ANGLING–Ms. 6768

ART OF PRINTING, 1728. 1874

ARTS AND CRAFTS EXHIBITION, London. 2062

ART SOCIETY PRESS, Wimbledon, est. 1953–Bibs. 1:**1240g**

ARUNDEL, Henry Fitzalan, 12th earl of, 1511–80 *see* FITZALAN, Henry, 12th earl of Arundel, 1511–80.

ARUNDEL CASTLE, Sussex–Libr. 7989

ARUNDEL LIBRARY (STAFFORD HOUSE). 2673

ARUNDELL, Henry, 3d baron Arundell, 1605–91–Libr. 13859
ASCHAM, Roger, 1515–68. **8311–12**
— Bibs. 1:**2350–1a**
— *Schoolmaster.* 8311–12 11492
ASHBEE, Charles Robert, 1863–1942 *see* ESSEX HOUSE PRESS, Chipping Camden, Glos., 1898–1909.
ASHBEE, Henry Spencer, 1834–1900. **8313–15**
ASHBURNE HALL, Manchester *see* MANCHESTER. UNIVERSITY. ASHBURNE HALL.
ASHBURNER, Anthony, Kendal, fl.1763–8. **3848**
ASHBURNER, George, fl.1798–1812. **3849**
ASHBURNER, James, fl.1766. 3849
ASHBURNHAM, Bertram, 4th earl of Ashburnham, 1797–1878–Libr. 1:383 427; 2314 2354 2539–40 3400–1
ASHBURTON, Francis Denzil Edward Baring, 5th baron, 1866–1938 *see* BARING, Francis Denzil Edward, 5th baron Ashburton, 1866–1938.
ASHENDENE PRESS, Chelsea, 1894–1923. **3850–9** 6083 6103 6325 6463 6475 6488 6502
— Bibs. 1:**1241–5f** 1353
— Type. 6610
ASHLEY, Robert, 1565–1641
— *Louis Le Roy's De la vicissitude.* 6359
ASHLEY LIBRARY *see* WISE, Thomas James, 1859–1937–Libr.; BRITISH MUSEUM. ASHLEY LIBRARY.
ASHMOLE, Elias, 1617–92–Libr. 2266 2874
ASHRIDGE PARK, Herts.–Libr. 2857
ASKEW, James, Preston, fl.1913. 10304
ASPERNE, James, fl.1802–22. **3860**
ASHPITEL, Arthur, 1807–69–Libr. 1:1539
ASHWOOD, Bartholomew, fl.1638–78–Bibs. 1:**2352**
ASPLEY, William, d.1640. 2:1031
'ASSEMBLED' PLAYS. 2:850 853 856 886; 7143 7146
ASSEMBLY OF GODS, 1498. 5472
ASSINGTON, Suff.–Librs. 1400
ASSOCIATION COPIES *see also* PRESENTATION COPIES. 479 703 775 924 1571 2276–7 2284 2287 2296 2331 2344 2346 2386 2389 3021 3294 4990 6852 6887b 7421 7767 9029 9548 10198 10211 10334 11281 11694 11840 12723 13921 14115 14255 14340
— Bibs. 1:432 577; 2316
— Collns. 2308 2852 3003 3021 3038 3071 3160 3245 11313
ASSOCIATION FOR THE REPEAL OF TAXES ON KNOWLEDGE. 3546

ASSOCIATION OF CORRECTORS OF THE PRESS, est. 1854. **3861**
ASSOCIATION OF HAND PRINTERS, LONDON, 20th cent. **3862**
ASSOCIATION OF MASTER PRINTERS OF LONDON. **3863**
ASTELL, Mary, 1666?–1731. **8316–17**
— Bibs. 1:**2352a–3**
— *Serious proposal to the ladies.* 8317
ASTLE, Thomas, 1735–1803. 3475
ASTLEY, Worcs.–Paper. 1429a
ASTON, Henry, fl.1822–1906. **3864**
ASTROLOGY. **6779**
— Bibs. 1:**2108 2241a**
— Mss. 6779
ASTRONOMY–Bibs. 1:**2110**
ATHENÆUM, THE. 7894
— Bibs. 1:1716k
ATHENIAN GAZETTE. 7667
ATHLONE, co. Westmeath. **1986**
— Bibs. 1:**1133–4**
— Ptg.–Bibs. 1:1133–4
ATHY, co. Kildare–Bibs. 1:**1090**
— Ptg.–Bibs. 1:1090
ATKYNS, sir Robert, 1647–1711. 1117a
ATLAS, THE. 7884
ATLAS, DOUBLE *see* PAPER–Double atlas.
ATLASES *see also* MAPS. 4940g 7510 7522 8140 8211
AUBREY, John, 1626–97. **8318–20**
— Bibs. 1:**2353p**
— Libr. 8128 8318–20
AUCHENDINNY MILL, Midlothian. 1712
AUCHMUTY MILL, Markinch. 5880
AUCKLAND, N.Z.
— PUBLIC LIBRARY–Collns. 1:549 614; 2:1463
— ST. JOHN'S COLLEGE. LIBRARY–Collns. 1:580
— UNIVERSITY. LIBRARY–Collns. 1:579
AUCTION AND SALE CATALOGUES *see also* SALE CATALOGUES.
— Bibs. 1:340 1189a **1443a–58**
AUCTIONEERS AND BIBLIOGRAPHICAL DESCRIPTION. 137 493
AUCTION SALES *see* SALES, AUCTION.
AUCTIONEERS *see also* BIBLIOGRAPHICAL DESCRIPTION AND AUCTIONEERS *and names of individual auctioneers, e.g.* S. BAKER; G. G. DES GRAZ; R. H. EVANS; E. HODGSON; S. PATERSON; PUTTICK AND SIMPSON; J. SOTHEBY; R. WILDE. 1265 3679 3684
AUDEN, Wystan Hugh, 1907–73. **8321–3**
— Bibs. 1:1597 **2354–9** 3785b
— *Poems.* 8322–3
— Ptg. 8323
— Text. 8321

Vol. **1** = *Bibliographies*   **2** = *Shakespeare*   **4** = 1–8221   **5** = 8222–14616

BACON, Francis, 1561–1626. *Letter written out of England*. 8368
— Libr. 8364
— Mss. 8362
— Paper. 8369a
— Ptg. 6093 8366
— *Works*. 11409 11420
BACON, sir James, 1798–1895. **8370**
— *Memoirs of Byron*. 8370
BACON, Nathanael, fl.1669. **8371**
BACON, Richard McKenzie, Norwich, d.1844. 1306
BACONIANA–Bibs. 2:30 72 79
BADIUS ASCENSIUS, Jodocus, 1462–1535. 627
BAD QUARTOS *see* QUARTOS, BAD.
BAGE, Robert, 1728–1801–Bibs. 1:**2375**
BAGEHOT, Walter, 1826–77. **8372**
— Bibs. 1:**2376**
— *English constitution*. 8372
— Text. 8372
BAGFORD, John, 1650–1716. 2055 2058 2541 2600 2640 3111 3475 5168
BAGGULEY, G. T., Newcastle-under-Lyme, fl.1897. 2050 2123
BAGNELLS AND KNIGHTS, Cork, est. 1762. **3875**
BAGSTER, Samuel, 1772–1851. 1294 **3876**
BAILDON, John, fl.1531. 9865
BAILDON, William Paley, 1859–1924.
— *Baildon and the Baildons*. 6937a
BAILEY, Benjamin, 1791?–1853. 11691
BAILEY, Carolyn Sherwin, 1875–1961–Libr. *see* HILL, Carolyn Sherwin (Bailey), 1875–1961–Libr.
BAILEY, Frank, fl.1845–92. **3877**
BAILEY, John Eglington, 1840–88–Libr. 1:**2279h** 3367
BAILEY, Nathaniel. d.1742. **8373–4**
— *Dictionary*. 8373–4 11443
— Publ. 11443
BAILEY, Philip James, 1816–1902. **8375–6**
— Bibs. 1:**2377**
— Collns. 8375
— *Festus*. 997 8376
— — Bibs. 1:2377
BAILEY, Walter, c.1529–92. **8377–9**
— Bibs. 1:**2406**
BAILLIE, Joanna, 1762–1851.
— Bibs. 1:**2378**
— *Collection of Poems*. 8380
BAILLIE, William, 1723–1810. **3878**
BAILY, Walter, c.1529–92 *see* BAILEY, Walter, c.1529–92.
BAIN, Alexander, 1810–77–Bibs. 1:**2379**
BAIN, Andrew, 1810–58–Libr. 1:**1002a**
BAIN, James, 1794–1866. **3879**
BAIN, James Stoddart, fl.1940. 3879

BAINBRIDGE, John, 1582–1643.
— *Canicularia*. 6421
— *Proclus and Ptolemy*. 896a
— Ptg. 6421
BAINBRIGG, Reginald, 1545–1606–Libr. 2999
BAINE, John, Edinburgh, fl.1732–86. **3880**
BAINES, sir Edward, 1800–90–Bibs. 1:**2380**
BAKER, David Augustine, 1575–1641–Bibs. 1:**2380q**
BAKER, David Erskine, d.1782. **8381–2**
— *Biographia dramatica*. 7217 8381–2
BAKER, Frank, 1910– –Libr. 14293
BAKER, Henry, 1698–1774. **8383–4**
— Collns. 8384
— Letters. 9927
— Mss. 8383–4
— *The universe*. 8384
BAKER, James, fl.1795–1803. **3881**
BAKER, James Franklin Bethune–, 1861–1951–Bibs. 1:**2381**
BAKER, Samuel, 1712–78. 5706–a
BAKER, Thomas, fl.1622–60–Bibs. 1:**2382**
BAKER, Thomas, Southampton, fl.1774–1805–Bibs. 1:**1246**
BALA, Merion.–Ptg. *see* JONES AND COMPANY, 1803–4.
'BALAAM'. 3605
BALDWIN, archbp., d.1190.
— *Sermo de altaris sacramento*. 5645
BALDWIN, Anne, fl.1699–1713. 3471 3882
BALDWIN, Charles, fl.1799–1853. 9537
BALDWIN, Richard, c.1653–98. 3471 3882
BALDWIN, Robert, fl.1749–1810. 1294 3639a
BALDWIN, William, fl.1547–71. **8385**
— *Treatise of moral philosophy*. 8385
BALE, bp. John, 1495–1563 *see also* BALE PRESS, Marburg, fl.1528–46. 835 7141 **8386–91**
— Bibs. 1:**2383–4**
— *King John*. 8386–7 8390
— Libr. 8388
— *Resurrection of the mass*. 8389 8391
— Text. 8386
BALE PRESS, Marburg, fl.1528–46–Bibs. 1:**742** **1247–f**
BALES, Peter, 1547–1610? **8392–3**
— *Brachygraphy*. 2:421; 8393
— *Writing schoolmaster*. 8392 14265
BALFOUR, Arthur James, 1st earl of Balfour, 1848–1930–Bibs. 1:**2385**
BALL, Henry William, Barton-upon-Humber, 1833–1914. **3883**
BALL, William, fl.1642–51.
— *Brief treatise concerning the regulating of printing*. 3559

BAPTIST MISSIONARY SOCIETY. LIBRARY. 3052

BARBAULD, Anna Lætitia (Aikin), 1743–1825. 7000a 14613
— Bibs. 1:2386f

BARBER, Mary, 1690?–1757. 8398–9
— True tale. 8398

BARBOUR, John, 1316?–95. 8400
— Bibs. 1:2387–8
— Bruce. 8400
— — Bibs. 1:2388

BARCLAY, Alexander, 1475?–1552. 8401

BARCLAY, John, 1582–1621. 8402
— Argenis. 8402
— — Bibs. 1:2388m 2388q
— Bibs. 1:2388m–q

BARCOMBE, Sussex–Paper. 1412

BARFORD, Hants–Paper. 1132a

BARHAM, Richard Harris, 1788–1845 see INGOLDSBY, Thomas, pseud.

BARING, Francis Denzil Edward, 5th baron Ashburton, 1866–1938–Libr. 2556

BARING, Maurice, 1874–1945. 8403
— Bibs. 1:684 2389–90

BARKER, Christopher, fl.1640–80. 3892

BARKER, Harley Granville, 1877–1946–Bibs. 1:2390m–n

BARKER, mrs. Jane, fl.1688–1736. 8404–5

BARKER, Robert, fl.1589–1645. 3892 5011 6887 8366

BARKER, William, fl.1539–72. 871b
— Bibs. 1:2391

BARKING, Essex. ABBEY. LIBRARY. 3375

BARKSDALE, Clement, 1609–87. 1117a

BARKSTEAD, sir John, d.1662. 708

BARLAS, John Evelyn, 1860–1914. 8406
— Bibs. 1:2391n

BARLEY, William, fl.1586–1614. 3893–5

BARLOW, Francis, 1626?–1702. 3896–7
— Bibs. 1:1248k

BARLOW, George, 1847–1913–Bibs. 1:2392

BARLOW, John, d.1629–Bibs. 1:2393

BARNARD, William, 1774–1849. 3898

BARNBOUGLE CASTLE, Edinburgh–Libr. 3323 8489a

BARNES, Joseph, Oxford, fl.1584–1618. 1373 3899

BARNES, Robert, 1495–1540. 8407–8
— Supplication unto king Henry. 8408

BARNES, Robert, 1840–95. 7420a

BARNES, William, 1801–86. 3900
— Bibs. 1:2394–a

BARNSLEY, Yorks.
— Bibs. 1:948
— Ptg.–Bibs. 1:948

BARNSTAPLE, Devon.–Paper. 1101x

BARODA. CENTRAL LIBRARY–Collns. 2:42

BARON, Bernard, 1700–62. 3901

BARRET, John, d.1580? 8409
— Alveary. 8409

BARRETT, Charlotte (Francis), fl.1904–Libr. 9001

BARRETT, Eaton Stannard, 1786–1820. 8409a
— Bksllng. 8409a
— Letters. 8409a

BARRETT, Elizabeth, 1806–61 see BROWNING, Elizabeth (Barrett), 1806–61.

BARRETT, William, fl.1597–1624.
— Southwell's Short rule. 13549

BARRIE, sir James Matthew, 1860–1937. 758 778 783 8410–24
— Auld licht idylls. 8413
— Better dead. 8420
— Bibs. 1:684 1597 2395–9a
— Collns. 8421 8423–4
— Courage. 8412
— Dear Brutus. 8418
— Jane Annie. 8415
— Libr. 8417
— Mss. 781 8411
— Superfluous man. 8416
— Tillyloss scandal. 8419
— Twelve pound look. 8411
— Wedding guest. 8422

BARRINGTON, sir Thomas, fl.1602–44–Libr. 2980

BARROIS, Pierre-Théophile, Paris, fl.1776–83. 3652

BARROW, Isaac, 1630–71. 884

BARROW-IN-FURNESS, Lancs. 1180a

BARRY, Michael Joseph, 1817–89–Bibs. 1:2399t

BARTHOLOMÆUS ANGLICUS, fl.1230–50. 6026 8425
— De proprietatibus rerum. 8425

BARTHOLOMEW, Augustus Theodore, 1882–1933–Libr. 1:2668

BARTLET, John, 1716–72.
— Gentleman's farriery. 5443

BARTLETT, Roger, Oxford, c.1630–1712. 3902–5

BARTLETT, William, 1679–1720–Bibs. 1:2400

BARTOLOZZI, Francesco, 1726–1815. 3906

BARTON, Thomas Pennant, 1803–69–Libr. 2:329 608; 610

BARTON-UPON-HUMBER, Lincs.
—Bksllng. see BALL, Henry William, 1833–1914.

BASEL, Switzerland. 840 865 8038
— PUBLIC LIBRARY–Collns. 2:648
BASIA. 612

BEAUMONT, Cyril William, 1891–1976. **3967**
— Bibs. 1:**1261–2**
BEAUMONT, Francis, 1584–1616, and John FLETCHER, 1579–1625. 167 **8443–77**
— *Beggar's bush.* 8466
— Bibs. 1:**2411–13a**
— *The captain.* 8471
— *The coxcomb.* 8466
— *Cupid's revenge.* 8466
— *King and no king.* 8447 8461 8466 8474
— *Knight of the burning pestle.* 8466
— *Love's cure.* 8471
— *Love's pilgrimage.* 8466
— *Maid's tragedy.* 8445 8465–6 8469 8475
— Mss. 8455
— *Noble gentleman.* 8466
— *Philaster.* 8443 8459 8466 8470
— Ptg. 8451 8455–8 8469–70 8472 8474 8476–7
— *Scornful lady.* 8466
— *The sun which doth the greatest comfort.* 8460
— *Tamer tamed.* 2:1880
— Text. 8443–50 8459 8472 8475
— *Thierry and Theodoret.* 8447 8466 8472
— *Woman hater.* 8466
— *Works, 1647.* 8451–2 8455–8 8476–7 11819 14125
— *Works, 1679.* 8453
BEAUMONT PRESS, est. 1917 *see* BEAUMONT, Cyril William, 1891–1976.
BEAUTIES OF MAGAZINES. 1623
BEAUTIES OF THE PRESS, 1800. 1753
BECCLES, Suff.–Librs. 1400
BECKE, Edmund, fl.1550. 6808
BECKET, Thomas, fl.1760–76. 3639a 6510a
BECKETT, Samuel Barclay, 1906– . **8477a**
— Bibs. 1:1597 **2413y–14k**
— Collns. 8477a
— *Whoroscope.* 4897e
BECKFORD, William, 1759–1844. **8478–92**
— *Al Raoui.* 8479 8484
— Bibs. 1:**2414y–18a**
— Bndng. 8486
— Collns. 2374 3879 8481 8485
— Letters. 8487
— Libr. 2314 8489a–90
— Publ. 8487
— *Vathek.* 8478–a 8480 8481a–2 8488–9 8492
BECKS, Alfred, 1845–1925–Libr. 7091
BECKS, George, 1834–1904–Libr. 1:1587d
BEDE, The venerable, 673–735. 3350a **8493–5**
— Bibs. 1:**2420**
— Handwr. 8495
— *Life of St. Cuthbert.* 8494
— Ptg. 8494

BEDE, Cuthbert, *pseud. of* Edward Bradley, 1827–89. **8496**
— Bibs. 1:**2421**
BEDELL, bp. William, 1571–1642. 8729
BEDFORD, Beds.
— Librs. 2952
— COLLEGE OF EDUCATION. LIBRARY–Collns. 1:1573g
— PUBLIC LIBRARY–Collns. 1:2613
BEDFORD, Francis, 1799–1883. 2028 **3968–70**
BEDFORD, Francis Russell, 2d earl of, 1527?–85 *see* RUSSELL, Francis, 2d earl of Bedford, 1527?–85.
BEDFORDSHIRE. **1038**
— Bibs. 1:**872–a**
BEDHAMPTON, Hants.–Paper. 1132a
BEE, THE. 10763 10774
BEECHING, Henry Charles, 1859–1919.
— Bibs. 1:**2422**
— *Selection from Daniel and Drayton.* 9794
BEERBOHM, sir Henry Maximilian, 1872–1956. 471 **8497–502**
— Bibs. 1:684 **2425–33**
— *Carmen becceriense.* 8500
— *Happy hypocrite.* 8498
— *Works.* 8497
BEES. 6729 **6797–8**
— Bibs. 1:**2111–12**
BEESTON, Ches. 6824
BEETHOVEN, Ludwig van, 1770–1827–Bibs. 1:1839 2068
BEETON, Isabella Mary (Mayson), 1836–65. 5941b
BEEVER, John, Coniston, 1793–1857. 1165a
BEGGS, Thomas, 1789–1821–Bibs. 1:**2434**
BEHAN, Brendan, 1923–64–Bibs. 1:1597
BEHN, Aphra (Amis), 1640–89. **8503–4**
— *Emperor of the moon.* 8503
— *Lycidus.* 8504
— *Remains.* 10804
BEILBY, Ralph, Newcastle-upon-Tyne, 1744–1817. 4040
BEILBY AND BEWICK, Newcastle-upon-Tyne, 1777–97. 4040
BEINECKE, Edwin John, 1886–1970–Libr. 1:4813; 7174
BEINECKE, Walter, 1918– –Libr. 8424
BELDORNIE PRESS, Ryde, 1840–3. **3971–a**
BELFAST, co. Antrim *see also* BOOK TRADE, LISTS–Belfast. **1846–50**
— Bibs. 1:**1026–3of**
— Librs. 1850 2450
— Newspapers–Bibs. 1:1026–8
— Ptg. 1849
— — Bibs. 1:1026–30 103of
— MUSEUM. LIBRARY–Collns. 1:1030

BENTLEY, George, 1828–95. **3994** 3995
10053
BENTLEY, John, fl.1588–95. **8518**
BENTLEY, Richard, d.1697. 3995
BENTLEY, Richard, 1662–1742. 4162 4171
5870 **8519–21**
— Bibs. 1:**2449–a**
— Bksllng. 8519
— *Dissertation on the letters of Philaris.* 7338
— *Milton's Paradise lost.* 8520 12348
BENTLEY, Richard, 1708–82.
— *Gray's Poems.* 10850
BENTLEY, Richard, 1748–1871–Bibs.
1:**1264p**
BENTLEY, Richard, 1794–1871 *see also*
BENTLEY'S MISCELLANY; BENTLEY'S
QUARTERLY REVIEW; BENTLEY'S
STANDARD NOVELS; COLBURN AND
BENTLEY, 1829–98. 2374 **3995–4004** 9991
10076 10088 10103 10131 10143
BENTLEY, Richard, 1854–1936. **4005**
BENTLEY, Samuel, 1785–1868. 3995
BENTLEY, William, fl.1639–55. 3995
BENTLEY HOUSE, C.U.P. *see* CAMBRIDGE
UNIVERSITY PRESS. BENTLEY HOUSE.
BENTLEY MILL, Binsted. 1132a
BENTLEY'S MISCELLANY. 9991 10090
— Bibs. 1:1716k
BENTLEY'S QUARTERLY REVIEW–Bibs.
1:1716k
BENTLEY'S STANDARD NOVELS. 3996
BENTON, Josiah Henry, 1843–1917–Libr.
1:1251n 1515–16
BEOLEY, Worcs.–Paper. 1429a
BERE MILL, Whitchurch. 1132a
BERESFORD, John Davys, 1873–1947–Bibs.
1:681 **2450**
BERG, Albert Ashton, 1872–1950 *see* NEW
YORK. PUBLIC LIBRARY. BERG
COLLECTION.
BERKELEY, bp. George, 1685–1753. **8522–33**
— Bibs. 1:**2451–4b**
— Collns. 8524
— Handwr. 8532
— *Irish patriot.* 8525
— Letters. 8527
— — Bibs. 1:2451c
— Libr. 8526–9
— Mss. 8525
— — Bibs. 1:2452
— *Queries relating to a national bank.* 8522
— *The querist.* 8523 8533
— *Siris.* 8530
— Text. 8533
BERKELEY, sir William, 1609–77. **8534**
— *Lost lady.* 8534
BERKENHEAD, sir John, 1617–79–Bibs.
1:**2454g**

BERKSHIRE. **1039–42**
— Bibs. 1:**873–4**
— Newspapers. 1039–40
BERLIN. STAATSBIBLIOTHEK–Collns.
2:613
BERNARD, Francis, 1627–98–Libr. 3670
BERNARD, Richard, 1568–1642–Bibs.
1:**2455–6**
BERNE, Switz. CITY AND UNIVERSITY
LIBRARY. 3254 3278
BERNERS, Juliana, b.1388? **8535**
— *Book of St. Albans.* 5607 6029 6192 7089
8535
— Illus. 6192
— *Treatise on fishing.* 3857
BEROL, Alfred C., 1892–1974–Libr. 1:674m
4483a
BERROW'S WORCESTER JOURNAL. 1431
BERRY, William, fl.1670–1700. 6550
BERTHELET, Thomas, fl.1510–55. **4006–11**
5461 6056 6081
— Bibs. 1:**1265**
— Bndng. 4007
— Type. 4008
BERTRAM, George, Edinburgh, fl.1808–78.
3785 4011g
BERTRAM, William, Edinburgh, est. 1821.
3785 **4011g**
BERWICK, Nthmb. **1317**
— Ptg. 1317 4210
BERWICKSHIRE– Bibs. 1:**986–8**
— Ptg.–Bibs. 1:986
BESANT, Annie (Wood), 1847–1933–Bibs.
1:**2457**
BESANT, sir Walter, 1836–1901.
— Collns. 7322a
— Illus. 7420
— *Westminster.* 7420
BESSEMER, Anthony, fl.1766–1832. **4012**
BEST, Paul, 1590?–1657.
— *Mysteries discovered.* 12410
BETA-RADIOGRAPHY. 3784 3809
BETHLEHEM, Pa. LEHIGH UNIVERSITY
see LEHIGH UNIVERSITY, Bethlehem,
Pa.
BETHUNE-BAKER, James Franklin,
1861–1951 *see* BAKER, James Franklin
Bethune-, 1861–1951.
BETJEMAN, sir John, 1906– . **8536**
BETLEY HALL, Staffs.–Libr. 754
BETSON, Thomas, fl.1500. 568 3202
BETTERTON, Thomas, 1635?–1710. **8537**
— *The prophetess.* 8537
— *Shakespeare's Hamlet.* 2:1193
BEVAN, Joseph Gurney, 1753–1814. 8097
BEVAN, Paul, 1783–1868–Libr. 8097
BEVERLEY, Robert MacKenzie, d.1868–Bibs.
1:**2457m**

Vol. **1** = *Bibliographies*   **2** = *Shakespeare*   **4** = 1–8221   **5** = 8222–14616

BEVIS OF HAMPTON. 1:539b
BEW, John, fl.1774–9. 1294 **4013**
BEWICK, John Newcastle-upon-Tyne, 1760–95. **4014**
BEWICK, Thomas, Newcastle-upon-Tyne, 1753–1828. 274 4514 6201 6207 6220 7022
— Bibs. 1:**2458–9**
— *Fables of Æsop.* 4023
— — Bibs. 1:2459
— *Chillingham bull.* 4028
— Collns. 4041
— *General history of quadrupeds.* 4036
— — Bibs. 1:2459
— *History of British birds.* 4031
— — Bibs. 1:2459
— *History of Pamela.* 4035 4038
— Letters. 4047
— *New invented hornbook.* 4018
— *Water birds.* 6712
BEYNON, Thomas, fl.1763–7–Libr. 3216
BIBLE *see also* BOOK TRADE, LISTS–Bible; TAYLOR, John, 1578–1653. 2:1005; 2343 6260 **6799–894**
— Alnwick. 4514
— Bibs. 1:756 920 1028 **1468z–506d**
— Birmingham. 3912 3929
— Bksllng. 3692–3
— Bndng. 5700 9391
— Cambridge. 1062 4165 6816 6865 6866 6891
— Collns. *see also* BRITISH AND FOREIGN BIBLE SOCIETY, London. LIBRARY. 3039 3052 6807 6811–12 6823 6835–6 6850 6856 6859 6868 6878 6881 6888 6893 6894 12323 12380
— Copyright. 3540
— Illus. 5851 6825 6872 6874 6884
— Ireland. 1748 4084 6858a 6867a 8729
— — Bibs. 1:1028
— Oxford. 2156 2176 3719 5333 5362 6447 6818 6851 6868 6891
— Ptg. 5333 5362 6116 6121b 6195–6 6447 6848 6851 6863 6865 6867a 6868 6873 6882 6889 6892 11956
— Publ. 3540 6891
— Scotland. 1565 1572 1703
— Versions. 6868 6886
— — Bibs. 1:1468z
— — Authorized. 6799 6802 6834 6837 6840 6844 6865 6873 6880 6887
— — — Bibs. 1:1469
— — Becke's. 6808
— — Bishops'. 6804a 6828 6868 6890
— — Catholic. 6873
— — Coverdale's. 6800–1 6803 6819 6821 6829 6839 6860–4 6868 6874
— — — Bibs. 1:1483g–h

— — Cranmer's *see* Great.
— — Cromwell's. 6810 6815
— — Douai *see* Rheims and Douai.
— — Geneva. 6804 6867a 6868 6873 6887b 6889
— — Great. 6800 6810 6815 6817 6868 6871 6874
— — Hieroglyphic. 6809
— — John Bull's. 6830
— — King James' *see* Authorized.
— — 'Leap frog'. 6813
— — Matthew's. 6868–a
— — — Bibs. 1:1485i
— — 'Mayflower'. 6887b
— — New Cambridge. 6866
— — New English. 3540
— — Polyglot. 6877
— — — Bibs. 1:1471
— — Printer's. 6833 6876
— — Revised. 6865 6868
— — Rheims and Douai. 6858a 6868 8364
— — — Bibs. 1:1481d
— — Scattergood's. 6826
— — 'She'. 6802
— — — Bibs. 1:1469
— — Soldiers'. 6814
— — Taverner's *see* Cromwell's.
— — Thumb *see* TAYLOR, John, 1578–1653. *Verbum sempiternæ.*
— — Tomson's. 6887b
— — 'Treacle'. 6820 6847
— — Tyndale's. 6857 6873
— — Universal family. 6853
— — 'Vinegar'. 6818 6868
— — Vulgate. 6869
— — 'Wicked'. 6799 6887
— Wales *see also* BIBLE, WELSH. 1517
— 1475–1640. 4781 5132 6195–6 6799–804a 6808 6810 6815 6817 6819 6821–2 6823–4 6828–9 6832–4 6837 6839–40 6842–5 6847 6854 6857 6860–3 6865 6867–8a 6871 6873–4 6876 6879–80 6884–5 6887–b 6889–90 6892–3
— 1475–1700. 258 860 6121b 8729
— 1640–1700. 1062 2176 6814 6816 6826 6849 6877
— — 1701–1800. 1317 1449a 3912 3929 5851 6121b 6818 6821 6831 6848 6851 6865 6868 8821
— 1801–1900. 2156 4514 5700 6846 6865 6883
— 1901– . 4588–9 6447 6866 6891
BIBLE. O.T. **6895–904**
— — Versions.
— — — Tyndale's. 6895
— — — BOOKS OF SOLOMON. 6897
— — — PENTATEUCH. 6895

BIBLE. O.T. PSALMS. 6898–904 8068
14471
— — — Bibs. 1:**1505–6** 1513–14 1517 1733
— — — Collns. 6898
— — — Mss. 6904
— — — Scotland. 1569 1651
— — — — Bibs. 1:1513
— — — Wales. 1476
— — — 1475–1640. 4522 4843 5079a
6899–901
— — SEPTUAGINT. 6896
— N.T. 829 834 **6905–16** 10443
— — Bibs. 1:1507a
— — Bndng. 2000
— — Ireland. 1879 1932–3 6858a
— — — Bibs. 1:1481d
— — Scotland. 8087
— — — Bibs. 1:965–1009 2290
— — Versions.
— — — Bishops'. 6911–12
— — — Douai see Rheims and Douai.
— — — Rheims and Douai. 6858a 6914–16
— — — Tomson's. 6867a
— — — Tyndale's. 6868 6905–6 6908–9
— — 1475–1640. 6905–9 6911–12 6914 6916
— — 1641–1700. 6913 8177
— — 1701–1800. 6914–15
— — 1801–1900. 6858a 6915
—, LITHUANIAN. 957–9a
—, WELSH see also WALES–Bible. 1449a
1453 4506 5557
— Bibs. 1:**1507–a**
BIBLE IN LITERATURE–bibs. 1:1589f
1596
BIBLE PATENT. 1285
BIBLIOGRAPHER, THE. 1:85
BIBLIOGRAPHERS AND EDITORS see also
individual bibliographers, e.g. Adam, R.;
Aitken, G. A.; Ames, J.; Anderson, J.;
Ashbee, H. S.; Beattie, W.; Bennet, T.;
Birkbeck, M.; Blacker, B. H.; Blades, W.;
Bohn, H. G.; Bradshaw, H.; Brushfield, T.
N.; Capell, E.; Carter, H. G.; Carter, J.
W.; Chalmers, G.; Chapman, R. W.;
Christie, R. C.; Clarke, A.; Cole, G. W.;
Collier, J. P.; Collier, R. G. C.; Copinger,
W. A.; Courtney, W. P.; Cox, E. M.;
Crone, J. S.; Davies, J. H.; De Morgan,
A.; De Ricci, S. M. R. R.; Dibdin, T. F.;
Dix, E. R. McC.; Duff, E. G.; Edmond, J.
P.; Fulton, J. F.; Furness, H. H.; Garnett,
R.; Gibson, S.; Gollancz, sir I.; Greg, sir
W. W.; Hayward, J. D.; Hazlitt, W. C.;
Heawood, E.; Herbert, W.; Hobson, G.
D.; Horne, T. H.; Isaac, F. S.; Jackson, W.
A.; Johnson, A. F.; Johnson, S.; Jones, J.
I.; Keynes, sir G. L.; Kirkpatrick, T. P. C.;
Laing, D.; London, W.; Lowndes, W. T.;

Macalister, sir J. Y. W.; McKerrow, R. B.;
Madan, F.; Madden, sir F.; Malone, E.;
Martindell, E. W.; Munby, A. N. L.;
Nixon, H. M.; Nowell-Smith, S.
H.; ÓCasaide, S.; O'Hegarty, P. S.; Osler,
sir W.; Paton, G.; Peet, W. H.; Petherick,
E. W.; Pollard, A. W.; Pollard, H. G.;
Povey, K.; Prideaux, W. F.; Quaritch, B.;
Reed, T. B.; Ritson, J.; Roberts, sir S. C.;
Roberts, W.; Rowe, N.; Sadleir, M. T. H.;
Savage, E. A.; Sayle, C. E.; Shepherd, R.
H.; Sherrington, sir C.; Scholderer, J. V.;
Scott, J.; Sisson, C. J.; Slater, J. H.; Smith,
J.; Steevens, G.; Watt, R.; Whiting, J.;
Williams, sir H. H.; Wilson, F. P.; Wor-
mald, F.; Worthington, G. **1–96** 188 7090
BIBLIOGRAPHERS–Bibs. *see* Bennett, H. S.;
Bigger, F. J.; Blades, W.; Crone, J. S.;
Dibdin, T. F.; Dix, E. R. McC.; Duff, E.
G.; Greg, sir W. W.; Hazlitt, W. C.;
James, M. R.; Johnson, A. F.; Keynes, sir
G. L.; McKerrow, R. B.; Madan, F.;
Mores, E. R.; Morison, S. A.; Plomer, H.;
Pollard, A. W.; Povey, K.; Sadleir, M. T.
H.; Sayle, C.; Scholderer, J. V.; Simpson,
P.; Wilson, J. D.; Wise, T. J.
BIBLIOGRAPHERS OF SCIENCE. 8144
8153
BIBLIOGRAPHICAL ARRANGEMENT.
98–9 110–11 134 164 188 254 259 266 269
272 1015
BIBLIOGRAPHICAL DESCRIPTION *see also*
BIBLIOGRAPHY–Terms and concepts. 7
97–174 183 257–9 266–7 269–72 2300 8501
9925
— Advertisements. 149 153–4
— Bndngs. 97 124 128 149 169 2119 2192
2240 2242
— Books–1475–1500. 97 100 116–17 126 128
131 133 143 156
— — 1475–1640. 101 103 6055
— — 1475–1700. 143–4 255 2978
— — 1701–1800. 143 162 9925
— — 1801–1900. 143 149 2374
— — 1901– 127 143
— Books in parts. 149
— Botanical books. 158 162–3 368
— Cancels. 149 257
— Catchwords. 97 128 143
— Centre rules. 140
— Chainlines. 155
— Collations. 124 130 143 254
— Colophons. 134 143 254
— Colour. 128 169
— Columns. 128
— Corrections. 128
— Dates. 97 128 254 257
— Explicits. 143

BIBLIOGRAPHY AND LINGUISTICS. 236
— AND LITERATURE. 189 229–30 268 298
— AND MUSIC. 7615a 7617a–b 9166
— AND NATURAL HISTORY. 239
— AND SCIENCE. 221 8144 8153 8159
— AND SCHOLARSHIP. 193
— AND TEXTUAL CRITICISM. 234
— AND TYPOGRAPHY. 6637 6650 6716
— AS SCIENCE. 134 209 225
— IN WALES. 1450 1455
BIBLIOTHECA CLASSICA. 3974
BIBLIOTHECA DRUMMENIANA. 2672
BIBLIOTHECA HARLEIANA, 1745. 11398
BIBLIOTHECA ILLUSTRATA. 6510a
BIBLIOTHECA JACKSONIANA *see* JACKSON, William, 1823–90–Libr.
BIBLIOTHECA LINDESIANA. 100 2570 2685 3095
— Bibs. 1:1760e
— Collns. 1:337 1460 1534 1870 2045–6; 1994 8171 8178
BIBLIOTHECA LLWYDIANA *see* LLOYD, John, 1750–1815–Libr.
BIBLIOTHECA MEADIANA *see* MEAD, Richard, 1673–1754–Libr.
BIBLIOTHECA MEDICI. 542
BIBLIOTHECA PEPYSIANA see CAMBRIDGE. UNIVERSITY. MAGDALENE COLLEGE. PEPYSIAN LIBRARY.
BIBLIOTHECA RABBINICA, 1629. 2855
BIBLIOTHECA UNIVERSALIS, 1688. 9498
BICKHAM, George, 1684–1758
— *Musical entertainer.* 7615a
BICKHAM, George, 1735–67.
— *Birds-eye views.* 7525
BICKHAM, George, d.1769. 8538–40
— *British monarchy.* 7525
— *Universal penman.* 8538–40
BIELEFELD. STADTBÜCHEREI–Collns. 2:135a
BIERCE, Ambrose, 1842–1914?
— *Fiend's delight.* 1005
— *Nuggets and dust.* 1005
BIGGER, Francis Joseph, 1863–1926–Bibs. 1:2459r
BIGGES, Walter, d.1586.
— *Drake's West Indian voyage.* 10313
BIGLAND, Ralph, 1711–84. 1117a
BIJOU ALMANAC. 7827
BILDERBECK, James Bourdillon, fl.1902–11. 9419a
BILL, John, 1576–1630. 4048–9
BILLINGSLEY, sir Henry, d.1606. 884
BILL MILLS, Herts. 1138
BILLS *see* POSTERS.
BILSON, Thomas, 1547–1616. 8541
— *True difference.* 8541

BINDERS, etc. *see* BOOKBINDERS.
BINDING *see* BOOKBINDING.
BINSTED, Hants.–Paper. 1132a
BINYON, Robert Laurence, 1869–1943–Bibs. 1:2460
BIOGRAPHIES AND AUTOBIOGRAPHIES–Bibs. 1:1508–11c 1668c
BIOGRAPHY AND BIBLIOGRAPHY. 11111
BIOREN AND MADAN SHAKESPEARE. 2:793
BIRCH, Thomas, 1705–66. 11506
— *General dictionary.* 7082
BIRCH HALL, Essex–Libr. 2816
BIRCHLEY HALL PRESS, Wigan, 1604–36. 4050–1
— Bibs. 1:1266
BIRD, Cuthbert Hilton Golding-, 1848–1939–Bibs. 1:2461
BIRDS. 6917–21
— Bibs. 1:2114–21
BIRDSALL AND SON, Northampton, fl.1890. 4052
BIRKBECK, George, 1776–1841. 2443
BIRKBECK, Morris, 1734–1816. 17
BIRKENHEAD, Frederick Edwin Smith, 1st earl of, 1872–1930 *see* SMITH, Frederick Edwin, 1st earl of Birkenhead, 1872–1930.
BIRKHEAD, Henry, 1617?–96. 8542
— *Female rebellion.* 8542
— Mss. 1:1606b
BIRLEY, sir Robert, 1903– . 3332
BIRMINGHAM, Warws. 1415–20
— Bible. 3912 3929
— Bibs. 1:945–6a
— Bksllng. 1415–17
— Librs. 1415 2452
— Newspapers. 1418 1420
— — Bibs. 1:1923
— Paper *see also* HUTTON, William, 1723–1815. 1419
— Ptg. 1416 6066
— — Bibs. 1:946–a
— Type *see* BASKERVILLE, John, 1706–75.
— CENTRAL SCHOOL OF ARTS AND CRAFTS. SCHOOL OF PRINTING. 4919–20
— — Bibs. 1:1266d
— ORATORY. 11145
— PUBLIC LIBRARIES.
— — Collns. 1:479 946–a 1252b 2032 3846–7; 2:237; 7026
— — SHAKESPEARE MEMORIAL LIBRARY. 2:270a 273b 301 312–13 320 326 330 341
— — — Collns. 2:177 238
— THEATRE ROYAL *see* THEATRE ROYAL, Birmingham.

BIRMINGHAM. UNIVERSITY. LIBRARY.
— — — Collns. 1:1255 3385–6; 3274
— — SHAKESPEARE INSTITUTE. LIBRARY. 2:326
BIRMINGHAM, George A., *pseud. of* James Owen Hannay, 1865–1950–Bibs. 1:2462
BIRMINGHAM BOOK CLUB. 2452
BIRMINGHAM GAZETTE. 1418
BIRMINGHAM LIBRARY. 3376b
— Collns. 11499
BIRMINGHAM SCHOOL OF LIBRAR-IANSHIP PRESS *see* MORENARDO PRESS, Birmingham, est. 1960?
BIRMINGHAM SCHOOL OF PRINTING *see* BIRMINGHAM. CENTRAL SCHOOL OF ARTS AND CRAFTS. SCHOOL OF PRINTING.
BIRR, co. Offaly–Bibs. 1:1112
BIRRELL, Augustine, 1850–1933–Bibs. 1:2463
BISHOP, Cortland Field, 1870–1935–Libr. 2983
BISHOP, Edmund, 1846–1917–Bibs. 1:2463d
BISHOP, John, 1665–1737. 8543
BISHOP LONSDALE COLLEGE OF EDUCATION, Derby. LIBRARY–Collns. 1:1573e
BISHOPS' BIBLE, 1560 *see* BIBLE–Versions–Bishops'; BIBLE. O.T.–Versions–Bishops'.
BISHOP'S STORTFORD, Herts.–Librs. 2593
BISHOPSTONE, Sussex–Ptg. 1408
BISHOP'S WARS–Bibs. 1:719
BISSET, James, 1762?–1832.
— *Lines written on hearing.* 8638
BITTON, Glos.–Paper. 1120a
BLACK, Adam, 1784–1874. 4053–a
BLACK, Charles, 1807–54. 4053–a
BLACKBURN, Charles Francis, 1828–96. 8544
BLACKBURNE, Francis, 1782–1867.
— Bndngs. 2245
— *Considerations.* 2245
Blackburne, Harriott Elizabeth, fl.1881 8545
— *Hale hall.* 8545
BLACKER, Beaver Henry, 1821–90. 30
BLACKIE, John, Glasgow, 1782–1874. 4054–7
BLACKIE, Walter Graham, Glasgow, 1816–1906. 4055–6
BLACK-LETTER *see* PRINTING IN BLACK-LETTER; TYPEFACES–Black letter.
BLACKLEY, Lancs. 1164a
— Ptg. 1164a
BLACKLOCK, William, d.1870 *see* BRADSHAW AND BLACKLOCK, fl.1869–71.

BLACKMORE, sir Richard, c.1655–1729–Bibs. 1:2464
BLACKMORE, Richard Doddridge, 1825–1900. 8546–50
— Bibs. 1:662 2465–6
— *Fringilla.* 8550
— Illus. 8547
— *Kit and Kitty.* 8549
— Mss. 8546
— *Poems by Melanter.* 8548
BLACKSTONE, sir William, 1723–80. 2:1656; 5360 5363 8551–4
— Bibs. 1:2467
— Bksllng. 8554
— *Commentaries.* 8554
— — Bibs. 1:2467
BLACKWELL, sir Basil Henry, Oxford, 1889– . 4826
— Bibs. 1:1339
BLACKWELL, Henry, 1851–1928–Libr. 3018 3099
BLACKWOOD, Alexander, Edinburgh, 1806–45. 4068
BLACKWOOD, George William, Edinburgh, 1876–1942. 4068
BLACKWOOD, James Hugh, Edinburgh, 1878–1951. 4068
BLACKWOOD, John, Edinburgh, 1818–79. 4061 4068
BLACKWOOD, Robert, Edinburgh, 1808–52. 4068
BLACKWOOD, William, Edinburgh, 1776–1834 *see also* BLACKWOOD'S EDINBURGH MAGAZINE. 4058–73 5250
— Bibs. 1:1266m–n
BLACKWOOD, William, Edinburgh, 1836–1912. 4068 6510a
BLACKWOOD AND SONS, Edinburgh. 4058 4061 4062a–c 4068
— Collns. 4066 4073
— Mss. 4066 4073
BLACKWOOD'S EDINBURGH MAGAZINE. 4059 4062–5 4067 4069–72 12038 13164 13180
— Bibs. 1:1716k 1927 1938 1939b–41 1944 3019 4353a 4714s 4730
BLADES, William, 1824–90. 2 4074–82 6637
— Bibs. 1:1266p–q
— Libr. 1:1142; 4078–9 4081
— *Life of Caxton.* 4081 4262 4317
BLAIKIE, Walter Biggar, Edinburgh, 1847–1928. 4082k 5527
— Libr. 1:719a
BLAIR, Eric, 1903–50 *see* ORWELL, George, *pseud.*
BLAIR, Hugh, 1718–1800. 8555–8
— Bibs. 1:2468
— Collns. 3050

BLAIR, Hugh, 1718–1800. *Critical dissertation on Ossian.* 8555–6
— Mss. 8555
— Sermons. 8557
— *Shakespeare's Works.* 2:757
BLAIR, Robert, 1699–1746.
— *Grave.* 8575 8625a
— Illus. 8575 8625a
BLAIR, Thomas Marshall Howe, 1901– .
— *Banks' Unhappy favorite.* 8396
BLAIRS. ST. MARY'S COLLEGE *see* ST. MARY'S COLLEGE, Blairs.
BLAKE, ENGRAVERS NAMED. 6210b
BLAKE, Martin, c.1596–1673–Bibs. 1:**2469**
BLAKE, Nicholas, *pseud., see* LEWIS, Cecil Day-, 1904–72.
BLAKE, William, 1757–1827. 2:654 659; 479 770 7000a 7026 **8559–645** 14604
— *America.* 8630 8636
— *Bible of hell.* 8572
— Bibs. 1:402 **2470–89**
— *Bisset's Lines written on hearing.* 8638
— *Blair's Grave.* 8575 8625a
— Bndng. 8627
— *Bonnycastle's Mensuration.* 8626
— *Book of Job.* 8593 8595 8598
— *Book of Thel.* 8606 8632
— *Bunyan's Pilgrim's progress.* 8645
— Collns. 786 8561 8570–1 8606 8608 8615 8618 8624 8641
— *Dante.* 8642–4
— *Descriptive catalogue.* 8597
— *Europe.* 8590
— *A fairy stepd.* 8587
— *Four Zoas.* 8572 8613 8627
— *Fench revolution.* 8639
— *Gray's Poems.* 8566
— Handwr. 8609
— *Hesiod.* 8631
— *He who binds.* 8583
— *Holy Thursday.* 8623
— *Infant sorrow.* 8579
— *Jerusalem.* 8599 8610 8628 8633
— — Bibs. 1:2486
— *Laughing song.* 8565
— Libr. 8616 8620 8622
— *Little Tom the sailor.* 8640
— — Bibs. 1:2488
— *Marriage of heaven and hell.* 8576
— *Milton.* 470 8569 8574 8580
— Mss. 8565 8568 8581 8598 8600 8607 8621 8635 8638
— Paper. 8635
— *Percy's Reliques.* 8612
— *Pickering ms.* 8635
— *Poetical sketches.* 8567 8589 8601 8637
— — Bibs. 1:2475 2480
— Ptg. 8601–2 8604 8636

— Publ. 8614
— *Remember me!* 8645
— *Rossetti ms.* 8581 8621
— *Songs of innocence and experience.* 8563 8582 8584 8595 8602 8639a 8641
— *Taylors' City scenes.* 8623
— Text. 8567 8573 8581 8583 8587 8599 8601 8628–9 8639
— *Vala see Four Zoas.*
— *Young's Night thoughts.* 8592 8611 8617
— AS ILLUSTRATOR. 6192 6201 6207 6220 8562 8564 8566 8575 8577 8590–4 8596 8598 8611 8617 8619 8623 8625a–6 8631 8634 8642–4 8645
BLAKENEY, Edward Henry, d.1955. 5578–9
BLAKEWAY, John Brickdale, 1756–1826. **8646–7**
— Mss. 8647
BLANCHARD, Edward Litt Laman, 1820–89 –Libr. 1:380
BLANDFORD FORUM, Dorset.
— Bksllng. *see* HUNT, Christopher, fl.1585–1638; SIMMONS, Samuel, fl.1763–1828.
— Librs. 5661
BLANK LEAVES. 2350 6278
BLANTYRE, Lanark.–Librs. 1685
BLESSINGTON, Marguerite (Power), countess, 1789–1849 *see* GARDINER, Marguerite (Power), countess Blessington, 1789–1849.
BLICKLING HALL, Norfolk–Libr. 2907
BLIGHT, Francis James, 1858–1935. 4805a
BLIND-TOOLED BINDINGS *see* BOOKBINDINGS, BLIND-TOOLED.
BLISS, Philip, 1787–1857. **8648**
— Bibs. 1:**2490–1**
— *Griffin's Fiedessa.* 10891
BLOCK, Gordon A., fl.1936–Libr. 801
BLOCKS, HALF-TONE *see* ETCHING, PHOTOGRAPHIC.
—, PROCESS *see* PROCESS BLOCKS.
BLOMEFIELD, Francis, 1705–52–Bibs. 1:**2492**
BLOMEFIELD, Miles, 1525–74?
— Bibs. 1:**2493**
— Libr. 3364a
BLOODY BANQUET, 1639. 609
BLOOMFIELD, Leonard Lionel, d.1916– Libr. 1:444d 480
BLOOMFIELD, Robert, 1766–1823. **8649–52**
— Bibs. 1:**2494–7**
— *Rural tales.* 8649 8651
— — Bibs. 1:2497
BLORE, Thomas, 1764–1818.
— Libr. 7421
BLOTTING PAPER *see* PAPER, BLOTTING.

BLOUNT, Charles, 1654–93–Bibs. 1:**2498**
BLOUNT, Edward, 1564–1632. 2:951; 684
4083
BLOW, James, Belfast, d.1759. **4084–5**
BLOWER, Elizabeth, fl.1763–88. 7289
BLOWER, Ralph, fl.1600–16.
— *Dekker's Looking glass.* 9947
BLUDDER, sir Thomas, c.1597–1655–Libr.
3174 3396a
BLUEBELL, co. Dublin. **1943**
— Ptg. 1943
'BLUE PENCIL'. 3592
BLUM, W. Robert, fl.1916–58–Libr. 806
BLUNDEN, Edmund Charles, 1896–
1974–Bibs. 1:**2499–c**
— Libr. 3283
BLUNSON, Henry James, fl.1843–92. **4086**
BLUNT, Wilfrid Scawen, 1840–1922–Bibs.
1:**2500–d**
BOARDS *see* BOOKBINDINGS–Boards.
BOAR'S HEAD PRESS, Manaton, est. 1931.
4087
BOASE, George Clement, 1829–97. **8653**
BOATE, Gerrard, 1604–50.
— *Ireland's natural history.* 1793
BOBBIN, Tim, *pseud. of* John Collier,
1708–86. **8654–5**
BOCCACCIO, Giovanni, 1313–75. 3853
BOCHUM. STADTBÜCHEREI–Collns.
2:153
— UNIVERSITÄT. BIBLIOTHEK–Collns.
2:153
BOCQUET, Edward, fl.1811.
— *Letters of Junius.* 11635
BODEDERN, Anglesey–Ptg. 1517
BODEN, Nicholas, Birmingham, fl.1769–70.
4088
BODENHAM, John, fl.1600. 12545
BODIES, TYPE *see* TYPE BODIES.
BODKIN, Thomas Patrick, 1887–1961–Bibs.
1:**2500g–h**
BODLEIAN LIBRARY PRESS, est. 1921.
4089–90 4494 4496 6320 6325
BODLEY, sir Thomas, 1545–1613 *see also*
OXFORD. UNIVERSITY. BODLEIAN
LIBRARY. 2266 2591 2737 6454
BODLEY HEAD PRESS, est. 1887. **4091–a**
BODMER, Martin, 1899– –Libr. 2:305
308–9 317 1976
BODUIL MILL, Liskeard. 1083b
BOECE, Hector, 1465?–1536. **8656–7**
— *History of Scotland.* 8656
— Libr. 8657
— Mss. 8656
BOETHIUS, d.524. 892 1103 4258 4260
10447
BOGSMILL, Midloth.–Paper. 1712
BOG-WITTICISMS. 7465

BOHN, Henry George, 1796–1884. 3973–4
4091b–c 12056
— Bibs. 1:**1267**
— *Guinea catalogue.* 4091c
— *Milton's prose.* 12345
BOILEAU DESPRÉAUX, Nicolas,
1636–1711–Bibs. 1:**809**
BOKBINDÄRMASTAREFÖENINGEN I
STOCKHOLM. 2239a
BOLEYN HOUSE, Essex *see* GREEN-
STREET HOUSE, East Ham.
BOLINGBROKE, Henry St. John, 1st
viscount, 1678–1751 *see* St. John, Henry,
1st viscount Bolingbroke, 1678–1751.
BOLT, Robert, 1924– –Bibs. 1:**1597**
BOLTON, Lancs.–Bibs. 1:**904**
— Newspapers. 5856–7
— Ptg. *see* TILLOTSON, John, fl.1834–
1915; TILLOTSON, William Frederick,
1844–99.
— PREMIER BOX COMPANY *see*
PREMIER BOX COMPANY, Bolton.
— PUBLIC LIBRARIES–Collns. 2:43
BOLTON, Edmund, 1575?–1633? **8658**
— *Hypercritica.* 8658
— Mss. 8658
— *Nero Caesar.* 2589
BOLTON, Sheila, fl.1959–Libr. 10915
BOLTON EVENING NEWS. 5856–7
BOMBAY ARTILLERY REGIMENT–Bibs.
1:**2232–3**
BONAPARTE, prince Louis-Lucien,
1813–91. **4092**
— Collns. 3288 3349a
— Libr. 2513 2519 2532 2535 2538 2829
3302
BONAPARTE, Napoleon (Napoleon I),
1769–1821. 5565
— Collns. 1:**1536t**; 2650 2804 2914
3005
BONAVENTURA, saint, 1221–74.
— Ptg. 6012–13 6022
— *Speculum vitæ Christi:* 6012–13 6022
BOND, Richmond Pugh, 1899– –Libr.
1:**1894–a**
BONE, sir David William, 1874–1959–Bibs.
1:**2501**
BONMAHON, co. Waterford–Bibs. 1:**1132d**
— Ptg. *see* DOUDNEY, David Alfred,
1811–94.
— — Bibs. 1:**1132d**
BONNELL, Henry Houston, fl.1859–
1932–Libr. *see* BRONTË SOCIETY–
Bonnell collection.
BONNYCASTLE, John, 1750?–1821.
— Illus. 8626.
— *Introduction to mensuration.* 8626
'BOOK'. 3594

BOOK, PARTS OF THE *see also* BLANK LEAVES; BOOKBINDINGS; BOOK LABELS; BOOK-PLATES; COLOPHONS; COLUMNS; DATES IN BOOKS; DEDICATIONS; ENDPAPERS; ERRATA LISTS; EXPLICITS; FOLIATION; FRONTISPIECES; HALF-TITLES; HEADLINES; HEADTITLES; ILLUSTRATIONS; IMPRINTS; IMPRIMATURS; INDEXES; MARGINS; PAGINATION; PREFACES; PRESS-FIGURES; PRIVILEGES; REGISTER; RUBRICS; RULES; RULINGS; RUNNING-TITLES; SIGNATURES; SUBSCRIPTION LISTS; TITLEPAGES; TITLES; TITLES, FORE-EDGE; WRAPPERS. 256–7 267 269 2300 **6260–311**

'BOOKBINDER'. 3597

BOOKBINDERIES. 2091 2094 2234

BOOKBINDERS. 2189 2197–8 2218

— Apprentices. 5700

— Labels *see* LABELS, BOOKBINDERS'.

— Tickets. 2137 2182 4117 5503

—, GERMAN. 2187

—, LIST OF *see* BOOKTRADE, LISTS–Bkbndrs.

BOOKBINDERS CASE UNFOLDED, c.1695. 2230

BOOKBINDERS' SOCIETIES *see* GUILD OF CONTEMPORARY BINDERS; GUILD OF WOMEN BINDERS, 1898–1904; LONDON JOURNEYMEN BOOKBINDERS; MASTER BINDERS' ASSOCIATION; NATIONAL UNION OF PRINTING, BOOKBINDING AND PAPER WORKERS, amalgamated 1921; SOCIETY OF LONDON BOOK-BINDERS, est. 1780; SOCIETY OF WOMEN EMPLOYED IN THE BOOKBINDING AND PRINTING TRADES; VELLUM BINDERS' SOCIETY, est. 1823.

BOOKBINDING. 256 259 263 269 282 **1993–2263** 2276 2347 3437 3452 5388

— Bibs. 1:1139g 1139m **1139m–x** 1143 1149f 1150 1154

— Bibs. (*as in Volume I*) 2004 2016–17 2056 2083 2091 2093 2105 2194 2215 2244

— Forwarding. 2021 2234

—, Gilding *see also* GWYNN FAMILY, 1842–1962. 2234

— Guidelines. 6249

— Newspapers and periodicals–Bibs. 1:1139s

— Prices. 1053 2021 2158 2169a 3690 5381 5392

— Terms and concepts. 2030 2038 2153 2192 2242 3588 3590 3607

— Tools. 2200

— 1475–1500. 1053 1620 2021 2091 2093–4 2154 2226 3436

— 1475–1640. 4007

— 1475–1700. 2021 2091 2093 2152

— 1501–1640. 1050 1053 1620 2021 2023a 2093 2112 2122 2125 2144–5 2154 2167 2184–5 2201 2211 2228 2236 2238a–b 2239a 2248 4576 5168

— 1641–1700. 2176 2179 2187 2212a 2230 2248 2874

— 1701–1800. 2039 2093 2153 2186 2212–3 2250 5382

— 1801–1900. 1993 2001 2036–8 2041 2045 2057 2063–4 2081 2084–5 2097–8 2104 2106 2114 2116 2118–19 2124 2126 2130 2133 2136 2150 2153 2178 2192 2202 2227 2242 2246 5334

— 1901– . 4089

—, PROVINCIAL.

— Aberdeenshire. Aberdeen *see* VAN HAGEN, Francis, fl.1626–36; VAN HAGEN, Francis, fl.1659–69; WILSON, James, 1836–1916.

— Buckinghamshire.

— — Eton. 5394

— Cambridgeshire.

— — Cambridge *see also* BOYSE, Daniel, fl.1616–28; MOORE, Ed., fl.1740–60; SPIERINCK, Nicolaus, fl.1514–45; STOAKLEY, George Frederick, fl.1846–91; TILLET, Titus, fl.1677; UNICORN BINDER, 15th cent. 1050–3 1056 1058 1066 1068 2093 2161 4168 4751

— Cardiganshire. 1522

— Cork.

— — Youghal *see* LARKING, Bartholomew, fl.1638.

— Derbyshire. 1091

— — Derby *see also* BEMROSE, sir Henry Howe, fl.1827–93; BEMROSE, William, 1792–1880. 1091

— — Dublin *see also* GALWEY, Arthur Francis, fl.1828–93. 1880 1913 1928

— Durham. 1313

— Fifeshire.

— — St. Andrews. 1676

— Huntingdonshire *see* LITTLE GIDDING BINDERY, 1625–7.

— Ireland *see also* BOOKBINDINGS, IRISH. 1768 1808–9 1820 1828 1830 1843

— — 1475–1700. 1825

— — 1701–1800. 1751 1825 1836

— Lancashire.

— — Liverpool *see also* FAZAKERLEY, John, fl.1877–91; FAZAKERLEY, Thomas, fl.1813–77. 1173 4158

BOOKBINDING. Lancashire. Manchester *see* FALKNER, George, fl.1891; FRYE, Bartholomew, fl.1818.
— London *see also* ST. ANN'S STEAM BINDING WORKS, London. 1190 1192 2163 2175 2186–7 2239b 5175 5489–90
— — 1475–1500. 1215
— — 1475–1640. 1189–90 1192 2175
— — 1641–1700. 1259 1276 4638 4678–9
— — 1701–1800. 1272 1276–7 1283 2234 4833
— — 1701–1800. 1272 1276–7 1283 2234 4833
— — 1801–1900. 1272 1276–7 1283 5060 5120k
— — Hammersmith *see* DOVES PRESS, 1900–16–Bndng.
— — Hampstead *see* HAMPSTEAD BINDERY, 1898–1904.
— Midlothian.
— — Edinburgh *see also* GOURLAW, Robert, d.1585; HUNTER, William, Edinburgh, fl.1824–1918; LIVINGSTONE, Edward, 1832–1905; LOWES, sir Patrick, fl.1494; SMYTH, Robert, fl.1564–1602. 1700 1720a
— Northamptonshire.
— — Northampton *see* BIRDSALL AND SON, fl.1890.
— Northumberland. 1313
— — Newcastle-upon-Tyne *see* FLEMING, James, fl.1740–66; LUBBOCK, William, fl.1808–22; MAPLISDEN, Peter, fl.1710.
— Nottinghamshire.
— — Nottingham. 1342 1344
— Oxfordshire.
— — Oxford *see also* BARTLETT, Roger, c.1630–1712; BLACKWELL, sir Basil Henry, 1889– ; DAVIS, Richard, 1619–88?; SEDGLEY, Richard, 1647–1719. 1353 1356 1369 1374 2248 4089 4576 5333–4 6778
— Perthshire.
— — Perth. 1735–6
— Scotland *see also* BOOKBINDINGS, SCOTTISH. 1:712e 725 1564 1581–2 1590 1592 1606 1609 1615 1620 1636
— Somerset.
— — Bath *see* CHIVERS, Cedric, fl.1853–92.
— Staffordshire.
— — Newcastle-under-Lyme *see* BAGGULEY, G. T., fl.1897.
— Wales. 1467
— Worcestershire.
— — Worcester *see* HOLL, John, fl.1790.
— Yorkshire.

— — Halifax *see* EDWARDS, William, 1723–1808.
— — York. 1443
BOOKBINDING OF ANNUALS. 2119
BOOKBINDING OF BIBLES. 5700 9391
BOOKBINDING OF NEW TESTAMENTS. 2000
BOOKBINDING OF NOVELS. 2119
BOOKBINDING PATENTS *see* PATENTS, BINDING.
BOOKBINDINGS *see also* PAPER COVERS. 2:793; 2272 2375 3473
— Bibliogr. descr. 97 124 128 149 169 2119 2192 2240 2242
— Boards. 2097–8 2108 2234
— Ciphers. 2091
— Collns. (Institutional). 2006 2008–a 2020 2022 2027 2043 2053 2080 2086 2093 2123a 2126 2128 2131 2144 2162 2164 2168 2170 2195 2199 2204 2214 2219 2222–3 2231 2237 2238 2239a 2247–8 2251–2 2663 2811 2852 2991 3051 3254 3258 3278
— — (Personal). 1994–6 1999 2028 2054 2066 2073 2090–1 2110–13 2121 2139 2143–4 2149 2169 2187–8 2199 2203 2205 2239 2241 2247 2251–2 2575 2669 2990 2998 3142 3254 3258 3278 3380a
— Edges *see also* FORE-EDGE PAINTING; TITLES, FORE-EDGE. 2021 2234
— Endpapers. 1720a 2190 2234 2375 3727 6265 6274 6279 6281 6291 6293 6303 6913
— Labels *see* LABELS, BOOKBINDERS'.
— Linings. 2092 2234 4416
— Methods. 2234
— Monograms. 2093 2112 2122
— Ordinaries. 2219
— Pastedowns. 1374 5183 7985
— Stamps *see* BOOKSTAMPS.
— 1475–1500. 2094
— 1475–1640. 1606 1997 2002 2007 2181 4049
— 1801–1900. 3453 6229
—, ARMORIAL *see also* BOOKSTAMPS. 279 1581–2 1592 2034 2047 2054 2069 2089–90 2109 2112 2117 2123a 2131 2139–40 2142 2144 2147 2162 2191 2217 2219 2222 2233 3124 3233 5624
—, ARTISTIC. 2012a 2020 2027–8 2036–7 2039 2041 2073 2140 2187 2234 2244 2248 4814–16
—, BANDED *see also* 'BANDED BINDING'. 4376
—, BLIND-TOOLED *see also* BOOKBINDINGS, STAMPED. 1997 2048 2080 2135 2154 2165 2177 2217
—, BOOKSELLERS'. 2102 2133
—, CAMEO. 2072

BOOKS–1475–1640–Bookselling–London.
1189 1215 1255 1291 3255

— — Booktrade. 841 1281 1285 3405
3410–12 3414–15 3419 3421 3431 3433
3435 3441 3454 3458 3466 3470 3478–9
3553–5 3560 3562–4 3575 3576a 3625 6106
8920

— —Booktrade, Lists. 1:491–2 500 502 512
516 523–4 530 1608 2256; 1189 1291 1353
1620 1710 3255 3411 3414 3422 46662b
5726 5744 5747 6129 6588 6661 6670

— — Broadsides. 3871 5474 6975 8070

— — Cancels. 647 968 6148 10882 11116
11579 14160 14371

— — Catalogues, Book. 678

— — Catholic books–Bibs. 1:2256–9 2264–5

— — Censorship. 626 3476 3497 3507 5742
7133 8455 10721 14371

— — Collns. 2663 3380a

— — Composition. 11803 12178 12273–4
12282–3 12442 12687

— — Copyright. 1281 3515–17 3521 3525
3528–31 3533 3536 3538 3542a 5873a 7172
7184 11083 12153

— — Dictionaries. 7073 7079 7081 7086
8072

— — Drama. 4611 **7104–92** 14431 14435
14437 14440

— — — Bibs. 1:**1599–601t**

— — Engraving. 7404 7523

— — Facsimiles–Bibs. 1:555

— — Foreign books. 871–2 873 875 883 884
889 891 896a–7 898 900a 915 932 935–6
939 947–8 960 963 966–70 973 974 3458
3470 3479

— — Forgeries. 554 7340 8917 9362 9811

— — Geography–Bibs. 1:2188–9

— — Illustrated books. 653 935 7382

— — — Bibs. 1:1747h–i

— — Illustration processes. 653

— — Libraries. 2445

— — Literature–Bibs. 1:2 46–7 84 490b

— — Indulgences–Bibs. 1:1534d

— — Manuscripts. 2:300; 637–8 657 7156

— — Medicine–Bibs. 1:2216 2219–20 2227

— — Military books–Bibs. 1:2231 2235–8

— — Music. 7583 7585 7587–9 7592 8861

— — — Bibs. 1:1830 1832 1841b 1841m

— — Oxford U.P. 5347 5355

— — Pamphlets–Bibs. 1:**1965–6**

— — Paper. 3701 3731

— —Papermaking. 3709–10 3764 3765a
3779

— — Patronage. 3413 3458 3470 3476 3479

— — Presentation books–Bibs. 1:2035a–7

— — Prices of books. 2681 3343 3433
3692–3 3695–6 4009 10320

— — Primers–Bibs. 1:2040

— — Printers. 3407 3409 3458 6054 6056–7
6059 6074 6086 6091 6143 6147 8819

— — Printing. 3425 3431 3448 3454 3458
3470 3479 3559 3564 3568–9 6055 6063–5
6068 6073 6093 6103 6106 6118 6121
6121b 6124 6128–31 6133a 6141–4 6147a
6174–6 6181 6240 6249 6343 6350 6359
6362 6365 6369 6400 6409 6456–7 8105

— — — Ireland. 1757 6063

— — — London. 1189 1199 1215 1222 1255
1257 1284 1287 1289 1291

— — — Scotland. 264 1561–3 1591 1619
1624 1627 1629 6063 6081 6124

— — Proclamations. 963 8069–71

— — — Bibs. 1:2048

— — Proofcorrection. 5660 6396 6398–400
6411–13

— — Publishing. 3476 6512 6535 6545–6
6562

— — — London. 1281

— — Religious books–Bibs. 1:2252

— — Schoolbooks–Bibs. 1:2277 2279

— — Science–Bibs. 1:2279g

— — Sermons–Bibs. 1:2062–3

— — Stationers' company. 1189 1281 3538
3542a 3566 3569 5684 5746 5733 5741–2
5744 5747–9 5755–6 5758–9 5765–6 5835
6002 6129 13058

— — Statutes. 4006 7471 7475 7477 7479
7953

— —Textual criticism. 401

— —Translations into English–Bibs. 1:771–4
827 839

— — Type. 653 6147a 6451 6564a 6572 6575
6582 6583 6588 6590 6598 6617 6620
6657–8a 6660–1 6662 6670–2 6683 6685
6691 6693–5a 6713

— — Typography. 6589

— — Watermarks. 1712 3730–1 3793 3806

— **1475–1700** see also 1641–1700. 256 271
487 **695–702** 884 1019 1409 2506

— — Accounting–Bibs. 1:2083 2085

— — Agriculture. 6727–32

— — — Bibs. 1:2098

— — Alchemy–Bibs. 1:2100d

— — Architecture–Bibs. 1:2106

— — Art–Bibs. 1:2105–6

— — Auction catalogues–Bibs. 1:1446

— — Authors. 6405

— — Ballads–Bibs. 1:1460 1463

— — Bibles. 258 860 6121b 8729

— — Bibliogr. descr. 143–4 255 2978

— — Bibs. 1:351e **560–93** 804

— — Biographies–Bibs. 1:1508

— — Books in parts–Bibs. 1:1532

— — Bookcollecting in. 2248 2314 7619

— — Bookselling. 3453 3493 3615–17 3629

— — — London. 1191 1209–10 1216 1224

BOOKSELLING–Inverness-shire.
— — Inverness *see also* DOUGLAS, Kenneth, d.1860; ETTLES, William, d.1819; LUSK, Robert Baillie, fl.1823; SMITH, James, fl.1811–51; YOUNG, John, fl.1807–15. 1683
— Ireland *see also* KING'S STATIONERS IN IRELAND. 1782
— Kent.
— — Canterbury. 1160
— Lanarkshire.
— — Glasgow *see also* BRASH, James, 1758–1835; BRASH AND REID, fl.1788–1835; MOORE, Dugald, 1805–41; REID, William, 1764–1831; SMITH, John, 1724–1814. 1580 1687
— Lancashire.
— — Lancaster *see* HOPKINS, Christopher, d.1742.
— — Manchester *see also* BELL, John Gray, 1823–66. 1174 1179
— — Warrington. 1182
— Lincolnshire.
— — Barton-upon-Humber *see* BALL, Henry William, 1833–1914
— London. 1206 1213 1234 1249 1252 1258a 1265 3616
— — Little Britain. 3616
— — 1475–1500. 1215 3423
— — 1475–1640. 1189 1215 1255 1291 3255
— — 1475–1700. 1191 1209–10 1216 1224
— — 1641–1700. 1259–60 3991
— — 1701–1800. 1261–3 3475 3991 6994
— — 1801–1900. 1191a 1200 1282 1290 4897hh 6994
— Louth. 1958b
— Midlothian.
— — Edinburgh *see also* DONALDSON, Alexander, fl.1750–94; GRAY, William, fl.1763–85; HISLOP, Archibald, fl.1668–78; MENZIES, John, 1808–79; RAMSAY, Allan, 1686–1758; SIBBALD, James, 1745–1803; STILLIE, James, fl.1800–89; THIN, James, 1823–1915. 1255 1580 1701 1711 1716
— — Lasswade. 1716
— Norfolk. 1304
— Northamptonshire. 1310–11
— Northumberland.
— — Alnwick *see* GRAHAM, Alexander, fl.1746–86.
— — Newcastle-upon-Tyne *see also* MAPLISDEN, Peter, fl.1710; RANDELL, Richard, fl.1676–1714. 1320
— Nottinghamshire.
— — Newark. 1329–30
— — Nottingham. 1342 1344

— — Oxford *see also* BOWMAN, Francis, fl.1634–47; DORNE, John, fl.1520; FIRTH, Richard, fl.1797; PRINCE, Daniel, fl.1750–96. 3467
— Perthshire.
— — Perth *see also* COWAN, Samuel, 1835–1914. 1735–6
— Scotland. 1556 1604 1624 1627 1629 4605
— Shropshire. 1385
— Somerset.
— — Bath *see also* MEEHAN, John Francis, d.1913. 1392
— Staffordshire.
— — Lichfield *see* JOHNSON, Michael, 1657–1732.
— — Wolverhampton. 1398
— Suffolk.
— — Ipswich *see* CRAIGHTON, William, fl.1739–61.
— Surrey.
— — Richmond. 1406
— Warwickshire.
— — Birmingham *see also* HUTTON, William, 1723–1815; LLOYD, Robert, 1778–1811; UNWIN, Matthew, d.1750; WILSON, James, 1850–1917. 1415–17
— — Stratford-upon-Avon. 1422
— — Warwick *see* TONGE, George, fl. 1682.
— Westmorland.
— — Kendal *see* ASHBURNER, Anthony, fl.1763–8.
— Wiltshire.
— — Salisbury *see* COLLINS, Benjamin, fl.1729–85.
— Yorkshire.
— — Bradford. 1438
— — Halifax *see* EDWARDS, James, 1756–1816.
— — Hull. 1440a
— — Leeds. 1441
— — York *see also* FOSTER, Mark, fl.1642–4; GENT, Alice (Guy), fl.1700–70; HILDYARD, Francis, 1682–1731; HILDYARD, John, fl.1731–7; HINXMAN, John, fl.1757–61; SOOTHERAN, Henry, d.1813; SUNTER, Robert, 1795–1873; TODD, George W., fl.1811–34; TODD, John, 1737?–1811; TODD, John, 1770–1837. 1443 1445–8
—, RAILWAY *see also* MENZIES, John, Edinburgh, 1808–79; SMITH, W. H. AND SON, est. 1792; SMITH, William Henry, 1825–91. 6524
—, RARE *see* BOOKSELLING, ANTIQUARIAN.
BOOKSELLING AND FORGERIES. 13961

Vol. **1** = *Bibliographies*   **2** = *Shakespeare*   **4** = 1–8221   **5** = 8222–14616

BOOKSELLING OF BIBLES. 3692–3
BOOKSELLING OF MUSIC see MUSIC SELLING.
BOOKSELLING OF NATURAL HISTORY. 8145
BOOKSELLING OF SCIENCE BOOKS. 8144–5 8153
BOOKS IN CHAINS see LIBRARIES, CHAINED.
BOOKS IN PARTS see also BOOK TRADE, LISTS–Books in parts. 1207 **6937–a** 6947 6978 6983–4 9878 10050 10058 10075 10115 10142 10890 11443 12055 12246 12484 13587 14253
— Bible. 6831
— Bibliogr. descr. 149
— Bibs. 1:**1529–33**
BOOKS IN SERIES see also individual series, e.g. ALDINE EDITION OF BRITISH POETS; BELL'S BRITISH POETS; BENTLEY'S STANDARD NOVELS; BOYS' FRIEND LIBRARY; CHAPMAN'S QUARTERLY SERIES; CHEAP REPOSITORY TRACTS; CRANFORD SERIES (MACMILLAN'S); DENT'S ILLUSTRATED ESSAYS; ENGLISH BIJOU ALMANACS; ENGLISH LIBRARY; FAMILY LIBRARY; KEYNOTE SERIES; LIBRARY OF IRELAND; LILLIPUTIAN LIBRARY, MACMILLAN'S ILLUSTRATED STANDARD NOVELS; PARLOUR LIBRARY, PRANCERIANA; SERVICE & PATON'S ILLUSTRATED ENGLISH LIBRARY; STANDARD PLAYS; TALES FROM BLACKWOOD. 288 **6938–43** 7326a 9886 9895
— Bibs. 1:1746
BOOKSISE, David, Carmarthen, d.1726 see THOMAS, David, Carmarthen, d.1726.
BOOKS OF HOURS see PRIMERS.
BOOKS OF SOLOMON see BIBLE. O.T. BOOKS OF SOLOMON.
BOOKS ON VELLUM see PRINTING ON VELLUM.
BOOKS PUBLISHED ABROAD see BRITISH BOOKS PUBLISHED ABROAD.
BOOKSTAMPS see also BOOKBINDINGS, BLIND-TOOLED. 2034 2047 2054 2069 2072 2091 2093–4 2096 2117 2139 2142 2147 2162 2200 2297 2663 3393a
BOOK THIEVES see also BOWTELL, John, 1753–1813; JUSTICE, Henry, fl.1716–63; LIBRI, count, 1803–69; LYTE, Henry Francis, 1793–1847; NICHOLS, Philip, fl.1562; PHILLIPPS, James Orchard Halliwell-, 1820–89; RIMBAULT, Edward Francis, 1816–76; WISE, Thomas James, 1859–1937. 2269 2352 2665 2935 3152

3271 9051
BOOK TRADE see also specific activities, e.g. BOOKSELLING; PRINTING; PUBLISHING. 3453 3469 3480a 3650
— Aliens. 3411 3414
— Associations see SOCIETIES; STATIONERS' COMPANIES.
— Collns. 3447 3493
— Directories. 3462 3651
— Durham–Bibs. 1:926k
— Newspapers–Bibs. 1:1186b
— Northumberland–Bibs. 1:926k
— Northumbria. 1031–2
— Piracy see BOOKS, PIRATED.
— Regulation see also ENTRANCE (STATIONERS' REGISTER). 1281 3458 3470 3479 **3545–76a** 5746 8920
— Terms and concepts see also 'Book', 'Bookbinder'; 'Bookseller'; 'Chapel'; 'Copy, Fair'; 'Drawback'; 'Editor'; 'Offprint'; 'Out of print'; 'Parchment'; 'Picked copies'; 'Printed for'; 'Publisher'; 'Remainder'; 'Second hand'; 'Short copy'; 'Stationer'; 'Vellum'. **3577–611**
— Wales. 1516
— 1475–1500. 3423–4 3436 3467 4318
— 1475–1640. 841 1281 1285 3405 3410–12 3414–15 3419 3421 3431 3433 3435 3441 3454 3458 3466 3470 3478–9 3553–5 3560 3562–4 3575 3576a 3625 6106 8920
— 1475–1700. 3471 3546
— 1641–1700. 1285 3457 3565
— 1701–1800. 3439–40 3445 3457 3475 3546
— 1801–1900. 1290 3440 3442 3465 3546
BOOK TRADE, LISTS OF PERSONS CONNECTED WITH see also OWNERS, LISTS OF. 2187 2375
— Aliens. 3414 3422
— Apprentices. 4662b 6129
— Ballads. 1:1460–1 1468b 1541
— Belfast. 1:1026–8
— Bible. 1:1495
— Bkbndrs. 1:440 885 930 1006; 1058 1086–7 1091 1180a 1189 1259 1276 1283 1342 1344 1353 1590 1620 1735–6 2012a 2076 2091 2093 2187 2197 2205 2248 3411 3462
— Bksllrs. 1:491 516 523–4 596 602 716 731 885 896 930 950 1006 1460 1535 1541–2 1608 1750–1 1753 2066–7 2136 2373; 1086–7 1091 1173 1180a 1189 1261–3 1290 1320 1342 1385 1422 1424 1624 1627 1629 1735–6 1908 2091 2093 2322 3417 3422 3434 3444 3462 3641 3991 5541 6661 6670 6943
— Books in parts. 1:1532
— Broadsides. 1:1534–5
— Butterflies and moths. 1:2136

BOONE, William, 1794–1869. 4623
BOOTH, Constance Georgine Gore-, 1868–1927 see MARKIEVICZ, Constance Georgine (Gore-Booth), 1868–1927.
BOOTHBY, sir William, d.1707–Libr. 4937
BOOTS BOOKLOVERS LIBRARY. 3367
BORDE, Andrew, 1490?–1549. **8659–61**
— Compendious regimen. 8661
— Introduction to knowledge. 8659–60
— Ptg. 8659
BORDERS see TYPE–Borders.
BOROWITZ, David, 1906– –Libr. 1:2935g
BORROW, George Henry, 1803–81. 482 755 **8662–71**
— Bibs. 1:**2502–6e**
— Collns. 3090 8666
— Death of Balder. 8664 8667 8671
— Dust and ashes. 8665
— Klinger's Faustus. 8662 8670
— Lavengro. 5407 8663 8670
— Libr. 8665
— Mss. 8665–6 8668
— Publ. 5250 5407 8671
— Tales of the wild and wonderful. 8669 14432
— The Zincali. 8668
BOSCOBEL TRACTS–Bibs. 1:947
BOSTON, Lincs. ST. BOTOLPH'S CHURCH. 5476
— Bibs. 1:1385m
BOSTON, Mass. 11282
— PUBLIC LIBRARY–Collns. 1:371d 2990 3200a; 2:190 329 608 1004; 544 610 737 6864 6868 8903 9229 9539 9891 10164 11305 11759–61 12362 12525 12572 13811 13996
BOSTON COLLEGE, Boston, Mass. LIBRARY–Collns. 1:4212 4946
BOSWELL, Alexander, ld. Auchinleck, 1707–82–Libr. 9139
BOSWELL, James, 1740–95. **8672–719** 11452
— Account of Corsica. 8684 8689
— Bibs. 1:**2507–8g** 3840e
— Collns. 2990 3036 3039 3380a 8698 8708 8710
— Journal of a tour to the Hebrides. 11383 11386
— Letters. 4570 8693 8713
— Letters of lady Jane Douglas. 8683
— Libr. 8695 8718
— Life of Johnson. 8672–a 8676 8679 8681 8690–2 8696 8706 8711 8714 8716–17 11442 12785–6
— Mss. 8687 8693 8697–700 8704–5 8708
— — Bibs. 1:2508a–d
— Observations on The minor. 8678 8685
— Ptg. 6357 8672a–4 8679–80 8686 8701 8714
— Publ. 8688 8696 8709

— Shrubs of Parnassus. 8675
— Text. 8714–15 11442
— Tour to the Hebrides. 8677 8680 8699 8701
— Verses in the character of a Corsican. 8682
— View of the Edinburgh theatre. 8678
BOTANICAL MAGAZINE. 6955 6958a
BOTANY see also AGRICULTURE; FLOWER BOOKS; GARDENING; HERBALS. **6944–68**
— Bibliogr. descr. 158 162–3 368
— Bibs. 1:1749f **2125–30**
— Collns. 6944 6950 6952
— Illus. 6958a
— Mss.–Bibs. 1:2129
— Newspapers and periodicals. 7327 7914
BOTESDALE BOOK CLUB. 2452
BOTHE, bp. Charles, d.1535–Libr. 3143 3336
BOTLEY, Hants.–Paper. 1132a
BOTTOMLEY, Gordon, 1874–1948–Bibs. 1:**2508h**
BOUCICAULT, Dion, 1820?–90.
— Corsican brothers. 7229
BOUKHOUT, Adrian Kempe van, fl.1536–7 see KEMPE, Adrian van Boukhout, Antwerp, fl.1536–7.
BOULTER, Robert, fl.1666. 3432
'BOUNTY', MUTINY ON THE–Bibs. 1:**2133**
BOURGUIGNON, Hubert François, 1699–1773 see GRAVELOT, Hubert François, 1699–1773.
BOURNE, Henry, 1694–1733.
— History of Newcastle-upon-Tyne. 1319
BOURNE, Nicholas, c.1580–1660. 3471 4149 7675
— Bibs. 1:1873c
BOURNE END, Herts.–Paper. 1139
BOURNEMOUTH, Hants. RUSSELL-COTES ART GALLERY AND MUSEUM see RUSSELL-COTES ART GALLERY AND MUSEUM, Bournemouth.
BOWBER, Thomas, fl.1663–95–Bibs. 1:**2509**
BOWDLER, Henrietta Maria, 1754–1830. 3509
— Shakespeare's Works. 2:805
BOWDLER, Thomas, 1754–1825. 2:785 787; 3509
— Shakespeare's Works. 2:785 805
BOWEN, Elizabeth Dorothea Cole (mrs. A. C. Cameron), fl.1927– –Bibs. 1:**2510**
BOWEN, Emmanuel, fl.1752.
— Britannia depicta. 6551
BOWEN, Ewart, fl.1935–40 see Gregynog press, Newtown, est. 1922.
BOWEN, Marjorie, pseud. of Gabrielle Margaret Vere (Campbell) LONG, 1888–1952–Bibs. 1:**2511**

Vol. **1** = Bibliographies   **2** = Shakespeare   **4** = 1–8221   **5** = 8222–14616

BOWER, Patrick, St. Andrews, 1723–1814. **4093**
BOWERS, Fredson Thayer, 1905– . 224
BOWES, Robert, Cambridge, 1835–1919. **4094**
BOWES AND BOWES, Cambridge. 1060
BOWKER, Robert Alfred, fl.1857–92. **4095**
BOWLES, William Lisle, 1762–1850–Bibs. 1:**2512**
BOWLES AND CARVER, fl.1793–1832. **4096**
BOWMAN, Francis, Oxford, fl.1634–47. 10238
BOWREY, Thomas, fl.1771–Libr. 2880
BOWTELL, John, 1753–1813. **4097–8**
— Libr. 4097–8
BOWTELL, John, 1777–1855. 4097
BOWYER, WILLIAM, 1663–1737. 171 919 **4099**
— Bibs. 1:635
BOWYER, William, 1699–1777. 3475 3622 **4099–102** 6116
— Bibs. 1:**1268–9**
— Bible. 6848
— Paper. 4100
— Somerville's The chase. 13522
BOXED BOOKS see BOOKS, BOXED.
BOXES see CARTONS.
BOXING. 6969
— Bibs. 1:1465d **2135**
BOX RULES see RULES, BOX.
BOYCE, Samuel, d.1775. **8720**
— Poems on several occasions. 8720
BOYD, Mark Alexander, 1563–1601. **8721**
— Sonnet. 8721
— Text. 8721
BOYD, Zachary, 1585?–1653. **8722**
— Bibs. 1:**2513**
— Form of catechising–Bibs. 1:2513
— Last battle of the soul. 8722
BOYDELL, John, 1719–1804. 3475 **4103–5**
— Shakespeare's Works. 2:733 755
BOYDELL, Josiah, 1752–1817. 4103
BOYES, John Frederick, 1811–79–Libr. 13970
BOYLE, co. Roscommon–Bibs. 1:1113
— Ptg.–Bibs. 1:1113
BOYLE, Eleanor Vere (Gordon) (mrs. Richard Boyle), 1825–1916. 7420a
BOYLE, John, 5th earl of Cork, and Orrery, 1707–62. **8723**
— Collns. 3007
— Remarks on the life of Swift. 8723
BOYLE, Robert, 1627–91. 775 **8724–32**
— Bibs. 1:**2514–18**
— Handwr. 8732
— Letters. 8730
— — Bibs. 1:2517c
— Libr. 8726 12590

— Mss. 8724
— Ptg. 8728 8731
— Sceptical chemist. 8725 8731
— Tracts. 8728
BOYLE, Roger, 1st earl of Orrery, 1621–79. **8733–5**
— Bibs. 1:**2519–a**
— The general. 8733
— Mss. 8733
— Parthenissa–Bibs. 1:2519a
— Zoroastres. 8733
BOYS, alderman, fl.1802. 2:733
BOYS, John, 1571–1625. **8735**
— Exposition of the last psalm. 8735
— Publ. 8735
BOYS, Thomas Shotter, 1803–74. 6202
— Bibs. 1:**1269g**
— Picturesque architecture in Paris. 6209
BOYSE, Daniel, Cambridge, fl.1616–28 **4106**
BOYS' FRIEND LIBRARY–Bibs. 1:15586b
BOYS' LITERATURE see CHILDREN'S LITERATURE.
BOYS OF ENGLAND. 7024
BOY'S OWN PAPER. 5518
BRACKETS see TYPE–Individual sorts–Brackets.
BRADBURY, Henry, 1831–60–Bibs. 1:**1270**
BRADBURY AND EVANS, 1831–72. 9991
BRADDILL, Thomas, fl.1680–1704 see BRADDYLL, Thomas, fl.1680–1704.
BRADDON, Mary Elizabeth (mrs. John Maxwell), 1837–1915. **8736–40**
— Bibs. 1:**2519b–c**
— Black band. 8738 8740
— Circe. 8739
— Collns. 7322a
— Lady Audley's secret. 8736
BRADDYLL, Thomas, fl.1680–1704. 5435
— Bunyan's Pilgrim's progress. 8937–8
BRADFORD, Yorks. **1437–8**
— Bibs. 1:**949**
— Bksllng. 1438
— Newspapers. 1437–8
— — Bibs. 1:949
— Ptg. 1438
BRADFORD ANTIQUARY–Bibs. 1:2938
BRADFORD LIBRARY AND LITERARY SOCIETY. 2628
BRADFORD MECHANICS' INSTITUTE. LIBRARY. 2622
BRADFORD SCIENTIFIC JOURNAL–Bibs. 1:2938
BRADFORTH, John, fl.1554–7. 7946
BRADING, Nathaniel, fl.1645–8–Libr. 2674
BRADLEY, Andrew Cecil, 1851–1935–Bibs. 1:**2519h**
BRADLEY, Basil, 1842–1904. 7420a

BRADLEY, Edward, 1827–89 *see* BEDE, Cuthbert, *pseud.*
BRADLEY, Francis Herbert, 1846–1924–Bibs. 1:2520
BRADLEY, Henry, 1845–1923–Bibs. 1:2520a
BRADLEY, Katherine Harris, 1846–1913 *see* FIELD, Michael, *pseud. of* Katherine Harris Bradley and Edith Emma Cooper.
BRADOCK, Richard, fl.1581–1615.
— *Chapman's Widow's tears.* 9383
BRADSHAW, Christopher, fl.1960 *see* SMOUT PRESS, fl.1960.
BRADSHAW, George, Manchester, 1801–53. 2291 8074 8076–7
BRADSHAW, Henry, 1831–86. 8 11 39 40 57 1755 1910 6637
— Libr. 1:731
BRADSHAW, John, 1602–59–Libr. 2718
BRADSHAW AND BLACKLOCK, Manchester, fl.1869–71. 6202
— Bibs. 1:1270d
BRADSHAWE, Nicholas, d.1655. **8741**
— *Canticum evangelicum.* 8741
BRADSHAW-ISHERWOOD, Christopher William, 1904– *see* ISHERWOOD, Christopher William Bradshaw-, 1904–.
BRAGG, sir William Henry, 1862–1942–Bibs. 1:2520n
BRAGGE, William, 1823–84–Libr. 8199
BRAMAH, Ernest, *pseud. of* Ernest Bramah Smith, 1868–1942–Bibs. 1:2520x–2a
BRAILLE *see* PRINTING IN BRAILLE.
BRAMBLETON HALL, 1818. 13492
BRAMSHOTT, Hants.–Paper. 1132a
BRAMSTON, sir John, 1611–1700–Libr. 1:1960
BRANAR, AN. 1799
BRANDE, William Thomas, 1788–1886–Bibs. 1:2523
BRASCH, Frederick Edward, 1875– –Libr. 12579
BRASH, James, Glasgow, 1758–1835. 4107
— Bibs. 1:2022
BRASH AND REID, Glasgow, fl.1788–1835. **4107**
BRASIL *see* SHAKESPEARE, William, 1564–1616–WORKS IN BRASIL.
BRASSEY INSTITUTE, Hastings. LIBRARY–Collns. 1:2060
BRASS RULES *see* RULES, BRASS.
BRATHWAITE, Richard, 1588?–1673. **8742–4**
— Bibs. 1:2523j
— *Drunken Burnaby.* 8744
— *Good wife.* 8742
— *Shepherds' tales.* 8743
BRAWDERS, William, Dublin, 1815–62. **4108**

BRAW LADS OF GALLA WATER. 9021
BRAY, Anna Eliza (Kempe), 1790–1883–Collns. 7322a
BRAY, Horace Walter, fl.1923–31 *see* RAVEN PRESS, Harrow Weald, est. 1931.
BRAY, John Francis, fl.1839–Bibs. 1:(2523q)
BRAY, Thomas, 1656–1730. 2411 2448a 2455 2568 2665 2675 3155
BRECKNOCKSHIRE. **1518–19**
BRECON, Brecknocks. **1518**
— Librs. 1510 1518
BRENT ELEIGH, Suff.–Librs. 1400
BRENTFORD. PUBLIC LIBRARY–Collns. 2771
BRERETON, Richard, d.1558–Libr. 2509
BREREWOOD, Francis, d.1781?
— Mss. 7215
— *The retaliator.* 7215
BRETON, Nicholas, 1545?–1626? **8746–53**
— Bibs. 1:2524–a
— *Flourish upon fancy.* 8746
— *I would and would not.* 8753
— *Passions of the spirit.* 8747
— *Post with a packet.* 8749
— *Soul's heavenly exercise.* 8751
BRETT, Edwin J., d.1895. **4109–10**
BRETT, Oliver Sylvain Baliol, 3d viscount Esher, 1881–1963. 2377
— Libr. 1:666; 2989
BREVIARIES. 8053
BREWER, Luther Albertus, 1858–1933–Libr. 1:3763 3765; 11270 11272 11278
BREWHOUSE PRESS, Wymondham, Leics., est. 1962. 4111
BREWSTER, sir David, 1781–1868. 1705 1707 1720
BREWSTER, William, 1560?–1644. **4112**
BREWSTER, William, 1665–1715. 3351
BREYDENBACH, Bernhard von, d.1497. 9136
BRICK ROW BOOKSHOP, New York. 8811
BRIDGEMAN, sir Orlando, 1606?–74–Libr. 14085
BRIDGE MILL, Maidstone. 1161a
BRIDGEPORT, Conn. SACRED HEART UNIVERSITY *see* SACRED HEART UNIVERSITY, Bridgeport, Conn.
BRIDGES, John, 1666–1724.
— *History of Northamptonshire.* 7381
BRIDGES, Robert Seymour, 1844–1930. 783 **8754–66**
— Bibs. 1:2525–9g
— *Case of thickening of the cranial bones.* 8760
— Collns. 3025 8761
— Handwr. 8763
— *Hopkins' Poems.* 11205
— Libr. 1:3703b; 11145
— *Poems.* 8758–9

Vol. **1** = *Bibliographies* **2** = *Shakespeare* **4** = 1–8221 **5** = 8222–14616

BRIDGES, Robert Seymour, 1844–1930. Ptg. 6098 8754 8765
— Publ. 8763 8766
— *Shorter poems.* 8755 8757
— Type. 8762
BRIDGEWATER, Frances Stanley, countess of, 1583–1636 *see* STANLEY, Frances, countess of Bridgewater, 1583–1636.
BRIDGEWATER HOUSE, Som. *see* EGERTON, Francis, 1st earl of Ellesmere, 1800–57–Libr.
BRIDGEWATER LIBRARY. 2836 2857 2939
BRIDIE, James, *pseud. of* Osborne Henry MAVOR, 1888–1951. 8767
BRIEFS. 1069
BRIGGS, Henry, 1561–1630. 884
BRIGHAM YOUNG UNIVERSITY, Provo, Utah. LIBRARY–Collns. 1:5000q
BRIGHT, Mary Chavelita (Dunne), 1859–1945 *see* EGERTON, George, *pseud.*
BRIGHT, Timothy, 1550–1615. 8170 8392 **8769–71**
— Bibs. 1:**2530**
— *Charactery.* 2:420 425–6 1433 1437 1564 1670; 8171 8769–70
— Mss. 8771
BRIGHTLAND, John, d.1717.
— *Isaac Bickerstaff's grammar.* 7356
BRIGHTON, Sussex.
— Publ. *see* PIKE, W. T., fl.1898–1911.
— PUBLIC LIBRARIES–Collns. 1:480 444d 1479
BRINDLEY, John, 1692?–1758. **4113** 4623
BRISCOE, Samuel, fl.1691–1705. **4114**
BRISTOL, Glos. **1122–7**
— Bibs. 1:892–5 895b **896p** 2270a
— Bksllng. 1124–5
— Collns. 1127
— Librs. 1124 2459
— Maps. 7485
— Newspapers–Bibs. 1:896p 1855
— Paper *see also* ROBINSON, Elisha Smith, 1817–85. 1120a.
— Ptg. 1017 1019 1125 1300 14510
— BAPTIST COLLEGE. LIBRARY. 3360
— — Collns. 4218a
— PUBLIC LIBRARIES–Collns. 1:421 543 610 896p 1152 1484 1494 1855 4741
— UNIVERSITY. 3847
— — LIBRARY–Collns. 7098
BRISTOL LIBRARY. 13529 13539
BRITISH ACADEMY–Bibs. 1:**1270g**
BRITISH ALBUM, 1790. 9068
BRITISH AND FOREIGN BIBLE SOCIETY, London. 6442
— LIBRARY. 3225 6807 6811
— — Collns. 1:1471 1500

BRITISH AND FOREIGN REVIEW. 7881
— Bibs. 1:4923
BRITISH APOLLO. 7703 7793
BRITISH BOOKS PUBLISHED ABROAD *see also* WELSH BOOKS PRINTED ABROAD *and individual foreign printers and publishers.* 188 279 **829–70** 8389 8391 11036–7 13985
— Bibs. 11502 540 700h **740–65** 3499
— Belgium *see also* BRUGES–Ptg. 868 5477 14349 14351
— Denmark. 864
— France. 831–3 838 841 844 858 866 870 5135 6928 7228 8057 8067 8478a 9108 9390 9899 11193 12020 12499 12504 13209
— — Bibs. 1:741 760 1691k 2679d 2877c 3185e–ea 3257g 3306 3412 4179 4221c 4270f 4332c 4442a 4829c 4894 5157y
— Germany. 829a 831a 834–7 843 845–6 847a 849 851 854 870 9900 10005 10695 13785 13857
— — Bibs. 1:743a 752–3 763–5 2677g 2975t 2984 3034 3066 3617a 4871 4107 5215
— Greenland. 9904
— Holland *see* Netherlands.
— Hungary–Bibs. 1:2680g 2858f
— Iceland. 12215
— — Bibs. 1:4175a
— India. 13002
— Italy. 11382 13854
— — Bibs. 1:2689k 2858h 3261 4869d 5089e
— Japan. 9110
— Netherlands. 842 848 850 852 854–6 862–3 866a–9 4112 7506 7684 7691 9393a 9886 10883 11429 11510
— — Bibs. 1:745 755–8 761 1729–30 2976b
— Poland. 13855
— — Bibs. 1:2868m 3085 4869e
— Rumania–Bibs. 1:3098d
— Russia. 859 10817 10967–8
— — Bibs. 1:2858e 3095c 3600–1 4217c 5053w
— Spain. 11731
— — Bibs. 1:2679e 3097e 3504a 4601
— Sweden. 10310
— — Bibs. 1:2878a 3185d
— Switzerland. 840 865 8038 8480 8481a–2 8488
— — Bibs. 1:759
— United States. 857–a 861 8116 8242 8286 8298 8304 8307 8342 8350 8352 8376 8492 8575 8585–6 8774 8786 8817a 8872 8900 8961–2 9010 9032 9048 9067 9072 9141 9207 9284 9309 9313 9327 9986 9994 9996–7 9999 10007 10105 10111 10150 10160 10187 10297 10309 10399 10828 10956 10958 10982 11220 11226 11229 11265 11282 11292 11479 11588 11630–1

BRITISH BOOKS PUBLISHED ABROAD.
United States–*cont.*
11634 11636 11672 11729 11739 11751–2
11788 11806 11853–4 11857 11886 11935
11954 11973 12169 12487 13206 13231
13318 13327 13804 13809 13813 14278–9
14315 14319 14322 14461 14489 14592
— — Bibs. 1:754 1495 1556a 1928u–v
2258–61 2341 2377 2398 2467 2542 2588
2618 2709 2986 3057 3076 3087 3095b
3216 3326 3283 3392 3469 3508 3593 3595
3718a 3940d 3960 4094f 4196 4274d 4443a
4606 4714 4853 4896 4911 5075 5104d
5171b 5177 5199 5203 5216–18
BRITISH CATALOGUE OF BOOKS. 3486
BRITISH CHRONOLOGIST, 1775. 728
BRITISH COLUMBIA. UNIVERSITY.
LIBRARY–Collns. 1:2736; 2:477
BRITISH CRITIC. 7927
— Bibs. 1:1925a
BRITISH DRAMA LEAGUE, London.
LIBRARY–Collns. 1:1589b–c
BRITISH EMPIRE. 792
BRITISH FIELD SPORTS, 1807–8. 8192
BRITISH INSTITUTION, 1806–68. 4749
BRITISH LETTER FOUNDRY, 1788–9. 3977
BRITISH LIBRARY *see* BRITISH MUSEUM.
LIBRARY.
BRITISH LIBRARY OF POLITICAL AND
ECONOMIC SCIENCE, London–Collns.
1:107; 3447
BRITISH MUSEUM. 8 2678
— LIBRARY. 2443 3184 3381a
— — Catalogues. 188 2550–1 6637
— — Collections. 1:507 1149f 1154 1462
1474 1520 1837 2137 3568 4469 5115
5192; 2:207 271 300 338; 525 550 572 576
630 685 2022 2027 2080 2214 2231 2614
2651 2803 4222 4299 4303 4382 4883 5622
6442 7100 7223 7231 7457 7624 8111 8338
9156 9158 9872 9497 9548 10170 10278
10290 10438 10612 10687 10719 10994
11159 11411 11652 11763 12528 12925
13278 13541 13684 13784
— — — Britwell. 2821 2833
— — — Clumber. 2984
— — — Croker. 2632 3005
— — — Davies. 2247 2251–2
— — — Gimson. 2943
— — — Ham house. 2985
— — — Harleian. 4620k
— — — Holkham hall. 3142 3147 3257
— — — Kipling. 11768
— — — Luttrell. 2957
— — — Meyerstein. 3163
— — — Peters. 2930
— — — Phillipps. 2758
— — — Sloane. 3154

— — — Smith. 785
— — — Spencer. 2951
— — — Moore. 2128
— — — Perrins. 3262
— — — Thomason *see* DEPT. OF PRINTED
BOOKS–THOMASON COLLECTION.
— — — Thompson. 3102
— — — Upcott. 2758
— — COTTONIAN LIBRARY. 3318
— — DEPT. OF MANUSCRIPTS–Bibs.
1:1760k
— — — Collns. 1:1650c 2033k; 2:1944–5
— — DEPT. OF PRINTED BOOKS–Bibs.
1:1760h
— — — Collns. 1:102 418–20 431 476 481
491 548 609 855 881m 1283 1448 1573f
1795m 1848 1873 2587a 2613a 2636 2679
2690a 2781d 2835 2985 3073 3098 3955
5125 5139 5142; 2:173 239 592 654 659
— — —ASHLEY LIBRARY *see also* WISE,
Thomas James, 1859–1937–Libr. 14400–1
14405
— — — THOMASON COLLECTION *see*
also THOMASON, George, d.1666–Libr.
— — — Collns. 1:1873 1972; 5845–7
— — KING'S LIBRARY. 2688 3222 7520
10201
— — KING'S MUSIC LIBRARY. 3246–7
7619
— — — Collns. 3290
— — LUMLEY LIBRARY. 3205
BRITISH PRINTER. 6136
BRITISH QUARTERLY REVIEW–Bibs.
1:1716k
BRITISH STAR. 1228
BRITTON, John, 1771–1857. 1428
BRITTON, Thomas, 1654?–1714–Libr. 2756
BRITWELL COURT, Bucks.–Libr. *see also*
MILLER, William Henry, 1789–1848–Libr.
2:274; 465 753 763 774 2354 2736 2751
2761–2 2772 2775–7 2787 2790 2797–8
2807 2812 2818 2820–1 2825 2831 2833
2839 3086 7670
BROAD, Charlie Dunbar, 1887–1971–Bibs.
1:2530s
BROADLEY, Alexander Meyrick, 1847–1916.
7456
BROADLEY, T. W., fl.1930–Libr. 12082
BROADSIDES *see also* BALLADS; BOOK
TRADE, LISTS–Broadsides;
PAMPHLETS; PROCLAMATIONS. 523
1021 1299 1311 1320 1344 1372 1414 1875
3707 4737 5426 5474 5750 **6970–7** 8070
13783
—Bibs. 1:570 573 1139z **1534–6v** 2270b
— Collns. 6970 6973a 6976
— Ireland. 6436
— Scotland. 1588 1638

BROADSIDES–Wales. 1484 3871
— 1475–1500. 6971
— 1475–1640. 3871 5474 6975 8070
— 1641–1700. 1299 1372 3707 5750
— 1701–1800. 1311 1414 1875 3707 4737 5426 13783
— 1801–1900. 5426
BROADWAY, Worcs.–Librs. *see* MIDDLE HILL.
BROCAS, John, Dublin, fl.1696–1707. 1907
BROCK, Arthur Clutton–, 1868–1924–Bibs. 1:**2531**
BROCK, Charles Edmund, 1870–1938. 7408
BROCK, Henry Matthew, 1875–1960. 7408
BROCKWEIR, Mons.–Ptg. *see* TINTERN PRESS, 1934–6.
BRODIE, Alexander, 1697–1754–Libr. 3307
BRODRIBB-IRVING, sir John Henry, 1838–1905 *see* IRVING, sir John Henry Brodribb-, 1838–1905.
BROGYNTN CASTLE, Shrop.–Libr. 1:470; 3009 3082
BROME, Alexander, 1620–66. 9475
— *Horace.* 897a
BROME, Richard, d.1652? 5318 7159 **8773**
— Bibs. 1:**2532**
— Mss. 1:1606b
— *Northern lass.* 8773
BROMLEY, Kent–Newspapers–Bibs. 1:901
BROMSBERROW, Glos.–Paper. 1120a
BRONTË, Anne, 1820–49. **8790–1**
— *Narrow way.* 8791
— *Tenant of Wildfell hall.* 8790
BRONTË, Charlotte (mrs. A. B. Nicholls), 1816–35. **8792–800**
— Bibs. 1:**2532b–cb**
— Handwr. 516
— *Jane Eyre.* 2342 8776
— Mss. 785 8792 8794 8797 8799
— — Bibs. 1:2532b
— *The professor.* 8799
— Publ. 5675 5680 8796
— *Shirley.* 8796 8798 8800
— — Bibs. 1:2532cb
— *Villette.* 8798
— — Bibs. 1:2532cb
BRONTË, Emily, 1818–48. **8801–9**
— Bibs. 1:**2532d**
— Mss. 785 8802–3
— *Poems.* 8801–2 8805–6
— *There let thy bleeding branch.* 8803
— *Wuthering heights.* 8776 8807–8
— — Bibs. 1:2532d
BRONTË FAMILY. **8774–88**
— Bibs. 1:**2533–42**
— Bndng. 8784
— Collns. 2849 3090 8777–9
— Handwr. 8785

— *History of Angria.* 8782
— Mss. 8777 8779 8781–2
— — Bibs. 1:2541d
— *Poems by Currer, Ellis and Acton Bell.* 8774 8780 8784 8786–8
— — Bibs. 1:2533x 2542
— Publ. 8788
— *Rockingham or the younger brother.* 8783
BRONTË SOCIETY. MUSEUM AND LIBRARY, Haworth–Collns. 1:2538 2540
— Bonnell collection. 8778
BROOKE, Frances (Moore), 1723–89–Bibs. 1:**2544**
BROOKE, sir Fulke Greville, 1st baron, 1554–1628 *see* GREVILLE, sir Fulke, 1st baron Brooke, 1554–1628.
BROOKE, Henry, 1703–83. **8810**
— *Gustavus Vasa.* 8810
BROOKE, sir John Arthur, 1844–1920–Libr. 2763
BROOKE, Leonard Leslie, 1862–1940. 5944
BROOKE, Ralph, 1553–1625. 4914
BROOKE, Rupert, 1887–1915. **8811–17a**
— Bibs. 1:684 **2545–50**
— *Collected poems.* 8815
— Collns. 8813
— *Letters from America.* 8814
— Libr. 8811–12
— Mss. 8816
— — Bibs. 1:2550
— *1914 and other poems.* 8817a
BROOKE, Stopford Augustus, 1832–1916
— Bibs. 1:**2551**
— Libr. 2654
BROOKE, Zachary Nugent, 1883–1946–Bibs. 1:2551g
BROOKFIELD, co. Down. **1867**
— Ptg. 1867
BROOKFIELD AGRICULTURAL SCHOOL, Moira. 1867
BROOK-JACKSON, Edwin, 1877–1936 *see* JACKSON, Edwin Brook-, 1877–1936.
BROOKLYN. PUBLIC LIBRARY–Collns. 1:2576 3033 3319 3457 3832 4885 4905
BROOKMAN, George, Glasgow, fl.1827–37. 4746
BROOKS, Maria (Gowen), 1795–1845.
— *Zóphiël.* 13530
BROOKS, VINCENT, DAY AND SON, 1867–85. 6202
BROOKS PRESS, Wirksworth, fl.1904–21. **4115**
BROOME, Michael, 1700–75. **4116**
BROOME, William, 1689–1745. **8818**
BROOMHILL HOUSE, Great Brickhill, Bucks.–Libr. 2870

BROTHERTON, Edward Allen, 1st baron
Brotherton of Wakefield, 1855–1930–
Libr. *see also* LEEDS. UNIVERSITY.
BROTHERTON LIBRARY. 1:343a 530
BROUGHAM, Henry Peter, baron
Brougham and Vaux, 1778–1868–Bibs.
1:**2552**
BROUGHTON, Lancs. 1180a
BROUGHTON, Hugh, 1549–1612. **8819**
— Ptg. 8819
BROUGHTON, Richard, d.1634–Bibs.
1:**2553**
BROUGHTON DE GYFFORD, John Cam
Hobhouse, baron, 1786–1869 *see*
HOBHOUSE, John Cam, baron
Broughton de Gyfford, 1786–1869.
BROWN, A. Curtis, 1866–1945. 3477
BROWN, Alfred Reginald Radcliffe-,
1881–1955–Bibs. 1:**2553m**
BROWN, Anne (Gordon), 1747–1810–Libr.
1635
BROWN, Christopher, d.1807. 1294
BROWN, Ford Madox, 1821–93. 7420a
BROWN, Frances, d.1879–Bibs. 1:**2553r**
BROWN, Hugh, Glasgow, fl.1714. 4746
BROWN, John, 1715–76. **8820**
— Bibs. 1:**2554**
BROWN, John, 1722–87. **8821**
— *Self-interpreting Bible.* 8821
BROWN, John, 1810–82–Bibs. 1:**2555**
BROWN, John Alexander Harvie-,
1844–1916–Bibs. 1:**2556**
BROWN, Meredith John Barry,
1885–1973–Libr. 3077
BROWN, Thomas, 1663–1704. **8822**
— Bibs. 1:**2557**
— Ptg. 8822
— *The weesils.* 8822
BROWN, Thomas, fl.1685–1713. 1517
BROWN, Thomas Edward, 1830–97–Bibs.
1:**2558–61**
BROWNE, Edward, 1644–1708.
— Bibs. 1:**2562** 2566b
— *Travels.* 8207
BROWNE, Gordon Frederick, 1858–1932.
7409
BROWNE, Hablôt Knight, 1815–82. 2297
6192 9983 9997a
— Bibs. 1:**1270m**
— *Dickens' Bleak house.* 10123
— *Dickens' David Copperfield.* 10118
— *Dickens' Dombey and son.* 10117
— *Dickens' Pickwick papers.* 9982 10082
— *Smollett's Works.* 13498
BROWNE, James P., fl.1869–85. 13498
BROWNE, John, fl.1610? **4117**
BROWNE, Leigh, d.1936–Libr. 13008
BROWNE, Moses, 1704–87.

— *Fletchers' Works.* 10562
BROWNE, Samuel, 1611?–65. 854 3396a
— Bibs. 1:**1271**
BROWNE, Simon, 1680–1732.
— *Defence of nature.* 13546
BROWNE, sir Thomas, 1605–82. **8823–55**
— Bibs. 1:**2563–6b**
— *Christian morals.* 8830
— Collns. 1306a 8851
— *Garden of Cyrus.* 8834 8843
— *Hydriotaphia.* 8832 8853a
— — Bibs. 1:2566ae
— *Letter to a friend.* 8840
— Letters. 8838
— Libr. 8835 8847 8855
— Mss. 8843 8847 8852
— *Musæum clausum.* 8837
— *Posthumous works.* 8848
— *Religio medici.* 8823–5 8827 8829 8831 8846
8849 8854
— — Bibs. 1:2563–a
— Text. 8823 8834
— *Urn burial.* 8834 8836 8839 8841–2 8844–5
8850
— — Bibs. 1:2566a
BROWNE, Thomas, Dublin, fl.1730–50.
4118–20
BROWNE, William, 1591–1643. **8856–62**
— *Britannia's pastorals.* 8856–60
— *Inner temple masque.* 8861
— Libr. 12651–3
— Mss. 8862
— Text. 8859–60
BROWNING, Elizabeth (Barrett), 1806–61.
8863–84 8886 14837
— Bibs. 1:652 **2567–72**
— *Battle of Marathon.* 8863–4
— Collns. 3061 8883
— Handwr. 8879
— Letters. 8865 8869
— — Bibs. 1:**2572**
— Libr. 8874
— Mss. 785 8876 8883
— *On a poem by E. B. B.* 8884
— Publ. 5226
— *Runaway slave.* 8881
— *Sonnets from the Portuguese.* 8866–8 8870–2
8876–7 14387 14406 14417 14436
— — Bibs. 1:**2569**
— Text. 8869
— *To Robert Lytton.* 8875
BROWNING, Robert, 1812–89. 831a 2322
8885–913 13454 14115 14387 14406 14436
— Bibs. 1:672 **2576–91**
— Bndng. 8894
— *Cardinal and the dog.* 8909
— Collns. 3061 8888 8892 8903 8905 8907
8910 8913

BROWNING, Robert, 1812–89. *Complete works* (Ohio U.P.). 8908
— *Fifine at the fair.* 8893
— Handwr. 8879
— *Helen's tower.* 8895
— *Home-thoughts.* 8912
— Illus. 8909
— Letters. 8889–90 8904 8913 13815
— — Bibs. 1:2589d
— Libr. 2344 8898 8901 13921
— *Lines to the memory of his parents.* 8899
— Mss. 785
— *Pacchiarotto.* 8896
— *Paracelsus.* 8897
— *Pauline.* 8891 14417
— *Pied piper*–Bibs. 1:2591
— *Poems.* 8900 8910a
— *Prince Hohensteil-Schwangau.* 8894
— Publ. 5226 5680 8893 8896
— *Ring and the book.* 8885
— — Bibs. 1:2577a 2520af
— Text. 8887 8906 8908
BROWNLOW, Arthur, formerly CHAMBERLAINE, 1644–1710–Libr. 2958
BROWN PAPER *see* PAPER, BROWN.
BROWN UNIVERSITY, Providence, R. I. LIBRARY–Collns. 1:1355; 2:236
BROXBOURNE, Herts.–Ptg. *see* WATTS, Richard, fl.1810–15.
BROXBOURNE LIBRARY *see* EHRMAN, Albert, 1890–1969–Libr.
BRUCE, George, fl.1738–Libr. 1668
BRUCE, George, fl.1775–1820. 8914
BRUCE, John Collingwood, 1805–92. 5518j
BRUDNELL, Thomas, fl.1621–47. 4121
BRUGES, Belgium–Ptg. 4240 4261 4273 4312
BRUMBAUGH, Thomas Bredle, 1921– –Libr. 11894
BRUNFELS, Otto, 1488–1534.
— *Prayers of the Bible.* 5516–17 8067
BRYAN, Stephen, Worcester, d.1748. 1432
BRYANT, A., fl.1822. 4122
BRYANT, Jacob, 1715–1804. 3078
— Libr. 1:1284; 4302
BRYANT, Thomas, 1828–1914–Bibs. 1:2595
BRYANT, William, fl.1782–1807–Libr. 2688–9
BRYCE, James, viscount Bryce, 1838–1922–Bibs. 1:2596
BRYDGES, sir Francis Egerton, 1762–1837 *see also* LEE PRIORY PRESS, Kent, 1813–22. 5048
BRYDGES, sir Samuel Egerton, 1762–1837–Bibs. 1:2597–8
— Libr. 2866
BRYSON, Martin, Newcastle-upon-Tyne, fl.1722–59. 1322

BUBWITH LIBRARY *see* WELLS. CATHEDRAL. LIBRARY.
BUC, sir George, d.1623. 8915–20
—*Commentary upon the new roll of Winchester.* 8915 8919
— *Daphnis polustephanos.* 8917
— Mss. 8915 8919
BUCHAN, John, baron Tweedsmuir, 1875–1940. 8921–2
— Bibs. 1:2598a–600
— Collns. 8922
— *Huntingtower.* 8921
BUCHAN, Peter, Peterhead, 1790–1854. 4123
— Bibs. 1:1272
BUCHANAN, George, 1506–82. 8923–5
— Bibs. 1:2604–5
— *Commentary on Virgil.* 8924
— *Latin poems.* 8925
— Libr. 1:2605; 8923
— Mss. 8924
— — Bibs. 1:2604
BUCHANAN, James, fl.1766.
— *British grammar.* 7353
BUCHANAN, Robert Williams, 1841–1901–Bibs. 1:2606–7
BUCHANAN, Thomas Ryburn, 1846–1911–Libr. 2149
BUCHANSTOWN, Aber. 4123
BUCK, sir George, d.1623 *see* BUC, sir George, d.1623.
BUCKINGHAMSHIRE. 1043–6
— Bibs. 1:874t–6 3505a
— Maps–Bibs. 1:1775
— Paper. 1043–6 3767a
BUCKLER, Edward, 1610–1706. 8926–8
— Bibs. 1:2608
— *Buckler against the fear of death.* 8928
— — Bibs. 1:2608
— *Midnight's meditations.* 8926
BUCKLEY, William Edward, 1817?–92–Libr. 2501
BUDGELL'S BEE. 7807
BUFFALO. UNIVERSITY. LIBRARY–Collns. 1:3883 3890; 11607
BUFFON, Georges Louis Leclerc, comte de, 1707–88 *see* LECLERC, Georges Louis, comte de Buffon, 1707–88.
BULKLEY, Stephen, fl.1630–80. 4124
BULL, Edward, 1798–1843. 4125
BULL, G. P., Roundwood, fl.1817. 4126
BULL, John, 1562–1628–Bibs. 1:2609
BULLEIN, William, d.1576–Libr. 4905
BULLEN, Arthur Henry, 1857–1920 *see also* SHAKESPEARE HEAD PRESS, Stratford-upon-Avon, 1904–42. 5631–2
— *Beaumont and Fletcher.* 8454
BULLEN, George, fl.1840–76. 5379

BULLOCK, Henry, d.1526–Libr. 4170
BULLOKAR, William, fl.1550–86.
— *Brief grammar.* 7354
BULLOUGH, Edward, 1880–1934–Bibs. 1:2509m
BULMER, John, Haverfordwest, 1784–1857. 4127
BULMER, William, 1757–1830. 1931 4128–39
— Bibs. 1:1273–6h
— Collns. 4138
— *Poems of Goldsmith and Parnell.* 4135
— Type. 4132 4138
BULWER-LYTTON, Edward George Earle Lytton, 1st baron Lytton, 1803–73 *see* LYTTON, Edward George Earle Lytton Bulwer-, 1st baron Lytton, 1803–73.
BULWER-LYTTON, Edward Robert, 1st earl of Lytton, 1831–91 *see* LYTTON, Edward Robert Bulwer, 1st earl of Lytton, 1831–91.
BULWER-LYTTON, Rosina (Wheeler), lady Lytton, 1802–82 *see* LYTTON, Rosina (Wheeler) Bulwer-, lady Lytton, 1802–82.
BUMPUS, J. & E., bksllrs., Cambridge. 2328 2334 12008 13197
BUNGAY, Suff.–Ptg. *see* CLAY, Richard, 1840–91.
BUNTING, Percy William, 1836–1911. 8288
BUNYAN, John, 1628–88. 8929–63
— *Barren fig-tree.* 8935 8957
— — Bibs. 1:2615
— Bibs. 1:1385k 2610–18
— *Book for boys and girls.* 8943
— Collns. 1:2610; 8960
— *Discourse of the building.* 8945
— *Grace abounding.* 8954
— Handwr. 8958–9
— Illus. 8645 8930 8951 8962
— Libr. 8958
— *Pilgrim's progress.* 480 2309 3638 5435 5436 8645 8929–34 8936–42 8944 8946 8949–53 8956 8961–2
— — Bibs. 1:2611 2614 2617
— *Pilgrim's progress, second part.* 8931 8947–8
— Publ. 5435 5436 8937–8 8942 8948
BUNYAN MEETING LIBRARY AND MUSEUM, Bedford–Collns. 1:2616
BURBY, Cuthbert, d.1607. 5749
BURCH, Edward, fl.1771. 5975
BURDENS. 523
BURDON-MULLER, Rowland, fl.1939 *see* MULLER, Rowland Burdon-, fl.1939.
BÜRGER, Gottfried August, 1747–94–Bibs. 1:821a
BURGES, Francis, Norwich, d.1706. 1306
BURGESS, Frederick, fl.1860–91–Libr. 2491 2511

BURGHES, Alexander Macleod, fl.1881–1912. 3477
BURGHLEY, William Cecil, baron, 1520–98 *see* CECIL, William, baron Burghley, 1520–98.
BURGON, John William, 1831–88. 8964
— *Petra.* 8964
BURIN ENGRAVING *see* ENGRAVING, BURIN.
BURKE, Edmund, 1729–97 *see also ANNUAL REGISTER.* 8965–83
— Bibs. 1:2620–2 3841
— Collns. 3046 8981
— *Essay towards an abridgement of the English history.* 8977 8980
— Handwr. 8982
— Letters–Bibs. 1:2621d
— Libr. 8973
— Mss. 8981
— *On the sublime and beautiful.* 8966–7
— *Philosophical enquiry into . . . ideas.* 8975
— Ptg. 8974
— Publ. 4559a
— *Reflections on the French revolution.* 8968 8974 8978
— — Bibs. 1:2621
— *Speech on the Nabob of Arcot's private debts.* 8972
— Text. 8965
— *Third letter on a regicide peace.* 8965
— *Vindication of natural society.* 8969
BURKE, bp. Thomas, 1710?–76. 8984–8
— *Hibernia Dominicana.* 8984–8
— Ptg. 8985
BURKE, Thomas, 1749–1815. 4140
BURKE, Thomas, 1886–1945–Bibs. 1:2623
BURLESQUE NOVELS *see* NOVELS, BURLESQUE.
BURLESQUE POETRY *see* POETRY, BURLESQUE.
BURLESQUES. 6752 6759
— Bibs. 1:1587b 1710 2003
BURLEY, Walter, d.1345? 8989–90
— *De vita et moribus philosophorum.* 8989
BURMAN, Charles Clark, 1855–1917–Libr. 1:926m; 6988
BURN, James and son, est. 1781. 4141–3
BURN, James Robert, fl.1842–90. 4142
BURNABY, Eustace, fl.1677–98. 4144
BURNE-JONES, sir Edward Coley, 1833–98 *see* JONES, sir Edward Coley Burne-, 1833–98.
BURNET, bp. Gilbert, 1643–1715. 8991–3
— Bibs. 1:2624–6
— Mss. 8991
— *Vindication.* 1692
BURNET, sir Thomas, 1694–1753. 8996
— *Second tale of a tub.* 8996

BURY, William, fl.1415–23. 3151
BURY ST. EDMUNDS, Suff.
— Librs. 1400 2663
— Paper see DUXBURY, Yates, 1818–91.
— KING EDWARD VI SCHOOL.
  LIBRARY. 2663
BUSBY, John, fl.1576–1612. 4146
BUSBY, John, fl.1607–31. 4146
BUSHEY, Herts.–Paper. 1139
BUSHILL, Thomas, Coventry, 1833–78. 4147
BUSS, Robert William, 1804–75. 9983
— Dickens' Pickwick papers. 9982
BUSSELL, F. R., fl.1946–Libr. 1:1559
BUTE, John Patrick Crichton Stuart, 3d
  marquis of, 1847–1900 see STUART, John
  Patrick Crichton, 3d marquis of Bute,
  1847–1900.
BUTLER, Edward Joseph Aloysius
  ('Cuthbert'), 1858–1934–Bibs. 1:2568g
BUTLER, Edward K., fl.1922–Libr. 1:4854;
  462
BUTLER, H. T., d.1933–Libr. 2923
BUTLER, Henry Montague, 1833–1918. 9143
— Tennyson's Crossing the bar. 9143
BUTLER, John, fl.1529. 6056 6081
BUTLER, Michael, Kilkenny, d.1779. 8935
BUTLER, Nathaniel, fl.1619–49.
— History of the Bermudas. 8200
BUTLER, mrs. Pierce, 1809–93 see KEMBLE,
  Frances Anne (mrs. Pierce Butler),
  1809–93.
BUTLER, Richard, 1794–1862–Bibs. 1:2658s
— Some notices ... Trim–Bibs. 1:2658s
BUTLER, Samuel, 1612–80. 9144–51
— Bibs. 1:1982 2660–4
— Hudibras. 9144–5 9147–51
— — Bibs. 1:2660–1a 2663–4
— Illus. 9144 9150
— Mss. 9148 9151
— Publ. 9149
— True and perfect copy of the lord Roos his
  answer. 9146
BUTLER, Samuel, 1835–1902. 469 756 758
  9152–62 11388
— Bibs. 1:2665–70
— Collns. 9156 9158 9162
— Erewhon. 9159
— Mss. 9153 9156 9158 9160–1
— Publ. 9157
— Text. 9159
— Way of all flesh. 9152 9157 9161
BUTLER, Thomas, 1765–93–Libr. 2:653
BUTLER AND TANNER, Frome, est. 1795.
  4148
BUTT, Isaac, 1813–79–Bibs. 1:2671
BUTT, John Everett, 1906–65–Bibs. 1:2671d
BUTTER, Nathaniel, c.1583–1664. 3471 4149
— Bibs. 1:1873c

— Certain (weekly) news. 7656
BUTTERFIELD, sir Herbert, 1900– –Bibs.
  1:2671h
BUTTERFLIES AND MOTHS see also BOOK
  TRADE, LISTS–Butterflies and moths.
  6978–84
— Bibs. 1:2136
BUTTERFLY–Bibs. 1:1721
BUTTERWORTH, Joseph, 1770–1826. 4150
BUXTON, sir Thomas Fowell, 1786–1845.
  5250
BUXTON FAMILY–Bibs. 1:2672
BYDDELL, John, fl.1535–45. 4151 6056
BYD Y BIGAIL. 1472
BYERS, sir John William, d.1920–Bibs.
  1:2673
BYNG, John, 5th viscount Torrington,
  1743–1813.
— Libr. 2922
— Tour into Kent. 1157
BYNNEMAN, Henry, d.1583. 4152–3
BYRD, William, 1538?–1623. 9163–7
— Cantiones sacræ. 9166
— Gradualia. 9166
— Masses. 9166–7
— Psalms, sonnets and songs. 9165–6
— Parthenia. 9163–4
— Songs of sundry natures. 9166
BYROM, John, 1692–1763–Bibs. 1:2674
BYRON, Ada Augusta, 1815–52. 9224
— Bibs. 1:2694
BYRON, Anne Isabella (Milbanke), lady,
  1792–1860. 9224
— Bibs. 1:2694
BYRON, Catherine (Gordon), lady, d.1811.
  9224
— Bibs. 1:2694
BYRON, George Gordon de Luna, pseud.,
  fl.1809–52. 9168–70 13335 13339
BYRON, George Gordon, afterwards Noël,
  baron Byron of Rochdale, 1788–1824. 478
  2322 8370 9171–248 14406 14417
— Beauties of English poets. 9180
— Beppo. 9197
— Bibs. 1:54–5 672 928 2675–94b 4432d
— Bndng. 9188
— Bride of Abydos. 9178
— Cain. 9248
— Childe Harold. 9173 9185 9193 9203
— Churchill's grave. 9210
— Collns. 3017 9195 9219–20 9223–4 9229
  9232 9234 9238 9244 9247
— The Corsair. 9211 9236
— Don Juan. 9181 9184 9222 9226–7 9230
  9240
— English bards and Scotch reviewers. 9171 9174
  9235
— Fugitive pieces. 9183 9206 9208

Vol. 1 = Bibliographies   2 = Shakespeare   4 = 1–8221   5 = 8222–14616

BYRON, George Gordon, 1788–1824–
Handwr. 516 9175 9239
— *Hebrew melodies.* 9192
— *Hours of idleness.* 9187 9231
— *Irish avatar.* 9177
— *Lava.* 9207
— *Letter to the editor of my grandmother's review.*
9209
— Letters. 7333 7338 9168 9186 9202 9219
9243
— — Bibs. 1:2692 2694
— Libr. 9201 9239a 9245
— *Manfred.* 9194 9198
— — Bibs. 1:2685
— *Memoirs.* 9212
— Mss. 492 5250 9172 9175 9192 9196–7
9200 9219–20 9222–4 9226–7 9230 9234
9235–a 9238 9241–2 13908a
— — Bibs. 1:2963–4b
— *Observations on an article in Blackwood's.*
9221
— *Ode to Napoleon.* 9200
— *On . . . Hoppner.* 9191
— *On Job.* 9246
— *On the death of the duke of Dorset.* 9228
— *Ossian's address to the sun.* 9218
— *Prefaces.* 9194
— *Prophesy of Dante.* 9235a
— Ptg. 9193
— Publ. 5250 5251 9213 9237 9240 9248
— *Sardanapalus.* 13908a
— *Select works.* 9217
— — Bibs. 1:2691
— *Sketch from private life.* 9204
— *Sonnet to countess Guiccioli.* 9235a
— Text. 9173 9185–6 9202 9210 9218 9230
— *Translation of a Romaic love song.* 9213
— *Werner.* 9194
— — Bibs. 1:2685
— *When I asked for a verse.* 9225
— *Works.* 5250 9188
BYSSHE, Edward, fl.1712. **9249**
— *Art of English poetry.* 9249

C., J., fl.1654.
— *Melancholy cavalier.* 13104
C., W., fl.1623.
— *The fatal vesper.* 10726
CABLE, Matthew, 1874–1961–Libr. 9773
CABRA, co. Dublin. **1944**
— Ptg. 1944
CADELL, Robert, Edinburgh, 1788–1849.
13242
CADELL, Thomas, 1773–1836. 3639a **4154–8**
CADELL AND DAVIES, 1791–1836. 4154–6
4158 9056 11880 12743
— Letters. 4155

CÆDMON, saint, fl.670. 11643–6
CAERMARTHENSHIRE *see* CARMAR-
THENSHIRE.
CAERNARVONSHIRE *see* CARNARVON-
SHIRE.
CÆSAR, G. Julius, 100–44 B.C.
— *Gallic wars.* 2:1018
— *Works.* 5866
CAESAR, sir Julius, 1558–1636–Libr. 2507–8
CÆSAR'S REVENGE, 1607. 7122
CAINE, sir Thomas Henry Hall, 1853–
1931–Bibs. 1:**2695**
CAIRNES, John Elliott, 1823–75–Bibs.
1:**2696**
CAITHNESS, Caith. **1671**
— Bksllng. 1671
— Newspapers. 1671
— Ptg. 1671
CAITHNESS-SHIRE. **1671**
— Bibs. 1:**989–90**
— Ptg.–Bibs. 1:990
CAIUS, John, 1510–73.
— *De antiquitate Cantabrigiensis.* 1073a
— *Of English dogs.* 7089
CALDECOTT, Randolph, 1846–86. 5944
6192
— Bibs. 1:**1276t**
— Collns. 770
— Mss. 770
— Publ. 5944
CALDERÓN DE LA BARCA, Pedro,
1600–81. 10555
— Bibs. 1:**843h**
CALEDON, EARLS OF–Libr. *see* CALEDON
HOUSE, co. Tyrone–Libr.
CALEDON HOUSE, co. Tyrone–Libr.
2:1976; 12756
CALEDONIAN MERCURY. 8702–3
CALENDAR OF SHEPHERDS. 4411 4413
4415 4416a 5311
CALICO PRINTING. 6367
CALIFORNIA. STATE LIBRARY, Sacramen-
to. SUTRO BRANCH, San Francisco
–Collns. 1:1965 4047d; 2:321
— UNIVERSITY. UNIVERSITY AT LOS
ANGELES. BIOMEDICAL LIBRARY
–Collns. 1:4347
— — — LIBRARY–Collns. 1:1668 1715
3225 3778e
— — — WILLIAM ANDREWS CLARK
LIBRARY–Collns. 1:574 605 664 1998
5104f; 716 736 794 811 7320 11290
CALKIN, P. AND A. E., bndrs., fl.1890.
5549
CALLCOTT, Maria (Dundas), formerly
Graham, lady, 1785–1842–Publ. 5250
CALLENDER'S PAPER COMPANY,
Celbridge. 3756

CALLOW END, Worcs.–Ptg. *see* STAN-
BROOK ABBEY PRESS, est. 1876.
CALSTOCK, Cornw.–Paper. 1083b
CALVERLEY, Charles Stuart (formerly
Blayds), 1831–84. **9250**
— Bibs. 1:**2697–b**
— Collns. 9250
— Mss.–Bibs. 1:2697b
CALVERT, Elizabeth, d.1674. **4159** 4160
CALVERT, Giles, d.1663. **4160–a**
CALVIN, Jean, 1509–64. 924 5898
CALWELL, Robert, 1780–1816–Libr. 1778
CAMBRENSIS, Giraldus de Barri,
1146?–1220? *see* GIRALDUS DE BARRI,
Cambrensis, 1146?–1220?
CAMBERWELL. MINET PUBLIC LIBRARY
see MINET PUBLIC LIBRARY,
Camberwell.
CAMBRIDGE, Cambs. *see also* BOOK
TRADE, LISTS–Cambridge. **1047–74**
— Bibs. 1:**878t–82**
— Almanacs. 1057
— Bible. 1062 4165 6816 6865 6866 6891
— Bndg. 1050–3 1056 1058 1066 1068 2093
2161 4168 4751
— Bksllg. 1047 1051–3 1055–6 1058–60 1063
1065 1067
— Guidebooks. 1058
— Librs. 1054 1071 2441 2445
— Newspapers. 1049 1064
— Ptg. 1017–18 1025 1048 1051–3 1055–8
1061 1070
— — Bibs. 1:877 879 881m
— UNIVERSITY *see also* BOOK TRADE,
LISTS–Cambridge. 251 1058 **1073–4** 4161
6891
— — Bibs. 1:**881m–2**
— — CHRIST'S COLLEGE. LIBRARY.
2637
— — — — Collns. 1:2951 4224 4229
— — CLARE COLLEGE. LIBRARY–Collns.
1:448
— — CORPUS CHRISTI. LIBRARY. 2490
3300 3304
— — — — Collns. 1:451
— — EMMANUEL COLLEGE. LIBRARY.
1:438–9 512
— — — — Collns. 6935
— — FITZWILLIAM MUSEUM–Collns.
1:351 444
— — — LIBRARY. 3089
— — KING'S COLLEGE. 3213 3252 3303
3392
— — — LIBRARY. 3068 3126 3179 3228
— — — — Catalogues. 3179
— — — — Collns. 1:432; 3091 12584
— — KING'S HALL. LIBRARY. 2794
— — LIBRARY. 156 2266 2706 3168 3229

— — — Catalogues. 3145 3353
— — — Collns. 1:329 472 500–1 581c 731
878; 558 1571 2378 4098 6308 6720 8608
13361 13753
— — MAGDALENE COLLEGE. PEPYSIAN
LIBRARY. 12702 12704–5 12709
— — — — Catalogues. 12710–11
— — — — —Collns. 1:510; 2240w 2280 7628
14265
— — PEMBROKE COLLEGE. **1074**
— — — LIBRARY–Collns. 1:426; 10847
— — PETERHOUSE–Bibs. 1:**882**
— — — LIBRARY–Collns. 1:443
— — QUEEN'S COLLEGE. LIBRARY–
Collns. 1:435
— — ST. CATHERINE'S COLLEGE. LIB-
RARY–Collns. 1:440
— — ST. JOHN'S COLLEGE. LIBRARY–
Collns. 1:441 2666; 6871
— — SANDARS LECTURES. 224 243 246
567 2159 2249 2355 3456 3476a 4169 6547
7617
— — SELWYN COLLEGE. LIBRARY–
Collns. 1:461
— — SIDNEY SUSSEX COLLEGE. LIB-
RARY–Collns. 1:452
— — TRINITY COLLEGE. LIBRARY. 3135
— — — — Collns 1:492 504; 2:178 304
— — TRINITY HALL. LIBRARY. 3132
— — — — Collns. 1:433
CAMBRIDGE, Richard Owen, 1717–
1802–Bibs. 1:**2697m**
— Mss.–Bibs. 1:**2697m**
CAMBRIDGE BIBLIOGRAPHICAL
SOCIETY. 327
CAMBRIDGE CHRONICLE. 1049
CAMBRIDGE INDEPENDENT PRESS.
1049
CAMBRIDGE INTELLIGENCER. 1049
CAMBRIDGE INTER-COLLEGIATE
CATALOGUE. 623
CAMBRIDGE SHAKESPEARE. 2:693 1197
1650f
CAMBRIDGESHIRE. **1047–74**
— Bibs. 1:**877–82**
— Maps–Bibs. 1:1**776**
CAMBRIDGE UNIVERSITY PRESS, est.
1521 *see also individuals associated with the
Press, e.g.* BASKERVILLE, John, 1706–75;
BENTLEY, Richard, 1662–1742;
CATCHPOLE, P.A., fl.1882–1932;
DANIEL, Roger, fl.1627–66; LEGATE,
John, d.1620?; LEWIS, Walter,
1878–1960; ROBERTS, sir Sydney Castle,
1889–1966; SIBERCH, John (Johann Lair),
fl.1521–2; THOMAS, Thomas, 1553–88.
4161–79 5648
— Bibs. 1:**1277–9**

Vol. **1** = *Bibliographies*   **2** = *Shakespeare*   **4** = 1–8221   **5** = 8222–14616

CAMBRIDGE UNIVERSITY PRESS, est. 1521–Bndng. 4168
— Collns. 1269
— *New Cambridge Bible.* 6866
— Paper. 4168
— *Suidæ lexicon.* 6340
— Type. 4161 4167a 4168 4824 6610
— BENTLEY HOUSE. 4165
— PITT PRESS *see* PITT PRESS, Cambridge, est. 1833.
— SYNDICATE. 4162 4178
— SYNDIC'S LIBRARY–Collns. 1:589 1153 1245f
CAMBERWELL *see* LONDON. CAMBERWELL.
CAMBUSNETHAN, Lanark.–Librs. 1633
CAMDEN, William, 1551–1623. **9251–5**
— *Annals of Elizabeth.* 9251
— *Britannia.* 9253
— Mss. 9255
— *Remains concerning Britain.* 9252 9254
CAMDEN SOCIETY *see* LONDON. CAMDEN SOCIETY.
CAMEO BINDINGS *see* BOOKBINDINGS, CAMEO.
CAMERARIUS, Philip, *pseud. of* John MOLLE, d.1638? 2414
CAMOËNS, Luis de, 1524–80. 10471–2
CAMPBELL, Archibald, marquis of Argyle and 8th earl, 1598–1661. 1574
CAMPBELL, Archibald, 9th earl of Argyle, d.1685. **9256**
— Bibs. 1:**2698**
— *Declaration and apology.* 9256
CAMPBELL, George, 1761–1817–Bibs. 1:**2699**
CAMPBELL, Hugh, fl.1927–Libr. 2840
CAMPBELL, John, 1st baron Campbell, 1779–1861–Publ. 6523
CAMPBELL, Joseph, 1879–1944–Bibs. 1:**2700**
CAMPBELL, Thomas, 1733–95. **9257**
CAMPBELL, Thomas, 1763–1854. **9258–60**
— Bibs. 1:**2701**
— *Exile of Erin.* 9260
— *Lochiel's warning.* 9258
— Mss. 9258
— Publ. 9260
— *Soldier's dream.* 9259
CAMPBELL, Thomas, 1777–1844–Publ. 5226 5250
CAMPBELTOWN, Argyllshire. 1577
— Librs. 1633
— Ptg. 9256
CAMPION, Edward, fl.1540. **4180**
CAMPION, Edmund, 1540–81–Bibs. 1:**2702**
CAMPION, Thomas, d.1619. **9261**
— *Poemata.* 9261

CAMUS, Albert, 1913–60–Bibs. 1:**810**
CANBERRA. NATIONAL LIBRARY OF AUSTRALIA *see* AUSTRALIA. NATIONAL LIBRARY, Canberra.
CANCEL BINDINGS *see* BOOKBINDINGS, CANCEL.
CANCELLATION. **6148–58**
CANCELS. 267 2375 6149–50 6152 6156
— Bibliogr. descr. 149 257
— 1475–1640. 647 968 6148 10882 11116 11579 14160 14371
— 1641–1700. 6151 8728 8731 10381 11585 12224 12364–5 13523a 13524d 13689
— 1701–1800. 4560 6151 6154–5 8015 8680 8686 8691 8701 9037 11444 11449 11511 11529 12695 12745 12751 13795 14363
— 1801–1900. 6153 6158 9769 9815 10761 11481 11831 12111 13208 13220 13807 14093 14526
— 1901– . 10946
CANCEL SIGNATURES *see* SIGNATURES, CANCEL.
CANCEL SLIPS. 6157
CANCEL TITLEPAGES *see* TITLEPAGES, CANCEL.
CANDISH, Richard, fl.1556–1601 *see* CAVENDISH, Richard, fl.1556–1601.
CANDY, Hugh Charles Herbert, 1859–1935–Libr. 1:**4234**
CANNAN, Charles, Oxford, 1858–1919. **4181**
CANNING, Elizabeth, 1734–73–Bibs. 1:**2703**
CANNING, George, 1770–1827. 7438
— Bibs. 1:**2704**
— Libr. 7767
CANONMILLS, Edinburgh–Paper. 1710
CANTERBURY, Kent. **1159–60**
— Bksllng. 1160
— Librs. 1160–a
— Newspapers. 1152 1159
— Paper. 3778
— Ptg. 1017 1025
— CATHEDRAL. LIBRARY. 2412a 2620
— KING'S SCHOOL. LIBRARY–Collns. 3331
CANTERBURY COLLEGE OF ART PRESS, fl.1960. 6495
CANVAS BINDINGS *see* BOOKBINDINGS, CANVAS.
CAPELL, Arthur, earl of Essex, 1631–83. **9262**
CAPELL, Edward, 1713–81. **9263**
— Libr. 1:504; 2:178
— *Notes and various readings.* 9263
— *Prolusions.* 2:791
— *Shakespeare's Works.* 2:735 791–2
CAPES, William Wolfe, 1834–1914–Bibs. 1:**2704g**

CAPE TOWN, S. A. PUBLIC LIBRARY
—Collns. 2:584 656; 3138 3298
CAPITALIZATION. 6180
CARADOC PRESS, Chiswick, 1900–9. 4182
6463
CARBONDALE. SOUTHERN ILLINOIS
UNIVERSITY see ILLINOIS. SOUTHERN
ILLINOIS UNIVERSITY, Carbondale.
CARDANO, Girolamo, 1501–76. 2329
CARDENIO see THEOBALD, Lewis,
1688–1744.
CARDIFF, Glam. 1543–4
— Librs. 1544
— Ptg. see LEWIS, William, 1833–1920.
— PUBLIC LIBRARIES—Collns. 1:953 1475
1485 2125; 2:191 208
CARDIGANSHIRE. 1522–30
— Bibs. 1:962–c
— Bndng. 1522
— Librs. 3110
— Maps–Bibs. 1:1813
— Ptg. 1523
CARDONNEL-LAWSON, Adam Mansfeldt,
formerly DE CARDONNEL, d.1820 see DE
CARDONNEL, Adam Mansfeldt,
afterwards CARDONNEL-LAWSON,
d.1820.
CARDS, PLAYING. 7251
CARDS, TRADE see also BOOKSELLERS'
TRADE-CARDS. 3474 3493 3646 6036
7248
CAREW, Bamfylde Moore, 1693–1770?
9264–5
— Accomplished vagabond. 9265
— Life. 9264
— Publ. 9264
CAREW, George, baron Carew of Clopton
and earl of Totnes, 1555–1629. 1957
— Libr. 2627
CAREW, John, d.1660. 708
CAREW, mrs. Mary Amelia, fl.1937–Libr.
10628
CAREW, Richard, 1555–1620. 9266–7
— Survey of Cornwall. 1085
— Tasso's Jerusalem delivered. 9266–7
— Text. 9266–7
CAREW, sir Richard, d.1643? 9268
— Excellency of the English tongue. 9268
CAREW, Thomas, 1598?–1639? 9269
CAREY see also CARY.
CAREY, George, 2d baron Hundson,
1547–1603. 3187
CAREY, Henry, d.1743. 9270–1
— Dissertation on old women. 9271
CAREY, Mathew, Dublin, 1760–1839. 1929
CAREY, William, 1761–1834–Bibs. 1:2704a
CARGILL, Donald, 1619?–81–Libr. 6875
CARICATURES. 4512 4514 5565 6193

CARION, Johann, 1499–1537. 9272
— Bndng. 5488
— Three books of chronicles. 5488 9272
CARK, Lancs. 1180a
CARLELL, Lodowick, fl.1629–64. 9273
— Arviragus and Philicia. 9273
— Mss. 9273
CARLETON, William, 1794–1869.
— Bibs. 1:2705
— Collns. 7322a
CARL F. PFORZHEIMER LIBRARY,
N.Y.–Collns. 1:4657–8
CARLILE, Richard, 1790–1843. 4182a–b
5909
CARLISLE, Cumb. see also BOOK TRADE,
LISTS–Carlisle. 1086–8
— Ptg. 6988
— CATHEDRAL. LIBRARY. 3374
CARLISLE, EARLS OF–Libr. see CASTLE
HOWARD, Yorks.–Libr.
CARLOW. 1852
— Bibs. 1:1040 1129
— Ptg. 1770 1852
— — Bibs. 1:1039–40 1129
CARLTON, William John, 1886– –Libr.
8179
CARLYLE, Alexander, 1722–1805–Collns.
3050
CARLYLE, Thomas, 1795–1881. 831a 2443
3033 9274–94 9771 10056 11360
— Bibs. 1:661 1939b 2706–12
— Bksllng. 9280
— Collns. 9276–7
— Frederick the great. 9286
— French revolution. 9287
— Handwr. 9291
— Lectures on literature. 9274
— Letters. 9289 9293
— — Bibs. 1:2711b
— Memorandum in support of L. Hunt. 9294
— Mss. 9274 9281–2 9285–8 9290 9292
9294
— — Bibs. 1:2706r–s
— Past and present. 9281–2 9288
— Publ. 5250 6523
— Reminiscences of my Irish journal. 9290 9292
— Sartor resartus–Bibs. 1:2711
— Text. 9285 9288 9293
CARLYLE'S HOUSE, London. 9276–7
CARLYLE'S HOUSE MEMORIAL
TRUST–Collns. 1:2706r–s
CARMARTHEN, Carms. 1533–8
— Bibs. 1:962q 1280
— Bksllng. see THOMAS, David, d.1726.
— Librs. 1535–6
— Ptg. 1533–4 1537–8
— — Bibs. 1:962q 1280
— GRAMMAR SCHOOL. LIBRARY. 1536

CARMARTHENSHIRE. **1531–40**
— Bibs. 1:**962q**
— Librs. 1532
— Ptg.–Bibs. 1:**962q** 1280
CARMICHAEL, Alexander, Glasgow, fl.1724–36. 4746
CARNAN, Thomas, d.1788. **4183–a**
— Bibs. 1:1573–a
CARNARVONSHIRE. **1540f–g**
— Bibs. 1:**962s–t**
CARNIE, Alfred, d.1898. **9295**
CAROGH ORPHANAGE PRESS, Naas, fl.1877–86. 6466
CARPENTER, Edward, 1844–1929–Bibs. 1:**2713–15**
CARPENTER, John, 1570–1620–Bibs. 1:**2716**
CARPENTER, Nathanael, fl.1605–35–Bibs. 1:**2717**
CARPENTER, Richard, 1577?–1627–Bibs. 1:(2718)
CARPENTER, William, fl.1625–1710. **9296**
— Jura cleri. 9296
CARPENTER, William, 1797–1874.
— Political letters. 3546
CARR, Ralph, fl.1594–1600. **9297**
— Troublesome and hard adventures in love. 9297
CARRICK-ON-SHANNON, co. Leitrim–Bibs. 1:1094
— Ptg.–Bibs. 1:1094
CARRICK-ON-SUIR, co. Tipperary–Bibs. 1:1129
— Ptg.–Bibs. 1:1129
CARRINGTON, George, fl.1833–1905–Libr. 2:395
CARROLL, Lewis, pseud. of Charles Lutwidge Dodgson, 1832–98. 475 775 7015 **9298–339**
— Alice in Wonderland. 479 766 768 778 828 2309 9298 9301–3 9305 9307–10 9312 9314–15 9318–21 9323 9325 9327 9329 9331 9335–7
— — Bibs. 1:**2735**
— Bibs. 1:674m 684 **2720–36**
— Collns. 9323 9328
— Endowment of the Greek professorship. 9311
— Garland of Rachel. 9316
— Hunting of the snark. 9299
— Lanrick, a game. 9332
— Letters. 9338
— Libr. 11718
— Mss. 828 9303 9307 9318 9322 9326
— Phantasmagoria. 9333
— — Bibs. 1:2732
— Ptg. 9314 9316
— Publ. 9301 9327
— Symbolic logic. 9339

— Text. 9304 9327
— Through the looking glass. 9304
CARSON, Hampton Lawrence, 1852–1929–Libr. 3236
CARTER, Cornelius, Dublin, fl.1696–1727. 1906–7 **4184**
CARTER, Frederick, fl.1926–32–Bibs. 1:**2740**
CARTER, Harry Graham, fl.1930– . 3476a 6651
CARTER, Isaac, Carmarthen, fl.1718–41–Bibs. 1:**1280**
CARTER, John Waynflete, 1905–75–Libr. 1:**3731**; 2241 3285 11218
CARTER, Will, 1912– , see RAMPANT LION PRESS, Cambridge, est. 1934.
CARTERET, John, earl Granville, 1690–1763–Libr. 1828 2206
CARTMEL, Lancs. 1180a
— PRIORY CHURCH. LIBRARY. 3215 3276
CARTONS. 4147
CARTWRIGHT, Thomas, 1535–1603. 851
CARTWRIGHT, William, 1611–43. **9340**
— Comedies, tragicomedies, with other poems. 9340
CARUCCI, Guglielmus Timoleon, count Libri-, 1803–69 see LIBRI (Guglielmus Brutus Icilius Timoleon, count Libri-Carruci dalla Somaja), 1803–69.
CARY see also CAREY.
CARY, Arthur Joyce Lunel, 1888–1957. **9341–2**
— Bibs. 1:**2741–4b**
— Horse's mouth. 9342
— Mss.–Bibs. 1:2744
— Text. 9342
— Verse. 9341
CARY, Henry Francis, 1772–1844. **9343–4**
— Dante. 9343–4
CARY, John, c.1754–1835. **4185** 8140
— Bibs. 1:**2745**
CARYE, Christopher, fl.1555–64–Libr. 3363
CARYE, William, d.1573–Libr. 3363
CARYLL, John, 1625–1711. **9345**
— Sir Salomon. 9345
CARYSFORT FAMILY–Libr. 757a 2789
CASANOVA DE SEINGALT, Giacomo, 1725–98. 944
CASE, John, d.1600. **9346**
— Praise of music. 9346
CASEMENT, Roger David, 1864–1916–Bibs. 1:**2746**
CASE OF THE CATHOLICS OF IRELAND, 1755. 1929
CASE OF THE PLANTERS OF TOBACCO, 1733. 738
CASES, TYPE see TYPECASES.

CASHEL, co. Tipperary. **1966–70**
— Bibs. 1:**1119** 1128–9
— Newspapers. 1968
— Ptg. 1967
— — Bibs. 1:1119 1128–9
— CATHEDRAL. LIBRARY. 1966 1969–70
— — — Collns. 1:456a
CASLON, H. W. AND COMPANY, fl.1849–
1930. 4198 6648–9
CASLON, William, 1692–1766. 3475 3819
4186–203 6083 6086 6121a 6123 6572 6613
6716 11506
— Letters. 4189
CASLON, William, 1720–88. 4197 5984
CASLON, William, 1754–1833. 6613
CASLON, William, fl.1803–69. 6613
CASSELL, John, 1817–65. **4204–7** 5998
— Bibs. 1:**1280n**
CASSELL AND COMPANY, London, est.
1848. 4204–a 4205 4207
— *Defoe's Robinson Crusoe.* 9884
CASSIOBURY PARK, Watford, Herts.–Libr.
2779
CASSY, Peter, d.1784–Libr. 2522
CASTELVETRO, Giacopo, fl.1546–1611.
4208–9
CASTERA, Jean Henri, 1749–1838.
— *History of Catherine II.* 6289
CASTILLO SOLÓRZANO, Alonso de,
1584–1648. 971
CASTLEBAR, co. Mayo–Bibs. 1:1106b
— Ptg.–Bibs. 1:1106b
CASTING-OFF *see* PRINTING–Casting-off.
CASTLE CONGER. 3991
CASTLECRAIG, Peebleshire–Libr. 2862
CASTLE HORNECK MILL, Penzance. 1083b
CASTLE HOWARD, Yorks.–Libr. 3053
CATALOGUE OF LONDON PLANTS. 6956
CATALOGUES, AUCTION *see* AUCTION
AND SALE CATALOGUES
CATALOGUES, BOOK. 208 1792 1806 2269
3481–94
— 1475–1640. 678
— 1641–1700. 3204
—, BOOK FAIR. 3490–1 3493
—, BOOKSELLERS'. 2272 3640 3677–8
3682 5328 5997
—, LIBRARY *see also* CAMBRIDGE INTER-
COLLEGIATE CATALOGUE;
LIBRARIES, PERSONAL–Catalogues;
OXFORD INTER-COLLEGIATE
CATALOGUE. 2422 2436 2441 2456 3493
— Bibs. 1:**1760d–p** 4421
— Birmingham. 3376b
— British museum. 188 2550–1 6637
— Cambridge. 623 3179 3145 3304 3353
12710–11
— Cartmel. 3215

— Durham. 2811
— Hereford. 3355
— Holkham hall, Norf. 3358
— Houghton-le-Spring. 2638
— London. 3016 3271
— More, Salop. 2643
— National library, Scotland. 1726 1730
— Oxford. 2704 2708 2717 2723 2729 2757
2773 2788 2806 2842 2855 2988 3062 3075
11038 11322 12024
— St. Andrews. 1677
— Scotland–Bibs. 1:1760f 1760j 1760p
—, MAPSELLERS'. 5329
—, MUSIC *see* MUSIC–Catalogues.
—, PRINTERS'. 3493–4 4915
—, PUBLISHERS'. 5826 6510 6528 6537
—, SALE *see* SALE CATALOGUES.
—, TERM. 3484–5 3488–9 3636 12583
CATALOGUING *see* BIBLIOGRAPHICAL
DESCRIPTION.
CATCHPOLE, P. A., Cambridge, fl.1882–
1932. 4163
CATCHWORDS. 267 6342
— Bibliogr. descr. 97 128 143
CATCOTT, George, fl.1792. 9402
CATECHISMS *see* PRIMERS.
—, MASONIC–Bibs. 1:2183a
CATHEDRAL LIBRARIES *see* LIBRARIES,
CATHEDRAL.
CATHERINE OF ARRAGON, queen,
1485–1536–Libr. 2193 2233
CATHERINE PARR, queen, 1512–48–Libr.
4009
CATHOLIC BOOKS *see also* BIBLE–
Versions-Catholic; BIBLE–Ver-
sions–Rheims and Douai; BIBLE–Ver-
sions–Vulgate; BIBLE. N.T.–Ver-
sions–Rheims and Douai; BOOK TRADE,
LISTS–Catholic books; MISSALS. 855
1521 **8081–8** 8952
— Bibs. 1:1853 2064 2255–66a 3542 4282
— Collns. 8088
— Newspapers–Bibs. 1:1853
— Ptg. 8082 8084 8086
CATHOLIC DEAF AND DUMB INSTI-
TUTION, Cabra. 1944
CATHOLIC PRINTERS, PUBLISHERS,
ETC. 1929 1953 4591 5829 5848a
CATHOLICS–Librs. 3396a
CATLIN, George, 1796–1872. 3391
CATNACH, James, 1792–1841. 4045
4210–12 5426 6994
CATNACH, John, 1769–1813. 4210 4514
CATTERMOLE, George, 1800–68. 9983
CATTLE. 6729
CATULLUS, Gaius Valerius, 87–54 B.C. 893
1444 14332
— Bibs. 1:777x

CELBRIDGE, co. Kildare–Paper *see* CALLENDER'S PAPER COMPANY, Celbridge.
CELESTINA see ROJAS, Fernando de, c.1465–1541.
CELLINI, Benvenuto, 1500–71. 943
CENSORSHIP *see also* BOOKS, SUPPRESSED; BOOKTRADE–Regulation. **3495–509a**
— Drama. 3499 7133 8455 12091
— Newspapers. 3503–5 3556 3559 7691
— Scotland. 1570
— 1475–1500. 128
— 1475–1640. 626 3476 3497 3507 5742 7153 8455 10721 14371
— 1641–1700. 3501 3508 12388 12395
— 1701–1800. 12091
— 1801–1900. 9233 10498 10516 10519 11895 12167
— 1901– . 3853 11625
—, MORAL. 3499 3502 3509–a 10498 10516 10519 11625 12167
—, POLITICAL. 3499 3502 3509a 12388 12395 14371
—, RELIGIOUS. 3498–500 3509a
CENTLIVRE, Susanna (Freeman), 1667?–1723. **9350–2**
— Bibs. 1:**2749–50**
— *To the army.* 9351
— *The wonder.* 9350
CENTRE-PIECE BINDINGS *see* BOOKBINDINGS, CENTRE-PIECE.
CENTRE-RECTANGLE BINDER. 2243a
CENTRE RULES *see* RULES, CENTRE.
CERTAIN BRIEF RULES, 1538. 7358
CERTAIN QUESTIONS CONCERNING MASONRY, 1460. 554
CERTAIN (WEEKLY) NEWS. 7656
CERVANTES SAAVEDRA, Miguel de, 1547–1616. 962 966–8 970 972 3854 3857–8 5780 13501 13511
— Bibs. 1:**844**
CHABOT, Phillipe Ferdinand Auguste de Rohan-, count de Jarnac, d.1875. 8783
CHAINED BOOKS *see* LIBRARIES, CHAINED.
CHAINLINES *see* FORMAT–Turned chainlines; PAPER–Chainlines.
CHALES, Claude François Milliet de, 1621–78 *see* MILLIET DE CHALES, Claude François, 1621–78.
CHALFORD, Glos.–Paper. 1120a
CHALLONER, bp. Richard, 1691–1781. 6915
CHALMERS, George, fl.1620. **9353**
— *Sylva leochæo suo sacra.* 9353
CHALMERS, George, 1742–1825. 5574 9928
— *Historical account of printing in Scotland.* 1585

CHALMERS, James, Aberdeen, 1764–1810. 4352
CHALMERS, Thomas, 1780–1847–Bibs. 1:**2751**
CHAMBER, John, 1546–1604.
— *Treatise against judicial astrology.* 6779
— Mss. 6779
CHAMBERLAIN, Robert, fl.1638. 6427
CHAMBERLAINE, Arthur, afterwards BROWNLOW, 1644–1710 *see* BROWNLOW, Arthur, formerly CHAMBERLAINE, 1644–1710.
CHAMBERLAYNE, Edward, 1616–1703.
— *Angliæ notitia.* 7240
— Bibs. 1:**2751k**
CHAMBERLEN, Hugh, fl.1630–1720–Bibs. 1:**2752**
CHAMBERS, Charles Edward Steuart, 1859–1936–Libr. 1:**2754–5**
CHAMBERS, David, fl.1950 *see* CUCKOO HILL PRESS, Pinner, est. 1950.
CHAMBERS, John, Dublin, 1754–1837. **4353–4**
CHAMBERS, Raymond Wilson, 1874–1942–Bibs. 1:**2753**
CHAMBERS, Robert, 1571–1624?
— *Christian reformation of Nosce teipsum.* 9848
CHAMBERS, Robert, Edinburgh, 1802–71. 4356–7
CHAMBERS, Robert, 1802–71–Bibs. 1:**2754–5a**
— *Traditions of Edinburgh.* 4356b
CHAMBERS, W. AND R., Edinburgh, fl.1860–90. 4355 4356a
CHAMBERS, William, Edinburgh, 1800–83. **4355–7**
— Bibs. 1:(1285x)(**2756**)
— *Encyclopædia.* 7243
— *Memoirs.* 6522
CHAMPION, THE. 7750 7785–6 7789 7913 10487 10493 10513
CHANCE FAMILY, Gloucester, 1872–1922. 1120
CHANCERY *see* ENGLAND. COURT OF CHANCERY.
CHANDLER, Elmer E., fl.1925–Libr. 13608
CHANNEL ISLANDS. **1992**
— Librs. 2754
— Ptg. 1992
CHAN TOON, Mabel (Cosgrove), 1872– .
— *For love of the king.* 14325
CHAPBOOKS *see also* BOOK TRADE, LISTS–Chapbooks. 1021 1186 1311 1320 1328 1344 3408 4514 4542 5200 5426 **6985–94** 6995 7000a 7011 7015 11850 13239 13241 14505
— Aberdeen–Bibs. 1:**1541d**
— Banbury. 1414 6985

CHAPBOOKS–Bibs. 1:1286 **1537–48** 1291k
1573c 3486 3985 4613
— Cumberland–Bibs. 1:1540
— Collns. 6986–8 6993 13234
— Ireland. 1761 1781
— Newcastle-upon-Tyne–Bibs. 1:1548
— Nottinghamshire–Bibs. 1:1538
— Penrith. 6988
— Ptg. 5882 6991 6994
— Scotland. 6991
— — Bibs. 1:1540a 1545
'CHAPEL'. 3610
CHAPEL-EN-LE-FRITH, Derbys.–Paper *see*
IBBOTSON, John, fl.1830.
CHAPELS, PRINTERS'. 5546 6057 6122
6146–7
CHAPIN LIBRARY *see* WILLIAMS
COLLEGE, Williamstown, Mass. CHAPIN
LIBRARY.
CHAPMAN, Edward, 1804–80 *see also*
CHAPMAN & HALL, est. 1830. **4358–9**
CHAPMAN, Frederick, 1823–95. 4358–9
CHAPMAN, George, 1559?–1634. 2:1019
1898; **9354–87** 13381
— *All fools.* 9354 9381 9571
— *Alphonso.* 9357
— Bibs. 1:**2757–61a**
— *Blind beggar of Alexandria.* 9386
— *Bussy d'Ambois.* 9356 9371 9374 9376
— *Cæsar and Pompey.* 9357
— *Conspiracy of Byron.* 9358 9377 9380
— *Eastward ho.* 9359–60
— — Bibs. 1:2757
— *Gentleman usher.* 9379
— *Homer's Iliad.* 9361 9366 9370 9373
9375
— — Bibs. 1:2760
— *Homer's Odyssey.* 9361 9366 9370
— *Humorous day's mirth.* 2:1200; 9384–5
— *Masque of the twelve months.* 9372
— *May-day.* 9382
— *Memorable masque of the Middle temple.* 9387
— *Monsieur D'Olive.* 9365 9378
— Mss. 9362
— Ptg. 9365 9378–9 9381–7
— Publ. 8920 9359
— *Rollo, duke of Normandy.* 8471
— Text. 8471 9355–8 9364 9366–7 9369
9373–4 9377 9380 9385–6
— *Widow's tears.* 9383
CHAPMAN, John, 1822–94 *see also*
CHAPMAN BROS., fl.1846–7; *CHAP-
MAN'S QUARTERLY SERIES.* **4359a–60**
6523 7918
CHAPMAN, Livewell, fl.1643–61. 3471
CHAPMAN, Robert William, 1881–1960. 69
85 87 14436
— Libr. 8329

CHAPMAN, Thomas, 1798–1885–Libr. 2523
CHAPMAN, William, 1815–92. **4361**
CHAPMAN AND HALL, est. 1830. 4358–9
9991 10155 12245
— *Dickens' Collected works.* 1:3056h
— *Dickens' Pickwick papers.* 10079
CHAPMAN BROS., pub., fl.1846–7. 977
CHAPMAN'S QUARTERLY SERIES. 4360a
CHAPPELL, Edwin, 1883– –Libr. 4412–13
CHAPTER COFFEE-HOUSE, London.
3639a
CHARACTERS–Bibs. 1:**1549–51** 4382
*CHARACTERS AND CRITICISMS UPON ...
ORATORS, 1705.* 728
CHARD, Thomas, fl.1577–1618. **4362–5**
— Letters. 4362–3
CHARLES I, king of Great Britain and
Ireland, 1600–49. **9388–93a**
— Bibs. 1:**2762–4**
— *Eikōn basilikē.* 520 3475 7333 7338 9388–90
9392–3a 12416 12443
— — Bibs. 1:2762–a 2764
— Libr. 2:657; 9391–b
— Publ. 9393a
CHARLES II, king of Great Britain and
Ireland, 1630–85. 2626 2677 5168
— Bibs. 1:**2770–2**
CHARLES V, king of France, 1337–80–Libr.
2882
CHARLES, Thomas, 1755–1814. **9394**
CHARLEWOOD, John, d.1592. 947
CHARLTON, Kent–Paper *see* DICKINSON,
George, fl.1834.
CHARTERHOUSE SCHOOL, Godal-
ming–Bibs. 1:**917**
CHARTERIS, Henry, Edinburgh, fl.1544–99.
1591
CHARTERIS, Robert, Edinburgh,
fl.1596–1610. 1591
CHARTHAM MILL, Canterbury. 3778
CHARTS *see also* MAPS. 7517 7630
— Bibs. 1:861 1765g 1772 1795m 2879d
— Copyright. 7517
— Publ. 7517 7630
CHASE, James Hadley, *pseud.* of René Ray-
mond, 1906– –Bibs. 1:**2774**
CHASTISING OF GOD'S CHILDREN, 1492?
6024
CHATSWORTH HALL, Derbysh.–Collns.
1:476 548; 2533
— — Collns. 580
CHATTERTON, Thomas, 1752–70. 7333
9395–410
— Bibs. 1:896p **2775–7**
— *Elegy Oct. 29.* 9397
— *Execution of sir Charles Bawdin.* 9399 9403
— Handwr. 9407
— *Heccar and Gaira.* 9406

CHATTERTON, Thomas, 1752–70. *Merry tricks of Lamingtown.* 9405
— Mss. 9397 9404–6
— *Miscellanies in prose and verse.* 9409 9958
— Ptg. 9399
— *Rowley poems.* 9402 9408
— *To Clayfield.* 9404
— *To miss C. on hearing her play.* 9410
CHATTO AND WINDUS, est. 1873. 4897b
CHATTO AND WINDUS FACSIMILE. 2:519
CHAUCER, Geoffrey, 1340?–1400. **9411–31**
— Bibs. 1:**2779a–82a**
— *Canterbury tales.* 9416 9419–21 9425 9428
— Collns. 3113
— *Complaint to his purse.* 9424
— *Envoy to Alison.* 9427
— *House of fame.* 9423
— Illus. 9428
— *Jack Upland.* 9430
— *Lack of steadfastness.* 9426
— *Legend of good women.* 9419a
— Mss. 768 9419a 9422 9426 9429 9431
— *Proverbs.* 9429
— Ptg. 9416 9421
— Text. 9416 9419–20 9424 9427
— *Works.* 4974 4978 4990 4995 6610 9413–14 9419a 9431 11642
CHAUCER SOCIETY, est. 1868. 9419a
CHEAP BOOKS *see* BOOKS, CHEAP.
CHEAP REPOSITORY TRACTS. 12488
— Bibs. 1:4274d
CHELMSFORD. CATHEDRAL. LIBRARY. 2592a
CHELSEA *see* LONDON. CHELSEA.
CHELTENHAM, Glos.
— Newspapers. 13760
— Ptg. 1119
CHELTENHAM JOURNAL. 13760
CHENEY, John, Banbury, 1732–1808. 1414 **4366–8**
— Bibs. 1:**1286**
CHEPMAN, Walter, Edinburgh, 1473?–1538? **4369–72**
— *Henry the minstrel's Wallace.* 11034
CHEPSTOW, Mons.–Paper. 1298a
CHEQUE PAPER *see* PAPER, CHEQUE.
CHERBURY, Edward Herbert, 1st baron, 1583–1648 *see* HERBERT, Edward, 1st baron of Cherbury, 1583–1648.
CHESHIRE. **1075–81**
— Bibs. 1:**883–d** 902
— Librs. 1162
— Maps. 7487
— — Bibs. 1:**1777–8**
— Newspapers–Bibs. 1:1862
CHESTER, Ches. *see also* BOOK TRADE, LISTS–Cheshire. **1075–81**
— Bibs. 1:**883d** 1462a

— Ballads. 1075
— Bksllng. 1077 1079–80
— Newspapers. 1076 1078
— Ptg. 1019 1075 1081
— — Bibs. 1:**883d**
— Publ. *see* CODDINGTON, William, 1770?–1804.
— STATIONERS' COMPANY *see* STATIONERS' COMPANY OF CHESTER, est. 1534.
CHESTERFIELD, Philip Dormer Stanhope, 4th earl of, 1694–1773 *see* STANHOPE, Philip Dormer, 4th earl of Chesterfield, 1694–1773.
CHESTERTON, Gilbert Keith, 1874–1936. **9432**
— Bibs. 1:681 **2784–7a**
CHESTER WEEKLY JOURNAL. 1076 1078
CHETHAM, Humphrey, 1580–1653 *see* CHETHAM HOSPITAL AND LIBRARY, Manchester.
CHETHAM HOSPITAL AND LIBRARY, Manchester. 2467 2561 2785 3058 3200 3206 3340
CHETTLE, Henry, 1560?–1607? 2:1722; **9433–8**
— Bibs. 1:**2787d**
— *Blind beggar of Bednal green.* 9433 9435
— *England's mourning garment.* 9434
— *Green's groatsworth of wit.* 9438
— Handwr. 2:1892 1909
— *Kind heart's dream.* 9438
— Letters–Bibs. 1:**2787d**
— Ptg. 9435 9438
— Text. 9433 9435–6
— *Tragedy of Hoffman.* 9436–7
— AS PRINTER. **4373**
CHETWIND, Philip, fl.1619–67. **4374**
— *Shakespeare Third folio.* 2:675
CHETWOOD, William Rufus. d.1766. **9439**
— *Voyage of Richard Castleman.* 9439
CHEVY CHASE. 6784
— Bibs. 1:**1464–b**
CHEW, Beverly C., 1850–1924–Libr. 1:396 493; 475
CHEYNE, George, 1671–1743. **9440**
CHEYNELL, Francis, 1608–65. **9441**
— *Man of honour.* 9441
CHEYNEY, Peter, 1891–1951. **9441f**
— *Poems of love and war.* 9441f
— *To Corona.* 9441f
CHICAGO. NEWBERRY LIBRARY *see* NEWBERRY LIBRARY, Chicago.
— PUBLIC LIBRARY–Collns. 1:3269; 2:44
— UNIVERSITY. LIBRARY–Collns. 1:1610
CHICHESTER, Sussex.
— Paper. 1412
— Ptg. *see* COCK ROBIN PRESS, est. 1932.

CHILCOTT, William, 1664–1711–Bibs. 1:**2788**

CHILD, Francis James, 1825–96. 4123

CHILD, Isabella, fl.1850. 6825

CHILD, sir Josiah, 1630–99. **9442**
— Bibs. 1:**2789–90b**
— *New discourse of trade.* 9442
— — Bibs. 1:2790

CHILDE, Timothy, fl.1690–1711. 11027

CHILDE, Vere Gordon, 1892–1957–Bibs. 1:**2790w**

CHILDERS, Robert Erskine, 1870–1922–Bibs. 1:**2791**

CHILDREN, EMPLOYMENT OF. 1514 6113

CHILDREN AS AUTHORS. 6996 7006

CHILDREN OF THE CHAPEL see LEITH, Mary Charlotte Julia (Gordon), fl.1875–1917.

CHILDREN's LITERATURE *see also* A.B.C. BOOKS; BOOK TRADE, LISTS–Children's books; BOYS' LITERATURE; CHAPBOOKS; DRAMA, JUVENILE. **6995–7061** 8063
— Bibs. 1:1374b–c 1417–18 **1552–738** 1737 1749
— Collns. 7010 7014 7022a 7026–7 7041 7048 7053 7056
— Illus. 6210 6213 6995 7013 7039 7443 7453
— Newspapers. 5518 6999 7002–3 7005 7009 7024 7037–8 7040 7045
— — Bibs. 1:1560 1857
— Ptg. 6192 6210 7000a 7039
— Publ. 4752 4859 5279 5283 7000a 7015 7022–3 7042–3
— 1701–1800. 5279 5283 6229 6995 7012 7047 9720 13030 13509
— 1801–1900. 844 3450 4425–6 4752 5133–7 6192 6210 6229 6995 7000–4 7007 7029 7039 7060–a 7443 7453

CHILDREN'S WELFARE EXHIBITION, Olympia, London. 10008–9

CHILDS, George, fl.1837. **4375**

CHILD'S OWN BOOK. 7001

CHINTZ BINDINGS *see* BOOKBINDINGS, CHINTZ.

CHIPPING CAMDEN, Glos.–Ptg. *see* ALCUIN PRESS, est. 1928; ESSEX HOUSE PRESS, 1898–1909.

CHIPPING NORTON, Oxon.
— Librs. *see* HEYTHROP COLLEGE. LIBRARY.
— HEYTHROP COLLEGE *see* HEYTHROP COLLEGE, Chipping Norton.

CHIRM, Silvanus, fl.1767–86. **4376**

CHISHULL, John, d.1674?–Bibs. 1:**2792**

CHISWELL, Richard, 1639–1711. 3432

CHISWICK *see* LONDON. CHISWICK.

CHISWICK PRESS, 1844–1962. 3974 **4377–82** 6123a 6142 6192 6194 6229
— Type. 6631

CHIT-CHAT–Bibs. 1:**4774**

CHIVERS, Cedric, Bath, fl.1853–92. **4383**

CHODERLOS DE LACLOS, Pierre Ambroise François, 1741–1803. 920

CHOLMONDELEY, George Horatio Charles, 5th marquess Cholmondeley, 1883–1968–Libr. 3021

CHRISTIAANS, Willem, Leiden, fl.1631–43. 862
— Bibs. 1:757 (1287)

CHRISTIAN HISTORY. 5069

CHRISTIAN MAGAZINE. 5271 9613

CHRISTIE, dame Agatha Mary Clarissa (lady Max Mallowan), 1890–1976–Bibs. 1:1597 **2792a**

CHRISTIE, James C., Dublin, fl.1813–44. 6442

CHRISTIE, Jonathan Henry, fl.1793–1876. 800
— Bibs. 1:4592

CHRISTIE, Richard Copley, 1830–1901. 6
— Bibs. 1:**2792b**
— Libr. 2471 2579

CHRISTIE-MILLER, Sydney Richardson, 1874–1931 *see* MILLER, Sydney Richardson Christie, 1874–1931.

CHRISTINE DE PISAN, fl.1363–1431. 4289 4306

CHRISTMAS, Henry, afterwards Noel-Fearn, 1811–68. 2694

CHRISTMAS BOOKS. 3426

CHRISTMAS CAROLS, 1570? 7597

CHRISTOPHERSON, bp. John, d.1558. **9443**
— *Tragedy of Jephte.* 9443

CHRIST'S KIRK ON THE GREEN, 1643. 1637

CHROMOLITHOGRAPHY. 5688 6123b 6192 6194 6200 6202 6206 6209 6229

CHROMO-XYLOGRAPHY. 6194

CHRONICLES. 664

CHUBB, Ralph Nicholas, 1892–1960. **4384**
— Bibs. 1:**1287f**

CHUBB, Thomas, 1679–1747–Bibs. 1:**2792d**

CHURCH, Elihu Dwight, 1835–1908–Libr. 1:387 493

CHURCHES, PRINTING IN *see* PRINTING IN CHURCHES.

CHURCHILL, Charles, 1731–64–Bibs. 1:**2793–5**

CHURCHILL, sir Winston Leonard Spencer, 1874–1965. **9444–7**
— Bibs. 1:**2796–800**
— *Savrola.* 9444 9446

CLARKE, Mary Anne, 1810–52–Bibs. 1:2812n

CLARKE, Mary Victoria (Novello) Cowden-, 1809–98–Collns. 5313

CLARKE, Samuel Dacre, fl.1856. 4387

CLARKE, Thomas James, fl.1916–Bibs. 1:2813

CLARKE, William, 1800–38. 8119

CLARKE AND BEDFORD, 1841–50. 2028

CLARKSON, Thomas, 1760–1846–Bibs. 1:2813e

CLARY, William Webb, 1888–1971–Libr. 1:934–a

CLASSICAL LITERATURE *see* FOREIGN BOOKS PUBLISHED IN BRITAIN–Classical.

CLASSICAL TRADITION–Bibs. 1:348d 573c 673a

CLASSICAL TRADITION AND SHAKESPEARE–Bibs. 2:154

CLASSIFICATION OF TYPES *see* TYPES–Classification.

CLATFORD, Hants.–Paper. 1132a

CLATTERFORD, I.O.W.–Paper. 1132a

CLAVELL, Robert, d.1711. 3845

CLAVERING, Molly ('Mary'), 1900– . 9468
— *Lairds of Fife.* 9468

CLAWSON, John Lewis, 1865–1933–Libr. 1:517–18 538d; 467 610 2824

CLAY, Richard, Bungay, Suffolk, 1840–91. 4388

CLEEVE, Alexander, fl.1678–90. 2187 4388a

CLELAND, John, 1709–89. 9469–73a
— *Fanny Hill.* 9469–73a
— *Venus in the cloister.* 9473a

CLEMENT, Francis. fl.1587.
— *Petty school.* 5902

CLEMENT, John, d.1572–Libr. 2826

CLEMENTS, Henry, 1686–1719. 3991

CLEMENTS, Henry John Beresford, 1869– –Libr. *see also* VICTORIA AND ALBERT MUSEUM, South Kensington, London. CLEMENTS COLLECTION. 2144

CLERGYMAN'S COMPANION, c.1708. 1469

CLERGYMEN. 2408

CLERK, sir John, 1684–1755. 9474

CLERKE, Anthony, fl.1540–61. 4389

CLERK OF TRANENT, c.1450?–Bibs. 1:2814

CLEVELAND. MEDICAL LIBRARY–Collns. 1:2195
— PUBLIC LIBRARY–Collns. 1:4295
— ROWFANT CLUB *see* ROWFANT CLUB, Cleveland.

CLEVELAND, John, 1613–58. 9475–8
— Bibs. 1:2815–16a
— Text. 9476 9478

CLEVERDON, Thomas Douglas James, 1903– . 3682

CLINT, George, 1770–1854. 4390

CLINTON, Henry Pelham Fiennes Pelham, 4th duke of Newcastle, 1785–1851–Libr. 2965–7 2976 2982 2984

CLOISTER PRESS, Heaton Mersey, est. 1921. 4391

CLONMEL, co. Tipperary. 1971–2
— Bibs. 1:1120–1 1129
— Ptg. 1971–2
— — Bibs. 1:1120–1 1129

CLOPPENBERG, Jan Evertz., Amsterdam, 1581–1647. 863
— Bibs. 1:758 (1288)

CLOTH BINDINGS *see* BOOKBINDINGS, CLOTH.

CLOUGH, Arthur Hugh, 1819–61. 9479–85b
— Bibs. 1:652 1:2817–19
— Bndng. 9485a
— *Longest day.* 9485b
— Mss. 9479–80 9482 9485
— *Poems.* 9483 9485a
— *Say not the struggle.* 9479–81
— *Solvitur aeris hiems.* 9485
— Text. 9481

CLOWES, William, 1779–1847. 4392

CLOWES, William, 1807–83. 4392

CLUBS, BOOK *see* BOOK CLUBS.

CLUMBER PARK, Worksop–Libr. 2965–7 2976 2982 2984

CLUTTON-BROCK, Arthur, 1868–1924 *see* BROCK, Arthur Clutton-, 1868–1924.

CLYMER, George, 1754–1835. 6333

COALVILLE, Leics.–Ptg. *see* MOUNT ST. BERNARD ABBEY PRESS, est. 1952?

COATES, Adrian, fl.1929–52–Libr. 3238

COBBETT, William, 1762–1835 *see also* COBBETT'S WEEKLY POLITICAL REGISTER. 3860 9486–95
— Bibs. 1:2820–1d
— Collns. 3012 9491 9493
— *Grammar.* 9495
— Letters. 9491
— — Bibs. 1:2821b
— *Life.* 9486
— Mss. 9487
— *Poor man's Bible.* 9487
— *Rural rides.* 9489
— *Three letters.* 9488

COBBETT'S WEEKLY POLITICAL REGISTER. 3012

COBDEN, Richard, 1804–65. 9496–7
— Bibs. 1:2822
— *Incorporate your borough.* 9496
— Mss. 9497

COBDEN-SANDERSON, Richard, fl.1920 *see* SANDERSON, Richard Cobden-, fl.1920.

COBDEN-SANDERSON, Thomas James, 1840–1922 *see* SANDERSON, Thomas James Cobden-, 1840–1922.

COBTREE, Kent–Paper. 1161a

COCHRAN, Elizabeth, fl.1730?–Libr. 1635

COCK, Alfred, 1849–98–Libr. 1:4279; 12501

COCKBURN, John, 1652–1729. **9498**

COCKER, Edward, 1631–75. **9499–503**
— Bibs. 1:**2833–a**
— *Arithmetic.* 9499–501 9503
— — Bibs. 1:2823–a
— *English dictionary.* 9502
COCKER, THE, 1743. 8016

COCKERELL, Douglas Bennett, 1870–1945. **4393**

COCKERELL, John Pepys-, fl.1931–Libr. 2889

COCKERELL, sir Sydney Carlyle, 1867–1962.
— Bibs. 1:**2824**
— Libr. 3093

COCKFIGHTING–Bibs. 1:**2138–e**

COCK LOREL'S BOAT, 1518? 519 6035

COCK ROBIN. 7010

COCK ROBIN PRESS, Chichester, est. 1932. **4394**

CODDENHAM, Suff.–Librs. 1400

CODDINGTON, William, Chester, 1770?–1804. 7075

CODEX SINAITICUS. 4393

CODRINGTON, Robert, d.1665. 9297

COE, William Robertson, 1869–1955–Libr. 1:2120

COFFEE HOUSES. 2459

COGAN, Francis, fl.1730–54. 12963
— *Addison's Miscellaneous works.* 8224

COGGESHALL, Edwin Walter, 1842–1929–Libr. 1:3066b

COHN, Albert Mayer, fl.1914–24–Libr. 1:2931; 4440

COKAYNE, sir Aston, 1608–84. **9504–5**
— *Chain of golden poems.* 9504

COKAYNE, sir Thomas, 1519?–92. **9506**
— *Short treatise of hunting.* 9506

COKE, sir Edward, 1552–1634. 3236
— Libr. *see also* HOLKHAM HALL, Norf.–Libr. 3084–5 3107

COKE, Gerald Edward, 1907– –Libr. 10933

COKE, Thomas, earl of Leicester, 1697–1759–Libr. 3268

COKE, Thomas William, 1st earl of Leicester, 1752–1842–Libr. *see* HOLKHAM HALL, Norf.–Libr.

COKE, Thomas William, 2d earl of Leicester, 1822–1909–Libr. *see* HOLKHAM HALL, Norf.–Libr.

COLBURN, Henry, fl.1807–55. 10208 11880

COLBURN AND BENTLEY, 1829–90. 4002a

COLBY COLLEGE, Waterville, Me. LIBRARY–Collns. 1:1351w 1352 2309 3326 3504b 3588 3590 3592 3595 3599 4362 4443 4783c 4809 4868; 8237 10931 12845 13660 13851 13923

COLCHESTER, Essex.
— Ptg. *see* GEMINI PRESS, 1934–6.
— PUBLIC LIBRARY–Collns. 3359

COLE, Francis, fl.1642. 9698

COLE, George Douglas Howard, 1889–1959–Bibs. 1:**2824d**

COLE, George Watson, 1850–1939. 45

COLE, sir Henry, 1808–82. 3974

COLEMAN, Thomas, 1598–1647. **9507**
— *Hopes deferred.* 9507

COLEMAN STREET PRESS, 1643–5. 6067
— Bibs. 1:595a

COLERAINE, co. Derry. **1865–6**
— Bibs. 1:**1055**
— Ptg. 1865–6
— — Bibs. 1:1055

COLERIDGE, Hartley, 1796–1849–Bibs. 1:**2824m–n**

COLERIDGE, Henry Nelson, 1798–1843. 9529

COLERIDGE, Samuel Taylor, 1772–1834 *see also THE FRIEND; THE WATCH MAN; WORDSWORTH, William, 1770–1850. Lyrical ballads.* 784 1280 8258 **9508–68** 11106 11840 13529 13539
— *Absence.* 9520
— *Ancient mariner.* 14546
— Bibs. 1:**2826–36**
— *Biographia literaria.* 9551
— *Christabel.* 9514 9539
— Collns. 9195 9523 9531 9534 9539 9541 9547 14533
— *Dejection.* 9518
— *Epitaphium testamentarium.* 9517
— *God omnipresent.* 9555
— Handwr. 9549
— *Kubla Khan.* 9532 9546 9559–60
— *Lewti.* 14529 14546
— Libr. 9515 9529 9533–4 9545 9557 9568
— *Lines to Thelwall.* 9565
— Mss. 9510–11 9522 9528 9531–2 9546 9548 9552–3 9559–61 9564–5 9567 14492 14507
— — Bibs. 1:2824m 5166t
— *Poems.* 9527 9540
— Publ. 5226 5250
— *Remorse.* 9558 9567
— *Sibylline leaves.* 9525 9535
— *Some notes on The ancyent marinere.* 14546
— Text. 9512 9518 9521 9527 9529–30 9535 9551 9554 9556 9563 9567 14546
— *Wandering of Cain.* 9516

COLES, Abraham, 1813–91? 2:778

COMPOSITION, MECHANICAL *see* COMPOSING MACHINES.
—, PHOTOGRAPHIC. 6163–71
COMPOSITORS *see also* BOOK TRADE, LISTS–Compositors. 257 5092
— Wages. 1275 5092
COMPOSITORS AND COPY. 257 4338 6064 7148 12252 14084 14372
COMPTON, James, 3d earl of Northampton, 1622–81–Libr. 3396a
COMPUTER-AIDED BIBLIOGRAPHY. 168 170
COMPUTER-AIDED COMPOSITION *see* COMPOSITION, COMPUTER-AIDED.
COMPUTERS. 7187
COMPUTER TYPESETTING *see* COMPOSITION, COMPUTER-AIDED.
COMYN, John, fl.1967–Libr. 9001
CONACHT *see* CONNAUGHT.
CONCORDANCES–Bibs. 1:**1574**
CONCURRENT PRINTING *see* PRINTING, CONCURRENT.
CONDITION, ORIGINAL *see* BOOK COLLECTING–Condition.
CONDUITT, John, 1688–1737. 12584
CONE MILL, Woolaston. 1120a
CONGERS. 3991 4605 6104
CONGRATULATIONS *see also* COMMENDATIONS. 1068
CONGREGATIONALIST BOOKS–Bibs. 1:**2266k**
CONGREGATIONAL LIBRARY, London *see* LONDON. CONGREGATIONAL LIBRARY.
CONGREVE, William, 1670–1729. **9625–34**
— *Amendments of mr. Collier's citations.* 6151
— Bibs. 1:1597
— *Double dealer.* 9630
— Handwr. 9634
— *Impossible thing.* 9625
— Libr. 9628–9 9633
— Mss. 9626 9632 13135
— Ptg. 6151 6703 9630
— *School for scandal.* 9632
CONGREVE, sir William, 1772–1828. 3732 6228
CONISTON, Lancs. **1165a**
— Ptg. 1165a 1180a
CONJURING *see also* MAGIC.
— Bibs. 1:2139–41a
— Scotland–Bibs. 1:2139
CONNAUGHT.
— Bibs. 1:**1055q**
— Ptg. 1788
CONNECTICUT. SOUTHERN CONNECTICUT STATE COLLEGE, New Haven. LIBRARY–Collns. 1:1572a

CONRAD, Joseph, *pseud. of* Teodor Józef Konrad Korzeniowski, 1857–1924. 194 481 779 11875
— *Almayer's folly.* 9651 9667
— Bibs. 1:684 **2855m–74b**
— Chance. 779 9635 9639 9655 9659a 9660 9667 14417
— Collns. 477 3024 9641–3 9648–50 9656 9661 9663 11783
— *Congo diary.* 9645
— Libr. 1:2866g; 472 9644 9666
— Mss. 470 472 9640–4 9651 9657 9664 9666a 9667
— — Bibs. 1:2866g–i 2874
— *Nature of a crime.* 9645
— *Nigger of the Narcissus.* 779
— *Nostromo.* 9657 9662
— *Notes on seige and fall of Paris.* 9667
— Ptg. 9659
— Publ. 4858a 9659b 9660
— *The rescue.* 9646 9659
— *The rover.* 9654
— *Set of six.* 9638
— *Some reminiscences.* 9653
— *Suspense.* 9658
— Text. 9652 9662
— *Victory.* 9665
CONSTABLE, Archibald, Edinburgh, 1774–1827 *see also* CONSTABLE'S MISCELLANY. 3440 **4402–4** 5250 13242
CONSTABLE, Henry, 1562–1613. **9668**
— Mss. 9668
CONSTABLE, T. & A., Edinburgh, est. 1760. 4404
CONSTABLE AND COMPANY, London, est. 1890. 1001
CONSTABLE'S MISCELLANY. 7817
CONSTANTINOPLE. 5180 5182
CONTEMPORARY REVIEW–Bibs. 1:1927
CONTENTION OF YORK AND LANCASTER, 1594. 5658 5660
CONWAY, Edward, 2d viscount, 1594–1655–Libr. 2608 3396a
CONWAY, sir John, d.1603 **9669**
— Ptg. 9669
CONYBEARE, John, 1691–1755–Bibs. 1:**2875**
CONZATTI, Zachary, Dublin, fl.1686. **4405**
COOK, Benjamin, fl.1734. **4406**
COOK, Davidson, fl.1874–1938 *see* COOK, T. Davidson, fl.1874–1938.
COOK, James, 1728–79. **9670–4**
— Bibs. 1:**2876–9d**
— Collns. 9674
— Mss. 9671–2
— *Voyages.* 9673
COOK, T. Davidson, fl.1874–1938–Libr. 9098

COOKE, Charles, 1766–1816. 1294 3639a
COOKE, George Alexander, 1781–1834. 4407
COOKE, James, 1614–88.
— Supplementum chirugiæ. 7556
COOKE, John, d.1660. 708
COOKE, Thomas, 1703–56. 9675
— Mss. 9675
COOKE, William, fl.1632–41. 13418
COOKERY. 491 7063–6
— Bibs. 1:2141b–5
— Collns. 3011 7065–6
COOKSTOWN, co. Tyrone–Bibs. 1:1122
— Ptg.–Bibs. 1:1122
COONEY, Peter, Dublin, fl.1789. 4408
COOPER, Anthony Ashley, 3d earl of Shaftesbury, 1671–1713. 9676–7
— Bibs. 1:2880–a
— Characteristics. 9677
— — Bibs. 1:2880a
— Moralists. 9676
COOPER, Charles Purton, 1793–1875–Libr. 3227
COOPER, Edith Emma, 1862–1914 see FIELD, Michael, pseud.
COOPER, John Gilbert, 1723–69. 9611
— Bibs. 1:2880d
COOPER, Richard, 1705–64. 4409
COOPER, Richard, 1740?–1815? 4409
COOPER, Samuel, 1609–72. 9678
— Mss. 9678
COOPER, bp. Thomas, 1517?–94. 11367
COOPER, William, fl.1675–89. 3670 3684
COOSEBEAN, Cornw.–Paper. 1083b
COOTE, Edmund, fl.1597.
— English schoolmaster. 5749
COOTEHILL, co. Cavan–Bibs. 1:1044
— Ptg.–Bibs. 1:1044
COPE, Richard Whittaker, d.1830? 4410
COPE'S TOBACCO PLANT. 7911
COPIES, ANNOTATED see ANNOTATED COPIES.
—, ASSOCIATION see ASSOCIATION COPIES.
—, COPYRIGHT DEPOSIT see COPYRIGHT DEPOSIT COPIES.
—, DEDICATION see DEDICATION COPIES.
—, EXTRA-ILLUSTRATED see EXTRA-ILLUSTRATED COPIES.
—, FINE PAPER see FINE PAPER COPIES.
—, INTERLEAVED see INTERLEAVED COPIES.
—, LARGE PAPER see LARGE PAPER COPIES.
—, PRESENTATION see PRESENTATION COPIES.

COPINGER, Walter Arthur, 1847–1910. 16 1718 11605
— Libr. 1:417g; 6812
COPLAND, Robert, fl.1508–47. 4411–17 6056 6081
— Bibs. 1:2880h
— Borde's Introduction to knowledge. 8659
— Calendar of shepherds. 4411 4413 4415 4416a
— — Bibs. 1:2880h
— Complaint of them that be too late married. 4414
— The seven sorrows. 4416
COPLESTON, bp. Edward, 1776–1849. 9679–80
— Advice to a young reviewer. 9679–80
COPPARD, Alfred Edgar, 1878–1957. 9681
— Bibs. 1:2881–2
— Cherry ripe. 9681
COPPERPLATE ENGRAVING see ENGRAVING, COPPERPLATE.
COPPER PLATERS see BOOK TRADE, LISTS–Copper plate makers.
'COPY, FAIR'. 3587
—, PRINTERS'. 257 367a 4348 4563 4663 5471 5833 6018 6026 6357 6361 6388 6405 6418 8494 9282 9421 9425 10752 11527 12060 12069 12205 13530 13876 13984 14091 14553
COPY, PRINTERS AND see COMPOSITORS AND COPY.
COPYBOOKS. 7067–70
— Bibs. 1:1575
— Collns. 7068–9
— Wales. 1481
COPYBOOKS, PRINTERS' see PRINTERS' COPYBOOKS.
COPY OF A LETTER SENT BY JOHN BRADFORTH. 7946
COPYRIGHT see also BOOKS, PIRATED. 174 612 3510–44
— Bibs. 1:1139m 1161
— Ireland. 1915
— Scotland. 1552 1599 1680
and in relation to the following:
— Allott. 4374
— Boswell. 8696 8709
— Bunyan. 8937–8
— Burns. 9086
— Byron. 9248
— Campbell, T. 9260
— Collins. 3523
— Dickens. 10056 10070–1 10116
— Flecker. 10559
— Gay. 10646 10651
— Heywood, T. 11083
— Housman. 11186
— Hudson. 11239

CORRECTORS OF THE PRESS *see also* LOWIS, David, fl.1496; ROBERTS, Michael, fl.1630; ROBINSON, Humphrey, fl.1623–70.
CORRECTORS OF THE PRESS. 6405 6407
— Fees. 6405
CORRESPONDENCE *see* LETTERS.
CORVINUS PRESS, fl.1936–7–Bibs. 1:1289
CORVO, baron, *pseud., see* ROLFE, Frederick William Serafino Austin Lewis Mary ('baron Corvo'), 1860–1913.
CORY, William Johnson, 1823–92. 9684
— Bibs. 1:2883–4
— *Ionica.* 518 9684
CORYATE, Thomas, 1577?–1617. 9685
— *Crudities.* 9685
COSIN, bp. John, 1594–1672. 9686
— Bibs. 1:2885
— *Collection of private devotions.* 9686
— — Bibs. 1:2885
— Libr. 2:612
COSTS *see* PRICES.
COTES, Thomas, fl.1606–41. 141
COTES'S WEEKLY JOURNAL. 7745 7803
COTGRAVE, Randle, d.1634. 2:880
COTTERAMS MILL, Maidstone. 1161a
COTTESFORD, Thomas, d.1555. 9687
— *Two very godly letters.* 9687
COTTINGHAM, Lewis Nockalls, 1787–1847–Libr. 3030
COTTON, Charles, 1630–87. 9688–91
— Bibs. 1:5010–11 5013
— Collns. 14222
— *Complete gamester.* 9688
— *Contentation of anglers.* 9691
— Mss. 9689 9691
— Text. 9690
COTTON, John, 1802–49–Bibs. 1:2886
COTTON, sir Robert Bruce, 1571–1631. 9692–3
— Libr. *see also* BRITISH MUSEUM. COTTONIAN LIBRARY. 2266 2445 9693
— *Short view of Henry the third.* 9692
— Text. 9692
COTTRELL, Thomas, fl.1757–85. 3475 6613
COTTRELL-DORMER, Charles, 1801–74 *see* DORMER, Charles Cottrell-, 1801–74.
COUCH, Jonathan, 1789–1870.
— *History of British fishes.* 4650
COULL, Thomas, fl.1861. 1223
COULTON, George Gordon, 1858–1947–Bibs. 1:2886e
COUNTERFEITING *see* FORGERIES.
COUNTERMARKS *see* WATERMARKS–Countermarks.
COURAGE, Archibald, Aberdeen, 1804–71. 4420
COURIER–Bibs. 1:5179

COURIERS, PROOF *see* PROOF COURIERS.
COURT AND CITY REGISTER–Bibs. 1:1902c
COURTESY BOOKS. 4611
— Bibs. 1:2146–52
COURTHOPE, William John, 1842–1917–Bibs. 1:2887
COURT MAGAZINE–Bibs. 1:4723b
COURTNEY, William Prideaux, 1845–1913. 19
COURT OF CIVIL COURTESY, 1577. 579
COURT OF FANCY, 1762. 872
COURT OF VENUS, 1537? 14571
COUSINS, James Henry Sproull, 1873–1956–Bibs. 1:2887d
COUSINS, Margaret E. (Gillespie), 1878–1954–Bibs. 1:2887d
COUSTILLAS, Pierre, fl.1968–Libr. 10708
COUTTS, Angela Georgina (mrs. William L. Ashmead-Bartlett), baroness Burdett-Coutts, 1814–1906–Libr. 2:536 540 1820; 2778
COVENT GARDEN LADIES see LIST OF COVENT GARDEN LADIES.
COVENTRY, Warws.
— Ptg. *see* BUSHILL, Thomas, 1833–78; TURNER, John, 1773–1863.
— PUBLIC LIBRARIES–Collns. 1:2866f 3248f 4628e
COVENY, Christopher, 1846–1941.
— *Dickens' Pickwick papers.* 9982
COVERDALE, Miles, 1488–1568. 4781
— Bible. 6800–1 6803 6819 6821 6829 6839 6860–4 6868 6874
— — Bibs. 1:1483g–h
COVERS, PAPER *see* PAPER-COVERS.
COWAN, Samuel, Perth, 1835–1914. 4420a
COWAN, William, 1851–1929–Libr. 1:1506 1512–13 1733
COWARD, sir Noël Pierce, 1899–1973–Bibs. 1:1597 2887j–k
COWBRIDGE, Glams.–Ptg. *see* THOMAS, Daniel, fl.1771; THOMAS, Rhys, d.1790; WALTERS, Henry, 1766–1829; WALTERS, John, 1721–97.
COWBRIDGE BOOK SOCIETY. 2450
COWDEN-CLARKE, Charles, 1787–1877 *see* CLARKE, Charles Cowden-, 1787–1877.
COWDEN-CLARKE, Mary Victoria (Novello), 1809–98 *see* CLARKE, Mary Victoria (Novello) Cowden-, 1809–98.
COWELL, John, c.1554–1611–Bibs. 1:2888
COWIE, Alfred T., fl.1948–58–Libr. 11599
COWLEY, Abraham, 1618–67. 9694–700
— Bibs. 1:2889–91
— *The guardian.* 9698
— *The mistress.* 9695
— *On hope.* 9700a–b

COWLEY, Abraham, 1618–67. *Plantarum libri duo.* 9696
— *Poems composed into songs.* 9694
— Publ. 9700
— *Puritan and the papist.* 9697
— Text. 9476 9695 9697
— *Verses on several occasions.* 9699
— *Vision.* 9700
— — Bibs. 1:2890
COWLEY, Hannah (Parkhouse), 1743–1809. **9701–2**
— *Belle's stratagem.* 9701
— Bibs. 1:**2892–3**
— Ptg. 9702
COWPER, Edward, fl.1815–52. 6312 7903
COWPER, William, 1731–1800. **9703–25**
— Bibs. 1:**2894–6d**
— Handwr. 9718
— Illus. 9707 9711–12
— *John Gilpin.* 9707 9711–12 9720
— Letters. 9706 9709–10
— — Bibs. 1:2895p
— Libr. 9713 9715 9717 13468
— Mss. 472 9722 9725
— — Bibs. 1:2896d
— *On the benefit from sea-bathing.* 9716
— *Poems.* 9724
— Publ. 9723
— *The rose.* 9721
— Text. 9705–6
— *To the immortal memory of the halibut.* 9705
COWPER AND NEWTON MUSEUM, Olney, Bucks. 9722
— Collns. 1:2896d
COWSE, James, Exeter, fl.1682. **4421**
COX, capt., fl.1575–Libr. 581 591
COX, Edwin Marion, fl.1915–25. 50
— Libr. 2711
COX, James Stevens, fl.1947–9–Libr. 3314
COX, Morris, fl.1957 *see* GOGMAGOG PRESS, Stratford, London, est. 1957.
COX, Nicholas, fl.1673–1721. 11903
COX, Thomas, d.1734.
— *Magna Britannia et Hibernia.* 1414
COX, Thomas, d.1754.
— *Defoe's Robinson Crusoe.* 9887
COX, Walter, c.1770–1837. **9726**
— Bibs. 1:**2897**
— *Observations on a pamphlet.* 9726
COXE, Henry Octavius, 1811–81–Bibs. 1:**2898**
COYET, Peter Julius, 1618–67–Libr. 2:650a
COYKENDALL, Frederick, 1872–1954–Libr. 1:2528
COZZENS, James Gould, 1903–78. 1002
CRAB, Gilbert, fl.1515.
— *Aristoteles de convenientia politice.* 1650
— Bibs. 1:4112k

CRABBE, George, 1754–1832. **9727–39**
— Bibs. 1:**2898a–904**
— Collns. 3046
— *Inebriety.* 9737
— Mss. 9727 9729
— — Bibs. 1:2903
— Publ. 5250 9730 9735–6
— *Tales.* 9731 9733–4
— — Bibs. 1:2902
— *The village.* 9732
— *Works.* 9730 9735
CRACKANTHORPE, Hubert, 1870–96–Bibs. 1:**2910–12**
CRAFTSMAN, THE. 7697 7783
CRAGHEAD, Robert, 1648–1738.
— *Advice for assurance of salvation.* 6913
CRAIG, Edward Gordon, 1872–1966. **9740–1**
— Bibs. 1:**2912c–f**
— Collns. 9740–1
— Ptg. 6098
CRAIG, James Thomson Gibson, 1799–1866–Libr. 1995
CRAIG, Robert, Airdrie, est. 1820. **4421m**
CRAIGHTON, William, Ipswich, fl.1739–61. **4422**
CRAIGIE, Dorothy (Glover), fl.1966–Libr. 1:1720
CRAIGIE, Pearl Mary Teresa (Richards), 1867–1906 *see* HOBBES, John Oliver, *pseud.*
CRAIGIE, sir William Alexander, 1867–1957–Bibs. 1:**2913**
CRAIK, Dinah Maria (Mulock), 1826–87. **9742**
— Bibs. 1:**2914**
— Collns. 3061
— *Head of the family.* 9742
CRAMPTON, John, Sawston, 1833–1910. **4423**
CRANACH PRESS, Weimar, est. 1913.
— Type. 6610 6645
CRANE, Elizabeth (Hussey), fl.1588–9. 5152
CRANE, Hart, 1899–1932.
— *The bridge.* 1008
CRANE, Ralph, fl.1575–1632. 2:615 909 943 948; 650 **9743–9**
— *Jonson's Pleasure reconciled.* 11568
— *Middleton's Game at chess.* 12269
— *Middleton's The witch.* 2:953; 12268
— *Shakespeare's Winter's tale.* 2:1861 1863
CRANE, Stephen, 1871–1900. 1003 1009
CRANE, Walter, 1845–1915. **4424–6** 6192 7420a
— Bibs. 1:**2914y–15**
CRANFORD SERIES (MACMILLANS). 7295 7297
— Bibs. 1:1746

CRANMER, archbp. Thomas, 1489–1556. **9750–4**
— *Bible.* 6800 6810 6815 6817 6868 6871 6874
— *Catechismus.* 9754
— Libr. 9750–3
CRANSTON, David, fl.1509–26–Bibs. 1:4112k
CRANSTON, William, fl.1515–40?–Bibs. 1:4112k
CRASHAW, Richard, 1612?–49. 8259 **9755–63**
— Bibs. 1:**2915g**
— Bndngs. 9762
— *Hymn to Saint Teresa.* 9761
— Mss. 9755 9759 9761 9763
— *Poemata et epigrammata.* 9757
— *Poems.* 9756
— *Steps to the temple.* 9756 9758 9760
— *Upon the bleeding crucifix.* 9759
CRASHAWE, William, 1572–1626. **9764–5**
— Bibs. 1:**2916**
— Letters–Bibs. 1:2916
— Libr. 9764–5
CRAWFORD, Alexander William Lindsay, 25th earl of, 1812–80 *see* LINDSAY, Alexander William, 25th earl of Crawford, 1812–80.
CRAWFORD, David, 1665–1726.
— *Several letters containing the amours.* 7278
CRAWFORD, Francis Marion, 1854–1909–Bibs. 1:**2917**
CRAWFORD, James Ludovic Lindsay, 26th earl, 1847–1913 *see* LINDSAY, James Ludovic, 26th earl of Crawford, 1847–1913.
CRAWFORD, William Horatio, 1818–88–Libr. 2703
CRAWFURD, David, d.1708. 1638
CRAYON ENGRAVING *see* ENGRAVING, CRAYON.
CREDITON. HOLY CROSS CHURCH. LIBRARY–Collns. 2233
CREECH, William, Edinburgh, 1745–1815. **4427–8** 9115–16
CREEDE, Thomas, d.1616. **4429**
— *Chapman's Monsieur D'Olive.* 9378
— *Shakespeare's Romeo and Juliet.* 2:1735
CREIFF, Perth.–Librs. 1731
CREIGHTON, bp. Mandell, 1843–1901–Bibs. 1:2918–b
CRICKET. **7071**
—Bibs. 1:**2153–7**
CRICKET FICTION *see* FICTION, CRICKET.
CRITICAL BIBLIOGRAPHY *see* BIBLIOGRAPHY, ANALYTICAL.

CRITICAL REVIEW. 7710 7718 7781 13513
— Bibs. 1:3469a 4721i–j 4723a–4 4738
CRITICISM, LITERARY. 6775
CRITICS, THE. 7735
CROATIA *see* SHAKESPEARE, William, 1564–1616–WORKS IN CROATIA.
CROCHET. 7470
— Bibs. 1:2200
CROCKER, Templeton, 1884–1948–Libr. 1:4898
CROCKER, William Henry, 1861–1937–Libr. 2:604
CROCKETT, Samuel Rutherford, 1860–1914–Bibs. 1:**2919**
CROESSMAN, Harley K., fl.1957–Libr. 1:3887
CROKE, sir George, 1560–1642. **9766**
— Ptg. 9766
— *Reports.* 9766
CROKER, John Wilson, 1780–1857.
—Bibs. 1:**2920**
— *Boswell's Johnson.* 5250
— Letters. 13190
— Libr. 2632 2683–4 3005
CROMEK, Robert Hartley, 1770–1812. 8578 8625a 9084 **9767–9**
— Ptg. 9769
— *Reliques of Robert Burns.* 9768–9
CROMWELL, Oliver, 1599–1658. **9770–3** 13579
— Bibs. 1:**2920d–2**
— Collns. 9773
— Letters. 2996
— Libr. 2221 5071 9770
CROMWELL'S BIBLE, 1539 *see* BIBLE –Versions–Cromwell's.
CRONE, John Smyth, 1858–1945. 34 56 58 60–1
— Bibs. 1:**2922h**
— Libr. 1815
CRONIN, Archibald Joseph, 1896– . **9774**
— *Hatter's castle.* 9774
CROOKE, Andrew, fl.1629–74. 13418
CROOKE, John, Dublin, d.1669. 1907 **4430** 13418
CROOKE, William, 1848–1923–Libr. 466
CROOM-JOHNSON, Norman, fl.1921 *see* JOHNSON, Norman Croom-, fl.1921.
CROSBY, Sumner McKnight, 1909– –Libr. 12192
CROSE, Jean Cornand de la, fl.1681–93 *see* LA CROSE, Jean Cornand de, fl.1681–93.
CROSS, George, fl.1825–93. **4431**
CROSS, Mary Ann (Evans), 1819–80 *see* ELIOT, George, *pseud.*
CROSS, Thomas, fl.1632–82. **4432**

CROSSE, Henry, fl.1603. **9775**
— Bibs. 1:**2923**
— *Virtue's commonwealth.* 478 9775
CROSSGROVE, Henry, 1683–1744. **4433**
CROSS PETITION–Bibs. 1:718
CROUSAZ, Jean Pierre de, 1663–1750. 11430
11466
CROWLEY, Edward Alexander ('Aleister'),
1875–1947–Bibs. 1:**2923n–q**
— Collns. 2339
— Mss.–Bibs. 1:2923p
CROWLEY, Robert, 1518?–88. **4434–a**
— *Fable of philargyry.* 4434
— *One and thirty epigrams.* 4434a
CROWNE, John, 1640?–1703?–Bibs. 1:**2924**
CROWQUILL, Alfred, *pseud. of* Alfred Henry
(1804–72) and Charles Robert (1803–50)
FORRESTER.
— *Dickens' Pickwick papers.* 9982
CROXLEY MILLS, Herts. 1139 4544
CRUDEN, Alexander, 1701–70. **4435–b**
— *Biblical concordance.* 4435b
— Bibs. 1:**2925**
CRUEL WAR, 1643. 7945
CRUIKSHANK, George, 1792–1878. 2:196;
755 764 2297 3496 4875 **4436–55** 6192
9983
— *Artist and the author.* 4451–2
— — Bibs. 1:5143
— *Bee and the wasp.* 4453
— Bibs. 1:1744–5 **2926–35g** 5143
— Collns. 4440 4444 4448–9
— *Comic almanack.* 5909
— *Dickens' Lord Bateman.* 10111
— *Dickens' Oliver Twist.* 10016
— *Drunkard's children.* 4450
— *German popular stories.* 4454a
— Mss.–Bibs. 1:2935g
— *My sketch book.* 4445
— *Punch and Judy.* 9582 9595
— Publ. 4447
— *Table-book.* 4443
CRUIKSHANK, Isaac, 1756?–1811? **4456**
7418
— Bibs. 1:2927 2929 2931
CRUIKSHANK, Isaac Robert, 1789–1856.
4457 6192 7418
— Bibs. 1:2927 2929 2931
CRUIKSHANK, Percy, fl.1851–76. 6204
CRUYS, Francis, fl.1698.
— *Ars nova natandi..* 1126
CRYPTOGRAMS. 518
CUALA PRESS, Dundrum, est. 1903. 1842
4458–63 4597 4599 6463
— Bibs. *see also* DUN EMER PRESS,
Dublin, 1903–7–Bibs. 1:**1289v–92** 5207
5209b
CUCKFIELD PARK, Sussex–Libr. 7478

CUCKOO HILL PRESS, Pinner, est. 1950.
4464–6 6495
CUDWORTH, Ralph, 1617–88. 1:**2936–a**
CUDWORTH, William, 1717–63–Bibs.
1:**2937**
CUDWORTH, William, 1830–1906–Bibs.
1:**2938**
CULLEN, William, 1710–90. 1623 **9776**
— *First lines of the practice of physic.* 9776
CULVERWEL, Nathaniel, d.1651–Bibs.
1:**2938m**
CUMBERLAND. **1086–8**
— Bibs. 1:**884**
— Chapbooks–Bibs. 1:1540
— Maps–Bibs. 1:**1779**
— Newspapers–Bibs. 1:1854
CUMBERLAND, George, 1754–1848–Bibs.
1:**2939**
CUMBERLAND, John, fl.1826–42. 9418
CUMBERLAND, prince Rupert, duke of,
1619–82 *see* RUPERT, prince, duke of
Cumberland, 1619–82.
CUMBERLAND, Richard, 1732–1811.
— Bibs. 1:**2940**
— *The brothers.* 11135
CUMBERLEGE, Stephen Austen, 1747–1828.
4467
CUMMING, John, Fintray, 1820–1900.
4468–a
— Bibs. 1:**1291k**
CUNARD, Nancy, 1896–1965 *see* HOURS
PRESS, Réanville, 1928–31.
CUNDALL, Joseph, 1818–95. 3974 **4469**
6229
— Bibs. 1:**1292**
CUNINGHAM, Henry, fl.1899–1922. 2:1168
CUNLIFFE, Rolf, baron Cunliffe,
1899–1963–Libr. 1:538
CUNNINGHAM, A. C., *pseud.* 2:740; 4490
CUNNINGHAM, Allan, 1784–1842. 4490
9777
— *King of the peak.* 9777
— Publ. 5250
CUNNINGHAM, John, 1729–73. **9778**
— *Day.* 9778
— Illus. 9778
CUNNINGHAM, Peter, 1816–69. **9779–89**
CUPAR, Fife.–Ptg. *see* TULLIS, George
Smith, 1805–48; TULLIS, Robert,
1775–1831; WESTWOOD, A., AND SON,
1862–95.
CUPID AND PSYCHE. 612
CURDRIDGE, Hants.–Paper. 1132a
CURLE, Richard Henry Parnell,
1883–1968–Bibs. 1:2855m **2941–c**
— Letters–Bibs. 1:2941c
— Libr. 1:2866h 5053a; 9648–50
CURLING, Henry, 1803–64–Bibs. 1:**2942**

CURLL, Edmund, 1675–1747. 3506 3616 3639a **4470–7** 4604 8405 14616
— Bibs. 1:**1292a–3**
— *Faithful memoirs of mrs. Oldfield.* 4470a
— *Shakespeare's Poems.* 2:1938
CURRENT INTELLIGENCE. 7659
CURRIE, miss C. B., fl.1890–1930. 7444
CURRIEHILL, sir John Skene, ld., 1543?–1617 *see* SKENE, sir John, ld. Curriehill, 1543?–1617.
CURTIS, Samuel, 1779–1860. 7327
CURTIS, William, 1746–99. 6955–6
— *Flora Londoniensis.* 6958 6964
CURWEN, Harold, 1886–1949 *see also* CURWEN PRESS, Plaistow, est. 1918. 4483 4486
CURWEN, Henry, 1845–92.
— *History of booksellers.* 5554
CURWEN PRESS, Plaistow, est. 1918. **4478–87** 6098 6490
— Bibs. 1:**1294–8** 3360b
— Type. 4479–80 4487
CURZON, Robert, 14th baron Zouche, 1810–73. 3391
CURZON-HOWE, Richard William Penn, 3d earl Howe, 1822–1900 *see* HOWE, Richard William Penn Curzon-, 3d earl Howe, 1822–1900.
CUSACK, Mary Frances, 1830–99–Bibs. 1:**2943**
CUSOP, Herefs.–Paper. 1138
CUSTOMS, PRINTERS' *see* PRINTERS' CUSTOMS.
CUTHILL, bksllr., 19th cent. 3618b
CUVIER, Georges, baron, 1769–1832. 8160
CYCLING–Bibs. 1:**2157p**
— Newspapers–Bibs. 1:**2157p**
CYLINDER PRESSES *see* PRESSES, CYLINDER.
CYMDEITHAS LLEN CYMRU, est. 1900? **4489**
CYMRU. 1512
CYNTHIA'S REVENGE, 1613. 7111
CZECHOSLOVAKIA *see* SHAKESPEARE, William, 1564–1616–WORKS IN CZECHOSLOVAKIA.

D., J.
— *Knave in grain.* 7165
DACOMB, sir Thomas, 1496–1572?–Libr. 2791 3344
DAEDALUS PRESS, est. 1964–Bibs. 1:**1298g**
DAILY ADVERTIZER. 7728
DAILY CHRONICLE. 5527
DAILY JOURNAL. 5546
DAILY NEWS. 7894
— Bibs. 1:4141

DAILY TELEGRAPH. 7837 7860 7894
DAILY UNIVERSAL REGISTER. 7742
DALDY, Frederick Richard, fl.1854–1925. 3974
DALE, Robert, d.1722. 703
— *Exact catalogue of nobility.* 703
DALHOUSIE UNIVERSITY, Halifax, Nova Scotia. LIBRARY–Collns. 1:3956
DALKEITH SUBSCRIPTION LIBRARY. 1633
DALLAS. SOUTHERN METHODIST UNIVERSITY. PERKINS SCHOOL OF THEOLOGY. BRIDWELL LIBRARY. 6893
— Collns. 1:1497d
DALLAS, Eneas Sweetland, 1828–79. **9790**
— *Kettner's Book of the table.* 9790
DALLASTYPE SHAKESPEARE. 2:499
DALRY MILLS, Edinburgh. 1710 1712
DALRYMPLE, sir David, ld. Hailes, 1726–92. **9791**
— *Ancient Scottish poems.* 12750
— Bibs. 1:**2944**
DALTON, Lancs. 1180a
DALTON, John, 1766–1844. **9792–3**
— Bibs. 1:**2944y–5**
— Publ. 9792
D'ALTON, John, 1792–1867–Libr. 2851
DALY, Augustin, 1838–99–Libr. 2563
DALY, Charles, fl.1835–55. 2:740; **4490**
— *Cunningham's Shakespeare.* 2:740
DALY, Denis, 1747–91–Libr. 3158 3162
DALZIEL, Edward, 1817–1905. 4491 6229 7420a
DALZIEL, Edward George, 1849–88. 7420a
DALZIEL, George, 1815–1902. **4491–2** 6229
— Bibs. 1:**1298q**
— Collns. 4492
DALZIEL, Thomas Bolton Gilchrist Septimus, 1823–1906. 7420a
DAMAGED TYPE *see* TYPE, DAMAGED.
DAMASINE PRESS, Leeds, fl.1960. 6495
DAMPER, W. G., fl.1931–Libr. 2:1651
DAMPIER, William, 1651–1715.
— *Voyage round the world.* 13718
DANCE, James, 1722–74 *see* LOVE, James, pseud.
DANCEY, Charles Henry, 1838–1913–Libr. 1:895a
DANDY'S BALL. 7001
DANESCOOMBE, Cornw.–Paper. 1083b
DANIEL, Charles Henry Olive, Oxford, 1836–1919. **4493–505** 5345 6320 6475 6502 8765
— Bibs. 1:**1299–1302**
— *Carroll's Garland of Rachel.* 9316
— Type. 4499

DANIEL, George, 1789–1864–Libr. 2:506 536 540; 6782

DANIEL, John, Carmarthen, 1784–1823. **4506–7**

— Bibs. 1:**1298t**

DANIEL, Roger, Cambridge, fl.1627–66. 4162

DANIEL, Samuel, 1562–1619. **9794–812** 11566

— Bibs. 1:**2946–8b**

— *Breviary of the history of England.* 9806

— *Civil wars.* 9797 9803–4 9807 9810 9812

— *History of England.* 9809

— *Hymen's triumph.* 9795

— Letters. 9811

— Mss. 9795 9804 9812

— *Panegyric congratulatory.* 9805

— Ptg. 6354

— *Sonnets to Delia.* 9794 9796 9808

— Text. 9801–2 9808

— *Works.* 6354 9800

DANIELL, William, 1769–1837.

— *Voyage around Great Britain.* 5260–a

DANIEL PRESS, 1845?–1903 *see* DANIEL, Charles Henry Olive, 1836–1919.

DANISH LITERATURE *see* FOREIGN BOOKS PUBLISHED IN BRITAIN–Denmark.

DANSKIN, Henry, d.1625. **9813**

— *De remoris.* 9813

DANTE ALIGHIERI, 1265–1321. 942 945–6 8616 9343–4 13319–20 13358

— Bibs. 1:**827b–31a**

DANTER, John, fl.1565–99. 2:918

— Bibs. 1:**1302g**

— *Shakespeare's Romeo and Juliet.* 2:1714 1717 1720 1722 1737

DAOUST, Edward C., fl.1929–Libr. 1:3076c

D'ARBLAY, Frances (Burney), 1752–1840 *see* BURNEY, Frances (mrs. D'Arblay), 1752–1840.

DARBY, John, fl.1662–1704. 12691

DARIEN COMPANY–Bibs. 1:**2158–61**

DARLEY, George, 1795–1846. **9814–15**

— Bibs. 1:**2949–50**

— *Poems.* 9814

— Ptg. 9815

— *Sylvia.* 9815

DARLINGTON, Frank Graef, 1859–1918–Libr. 1:4006

DARMESTETER, Agnes Mary Frances (Robinson), later Duclaux, 1857–1944 *see* DUCLAUX, Agnes Mary Frances (Robinson), formerly Darmesteter, 1857–1944.

DARTFORD, Kent. **1161**

— Paper. 1161

DARTMOOR, Devon. **1102**

DARTMOUTH COLLEGE. LIBRARY–Collns. 1:3491; 5510 8812 9098

DARTON, HARVEY AND DARTON, 1813–38. 11880

DARTON, William, 1755–1819–Bibs. 1:**1303**

DARTON AND HARVEY, fl.1810. 8099

DARWIN, Charles Robert, 1809–82. **9816–26**

— Bibs. 1:**2951–7**

— Bndng. 9824

— *Manual of geology.* 9819

— *Origin of species.* 9816–7 9820–1 9823–6

— — Bibs. 1:**2952–4 2956**

— Publ. 9821 9824

DASHWOOD, Edmée Elizabeth Monica (de la Pasture), 1890–1943 *see* DELAFIELD, E. M., *pseud.*

DATES IN BOOKS. 663 739 6128 6288 6525

— Bibliogr. descr. 97 128 254 257

DATES IN WATERMARKS *see* WATERMARKS–Dates.

DATING. 3793 6671 8514

DAUNCE, Edward, fl.1585. **9827**

— *Praise of nothing.* 9827

DAVENANT, Charles, 1656–1714. **9828–9**

— Bibs. 1:**2960**

— *Essays upon peace.* 9828

D'AVENANT, sir William, 1606–68. **9830–6**

— Bibs. 1:**2961**

— *Gondibert.* 9831–6

— *Luminalia.* 9830

— *Macbeth.* 2:1507

— Publ. 6535

— *Salmacida spolia.* 6535

— *Shakespeare's Hamlet.* 2:1175

— Text. 9835

DAVENPORT, Robert, fl.1623. 7159

DAVEY, NORMAN, 1888– –Bibs. 1:**2961j**

— Collns. 2329

DAVID AP GWILYM, 14th cent. **9837**

— *Barddoniaeth.* 9837

DAVIDSON, John, 1549?–1604–Bibs. 1:**2961p**

— Mss.–Bibs. 1:2961p

DAVIDSON, John, 1857–1909. **9838–41**

— Bibs. 1:684 **2962–4**

— Collns. 9838–40

— Mss. 9838

— Publ. 9838

DAVIDSON, Thomas, Edinburgh, fl.1541. 1591

DAVIDSON, William, 1756?–95? 6053

DAVIES-JONES, sir Evan, 1859–1949 *see* JONES, sir Evan Davies-, 1859–1949.

DAVIES, Godfrey, 1892–1957–Libr. 1:605

DAVIES, Gwendoline Elizabeth, d.1951 and Margaret S. DAVIES *see also* GREGYNOG PRESS, Newtown, est. 1922. 4797 4802

DENBIGH, Denbigh.–Ptg. *see* JONES, Thomas, 1756–1820.
DENBIGHSHIRE. **1541**
— Bibs. 1:**963**
DENDRITIC MARKINGS *see* PAPER–Dendritic markings.
DENHAM, Henry, fl.1560–87. 3873 **4531**
DENHAM, sir James, formerly Steuart, 1712–80–Bibs. 1:**3010d**
DENHAM, sir John, 1615–69. **9950–2**
— Bibs. 1:**3011–a**
— *Cooper's hill.* 9951
— — Bibs. 1:**3011–a**
— Mss. 9950
— — Bibs. 1:**3011**
DENMARK, BRITISH BOOKS PUBLISHED IN *see* BRITISH BOOKS PUBLISHED ABROAD–Denmark; SHAKESPEARE, William, 1564–1616–WORKS IN DENMARK.
DENN, Patrick, 1756–1828–Bibs. 1:**3011q**
DENNIS, John, 1657–1734. **9953**
— Bibs. 1:**3012**
— *Causes of the decay and defects.* 9953
— Mss. 9953
DENNY, Stirlingshire–Paper *see* LUKE, John, fl.1800.
DENNY, sir William, d.1676.
— *Pelecanicidium.* 3897
DENNYS, John, d.1609. 1117a
DENT, Edward Joseph, 1876–1957–Bibs. 1:**3013**
DENT, J. M. AND SONS, est. 1888. 4534–5
DENT, Joseph Mallaby, 1849–1926 *see also* DENT'S ILLUSTRATED ESSAYS. **4532–5**
DENT'S ILLUSTRATED ESSAYS. 7426
— Bibs. 1:1746
DE OCTO ORATIONIS PARTIUM CONSTRUCTIONE, *c.*1521. 1048
DE PIENNE, Peter, Waterford, fl.1647–55 *see* PIENNE, Peter de, Waterford, fl.1647–55.
DE PLANCHE, John, fl.1572 *see* PLANCHE, John de, fl.1572.
DEPOSIT COPIES *see* COPYRIGHT DEPOSIT COPIES.
DE QUINCEY, Thomas, 1785–1859. **9954–63** 14513
— Bibs. 1:**3014–19**
— Collns. 9954
— *Confessions of an English opium eater.* 9957 9962
— Handwr. 9963
— Letters. 9960
— Libr. 9958
— Mss. 9959 9961
— Publ. 9960
— *Street companion.* 9956
— Text. 9530 9962

DERBY, Derbys. *see also* BOOK TRADE, LISTS–Derby. **1092–4**
— Bksllng. 1091–2
— Bndng. 1091
— Newspapers. 1093
— Ptg. 1091–2 1094
— Publ. 1091
— BISHOP LONSDALE COLLEGE OF EDUCATION *see* BISHOP LONSDALE COLLEGE OF EDUCATION, Derby.
DERBY, Charles Stanley, 8th earl of, fl.1669 *see* STANLEY, Charles, 8th earl of Derby, fl.1669.
DERBY, EARLS OF–Libr. *see* KNOWSLEY HALL, Lancs.
DERBY, Edward Henry Stanley, 15th earl, 1826–93 *see* STANLEY, Edward Henry, 15th earl of Derby, 1826–93.
DERBY, William George Richard Stanley, 9th earl of, 1664–1702 *see* STANLEY, William George Richard, 9th earl of Derby, 1664–1702.
DERBY, William Stanley, 6th earl of, *c.*1561–1642 *see* STANLEY, William, 6th earl of Derby, *c.*1561–1642.
DERBYSHIRE *see also* BOOK TRADE, LISTS–Derbyshire. **1089–94**
— Bibs. 1:**884x–5**
— Bndg. 1091
— Librs. *see* CHATSWORTH HALL.
— Ptg. 1089–91
— — Bibs. 1:**884x–5**
— Publ. 1091
DE RICCI, Seymour Montefiore Roberto Rosso, 1881–1942. 53 2292
— *Census of Caxtons.* 4302
DERING, sir Edward, 1598–1644. 2:372 1277–9
— Libr. 7191
DERRY. **1861–6**
— Bibs. 1:**1053–5f**
— Librs. 1864
— Ptg. 1861
— — Bibs. 1:1053–4
— ST. COLUMB'S COLLEGE *see* ST. COLUMB'S COLLEGE, Derry.
DERRY AND SONS, Nottingham, est. 1867. **4536**
DE SAINLIENS, Claude, fl.1568–97 *see* HOLYBAND, Claude, *pseud.*
DE SAUTY, A., fl.1890–1914. **4537**
DESCHAMPS, François Michel Chrétien, 1683–1747. 909
DESCRIPTION, BIBLIOGRAPHICAL *see* BIBLIOGRAPHICAL DESCRIPTION.
DES GRAZ, Charles Geoffrey, 1893–1953. **4538**
DESIDERIUS. 1164a

DE SOLEMNE, Anthony, Norwich, fl.1565–80 *see* SOLEMNE, Anthony de, Norwich, fl.1565–80.

DE STAËL, Anne Louise Germaine, 1766–1817 *see* STAËL, Anne Louise Germaine de, 1766–1817.

DETECTIVE FICTION *see* FICTION, DETECTIVE.

DETECTIVES IN FICTION–Bibs. 1:1720

DETROIT. WAYNE STATE UNIVERSITY *see* WAYNE STATE UNIVERSITY.

DEUTSCHE SHAKESPEARE-GESELL-SCHAFT. BIBLIOTHEK. 2:336–7

— — Collns. 2:33 35 81–2 98

DEUTSCHE SHAKESPEARE-GESELL-SCHAFT WEST. BIBLIOTHEK –Collns. 2:153

DE VALERA, Eamonn, 1882–1975. **9964**

DE VERE, Aubrey Thomas, 1814–1902–Bibs. 1:**3024–6b**

DE VERE, Edward, 17th earl of Oxford, 1550–1604. 2:**1029–a**

— Bibs. 2:88

DEVEREUX, Robert, 2d earl of Essex, 1566–1601. 2782 3281

— Libr. 2482

— Mss. 9597

DEVEREUX, Robert, 3d earl of Essex, 1591–1646–Libr. 3377

DEVICES, PRINTERS'. 258 279 2224 4008 4118–19 5332 5492a 5644 6042 6655–6 6659–61 6664 6668 6671 6677 6681 6685 6689 6691 6693 6695

— Bibliogr. descr. 97 128 254

—, PUBLISHERS'. 1264 1368 5416 5777 6660–1 6664 6685 6695

DEVIL OF A DUKE, 1733. 6786

DEVILS, PRINTERS' *see* PRINTERS' DEVILS.

DE VINNE, Theodore Low, 1828–1914–Libr. 1:394

DEVONSHIRE. **1095–103**

— Bibs. 1:**886–b**

— Bksllng. 1099

— Librs. 1097

— Paper. 1098 1099a–c 1100b–f 1101x

— Ptg. 1099–100

DEVONSHIRE, DUKES OF *see* CHATSWORTH HALL, Derbys.–Libr.

DEVONSHIRE, Georgiana Cavendish, duchess of, 1757–1806 *see* CAVENDISH, Georgiana, duchess of Devonshire, 1757–1806.

DEVONSHIRE HOUSE. REFERENCE LIBRARY. 8090

DEVOTIONAL BINDER. 2234a

DE WALPERGEN, Peter, Oxford, 1646?–1703 *see* WALPERGEN, Peter de, Oxford, 1646?–1703.

D'EWES, sir Simonds, 1602–50–Libr. 3199 3343 3379 9869

DE WITT, Johannes, fl.1596. 2:1842

DE WORDE, Wynkyn, d.1534? *see* WORDE, Wynkyn de (Jan van Wynkyn), d.1534?

DEXTER, Gregory, 1610–1700. **4539–41**

— Bibs. 1:**1305m**

DEXTER, Robert, fl.1580–1603. 5749

DIALECTS–Bibs. 1:2203

DIALOGUE BETWEEN VIATOR AND PISCATOR, 1577. 668

DIARIES. 7544

— Bibs. 1:**1575x–6d**

DIBDIN, Charles, 1745–1814. **9965**

— Bibs. 1:**3027–8**

DIBDIN, Thomas Frognall, 1776–1847. 6060 6637 **9966–71**

— Bibs. 1:**3039–31a**

— Letters. 9969

— Libr. 659 9970–1

— *Library companion.* 9956

— Ptg. 6098 9967

DIBELIUS, Wilhelm, 1876– .

— *Wilson's Cobbler's prophesy.* 14373

DIBON, Roger, 1687–1777.

— *Description of the venereal diseases.* 13504

DICEY, William, Northampton, fl.1713–54. 1311 **4542**

DICKENS, Charles John Huffam, 1817–70 *see also ALL THE YEAR ROUND; HOUSEHOLD WORDS.* 467 478 747 757 831a 2322 3450 3496 3723 **9972–10188** 10707 10710 14587

— American ed. 9986 9994 9996–7 9999 10007 10105 10111 10150 10160 10187

— *American notes.* 9997 10187

— *Barnaby Rudge.* 9997a 10065 10106 10185

— *Battle of life.* 3496 9988 10020 10094 10175 10181

— Bibs. 1:663f 674m **3032–104** 3965t 4004f

— *Bleak house.* 9997a 10123

— *The chimes.* 10020

— *Christmas books.* 9983 9997a 10020 10030

— *Christmas carol.* 476 757a 10017 10020 10026–7 10035 10055 10061 10063 10080 10084 10096–8 10128 10159 10161 10171

— — Bibs. 1:3095a

— Collns. 752 2299 10004 10019 10024 10030 10032 10037–9 10043–4 10051 10059 10064 10067 10102–4 10108 10112–14 10130 10141 10163–4 10170 10173 10176

— *Cricket on the hearth.* 10020 10149

— *Curious dance round a curious tree.* 10186

— *David Copperfield.* 9997a 10105 10118 10124 10145

— *Dombey and son.* 9997a 10018 10117 10188

DICTIONARIUM LINGUA LATINA ET ANGLICANA, 1587. 5833
DICTIONARY OF CHRISTIAN BIOGRAPHY–Bibs. 1:4822b
DICTIONARY OF NATIONAL BIOGRAPHY. 5680
— Bibs. 1:4928
DIDOT, Pierre François, 1732–95. 3785 6637
DIDOT-SAINT-LEGER, Pierre François, 1767–1829. 3785 6637
DIGBY, Everard, fl.1590. **10191–3**
— *De arte natandi.* 10191
— *Theoria analytica.* 10192–3
DIGBY, John, fl.1722. **10194**
— *Philosophical account of nature.* 10194
DIGBY, sir Kenelm, 1603–65. **10195–8**
— Bibs. 1:**3139–42**
— Libr. 2266 10196 10198 10388
— Mss. 10197
DIGGES, Leonard, d.1571. **10199–201**
— *Prognostication everlasting.* 10199–200
DIGGES, Leonard, 1588–1635. 2:951
DIGGES, Thomas, 1546–95. **10202–3**
DILKE, Charles Wentworth, 1789–1864–Letters. 12033
DILKE, Emilia Frances (Strong), lady, 1840–1904–Libr. 2619
DILLY, Edward, 1732–79. 3639a
DINNIS, Enid Maud, 1873– –Bibs. 1:**3143**
DIOCESAN LIBRARIES *see* LIBRARIES, DIOCESAN.
DIPLOCK, John, Trowbridge, fl.1828–40. **4548**
DIPLOCK, W., *pseud.* of Mary Matilda Howard, 1804–93.
— *Ocean flowers.* 8158
DIPROSE BROTHERS, fl.1891. **4550**
DIRECTORIES. 1016 3462
— Bath–Bibs. 1:940–a
— Dublin. 1743 1899 1903–4
— England–Bibs. 1:865
— Ireland. 1743 1808
— Lancashire–Bibs. 1:903a
— Liverpool. 1170 1173
— — Bibs. 1:905x
— London. 1188 1201 1232 1247 1274 1292 3462
— — Bibs. 1:914
— Manchester. 1176
— Nottinghamshire–Bibs. 1:928
— Staffordshire–Bibs. 1:941a
— Wales–Bibs. 1:865
—, BOOK-TRADE. 3462 3651
—, ECCLESIASTICAL. 1743
—, MEDICAL. 1743
DIRECTORY FOR THE PUBLIC WORSHIP OF GOD, 1644. 1473

DISCOURS DU GRAND ... TRIUMPHE, 1558. 1601
DISCOURSE OF THE USAGE, 1595. 601
DISPENSATORIES. 1713 1714a
DISPLAY PRINTING *see* LEICESTER FREE STYLE.
DISRAELI, Benjamin, 1st earl of Beaconsfield, 1804–81. 831a 3879 **10204–8**
— Bibs. 1:**3146–9**
— *Coningsby.* 10208
— Mss. 10204
— Publ. 5250 10207–8
— *Sybil.* 10208
— *Tancred.* 10208
— *Vivian Grey.* 10204 10207
D'ISRAELI, Isaac, 1766–1848. **10209**
— Bibs. 1:**3149d**
— Libr. 786
— Publ. 5250
DISSENTERS. 3502
— Librs. 2459
DISSERTATIONS *see also* THESES.
— Bibs. 1:10–11 657 1630–b 2858
'DISTRIBUTE'. 3589
DITCHLING, Sussex–Ptg. *see* ST. DOMINIC'S PRESS, est. 1916.
DITTON, Kent–Paper. 1161a
DIVES ET PAUPER see PARKER, Henry, d.1470.
DIVINE MUSICAL MISCELLANY, 1754. 7377
DIX, Ernest Reginald McClintock, 1857–1936. 22 42–4 1918
— Bibs. 1:**3149v**
— Libr. 1:1069–a
DIXEY, Harold Giles, Oxford, est. 1922–Bibs. 1:**1306**
DIXON, Richard Watson, 1833–1900–Bibs. 1:**3150**
DIXSON, sir William, 1870–1952–Libr. 1:2876
DOBELL, Bertram, 1842–1914. **4551–4**
— Bibs. 1:**1306d**
— Libr. 1:4962; 4554
DOBELL, Percy John, fl.1918–33–Libr. 10364
DOBRÉE, Bonamy, 1891–1969–Bibs. 1:**3150d**
DOBSON, Alban Tabor Austin, 1885–1962–Libr. 1:**3153–4**
DOBSON, Edward, fl.1643–4. 3396a
DOBSON, Henry Austin, 1840–1921. **10210–1**
— Bibs. 1:**3151–5**
DOBSON, William, fl.1750–8.
— *Milton's Paradise lost.* 12381
DOCK *see* PLYMOUTH.
DOCKWRA, Will, fl.1682–1716. **10212**

DORSET, Thomas Sackville, 1st earl of, 1536–1608 see SACKVILLE, Thomas, 1st earl of Dorset, 1536–1608.

DOUAI. BIBLIOTHEQUE MUNICIPALE –Collns. 2:371 398

DOUAI BIBLE see BIBLE–Versions–Rheims and Douai; BIBLE. N.T.–Versions–Rheims and Douai.

DOUGLAS, William, d.1819–Libr. 2873

DOUBLE ATLAS PAPER see PAPER, DOUBLE ATLAS.

DOUBLE CROWN CLUB. 321–2 328 4487 4799 4982 5398 6098 6119

DOUBLEDAY, Edward, 1811–49.
— Genera of diurnal lepidoptera. 6983

DOUBLEDAY, Frank Nelson, 1862–1934–Libr. 11782–3.

DOUBLEDAY, Henry, 1808–75.
— Synomic list of British lepidoptera. 6978

DOUCE, Francis, 1757–1834–Libr. 2066 2111 2925–6 2928

DOUDNEY, David Alfred, Bonmahon, 1811–94. **4577**

DOUGHTY, Charles Montagu, 1843–1926. **10277–80**
— Arabia deserta. 10279–80
— Bibs. 1:**3166**
— Mansoul. 10278
— Mss. 10278
— Under arms. 10277

DOUGLAS, I. O. M. MANX MUSEUM –Collns. 1:1796

DOUGLAS, ld. Alfred Bruce, 1870–1945–Bibs. 1:**3166r**

DOUGLAS, David, 1823–1916.
— Scott's Journal. 13207 13213

DOUGLAS, lady Eleanor (Touchet), d.1652–Bibs. 1:**3167**

DOUGLAS, Francis, Aberdeen, 1719–86. **4578–9**

DOUGLAS, bp. Gavin, 1474?–1522. **10281**
— Bibs. 1:**3168**
— Æneid. 5574 10281

DOUGLAS, James, 1675–1742–Bibs. 1:**3168k**
— Mss.–Bibs. 1:3168k

DOUGLAS, John, c.1690–1743–Bibs. 1:3168k

DOUGLAS, bp. John, 1721–1807–Collns. 3050

DOUGLAS, Kenneth, Inverness, d.1860. 1683

DOUGLAS, Norman, pseud. of George Norman DOUGLASS, 1868–1952. 783 **10282–6**
— Bibs. 1:681 684 3169–72
— Collns. 2339
— Old Calabria. 10283
— One day. 4897e

— Some limericks collected. 10282

DOUGLAS, sir Robert, 1694–1770.
— Peerage of Scotland. 7361

DOUGLASS, George Norman, 1868–1952 see DOUGLAS, Norman, pseud.

D'OUTRE-MEUSE, Jean, fl.1350 see MANDEVILLE, sir John, fl.1350.

D'OUVILLY, George Gerbier, fl.1661.
— False favorite disgrac'd. 6352
— Ptg. 6352

DOVASTON, John Freeman Milward, 1782–1854. 4047

DOVE COTTAGE, Ambleside–Collns. 1:5767

DOVER, Thomas, 1660–1742.
— Ancient physician's legacy. 7555

DOVES PRESS, Hammersmith, 1900–16. 754 **4580–9a** 5161 5588 5593 6083 6103 6463 6465 6475 6488 6502
— Bibs. 1:**1312–15e** 1353
— Bndng. 4580 4589a 5593 14453
— Collns. 4589a
— Type. 4588a 6488 6610

DOWDALL, John, fl.1693. **10287–8**
— Mss. 10287–8
— Traditionary anecdotes of Shakespeare. 10287–8

DOWDEN, Edward, 1843–1913.
— Bibs. 1:**3173–4**
— Mss. 2:784

DOWLAND, John, 1563?–1626? **10289**
— Bibs. 1:**3175**
— Ptg. 10289
— Second book of songs. 10289

DOWN. **1867–8**
— Bibs. 1:**1057–67**

DOWNES, Bartholomew, fl.1618–36–Bibs. 1:1873c

DOWNEY, Edmund, 1856–1937. 5859a

DOWNING, William, 1844–1900. **4590**

DOWN MILL, Whitchurch. 1132a

DOWNPATRICK, co. Down.–Bibs. 1:1057

DOWSON, Ernest Christopher, 1867–1900. **10290**
— Bibs. 1:684 **3176–9a**

DOYLE, sir Arthur Conan, 1859–1930. 4178 7265–6 8415 **10291–312**
— Adventures of Sherlock Holmes. 10291 10304
— Bibs. 1:684 **3179y–85ea**
— Boscombe valley mystery. 10297
— Cardboard box. 10301
— Case of identity. 10297
— Case of the golden blonde. 10306
— Case of the missing three-quarter. 10308
— Collns. 3024 10302 10305 10312
— Enquiry into the case of G. Edalji. 10293
— Hound of the Baskervilles. 10309
— Mss. 10307–8

DOYLE, sir Arthur Conan–Mss.–Bibs. 1:3181r 3181w
— *Plea for justice.* 10293
— Publ. 5680 10292 10294 10297 10304 10309
— *Red-headed league.* 10297
— *Scandal in Bohemia.* 10297
— *Sign of four.* 10304 10311
— *Study in scarlet.* 10292 10294 10296 10298 10306
— Text. 10295
— *Valley of fear.* 10295
— *Works.* 10299
DOYLE, Richard, 1824–83. 2297 7848 9983
— Bibs. 1:**1315k**
DRAKE, sir Francis, 1540?–96. **10313–14** 10907
— Collns. 10314
DRAKE, William Henry, 1857–1917.
— *Gaskell's Cranford.* 10640 10642
DRAMA *see also* 'ASSEMBLED' PLAYS; BOOK TRADE, LISTS–Drama; PLAYBILLS; PLAYS, LISTS OF; PROMPTBOOKS; THEATRE. **7090–234**
— Bibs. 1:**1585–654**
— Censorship. 3499 7133 8455 12091
— Collns. 3380a 7091–2 7095–101 7103 7126 7149–50 7153 7174 7176 7188 7191–2 7198a 7219–20 7223 7226 7231 7233 12797
— Copyright. 7172 7184
— Illus. 7390 13250
— Mss. *see also* REVELS MSS. 7095 7115 7131–2 7136 7154 7158 7162 7185 7190 7196 7205 7210 7218–20 7226
— — Bibs. 1:1606b–c 1607 1611b 1615 1633d–f 1635c 1650c
— Newspapers. 7102 7713 7745 7803 7930 7934–5
— — Bibs. 1:1586
— Ptg. 6372 7113 7121 7129 7133 7148 12174
— Publ. 2:434 844 855; 7127 7133 7172 7184 7745
— Regulation. 3499 7133 9632 14051
— Text. 372 395 398 401 7155
— 1475– –Bibs. 1:**1585–98** 2199
— 1475–1640. 4611 **7104–92** 14431 14435 14437 14440
— –Bibs. 1:**1599–601t** 5139 5142
— 1475–1700. 3380a 3499 **7193–8** 7390 12174
— — Bibs. 1:734 **1602–19** 1656d 5139 5142
— 1641–1700. 238 6372 **7199–212**
— — Bibs. 1:325 1464f **1620–6**
— 1701–1800. 3499 **7213–20** 7745 14051
— — Bibs. 1:634 1605 **1630–7**
— 1801–1900. 792 7021 **7221–33**
— — Bibs. 1:1417–18 1563 **1638–50c** 3090 3093 4022

— 1901– . **7234**
— — Bibs. 1:1638 **1651–3**
— Ireland. 1749
— — Bibs. 1:1589 1589g–h 1621p 1652 1652p 1652t 1653
— Scotland–Bibs. 1:1586 1652g
—, ACADEMIC–Bibs. 1:1599d
—, JUVENILE. 5371 7021 7023 7028–9 7032 7035 8603
— Bibs. 1:1417–18 1563
— Collns. 7026–7 7041 7056
— Illus. 7046
— Publ. 7021 7023 7030–1 7033–5 7042
— AND BIBLIOGRAPHY. 238
DRAMATIC INSPECTOR. 7930
'DRAWBACK'. 3608
DRAWINGBOOKS. 6192–3 7327
DRAWING-ROOM BOOKS *see* BOOKS, DRAWING-ROOM.
DRAWINGS, LINE. 6186
— Ptg. 6186
—, WASH. 6186 6200
— Ptg. 6186
DRAYTON, Michael, 1563–1631. **10315–28**
— *Battle of Agincourt.* 10326
— — Bibs. 1:3189a
— Bibs. 1:**3186–9a**
— Bksllng. 10320
— Bndng. 10320
— Collns. 10322
— *Endymian and Phoebe.* 10318
— *England's heroical epistles.* 10319
— *Harmony of the church.* 10316
— *Idea.* 9583
— *Letters.* 10328
— *The owl.* 10320–1
— Paper. 10326
— *Piers Gaveston.* 10317
— *Poems.* 10320 10323 10326
— — Bibs. 1:3189a
— *Polyolbion.* 10315 10320 10325 13878
— Publ. 10316–17
DREAM OF A QUEEN'S REIGN, 1843. 751
DREIER, Katherine Sophie, 1877– –Libr. 14321
DREXELIUS, Hieremias, 1581–1638. 11980
DRINKWATER, John, 1882–1937. 769 **10329–30**
— Bibs. 1:684 **3190–3**
— *Persuasion.* 10329
— — Bibs. 1:3192
— Publ. 10329
DRISCOLL, Charles B., 1885–1951–Libr. 7963
DROGHEDA, co. Louth. **1959**
— Bibs. 1:**1102–3**
— Ptg. 1959
— — Bibs. 1:1102–3

DROLLERIES. 11088
— Bibs. 1:1996
DROUESHOUT ENGRAVING. 2:530 569
572
DRUCE, Francis, fl.1913–38–Libr. 6950
DRUMMOND, David, 3d lord Maderty,
1611?–94–Libr. 2672 2846
DRUMMOND, William, 1585–1649. **10331–6**
— Bibs. 1:**3193e**
— *Conversations.* 10333
— Libr. 2672 9813 10273 10335
— *Poems.* 10336
DRUMMOND, William Hamilton,
1778–1865–Bibs. 1:**3194**
DRUMMOND CASTLE, Perth.
LIBRARY–Collns. 1:335
DRURY, George Thorn-, 1860–1931. 14469
— Libr. 1:600; 2892 2910
DRURY, John, 1590–1680–Bibs. 1:**3194a**
— Mss.–Bibs. 1:**3194a**
DRYDEN, N.Y. PUBLIC LIBRARY–Collns.
1:3203
DRYDEN, John, 1631–1700. 3453a 7159
10337–93 11957 12103
— *All for love.* 10349 10391–2
— — Bibs. 1:3208
— *Alexander's feast.* 10341
— Bibs. 1:579 597–8 600 1597 **3195–208**
— *Character of Polybius.* 10344
— *Character of St. Évremond.* 10347
— Collns. 10364
— *Conquest of Granada.* 10359 10363
— *Critical and miscellaneous prose.* 12111
— *Defresnoy's Art of painting.* 10339
— *Epilogue spoken to the king.* 10353
— *Epilogue to sir Fopling Flutter.* 10357
— *Essay of dramatic poesy.* 10355
— — Bibs. 1:3196a
— *Fables.* 3453a 3656
— Handwr. 10377
— *Heroic stanzas on the death of Cromwell.*
10393
— *Indian emperor.* 388 10372 10375
— — Bibs. 1:3204
— *King Arthur.* 10381
— Libr. 10366 10386 10388
— *MacFlecknoe.* 10383 10385
— *Miscellany poems.* 5870 10365
— Mss. 10356–7 10367–8 10375 10384–5
10393
— — Bibs. 1:3200
— Ptg. 10370–1 10379 10381 12111
— Publ. 5869–70 10342–3 10361–2 10378
10390
— *Religio laici.* 10189 10337
— *Shakespeare's Tempest.* 10368
— *State of innocence.* 10340 10356 10367
10379–80 10384

— — Bibs. 1:3205
— *Talent for English prose.* 10389
— Text. 10341 10348–9 10359 10363 10372
10374–5 10383–5 10389
— *Theodore and Honoria.* 10348
— *To the lady Castlemain.* 10352
— *To you who live in chill degree.* 10382
— *Triumphs of levy.* 10360
— *Troilus and Cressida.* 10370–1
— *Tyrannic love.* 10376
— *Virgil.* 3453a 10338 10361–2 10390
— *Wild gallant.* 10373
DRYDEN PRESS, fl.1869–1921 see DAVY,
John, fl.1834.
DRY POINT ENGRAVING see EN-
GRAVING, DRY POINT.
DU BARTAS, Guillame de Salluste, 1544–90.
915
DUBLIN. **1869–945**
DUBLIN, co. Dublin *see also* BOOK TRADE,
LISTS–Dublin. **1869–941**
— Almanacs. 1743 1882–3
— Ballads. 1924
— Bibs. 1:731 **1068–75**
— Bndng. 1880 1913 1928
— Bksllng. 1792 1871 1873 1902 1908 1925
— Directories. 1743 1899 1903–4
— Librs. 1873 1901 2450
— Maps. 1916
— Newspapers. 1763 1870 1878 1884–6 1888
1896 1900 1917 1920 1922 1930
— — Bibs. 1:1950 1952 1954
— Paper. 1817 1945
— Ptg. 920 1869 1872 1874 1876 1879 1881
1890 1892 1894–5 1897 1905–11 1918–19
1921 1927 1929 11967 12698 13583 14246
— — Bibs. 1:1068–73 1076 1427 1834 2278
2620s 3466 4408a
— Publ. 1914–15 1929 9886 9888 9894
12698 13026 13382 14190
— Type. 1893 5577
— ABBEY THEATRE see ABBEY THEATRE,
Dublin.
— BANK OF IRELAND see BANK OF
IRELAND.
— KILDARE PLACE SOCIETY see
KILDARE PLACE SOCIETY, Dublin, est.
1811.
— MILLTOWN PARK COLLEGE see
MILLTOWN PARK COLLEGE, Dublin.
— NATIONAL GALLERY see IRELAND.
NATIONAL GALLERY, Dublin.
— NATIONAL LIBRARY OF IRELAND see
IRELAND. NATIONAL LIBRARY,
Dublin.
— NATIONAL LITERARY SOCIETY see
NATIONAL LITERARY SOCIETY,
Dublin.

DUBLIN, co. Dublin. ROTUNDA
HOSPITAL. LIBRARY. 1898
— ROYAL DUBLIN SOCIETY see ROYAL
DUBLIN SOCIETY.
— ROYAL IRISH ACADEMY see ROYAL
IRISH ACADEMY, Dublin.
— SMOCK ALLEY THEATRE see SMOCK
ALLEY THEATRE, Dublin.
— SOCIETY OF STATIONERS see
SOCIETY OF STATIONERS, Dublin,
fl.1620–40.
— UNIVERSITY. 1934–41
— — MARSH'S LIBRARY. 1934–9
— — — Collns. 1:425 426a 2038a; 1934
1966 10318 13714
— — TRINITY COLLEGE. 1755 1940–1
— — — Bibs. 1:1076
— — — LIBRARY–Collns. 1:425 546 4834
4867 4869–70 5104 5205; 1825 8399 8981
14588
DUBLIN AND LONDON MAGAZINE. 1886
DUBLIN LIBRARY SOCIETY. 1901 2450
DUBLIN PENNY JOURNAL. 1763
DUBLIN REVIEW–Bibs. 1:1716k 1953
DUBLIN SATURDAY MAGAZINE. 1920
DUBLIN UNIVERSITY MAGAZINE. 1888
1917
— Bibs. 1:1953e 4117a
DUBLIN UNIVERSITY PRESS–Bibs. 1:1316
DUBLIN WEEKLY ORACLE. 1930
DUCK, Stephen, 1705–56. 10394
— Bibs. 1:3210–11
DUCKETT, James, d.1601. 4591
DUCLAUX, Mary, *pseud.* of Agnes Mary
Frances ROBINSON, 1856–1944–Bibs.
1:3211a
'DUCTUS LITTERARUM'. 371
DUDLEY, Owen Francis, 1882–1952–Bibs.
1:3211p
DUDLEY, Robert, earl of Leicester,
1532?–88. 1373
— Bibs. 1:2035c
— Libr. 2112
DUDLEY, Robert, fl.1858–91. 2227
DUDLEY BINDER, fl.1588. 4592
DUELLING see also FENCING. 7259
DUFF, Alexander William George, 1st duke
of Fife, 1849–1912–Libr. see MAR
LODGE, Aber.; SKENE HOUSE, Aber.
DUFF, Edward Gordon, 1863–1924. 31–2 62
— Bibs. 1:3212
— Libr. 472
DUFF, William, fl.1739–50. 10395
DUFFIELD, Howard, 1854–1941–Libr. 10059
10102
DUFFY, sir Charles Gavan, 1816–1903–Bibs.
1:3213
— Libr. 2690

DUFFY, James, Dublin, d.1871. 4593
DUGARD, William, 1606–62. 1198 3471
4594
— Bibs. 1:4230
— *Fuller's Life of Sidney.* 10609
— *Milton's Pro populo.* 12331
DUGDALE, sir William, 1605–86. 10396–7
— *Antiquities of Warwickshire.* 10396
— Bibs. 1:3214–15
— *History of inbanking.* 10397
DUIGNAN, William Henry, 1824–1914–Bibs.
1:3215a
DUKE UNIVERSITY, Durham, N.C.
LIBRARY. 14418
— — Collns. 1:1669a–b 1851 1978i 4544k;
7777 9232 12625 13088 13092 13099 13922
14293
DULLES, William Crothers, d.1912–Libr.
1:1740 1743
DULWICH COLLEGE, Camberwell.
LIBRARY. 2506 3182 9589
DUMAS, Alexandre, 1802–70. 912
DU MAURIER, George Louis Palmella
Busson, 1834–96. 7420a 10398–400
— Bibs. 1:3216–a
— Bndng. 10398
— *Peter Ibbetson.* 10398
— Publ. 10400
— *Trilby.* 2309
— — Bibs. 1:3216
— AS ILLUSTRATOR. 10400
DUMBARTON OAKS RESEARCH
LIBRARY AND COLLECTION. 11683
DUMFRIES, Dumf. 1673–4
— Librs. 1633
— Ptg. 1674
— *DUMFRIES MERCURY.* 1673
DUMFRIESSHIRE. 1672
— Bibs. 1:992–5
— Librs. 1672
— Ptg.–Bibs. 1:994
DUNBAR, William, 1465?–1530?–Bibs.
1:3217
DUNBLANE, Perth.–Librs. 2525a
DUNCAIRN PRESS, Belfast, fl.1850–70 see
MACRORY, Adam J., Belfast, fl.1850–77.
DUNCAN, Andrew, Glasgow, d.1840. 4746
DUNCAN, Edward, 1804–82. 4595
DUNCTON, Sussex–Paper. 1412
DUNDALK, co. Louth. 1959a
— Bibs. 1:1104–5
— Ptg.–Bibs. 1:1104–5
DUNDAS, Robert W., fl.1909–29–Libr. 2861
DUNDEE, Angus. 1665–8
— Bksllng. 1667
— Librs. 1571 1633 1668–9
— Newspapers. 1665–a
— — Bibs. 1:1930 1931a

DUNDEE, Angus–Ptg. 1665 1666
— CATHEDRAL. LIBRARY–Collns. 11089
— DOMINICAN LIBRARY. 1571
— HIGH SCHOOL. LIBRARY. 1668
— PUBLIC LIBRARY. 1633
— ST. MARY'S CHURCH. LIBRARY. 1669
DUNDRUM, co. Dublin.–Ptg. see CUALA PRESS, est. 1903.
DUNEDIN, N.Z. PUBLIC LIBRARY–Collns. 1:3101
DUN EMER PRESS, Dublin, 1903–7. 1842 4596–9
— Bibs. see also CUALA PRESS, Dundrum, est. 1903–Bibs. 1:1317
DUNFERMLINE, Fife see also BOOK TRADE, LISTS–Dunfermline.
— Bibs. 1:997
— Bksllng. see MILLER, George, 1771–1835; MILLER, James, 1791–1865.
— Publ. see MILLER FAMILY, 1771–1865.
— MURISON BURNS COLLECTION see MURISON, John, 1852–1921–Libr.
DUNFERMLINE NEWS. 3547
DUNFERMLINE PRESS see MILLER FAMILY, Dunfermline, 1771–1865.
DUNGANNON, co. Tyrone–Bibs. 1:1057 1122a–c
— Ptg.–Bibs. 1:1057 1122a–c
DUNLOP, Durham, 1812–82. 10401
DUNN, George, 1865–1922–Libr. 1:453
DUNNING, Thomas Joseph, fl.1840. 5700
DUNSANY, Edward John Moreton Drax Plunkett, baron, 1878–1957 see PLUNKETT, Edward John Moreton Drax, baron Dunsany, 1878–1957.
DUNS SUBSCRIPTION LIBRARY. 1633
DUNSYRE, Lanark.–Ptg. see WILD HAWTHORN PRESS, fl.1962.
DUNTON, Anne, fl.1778. 10402
— Discourse on justification. 10402
DUNTON, John, 1659–1733. 3432 3475 3616 3620 3639a 3659 3670 4600–6 4835b
— Dublin scuffle. 4602
— Sketches of the printers ... of London. 1259
DUNTON, Walter Theodore Watts-, 1832–1914. 10403–5 14406 14417
— Aylwin. 10403
— Bibs. 1:3218–19
— Letters. 10405
— Libr. 1:4849e; 10404
DUODECIMO FORMAT see FORMAT –Duodecimo.
DUODO BINDINGS see BOOKBINDINGS, DUODO.
DUPRÉ, Jean, Paris, fl.1481–1501. 8043
DUPRE DE SAINT-MAUR, Nicolas François, 1695–1774 see ST. MAUR, Raymond de, pseud.

DURDANS, Epsom–Libr. 2913 3258
D'URFEY, Thomas, 1653–1723. 10406–10
— Bibs. 1:3220–2
— Comical history of Don Quixote. 10406
— Cynthia and Endymion. 10409
— Love for money. 10408
— — Bibs. 1:3221
— Ode on the anniversary. 10407
— Ptg. 6155
— Richmond heiress. 10410
— — Bibs. 1:3222
— Tales tragical and comical. 6155
DURHAM. 1105–10
— Bibs. 1:887 926k
— Bndng. 1313
— Book collecting. 1105–7 2811
— Book trade–Bibs. 1:926k
— Librs. see LAMBTON CASTLE; RAVENSWORTH CASTLE.
— Maps–Bibs. 1:1780–1a
— Paper see also HUTTON, Robert, Sunderland, 1799–1865. 1109 5564q
— CATHEDRAL. LIBRARY. 2811 2822 3165 3350a
— — — Collns. 1:446 1842; 2811 6836
— COSIN'S LIBRARY. see DURHAM UNIVERSITY. LIBRARY.
— ST. OSWALD'S CHURCH–Collns. 1:446
— SURTEES SOCIETY see SURTEES SOCIETY, Durham, est. 1834.
— UNIVERSITY. ARMSTRONG COLLEGE, Newcastle-upon-Tyne–Collns. 2:209
— — KING'S COLLEGE. LIBRARY–Collns. 1:925 1455 1544 1581 2226
— — LIBRARY–Collns. 1:446 473–a 1453 1455 1780–1; 2:612; 2134 3201 3264
— USHAW COLLEGE see ST. CUTHBERT'S COLLEGE, Ushaw.
DURHAM, N.C. DUKE UNIVERSITY see DUKE UNIVERSITY, Durham, N.C.
DURHAM, James, 1622–58–Bibs. 1:3223
DURHAM, John Frederick Lambton, 5th earl of, 1884–1970 see LAMBTON, John Frederick, 5th earl of Durham, 1884–1970
DURHAM, Robert, fl.1824–36. 1680
DURIE, John, 1596–1680. 2403 2434
DURNING-LAWRENCE, sir Edwin, bart., 1837–1914 see LAWRENCE, sir Edwin Durning-, bart., 1837–1914.
DURRELL, Lawrence George, 1912– . 10411
— Bibs. 1:3223d–8
DURSLEY, Glos.–Paper. 1120a
— Ptg. 1119
DURSTON, Thomas, fl.1698. 4607
DUST JACKETS see WRAPPERS, BOOK.

DUTCH LITERATURE see BRITISH BOOKS PUBLISHED ABROAD–HOLLAND; FOREIGN BOOKS PUBLISHED IN BRITAIN–Holland.
DUTTON, Ann (Williams), 1692–1765–Bibs. 1:**3230**
DUTY see EXCISE.
DUVEEN, Denis I., fl.1960–Libr. 1:2230; 6739
DUVEEN, Louis, d.1920–Libr. 2:1011
DUXBURY, Yates, Bury, 1818–91. **4608**
DWIGGINS, William Addison, 1880–1956. 4196
DYCE, Alexander, 1798–1869.
— Libr. 2480
— Shakespeare's Works. 2:692
DYER, sir Edward, d.1607. 9827 **10412**
DYER, John, d.1713. 7695
DYER, John, 1699–1758. **10413**
— Publ. 10413
— Ruins of Rome. 10413
DYER'S MILL, Mons.–Paper. 1298a
DYMOTT, Richard, fl.1749–88. **4609**
DYSON, Humphry, d.1632–Libr. 2676 3097 8070

E., M. E. see EDWARDS, Mary Ellen, fl.1839–1908.
EALING. PUBLIC LIBRARY–Collns. 1:5081
EAMES, Wilberforce, 1855–1937–Libr. 1:384
EARLE, bp. John, 1601?–65. **10414**
— Bibs. 1:**3230a**
— Microcosmography. 9406 10414
— — Bibs. 1:**3230a**
— Mss. 9406
EARLOM, Richard, 1743–1822. **4610**
EARLY ENGLISH TEXT SOCIETY, est. 1864. **4611**
EASEBOURNE, Sussex–Ptg. 1408
EASON, Charles, Dublin, fl.1850–99. **4612**
EAST, Thomas, 1540?–1608? 3894 **4613**
— Bibs. 1:**1318**
— Mandeville's Travels. 12124 12126
EAST ANGLIA–Bibs. 1:**888–9**
EASTBOURNE, Sussex–Ptg. 1408
EASTE, William, fl.1591–1625–Bibs. 1:**3231**
EAST HAM, Essex–Ptg. see GREENSTREET HOUSE, East Ham.
EAST LOTHIAN–Bibs. 1:**996**
— Publ. 5191
EAST LOTHIAN PRESS see MILLER FAMILY, Dunfermline, 1771–1865.
EAST MALLING, Kent–Paper. 1161a
EASTON, Thomas, fl.1681–95–Bibs. 1:**3232**
EBSWORTH, Joseph, 1788–1868. **10415**
— Mss. 10415

ECCLESIASTICAL DIRECTORIES see DIRECTORIES, ECCLESIASTICAL
ECCLESIASTICAL TYPOGRAPHY see TYPOGRAPHY, ECCLESIASTICAL.
ECHARD, Laurence, 1670?–1730.
— History of England. 3991
ECKEL, John C., 1858– –Libr. 1:3082
ECHO, THE. 7826
ECCECTIC REVIEW. 7823
ECONOMICS see also DARIEN COMPANY; POOR LAWS; SOUTH SEA COMPANY. 1717
— Bibs. 1:1939a **2162–72**
ECKERSLEY, Arthur, 1875–1921–Libr. 8813
ECTON HALL, Northants.–Libr. 2805
EDDISON, Eric Rücker, 1882–1945–Bibs. 1:**3233**
EDEN, Richard, 1521?–76–Libr. 3118
EDGEGILDERS see GWYNN FAMILY, 1842–1962.
EDGES see BOOKBINDING–Edges; FORE-EDGE PAINTING; TITLES, FORE-EDGE.
EDGEWORTH, Maria, 1767–1849. 7000a 7011 7015 **10416–18**
— Bibs. 1:**3234**
— Castle Rackrent. 10416
— Parents' assistant. 10418
EDGEWORTH, Richard Lovell, 1744–1817. 7000a 7015 **10419**
— Practical education. 10419
EDINBURGH, Midloth. see also BOOK TRADE, LISTS–Edinburgh. 1600 **1695–730**
— Bibs. 1:2221a
— Bndng. 1700 1720a
— Bksllng. 1255 1580 1701 1711 1716
— Librs. 1633 1695 1701 1724–30
— Maps–Bibs. 1:**1817**
— Newspapers. 1600 1704 3886
— — Bibs. 1:1932–3 1943
— Paper see also WATKINS, Richard, d.1747. 1710 1712
— Playbills. 7232
— Ptg. 1255 1596 1696–7 1703 1708 1721–2 5418 9896 13423 13585
— Publ. 1711
— Type see BAINE, John, fl.1732–86; BERTRAM, George, fl.1808–78; MILLER, William, fl.1807–43.
— ADVOCATES' LIBRARY see SCOTLAND. NATIONAL LIBRARY, Edinburgh. ADVOCATES' LIBRARY.
— CATHEDRAL. LIBRARY–Collns. 1:442
— INSTITUTE OF CHARTERED ACCOUNTANTS OF SCOTLAND see INSTITUTE OF CHARTERED ACCOUNTANTS OF SCOTLAND, Edinburgh.

EDWARDS, Sydenham Teast, 1769?–1819.
6958a 7089
EDWARDS, Thomas, 1699–1757.
— Canons of criticism. 2:698 796
— Spenser's Faerie queene. 13569
EDWARDS, Thomas (Caerfallwch),
1779–1858. 1461
EDWARDS, William, Halifax, 1723–1808.
4616–18
EELES (Binder), fl.1818–59. 3983
EGAN, Pierce, 1772–1849. 8241 10420
— Sporting age. 7089
EGERTON, Francis, 1st earl of Ellesmere,
1800–57.
— Illus. 7394
— Libr. 2:592; 2857
— The mill. 7394
EGERTON, George, pseud. of Mary Chavelita
(Dunne) Bright, 1859–1945–Bibs. 1:3235
EGERTON, sir Thomas, baron Ellesmere
and viscount Brackley, 1540?–1617–Bibs.
1:2035b
EGERTON, Thomas, fl.1788–90. 8332
EGERTON, William, pseud., see CURLL, Ed-
mund, 1675–1747.
EGLINTOUN, sir Hew, c.1450?–Bibs.
1:3240
EGMONDT, Frederick, fl.1493–1521.
4619–20
EHRMAN, Albert, 1890–1969–Libr. 1:1186f
1209; 2205 2884 2998 3169 3493 3879
6720
EIKŌN BASILIKĒ see CHARLES I, king of
Great Britain and Ireland, 1600–49.
ELD, George, fl.1604–24.
— Chapman's All fools. 9981
— Chapman's Memorable masque. 9387
— Shakespeare's Sonnets. 2:1975
ELDER, Alexander, Aberdeen, 1790–1876 see
SMITH, ELDER AND COMPANY, Aber-
deen, 1816–1917.
ELDON, John Scott, 1st earl of, 1751–1838
see SCOTT, John, 1st earl of Eldon,
1751–1838.
ELECTROTINTING. 6228
— Bibs. 1:1163
ELECTROTYPING. 5333 6057 6348 6565
8596
ELEGY ON STELLA. 9026
ELIOT, George, pseud. of Mary Ann (Evans)
Cross, 1819–80. 732 831a 10421–9 14387
— Adam Bede. 10426
— Agatha. 10423 10428
— Bibs. 1:3245–50
— Bndngs. 10426
— Collns. 10427 10429
— Letters. 10424
— Mss. 759 10421 10424 10427

— — Bibs. 1:3248f
ELIOT, John, fl.1592.
— Ortho-epia Gallica. 7081
ELIOT, Thomas Stearns, 1888–1968.
10430–42
— Bibs. 1:1597 3251–62
— Bndng. 10433
— Collns. 10431 10438 10440
— Ezra Pound, his metric and poetry. 10437
— Gerontion. 10435
— Letters–Bibs. 1:3262
— Mss. 10430 10441–2
— — Bibs. 1:3258
— Publ. 10439
— Religious drama and the church. 10436
— Sacred wood. 10432
— Text. 10434–5
— Waste land. 10430 10433 10439 10442
ELIOT'S COURT PRESS, 1584–1674. 1243
1248
ELISIONS AND ABBREVIATIONS see
ORTHOGRAPHY.
ELIZABETH I, queen of England and
Ireland, 1533–1603. 2482 10443–8 13425
— Bibs. 2035a 3263
— Boethius' De consolatione. 10447
— Godly meditation. 10445
— Injunctions given. 10448
— Libr. 1996 2075 4904 10443–4
— Type. 6436
ELKINS, William McIntire, 1882–1947–Libr.
1:3094 3467; 10067
ELLESMERE, Francis Egerton, 1st earl of,
1800–57 see EGERTON, Francis, 1st earl
of Ellesmere, 1800–57.
ELLIOTT, Ebenezer, 1781–1849. 10449
— Bibs. 1:3265
— Mss.–Bibs. 1:3265
ELLIOTT, Thomas, fl.1703–62/3. 4620k
ELLIS, Alexander John, 1814–90. 5423
ELLIS, Edward S., 1840–1916–Bibs. 1:847
ELLIS, Frederick Startridge, 1830–1901.
4621–3 13085
ELLIS, George, 1753–1815. 7893
— Publ. 5250
ELLIS, Gilbert Ifold, 1858–1902. 4623
ELLIS, Henry Havelock, 1859–1939. 3506
— Bibs. 1:3265x–6
— Revaluation of obscenity. 4897e
ELLIS, Sarah (Stickney), 1812–72. 3974
ELLIS AND ELVEY, 1887–1905. 4621a–b
ELLIS-FERMOR, Una Mary, 1894–1958 see
FERMOR, Una Mary Ellis, 1894–1958.
ELLWOOD, Thomas, 1639–1713. 10450–1
— Bibs. 1:3366g–h
— Davideis. 10450–1
ELMSLEY, Peter, 1736–1802. 3639a
ELOISA EN DISHABILLE, 1822. 749

ELPHINSTONE, bp. William, 1431–
1514–Libr. 3248
ELSTOB, Elizabeth, 1683–1756. 3475
— Type. 6415
ELSTOB, William, 1673–1715. 3475
ELSTRACK, Renold, fl.1590–1630. 10448
ELTON, Charles Isaac, 1839–1900–Libr.
1:381
ELWES, Alfred Thomas, fl.1867–93. 4624
ELYAS (printer), fl.1495–1500. 4625
ELYOT, sir Thomas, 1490?–1546. 10452
— Bibs. 1:3267–8
— *Hermathena.* 10452
ELY PAMPHLET CLUB. 2452
ELYS, Edmund, fl.1655–1707.
— *Boethius' De consolatione.* 892
EMANUEL, Victor, 1898–1960–Libr. 1:5176
EMBLEMS. 4014 7235–6 9798–9
EMBROIDERED BINDINGS *see*
BOOKBINDINGS, EMBROIDERED.
EMDEN, Germany. 5186b
EMERSON, Ralph Waldo, 1803–82.
— *Poems.* 977
EMMET, Robert, 1778–1803–Bibs.
1:3269–70f
EMMETT, William Lawrence, fl.1870–80.
4110
EMPSON, William, 1906– –Bibs. 1:3270h
ENAMELLED BINDINGS *see* BOOK-
BINDINGS, ENAMELLED.
ENCHIRIDION LEGUM, 1673. 6513
ENCOMIA–Bibs. 1:1656e
ENCYCLOPÆDIA BRITANNICA. 7241 7244
— Bibs. 1:1529 4006
ENCYCLOPÆDIA METROPOLITANA, 1845.
9538 9562
ENCYCLOPEDIAS. 1707 1720 7237–45
— Bibs. 1:1656g–h 2250a
ENDPAPERS *see* BOOKBINDINGS–
Endpapers.
ENGAGEMENT CONTROVERSY–Bibs.
1:1973
ENGELMANN, Godefroi, 1788–1839. 6202
ENGLAND. 1013–448
— Bibs. 1:855–952
— Directories–Bibs. 1:865
— Illus. 6223
— Presses, Provincial–Bibs. 1:866–8
— Roadbooks and itineraries–Bibs. 1:870–1
— Topography–Bibs. 1:855–62
— COURT OF CHANCERY. 3625 6070
— COURT OF THE STAR CHAMBER.
3542a 3559 3571 6074 6613
— PRIVY PURSE. 3428
— ROYAL COLLEGE OF SURGEONS *see*
ROYAL COLLEGE OF SURGEONS OF
ENGLAND.
—, NORTHERN. 1031–2

—, NORTHWEST–Paper. 3768
—, SOUTHWEST–Paper. 3784
ENGLAND'S HELICON, 1600. 2:1487; 5075
ENGLISH BIJOU ALMANACS, 1836–46. 7577
ENGLISH CATALOGUE OF BOOKS. 1:663;
3486 8544
ENGLISH FOLK-DANCE AND SONG
SOCIETY. CECIL SHARP LIBRARY. 3139
ENGLISH FREEHOLDER. 7711
ENGLISH HISTORY–Bibs. 1:15–22 490a
594b 657j 679b
ENGLISH LIBRARY. 4547
ENGLISH LITERATURE. 181 184 188 200
258
— Bibliographies–Bibs. 1:25–35
— Bibliographies, Serial. 1:36–64
— — Bibs. 1:36–8
— General guides. 1:1–24
— 1475–1640–Bibs. 1:2 46–7 84 490b
— 1641–1700–Bibs. 1:2 48–50 594–b 623f
— 1701–1800–Bibs. 1:2 48–50 625–8a
— 1801–1900–Bibs. 1:2 51–63 628a 657a–c
657j 669f
— 1901– –Bibs. 1:2 64 677–9b
ENGLISHMAN, THE–Bibs. 1:4773
ENGLISH MERCURY, 1588. 7654
ENGLISH PILOT. 7630
— Bibs. 1:1767a
ENGRAVERS *see also* BLAKE, ENGRAVERS
NAMED; BOOK TRADE, LISTS–
Engravers, *and individual engravers, e.g.*
Austin, Richard, fl.1787–1830; Baillie,
William, 1723–1810; Barnard, William,
1774–1849; Barnes, William, 1801–86;
Baron, Bernard, 1700–62; Bartolozzi,
Francesco, 1726–1815; Beilby, Ralph,
Newcastle-upon-Tyne, 1744–1817; Beilby
and Bewick, Newcastle-upon-Tyne,
1777–97; Bewick, John, Newcastle-upon-
Tyne, 1760–95; Bewick, Thomas,
Newcastle-upon-Tyne, 1753–1828;
Bickham, George, 1684–1758; Bickham,
George, 1735–67; Blake, William,
1757–1827; Boydell, John, 1719–1804;
Boydell, Josiah, 1752–1817; Burke,
Thomas, 1749–1815; Cary, John,
c.1754–1835; Caslon, William, 1692–1766;
Cave, Henry, York, 1779–1836; Cave,
Henry, York, 1808–71; Cave, Richard,
York, 1802–73; Cave, William, York,
1751–1812; Cave, William, York,
1775–1865; Cave, William, York, fl.1818;
Clint, George, 1770–1854; Cooke, George
Alexander, 1781–1834; Cooper, Richard,
1705–64; Cooper, Richard, 1740?–1815?;
Corbutt, C., *pseud. of* Richard Purcell,
fl.1750–66; Cross, Thomas, fl.1632–82;
Duncan, Edward, 1804–82; Earlom,

ENGRAVERS—cont.
Richard, 1743–1822; Elstrack, Renold, fl.1590–1630; Evans, William Camden, 1777–1855; Faithorne, William, 1616–91; Fawcett, Benjamin, 1808–93; Fittler, James, 1758–1835; Flaxman, John, 1755–1826; Freeman, Samuel, 1775?–1857; Frye, Thomas, 1710–62; Gillray, James, 1757–1815; Green, Valentine, 1739–1813; Green, William, 1761–1823; Harris, John, 1791–1873; Harris, John, fl.1798–1857; Hibbert, Charles, d.1819; Hodges, Charles Howard, 1764–1837; Hoffman, Francis, fl.1706–25; Hogarth, William, 1697–1764; Hole, Henry Fulke Plantagenet Woolicombe, d.1820; Jackson, John Baptist, 1701–80?; Jenner, Thomas, fl.1618–72; Jewitt, Thomas Orlando Sheldon, 1799–1869; Kirkall, Elisha, 1682?–1742; Leech, John, 1817–64; Marshall, William, fl.1630–50; Medland, Thomas, fl.1777–1822; Ogborne, John, 1755–1837; Pether, William, 1738?–1821; Pine, John, 1690–1756; Pollard, Robert, Newcastle-upon-Tyne, 1755–1838; Purcell, Richard, fl.1750–66; Reid, Andrew, Newcastle-upon-Tyne, 1823–96; Rowlandson, Thomas, 1756–1827; Sandby, Paul, 1725–1809; Sherborn, Charles William, 1831–1912; Soiron, François, fl.1755–1813; Stadler, Joseph Constantin, fl.1780–1812; Stent, Peter, fl.1640–65; Strange, sir Robert, 1721–92; Sturt, John, fl.1809–20; Swain, Charles, Manchester, 1801–74; Taylor, Isaac, 1730–1807; Tompson, Richard, fl.1656–93; Turner, Charles, 1774–1857; Vertue, George, 1684–1756; Walker, William, 1729–93; Ward, James, 1769–1859; Ward, William, 1766–1826; Woollett, William, 1735–85. 3429–30 5541 6210a
—, LISTS OF. 1461a
ENGRAVING. 1189 1259 6207
— Bibs. 1:1163 1741–2
— Ireland. 1742 1808
— Scotland. 1593 1611
— Wales. 1482
— 1475–1640. 7404 7523
— 1641–1700. 6191 6220 7404
— 1701–1800. 6191 6207 6220 6223 7391 7406 7413
— 1801–1900. 6191 6202 6207 6223
—, BURIN. 6187
—, COPPERPLATE. 5419 6121b 6207 6210 6259
—, CRAYON. 6187 6202
—, DROUESHOUT see DROUESHOUT ENGRAVING.

—, DRY POINT. 6187
—, MEDAL. 6228
—, MEZZOTINT see also MEZZOTINTS. 6187 6191–2
—, STEEL. 6185 6191 6207 6210
—, STIPPLE. 6187 6192 6194 7391 7406
—, WOOD. 3842 4014 6186 6201 6207 6210 6220
ENGRAVINGS. 1623 4176 4715
— Bibs. 1:1735y 1738n 1739 1745d 1745f 2471k 2473b 2474p 2482 4138b
— Publ. 6550
—, COPPERPLATE. 6190 7404 7523 8596
—, LISTS OF. 1623 3963 6266 6284 7404
—, STEEL. 5046
—, WOOD see WOODCUTS.
ENIGMAS. 524
ENNIS, co. Clare. 1854
— Bibs. 1:1045
— Ptg. 1854 1955
— — Bibs. 1:1045
ENNISCORTHY, co. Wexford. 1987
— Bibs. 1:1137–8
— Ptg. 1987
— — Bibs. 1:1137–8
ENNISKILLEN, co. Fermanagh.
— Bibs. 1:1080–2
— Ptg. 1771–2
— — Bibs. 1:1080–2
ENQUIRY OF THE DEATH OF RICHARD HUNNE, 1539? 590
ENTERTAINING HISTORY OF GOODY GOOSECAP. 6997
ENTERTAINMENT AT RICHMOND. 7106
ENTICK, John, 1703?–73.
— Proposals for printing Chaucer. 9413
ENTRANCE (STATIONERS' REGISTER). 1281 3438 3446 3530 3563 5762 13058
ENUMERATIVE BIBLIOGRAPHY see BIBLIOGRAPHY, ENUMERATIVE.
EPHEMERA, PRINTED. 7246–57 7621 7624
— Bibs. 1:1979
— Collns. 5354 7249 7251
ENVELOPES. 3714 4545
EPICURE'S ALMANAC. 6742
EPISTLE TO JAMES BOSWELL, 1790. 8707
EPISTOLARY FICTION see FICTION, EPISTOLARY.
EPITAPH ON THE DUKE OF SCHOMBERG. 13705
EPITAPH UPON THE DEATH OF KING EDWARD, 1554. 6975
EPSOM, Surrey–Librs. see DURDANS.
EPWORTH PRESS, est. 1739 see METHODIST PUBLISHING HOUSE, est. 1739.

ERAGNY PRESS, 1894–1914. **4626–33** 6463
6502
— Bibs. 1:1245f **1319**
— Type. 6610
ERASMUS, Desiderius, 1466–1536. 933–4
936 938–40 2187
— Bibs. 1:**826–a**
— *Catechismus.* 937
— *De pueris instituendis.* 932
— *Enchiridion.* 4151
ERIE COUNTY, N.Y. BUFFALO AND ERIE
COUNTY PUBLIC LIBRARY–Collns.
1:554c 624e
ERLANGEN, Bavaria. UNIVERSITY.
ENGLISH SEMINAR LIBRARY. 9179
ERRATA. 6401 7738 8403 13306 13349
13598 14490
—, LISTS OF. 275 5345 5660
ERRORS, BIBLIOGRAPHICAL *see* BIB-
LIOGRAPHICAL ERRORS.
ERVE, Egidius van der, Emden, fl.1555. 843
— Bibs. 1:**1320**
ESHER, Oliver Sylvain Baliol, 3d viscount,
1881–1963 *see* BRETT, Oliver Sylvain
Baliol, 3d viscount Esher, 1881–1963.
ESKIMO. 9904
ESPARTO. 3700 3745a 3784 5564p–q
ESQUEMELING, Alexander Olivier,
fl.1662–79 *see* EXQUEMELIN, Alexandre
Olivier, fl.1662–79.
ESSAYS–Bibs. 1:**1657**
ESSEX. **1111–16**
— Bibs. 1:**890–1**
— Librs. 2452
— Maps–Bibs. 1:**1782–k**
— Ptg. 1111
ESSEX, Arthur Capell, earl of, 1631–83 *see*
CAPELL, Arthur, earl of Essex, 1631–
83.
ESSEX, Robert Devereux, 2d earl of,
1566–1601 *see* DEVEREUX, Robert, 2d
earl of Essex, 1566–1601.
ESSEX HOUSE PRESS, Chipping Camden,
Glos., 1898–1909. **4634–5** 6462–3 6502
13654
— Bibs. 1:**1321–2**
EST, Thomas, 1540?–1608? *see* EAST,
Thomas, 1540?–1608?
'ET AMICORUM'. 2447
ETCHING. 6186–7 6194 6207 6210
—, PHOTOGRAPHIC. 6206
ETCHINGS. 3496 6284
— Ptg. 5186
ETHEREGE, sir George, 1635?–91. **10453**
— Bibs. 1:**3271**
— Letters. 10453
ETHERIGE, Samuel, 1778–c.1840–Bibs.
1:**3272**

ETON, Bucks.
— Bndng. 5394
— Ptg. 1019
— COLLEGE. 8112 8115
— — Bibs. 1:**875–6**
— — LIBRARY. 2494 3197–8 3332
— — — Collns. 1:880 1613; 2:183a; 3198
3357 10830
ETTLES, William, Inverness, d.1819. 1683
EUCLID, 323–283 B.C. 884 7548
EUING, William, 1788–1874–Libr. 1:1460
1477; 6850
EURGRAWN CYMRAEG. 1458 1486
EURIPIDES, 480–406 B.C. 11166
EUROPEAN COPYRIGHT *see* COPY-
RIGHT, EUROPEAN.
EUROPEAN MAGAZINE–Bibs. 1:4350
EVANGELISM–Bibs. 1:1559d
EVANS, Adam, Machynlleth, 1819–96–Bibs.
1:963h
EVANS, Daniel, Swansea, fl.1781–1806. **4636**
EVANS, David Caradoc, 1878–1945.
— Bibs. 1:**3272f–g**
— Collns. 2329
EVANS, Edmund, 1826–1905. **4637** 6123b
6192 6194 6202 6229
— Bibs. 1:**3272q**
EVANS, Edward, 1831–1901. **10454**
— Bibs. 1:**3272t**
EVANS, Henry, fl.1650–76. **4638**
EVANS, John, 1792–1827. **10456**
EVANS, sir John, 1823–1908–Bibs. 1:**3273**
EVANS, Lewis, fl.1557–74.
— *Horace.* 897
EVANS, Margiad, *pseud. of* Peggy Eileen
Arabella Williams, 1909–58–Bibs. 1:**3273n**
EVANS, Robert Harding, 1778–1857.
4639–42
EVANS, Robert Harding, and co., ltd.–Bibs.
1:1443b
EVANS, Thomas, 1739–1803. 3622 3639a
EVANS, Thomas, 1742–84. **4642**
EVANS, Thomas, 1766–1833. 10456
— Bibs. 1:**3273r**
— Mss.–Bibs. 1:**3273r**
EVANS, Titus, Machynlleth, fl.1789–96–Bibs.
1:963h
EVANS, William Camden, 1777–1855. **4642a**
EVELYN, John, 1620–1706–Bibs. 1:**3274–6e**
EVELYN, John, 1655–99. 176 **10457–65**
— Bibs. 1:**3276a–7**
— *History of the three imposters.* 10464
— *Instructions concerning a library.* 10461
— *Kalendarium hortense.* 10462
— Letters. 8838
— Libr. 10460–1 10463
— *Life of mrs. Godolphin.* 10457
— *Memoirs.* 10458

EVELYN, John, 1655–99 Mss. 10457–8 10465
— *Public employment.* 10459
EVELYN, sir John, 1682–1763.
— Bibs. 1:**3278**
— Libr. 3108
EVENING NEWSPAPERS *see* NEWS-PAPERS, EVENING.
EVENING POST. 7644
EVERARD, Edmund, fl.1679–81.
— *Discourses on the present state.* 3572
EVERARD, Thomas, 1560–1633–Bibs. 1:**3279**
EVERGREEN–Bibs. 1:1721
ÉVREMOND, Charles de Marguetel de Saint-Denis de Saint-, 1616–1703 *see* SAINT-ÉVREMOND, Charles de Marguetel de Saint-Denis de, 1616–1703.
EWING, Juliana Horatia (Gatty), 1841–85. 3974
EXAMINER, THE. 7790 7894
— Bibs. 1:3993a
EXCEEDING TRUE AND HAPPY NEWS FROM . . . GLOUCESTER, 1642. 704
EXCISE.
— Bibs. 1:1139z
— Newspapers *see* NEWSPAPER STAMPS.
— Pamphlets. 7949
— Paper. 1514 1837 3546 3707 3717 3746 3765 3767–a 3769 4545 5359 5909 5935 5975
EXETER, Devon. **1102b–e**
— Bibs. 1:2224
— Bksllng. 1102b 1102e 3433
— Librs. 1102b
— Maps–Bibs. 1:**1782k**
— Ptg. 1019 1025 1102b 1102e
— CATHEDRAL. LIBRARY. 2549 2592 3101 3205a 3302a
— — — Collns. 1:2217
— UNIVERSITY. LIBRARY–Collns. 1:2834
EXHIBITION CATALOGUES *see* CAT-ALOGUES, EXHIBITION.
EXHIBITIONS *see also* SHAKESPEARE, William, 1564–1616–EXHIBITIONS. 505 1367 2062 8615 8618 8880 9103 9738 10032 10085 11025 12502 12715 14446–7 14480 **14595**
— Aberystwyth public library. 1:962c; 1524
— Aldeburgh festival. 1:2903
— Baylor university library. 1:2591
— Belfast public libraries. 1:4503 4505
— Bibliothèque nationale. 1:2912db; 533
— Birmingham public libraries. 1:479 3846–7
— Birmingham university library. 1:1255 3385
— Bodleian library. 1:608 1836 4282 4686 4943h; 528 7258 7464 7480–1 7563 7574 8049 10666 11427 11564 13431–2 13812
— Boston college library. 1:4212
— Boston public library. 1:1515 3909; 6864 8903 10164 11305 11759 12525
— Boussod, Jean, Manzi, Joyant & co. 2036–7
— Bridwell library, Southern Methodist university. 1:1497d
— Brighton public libraries. 1:1479
— Bristol public libraries. 1:1484 1494 4741
— British museum. 1:1149f 1154 1474 1520 1573f 2033k 3421 3568 4469 5192; 525 576 3437 3452 4886 5622 10438 12925
— Brooklyn public library. 1:4858
— Brotherton library, Leeds. 1:4538 4604d
— Brown university library.
— Bumpus, J. & E., bksllrs., Cambridge. 1:879 2728–9 4016e; 2328 2334 12008 13197
— Burlington fine arts club. 2010
— University of California library. 7320
— University of California at Los Angeles library. 1:1668 3778
— Cambridge university library. 8608 13753
— Cambridge university press. 1:1497
— Cardiff public libraries. 1:1475 1485 2125
— Carnegie institution, Pittsburgh. 1:2127
— Cassell and co. 1:1280n
— Caxton club, Chicago. 1:3321; 2038 2270
— Chapin library, Williams college. 1:2149 4248
— Chatsworth house library. 580
— Christ's college, Cambridge. 1:2951 4224
— Clements library, University of Michigan. 1:2126
— Colby college library. 1:3504a 3590 3592 4809; 13660 13923
— Columbia university library. 1:1139 2726; 2056 12319
— Connecticut college. 14525
— Cornell university library. 1:5174
— Corpus Christi college, Cambridge, library. 1:1173
— Coventry public libraries. 1:3248f
— Dickens' birthplace museum, Portsmouth. 1:3055 3065 3070g
— Dublin civic museum. 1:3569
— Durham university. 2134
— East Anglian master printers' alliance. 1:888
— Edinburgh public libraries. 1:2638 3171; 9096
— Essex chapter house. 1:2772
— Exeter memorial library. 1:2224
— Exeter university college. 1:2834
— Festival of Britain. 532
— Fine art society, London. 1:4893
— First edition club, Liverpool. 1:1229

EXHIBITIONS–First edition club, London.
1:681 1263 2684; 2086 7960
— Fitzwilliam museum, Cambridge. 1:351.
— Florida state university library. 1:2733
— Foyle's art gallery. 2203
— Francis Thompson society. 1:4954b
— Franklin club of St. Louis. 1:3058
— Geographical society of Ireland. 1:1818
— Gilbert White fellowship. 1:5079
— Glasgow bibliographical society. 1:1002
— Glasgow institute of the fine arts.
1:2630
— Glasgow university library. 1:1476–7
2604; 4690–2
— Gloucester public library. 1:1388b
— Grolier club, N.Y. 1:327–8 330–1 359e
368 486 495 552 1200a 1621 1718 2037d
2101 2431 2471 2508a 2781 3062–3 3173
3433 3591 3805g 3836 3951 4038 4222
4438 4552–3 4651 4756 4802–3 4888
4913–14; 538 2008a 2046 6714 8693
— Guildhall library. 1:4647
— Harvard university library. 1:3841d 3851;
11662
— Henry E. Huntington library. 1:1663 2216
2690; 7150 9103
— Holburne museum. 1:2418
— Houghton library, Harvard. 1:4520d
— Hull university. 1:1492 3360c
— Hunterian museum, Glasgow. 1:1329
2291 3793
— Illinois university library. 1:1728 4241
— Institute of contemporary arts. 11592
— International association of antiquarian
booksellers. 1:573
— University of Iowa. 13070
— J.B. Speed art museum, Louisville.
1:2935g
— Jews' college, London. 1:921
— John Rylands library, Manchester. 1:326
336 429 460 1472–3 1481–2 4223; 6894
8052 10173
— Johnson house, Lichfield. 1:3841bb
— King's college, London, library. 1:1496
— King's college, Newcastle, library. 1:2226
— King's Lynn festival. 1:1236m
— Lehigh university. 1:2952
— Leicester. 1:1259g
— Library company, Philadelphia. 1:4921
— Lilly library, University of Indiana.
1:4249a
— Little museum of La miniatura, Pasadena.
1:1351p 2476 4302c
— London university Council for psychical
investigation. 1:2244
— London university library. 1:4389; 2131
— Loughborough technical college. 6501
— McMurry college. 9661

— Mauchline Burns club. 9103
— Mitchell library, Glasgow. 1:725
— Napier tercentenary celebration. 1:4321
— National book league. 1:358 360 613 689
1559 1569 1590 1714 1754 1767 2118 2157
2175 2179 3006 4213 4632
— National gallery of Scotland. 1:4604
— National library of India. 1:359a
— National library of Ireland. 1:1828
— National library of Scotland. 1:367 712e
1266m 2130 3567; 3258 4066 9103
11101
— National library of Wales. 1:696 700
1507a; 7014 9853
— Nevada university library. 1:2641
— Newberry library. 1:1350m 1483 1656h
3881
— Newcastle-upon-Tyne university library.
1:1773 2121 5209ac
— New Dudley gallery. 9995
— New gallery, Belfast. 4569
— New York public library. 1:1480 2912f
4160; 2126 5348 7272 7978 8032
— — Berg collection. 1:355–6 361 368a
2444b 3097 3450 4634 4922 5175
— Norwich public libraries. 1:2492
— Nottingham castle. 2012a
— Nottingham mechanics institute. 1:2682
— Nottingham public library. 1:929 5085
— Nottingham university library. 1:4020
— Olympia. 10008–9
— Oxford university press. 1:1497; 11395
— Peabody institute library. 1:1725
— Pennsylvania university library. 1:2796
3671; 6860 11762
— Perkins school of theology. 6893
— Peterborough natural history, scientific,
and archæological society. 1:2807
— Philadelphia free library. 1:3094 3841c
4328; 11315
— Philadelphia museum of art. 1:2479
— Pierpont Morgan library. 1:1491 1562
3848; 507 672 2123a 5597a 6933 7048
7053 10684 11786
— Polish library, London. 1:2870
— Press club, London, library. 1:1852 1888;
13142
— Princeton university library. 1:363f 363h
2488c 3958; 540–1 792 3382 7192 12847
— Reading university library. 1:874
— Rosenbach company. 1:348k; 527
— Royal college of physicians. 1:3619
— Royal institution of chartered surveyors,
Surrey branch. 1:1806
— Royal Irish academy. 1:4358
— Royal library, Windsor castle. 2020
— St. Bride foundation institute. 1:1203
1250 1266q 1556

EXHIBITIONS–St. Marylebone public libraries. 1:2571 3182 4533
— St. Patrick's hospital, Dublin. 1:4838
— San Francisco public library. 1:4807
— Sheffield public libraries. 1:1487
— Signet library, Edinburgh. 1:720; 9091
— Society of arts. 1998
— Society of herbalists library. 1:2180
— Southern Illinois university library. 1:3887 4019
— Southwark public libraries. 1:3088; 2841a
— Stanford university library. 1:3436; 4589a
— Stationers' company. 3629
— Stoke Newington public libraries. 1:2988 4225 5039
— Swansea public library. 1:963e 4938; 1545
— Sweden. Kungliga bibliotekets. 2239a
— Temple university library. 1:3008
— Texas university humanities research center. 1:365 2640 3258 3398 4458c 4582b 5140
— Texas university library. 1:3981 4654 4837 4897 5137; 11835 12846 13755
— Times bookshop, London. 1:1236 3193; 6496
— Toronto public libraries. 1:1568
— Tregaskis, J. and M. L., London. 2014a 2023 2025a
— Trinity college, Dublin, library. 1:2454 4834 4869–70 5104 5205; 14588
— University college, London, library. 1:3728; 11202
— Victoria and Albert museum. 1:2912eb 3059; 8438 10004
— Victoria public library. 1:3089
— Virginia bibliographical society. 1:2128
— Virginia university library. 1:846
— Warwickshire county museum. 1:3215
— Wellcome historical medical museum. 1:3822 4065
— Wigan public library. 1:353 1521
— Wilberforce museum, Hull. 1:4144
— William Blake trust. 1:2486a
— William Morris society. 1:1354 4304; 12531
— William Morris society, Tokyo. 1:4302d
— Winchester college library. 1:2845; 9617
— Wisbech society. 1:1785
— Yale university library. 1:1478 2289dc 2417 3255 3468 3587 3833 3837 3842 5203; 6223 6780 7149 8027 8104 8281 8485 8524 10431 10750 11433 12011 12355 12526 12897 14537
EX LIBRIS BOOKS see ASSOCIATION COPIES.
EXPERIENCED FOWLER, 1697. 714

EXPLANATION OF THE SCOTS COMMISSIONERS, 1641. 1588
EXPLICATION–Bibs. 1:1981–d
EXPLICITS–Bibliogr. descr. 143
EXPORTATION OF BOOKS. 12583
EXPOSITION OF CERTAIN DIFFICULT AND OBSCURE WORDS, 1579. 7079
EXQUEMELIN, Alexandre Olivier, fl.1662–79.
— *Buccaneers of America.* 7958
EXTRACTS FROM THE CLASSICS, 1888. 907
EXTRA-ILLUSTRATED COPIES. 2:659 778 1123m; 1413 6846 6848 7381 7403 7414 7421 7437 7442 8692 8711 9983 10006 10588 10592 12693
— Bibs. 1:359
EXTRA-ILLUSTRATION. 7379 7384 7401–2 7405 7417 7423 7427 7449 7454 7626 9982 9997a
EXTRA-ILLUSTRATORS see BAXTER, John 1781–1858; BELL, John Gray, 1823–66; BROADLEY, Alexander Meyrick, 1847–1916; COLES, Abraham, 1813–91?; COLLINGS, Edward J., fl.1905–12; GRANGER, James, 1723–76; HARVEY, Francis, 1830–1900; MORICE, James, fl.1509–53.
EY ENSUYT UND CHANSON, 1818. 4134
EYHORNE MILL, Kent. 1161a
EYHORNE STREET, Kent–Paper. 1161a
EYRE AND SPOTTISWOODE, est. 1832. 4643 6891
— Bndng. 4643

F., I.
— *Christ's bloody sweat.* 686
F., P., fl.1590.
— *History of Faustus.* 7160
FABER, Frederick William, 1814–63–Bibs. 1:3280
FACETIAE, BIBLIOGRAPHICAL see FACETIAE, BIBLIOGRAPHICAL.
FACSIMILES see also SHAKESPEARE, William, 1564–1616–Facsimiles. 257 342 495–504 505 584 2352 2542 4837 5571 7117 7293 7335 8630 8639a 9022 9243 11285 11670 11701 13045 13229 14463
— Bibs. 1:330 555 1281a 2643 4823
—, PHOTOGRAPHIC. 495–7
—, TYPE. 498 11802 12196
FACTORY LIBRARIES see LIBRARIES, FACTORY.
FACTOTUMS see TYPE–Factotums.
FAIRBANK, Alfred John, 1895– –Bibs. 1:3280p
FAIRBURN, John, fl.1817–30. 7023

FAIRFAX, Edward, d.1635.
— *Tasso's Jerusalem delivered.* 9266
FAIRFAX, Thomas, 3d baron Fairfax of Cameron, 1612–71–Libr. 2266
FAIRFIELD, Cicily Isabel, (mrs. H. M. Andrews), 1892– *see* WEST, dame Rebecca, *pseud.*, 1892–.
FAIRIES. 7258
FAIRLEY, John A., fl.1907–27–Libr. 1:1541d
FAIRLEY, William, fl.1867–94.
— *Practical observations on the South Wales coalfield.* 8157
FAIR MAID OF BRISTOW, 1605. 7110a 7166
FAIR ROSAMOND. 6989
FAIRS. 3683
FAITHORNE, William, 1616–91. **4644–5**
FAKES AND FAKERS *see* FORGERS; FORGERIES.
FALCONAR, Maria, fl.1771–1802.
— *Poetic laurels.* 5938
— Ptg. 5938
FALCONER, Charles MacGregor, d.1907. 11897
— Libr. 1:4003 4006
FALCONER, William, 1732–69. **10466–7**
— *Nautical journal.* 10466
— *Shipwreck.* 10467
FALCONRY *see also* HAWKING.
— Bibs. 1:2120 2192 2193d
FALES, De Coursey, 1888–1966–Libr. 1:4614b 5043; 7317 7321
FALES LIBRARY *see* NEW YORK. UNIVERSITY. FALES LIBRARY.
FALKNER, George, Manchester, fl.1891. **4646**
FALKNER, John Meade, 1858–1932.
— Bibs. 1:**3281**
— Libr. 2909
FALKNER, Priscilla Susan, (mrs. Edward Bury), fl.1793–1867 *see* BURY, Priscilla Susan (Falkner), fl.1793–1867.
FAMILY LIBRARY. 5250
FAMILY SHAKESPEARE see BOWDLER, Henrietta Maria, 1754–1830.
FANCOURT, Samuel, 1678–1768. 2428
FANE, Mildmay, 2d earl of Westmorland, d.1666. **10468**
— Mss. 10468
FANFROLICO PRESS, 1926–30. **4647–9**
— Bibs. 1:1322b
FANN STREET FOUNDRY, 1808–20 *see also* THORNE, Robert, 1754–1820. 5518 6613
FANSHAWE, sir Richard, 1606–66. **10469–72**
— *Camoëns' Lusiads.* 10471–2
— Mss. 10470
— *Il pastor fido.* 10469
FANTASY PRESS, Oxford, est. 1951–Bibs. 1:**1322g**

FAQUES, Richard, fl.1509–38. 6056
FAQUES, William, fl.1504–8. 6056 6081
FARADAY, Michael, 1791–1867. 6381
— Bibs. 1:**3282**
FARLEY FAMILY, Bristol, fl.1699–1774. 1300
FARMER, Edward, fl.1817–Libr. 1810
FARMER, John Stephen, 1835–1908. 7117
— Bibs. 1:**3282g**
FARMER, Richard, 1735–97. 3310 12761
— Libr. 1:1018; 2639
FARMER, William, fl.1612. 1882
FARMING *see* AGRICULTURE.
FARNOL, John Jeffery, 1878–1952–Bibs. 1:**3282p**
FARQUHAR, George, 1678–1707. **10473**
— Bibs. 1:1597 **3282w**
— *Constant couple.* 10473
FARRAR, Frederick William, 1831–1903–Bibs. 1:**3283**
FAULKNER, George, Dublin, 1699?–1775. 13789
— *Swift's Gulliver's travels.* 13791
— *Swift's Works.* 13737 13746 13795
FAULKNER, Thomas William, fl.1794–1845. 1277 5700
FAUNTLEROY, Henry, 1785–1824–Libr. 2710
FAUSTUS (Ballad). 6789 6794–5
— Bibs. 1:1467
FAVYN, André, fl.1623.
— *Theatre of honour.* 2:558
FAWCETT, Benjamin, 1808–93. **4650–a** 6192 6194 6202 6229
— Bibs. 1:**1322m**
FAWCETT, Thomas, fl.1621–44. 3834
FAWKES, Francis, 1720–77. **10474**
— *Brown jug.* 10474
FAWNE, Luke, d.1665. **4651**
FAYETTE, Marie-Madeleine Pioche de la Vergue, comtesse de, 1634–92 *see* PIOCHE DE LA VERGUE, Marie-Madeleine, comtesse de Fayette, 1634–92.
FAZAKERLEY, John Liverpool, fl.1877–91. **4652**
FAZAKERELEY, Thomas, Liverpool, fl.1813–77. 4652
FEARN, Henry Noel-, formerly Christmas, 1811–68 *see* CHRISTMAS, Henry, afterwards Noel-Fearn, 1811–68.
FEARN, John Russell, 1908–60–Bibs. 1:**3283a–b**
FEES *see also* WAGES.
— Correctors. 6405
FEILING, sir Keith Grahame, 1884– –Bibs. 1:**3283d**

FELKIN, mrs. A. L., 1860–1929 *see*
FOWLER, Ellen Thorneycroft (mrs. A. L.
Felkin), 1860–1929.
FELL, Herbert Granville, 1872–1951. 7409
FELL, bp. John, 1625–86. **4653–61** 5355
— Bibs. 1:(1197) 1201a 1211 **3283g**
— Collns. 5357
— Letters. 5332
— Type. 4499 4654–61 5332 5342 5366 6572
6629
FELL, William, fl.1806–30. 4623
FELLOWS, Reginald Bruce, fl.1893–
1948–Libr. 8077
FEMALE FACTION, 1729. 6402
*FEMALE POEMS ON SEVERAL OCCASIONS,
1679.* 7997
FENCING *see also* DUELLING. **7259–a**
— Bibs. 1:**2176–8**
FÉNELON, François de Salignac de la
Mothe-, 1651–1715. 13500 13514
FENLANDS–Maps–Bibs. 1:1776 **1783–5**
FENN, George Manville, 1831–1909–Bibs.
1:**3283k**
FENN, sir John, 1739–94–Libr. 2602
FENNER, William, Cambridge, fl.1725–34.
6377
— Ptg. 6242
— *So short a catechism.* 6242
FENNING, Daniel, fl.1756–75.
— *Royal English dictionary.* 7076
FENTON, Edward, fl.1621.
FERGUSON, John, 1787–1856. 3050
FERGUSON, John, d.1915–Bibs. 1:**3284–5**
— Libr. 1:2100
FERGUSON, John, fl.1912–29–Bibs. 1:**3286**
FERGUSON, sir John Alexander,
1881–1969–Libr. 1:2876
FERGUSON, sir Samuel, 1810–86–Bibs.
1:**3287–8**
FERGUSSON, Robert, 1750–74. **10475–6**
— Bibs. 1:**3289**
— *Poems.* 9097 10476
FERMANAGH–Bibs. 1:**1080–2**
FERMOR, Una Mary Ellis-, 1894–1958–Bibs.
1:**3292**
FERMOY, co. Cork–Bibs. 1:**1051**
— Ptg.–Bibs. 1:**1051**
FERRAND, Jacques, fl.1612–40. 9123
FERRAR, Nicholas, 1592–1637 *see also*
LITTLE GIDDING BINDERY, 1625–47.
— Bibs. 1:**3641–2**
— Mss. 5087
FERRIER, Susan Edmonstone, 1782–1854.
9468
FESTIVAL OF BRITAIN, 1953. 532
FESTSCHRIFTEN–Bibs. 1:881m
FETTERCAIRN HOUSE, Kincardineshire.
8697 8700 8704

— Collns. 1:2508c
FICTION *see also* NOVELS. **7260–326**
— Bibs. 1:**1658–724p**
— Collns. 2992 7291 7306 7317 7320–1
7322a 7323 7325 14206
— Ireland. 1848
— — Bibs. 1:1719 1723k
— Publ. 7290
— Text. 383
— Wales–Bibs. 1:1717
— 1601– . **7260–74**
— — Bibs. 1:**1658–70**
— 1601–1700. **7275–8**
— 1475–1700–Bibs. 1:**1685–6; 1686d–9**
— 1701–1800. **7279–92**
— — Bibs. 1:**1368** 1685 **1690–701**
— 1801–1900. 859 1848 7265–6 **7293–325**
7426
— — Bibs. 1:1361 1368 1692 1697–8
1705–22c 1746 2199a–b
— 1901– . **7326–a**
— — Bibs. 1:1708–9 1716 **1723–4p**
—, CRICKET–Bibs. 1:2156y
—, DETECTIVE. 2327 2374 7265–6 7270–1
7273–4 7323
—, EPISTOLARY–Bibs. 1:1693 1695
1700
—, SCIENCE *see* SCIENCE FICTION.
—, SERIAL *see also individual series listed under*
BOOKS in SERIES. 2327 2992 7268 7294
7298
FICTITIOUS BOOKS *see* BOOKS, FICT-
IOUS.
FICTITIOUS NEWSPAPERS *see* NEWS-
PAPERS, FICTITIOUS.
FIELD, THE. 7833
FIELD, Barron, 1786–1846. 14552
FIELD, Guy Cromwell, 1887–1955–Bibs.
1:**3295**
FIELD, John, 1782–1837. **10477–8**
— Bibs. 1:**3296**
FIELD, Michael, *pseud. of* Katherine
Harris Bradley, 1846–1913 and Edith
Emma Cooper, 1862–1914–Bibs.
1:**3296m**
FIELD, Nathan, 1587–1620. **10479–82**
11537
— *Amends for ladies.* 10479 10481
— Bibs. 1:**3297**
— *Blind beggar of Bednall green.* 6410
— Ptg. 6410
— Text. 8467 10479 10481
— *Woman is a weathercock.* 10480
FIELD, Richard, 1589–1624. **4662–6**
— Bibs. 1:**1322p**
— *New testament.* 6907
FIELD, William B. Osgood, fl.1930–Libr.
1:4029 4039

FIELDING, Henry, 1707–54 *see also THE CHAMPION*. **10483–525**
— *Apology for T.C.* 10511
— *Amelia*. 10511 10523
— — Bibs. 1:3303
— *Apology for Cibber*–Bibs. 1:3303
— Bibs. 1:**3298–307**
— *Charge to the jury*. 10496
— *Coffeehouse politician*. 10506 10510
— — Bibs. 1:3302
— Collns. 3007 3380a 10497 10501
— *Complete history of the rebellion*. 10500 10508 10515
— *The coronation*. 10518
— *Dialogue between a gentleman and an honest alderman*. 10511
— — Bibs. 1:3303
— *Female husband*. 474
— *History of the present rebellion*. 10517
— — Bibs. 1:3305
— *Jonathan Wild*. 10486
— *Joseph Andrews*. 10522
— Libr. 277 10483 10485
— *Miscellanies*. 10492 10520–1
— *The miser*. 10495 10499 10524
— *Modern husband*. 10514
— Mss. 10505 10525
— — Bibs. 1:3307
— *Plain truth*. 10509
— Ptg. 10494 10521
— Publ. 10488 10507 10512–13 10520 10523
— *Stultus versus Sapientem*. 10502
— Text. 10503 10522 10524
— *Tom Jones*. 3649 10498 10503 10507 10516 10519
— *Voyage to Lisbon*. 10484 10489–91
FIELDING, sir John, 1721–80–Bibs. 1:3310
FIELDING, Sarah, 1710–68–Bibs. 1:**3311–a**
— *The governess*–Bibs. 1:3311a
FIELDS, OSGOOD AND COMPANY, Boston, est. 1866. 12992
FIFE, Fife. **1675**
— Librs. 1675
FIFE, Alexander William George Duff, 1st duke of, 1849–1912 *see* DUFF, Alexander William George, 1st duke of Fife, 1849–1912.
FIFESHIRE. **1675–94a**
— Bibs. 1:**996x–y**
— Paper. 5880
FIGGINS, Vincent, 1766–1836. **4667–8** 6613
— Type. 4667–8 6442
FIGGIS, Darrell, 1882–1925–Bibs. 1:**3312**
FILDES, sir Samuel Luke, 1844–1927. 7420a 9983 9997a
FILMER, sir Robert, 1588?–1669. **10526**
— Bibs. 1:**3312f**

FILMSETTING *see* COMPOSITION, PHOTOGRAPHIC.
FINCH, Anne, countess of Winchilsea, 1661–1720. **10527–9**
— Mss. 10529
— *Progress of life*. 10527
FINE PAPER COPIES. 8369a 10268 10326 10328
FINE PRINTING *see* PRINTING, FINE.
FINLASON, Thomas, Edinburgh, fl.1604–27–Bibs. 1:**1323**
FINLAY, George, 1799–1875–Bibs. 1:**1313**
FINN, Edward, Kilkenny, d.1777. **4669** 8985
FINSBURY, London *see* LONDON. FINSBURY.
FINTRAY, Aber. **1664a**
— Ptg. *see* CUMMING, John, 1820–1900.
FIRBANK, Arthur Annesley Ronald, 1886–1926. **10530–3**
— Bibs. 1:684 **3313x–15**
— Mss. 10531–2
— — Bibs. 1:3315
— *New rhythum*. 10531
— Text. 10533
— *Vainglory*. 10533
— *Valmouth*. 10532
FIREWORKS–Bibs. 1:570
FIRST BOOKS–Bibs. 1:356
FIRST EDITION CLUB, 1922–31. **4670–2** 7960
— Collns. 2086 2114
FIRTH, sir Charles Harding, 1857–1936–Bibs. 1:**3316**
FIRTH, Richard, Oxford, fl.1797. 7595
FISHER, Ann (mrs. Thomas Slack), fl.1745–56. 8117
FISHER, bp. John, 1459–1535. **10534–7**
— Bibs. 1:**3317–18c**
— Collns. 12502
— Letters. 10536
— Mss.–Bibs. 1:3318c
— *Sermons*. 10534–5 10537
FISHER, Sidney T., fl.1956–64–Libr. 2:233 235 241
FISHER AND SON, fl.1890. **4673–4**
FISHING *see* ANGLING.
FISKE, John Willard, fl.1930–Libr. 1:3203
FITCH, Walter Hood, 1817–92. 6958a
FITCHETT, John, 1776–1836. **10538**
— *King Alfred*. 10538
FITCHETT, William Henry, 1845–1928. 5680
FITTLER, James, 1758–1835. **4675**
FITZALAN, Henry, 12th earl of Arundel, 1511–80–Libr. 5176
FITZER, William, 1600?–71. 845 849
— Bibs. 1:3617a

FITZGERALD, Edward, 1809–83. 857a 7342 **10539–55**
— Bibs. 1:652 **3319–26**
— Bndng. 5599–600 5602 5778.
— *Euphranor.* 10539
— Illus. 3496 10545
— Ptg. 6098
— *Rubaiyât of Omar Kháyyám.* 258 2309 3496 5599–600 5602 5778 10541 10543–8 10550–4
— — Bibs. 1:3321–2 3324f–6f
— *Salaman and Absal.* 10549
— *Six dramas of Calderon.* 10555
FITZGERALD, Edward Marlborough, fl.1802–25. 10540
FITZGERALD, Percy Hetherington, 1834–1925–Bibs. 1:**3326y–7**
FITZHERBERT, sir Anthony, 1470–1538. **10556**
— Bibs. 1:**3328**
— *Grand abridgement*–Bibs. 1:3328
— *New natura brevium.* 3657
FITZMAURICE, George, fl.1914–Bibs. 1:**3329**
FITZPATRICK, William John, 1830–95–Bibs. 1:**3329m**
FLAHERTY, William Edward, 1807–78. **10557**
— *Annals of England.* 10557
FLAMBOYANT BINDER, fl.1540–5. 2238b
FLAMING WHIP FOR LECHERY, 1700. 712
FLAMSTEED, John, 1646–1719. **10558**
— *Historia cœlestis.* 10558
FLAPPER, THE. 7748
FLAUBERT, Gustave, 1821–80–Bibs. 1:**811g**
FLAVELL, John, 1630–91–Bibs. 1:**3329t**
FLAXMAN, John, 1755–1826. **4676** 8601 8619
— Bibs. 1:**3330**
FLECKER, James (formerly Herman) Elroy, 1884–1915. **10559**
— Bibs. 1:**3330f–h**
FLEMING, Abraham, 1552?–1607.
— *Holinshed's Chronicles.* 11119
FLEMING, Henry, fl.1679–Libr. 2606
FLEMING, Ian Lancaster, 1908–64–Libr. 3023 3360a
FLEMING, James, Newcastle-upon-Tyne, fl.1740–66. **4677**
FLESHER, Miles, fl.1611–64.
— *Shakespeare's King Lear.* 2:1442
FLETCHER, Andrew, 1655–1716. **10560**
— Bibs. 1:**3331**
FLETCHER, Giles, 1549?–1611. **10561**
— Bibs. 1:**3332**
— *Licia.* 10561
— Ptg. 10561
FLETCHER, Giles, 1588?–1623. **10562**

— *Of the Russe commonwealth.* 10909
FLETCHER, Harris Francis, 1892– .
— *Milton's complete poetical works.* 12398
FLETCHER, John, 1579–1625 *see also* BEAUMONT, Francis, 1584–1616, and John FLETCHER, 1579–1625. 2:1688 1912; 8537 **10563–6**
— *Barnavelt.* 8464
— Bibs. 1:1597 **3333**; 2:1877 1916
— *Bonduca.* 2:1688; 8444 8462
— *Custom of the country.* 8464
— *Double marriage.* 8464
— *Elder brother.* 8464
— *False one.* 8464
— *Four plays in one.* 8467
— *Henry VIII see* SHAKESPEARE, William, 1564–1616. *Henry 8.*
— *Honest man's fortune.* 8467
— *Knight of Malta.* 8467
— *Little French lawyer.* 8464
— *Lover's progress.* 8464
— *Maid in the mill.* 8468
— Mss. 2:1688; 10563 10565
— *Nice valour.* 8468
— *Night walker.* 8467
— *The prophetess.* 8464 10564
— — Bibs. 1:3333
— Ptg. 2:1912
— *Queen of Corinth.* 8467
— *Rollo, duke of Normandy.* 10566
— *Rule a wife.* 8446
— *Sea voyage.* 8464
— *Spanish curate.* 8464
— *Two noble kinsmen.* 2:943 1912 1915; 3689 8471
— *Very woman.* 8464
— *Wit without money.* 8467
FLETCHER, John, fl.1646–71. **4678–9**
FLETCHER, John, Chester, fl.1784–1831. **4680**
FLETCHER, Miles, fl.1611–64 *see* FLESHER, Miles, fl.1611–64.
FLETCHER, Phineas, 1582–1650. 10562 **10567**
— Mss. 10567
FLETCHER, W. H. B., 1847–1941–Libr. 6952
FLEURE, Herbert John, 1877–1969–Bibs. 1:**3334**
FLEURON, THE. 1:97; 4483 4487 6133
FLINTSHIRE. **1542**
— Librs. *see* GWYSANEY (SEAT); MOSTYN HALL.
— Paper. 1502 1542
— COUNTY LIBRARY, Hawarden–Collns. 1:**2349**
FLOOD, William Henry Grattan, 1859–1928–Bibs. 1:**3334n**
FLORA, OR THE DESERTED CHILD. 7324a

FLORES HISTORIARUM. 12659
FLORIDA. STATE UNIVERSITY, Tallahassee. LIBRARY–Collns. 1:1573db–dc 2733
— UNIVERSITY. LIBRARY–Collns. 1:4608
FLORIO, John, 1553?–1625.
— *Montaigne's Essays.* 2:1000a 1012 1016 1022 1027; 900a
— *World of words.* 2:1031
FLORISTS' MAGAZINE. 7914
FLOWER, Desmond John Newman, 1907––Libr. 2385 3170
FLOWER, Robert Ernest William, 1881–1946–Bibs. 1:3335
FLOWER, sir Walter Newman, 1879–1964–Libr. 1:3565
FLOWER BOOKS. **7327–30**
— Bibs. 1:1748 **2179–81**
— Illus. 7327 7329
— Ptg. 7327
FLOWERS, Type *see* TYPE–Flowers.
FLOYD, Thomas Hope, fl.1920–31–Libr. 3287
FOLGER, Henry Clay, 1857–1930 *see also* FOLGER SHAKESPEARE LIBRARY, Washington, D.C. 2:280a 325 576–7
FOLGER SHAKESPEARE LIBRARY, Washington, D.C. 2:279 280a 282–6 290–1 294 297–9 302 306–7 310 323–4 327 333–4 342 345; 2343 2978
— Collns. 1:519 597; 2:278 290–1 293 297–8 310 319 366 477–8 508 530 567 570 576 581 592 655 658 784 1030 1570 1659; 649 2148 2990a 3235 7183 7689 7934 8070 8534
FOLIATION–Bibliogr. descr. 128 143
FOLIO FORMAT *see* FORMAT–Folio; FORMAT–Quarto, folio–form.
FOLIOS. 662 6236 6892
— Bibliogr. descr. 140
— Bibs. 1:1621
FOLIO SOCIETY, est. 1947. **4681–2**
— Bibs. 1:**1323a–b**
FOLK DANCES–Collns. 3139
FOLKLORE IN SHAKESPEARE–Bibs. 2:34
FOLLIOTT, George, 1801–51–Libr. 2871
FONTENELLE, Bernard le Bouvier de, 1657–1757. 900
FOOLSCAP. 3704 3797
FOOLS IN SHAKESPEARE–Bibs. 2:111
FOOTE, Charles Benjamin, fl.1894–Libr. 1:382 4796; 2524 2531
FOOTE, Samuel, 1720–77–Bibs. 1:**3336**
FORBES, George Hay, Burntisland, 1821–75. 5424d
— Bibs. 1:1385
FORBES, James, 1629?–1712–Libr. 2848 3394ab

FORBES, James, 1749–1819. **10568**
FORBES, John, 1568?–1634. **10569**
— *Four sermons.* 10569
FORBES, John, 1570–1606–Bibs. 1:**3337**
FORBES, John, 1593–1648.
— *Mariner's everlasting almanac.* 6744
FORBES, John, d.1675. **10570**
— *Cantus.* 10570
FORBES, sir John, 1787–1861. 7566
FORBES, William, d.1595–Libr. 2920
FORBES, sir William, 1736–1806.
— Bibs. 1:2508c
— Mss. 8697
FORBES-LEITH MUSIC BOOKS. 1621
FORD, Charles, 1682–1743. 13797
FORD, Ford Madox (formerly Hueffer), 1873–1939. **10571–3**
— Bibs. 1:**3338–42**
— *Good soldier.* 10573
— Collns. 10571
— *It was the nightingale.* 10572
— Mss. 10572–3
— — Bibs. 1:**3340–1**
— Text. 10573
FORD, John, fl.1602–39. 7159 **10574–6**
— Bibs. 1:**3345–a**
— *Fame's memorial.* 10574
— *Laws of Candy.* 8468
— Mss. 10574–6
— *Perkin Warbeck.* 10575–6
— Text. 8468
FORD, Richard, 1796–1858. 5250
— Bibs. 1:**3346**
— *Handbook for travellers in Spain.* 8213
FORD, Simon, c.1619–99–Bibs. 1:**3347**
FORD, William Simpson, fl.1846. **4683**
— Collns. 7383
FORDHAM, sir Herbert George, 1854–1929–Bibs. 1:**3347h**
FORD MILL, South Hytton. 5564q
FORE-EDGE PAINTING AND DECORATION. 784 5070 7380 7385 7410 7444 7447–8 7460
FORE-EDGE TITLES *see* TITLES, FORE-EDGE.
FOREIGN BOOKS PUBLISHED IN BRITAIN. 870a–1012
— Bibs. 1:**770–851**
— Classical. **875–98a**
— — Bibs. 1:716g **772–801s** 1071 1073
— — Greek. 875 **879–85**
— — — Bibs. 1:**775–7** 1365a
— — Latin. 875 **886–98**
— — — Bibs. 1:**777m–801s**
— — Denmark. **899**
— — Bibs. 1:**802–3**
— France. 871 **900–24** 1895 7858 11356

FOREIGN BOOKS PUBLISHED IN BRITAIN–France–Bibs. 1:**804–18**
— Germany. 871 **925–31** 12088
— — Bibs. 1:**819–25** 1726a
— Holland see Netherlands.
— Hungary–Bibs. 1:**826g**
— Italy. **941–56**
— — Bibs. 1:**826d–33a**
— Lithuania. **957–9a**
— Netherlands. **932–40** 7958
— — Bibs. 1:**826–a**
— Norway–Bibs. 1:**833p**
— Poland. **960–1**
— — Bibs. 1:**834–6**
— Portugal–Bibs. 1:2199b
— Russia. **961**
— — Bibs. 1:**837–8a** 3968m
— Spain. **962–75**
— — Bibs. 1:**839–45** 2199b
— Switzerland. 10729
— — Bibs. 1:**845a**
— United States. **976–1012** 4004
— — Bibs. 1:**846–51**
— 1475–1640. 871–a 873 875 883–4 889 891 896a–7 898 900a 915 932 935–6 939 947–8 960 963 966–70 973 974 3458 3470 3479
— 1641–1700. 884 890 892–6 897a 918 949 957–9a 972 973a 975 7958
— 1701–1800. 872 877 879 882 888 898a 903 905–6 913–14 919–23 926 943 950 962 1895 10729 11356 12088
— 1801–1900. 880 899 907–8 911 927–8 931 944 951 954–5 961 977–91 994–1000 1003–7 1009–11 4004 7858
— 1901– . 992 1001–2 1008
FOREIGN REVIEW. 13531
FORESTALL, Kent–Paper. 1161a
FORESTER, Frank, *pseud.* of Henry William Herbert, 1807–58. 990
FORFAR LIBRARY. 1633
FORFARSHIRE see ANGUS.
FORGERIES see also BOOKS, FICTIOUS; NEWSPAPERS, FICTITIOUS. 257 386 2352 6093 **7331–42a** 7369 8215 8793 8931 8948 9216 9771 12266
— Bibs. 1:**1724x–5**
— 1475–1640. 554 7340 8917 9362 9811
— 1641–1700. 708 713 4159 12404
— 1701–1800. 3798 7331 9011 10744 10848 13508 13622 13632 14336
— 1801–1900. 3964c 7332 7337 8783 8794 9979–80 9982 10151 10175 10181 10291 10428 12787 13304–5 13313 13324 13336–7 13343 13352 13960–1 13989
— 1901– . 9636 9638 10947 11743 11769
—, BALLAD. 7332–3

—, ILLUSTRATION. 3906 3964c 7342 8435 9982
—, NEWSPAPER. 7654 7660 7665 7671 9105
—, PAPER. 3732 3798 3801 7256–a
—, SHAKESPEARIAN. 2:360b 361b; 7331 7333–4
FORGERIES AND BOOKSELLING. 13961
FORGERS see BYRON, George Gordon de Luna, *pseud.,* fl.1809–52; CHAN TOON, Mabel Cosgrove, 1872– ; CHATTERTON, Thomas, 1752–70; COLLIER, John Payne, 1789–1883; CROMEK, Robert Hartley, 1770–1812; FAUNTERLOY, Henry, 1785–1824; FORMAN, Henry Buxton, 1842–1917; HIBBERT, Charles, d.1819; IRELAND, William Henry, 1777–1835; LAUDER, William, d.1771; POWELL, Thomas, 1809–87; SIMONIDES, Constantine, 1824–67; SMITH, Alexander Howland ('Antique'), fl.1886–94; SQUIRE, William, fl.1770; WALKER, Henry, fl.1641–60; WARE, Robert, d.1696; WISE, Thomas James, 1859–1937.
FORMAN, Henry Buxton, 1842–1917. 2374 8284 14406 14415–17 14449
— *Building of the idylls.* 14419
— Letters. 14419
— Libr. 1:4650; 2354 2742–4 3045
— Mss. 14419
— *Tennysoniana.* 14419
FORMAN, Simon, 1552–1611. 2:1513 1523; **10577–83**
— *Books of plays.* 10577–83 12775
FORMAT see also IMPOSITION; SIZES OF BOOKS. 6147a 6249 6252 7813
— Agenda. 6245
— Bibliogr. descr. 124 134 143 148 257 267 6246
—Duodecimo (12°). 257 6241 6245 6345
— Folio (2°) see also FOLIOS. 6232
— Octavo (8°). 6233 6238 6253
— Octodecimo (18°). 6253
— Quarto (4°). 6232 6237–8
— Quarto, folio-form. 7616
— Turned chainlines. 6237 6243–4
— Twentyfours (24°). 257 6245 6248
'FORME'. 3606
FORMES see PRINTING–Formes.
FORRESTER, Alfred Henry, 1804–72 see CROWQUILL, Alfred, *pseud.*
FORRESTER, Charles Robert, 1803–50 see CROWQUILL, Alfred, *pseud.*
FORRESTER, James, fl.1734. **10584**
— *Polite philosopher.* 10584
FORSHAW, Charles F., fl.1885–92–Bibs. 1:**3347a**

FORSTER, Edward Morgan, 1879–1970. **10585**
— Bibs. 1:**3348–52**
FORSTER, John, 1812–76. 2319 **10586–8**
— Libr. 1:3050h; 2480 10067
— *Life of Dickens.* 10588
— Mss. 10587
FORTEY, William S., d.1901–Libr. 5426
FORTNIGHTLY REVIEW. 4359
— Bibs. 1:1716k
FORT WORTH. TEXAS CHRISTIAN UNIVERSITY *see* TEXAS CHRISTIAN UNIVERSITY, Fort Worth.
FORWARD, Charles John, fl.1814–91. **4684–5**
FORWARDING *see* BOOKBINDING–Forwarding.
FOSBROKE, Thomas Dudley, 1770–1842. 1117a
FOSCOLO, Ugo, 1778–1827. 954 5250
FOSTER, Benjamin Franklin, fl.1836–58–Libr. 6724a
FOSTER, Birket, 1825–99. 7420a
FOSTER, J. Herbert, fl.1910–20–Libr. 462
FOSTER, John, 1770–1843. 831a
FOSTER, John, baron Oriel, 1740–1828. **10589**
— *Strictures on the address.* 10589
FOSTER, Joseph, 1844–1905.
— *Alumni Cantabrigienses.* 1073
FOSTER, Mark, York, fl.1642–4. **4686**
FOSTER, Thomas, fl.1591–1614–Bibs. 1:**3355**
FOUL CASE *see* TYPECASES, FOUL.
FOULIS, Andrew, Glasgow, 1712–75. 4687 4691 4693–4 4746
— Bibs. 1:1325–7
FOULIS, Andrew, Glasgow, d.1829. 4693 4746
— Bibs. 1:1327
FOULIS, Robert, Glasgow, 1707–76. **4687–96** 4746
— Bibs. 1:**1324–7**
— Collns. 4690–2
— Letters. 4695
FOULIS ACADEMY OF ARTS, Glasgow. 4691
FOUL PAPERS. 7165
FOUNTAINE, Andrew, d.1873–Libr. *see* NARFORD HALL, Norf.
FOUR CARDINAL VIRTUES. 5185
FOURDRINIER, Henry, 1766–1854. 3757 3785 **4697–8**
FOURDRINIER, Sealy, d.1847. 3757
FOURDRINIER PAPER MACHINE. 3757 3760 3785
FOUR GOSPELS IN ONE NARRATIVE, 1854. 795
FOURNIER, George, 1595–1652. 884

FOURNIER, Pierre Simon, 1712–68. 6442 6637
FOWLER, Ellen Thorneycroft (mrs. A. L. Felkin), 1860–1929–Bibs. 1:**3356**
FOWLER, Henry Watson, 1858–1933. **10590**
— *Dictionary of modern English usage.* 10590
FOWLER, John Henry, 1861–1932–Libr. 2885
FOX, Augustus Henry Lane, afterwards Pitt-Rivers, 1827–1900 *see* RIVERS, Augustus Henry Lane Fox Pitt-, 1827–1900.
FOX, Charles, fl.1890. 4109
FOX, George, 1624–91. **10591–5**
— Bibs. 1:**3356k**
— Handwr. 10591
— Libr. 10593–5
— Mss.–Bibs. 1:**3356k**
FOX, Margaret (Askew) Fell, 1614–1702–Libr. 2963 3167.
FOXE, John, 1516–87. **10596–600**
— *Acts and monuments.* 10598–600
— Bibs. 1:**3357**
— *Commentarii rerum.* 10596
— *Locorum communium tituli et ordines.* 10597
— Ptg. 10599–600
FOXHUNTING–Bibs. 1:**2182**
FOXWELL, Herbert Somerton, 1849–1936–Bibs. 1:**3358**
FRAGOSA, KING OF ARAGON, 1618? 679
FRANCE *see also* BRITISH BOOKS PUBLISHED ABROAD–France; SHAKESPEARE, William, 1564–1616–WORKS IN FRANCE. 3441 3925 5877 6193 6609 10516 10519 12388
— ACADÉMIE ROYALE DE SCIENCES, Paris. 3948
— BIBLIOTHÈQUE NATIONALE, Paris.
— — Collns 1:357 2912db 4150
— — DÉPT. DES IMPRIMÉS–Collns. 2:227
FRANCIS, John Deffett, 1815–1901–Libr. 954
FRANCIS, sir Philip, 1740–1818. 11628–9
FRANCIS BACON FOUNDATION, Pasadena, Calif. LIBRARY. 8369
— — Collns. 1:545 611 2374f
FRANCISCAN BOOKS–Bibs. 1:**2264**
FRANCIS THOMPSON SOCIETY–Collns. 1:4954b
FRANCKTON, John, Dublin, fl.1600–18. 1907 **4699–704**
— Bibs. 1:**1328**
— Type. 4700–1 4703–4
FRANKENBERGK, Henry, fl.1482. **4705**
FRANKFURT, Germany. 845 854 6637
FRANKFURT BOOK FAIR. 2:551
FRANKFURT BOOK FAIR CATALOGUES. 3490–1 3493

FRANKLIN, Benjamin, Philadelphia, 1706–90. 5796
FRANKLIN, lady Jane (Griffin), 1792–1875–Libr. 795
FRANKLIN, sir John, 1786–1847–Bibs. 1:3359
FRANKS, sir Augustus Wollaston, 1826–97–Libr. 279 2054
FRASCATI SEMINARY PRESS, c.1800. 3130
FRASER, Claud Lovat, 1890–1921. 4480 4706–10 6098
— Bibs. 1:3360–c
— Gay's Beggar's opera. 4707
— Housman's Shropshire lad. 6098
— O'Connor's Luck of the bean rows. 4708
FRASER, Francis Arthur, fl.1869–83. 7420a
FRASER, James, d.1841. 5909
FRASER, sir William, 1816–98. 482
FRASER'S MAGAZINE. 13328 14000
— Bibs. 1:1716k 1918 4111 4920 4925
FRATERNITY OF VAGABONDS. 559
FRAZER, sir James George, 1854–1941–Bibs. 1:3361
FREDERICK LOUIS, prince of Wales, 1707–51–Libr. 12853
FREE, John, fl.1727–58.
— Certain articles. 3601
FREEBAIRN, Robert, Glasgow, fl.1701–47. 4712
FREE BRITON. 7763
FREEMAN, Edward Augustus, 1823–92–Bibs. 1:3362
FREEMAN, John, 1880–1929–Bibs. 1:3363
FREEMAN, Richard Austin, 1862–1943. 7300
— Bibs. 1:3364–a
FREEMAN, Samuel, 1775?–1857. 4713
FREEMAN'S JOURNAL. 7720
FREEMASONRY–Bibs. 1:2183–5 2241a
FREETH, John, 1731–1808. 10601
FREETHOUGHT. 7343
— Collns. 7343
FREIND, John, 1675–1728–Libr. 2562
FRENCH see PRINTING IN FRENCH.
FRENCH, Frederick, fl.1901–Libr. 2572
FRENCH GRAMMARS see GRAMMARS, FRENCH.
FRENCH LITERATURE see BRITISH BOOKS PUBLISHED ABROAD; FOREIGN BOOKS PUBLISHED IN BRITAIN.
FRENCH NEWSPAPERS see NEWSPAPERS, FRENCH.
FRENCH PROTESTANT HOSPITAL, London. LIBRARY. 2850 2921
FRESH DISCOVERY OF THE HIGH-PRESBYTERIAN SPIRIT, 1655. 3559
FRESNOY, Nicolas Lenglet du, 1674–1755 see LENGLET DU FRESNOY, Nicolas,

1674–1755.
FREWEN, John, 1558–1628. 10602
— Certain fruitful instructions. 10602
FRIEDMAN, Lee Max, 1871– –Libr. 737
FRIEND, THE. 9521 9536 9544
— Ptg. 9537
FRIENDS, SOCIETY OF see also BOOK TRADE, LISTS–Friends. 1547 6852 8089–99
— Bksllng. 1445 3615
— Collns. 8090 8096–8
— Newspapers. 1930
— Ptg. 8090–2 8094–5 8099
— Publ. 8093–4 8099
— REFERENCE LIBRARY. 2766 8098
FRIENDS BOOKS see also FRIENDS, SOCIETY OF.
— Bibs. 1:2267–70b
FRIENDS OF LITERATURE, 1805–11. 3622
FRIENDS OF NORTH NEWINGTON. 5474
FRITSCH, Thomas, Leipzig, fl.1703. 7202
FROBISHER, sir Martin, 1535?–94. 8208
FROG MILL, Curdridge. 1132a
FROGMORE MILL, Herts. 1139 5256
FROISSART, Jean, 1337?–1410–Bibs. 1:811m
FROME, Som.–Ptg. see also BUTLER AND TANNER, est. 1795. 4495
FRONTISPIECES. 1459 6306 7413 7810a 10123
— Bibs. 1:1735y
— Collns. 6266
FROST, John, 1784?–1877–Bibs. 1:3365
FROST, Robert, 1874–1963.
— Boy's will. 992
— North of Boston. 992
FROUDE, James Anthony, 1818–94. 10603
— Nemesis of faith. 10603
FRY, Christopher, 1907– –Bibs. 1:1597 3365d
FRY, Edmund, 1754–1835. 6613
FRY, Joseph, 1728–87. 6572 6613
FRYE, Bartholomew, Manchester, fl.1818. 4714
FRYE, Thomas, 1710–62. 4715
FULLER, Samuel, Dublin, fl.1720–36. 4716
FULLER, Thomas, 1608–61. 10604–9
— Abel redivivus. 10608
— Bibs. 1:3366–70
— Bndng. 6279
— Holy war. 2:1939; 6279
— Jacob's vow. 10604
— Life and death of Sidney. 10609
— Sermon preached. 10607
— Worthies of England. 10605–6
FULLWOOD, Francis, d.1693–Bibs. 1:3371
FULMAN, William, 1632–88. 13686
— Life of John Hales. 14218

FULTON, John Farquhar, 1899–1960. 3321
FUN–Bibs. 1:3432a 3434
FUNERAL POEM TO ...THE EARL OF LINCOLN, 1728. 741
FURLY, Benjamin, 1636–1714–Libr. 2698 3315–16
FURNACE, Herefs.–Paper. 1138
FURNESS, Horace Howard, 1833–1912. 2:287–8 343; 18
— *Variorum Shakespeare.* 2:724 731 745 750 779 804 1270
FURNISS, Harry, 1854–1925. 9997a
FURNIVALL, Frederick James, 1825–1910.
— Bibs. 1:3372–3
— *Leopold Shakspere.* 2:711
FUSELI, Henry (Johann Heinrich Fuessli), 1741–1825–Bibs. 1:3374–5

GABBERBOCCUS PRESS, 20th cent. 4717
GABLE, William F., 1856–1921–Libr. 9642
GADDESDEN, JOHN OF, 1280?–1361 *see* JOHN OF GADDESDEN, 1280?–1361.
GAELIC BOOKS *see also* PRINTING IN GAELIC. 13856
— Bibs. 1:4869f
GAELIC SOCIETY, London. LIBRARY. 3092
GAINSBOROUGH. PUBLIC LIBRARY– Collns. 1:4217d
GALASHIELS, Selkirkshire–Librs. 1633
GALBRAITH, Robert, d.1543. 10610
— Bibs. 1:4112k
— *Opus quadriperititum.* 10610
GALEN, 129–99? 5645–6 8657
GALFREDUS, Petrus, fl.1510–24.
— *Geneologia.* 4010
GALIGNANI, Giovanni Antonio, 1796–1873. 832 838 866
GALIGNANI FAMILY, bksllrs., Paris–Bibs. 1:760
GALLATIN, Albert Eugene, 1881–1952–Libr. 1:2407–8 2430 2432 4520d; 13847
GALLEY. 6174
GALSWORTHY, John, 1867–1933. 10611–23
— *Awakening.* 10615
— Bibs. 1:684 1597 3379–86
— *Bit o' love.* 10618
— Collns. 10623
— *Forsyte chronicles.* 10611–12 10614–15 10621
— *In Chancery.* 10615
— *Indian summer of a Forsyte.* 10614
— *Justice.* 10613
— *Man of property.* 10614 10619 10622
— Mss. 10612 10614–17
— *On Forsyte 'change.* 10617

— *Passers by.* 10617
— Publ. 10613 10618–19 10621
— *Silent wooing.* 10617
— *Silver spoon.* 10616
— *Swan song.* 10617 10620
— Text. 10614–17
— *To let.* 10615
— *White monkey.* 10616
GALT, John, 1779–1839. 783 10624.
— Bibs. 1:3390–2
— Collns. 7322a
— *The howdie.* 10624
— Mss. 10624
GALWAY. 1946–9
— Bibs. 1:1055q 1082a–7a
— Ptg.–Bibs. 1:1082a–4
GALWEY, Arthur Francis, Dublin, fl.1828–93. 4718
GAMBLE, John, 1770–1831.
— Bibs. 1:3392m
— Mss. 2:1974
GAMBLE, John, fl.1801. 3785
GAMBOLD, William, 1672–1728. 10625
GAMING. 8191
GAOL LITERATURE. 7344
GARBRAND, John, fl.1606–17–Libr. 1369
GARDENING *see also* HERBALS. 7345–8
— Bibs. 1:2186–7a
— Collns. 7347
GARDEN OF THE SOUL see HORSTIUS, Jacobus Merlo, d.1644.
GARDINER, Marguerite (Power), countess Blessington, 1789–1849–Bibs. 1:3393–4
GARDINER, Samuel Rawson, 1829–1902–Bibs. 1:3395
GARDINER, bp. Stephen, 1483?–1555–Bibs. 1:3395g
— Letters–Bibs. 1:3395g
— Mss.–Bibs. 1:3395g
GARDINER, sir Thomas, 1591–1652–Libr. 3396a
GARDINER, William Nelson, 1766–1814. 4719
GARDNER, Wells, fl.1857. 4719a
GARLANDS–Bibs. 1:1544
GARNET, Henry, 1555–1606–Bibs. 1:3396
GARNET, John, Sheffield, fl.1736–53–Bibs. 1:1328p
GARNETT, David, 1892– . 5305
GARNETT, Edward, 1868–1937–Libr. 1:2866i
GARNETT, Richard, 1835–1906. 4–5 12 14 2386
— Bibs. 1:3397–b
GARNETT, William, fl.1819–29. 5772a
GARNETT FAMILY–Bibs. 1:3398
GARRATT, J. E., fl.1893. 2:499
GARRET, John, fl.1667–1713. 6550

GARRICK, David, 1717–79. 779 **10626–31**
— Bibs. 1:**3399–a** 3841
— Collns. 10628
— *The fairies.* 10631
— *Jubilee.* 10626
— Libr. 2:300; 10627
— Mss. 10630
— — Bibs. 1:3399
— Publ. 4559a
— *Shakespeare's Hamlet.* 2:1195
— *Shakespeare's Romeo and Juliet.* 2:1705
— *To mr. Gray on his odes.* 10629
GARROD, Heathcote Williams, 1878–
1960–Bibs. 1:**3399k**
GARSTIN, John Ribton, fl.1836–1900–Libr.
2727
GASKELL, John Philip Wellesley, fl.1978 *see*
WATER LANE PRESS, Cambridge, est.
1952.
GARTER, Thomas, fl.1578. **10632**
— *Susanna.* 10632
GASCOIGNE, George, 1525?–77. **10633–7**
— Bibs. 1:**3400–1b**
— *Hundred sundry flowers.* 10633 10635–7
— Illus. 10637
— *Noble art of venery.* 10637
— Publ. 10636
GASCOYNE, David, 1916– –Bibs. 1:**3402**
GASELEE, sir Stephen, 1882–1943–Libr.
1:450; 558 3060 3105
GASKELL, Elizabeth Cleghorn (Stevenson),
1810–65. 831a **10638–44**
— Bibs. 1:**3403–13c**
— Collns. 10641
— *Cranford.* 10640 10642
— *The half-brothers.* 7294 10639
— Illus. 10640 10642
— *Life of Charlotte Brontë.* 10638
— *Lizzie Leigh.* 10644
— Publ. 5680
— Text. 10638
GASKELL, Charles George Milnes,
1842–1919–Libr. 470
GASKELL, Ernest, fl.1894–1920. 1:1511c
GASKELL, William, 1805–84–Bibs. 1:**3414**
GASKIN, Arthur Joseph, 1862–1928. **4720**
— *Good king Wenceslaus.* 4720
GATESHEAD, Nthmb.–Ptg. 1019
GATTY, Alfred, 1813–1900–Bibs. 1:**3414q**
GATTY, Margaret (Scott), 1807–73. 3974
GAUDEN, John, 1605–62–Bibs. 1:**3415**
GAUFFRECOURT, Jean-Vincent Capronnier
de, 1692–1766. 5999
GAVER, James, fl.1539. **4721**
GAWAIN. 382
GAWSWORTH, John, *pseud.* of Terence Ian
Fytton Armstrong, 1912– *see* ARM-
STRONG, Terence Ian Fytton, 1912– .

GAY, John, 1685–1732. **10645–54**
— *Beggar's opera.* 4707 10646 10649 10653
— Bibs. 1:1597 **3416–b**
— Collns. 10652
— *Fables.* 10645 10650
— — Bibs. 1:3416
— Illus. 4707
— Mss. 12862
— Music. 10649
— Ptg. 10653
— Publ. 10646 10651
— *True and faithful narrative.* 10654
GAYLARD, Doctor, fl.1721–36–Bibs.
1:**3416d**
— *Loyal observator revived*–Bibs. 1:3416d
GAYLEY, Charles Mills, 1858–1932.
— *Representative English comedies.* 7195
GAZETEER, THE. 7780 7798
GAZETTE DES LONDRES. 1195
GED, William, Edinburgh, 1690–1749. 3475
4722–9 8489
— Bibs. 1:**1329**
— *Sallust.* 4728
GEE, John, 1596–1639.
— *Foot out of the snare.* 3693
GEIKIE, sir Archibald, 1835–1924–Bibs.
1:**3416g**
GEMINI, Thomas, fl.1540–77. **4730**
— *Compendiosa.* 14138
GEMINI PRESS, Colchester, 1934–6. 4731
GEMS FROM THE POETS, 1859. 8029
GENEALOGY–Bibs. 1:856–7 902
*GENERAL CATALOGUE OF BOOKS
PRINTED IN IRELAND, 1791.* 1806
*GENERAL CONTENTS OF THE BRITISH
MUSEUM, 1761.* 2678
*GENERAL DICTIONARY, HISTORICAL AND
CRITICAL, 1734–41.* 7082
GENERAL TYPOGRAPHICAL ASSOCIA-
TION OF SCOTLAND, 1841. 5614
GENERYDES MS. 3309
GENEST, John, 1764–1839–Libr. 3116
GENEVA BIBLE, 1560 *see* BIBLE–
Versions–Geneva.
GENT, Alice (Guy), York, fl.1700–70. 3620
4732
GENT, Thomas, York, 1693–1778. 277 3620
3639a 3659 **4733–7**
— *Life of Thomas Gent.* 4736
GENTLEMAN, Francis, 1728–84. 2:701
GENTLEMAN'S MAGAZINE. 4214 5293a
5294a 7698 7702 7714 7721 7769 7797
7806 7812 11725 13705
— Bibs. 1:1716k 1902a 1910 3621d
4822b
GEOGRAPHY–Bibs. 1:**2188–9**
GEOLOGY. 8129 8132 8134 8140 8143
8157

Vol. **1** = *Bibliographies*   **2** = *Shakespeare*   **4** = 1–8221   **5** = 8222–14616

GEORGE III, king of Great Britain and Ireland, 1738–1820. 2218 2915 4891
— Libr. 2202 2558
GEORGE ALLEN AND UNWIN, est. 1914 *see* ALLEN AND UNWIN, est. 1914.
GEORGETOWN UNIVERSITY, Washington, D.C. LIBRARY–Collns. 1:540
GERARD, Alexander, 1728–95–Bibs. 1:(3417)
GERARD, Jane Emily (mrs. Miecislas de Laszowski), 1849–1905–Collns. 7322a
GERBIER, sir Balthazar, 1592?–1667–Bibs. 1:3417r
GERM, THE. 756
GERMAN LITERATURE *see* BRITISH BOOKS PUBLISHED ABROAD; FOREIGN BOOKS PUBLISHED IN BRITAIN.
GERMAN REVIEW. 7870
GERMANY *see also* SHAKESPEARE, William, 1564–1616–WORKS IN GERMANY.
— Type. 6641
— STAATSBIBLIOTHEK *see* BERLIN. STAATSBIBLIOTHEK.
GESNER, Conrad, 1516–65. 12347 12401
GHOST IN THE BANK OF ENGLAND, 1888. 12782
GHOSTS, BIBLIOGRAPHICAL. 191 514 585 644 1008 1608 2375 4342 4367 7619 11050 11766 13439 13469 14060 14158 14460
GIBBINGS, Robert John, 1889–1958. 4759 4762
— Bibs. 1:3418–19
GIBBON, Edward, 1737–94. 10655–77
— Bibs. 1:3420–3
— Bksllng. 10656
— Collns. 10666
— *Decline and fall.* 2342 10656–8 10661
— Handwr. 10675
— Libr. 10655 10662–3 10667–71 10674 10677
— *Mémoire justificatif.* 10673
— Mss. 1067
— — Bibs. 1:3421
— Publ. 10672
— Text. 10661
GIBBON, Lewis Grassic, *pseud. of* James Leslie Mitchell, 1901–35—Bibs. 1:3424–5b
GIBBON, Skeffington, fl.1796–1831. 10678–9
— Bibs. 1:3426
— *On the repeal of the union.* 10678–9
GIBBON, William Monk, 1896–ͨ–Bibs. 1:3426d
GIBBONS, Richard, 1550?–1632. 6916
GIBBS, Henry Hucks, 1st baron Aldenham, 1819–1907–Libr. 2492 2962
GIBSON, Strickland, 1877–1938. 59 78 81
GIBSON, Thomas, d.1562. 6056

GIBSON, Thomas Milner-, 1806–84. 3546
GIBSON, Walter, fl.1684–1710.
GIBSON, Wilfrid Wilson, 1878–1962–Bibs. 1:3427
GIFFARD, Henry, fl.1741. 10680
— *Pamela.* 10680
GIFFORD, George, d.1620–Bibs. 1:3428
GIFFORD, William, 1756–1826. 10681–2
— Bibs. 1:1925
— Publ. 5250
GIFT BOOKS *see also* PRESENTATION COPIES. 5909 6229 7931 8055
— Bibs. 1:1847a 2037
GIGANTOMACHIA, 1682. 718
GILBERT, Ann (Taylor), 1782–1866 *see* TAYLOR, Ann (mrs. Gilbert), 1782–1866.
GILBERT, sir John, 1817–97. 4738–9 7420a
— Bibs. 1:3428a
GILBERT, sir John Thomas, 1829–98.
— Bibs. 1:3429
— Libr. 2728 2734
GILBERT, Thomas A., fl.1927–Libr. 1:344; 2841a
GILBERT, William, 1544–1603–Bibs. 1:3429a–b
— *De magnete*–Bibs. 1:3429a–b
GILBERT, William, 1804–90–Bibs. 1:3429d
GILBERT, sir William Schwenck, 1836–1911. 10683–90
— *Bab ballads*–Bibs. 1:3432a–b
— Bibs. 1:3430–4
— Collns. 10684–5 10687
— *The gondoliers.* 10689
— *Grand duke.* 10690
— *More Bab ballads.* 10683
— Mss. 10685–7
— *Princess Ida.* 10688
— Ptg. 10690
— Publ. 10683
GILBERT AND RIVINGTON, fl.1830–52. 5555
GILBERTUS, Nicolai, 1463–1532 *see* NICOLAI, Gilbertus, 1463–1532.
GILBEY, Arthur N., fl.1940–Libr. 6766–7
GILDAS, 516?–70?
— *De excidio Britanniæ.* 12379
GILDERS *see* EDGEGILDERS.
GILDING *see* BOOKBINDING–Gilding.
GILDON, Charles, 1665–1724. 10691–4
— *Cato examined.* 10694
— *Les soupirs.* 10693
— *Memoirs of the life of Wycherley.* 10691
— *Shakespeare's Poems.* 2:1938
— *Stage-beaux tossed.* 10692
GILL, Arthur Eric Rowton, 1882–1940. 4740–4
— Bibs. 1:3434u–7c
— Mss.–Bibs. 1:3437

GILL, Arthur Eric Rowton, 1882–1940–Ptg. 6098–9
— Type. 4741 4743–4 6618 6641
GILL, Michael Henry, Dublin, fl.1856–72. 5113
GILLEMEAU, Jacques, 1550–1613–Bibs. 1:2219
GILLMAN, James, 1782–1839–Libr. 9195 9545
GILLRAY, James, 1757–1815. 7438 9492
GILMOUR, John Scott Lennox, 1906– –Libr. 1:3696; 7343
GILPIN, William, 1724–1804. **10695–9**
— Bibs. 1:**3438**
— *Essay upon prints.* 10696
— Illus. 10699
— *Practical illustration.* 10698
GILT PAPER *see* PAPER, GILT.
GIMBEL, Richard, fl.1920–59–Libr. 1:3100
GIMSON, Arthur, fl.1935–Libr. 2943
GINGER, William, 1727–1803. **4745**
GIPSIES *see* GYPSIES.
GIRALDUS DE BARRI, Cambrensis, 1146?–220?–Bibs. 1:**3439**
GIRSBY MANOR, Lindsey, Lincs.–Libr. 2:431–2
GISSING, George Robert, 1857–1903. 757 **10700–11**
— Bibs. 1:684 **3440–51**
— Collns. 2291 10701 10705–6 10708
— *Human odds and ends.* 10703
— Publ. 4002 10709
— *Thyrza.* 10702
— *Veranilda.* 10709
GLADSTONE, William Ewart, 1809–188 *see also* ST. DEINIOL'S THEOLOGICAL AND GENERAL LIBRARY, Hawarden. 778 831a 4852 4855 5250 **10712–19**
— Bibs. 1:**3455–7a**
— *Contributions towards the Glynne language.* 10716
— Libr. 10712–13 10718
— *Locksley hall.* 10719
— Mss. 10719
— Publ. 6523
— *Rock of ages.* 10715 10717
GLAMORGANSHIRE. **1543–6**
— Bibs. 1:**963e**
GLANVILL, Joseph, 1636–80. **10720**
— Bibs. 1:**3458**
— *Essay concerning preaching.* 10720
GLAPTHORNE, Henry, fl.1639. **10721**
— Text. 10721
— *Wit in a constable.* 10721
GLASGOW, Lanark. 188 **1686–94a**
— Bibs. 1:**1002–4**
— Bksllng. 1580 1687
— Librs. 1633 1694–a

— Newspapers. 1690–1 1693
— — Bibs. 1:1934x
— Ptg. 1596 1686–9 1692 4691 6066
— — Bibs. 1:1002–a 1726
— Publ. 1687
— Type. 4693
— ACADEMY OF THE FINE ARTS. 4691 4693
— ASSEMBLY–Bibs. 1:**1004**
— FOULIS ACADEMY OF ARTS *see* FOULIS ACADEMY OF ARTS, Glasgow.
— GLASGOW COLLEGE. LITERARY SOCIETY. 4693
— MAITLAND CLUB *see* MAITLAND CLUB, Glasgow, fl.1827–47.
— MITCHELL LIBRARY *see* MITCHELL LIBRARY, Glasgow.
— ROYAL INSTITUTE OF FINE ARTS *see* ROYAL GLASGOW INSTITUTE OF FINE ARTS.
— UNIVERSITY. HUNTERIAN MUSEUM. LIBRARY–Collns. 1:529 1329 2291 3168k 3793
— — LIBRARY. **1694–4a**
— — — — Collns. 1:717–19 1003 1362q 1460 1476–7 2100 2161; 670 1632 1694a 1836 2238 3297 3537 6850 8851 8923 9079
GLASGOW EXHIBITION, 1896. 9008
GLASGOW UNIVERSITY PRESS, est. 1638. 4693 **4746–7**
GLASSE, Hannah, fl.1747. **10722–4**
— Bibs. 1:**3458d**
— *Art of cookery.* 10722–4
GLAZED PAPER *see* PAPER, GLAZED.
GLEAVE, Joseoph James, fl.1907–Libr. 1:2536
GLEIG, George Robert, 1796–1888–Collns. 7322a
GLENDOWER, Owen (Owain ab Gruffydd), 1359?–1416?–Bibs. 1:**3459**
GLENRIDDELL mss. *see* RIDDELL, Robert, 1755–94–Libr.
GLOBE, THE. 7831
GLOBE CHAUCER, 1898. 9419a
GLOBE SHAKESPEARE. 2:703 953 1197 1444 1461
GLORY MILL, Wooburn Green. 3767a
GLOSSARIES *see* DICTIONARIES.
GLOUCESTER, Glos.
— Librs. 2848
— Paper. 1120a
— Ptg. 1119
— Publ. *see* CHANCE FAMILY, 1872–1922; RAIKES, Robert, 1690–1757; RAIKES FAMILY, fl.1722–1802; WALKER FAMILY, fl.1802–71.
— CATHEDRAL LIBRARY. 1119

GLOUCESTER, Glos. PUBLIC LIBRARY–Collns. 1:895a–b 896 1388b 4993
— SHIRE HALL–Collns. 1:896d
— SOUTHGATE CHAPEL. LIBRARY. 2848
GLOUCESTER, William Frederick, duke of, 1776–1834 see WILLIAM Frederick, duke of Gloucester, 1776–1834.
GLOUCESTER JOURNAL. 1118 1120–1 5495 7813
GLOUCESTERSHIRE see also BOOK TRADE, LISTS–Gloucestershire. 1117–36
— Bibs. 1:892–6p
— Bksllg. 1117
— Librs. 2452
— Maps–Bibs. 1:1786–7
— Newspapers. 1118 1120–1
— Paper see also ROBINSON, Elisha Smith, Bristol, 1817–85. 1120a
— Ptg. 1119
— — Bibs. 1:892 896
GLOVER, Dorothy see CRAIGIE, Dorothy (Glover), fl.1966.
GLOVER, Terrot Reaveley, 1869–1943–Bibs. 1:3458e
GLYNDE, Sussex.–Ptg. 1408
GLYNN, Richard, 1793–1838. 4748–9
GLYPHOGRAPHY. 6228
— Bibs. 1:1163
GNAPHEUS, Gulielmus, 1493–1568. 891
GOAD, Thomas, 1576–1638. 10725–6
— *Doleful evensong.* 10725–6
GOADBY, M., fl.1779. 4750.
GOADBY, Robert, 1721–78. 7727 9264
GODALMING, Surrey. CHARTERHOUSE SCHOOL see CHARTERHOUSE SCHOOL, Godalming.
GODFRAY, Thomas, fl.1532–5. 6056 6897 8067
GODFREY, Garrett, fl.1522. 4751
GODKIN, James, 1806–79–Bibs. 1:3459p
GODLY EXHORTATION, 1603. 682
GODTHAAB, Greenland. 9904
GODWIN, bp. Francis, 1562–1633. 10727
— Bibs. 1:1686d 3459n
— *Man in the moon.* 10727
— — Bibs. 1:3459n
GODWIN, M. J. AND COMPANY, fl.1809–20. 4752 7000a 11851
GODWIN, Mary Wollstonecraft (mrs. P. B. Shelley), 1797–1851.
— Bibs. 1:3460 4657
— Libr. 13350
— Mss.–Bibs. 1:4654d
— Publ. 5226
GODWIN, William, 1756–1836. 783 7000a 10728–9
— Bibs. 1:3461–2

— *Letters of Verax.* 10728
— *Wyss' Swiss family Robinson.* 10729
GOETHE, Johann Wolfgang von, 1749–1832–Bibs. 1:821b–2
GOFF, Thomas, 1591–1629–Bibs. 1:3463
GOGARTY, Oliver St. John, 1878–1957. 10730
— *Blight.* 10730
GOGMAGOG PRESS, Stratford, London, est. 1957. 4753–4 6502
— Bibs. 1:1329n
GOGOL, Nikolai Vasilevich, 1809–52. 961
GOLD, PRINTING IN see PRINTING IN GOLD.
GOLDBEATERS see BOOK TRADE, LISTS–Goldbeaters.
GOLDEN COCKEREL PRESS, Waltham St. Lawrence, Berks., est. 1921. 4115 4755–65 6099 6502
— Bibs. 1:873 1330–4
GOLDEN HEAD PRESS, est. 1955–Bibs. 1:1335
GOLDEN VALLEY MILL, Bitton. 1120a
GOLDING, Arthur, 1536?–1605?
— Bibs. 1:3463d–e
— *Cæsar's Martial exploits in Gallia.* 2:1018
GOLDING, William Gerald, 1911– –Bibs. 1:3463k
GOLDNEY, H., fl.1785. 1294
GOLDSCHMIDT, Ernst Philip, 1887–1954. 4766–71
— Bibs. 1:1335f
— Libr. 2091
GOLDSMITH, Oliver, 1728–74 see also THE BEE. 731 2289 7000a 7008 10731–82
— Bibs. 1:1597 3464–72 3840e
— Collns. 3039 10750 10758
— *Deserted village.* 10732–3 10739 10769 10777
— — Bibs. 1:3470
— *Edwin and Angelina.* 10781
— *English lives.* 10755
— *Essay on friendship.* 10771
— *Essays.* 10745 10767
— *Good natur'd man.* 10775
— — Bibs. 1:3471
— Handwr. 10776
— *History of England.* 10752
— Illus. 10741 10765 10779
— Libr. 274
— *Life of Bolingbroke.* 10778
— — Bibs. 1:3472
— *Little goody two-shoes.* 10736 10780
— — Bibs. 1:3469 3473
— *Memoirs of m. de Voltaire.* 10753
— *Memoirs of my lady B.* 10742
— *Millenium hall.* 10768
— Mss. 10744 10747–9 10751 10754 10762

Vol. 1 = *Bibliographies*   2 = *Shakespeare*   4 = 1–8221   5 = 8222–14616

GÖTTINGEN. UNIVERSITÄT. BIB-
LIOTHEK. 9526
GOUDAR, Ange, 1720–91. 913
GOUDY PRESSES *see* PRESSES, GOUDY.
GOUGE, William, 1578–1653.
— Ptg. 6399
— *Whole armor of God.* 6399
GOUGH, John, fl.1528–56. 8067
GOUGH, sir Richard, 1659–1728–Libr.
1:1536v; 6976
GOUGH, Richard, 1735–1809. 3475 11025
— Bibs. 1:**3485**
— *British topography*–Bibs. 1:**3485**
GOULD, John, 1804–81. 5778 **10794–5**
— Collns. 10795
GOULD, Robert, d.1709–Bibs. 1:**3485e**
GOULD, Samuel, 1710–83. **4779**
GOULDING, Frederick, 1842–1909. **4780**
— Bibs. 1:**1335k**
GOUPIL AND COMPANY, London/Paris.
2036–7
GOURLAW, Robert, Edinburgh, d.1585.
1255
GOVAN, Donald, Glasgow, fl.1714–19. 4746
GOVANE, John, 1608?–56–Libr. 3065
GOVERNMENTAL PRINTING *see*
PRINTING, GOVERNMENTAL.
GOWER, John, 1325?–1408.
— *De confessione amantis.* 2447 4348
GRACE, Sheffield, 1788?–1850–Libr. 2702
GRADUS AD PARNASSUM. 3991
GRAFTON, Richard, 1511?–73. **4781–4**
6056
GRAHAM, Alexander, Alnwick, fl.1746–86.
4785
GRAHAM, Dougal, 1724–79–Bibs. 1:**3486**
GRAHAM, mrs. Maria, 1785–1842 *see*
CALLCOTT, Maria (Dundas), lady,
1785–1842.
GRAHAM, Rigby A., 1931– . 5370
GRAHAM, Robert Bontine Cunninghame,
1852–1936. **10796**
— Bibs. 1:**3490–2**
— Collns. 10796
GRAHAM, Thomas Alexander Ferguson,
1840–1906. 7420a
GRAHAME, James, 1765–1811. **10797**
— *Fragments of a tour.* 10797
GRAHAME, Kenneth, 1859–1932. **10798–9**
— Bibs. 1:**3492a–b**
— *Wind in the willows.* 10799
GRAINGER, James, 1721?–66. **10800**
— Mss. 10800
— *Sugar cane.* 10800
GRAMMAR. 6178 6183
GRAMMARS. 670 3448 **7349–59a**
— Bibs. 1:843 954 1419 **1726–31**
—, FRENCH. 7352

—, LATIN. 7350
—, WELSH. 7359a
GRAND, Sarah, *pseud. of* Frances Elizabeth
(Clarke) McFall, 1862–1943.
— Bibs. 1:**3493**
— Publ. 4858a
GRAND MAGAZINE OF MAGAZINES. 7700
*GRAND MAGAZINE OF UNIVERSAL
INTELLIGENCE.* 7811
GRANGER, James, 1723–76. **10801–2**
— *Biographical history.* 10801–2
GRANGERISED BOOKS *see* EXTRA-
ILLUSTRATED COPIES.
GRANGERISERS *see* EXTRA-ILLUS-
TRATORS.
GRANT, Edward, 1540?–1601.
— *Græcæ linguæ spicilegium.* 7359
GRANT, Francis, 1834?–99–Libr. 2564
GRANT, James, 1822–87.
— Bibs. 1:**3494**
— Collns. 7322a
GRANT, James Gregor, fl.1847. **10803**
— *Madonna pia.* 10803
GRANTCHESTER, Cambs.–Ptg. *see* WID-
NALL, Samuel Page, 1825–94.
GRANTHAM, Lincs.–Librs. 2493 2504
GRANVILLE, B., 1709–75–Libr. 10929
GRANVILLE, George, baron Lansdowne,
1666–1735. **10804**
— *Behn's Remains.* 10804
GRANVILLE, John Carteret, earl, 1690–1763
see CARTERET, John, earl Granville,
1690–1763.
GRATAROLI, Guglielmo, 1516–68. 592
GRATIÆ THEATRALES. 7161
GRATTAN, Henry, 1746–1820–Libr. 2474
GRAUNT, John, 1620–74.
— Bibs. 1:(3494a)
— *Natural and political observations*–Bibs.
1:4417
GRAVELOT, Hubert François, 1699–1773.
4786
— Bibs. 1:**3495–6**
GRAVES, Alfred Perceval, 1846–1931–Bibs.
1:**3497**
GRAVES, Clotilda Inez Mary, 1863–1932 *see*
DEHAN, Richard, *pseud.*
GRAVES, John Woodcock, 1795–1886.
10805
— *Do ye ken John Peel.* 10805
GRAVES, Richard, 1715–1804. 888
— Bibs. 1:**3498**
GRAVES, Robert von Ranke, 1895– . 5617
10805–6
— Bibs. 1:**3498y–500**
— *I Claudius.* 10805
— Ptg. 10805
— *Ten poems more.* 4897e

Vol. **1** = *Bibliographies*   **2** = *Shakespeare*   **4** = 1–8221   **5** = 8222–14616

GRAVESEND, Kent–Ptg. *see* POCOCK, Robert, 1760–1830.
GRAY, Edward William, 1787?–1860.
— *History and antiquities of Newbury.* 4827
GRAY, George, fl.1900–Libr. 1:1272
GRAY, John, 1646–1717–Libr. 1:575; 1633
GRAY, John, 1724–1811. **10808**
GRAY, John, fl.1825–48–Bibs. 1:**3500f**
GRAY, John, fl.1893. **10809**
— *Silverpoints.* 10809
GRAY, John Edward, 1800–75.
— *Illustrations of Indian zoology.* 8136 8141
GRAY, John Henry, 1866–1934–Bibs. 1:**3501**
GRAY, Maria Emma (Smith), 1787–1876.
— *Figures of molluscous animals.* 8133
GRAY, Paul, 1848–68. 7420a
GRAY, Thomas, 1716–71. **10810–60**
— *The bard.* 10827
— Bibs. 1:**3501a–6**
— *The candidate.* 10841
— *Chronological tables.* 10845
— Collns. 3039 10838 10846
— *Elegy written in a country churchyard.* 2342 2979 2990 10810–11 10813–15 10817–18 10824 10828–31 10833 10835 10840 10844 10849 10853 10858 10860
— — Bibs. 1:3504–b 3506
— Handwr. 10857
— Illus. 8566 10850
— Letters. 10832 10839 14179
— Libr. 274 10825 10842 10847 10851
— *Long story.* 10845
— *Miscellaneous pieces.* 10860
— Mss. 10812 10823 10836–8 10845
— *Ode on the death of a favorite cat.* 10852 10854–6
— *Odes.* 10822 10843 10848
— *Poems.* 8566 10812 10816 10819 10821 10850
— *Progress of poesy.* 10836
— Publ. 4559a 10812 10853
— Text. 10813 10819 10822 10826 10829 10849 10859 14179
— *Vah, tenero.* 10859
— *Village blacksmith.* 10820
GRAY, William, d.1551.
— *A brief apology . . . Thomas Smith.* 629
GRAY, William, fl.1563. **10861**
— *Fantasies of idolatry.* 10861
GRAY, William, Edinburgh, fl.1763–85. 1633
GREAT BIBLE, 1539 *see* BIBLE–Versions–Great.
GREAT BRICKHILL, Bucks.–Librs. *see* BROOMHILL HOUSE.
GREAT BRITAIN. ADMIRALTY. LIBRARY–Collns. 1:2234
— BOARD OF ORDINANCE. 4203
— COMMISSIONERS OF EXCISE. 5975
— COURT OF CHANCERY. 3625 6070
— COURT OF HIGH COMMISSION. 6799
— EXCHEQUER. 3560
— FOREIGN OFFICE. LIBRARY–Collns. 1:588
— HISTORICAL MANUSCRIPTS COMMISSION. 2409
— INDIA OFFICE. LIBRARY. 2601 11847
— LORD CHAMBERLAIN'S OFFICE. 7223 7231
— MINISTRY OF AGRICULTURE AND FISHERIES. LIBRARY–Collns. 1:2093
— PARLIAMENT *see also* DEBATES, PARLIAMENTARY–Bibs. 3546 3551 3556 3559 3566 7467 **7952–6**
— — Bibs. 1:**2245**
— — *Directions of the Lords and commons assembled.* 715
— — HOUSE OF COMMONS. 4830 7956
— — — *Journal.* 1835
— — HOUSE OF LORDS. 3546
— PRIVY COUNCIL. 3548–9
— PUBLIC RECORD OFFICE. 12019
— — Collns. 1:1771; 2:126
— TREASURY. 3614
GREAT DANSEKER. 7943
GREATHEAD, Bertie, 1759–1826. **10862**
— *Arno miscellany.* 10862
GREAT TOTHAM PRESS, Essex, 1830–62. **4787**
— Bibs. 1:**1336**
GREAVES, John, 1605–52–Libr. 3396a
GREAVES, Thomas, fl.1787. **4788**
GREEK, PRINTING IN *see* PRINTING IN GREEK.
GREEK LITERATURE *see* FOREIGN BOOKS PUBLISHED IN BRITAIN–Classical–Greek; SHAKESPEARE, William, 1564–1616–WORKS IN GREEK.
GREEK NEWSPAPERS *see* NEWSPAPERS, GREEK.
GREEN, Charles, 1840–98. 7420a 10148
GREEN, Frank, 1835–1902. **4789**
GREEN, John, *pseud.* of Bradock Mead, fl.1730–47.
— *New general collection of voyages.* 8214
GREEN, John Richard, 1837–83–Bibs. 1:**3508**
GREEN, Joseph Henry, 1791–1863–Libr. 9545
GREEN, Matthew, 1696–1737. **10863**
GREEN, Roger Gilbert Lancelyn, 1918––Libr. 11901
GREEN, Thomas Hill, 1836–82–Bibs. 1:**3509**
GREEN, Valentine, 1739–1813. **4790**
GREEN, William, 1761–1823. **4791**
— *Guide to the lakes.* 4791

GREENAWAY, Catherine ('Kate'), 1846–1901. 6192 **10864**
— Bibs. 1:**3510–d**
— *Mother Goose.* 10864
— Publ. 5944
GREENE, Henry Graham, 1904– .
— Bibs. 1:1597 **3511–16**
— Libr. 1:1720
GREENE, Joseph, 1712–90. 2:1035
GREENE, Robert, 1560?–92. **10865–86**
— Bibs. 1:**3520–4**
— *Conny-catching.* 10879
— — Bibs. 1:3524
— *A disputation.* 10881
— *Friar Bacon and friar Bungay.* 10876
— *George-a-Greene.* 8918 9579 10886
— *Guydonius.* 10870
— *James IV.* 10872
— *Looking-glass for London.* 10869
— *Notable discovery of cosenage.* 10873 10879
— *Orlando furioso.* 7125 10871 10885
— *Planetomachia.* 10867 10875
— Ptg. 10882–3
— *Quip for an upstart courtier.* 10866 10868 10878 10880 10882–4
— — Bibs. 1:3522
— *Spanish masquerado.* 10877
— Text. 10865 10871 10874 10878 10882 10885
GREENFIELD, Flintshire–Paper. 1542
GREENHILL, George, fl.1814–36. 1680
GREENISLAND, co. Antrim–Ptg. 1770
GREENLAND, BRITISH BOOKS PUBLISHED ABROAD *see* BRITISH BOOKS PUBLISHED ABROAD–Greenland.
GREENOCK, Renfrew.
— Librs. 1633
— Ptg. *see* SIGNET PRESS, est. 1956.
GREENOUGH, Chester Noyes, 1874–1938–Libr. 7262
GREENSTREET HOUSE, East Ham–Ptg. 1018
GREENWICH *see* LONDON–GREENWICH.
GREENWOOD, Christopher, 1786–1855. 7519
— Bibs. 1:**3527**
GREENWOOD, Frederick, 1830–1909. 7908
GREENWOOD, James, d.1737.
— *London vocabulary.* 698d
GREENWOOD, Thomas, 1851–1908–Libr. 3270
GREG, sir Walter Wilson, 1875–1959. 79 80 82–4 324
— Bibs. 1:**3527g–h**
— *English literary autographs.* 11368
GREGG, mrs. H. *see* KIRBY, Mary (mrs. H. Gregg), 1817–93.

GREGORY I, saint, fl.540–604.
— *Dialogues.* 14482
GREGORY, COLLINS AND REYNOLDS, fl.1843–9. 6202
GREGORY, David, 1661–1708.
— *Euclid.* 7548
GREGORY, Edward John, 1850–1909. 6202
GREGORY, Isabella Augusta (Persse), lady, 1852–1932–Bibs. 1:**3528**
GREGYNOG PRESS, Newtown, est. 1922. 1492 **4792–803** 4826 6502
— Bibs. 1:**1337–8** 1339
— Bndng. 4796 4798 4802
— Type. 4794
GRENVILLE, Thomas, 1755–1846–Libr. 2314
GRESHAM COLLEGE, London *see* LONDON. GRESHAM COLLEGE.
GRESHAM MUSIC LIBRARY *see* LONDON. GUILDHALL. LIBRARY. GRESHAM MUSIC LIBRARY.
GRESHAM PRESS, est. 1826. 5886
GREVILLE, sir Fulke, 1st baron Brooke, 1554–1628. **10887–8**
— *Certain learned and elegant works.* 6354 10887
— *Life of Sidney.* 10888
— Mss. 10888
— Ptg. 6354
GREY, Edward, 1st viscount Grey of Fallodon, 1862–1933–Bibs. 1:**3530**
GREY, sir George, 1812–98.
— Bibs. 1:**3531**
— Libr. 2:584 656 1463; 3138 3149 3261 3298
GREY, Henry George, 3d earl Grey, 1802–94–Bibs. 1:**3532**
GRIBBEL, John, 1858–1937–Libr. 3036 9033 9060 9071
GRIEG, John, fl.1850. **10889–90**
— *Border antiquities.* 10889–90
GRIERSON, George, Dublin, 1709–53. 1932–3 4085 **4804**
— *Shakespeare's Hamlet.* 2:704
— *Shakespeare's Julius Caesar.* 2:704
— *Shakespeare's Othello.* 2:704
GRIERSON, sir Herbert John Clifford, 1866–1960. 10243
— Bibs. 1:**3531g**
GRIEVE, Christopher Murray, 1892–1978 *see* MACDIARMID, Hugh, *pseud.*
GRIFFIN, Bartholomew, fl.1596. **10891**
— *Fiedessa.* 10891
GRIFFIN, Charles, 1820–62. **4805–a**
GRIFFIN, William, fl.1764–76. 10757 10759
GRIFFITH, Arthur, 1872–1922–Bibs. 1:**3533**
GRIFFITH, Edward, 1790–1858.
— *Cuvier's Animal kingdom.* 8160

GRIFFITH, Elizabeth, 1720?–93–Bibs. 1:3534
GRIFFITH, bp. George, 1601–66. 1517
GRIFFITH, Reginald Harvey, 1873–1957–Libr. 12864
GRIFFITH, sir Richard John, 1st baronet, 1784–1878–Bibs. 1:1817q
GRIFFITH, William, fl.1652–9.
— Discourse on Bacon. 8367
GRIFFITHS, Ralph, 1720–1803. 3639a 4806 7795 10759
GRIGGS-PRÆTORIUS FACSIMILES. 2:390 1192
GRIMALD, Nicholas, 1519–62. 5874
GRIMALDI, Joseph, 1779–1837. 3496
GRIMM, Jacob Ludwig Carl, 1785–1863. 4454a 4897ca 13171
GRIMSTON, Elizabeth (Bernye), c.1563–1603. 10892 13867
— Miscellanea. 681 10892
GROBIANA'S NUPTIALS–Ms. 7158
GROCYN, William, 1446?–1519–Libr. 2479 2843
GROHMAN, William Adolf Baillie-, 1851–1921.
— New South Africa. 10904
GROLIER CLUB, New York. 539
— Collns. 1:327–8 552 1621 1660–1 1735y 2037d 2781 3062–3 3197 3591 3805g 3836 3951 4038 4222 4437–8 4552–3 4756 4802–3 4888 4913–14; 538 2008a 2046 6714
GROPALL, John, Exeter, d.1554? 4807
GROSART, Alexander Balloch, 1827–99. 10893–4
GROSE, John Henry, fl.1750–83.
— Voyage to East Indies. 8203
GROSSE, Alexander, d.1654–Bibs. 1:3535
GROSSMITH, George, 1847–1912. 10895
— Diary of a nobody. 10895
GROTE, George, 1794–1871–Bibs. 1:3536
GROTE, John, 1813–66. 10896
— Mss. 10896
GROVE, William, fl.1418–27. 3151
GROVE MILL, Presteigne. 1138
GROVE MILL, Eyhorne Street. 1161a
GROVER, Isaac, Dublin, d.1663. 4808
GROVER, Thomas, fl.1657–75. 4809
GRUB STREET JOURNAL. 2:705
— Bibs. 1:1900h
GRUFFYD, Owain ab, 1359?–1416? see GLENDOWER, Owen, 1359?–1416?
GRUFFYD, William John, 1881–1954–Bibs. 1:3536k
GRYPHUS, Petrus, fl.1509. 6017a
GRYMESTON, Elizabeth (Bernye), c.1563–1603 see GRIMSTON, Elizabeth (Bernye), c.1563–1603.

GUARANTEES see WARRANTIES.
GUARDIAN, THE. 8531
GUAZZO, Stefano, fl.1574–86–Bibs. 1:832
GUERNSEY see CHANNEL ISLANDS.
GUICCIOLI, Teresa, countess, 1803–73. 9224
— Bibs. 1:2694
GUIDEBOOKS. 1033
— Bibs. 1:878t 2103d
— Aberystwyth. 1526
— Cambridge. 1058
GUIDELINES see BOOKBINDING-Guidelines.
GUILD, William, 1586–1657–Libr. 2692
GUILDFORD, Surrey. 1404
— ROYAL GRAMMAR SCHOOL. LIBRARY. 2402
GUILD OF CONTEMPORARY BINDERS. 2239a
GUILD OF WOMEN BINDERS, 1898–1904. 4812–20
GUILLAN, Archibald, 1790–1891. 4821
GUILLE-ALLÈS LIBRARY, Guernsey. 2754
GUILLEMEAU, Jacques, 1550–1613. 7560 7564
GUINEY, Louise Imogen, 1861–1920–Bibs. 1:3537
— Mss.–Bibs. 1:3537
GULIELMUS, Laurentius, 1414?–1503. 4313a 4314
GULLICK, Norman, fl.1931–Libr. 1:3479d
GUN, Matthew, Dublin, fl.1695–6. 1906–7
GUNN, Neil Miller, 1891–1973–Bibs. 1:3538–9
GUNNEX MILL, Alfrick, Worcs. 1429a
GUNNING, Susannah (Minifie), 1740?–1800–Bibs. 1:3540
GUNNISLAKE, Cornw.–Paper. 1083b
GUNS–Bibs. 1:2190m–n
GUN'S MILL, Flaxley. 1120a
GUNST, Morgan Arthur, fl.1939–40–Libr. 4589a
GUNTHER, Charles Frederick, 1837–1920. 2:1004
GUPPY, Henry, 1861–1948–Bibs. 1:3540m
GUTHRIE, James Joshua, fl.1895–1952. 5396 5400
— Bibs. 1:3541
GUTHRIE, Stuart, fl.1932. 4394
GUTHRIE, Thomas Anstey, 1856–1934 see ANSTEY, F., pseud.
GUTHRIE, William, 1708–70. 10897
— History of England. 10897
GUTHRIE, sir William Tyrone, 1900–71–Bibs. 1:3541k
GUY, Alice, York, fl.1700–70 see GENT, Alice (Guy), York, fl.1700–70.

Vol. 1 = Bibliographies   2 = Shakespeare   4 = 1–8221   5 = 8222–14616

GUY, Thomas, 1644–1724 *see also* LONDON.
GUY'S HOSPITAL. 3475 3616 3620 3639a
4822–a
GUY OF WARWICK–Bibs. 1:539b
GWIN, Robert, fl.1591. 8085
GWINETT, Ambrose, fl.1770? **10898**
GWINNE, Matthew, 1558?–1627–Libr. 3124
GWYN, Robert, fl.1591 *see* GWIN, Robert,
fl.1591.
GWYN, Owen, fl.1605. 7186
GWYNN, Edward, d.1650–Libr. 2:397 413;
2594 2927
GWYNNETH, John, fl.1557–Bibs. 1:**3542**
GWYNN FAMILY, 1842–1962. **4823**
GWYSANEY (SEAT), Flintshire–Libr. 3134
GYLES, Arthur, fl.1886.
— *Directory of second-hand booksellers.* 3651
GYPSIES. **7360**
— Bibs. 1:**2191**
GYPSY NOVELS *see* NOVELS, GYPSY.

H., I.
— *Questiones Alberti de modis significandi.* 4902
H., J., fl.1669.
— *Miscellanea.* 7993
HAAS, Wilhelm, d.1800. 6332
HAAZ, John, fl.1592. **4824**
HABER, Louis J., fl.1909–Libr. 1:387d
HABERKORN, John, fl.1755–65. 923
HABERLY, Loyd, 1896– . **4825–6**
— Bibs. 1:**1339**
HACHETTE ET CIE, Paris, 19th cent. 10057
HACKER, Francis, d.1660. 708
HACKET, bp. John, 1590–1670. **10899**
— Libr. 2:466
— *Scrinia reserata.* 10899
HACK MILL, Wotton-under-Edge. 1120a
HACON AND RICKETTS *see* VALE PRESS,
1896–1904.
HADDINGTON, East Lothian–Librs. 1633
2488
HADDINGTON, George Baillie-Hamilton-
Arden, 11th earl, 1827–1917 *see* ARDEN,
George Baillie-Hamilton-, 11th earl of
Haddington, 1827–1917.
HADDON, Walter, 1516–72. **10900–1**
— Bibs. 1:**3543**
— *Poëmata.* 10900–1
HAFOD PRESS, Cardiganshire, 1803–10 *see*
JOHNES, Thomas, Hafod, 1748–1816.
HAGEN, Francis van, Aberdeen, fl.1626–36
see VAN HAGEN, Francis, fl.1626–36.
HAGEN, Francis van, Aberdeen, fl.1659–69
see VAN HAGEN, Francis, Aberdeen,
fl.1659–69.
HAGEN, Godfried van der, fl.1534–5. 829

HAGEN, Winston Henry, 1859–1918–Libr.
1:393 493
HAGGARD, sir Henry Rider, 1856–1925.
10902–5
— Bibs. 1:**3544–7**
— Collns. 1306a 10905
— *King Solomon's mines.* 10902–3
— Publ. 10902
— *She.* 11899
HAGUE, Netherlands. 854
— KONINKLIJKE BIBLIOTHEEK–Collns.
1:1353f; 4999
HAGUE, Louis, 1806–85. 6202
HAIGH HALL, Wigan *see* BIBLIOTHECA
LINDESIANA.
HAILES, sir David Dalrymple, ld., 1726–92
see DALRYMPLE, sir David, ld. Hailes,
1726–92.
HAKE, Edward, fl.1567–89.
— *Touchstone for this time present.* 932
HAKEWILL, George, 1579–1649.
— *Apology or declaration.* 2:1124
— Bibs. 1:**3548**
HAKLUYT, Richard, 1552?–1616. **10906–9**
14134
— Bibs. 1:**3548a–9**
— *Voyages.* 10906–9
— — Bibs. 1:**3548a–9**
HALDANE, John Burdon Sanderson,
1892–1964–Bibs. 1:**3549i–k**
HALDANE, John Scott, 1860–1936–Bibs.
1:**3549n**
HALE, Philip, fl.1847–81. 3136
HALES, John, d.1571. **10910**
— *Discourse of the commonwealth.* 10910
HALES, John Wesley, 1836–1914.
— *Keats's Eve of St. Agnes.* 11689
HALF-SHEET IMPOSITION *see* IM-
POSITION, HALF-SHEET.
HALF-TITLES. 6280 6287 6532 11421 13399
HALF-TONE BLOCKS *see* ETCHING,
PHOTOGRAPHIC.
HALIFAX, Yorks. **1439–40**
— Bibs. 1:**949j–k**
— Bndng. *see* EDWARDS, William, 1723–
1808.
— Bksllng. *see* EDWARDS, James, 1756–
1816.
— Librs. 1440
— Ptg. *see* MILNER, William, 1803–50.
HALIFAX, Nova Scotia. DALHOUSIE
UNIVERSITY *see* DALHOUSIE
UNIVERSITY, Halifax, Nova Scotia.
HALIFAX, George Savile, 1st marquis of,
1633–95 *see* SAVILE, George, 1st marquis
of Halifax, 1633–95.
HALIDAY, Charles, 1789–1866–Libr. 2713
HALL, Basil, 1788–1844. 5250

HALL, Charles, 1745?–1825?–Bibs. 1:3549q
HALL, David, 1714–72. 5796
HALL, Edward, d.1547. 10911–14
— *Chronicle.* 10911–14
HALL, J., fl.1627?–Libr. 2589
HALL, John, 1529?–66? 5875
— Bibs. 1:3550
— *Court of virtue*–Bibs. 1:3550
HALL, John, 1627–56.
— *Letter written to a gentleman.* 12363
HALL, John, 1764–1869. 3785
HALL, bp. Joseph, 1574–1656.
— *Defence of the humble remonstrance.* 12430
HALL, Marguerite Radclyffe, fl.1906–36. 10915
— Collns. 10915
HALL, Spencer Timothy, 1812–85.
— *Forester's offering.* 6172
— Ptg. 6172
HALL, Thomas, 1610–65. 10916
— Bibs. 1:3550q
HALL, Trevor Henry, 1910– –Libr. 7482
HALL, William, fl.1577–1614. 4828
HALL, William, fl.1781–93. 1277 5700
HALLAM, Arthur Henry, 1811–33. 10917–22
— Bibs. 1:3551–2
— *Poems.* 10917a 10920–1 13900 13928
— *Remains.* 10917 10919
HALLAM, Henry, 1777–1859. 5250
HALL AND MARSH, Newbury, fl.1839. 4827
HALLEY, Edmond, 1656–1742. 10923
— Bibs. 1:3552h–9
— *Apolonius.* 7548
HALLIARD, Jack, *pseud.*
— *Voyages and adventures.* 8202
HALLIWELL-PHILLIPPS, James Orchard, 1820–89 *see* PHILLIPPS, James Orchard Halliwell-, 1820–89.
HALLIWELL, James Orchard, afterwards HALLIWELL-PHILLIPPS, 1820–89
HALLIWELL-PHILLIPPS FACSIMILE. 2:592
HALL MILL, Awre. 1120a
HALSEY, Frederic Robert, 1847–1918–Libr. 1:493
HALSEY, sir Walter Johnston, 1868–1950–Libr. 2:467
HAM HOUSE, Richmond, Surrey–Libr. 2603 2985 3393a
HAMILTON, Anthony, comte de Grammont, 1646?–1720. 14182
— Bibs. 1:3560
HAMILTON, Emma (Lyon), lady, 1761?–1815. 4615
HAMILTON, Eugene Lee-, 1845–1907. 10924–6
— Bibs. 1:3560a–b
— Publ. 10924

HAMILTON, Gavin, 1753–1805. 9040
HAMILTON, Johan Abraham, 1734–95–Libr. 1:1604
HAMILTON, Joseph, fl.1825. 10927
HAMILTON, Rowan, fl.1890.
— *Lectures on quarternions.* 7552
HAMILTON, William, 1704–54–Bibs. 1:3561
HAMILTON, sir William, 1730–1803–Bibs. 1:3562
HAMMERMEN OF ST. ANDREWS. 1676
HAMMERSMITH *see* LONDON. HAMMERSMITH.
HAMMERTON, sir John Alexander, 1871–1949–Bibs. 1:3562
HAMMOND, Chris, fl.1906. 7409
HAMMOND, Henry, 1605–60.
— Bibs. 1:3562k
— Libr. 3401a
HAMMOND, James, 1710–42.
— *Love elegies.* 11458
HAMMOND, John Lawrence Le Breton, 1872–1949–Bibs. 1:3563
HAMMOND, William, 1719–83. 10928
— Mss. 10928
HAMPER MILL, Herts. 1139
HAMPSHIRE. 1131–6
— Bibs. 1:897–p
— Bksllng. 1131
— Newspapers. 1133 7768
— Paper *see also* PORTAL, Henri, Laverstoke, 1690–1747; PORTAL, John, Laverstoke, 1764–1848; PORTAL, Joseph, Laverstoke, 1720–93. 1132a
— Ptg. 1131
HAMPSTEAD *see* LONDON. HAMPSTEAD.
HAMPSTEAD BINDERY, 1898–1904. 4815 4817 4819
HAMPSTEAD LIBRARY. 2543a
HANBURY, Benjamin, 1778–1864–Libr. 2653
HANBURY, William, 1725–78. 3397
HANDCOCK, Matthew, fl.1790–Libr. 2:653
HAND COLOURING *see* COLOURING, HAND.
HANDEL, George Frederick, 1685–1759. 10927–37
— Bibs. 1:3564–71b
— Collns. 10929 10933 10937 12925
— *Messiah.* 10930 10933
— Mss. 10929
— — Bibs. 1:3571b
— Paper. 10935
— Publ. 5932 10932–3
HANDFUL OF PLEASANT DELIGHTS. 7983–4 7998
HANDMADE PAPER *see* PAPER, HANDMADE.
HAND PRESSES *see* PRESSES, COMMON.

HARRIS, Howell, 1714–73–Libr. *see also* TREVECCA LIBRARY. 3361a

HARRIS, James Edward, 5th earl of Malmesbury, 1872–1950–Libr. 2:470g 674

HARRIS, John, fl.1655. 7968

HARRIS, John, 1666–1719.
— *Lexicon technicum.* 7239

HARRIS, John, fl.1773. **4836**

HARRIS, John, 1791–1873. **4837** 12121

HARRIS, John, fl.1798–1857. **4838**

HARRIS, Richard, Maidstone, fl.1738. 5975

HARRIS, Vavasor, fl.1695–1705. 4835b

HARRIS, Walter, 1686–1761.
— *Ware's History of bishops.* 14236

HARRISON, Frank Mott, fl.1928–41–Libr. 1:2613

HARRISON, Frederic, 1831–1923–Bibs. 1:**3612–13**

HARRISON, James, 1730–69. 3639a **4839–41**

HARRISON, James William, 1830–1912. 4839

HARRISON, Jane Ellen, 1850–1928–Bibs. 1:**3613b**

HARRISON, sir John, c.1589–1669–Libr. 3396a

HARRISON, John, fl.1600–4. 6683

HARRISON, John, fl.1603–39. **4842**

HARRISON, John, d.1642–Libr. 3235a

HARRISON, Thomas, 1606–60. 708

HARRISON AND COMPANY. 1294

HARRIS PUBLIC LIBRARY, Preston–Collns. 1:1537c 4949 4951

HARROW WEALD, Middlesex.–Ptg. *see* RAVEN PRESS, est. 1931.

HARRY, Blind *see* HENRY THE MINSTREL (Blind Harry), fl.1470–92.

HARSNETT, archbp. Samuel, 1561–1631. 11015
— Libr. 3359

HART, Andrew, Edinburgh, d.1621. **4843**
— Bibs. 1:**1340–1**

HART, Elizabeth Anna (Smedley), fl.1822–88. **10989**
— *The runaway.* 10989

HART, Horace, Oxford, 1840–1916. 4658 5357 5366 6637
— *Rules.* 5357

HART, John, d.1574–Bibs. 1:**3613h**

HARTE, Francis Bret, 1836–1902–Bibs. 1:848

HARTE, Walter, 1709–74.
— *Poems on several occasions.* 6155
— Ptg. 6155

HARTING, James Edmund, 1841–1928–Bibs. 1:**3614**

HARTLEPOOL, Durham.–Ptg. *see* PROCTER, John, fl.1810–79.

HARTLEY, Leslie Poles, 1895– –Bibs. 1:**3414e**

HARTLEY VICTORIA COLLEGE, Manchester *see* MANCHESTER. HARTLEY VICTORIA COLLEGE.

HARTLIB, Samuel, d.1662–Bibs. 1:**3614p**

HARTWELL, Abraham, fl.1600–Libr. 2786

HARTWELL HOUSE, Bucks.–Libr. 2996

HARVARD COLLEGE.
— *Humble proposal.* 5285

HARVARD UNIVERSITY. 2:340
— GRADUATE SCHOOL OF BUSINESS ADMINISTRATION. BAKER LIBRARY. KRESS LIBRARY–Collns. 1:1536v 2166–71 4707; 6976
— LIBRARY–Collns. 1:110 1536t 1541 2019 2070b 2430 2432 2726 3030 3792 3841d 3949 3984 4436 4897b; 2:277a 340; 660 695 2944 2947 3897 6433 6441 7221 7262 7680 8070 8528 9523 9534 10067 11518 11662 11776 11848 12337 12564 12786 13347 13637 13933 14187 14189 14503
— — WIDENER COLLECTION *see* WIDENER, Harry Elkins, 1885–1912–Libr.

HARVEY, Christopher, 1597–1663. **10990**
— *The synagogue.* 10990

HARVEY, Francis, 1830–1900. **4844**

HARVEY, Gabriel, 1545?–1630? **10991–1001**
— Bibs. *see* HARVEY FAMILY.
— Letters. 10992 10993a 10995 10997 10999
— Libr. 10991 10993–4 10996 10998 11000–1
— Text. 10992

HARVEY, John, 1564–92 *see* HARVEY FAMILY.

HARVEY, Perry Williams, 1869–1932–Libr. 1:1253

HARVEY, Richard, 1560?–1623? *see* HARVEY FAMILY.

HARVEY, William, 1578–1657.
— Bibs. 1:**3617–19f**
— *De motu cordis.* 849
— — Bibs. 1:3617a
— Handwr. 11003
— Mss. 11002
— — Bibs. 1:3619f

HARVEY, William Henry, 1811–66.
— *Flora capensis.* 6951

HARVEY FAMILY–Bibs. 1:**3615–16**

HARVIE, Thomas, Glasgow, fl.1704–56. 4746

HARVINGTON, Worcs.–Paper. 1429a

HASKELL, Grace Clark, fl.1936–Libr. 5493a

HASLEWOOD, Joseph, 1769–1833. **11004** 13698
— *Prompter, The.* 7230a

HASSALL, Christopher Vernon, 1912–63. 3173

HASTED, Edward, 1732–1812.
— *History of Kent.* 1151
HASTINGS. BRASSEY INSTITUTE *see* BRASSEY INSTITUTE, Hastings.
— PUBLIC LIBRARY–Collns. 2:128
HATCHARD, John, 1768–1849. **4845–7**
HATCHARD, Thomas, 1794–1858. 4846–7
HATFIELD, Herts.–Paper. 1139
HATFIELD HOUSE, Herts.–Libr. 3329 3384
HATTON, sir Christopher, 1540–91–Libr. 3106 3233
HATTON, Christopher, 1st baron Hatton, 1605?–70.
— *Psalter of David.* 13873
HATTON, Edward, fl.1694–1722.
— *New view of London.* 1239
HATTON, Thomas, fl.1927–38–Libr. 1:3078 3074h; 10043 10064
HATTON HALL, Midloth. 2529
HAUPTMANN, Gerhart, 1862–1946–Bibs. 1:**822d**
HAVERFORD COLLEGE. LIBRARY–Collns. 1:541; 2:475
HAVERFORDWEST, Pembrokeshire. **1549–51**
— Bibs. 1:**964**
— Paper. 1551
— Ptg. 1549–50
— — Bibs. 1:**964**
HAVILAND, John, 1589–1638. **4848–a**
HAWARDEN, Flintshire.
— Librs. *see* ST. DEINIOL'S THEOLOGICAL AND GENERAL LIBRARY.
— FLINTSHIRE COUNTY LIBRARY *see* FLINTSHIRE COUNTY LIBRARY, Hawarden.
HAWES, Stephen, d.1523? **11005–6**
— *Conversion of swearers.* 11006
HAWICK, Roxb. **1739**
— Bibs. 1:1008
— Newspapers. 1739
HAWKER, Robert Stephen, 1803–75. **11007–8**
— Bibs. 1:**3620–1**
— *Ecclesia.* 11008
— Mss. 11007
HAWKESWORTH, John, 1715?–73–Bibs. 1:**3621d**
HAWKEY, John, 1703–59. 12348
HAWKING–Bibs. 1:**2192–3d** 2197d
HAWKINS, sir Anthony Hope, 1863–1933 *see* HOPE, Anthony, *pseud.*
HAWKINS, George, fl.1741–80. **4849**
— Bibs. 1:**1341g**
HAWKINS, Henry, 1762–1841–Bibs. 1:3621a
HAWKINS, John, fl.1530. 6081
HAWKINS, sir John, 1719–89–Bibs. 1:**3621k**

HAWKINS, John Sidney, 1758–1842–Bibs. 1:3621a
HAWKINS, Thomas, fl.1771. 2:761
HAWORTH. BRONTË SOCIETY MUSEUM AND LIBRARY *see* BRONTË SOCIETY. MUSEUM AND LIBRARY, Haworth.
HAWORTH, Adrian Hardy, 1768–1833–Bibs. 1:**3621p**
HAWTHORNE, Nathaniel, 1804–64. 1000
HAY, William, fl.1500–41–Libr. 3393
HAYDAY, James, 1796–1872. 2028 **4850**
HAYDN, Franz Josef, 1732–1809–Bibs. 1:**2068–9**
HAYDON, Benjamin Robert, 1786–1846. **11009**
— Libr. 13338
— *Paul's letters to his kinsfolk.* 11009
HAYE, George, fl.1850. **4851**
HAYEK, Friedrich August von, 1899– –Bibs. 1:3621w
HAYE MS.–Bndng. 5104–5
HAYES, William, fl.1794.
— *Portraits of rare and curious birds.* 6917a
HAYLE MILL, Maidstone. 1161a 3772
HAYLES, HOLY BLOOD OF see LITTLE TREATISE OF DIVERS MIRACLES … IN HAYLES.
HAYLEY, William, 1745–1820. **11010–12**
— Bibs. 1:**3622**
— *Genesis.* 8568
— Libr. 11010
— Mss. 8568
— *Memoir of Cowper.* 11011–12
— Publ. 11012
HAYMAN, Francis, 1708–76–Bibs. 1:**3623**
HAY MILL, Herefs. 1138
HAYWARD, Edward, fl.1656–60.
— *Sizes of riggings.* 8168
HAYWARD, sir John, 1564?–1627. **11013–15**
— Bibs. 1:**3624**
— *Life of Henry IV.* 6093 11013–15
— — Bibs. 1:**3624**
— Ptg. 6093
HAYWARD, John Davy, 1904–65. 92a
— Libr. 3373
HAYWARDS HEATH, Sussex–Ptg. 1408
HAYWOOD, Eliza (Fowler), 1693–1756. **11016**
— Bibs. 1:**3625**
HAZARD, Samuel, Bath, fl.1772–1806. 12488
HAZELL, Walter, 1843–1919. **4851–5**
HAZLITT, William, 1778–1830. **11017–24**
— Bibs. 1:661 **3626–8**
— *Human action.* 11019–20
— *Liber amoris.* 11022
— Libr. 11694
— Mss. 11017 11021
— *New and improved grammar.* 11018

HAZLITT, William, 1778–1830. *On the fear of death.* 11021
— *Outlines of grammar.* 11017
— Publ. 11019 11024
— *Spirit of the age.* 11024
— Text. 11023
HAZLITT, William Carew, 1834–1913. 1 3667
— Bibs. 1:**3628n**
— Libr. 2:203
HEAD, sir Francis Bond, 1st baronet, 1793–1875. 5250
HEAD, sir George, 1782–1855. 5250
HEADLEY, Hants.–Paper. 1132a
HEADLINES *see also* RUNNINGTITLES. 5117 6290
— Bibliogr. descr. 136
HEADPIECES *see* TYPE–Ornaments.
HEADTITLES–Bibliogr. descr. 143
HEAL, sir Ambrose, 1872–1959–Libr. 7068
HEALY, Timothy Michael, 1885–1931–Bibs. 1:**3628s**
HEARNE, Richard, fl.1632–46. 3501
HEARNE, Thomas, 1678–1735. **11025–7**
— Bibs. 1:**3629**
— *Ductor historicus.* 11027
HEATH, Charles, Monmouth, 1761–1831. **4856**
HEATH, sir John, fl.1643–Libr. 3396a
HEATH, William, 1795–1840 *see* PRY, Paul, *pseud.*
HEATON, Wallace E., fl.1939–Libr. 1:2185
HEATON MERSEY, Lancs.–Ptg. *see* CLOISTER PRESS, est. 1921.
HEAVY NEWS OF AN HORRIBLE EARTH-QUAKE, 1542. 656
HEAWOOD, Edward, 1863–1949. 3802–3
HEBER, Richard, 1774–1833–Libr. 2314 2652 2746 2986 3391
HEBREW BOOKS *see* JEWISH BOOKS; PRINTING IN HEBREW; SHAKESPEARE, William, 1564–1616–WORKS IN HEBREW; WORKS IN ISRAEL; TYPEFACES–Hebrew.
HEBREW LITERATURE *see* JEWISH LITERATURE.
HEBREW LYRICS, 1859. 11870
HEIDELBERG, Germany. 851 854 6843
HEIGHAM, John, St. Omer, fl.1568–1632. **4857**
HEINE, Heinrich, 1797–1856–Bibs. 1:822e
HEINEMANN, William, 1863–1920. 3477 **4858**–a 6522
HEINEMANN, William, est. 1890. 1:4016f
HELME, Elizabeth, d.1816. 7324a
HELPS, sir Arthur, 1813–75. 5680
HELSHAM, Samuel, Dublin, fl.1681–9. 1907
HELMINGHAM HALL, Suffolk–Libr. 3393a

HELVÉTIUS, Claude Arien, 1715–71. 923
HELY-HUTCHINSON, John Walter, fl.1953 *see* HUTCHINSON, John Walter, fl.1953.
HEMANS, Felicia Dorothea (Browne), 1793–1835–Bibs. 1:**3629q**
HEMINGE AND CONDELL. 2:531 534 550
HEMINGFORD GREY, Hunts.–Ptg. *see* VINE PRESS, est. 1956.
HEMPSTEAD *see* LONDON–HAMPSTEAD.
HENBLAS, Anglesey. 1517
HENDERSON, Alexander, 1583?–1646. 1678
HENDERSON, Alexander, 1791–1832–Libr. 3070
HENDERSON, Henry, 1820–79. **11028**
HENDERSON, James, 1823–1906. **4859**
HENDERSON, William, fl.1889. 7965
HENDERSON'S WEEKLY see YOUNG FOLKS.
HENHAM, Ernest George, fl.1907–25 *see* TREVENNA, John, *pseud.*
HENLEY, William Ernest, 1849–1903. **11029–30**
— Bibs. 1:**3630–1**
HENRIETTA MARIA, queen consort, 1609–69–Libr. 2000
HENRIETTA'S HEARTACHES. 802
HENRY VII, king of England, 1457–1509. 2985 3423 3428 4257
HENRY VIII, king of England, 1491–1547. 671 2233 4006–7 **11031–2** 11971
— *Assertio septem sacramentorum.* 11032
— Libr. 2201 11031
HENRY BENEDICT MARIA CLEMENT, card. York, 1725–1807–Libr. 3130
HENRY E. HUNTINGTON LIBRARY, San Marino, Calif. 113 495 2836 2868 2890 2903 3237; 2:311 344a 1210
— Collns. 1:372b 387 389 514–15 531 605 1522 1593 1633d 1633f 1663 1759 1835 1886 1998 2216 2286 2690 3091e 4467 4609 4842d 5134; 2:243 1355; 545 787 2836 2891 2939 4492 6098a 6904 7101 7150 7219–20 7509 9103 9541 9924 10067 10108 11309–10 11556 13215 13794
HENRY FREDERICK, prince of Wales, 1594–1612. **11033**
— Bibs. 1:**3632**
— Libr. 2068a 2187 2813
HENRY THE MINSTREL (Blind Harry), fl.1470–92. 11034
— Bibs. 1:1341 **3633–5**
— *Wallace.* 11034
— — Bibs. 1:**3634–5**
HENRYSON, Robert, 1430?–1506?–Bibs. 1:**3636**
HENSLOWE, Philip, d.1616.
— *Diary.* 7156–7 9570
HENSCHEL, Ernest, 1878– –Libr. 7624

HENTY, George Alfred, 1832–1902. **11035**
— Bibs. 1:**3637–8**
— *Out on the pampas.* 11035
HERALDRY. 2061 **7361–3**
— Bibs. 1:857 **2193m**
— Scotland. 7361–2
HERBALS *see also* FLOWER BOOKS. **7364–8**
— Bibs. 1:**2194–6**
— Collns. 6950 7962
— Illus. 7368
HERBERT, sir Alan Patrick, 1890–
1971–Bibs. 1:**3639**
HERBERT, Edward, 1st baron Herbert of
Cherbury, 1583–1648. **11036–42**
— *Autobiography.* 11039
— Bibs. 1:**3640**
— *De veritate.* 11036–7
— Libr. 2238a 11038
— Mss. 11039–41
— *Religio laici.* 11041–2
HERBERT, George, 1593–1633. **11043–8**
— Bibs. 1:**3640t–3**
— *The caller.* 11048
— Mss. 11046–8
— *Perigrinis almam matrem.* 11047
— *The temple.* 11043 11045
— Text. 11044
HERBERT, sir Henry, 1595–1673. 3499 7168
11049
HERBERT, Henry William, 1807–58 *see*
FORESTER, Frank, *pseud.*
HERBERT, sir William, d.1593. **11050**
— *Sidney or Baripenthes.* 11050
HERBERT, Mary (Sidney), countess of Pem-
broke, 1561–1621. 13427 13442
HERBERT, William, 3d earl of Pembroke,
1580–1630.
— *Poems.* 14216
HERBERT, William, 1718–95. 3475
HERBERT, William, 1771–1851.
— *Ames' Typographical antiquities.* 6060 6120
— *Entries of copies.* 5768a
HERBERT, William, 1778–1847.
— *Amaryllidaceæ.* 6960
HERBERT FAMILY–Bibs. 1:**3644**
— Libr. *see* POWIS CASTLE, Mont-
gomeryshire–Libr.
HERD, David, 1732–1810–Libr. 1635 6792
6796
HERDSFIELD, George, fl.1782–9. 4376
HEREFORD, Herefs.
— Bksllng. *see* LASLEY, Thomas, fl.1687;
WILLIAMS, Roger, fl.1695.
— Ptg. 1025 5373
— ALL SAINTS' CHURCH. LIBRARY. 3320
3327
— — — — Collns. 1:587
— CATHEDRAL. LIBRARY. 2429 2895

3079–80 3104 3137 3143 3146 3249 3299
3325 3336 3404
— — — Collns. 1:471 481a 587; 3313 3336
3355
— — — VICARS' CHORAL LIBRARY.
3143 3250 3336
— — — — Collns. 1:475a
HEREFORDSHIRE. **1137–8**
— Bksllng. 1137
— Paper. 1138
— Ptg. 1137
HERFORD, Charles Harold, 1853–1931, and
E. S. and P. SIMPSON.
— *Ben Jonson.* 11569
HERFORD, John, St.Albans, fl.1534–48.
6036
HERIOT, John, 1760–1833. **11051**
HERKOMER, sir Hubert von, 1849–1914.
7420a
HERMITAGE MILL, Stroud. 1120a
HERO AND LEANDER, 1783. 879
HERON, ptr., fl.1632–46 *see* HEARNE,
Richard, fl.1632–46.
HERON, Robert, 1764–1807.
— Bibs. 1:**3645**
— *Letters of Junius.* 11636
HERRICK, Robert, 1591–1674. **11052–61**
— Bibs. 1:**3646–50a**
— *Hesperides.* 11052–3 11055
— *Litany to the holy spirit.* 11056
— Mss. 11061
— *Noble numbers.* 11052
— Text. 11055–7
HERRINGMAN, Henry, 1627/8–1704. 4860
— Bibs. 1:**1342**
HERTFORD, Herts.
— Paper. 1139
— Ptg. *see* AUSTIN, Stephen, fl.1798–1818.
HERTFORDSHIRE. **1139**
— Librs. *see* ASHRIDGE PARK; HATFIELD
HOUSE.
— Maps–Bibs. 1:**1788–90**
— Newspapers–Bibs. 1:1856
— Paper *see also* TIDCOMBE, George, Wat-
ford, 1800–91. 1139 4544–5 5256
HERVET, GENTIAN, 1499–1584.
— *Treatise of household.* 624
HERVEY, Mary (Lepell), lady, 1700–68.
5250
HERVIE, Robert, fl.1611. **11062**
— *Health in a cup of wine.* 11062
HESELTINE, Philip Arnold, 1894–1930 *see*
WARLOCK, Peter, *pseud.*
HESLOP, Joseph, fl.1834. 1290
HESLOP, Richard Oliver, 1842–1916–Libr.
1:925 1581
HESSEY, James Augustus, 1785–1870. 5823
9960

HETHERINGTON, Henry, 1792–1849 see also *POOR MAN'S GUARDIAN*. 13310

HETLEY, sir Thomas, fl.1630.
— *Law reports*. 3787

HEUFFER, Ford Madox (later Ford), 1873–1939 see FORD, Ford Madox (formerly Hueffer), 1873–1939.

HEWELL, Worcs.–Paper. 1429a

HEWETT, John W., fl.1877–92. **4861**

HEWITSON, William Chapman, 1806–78.
— *Illustrations of exotic butterflies*. 6979 6984

HEWLETT, Maurice Henry, 1861–1923. **11063–4**
— Bibs. 1:684 **3651–5c**
— *Forest lovers*. 11064

HEYDON, sir John, d.1653–Libr. 3396a

HEYLYN, Peter, 1600–62. **11065–6**
— *Cosmography*. 4374
— *Observations on Charles*. 11065

HEYRICKE, Robert. 3754

HEYTESBURY, William, fl.1340. **11067**
— *Quædam consequentiæ subtiles*. 11067

HEYTHROP COLLEGE, Chipping Norton. LIBRARY. 3224

HEYWOOD, Lancs.–Bibs. 1:**905**

HEYWOOD, Abel, Manchester, est. 1832. **4861a**

HEYWOOD, James, 1687–1776. **11068**
— *Letters and poems*. 11068

HEYWOOD, Jasper, 1535–98. **11069**
— *Seneca's Troas*. 11069

HEYWOOD, John, 1497?–1580? **11070–3**
— Bibs. 1:**3656–7a**
— *Play of love*. 11070 11072
— *Play of the weather*. 7141 11073

HEYWOOD, Thomas, 1514?–1641. **11074–85** 12161 13381
— Bibs. 1:1597 **3658–9a**
— *The captives*. 2:951 1910
— *Escapes of Jupiter*. 11075a
— *Fair maid of the exchange*. 11082
— *Fair maid of the west*. 11084
— Handwr. 2:1892 1900 1910
— *Hierarchy of the blessed angels*. 11083
— *If you know not me*. 11074 11076–8
— *Iron age*. 11081
— *London's ius honorarium*. 11085
— Mss. 2:951; 11075a 11079
— Ptg. 11081–2 11085
— Publ. 4914 11083
— *Scourge of Venus*. 11075 11079
— *Sir Thomas Wyatt*. 11077
— Text. 11080 11084

HIBBERT, Charles, d.1819. **4862**

HIBBERT, Edward George, fl.1900–Libr. 2583

HIBBERT, Julian, 1801–34. **4863**
— Bibs. 1:**3660**

HICHENS, Robert Smythe, 1864–1950–Publ. 4858a

HICKES, George, 1642–1715. **11086–7**
— *Linguarum veterum thesaurus*. 11087
— Ptg. 11087

HICKES, James, fl.1642–68. 7666

HICKES, William, fl.1669–82. **11088**
— Bibs. 1:**3661**

HICKMOTT, Allerton Cushman, fl.1925–Libr. 3244

HICK SCORNER. 7141

HIEROGLYPHIC BIBLE see BIBLE–Versions–Hieroglyphic.

HIERON, Samuel, c.1572–1617–Bibs. 1:**3662**

HIFFERMAN, Paul, 1719–77–Bibs. 1:**3662g**

HIGDEN, Ranulf, d.1364.
— *Polychronicon*. 4282 6025 6036

HIGGIN, Anthony, fl.1608–24–Libr. 3319

HIGGINS, Frederick Robert, 1896–1941–Bibs. 1:**3663**

HIGHGATE see LONDON. HIGHGATE.

HIGH HOUSE PRESS, Shaftesbury, est. 1924. 4761 **4864–8**

HIGHWAYMEN–Bibs. 1:1542c

HIGH WYCOMBE, Bucks. **1046**
— Paper. 1046 3767a

HIGLETT, G. A., fl.1920–9–Bibs. 1:**3664**

HILDROP, John, d.1756. **11089**
— *Note on God's judgments*. 11089

HILDYARD, Francis, York, 1682–1731. 1448

HILDYARD, John, York, fl.1731–7. 1448

HILL, Abraham, 1635–1721. 7206

HILL, Arthur Frederick, 1860–1939–Libr. 7612

HILL, Carolyn Sherwin (Bailey), d.1961–Libr. 1:1572a

HILL, George Birkbeck Norman, 1835–1903.
— *Boswell's Life*. 8672 8676 8690
— *Johnsonian miscellanies*. 11375 11520
— *Johnson's Letters*. 11373 11375
— *Johnson's Lives*. 11375

HILL, Nicholas, 1570?–1610. **11090**
— Mss. 11090

HILL, Thomas, fl.1563–1600.
— Bibs. 1:**3664d**
— *Treatise teaching how to dress a garden*. 7348

HILL, Thomas, 1760–1840. 3123

HILLS, Henry, d.1689. **4869–70**

HILLS, Henry, d.1713. **4871–3** 7805 8021
— *Shakespeare's Julius Cæsar*. 2:1407

HILLS, John Waller, 1867–1938–Libr. 6763

HILLSBOROUGH, Down.–Ptg.–Bibs. 1:1057

HILSEY, bp. John, d.1539.
— *Manual of prayers*. 8067

HILTON, James, 1900–54. **11091**
— Bibs. 1:**3665**
— Bndng. 11091
— *Knight without armour.* 11091
HIND, Charles Lewis, 1862–1927–Bibs. 1:**3665p**
HINMAN COLLATORS. 415–18 423
HINSDON AND ANDREW REID, LTD., Newcastle-upon-Tyne *see* REID, Andrew, Newcastle-upon-Tyne, 1823–96.
HINXMAN, John, York, fl.1757–61. 1448
HIRD, Lewis A., fl.1953–Libr. 1:**3095d**
HIRSCH, Paul, 1881–1951–Libr. 7608
HIS/HER MAJESTY'S PRINTING OFFICE *see also* KING'S PRINTING HOUSE. 5013
HISLOP, Archibald, Edinburgh, fl.1668–78. **4877**
HISSEY, J. J., fl.1926. 482
HISTOIRE ANGLOISES–Bibs. 1:1691k
HISTORICAL BIBLIOGRAPHY *see* BIBLIOGRAPHY, HISTORICAL.
HISTORY *see* ENGLISH HISTORY; SCOTTISH HISTORY; WELSH HISTORY.
—, LOCAL *see* ENGLAND–Topography.
HISTORY AND SHAKESPEARE–Bibs. 2:112
HISTORY OF LITTLE GOODY TWO-SHOES, 1765? 10736 10780
HISTORY PLAYS–Bibs. 1:1611c–cb
H.M.S. CALEDONIA. 6053
H.M.S.O *see* HIS/HER MAJESTY'S PRINTING OFFICE.
HOBBES, John Oliver, *pseud. of* Pearl Mary Teresa (Richards) Craigie, 1867–1906–Bibs. 1:**3666**
HOBBES, Thomas, 1588–1679. **11092–4**
— Bibs. 1:**3667–9**
— *English works.* 11092
— *Leviathan.* 11093–4
HOBHOUSE, John Cam, baron Broughton de Gyfford, 1786–1869.
— Publ. 5250
HOBHOUSE, Leonard Trelawny, 1864–1929–Bibs. 1:**3669d**
HOBSON, Geoffrey Dudley, 1882–1949. 2160 2166
HOCKLIFFE, Frederick, 1833–1914–Libr. 1:1573g
HODGES, Charles Howard, 1764–1837. **4878**
HODGES, FIGGIS AND COMPANY, Dublin, est. 1844. **4878a**
HODGKIN, John Eliot, fl.1860–1914–Libr. 1:570
HODGKIN, Thomas, 1831–1913.
— Bibs. 1:**3670**
— *George Fox.* 10592

HODGKINS, John, Manchester, fl.1588–9. 5153
HODGSKIN, Thomas, fl.1825–32–Bibs. 1:**3670f**
HODGSON, Edmund, est. 1807. **4879–83**
HODGSON, John Evan, 1831–95. 8692
HODGSON, Orlando, fl.1825–44. 7023
HODGSON, Ralph, 1871–1962–Bibs. 1:**3671**
HODSON, James Lansdale, 1891–1956. **11095**
— Bibs. 1:**3671h**
— Mss. 11095
— — Bibs. 1:**3671h**
HODSON, James Shirley, 1819–99. 6194
HODSON, William, fl.1640. **11096**
— *Credo resurrectionem carnis.* 11096
HOE, Robert, 1839–1909–Libr. 1:388–9 493 572 629 1655; 2028 2983 11556
HOFFMAN, Francis, fl.1706–25. 7644
HOFFMANN, Heinrich, 1809–94. 930
HOFLAND, Barbara, 1770–1844–Bibs. 1:**3672**
HOGAN, Charles Beecher, 1906– –Libr. 8351
HOGAN, Francis Joseph, 1877–1944–Libr. 1:403 672a 1709 2023; 3001 3067
HOGAN, Michael, fl.1852–1924–Bibs. 1:**3673**
HOGARTH, William, 1697–1764. 3496 **4884–6** 7248
— Bibs. 1:**3674–8**
— *Butler's Hudibras.* 9150
— Collns. 4886
— *Works.* 4885
HOGARTH PRESS, est. 1918. **4887–9**
HOGG, Alexander, fl.1780. 1294
HOGG, James, 1770–1835 *see also* THE SPY. **11097–106**
— Bibs. 1:**3680–2d**
— *Chaldee manuscript.* 11105
— *The cherub.* 11106
— Collns. 11099 11101
— *Confessions of a justified sinner.* 11102
— *Domestic manners of Scotland.* 11103
— Letters. 11103 11105
— Mss.–Bibs. 1:**3681b**
— Publ. 5250
HOGG, Robert, 1864–1941–Libr. 3032
HOGG, Thomas Jefferson, 1792–1862. 11107–9
— *Memoirs of prince Alexy Haimatoff.* 11108–9
— Mss. 11107
HOGGARDE, Miles, fl.1557 *see* HUGGARDE, Miles, fl.1557.
HOLBEIN, Hans, 1497–1553. 6874
— *Emblems of mortality.* 4014
HOLBORN *see* LONDON. HOLBORN.

HOLBROOK, Ann Catherine, 1780–1837.
11110
— *Rebecca.* 11110
HOLCROFT, Thomas, 1745–1809. 11111–13
— Bibs. 1:3683–4
— *Follies of a day.* 11113
— — Bibs. 1:3684
— *The German hotel.* 11112
HOLDSWORTH, James Joseph, 19th cent.
4623
H O L E, Henry Fulke Plantagenet
Woolicombe, d.1820. 4890
HOLE, Richard, 1746–1803–Bibs. 1:3685
HOLE, William, 1709–91–Bibs. 1:3686
HOLFORD, sir George Lindsay, 1860–
1926–Libr. 2:1976; 2835 2847
HOLFORD, Robert Stayner, 1808–92. 2314
2837
HOLINSHED, Raphael, d.1580? 11114–19
— *Chronicle of England.* 2:1037 1358;
11115–19
— Illus. 11117
— Ptg. 11116 11118
— Text. 11115 11119
HOLKHAM HALL, Norf.–Libr. 1:346k;
2781 2887 3142 3156 3161 3268 3388
— Catalogues. 3358
— Collns. 2897 3106 3142 3147 3150
3257
HOLL, John, Worcester, fl.1790. 4891
HOLLAND *see* NETHERLANDS.
HOLLAND, Compton, fl.1612–26. 6550
HOLLAND, David Cuthbert Lyall, 1915–
–Libr. 3024
HOLLAND, Henry, 1583–1650? 4892 6550
— *Baziliologia.* 4892 7404
HOLLAND, Joseph, fl.1552–1605–Libr. 3048
HOLLAND, Michael, fl.1940–Libr. 3024
HOLLAND, Philemon, 1552–1637. 11120–2
— Bibs. 1:3687–8
— Libr. 11120
— *Livy's Roman history.* 11121
— *Suetonius' History of twelve Cæsars.* 11122
HOLLAND, sir Richard, fl.1450. 11123
— Bibs. 1:3689
— *Book of the Howlat.* 11123
HOLLAND, Robert, 1557–1622? 11124
HOLLAND HOUSE, Kensington–Libr. 2484
HOLLES, sir Thomas Pelham-, 5th baronet
Pelham, 1st duke of Newcastle, 1693–1768.
3561
HOLLINGBOURNE OLD MILL, Kent.
1161a 5975
HOLLINGBURY COPSE, Sussex *see*
PHILLIPPS, James Orchard Halliwell-,
1820–89–Libr.
HOLLINGWORTH'S, Maidstone, fl.1830.
3891

HOLLIS, Maurice Christopher, 1902– –Bibs.
1:3689m
HOLLIS, Thomas, 1720–74. 2647 3094 3115
3254 3278 3475
— Collns. 3267 3317 6441
— Libr. 2245 2947 2950 3267 5206
12560
HOLME, Constance, fl.1913. 11125
— *Beautiful end.* 11125
— Bibs. 1:3690–1
HOLME PIERREPONT, Notts.–Librs. 2609
H O L M E S, sir Maurice Gerald,
1885–1964–Libr. 8210
HOLMES, Sherlock *see* DOYLE, sir Arthur
Conan, 1859–1930.
H O L M E S, Thomas Rice Edward,
1855–1933–Bibs. 1:3692
HOLROYD, Henry North, 3d earl of
Sheffield, 1832–1909–Libr. 1:1535
HOLT, John, fl.1510. 11126–8
— *Lac puerorum.* 11126–8
HOLTBY, Winifred, 1898–1935. 11129
— Bibs. 1:3693
HOLYBAND, Claude, *pseud.* of Claude de
Sainliens, fl.1568–97. 11130–2
— *French Littleton.* 11130–2
— *French schoolmaster.* 9949 11130–2
HOLYOAKE, George Jacob, 1817–1906.
11133
— Bibs. 1:3694
HOLYROOD PRESS, Edinburgh, 1686–
8–Bibs. 1:1343
HOLYWELL, Flintshire–Paper. 1502
HOME, John, 1722–1808. 11134–5
— Bibs. 1:3695–a
— *Douglas.* 11134–5
HOME, William Douglas, 1912– –Bibs.
1:1597
HOME AND FOREIGN REVIEW–Bibs.
1:1927
HOME PARK MILL, Herts. 1139 4544–5
HOMER. 876 881 12805 12809 12826 12860
12872 12874
— Bibs. 1:776a
HONE, Joseph Maunsel, Dublin, 1882–1959.
5164
HONE, William, 1780–1842. 4893–5
— Illus. 4447
— *Political house that Jack built.* 4893
HONEYMAN, Robert B., fl.1920–59–Libr.
2:609
HONEYWOOD, Michael, 1597–1681 *see*
HONYWOOD, Michael, 1597–1681.
HONNOLD LIBRARY FOR THE AS-
SOCIATED COLLEGES, Claremont,
Calif.–Collns. 1:934–a 2656; 1346 9162
HONOURABLE SOCIETY OF LINCOLN'S
INN *see* LONDON. LINCOLN'S INN.

HONYWOOD, Michael, 1597–1681–Libr.
2903a–b 2584 6973a
HOOCHSTRATEN, Johannes, fl.1523–72 see
BALE PRESS, Marburg, fl.1528–46; LUFT,
Hans, pseud.
HOOD, Robin see ROBIN HOOD.
HOOD, Samuel, fl.1822. 1168
HOOD, Thomas, 1799–1845–Bibs. 1:3696
HOOD'S COMIC ANNUAL. 7830
HOOE, Sussex–Paper. 1412
HOOKE, Robert, 1635–1703.
— Bibs. 1:3697–8
— Libr. 12590
HOOKER, Richard, 1554?–1600. 11136
— Bibs. 1:3699
— Ecclesiastical polity. 11136
— — Bibs. 1:3699
HOOKER, Thomas, 1586–1647. 11137
— Soul's humiliation. 11137
HOOKER, sir William Jackson, 1785–1865.
6963
— Curtis' Flora Londoniensis. 6958
HOOKES, Nicholas, 1628–1712. 11138
— Amanda. 11138
HOOKHAM, Thomas, fl.1767–1830. 4896
HOOK MILL, Wolson bridge. 1132a
HOOLE, Charles, 1610–67. 11139
— Commenius' Visible world. 8108
— Corderius' School colloquies. 11139
HOOLE, Samuel, 1758–1839. 11140
— Leeuwenhoek's Select works. 11140
HOPE, Anthony, pseud. of sir Anthony Hope
Hawkins, 1863–1933. 11141
— Prisoner of Zenda. 11141
HOPE, Thomas, 1770?–1831. 5250
HOPE, Thomas Charles, 1766–1844–Mss.
8150
HOPE, sir William Henry St.John, 1854–
1919–Bibs. 1:3700
HOPKINS, Arthur, fl.1848–1901. 7420a
HOPKINS, Christopher, Lancaster, d.1742.
4897
HOPKINS, Gerard Manley, 1818–97. 11142
HOPKINS, Gerard Manley, 1844–89. 8765
11143–52
— Bibs. 1:3701–4
— Collns. 11145
— Handwr. 11147
— Journal. 11144
— Mss. 11145–6 11149–50
— — Bibs. 1:3703b 3703p
— Poems. 11205
— Publ. 11148
— Thee God I come from. 11152
— Spicilegium poeticum. 11142
HOPPNER, John, 1758–1810. 8578
HOPTON, Susanna (Harvey), 1627–1709.
11153

— Collection of meditations. 11153
— Libr. 14085
HORACE (Quintus Horatius Flaccus), 65–8
B.C. 887 897a 5419–20 12836
— Bibs. 1:778
HORÆ see PRIMERS.
HORÆ SUBSECIVÆ. 2414
HORMAN, William, d.1535.
— Bibs. 1:3706
— Libr. 5908
HORN BOOKS. 258 7000a 7010 7022a
7369–71
HORNBY, Charles Harry St.John, 1867–
1946 see also ASHENDENE PRESS,
1894–1923. 3859
HORNBY CASTLE, Yorks.–Libr. 2875
HORNE, John, 1614–76.
— Brief instructions for children. 7052
HORNE, Richard Henry (Hengist), 1803–84.
11154–5
— Bibs. 1:3710
— Orion. 11154–5
— Text. 11154
HORNE, Thomas Hartwell, 1780–1862.
6637
HORNIMAN MUSEUM AND LIBRARY,
London–Collns. 8134
HORSERIDING–Bibs. 1:2196f
HORSES. 6729 7372–3
— Collns. 7373
HORSFIELD, Thomas, 1773–1859.
— Descriptive catalogue of lepidopterous insects.
6980
HORSFIELD, Thomas Walker, d.1837.
— History of Sussex. 1413
HORSLEY, sir Victor Alexander Haden,
1857–1916–Bibs. 1:3710a–b
HORSTIUS, Jacobus Merlo, d.1644. 925
8065–7
HORTICULTURE see GARDENING.
HORTON MILL, Bucks. 1045
HORTULUS ANIMÆ see HORSTIUS, Jacobus
Merlo, d.1644.
HORWOOD, Richard, fl.1758–1803. 7484
7508
HOSKINS, John, 1566–1638. 11156
— Directions for speech. 11156
HOSPITAL OF INCURABLE FOOLS, 1600.
684
HOTMAN, Jean, sieur de Villiers Saint Paul,
1552–1636.
— The ambassador. 6546
— Casketful of rich jewels. 6546
— Publ. 6546
HOTTEN, John Camden, 1832–73. 1005
4897a–cb
— Bibs. 1:3711
— Dictionary of slang. 4897c

Vol. 1 = Bibliographies   2 = Shakespeare   4 = 1–8221   5 = 8222–14616

HUDSON, William Henry, 1841–1922.
Osprey. 11240
— Publ. 11238–9
— *Purple land.* 478 758
HUDSON-WILLIAMS, Thomas, 1873–1961
see WILLIAMS, Thomas Hudson-,
1873–1961.
HUEFFER, Joseph Leopold Ford Hermann
Madox, afterwards Ford Madox Ford,
1873–1939 *see* FORD, Ford Madox
(formerly Hueffer), 1873–1939.
HUGGARDE, Miles, fl.1557. 658
HUGHES, Arthur, 1832–1915. 7420a
HUGHES, George, 1603–67–Bibs. 1:3750
HUGHES, Hugh, 1790–1863. 4897g
— *Beauties of Cambria.* 4897g
HUGHES, John, 1677–1720.
— *Spenser's Works.* 13566
HUGHES, Richard Arthur Warren, 1900–
–Bibs. 1:3750k
HUGHES, Robert, Dublin, fl.1648–51. 1907
HUGHES, Thomas, 1822–96–Bibs. 1:3751–3
HUGHES, Thomas, fl.1853–75–Bibs. 1:3755
HUGHES, William A., fl.1924–59–Libr.
807
HUGHES AND SON, Wrexham, est. 1823.
4614a
HUGHES-STANTON, Blair, 1902– *see*
STANTON, Blair Hughes, 1902–
HUGHS, John, 1677–1720.
— *Shakespeare's Hamlet.* 2:1194
HUGO, Victor-Marie, 1802–85. 911 8898
HUGUENOTS. 3762
HUGUENOT SOCIETY. 3414
HUISH, Robert, 1777–1850–Bibs. 1:3755d
HULL, Yorks. 1440a
— Bksllng. 1440a
— Librs. 2455 2595
— Ptg. 1440a
HULL. PUBLIC LIBRARIES–Collns. 1:5094
HULL LYCEUM. LIBRARY. 2595
HULLMANDEL, Charles Joseph, 1789–1850.
6202
HULME, Thomas Ernest, 1883–1917–Bibs.
1:3755h–j
HUMAN SKIN AS BINDING *see* BOOK-
BINDINGS, HUMAN SKIN.
HUMBLE, George, d.1640. 6550
HUME, Alexander, 1560?–1609. 11248
— Bibs. 1:3756
— *Of the day estivall.* 11248
HUME, David, 1711–76. 11249–59
— Bibs. 1:3757–9
— *Essays.* 11249
— *Exposé succinct.* 11257
— *Four dissertations.* 11253 11259
— Handwr. 8532
— *History of England.* 11259

— — Bibs. 1:3757
— *Life.* 11255
— Mss. 11251 11256
— — Bibs. 1:3757
— Publ. 5796 11252
— Text. 11258–9
— *Treatise of human nature.* 11251 11254
11258
HUME, Fergus, 1859–1932.
— *Mystery of a hansom cab.* 7323
— Publ. 7323
HUME, Hugh, 3d earl of Marchmont,
1708–94–Libr. 2716
HUME, Joseph, 1777–1855. 11260
— Mss. 11260
HUME, sir Patrick, fl.1580–Bibs. 1:3760
HUME, sir Patrick, 1st earl of Marchmont,
1641–1724–Libr. 2716
HUME, Patrick, fl.1695.
— *Commentary on Paradise lost.* 12348
HUME, Tobias, d.1645. 11261
— *First part of airs.* 11261
HUMOROUS NEWSPAPERS *see* NEWS-
PAPERS, HUMOROUS.
HUMPHREY, duke of Gloucester, 1391–
1447–Libr. 1361 2266 2745 3354a
HUMPHREY, Hannah, fl.1778–1830. 4897h
HUMPHREY, John, 1621–1719. 11262
— *Proposition for the safety.* 11262
HUMPHREYS, Charles, b.1851. 4897hh
HUMPHREYS, Henry Noel, 1810–79. 6202
6229
HUNDRED SUNDRY FLOWERS see
GASCOIGNE, George, 1525?–77.
HUNGARIAN LITERATURE *see* BRITISH
BOOKS PUBLISHED ABROAD;
FOREIGN BOOKS PUBLISHED IN
BRITAIN; SHAKESPEARE, William,
1564–1616–WORKS IN HUNGARY.
HUNGARY, BRITISH BOOKS PUBLISHED
IN *see* BRITISH BOOKS PUBLISHED
ABROAD–Hungary.
HUNNIS, William, fl.1549–97–Bibs. 1:3760a
HUNDSON, George Carey, 2d baron,
1547–1603 *see* CAREY, George, 2d Hund-
son, 1547–1603.
HUNSDON HOUSE, London *see* LON-
DON. HUNSDON HOUSE.
HUNT, Christopher, Blandford,
fl.1585–1638. 4897i
HUNT, James Henry Leigh, 1784–1859 *see
also* LEIGH HUNT'S LONDON JOUR-
NAL. 2322 2523 7885 11263–82
— *Abou.* 11279
— Bibs. 1:54–5 661 672 3761–5
— Bndng. 11271
— Collns. 11270 11272 11278
— *Descent of liberty.* 11280

HUNT, James Henry Leigh, 1784–1859. *Feast of the poets.* 11282
— *Imagination and fancy.* 11277
— Letters. 11272
— — Bibs. 1:3765
— Libr. 11694
— *Love letters.* 11276
— *The palfrey.* 11271
— Publ. 5226 5250 11276–7
— *Sir Ralph Esher.* 11267–8
— *The town.* 11269
HUNT, John, 1775–1848. 9237
HUNT, Rachel McMasters (Miller), fl.1953–Libr. 1:2126–9
HUNT, Violet, 1866–1942. **11283**
— Mss. 11283
HUNT, William Holman, 1827–1910. 7420a **11284** 13898
— Mss. 11284
HUNTER, Alexander Gibson, fl.1804–11. 5250
HUNTER, Christopher, 1675–1759–Libr. 1319
HUNTER, John, 1728–93–Bibs. 1:**3770**
HUNTER, Joseph, 1783–1861. 3337 **11285**
— *Chorus vatum Anglicanorum.* 11285
HUNTER, William, 1718–83.
— Bibs. 1:**3771–2**
— *Lectures on the gravid uterus.* 7570
HUNTER, William, Edinburgh, fl.1824–1918. **4898**
HUNTING *see also* BOOK TRADE, LISTS–Hunting. 9506
— Bibs. 1:**2197–d**
— Collns. 4774
— Mss.–Bibs. 1:2197d
HUNTINGDON, Hunts. **1145–6**
— Bksllng. 1145
— Ptg. 1145
HUNTINGDON BOOK CLUB SOCIETY. 2452
HUNTINGDONSHIRE. **1140–50**
— Bibs. 1:**898–9b**
— Bndng. *see* LITTLE GIDDING BINDERY, 1625–7.
— Bksllng. 1140 1143
— Maps–Bibs. 1:**1790d**
— Newspapers. 1144
— Ptg. 1140 1143
— COUNTY RECORD OFFICE, Huntingdon–Collns. 1:1790d
HUNTINGTON, Henry Edwards, 1850–1927 *see also* HENRY E. HUNTINGTON LIBRARY, San Marino, Calif. 2:325; 2834 2890 3181 3402
HUNTINGTON LIBRARY *see* HENRY E. HUNTINGTON LIBRARY AND ART GALLERY, San Marino, Calif.

HUNTON, Anthony, 1560?–1624.
— *Guillemeau's worthy treatise of the eyes.* 7560 7564
HURCOTT, Worcs.–Paper. 1429a
HURD, bp. Richard, 1720–1808–libr. 2580
HURST, Thomas, fl.1800–5. 1294
HUTCHINS, John, 1698–1773.
— *History and antiquities of Dorset.* 5293
HUTCHINSON, John Walter Hely-, fl.1953–Libr. 2187
HUTCHINSON, Lucy (Apsley), b.1620. **11286–7**
— *Memoirs of colonel Hutchinson.* 11287
— Mss. 11286–7
HUTCHISON, Robert, Glasgow, fl.1827–38. 4746
HUTH, Alfred Henry, 1850–1910–Libr. 1:391 507 1462; 2486 2738 2747–8
HUTH, Edward, 1847– –Libr. 757a
HUTH, Henry, 1815–78–Libr. 1:390–2 1460; 2314 2483
HUTTON, Charles, 1737–1823. 8117
— *Miscellanea mathematica.* 7545
HUTT, David, fl.1960 *see* DAMASINE PRESS, Leeds, fl.1960.
HUTTON, Edward, 1875–1970–Bibs. 1:**3773**
HUTTON, George, fl.1627–48. **4899**
— Bibs. 1:**1345**
HUTTON, James, 1726–97.
— *Theory of the earth.* 8129 8143
HUTTON, Richard Holt, 1826–97. **11288**
— Bibs. 1:**3773d**
— *Essays theological and literary.* 11288
HUTTON, Robert, Sunderland, 1799–1865. **4900**
HUTTON, William, Birmingham, 1723–1815. 1419 3620 3639a 3659 **4901**
HUVIN, Jean, fl.1498. **4902**
HUXLEY, Aldous Leonard, 1894–1963. 481 **11289–93**
— Bibs. 1:681 684 **3774–8e**
— *Brave new world.* 11291
— Collns. 11290
— *Crome yellow.* 11293
— *Gioconda smile.* 11289
— *Leda.* 11292
— Letters. 11289
— Mss. 11289–90
— — Bibs. 1:3778e
— Text. 11291 11293
HUXLEY, Thomas Henry, 1825–95.
— Bibs. 1:**3779–d**
— Mss. 8131
— — Bibs. 1:3779b 3779d
HYDE, Donald Frizell, 1909–66. 3369 3378
— Libr. 1:3850 3851

HYDE, Donald Frizell, 1909–66 and Mary
Morley Crapo HYDE, 1912– –Libr. 3188
3380a 11465 11518
HYDE, Douglas, 1860–1949–Bibs. 1:**3780–1**
HYDE, Edward, earl of Clarendon, 1609–74.
11294–6
— *History of the rebellion.* 3991 11294
— Libr. 11295
— Mss. 11296
— Publ. 11294
HYETT, sir Francis Adams, 1844–1941–Libr.
1893–5 895b 896d 2775
HYMNS. **7374–8**
— Bibs. 1:698 949 **1732–3**
— Collns. 7378
— Scotland. 1575
— Wales. 4941 7376

-IAD (titles ending in)–Bibs. 1:346m
IBBOTSON, John, Chapel-en-le-Frith,
fl.1830. 3785
IBBOTSON, Richard, Staines, fl.1807–30.
3785
IBSEN, Henrik, 1828–1906. 4858a
ICELAND *see* SHAKESPEARE, William,
1564–1616–WORKS IN ICELAND.
ICELAND, BRITISH BOOKS PUBLISHED
IN *see* BRITISH BOOKS PUBLISHED
ABROAD–Iceland.
IDAHO. UNIVERSITY. LIBRARY–Collns.
1:4614
IDLER, THE see JOHNSON, Samuel,
1709–84.
ILIVE, Jacob, 1705–63. 3475
ILLINOIS. SOUTHERN ILLINOIS UNI-
VERSITY, Carbondale. LIBRARY–
Collns. 1:4019
— UNIVERSITY. LIBRARY.
— — — Collns. 1:1601p 1699 1728 1891
2980 4238 4241; 2:228; 3159 4001 14280
ILLUSTRATED BINDINGS *see* BOOK-
BINDINGS, ILLUSTRATED.
ILLUSTRATED BOOKS *see also* ART;
BIRDS; COPYBOOKS; EMBLEM
BOOKS; EXTRA-ILLUSTRATED
COPIES; FLOWER BOOKS; HERBALS;
ILLUSTRATORS; MAPS. 481 2375 7089
7379–463
— Bibs. 1:359 369 444 460 **1735–55** 2130
2179 2284 2532d 3052 3091 4239–40
4353b 4544 4844
— Collns. 3022 3025 7422 7434 7457
— Scotland. 1631
— — Bibs. 1:1754k
— Wales–Bibs. 1:1745d
— 1475–1640. 653 935 7382

— 1641–1700. 7413 7941
— 1701–1800. 479 729 950 7391 7406
7412–13 7429 7431 7441 7450
— 1801–1900. 1229 1231 5944 6229 7386
7389 7396–9 7420a 7425–6 7430 7433 7440
7443 7453 7455 7461 7613 7732 7829
ILLUSTRATED LONDON NEWS. 5909
ILLUSTRATION OF ANNUALS. 7430
ILLUSTRATION OF BIBLES. 5851 6825
6872 6874 6884
ILLUSTRATION OF BOTANICAL BOOKS.
6958a
ILLUSTRATION OF CHILDREN'S
LITERATURE. 6210 6213 6995 7013 7039
7443 7453
ILLUSTRATION OF DRAMA. 7390 13250
ILLUSTRATION OF FLOWER BOOKS.
7327 7329
ILLUSTRATION OF HERBALS. 7368
ILLUSTRATION OF JUVENILE DRAMA.
7046
ILLUSTRATION OF NATURAL HISTORY.
6193 8147
ILLUSTRATION OF NOVELS. 6229 7260
7286 7297 7435
ILLUSTRATION OF SPORT. 4650a 6193
ILLUSTRATION OF TRAVEL BOOKS.
7441
ILLUSTRATION PROCESSES *see also*
AEROGRAPHY; AQUATINTING;
CHROMOLITHOGRAPHY; CHROMO-
XYLOGRAPHY; COLOUR PRINTING;
ELECTROTINT; ENGRAVING;
ETCHING; EXTRA-ILLUSTRATION;
GLYPHOGRAPHY; LITHOGRAPHY;
LITHOTINT; NATURE-PRINTING;
PAINTINGS, OIL; PHOTOGRAPHS;
PHOTOGRAVURE; PHOTOLITHO-
GRAPHY; PLANOGRAPHY; SIDERO-
GRAPHY; WATERCOLOURING. 257 259
269 **6185–229**
— Bibs. 1:1139c 1139m 1151 1155 1735
1754 2130; 6095 6100
— 1475–1640. 653
— 1475–1700. 6194 6210
— 1641–1700. 3473 6213 6226
— 1701–1800. 6194 6210 6213
— 1801–1900. 792 6142 6194 6202 6208
6210 6212–13 6219a 6224 6229
ILLUSTRATIONS *see also* CARICATURES.
263 6192
— Bibliogr. descr. 143 256 6187
— Forgeries. 3906 7342 8435 9982
— Newspapers. 7389 7407 7430 7732 7753
7858
— Proofs. 6200 8590 9329 11828
ILLUSTRATIONS OF PRINTING PRESSES.
6313–14 6317 6329 10610 12105

ILLUSTRATORS *see also* BOOK TRADE, LISTS–Illustrators; ENGRAVERS, *and individual illustrators, e.g.* Alken, Henry Thomas, 1785–1851; Allan, David, 1744–96; Allingham, William, 1824–96; Armstead, Henry Hugh, 1828–1905; Baker, James, fl.1795–1803; Barlow, Francis, 1626?–1702; Barnes, Robert, 1840–95; Beardsley, Aubrey Vincent, 1872–98; Bell, Robert Anning, 1863–1933; Blake, William, 1757–1827; Boyle, Eleanor Vere (Gordon), 1825–1916; Boys, Alderman, fl.1802; Brock, Charles Edmund, 1870–1938; Brock, Henry Matthew, 1875–1960; Brown, Ford Madox, 1858–1932; Brooke, Leonard Leslie, 1862–1940; Browne, Gordon Frederick, 1858–1932; Browne, Hablôt Knight, 1815–82; Burney, Edward Francis, 1760–1848; Bury, Priscilla Susan (Falkner), fl.1793–1867; Buss, Robert William, 1804–75; Caldecott, Randolph, 1846–86; Cattermole, George, 1800–68; Cave, Henry, York, 1808–71; Childs, George, fl.1837; Chubb, Ralph Nicholas, 1892–1960; Clarke, Joseph Clayton, fl.1888–1912; Coveny, Christopher, 1846–1926; Crane, Walter, 1845–1915; Crowquill, Alfred, *pseud.* of Alfred Henry (1804–72) and Charles Robert (1803–50) Forrester; Cruikshank, George, 1792–1878; Cruikshank, Isaac Robert, 1789–1856; Cruikshank, Percy, fl.1851–76; Dalziel, Edward, 1817–1905; Dalziel, Edward George, 1849–88; Dalziel, George, 1815–1902; Dalziel, Thomas Bolton Gilchrist Septimus, 1823–1906; Day, William, fl.1813–45; De Witt, Johannes, fl.1596; Dickes, William Frederick, fl.1903–6; Dicksee, sir Francis Bernard, 1853–1928; Doyle, Richard, 1824–83; Drake, William Henry, 1857–1917; Du Maurier, George Louis Palmella Busson, 1834–96; E., M. E., i.e. Mary Ellen Edwards, fl.1839–1908; Elwes, Alfred Thomas, fl.1867–93; Engelmann, Godefroi, 1788–1839; Fell, Herbert Granville, 1872–1951; Fildes, sir Samuel Luke, 1844–1927; Flaxman, John, 1755–1826; Foster, Birket, 1825–99; Fraser, Claud Lovat, 1890–1921; Fraser, Francis Arthur, fl.1869–83; Furniss, Harry, 1854–1925; Fuseli, Henry (Johann Heinrich Fuessli), 1741–1825; Gaskin, Arthur Joseph, 1862–1928; Gibbings, Robert John, 1889–1958; Gilbert, sir John, 1817–97; Gill, Arthur Eric Rowton, 1882–1940; Graham, Thomas Alexander Ferguson, 1840–1906; Gravelot, Hubert François, 1699–1773; Gray, Paul, 1848–68; Green, Charles, 1840–98; Greenaway, Catherine ('Kate'), 1846–1901; Hague, Louis, 1806–85; Hammond, Chris, fl.1906; Hayes, William, fl.1794; Hayman, Francis, 1708–76; Herkomer, sir Hubert von, 1849?–1914; Hopkins, Arthur, 1848–1901; Hopkins, Gerard Manley, 1818–97; Houghton, Arthur Boyd, 1836–75; Hughes, Arthur, 1832–1915; Hughes, Hugh, 1790–1863; Hullmandel, Charles Joseph, 1789–1850; Humphreys, Henry Noel, 1810–79; Hunt, Henry Holman, 1827–1910; Jones, sir Edward Coley Burne-, 1833–98; Jones, Owen, 1809–74; Keene, Charles Samuel, 1823–91; Kent, William, 1684?–1748; Kipling, John Lockwood, 1837–1911; Lambourn, Peter Spendelowe, 1722–74; Landseer, sir Edwin Henry, 1802–73; Lawless, Matthew James, 1837–64; Lawson, Cecil Gordon, 1851–82; Lawson, Francis Wilfred, 1842–1935; Lawson, John, fl.1865–1902; Le Blond, Abraham, 1819–94; Leech, John, 1817–64; Leighton, Frederic, baron Leighton of Stretton, 1830–96; Lewis, Charles George, 1808–80; Lewis, John Frederick, 1805–76; Linton, sir James Drogmole, 1840–1916; Linton, William James, 1822–97; Lydon, Alexander Francis, 1836–1917; Maclise, Daniel, 1806–70; Macready, William, 1832–71; Mahoney, James, fl.1866–1910; Marks, Henry Stacey, 1829–98; Marmion, Edmund, fl.1653; Martin, John, 1789–1854; Martin, Jonathan, 1782–1838; Martin, William, 1772–1851; Meadows, Joseph Kenny, 1790–1874; Millais, sir John Everett, 1829–96; Minton, Francis John, 1917–57; Moore, Albert Joseph, 1841–93; Morten, Thomas, 1836–66; Nash, Joseph, 1809–78; Nash, Paul, 1889–1946; North, John William, 1841–1924; Onwhyn, Thomas, d.1886; Orchardson, sir William Quiller, 1832–1910; Paget, Henry Marriot, 1856–1936; Pailthorpe, Frederick W., fl.1870–86; Palmer, Samuel, 1805–81; Park, Arthur, d.1863; Partridge, sir J. Bernard, 1861–1945; Paton, sir Joseph Noel, 1821–1901; Peake, Mervyn Laurence, 1911–68; Pettie, John, 1839–93; Pickersgill, Frederick Richard, 1820–1900; Pinwell, George John, 1842–75; Potter, Helen Beatrix, 1866–1943; Poynter, sir Edward John, 1836–1919; Pry, Paul, *pseud. of* William Heath, 1795–1840; Rackham, Arthur, 1867–1939; Rossetti, Dante

ILLUSTRATORS–*cont.*
Gabriel, 1828–82; Rutherston, Albert Daniel, 1881–1953; Sambourne, Edwin Linley, 1844–1910; Sandys, Anthony Frederick Augustus, 1829–1904; Sargeant, Waldo, fl.1900; Scott, John, 1774–1827; Seymour, Robert, 1800?–36; Shields, Frederic James, 1833–1911; Sibson, Thomas, 1817–44; Small, William, 1843–1929; Sneyd, Ralph, fl.1815; Soloman, Simeon, 1840–1905; Stanfield, Clarkson, 1793–1867; Stern, Lewis, fl.1772; Stone, Frank, 1800–59; Stothard, Thomas, 1755–1834; Strutt, Joseph, 1749–1802; Sullivan, Edmund Joseph, 1869–1933; Tenniel, sir John, 1820–1914; Thackeray, William Makepeace, 1811–63; Thomas, George Housman, 1824–68; Thomson, Hugh, 1860–1920; Thornhill, sir James, 1676–1734; Thurston, John, 1774–1822; Topham, Francis William, 1808–77; Vanderbank, John, 1694–1739; Van der Gucht, Gerard, 1696–1776; Van der Gucht, Michael, 1660–1725; Vizetelly, Henry Richard, 1820–94; Wale, Samuel, 1721?–86; Walker, Anthony, 1726–65; Walker, Frederick, 1840–75; Watson, John Dawson, 1832–92; Watts, George Frederic, 1817–1904; Weir, Harrison William, 1824–1906; Whistler, James Abbott McNeill, 1834–1903; Whistler, Reginald (Rex) John, 1905–44; Wright, John Buckland, 1897–1954; Yeats, Jack Butler, 1871–1957. 2375
IMAGE OF PITY. 545a
IMAGINARY VOYAGES *see* VOYAGES, IMAGINARY.
IMITATIONS *see also* PARODIES. 10814
— Bibs. 1:777m 1981e 2001 2330 2566 2622 2655 2660 2844a 3033b 3506 4829 4833
IMPORTATION OF BOOKS. 841 847 965 3435 3441 3559 5877 11911 12583
IMPORTATION OF PAPER *see* PAPER, IMPORTATION OF.
IMPOSITION *see also* FORMAT. 257 5945 6238 9659
—, HALF-SHEET. 120 142 6240–2 6245 6250–1 8822
—, INVERTED. 6247
—, QUADRUPLE. 10770
—, SINGLE-PAGE. 10599–600
IMPRESSIONS *see also* EDITION, IMPRESSION, ISSUE, AND STATE; SIZES OF IMPRESSIONS. 157
IMPRIMATURS *see also* PRIVILEGES, PUBLISHING. 3550 3567 3572 3574
IMPRINT, THE. 6635
IMPRINTS. 1281 1790 1919 3578 3601 3633

4008 4855 5096–7 5335 5554–5 6272–3 6292 6300 6304–5 12012
— Bibliogr. descr. 134
INCHBALD, Elizabeth (Simpson), 1753–1821–Bibs. 1:3782
INCUNABULA *see* BOOKS–1475–1500.
'INCUT'. 3588
INDEPENDENT LABOUR PARTY–Bibs. 1:691
INDEXES. 2375
INDEX INTELLIGENCER. 7655
INDEX LIBRORUM PROHIBITORUM. 3498 3500
INDIA *see also* SHAKESPEARE, William, 1564–1616–WORKS IN INDIA. 3717 4871 13002
— NATIONAL LIBRARY, Calcutta–Collns. 2:128a
—, BRITISH BOOKS PUBLISHED IN *see* BRITISH BOOKS PUBLISHED ABROAD–India.
INDIANA. UNIVERSITY. LIBRARY–Collns. 1:368 3724 3731 4006 4249a 4904b 5207
— — LILLY LIBRARY. 3232 14129
— — — Collns. 7233 11218 13968
INDIAN LITERATURE *see* ANGLO-INDIAN LITERATURE.
INDIA PAPER *see* PAPER, INDIA.
INDUCTIONS–Bibs. 1:1601c 1601r–t
INDUSTRIALIZATION. 1046 1161b 1165 1256 1277 3767a 5700 6145
INDULGENCES. 545a 550 660 1934 5462 5468 5650 6015 6034
— Bibs. 1:1534d
INFANT MINSTREL, 1816. 7060–1
INFANT'S LIBRARY. 5133–7
— Bibs. 1:1564 1565a–b
INGE, William Ralph, 1860–1954–Bibs. 1:3782m
INGLEBY, Holcombe, 1854–1926–Libr. 2:467
INGLIS, Esther (mrs. B. Kello), formerly Langloiş, 1571–1624. 11297–9
— Bibs. 1:3782t–u
— Mss. 11297–9
INGLIS, John Bellingham, 1780–1870–Libr. 2565
INGLIS, Robert, fl.1849–88. 2:716
INGOLD, Ernest, 1885–1977–Libr. 2:228
INGOLDSBY, Thomas, *pseud. of* Richard Harris Barham, 1788–1845. 11300–1
— Bibs. 1:3783b
— *Ingoldsby legends.* 11300
INGRAM, Herbert, 1811–60. 6202
INGRAM, John Kells, 1823–1907–Bibs. 1:3783
INGRAM, sir William James, 1811–1902. 4903

INITIAL BINDER, fl.1563. **4904–5**
INITIALS (Letters) *see* TYPE–Initials.
INITIALS (Names). 677 6693
INK–Bibs. 1:1139m **1139y–ya**; 6256–7
—, COLOURED. 6259
—, PRINTING. 97 4129a 5982 6255 6257 6259 6348
INKING. 6258 6312
— Balls. 6259
— Rollers. 6259
INK ON BINDINGS. 2097
INNERPEFFRAY, Perth.–Librs. 1633 1731–2 2459 2846
INNES, Cosmo, 1798–1874–Bibs. 1:**3783d**
INNS OF COURT, London *see* LONDON. INNS OF COURT.
INNYS, John, fl.1713–32–Libr. 7497
INNYS, William, fl.1711–32. **4906**
INQUIRER, THE–Bibs. 1:5091v
INQUISITOR, THE. 7885
INSHEWAN, Angus–Libr. 1633
INSOLUBILIA, 1517. 1359
INSTITUTE OF CHARTERED ACCOUNTANTS IN ENGLAND AND WALES. LIBRARY–Collns. 1:2080–1
INSTITUTE OF CHARTERED ACCOUNTANTS OF SCOTLAND, Edinburgh. LIBRARY–Collns. 1:2084
INSTITUTE OF CONTEMPORARY ARTS, London. 11592
INSTITUTE OF SHORTHAND WRITERS, London. LIBRARY–Collns. 1:2279i
INSTITUTO BRITÂNICO EM PORTUGAL, Lisbon–Collns. 2:129
INSTRUCTION, BIBLIOGRAPHICAL *see* BIBLIOGRAPHY–Instruction.
INSTRUCTIONAL PRESSES *see* PRESSES, INSTRUCTIONAL.
INSTRUMENTAL TUTORS *see* TUTORS, INSTRUMENTAL.
INTAGLIO. 6187 6194
INTELLIGENCER. 7715
INTERLEAVED COPIES. 14023
INTERLUDE OF JOHN THE EVANGELIST. 7110
INTERLUDE OF THE FOUR ELEMENTS, 1538. 7134
INTERLUDES. 5185
INTRODUCTION FOR TO LEARN TO RECKON, 1537. 7549
INVENTORIES.
— Paper. 3725 5359
—, BOOKSELLERS' *see* BOOKSELLERS–Inventories.
INVERNESS, Inver. **1682–4**
— Bksllng. 1683
— Librs. 1683
— Newspapers. 1684

INVERNESS COURIER. 1684
INVERNESS JOURNAL. 1683
INVERNESS-SHIRE. **1682–4**
— Bibs. 1:**1001**
— Newspapers–Bibs. 1:1931
INVERTED IMPOSITION *see* IMPOSITION, INVERTED.
INVINCIBLES. 1924
IOWA. STATE UNIVERSITY, Ames. LIBRARY–Collns. 11278 11310
— UNIVERSITY. LIBRARIES–Collns. 1:4317p 5127b; 12549 13070 14365–6
IPING, Sussex–Paper. 1412
IPSWICH, Suff. **1401–3**
— Bksllng. *see* CRAIGHTON, William, fl.1739–61.
— Librs. 1400 1402 2607
— Ptg. 1017 1019 1025 1401 1403
— Publ. 1403
IPSWICH OLD TOWN LIBRARY. 1400 2607 3103
IRELAND *see also* ANGLO-IRISH LITERATURE; BOOK TRADE, LISTS–Ireland; PRINTING IN GAELIC; SHAKESPEARE, William, 1564–1616–WORKS IN IRELAND. *For Irish books arranged by period see* BOOKS–Ireland. **1742–991**
— Almanacs. 1743 1764 1796 1800 1882–3
— — Bibs. 1:1427
— Auction sales. 3671
— Ballads. 1786
— — Bibs. 1:1465d
— Bible. 1748 4084 6858a 6867a 8729
— — Bibs. 1:1028 1481d
— — N.T. 1879 1932–3 6858a
— — — Bibs. 1:1481d
— Bibs. 1:**1010–139**
— Bndng. 1768 1808–9 1820 1828 1830 1843
— Book collecting. 2266
— Bndng.
— — 1475–1700. 1825
— — 1701–1800. 1751 1825 1836
— Book of common prayer. 1876
— Bksllng. 1782
— Broadsides. 6436
— Chapbooks. 1761 1781
— Collns. 2764
— Copyright. 1915
— Directories. 1743 1808
— Drama. 1749
— — Bibs. 1:1589 1589g–h 1621p 1652 1652p 1652t 1653
— Economics–Bibs. 1:2163
— Engraving. 1742 1808
— Fiction. 1848
— — Bibs. 1:1719 1723k

ISSUE see EDITION, IMPRESSION, ISSUE, AND STATE.
—, SIZE OF see SIZES OF ISSUES.
ITALIAN BOOKS see also PRINTING IN ITALIAN.
— Collns. 956
ITALIAN LITERATURE see BRITISH BOOKS PUBLISHED ABROAD; FOREIGN BOOKS PUBLISHED IN BRITAIN; SHAKESPEARE, William, 1564–1616–WORKS IN ITALY.
ITALY, BRITISH BOOKS PUBLISHED IN see BRITISH BOOKS PUBLISHED ABROAD–Italy.
ITINERARIES see ROADBOOKS AND ITINERARIES.
ITINERARY BOOKSELLING see BOOK-SELLING, ITINERARY.
ITTON, Chepstow–Paper. 1298a
ITTON COURT, Mons.–Paper. 1298a
IVIE, John, fl.1661.
— Declaration. 720
IVY MILL, Kent. 1161a

JACK AND THE BEANSTALK. 7017
JACKETS, BOOK see WRAPPERS, BOOK.
JACK JUGGLER. 7119
JACKSON, Edwin Brook-, 1877–1936–Libr. 2804
JACKSON, Holbrook, 1874–1948. 11313–15
— Bibs. 1:3785d
— Collns. 11315
— Libr. 11313–14
JACKSON, John, Louth, fl.1797. 1958b
JACKSON, John Baptist, 1701–80? 6192
JACKSON, Joseph, 1733–92. 3475 6613
JACKSON, Richard Charles, fl.1851–1902–Bibs. 1:3785g
JACKSON, Thomas, 1579–1640. 12285
— Publ. 6552
— Works. 6552
JACKSON, William, 1823–90. 1:1540
— Libr. 6986 6988
JACKSON, William Alexander, 1905–64. 91 93 295a 5768a
JACKSON, Zachariah, fl.1818–20.
— Few concise examples. 2:1704
JACKSON'S OXFORD JOURNAL. 1376 7771
JACOB AND ESAU, c.1558. 691
JACOBI, Charles Thomas, 1853–1933. 4908
JACOBI, Henry, fl.1505–14. 1197
— Bibs. 1:920a
JACOBITISM. 1176 1574 1597 1618
JACOBS, William Wymark, 1863–1943. 11316–17
— Bibs. 1:3786–7

JACOBSON, Walter Hamilton Acland, fl.1877–1907–Bibs. 1:3788
JACOBUS DE VORAGINE, archbp., 1230–98. 4305 4309 4325 5817
JAGGARD, Dorothy (Weaver), later Fawne, d.1666. 2:551a; 4651
JAGGARD, William, fl.1568–1623 see also SHAKESPEARE, William, 1564–1616–QUARTOS, PAVIER. 2:547 551–a 574b 918; 3494 4651 4909–17
— Catalogue of English books. 3494 4915
— Deloney's Ballad of king Arthur. 6791
— Deloney's Thomas of Reading. 2:617
— Favyn's Theatre of honour. 2:558
— Passionate pilgrim. 4913–14
— Shakespeare's First folio see SHAKESPEARE, William, 1564–1616–FOLIO, FIRST–Ptg.
— Vincent's Discovery of errors. 2:558; 14159–60
JAGGARD PRESS, fl.1594–1627–Bibs. 1:1345a–b
JAMES I, king of England, 1566–1625. 10597 11318–24
— Basilicon doron. 11323
— — Bibs. 1:3790 3792
— Bible see BIBLE–Versions–Authorized.
— Bibs. 1:3789–93
— Libr. 4049 10253 11318–21
— Opera. 11324
— — Bibs. 1:3791
JAMES I, king of Scotland, 1394–1437. 11325
— Christ's kirk on the green see CHRIST'S KIRK ON THE GREEN, 1643.
— King's quair. 11325
— Poetical remains. 9075
JAMES II, king of England, 1633–1701. 11326
— Libr. 2122
— Memoirs. 11326
JAMES IV, king of Scotland, 1473–1513. 1591 2626
JAMES VI, king of Scotland, 1566–1625 see JAMES I, king of England, 1566–1625.
JAMES, Edwin Oliver, 1888–1972–Bibs. 1:3793g
JAMES, George, 1683–1735. 3475
JAMES, George Payne Rainsford, 1799–1860. 11327–8
— Bibs. 1:3794–5
— Revenge. 11327
JAMES, Harold E., fl.1958–Libr. 3245
JAMES, Henry, 1843–1916. 11329–52
— The ambassadors. 11335 11340 11342 11346
— The American. 11334
— At Isella. 11331
— Awkward age. 11331
— Bibs. 1:3796–810

JAMES, Henry, 1843–1916–Collns. 11339
— *Future of the novel.* 11351
— Letters. 11341
— — Bibs. 1:3806
— Libr. 11348 11350
— Mss. 11343 11349
— *Portrait of a lady.* 11352
— Ptg. 11330
— Publ. 4858a 11341 11346–7
— *Roderick Hudson.* 11344
— *Spoils of Poynton.* 11347
— Text. 11331–2 11335 11338 11340 11342 11344–5 11347 11352
— *Tragic muse.* 11343
JAMES, John, d.1772. 3475 6613 6627
JAMES, Montague Rhodes, 1862–1936. **11353**
— Bibs. 1:**3815–16a**
— *Casting the runes.* 11353
JAMES, Richard, 1592–1638. 2:551a–2
JAMES, Thomas, 1573?–1629. **11354–5**
— Bibs. 1:**3816m**
— *Concordantiae sanctorum patrum.* 11354–5
JAMES, Thomas, fl.1710–38. **4918** 6613
JAMIESON, Robert, 1780?–1844–Libr. 1634
JANNER, Oswald, fl.1905–7. 5601
JANSSON, Jan, 1588–1664? 7486
JANUS OR THE EDINBURGH LITERARY ALMANACK. 1699
JAPAN *see* SHAKESPEARE, William, 1564–1616–WORKS IN JAPAN.
—, BRITISH BOOKS PUBLISHED IN *see* BRITISH BOOKS PUBLISHED ABROAD–Japan.
JAPANNING. 3929 3934
JARMAN, John Boykett, 1782?–1864–Libr. 3394
JARNAC, Phillipe Ferdinand Auguste de Rohan-Chabot, count de, d.1875 *see* CHABOT, Phillipe Ferdinand Auguste de Rohan–, count de Jarnac, d.1875.
JARRY, Francis, 1733–1807. **11356**
— *Moniteur.* 11356
JARVIS, Charles, 1675?–1739.
— *Don Quixote.* 962
JAY, Leonard, 1888– . **4919–20**
— Bibs. 1:**1345b**
JAYE, Henry, d.1643. 856
— Bibs. 1:**1346**
JEALOUS COMEDY, THE. 2:1573
JEANS, sir James Hopwood, 1877–1946–Bibs. 1:**3816q**
JEDBURGH, Roxb. **1740**
— Bibs. 1:**1009**
— Ptg. 1740
JEFFERIES, John Richard, 1848–87. 480 **11357–9**

— Bibs. 1:**3817–20a**
— Bndng. 2124
— *Land.* 11357
— *Scarlet shawl.* 2124
JEFFREY, Francis, ld. Jeffrey, 1773–1850. **11360–1**
— Bibs. 1:2676d
JEFFREYS, George, 1st baron Jeffereys of Wem, 1648–89–Libr. 2859
JELINGER, Christopher, d.1685–Bibs. 1:**3820n**
JENKINS, John Edward, 1838–1910–Collns. 7322a
JENKINS, Robert Thomas, 1881–1969–Bibs. 1:**3820t**
JENKINSON, Richard C., 1853–1930–Libr. 1:1226m
JENKS, Edward, 1861–1939–Bibs. 1:**3821**
JENNENS, Charles, 1700–73.
— *Shakespeare's Tragedies.* 2:742
JENNER, Edward, 1749–1823.
— Bibs. 1:**3822–3**
— Mss.–Bibs. 1:**3822**
— *Origin of the vaccine inoculation.* 7568
JENNER, Thomas, fl.1618–72. 6550
JENNINGS, Richard, 1881–1953. 3164 3272 14434
— Bibs. 1:**3824**
JENSEN, Bent Juel–, fl.1953–70–Libr. 687a
JEPHSON, Robert, 1736–1803–Bibs. 1:**3825**
JERDAN, William, 1782–1869. **4921**
JERMIN, Michael, c.1591–1659–Bibs. 1:**3826**
JEROME, 'OXFORD' *see* RUFINUS, Tyrannius, Aquileiensis, fl.345–410.
JEROME, Jerome Klapka, 1859–1927.
— Bibs. 1:1597
— Illus. 4711
— *Three men in a boat.* 4711
JERROLD, Douglas William, 1803–57. 5909 **11362**
— Bibs. 1:**3826a**
JERSEY CITY, N.J. PUBLIC LIBRARIES–Collns. 2:45
JERUSALEM INFIRMARY, 1749. 7217
JERVISE, Andrew, 1820–78–Libr. 2961
JESSE, George Richard, 1820–98. 7089
JESSEL, Frederic, 1859– –Libr. 7251
JESSEY, Henry, 1601–63. 708
JEST BOOKS. **7464–6**
— Bibs. 1:**1757–9**
— Collns. 7464
JESUIT BOOKS–Bibs. 1:**2265–6a**
JEVON, Thomas, 1652–88. **11363–4**
— Bibs. 1:**3827**
— *Devil of a wife.* 11363–4
— *Devil to pay*–Bibs. 1:**3827**
JEWEL, bp. John, 1522–71. **11365–8**
— *Apology of private mass.* 11367

Vol. 1 = *Bibliographies*   2 = *Shakespeare*   4 = 1–8221   5 = 8222–14616

JEWEL, bp. John, 1522–71. *Certain sermons.* 3152
— Libr. 11365
— Mss. 11366 11368
JEWISH BOOKS *see also* JEWISH LITERATURE; PRINTING IN HEBREW; SHAKESPEARE, William, 1564–1616– WORKS IN HEBREW; – WORKS IN ISRAEL; TYPEFACES–Hebrew. 7467–9
— Collns. 2855 3074
— Newspapers–Bibs. 1:1861
JEWISH HISTORICAL SOCIETY OF ENGLAND. MOCATTA LIBRARY. 3047
JEWISH LITERATURE–Bibs. 1:1861 4872
JEWITT, Llewellyn Frederick William, 1816–86. 2:1030
JEWITT, Thomas Orlando Sheldon, 1799–1869. 4922
JEWS' COLLEGE, London *see* LONDON. UNIVERSITY. JEWS' COLLEGE.
JEWS IN LITERATURE–Bibs. 1:2197x–9c
JINKABOUT MILL, Midloth. 1712
JOACHIM, Harold Henry, 1869–1938–Bibs. 1:3827c
JOANNES DE GIGLIIS, fl.1478–98. 6971
JOANNES SULPITIUS, 15th cent. *see* SULPITIUS, Joannes, Verulanus, 15th cent.
JOBBING PRINTING *see* PRINTING, JOBBING.
JOHANNESBURG. PUBLIC LIBRARY– Collns. 1:1232
JOHANNES PECHAM, fl.1279–92 *see* PECHAM, John, fl.1279–92.
JOHN, John, 1698–1770. 11369
— *Miscellaneous observations upon authors.* 11369
JOHN BULL. 7825 7894
JOHN BULL'S BIBLE *see* BIBLE–Versions– John Bull's.
JOHNES, Thomas, Hafod, 1748–1816. 4923–7
JOHNISTOUN, Patrick, fl.1450?–Bibs. 1:3828
JOHN OF BORDEAUX–Ms. 7170 7175
JOHN OF GADDESDEN, 1280?–1361. 11370–1
— Bibs. 1:3827k
— *Rosa Anglica.* 11370–1
— — Bibs. 1:3827k
JOHN O'LONDON'S WEEKLY. 14010
JOHN RYLANDS LIBRARY, Manchester. 62 2495 2499 2552–3 2570 2648
— Collns. 1:326 336–7 429 458 460 498 1472–3 1481–2 3841b 4223; 2:193 339; 550 1780 3295 3314a 6894 6993 8052 9969 10173 11284 11417 13119 13121
JOHNSON, Alfred Forbes, fl.1922–70. 67a
— Bibs. 1:3828a

JOHNSON, Charles, fl.1724–36–Bibs. 1:3829
JOHNSON, Esther, 1681–1728–Handwr. 13729
JOHNSON, James, Edinburgh, d.1811. 4929
JOHNSON, John, d.1747. 11506
JOHNSON, John, 1777–1848. 4930
— *Typographia.* 4930
JOHNSON, John de Monins, Oxford, 1881–1956. 4931 5353
JOHNSON, Joseph, 1738–1809. 3639a 4932–3
JOHNSON, Lionel Pigot, 1867–1902. 11372
— Bibs. 1:3830
— *Complete poems.* 11372
— Text. 11372
JOHNSON, Michael, Lichfield, 1657–1732. 3622 4934–7
JOHNSON, Norman Croom-, fl.1921–Libr. 11778
JOHNSON, R., fl.1510–Libr. 3133
JOHNSON, Richard, 1734–93. 4938
— Bibs. 1:3831
JOHNSON, Robert, fl.1600–12.
— *Traveller's breviate.* 8206
JOHNSON, Samuel, 1709–84 *see also THE RAMBLER.* 2:735 783 790 795; 482 731 778 2299 3475 3532 3535 8557 9503 11373–525
— *Ascham's Schoolmaster.* 11492
— *Beauties of Johnson.* 11438
— Bibs. 1:402 3832–54
— Bksllng. 11482 11500
— Collns. 2360 2990 3039 3188 3380a 4178 11395 11417 11427 11432–3 11436 11460 11465 11518
— *Crousaz on Pope.* 11430 11466
— *Dictionary.* 2:775 781; 2309 5796 11400 11412 11443 11463 11476 11478 11488 11491 11497 11512 11515 13010
— *False alarm.* 11428 11483 11496
— Handwr. 11477
— *Harleian miscellany.* 11486
— *History of the council of Trent.* 11501 11506
— *The idler.* 11405 11457 11510
— *Journey to the Western Islands.* 11383 11386–7 11415 11419 11449 11474 11487 11511 11514
— Letters. 5097 11373 11375 11379 11391 11393–4 11410 11417 11435 11442 11445–6 11450–3 11513
— — Bibs. 1:3841 3842b 3844 3850f
— Libr. 2:504 727; 276 1683 11374 11384 11399 11402 11409 11420 11454–6 11458 11472 11493 11495 11498–9
— *Life of Blake.* 11434
— *Life of Goldsmith.* 11424

JONES, Thomas, Denbigh, 1756–1820 see also JONES AND COMPANY, Bala, 1803–4. **11534**
— Bibs. 1:**1347b**
— Mss. 11534
JONES, Thomas, c.1820–1913?–Bibs. 1:**3860**
JONES, Thomas, 1870–1955. 4802
JONES, Thomas Gwynn, 1871–1949–Bibs. 1:**3861**
JONES, William, fl.1587–1626. **4944**
— Bibs. 1:**1347d**
JONES AND COMPANY, Bala, 1803–4. 11534
JONES, sir William, 1566–1640. 1517
JONES, sir William, 1746–94–Bibs. 1:**3862**
JONES, William Henry, fl.1889–1922. **11535**
— *Brief account of Foxwist.* 11535
JONES'S EVENING NEWS-LETTER. 4519
JONSON, Benjamin, 1573?–1637. 2:943 1981; 9375 **11536–84**
— *The alchemist.* 11557 11579
— *Art of poetry.* 11567
— *Bartholomew fair.* 11582
— Bibs. 1:1597 **3863–7**
— *Case is altered.* 11575
— *Catiline.* 11576
— Collns. 11564
— *Cynthia's revels.* 11574
— *English grammar.* 11536
— *Epicœne.* 11538 11541 11559
— *Every man out of his humour.* 6350 11540 11548 11550 11565
— *Fountain of self-love.* 11562
— *Gypsies metamorphosed.* 11555 11558 11560
— *Hymn to God.* 11576
— *King's entertainment.* 11571
— Libr. 11539 11547 11551 11572 11583
— *Masque of augurs.* 11576
— Mss. 11544
— *Pleasure reconciled to virtue.* 11568
— *Poetaster.* 11580
— Ptg. 6350 11571 11579
— *Sejanus.* 11538 11563 11580
— *Shakespeare First folio.* 2:534 951
— Text. 8471 11540 11546 11552 11557–8 11560 11563 11565 11569–70 11573–4 11580
— *Timber.* 11549
— *Volpone.* 11537
— *Works.* 2:472 843b; 11540 11542–5 11554 11556 11561 11573
JORDAN, Thomas, 1612?–85. **11585–7**
— *Money is an ass.* 11585
— Mss. 11586–7
— Ptg. 11585
JORDANUS NEMORARIUS, fl.1230. 1555
JOSEPH, Horace William Brindley, 1867–1943–Bibs. 1:**3869**

JOSEPHUS, Flavius, 37–c.98. 11975
JOSIPPON see *YOSIPPON.*
JOURNAL OF AUCTIONS AND SALES. 7846
JOURNAL POLITIQUE ET LITTERAIRE D'ANGLETERRE. 7776
JOYCE, James Augustine, 1882–1941. **11588–625**
— Bibs. 1:1597 **3870–91**
— Collns. 1:3879ah; 11592 11594 11599 11603 11618
— *Dubliners.* 11606 11615
— *Exiles.* 11610–1
— *Finnegan's wake.* 11589 11593 11596 11601 11605 11613
— — Bibs. 1:3886
— Handwr. 11602
— Letters. 11607
— Libr. 11595
— Mss. 11593 11603 11607 11610–11
— — Bibs. 1:3879ah 3885 3890
— *Portrait of the artist.* 11612 11619
— Ptg. 11608 11619
— Publ. 5529 11605 11621
— Text. 11589 11596 11598 11600–1 11606 11609 11612–15 11623–4
— *Ulysses.* 11588 11590 11597–8 11600 11604 11608–9 11620–5
JOYE, George, d.1553. 6873
— *Horstius' Garden of the soul.* 8065–7
JOYFUL RECEIVING OF JAMES VI, 1590. 615
JOYNSON William, St. Mary Cray, fl.1839–60. 3757
JUDSON, Thomas, fl.1581–1600. 6683
JUGGE, Richard, fl.1531–77? 3091 **4945–6**
— Bibs. 1:1366
JUNIUS, *pseud.* 5192 **11626–41**
— Bibs. 1:**3895–900a**
— Collns. 11632 11638 11640
— Handwr. 11626–7
— Illus. 11635
JUNIUS, Franciscus, 1589–1677. **11642–6**
— *Cædmonis monachi paraphrasis.* 11643–6
— *Chaucer.* 11642
— Ms. 11642
JUPP, Edward Basil, 1812–77–Libr. 4038
JUPP, Ralph Tennyson, fl.1922–Libr. 1:3068p 3070f; 10019 10141
JUSTICE, Henry, fl.1716–63–Libr. 3135
JUSTIFICATION. 6183
JUVENILE DRAMA see DRAMA, JUVENILE.
JUVENILE LITERATURE see CHILDREN'S BOOKS.
JUVENILE LITERATURE see CHILDREN'S LITERATURE; DRAMA, JUVENILE
JUVENILE LIBRARY. 6999

KALEIDOSCOPE, THE. 7924
KALM, Pehr, 1716–79. 12967
KALTHOEBER, Christian Samuel, fl.1782–1817. **4947**
KANE, GRENVILLE, 1854–1943–Libr. 531
KANSAS. STATE UNIVERSITY, Lawrence. LIBRARY–Collns. 2:1124
— UNIVERSITY. LIBRARIES–Collns. 1:2196 3427 3881 4865 5202 5206; 3307 4041 7969 8023 8181 10795 11594 12611 12982 13852
KARSLAKE, Frank, 1851–1920. **4948**
KASTNER, J. Const., fl.1853. **11647**
KASTNER, Leon Emile, fl.1903–36.
— *Drummond's Poems.* 10336
KAVANAGH, Patrick Joseph Gregory, 1931––Bibs. 1:**3900d**
KAY, Arthur, d.1939–Libr. 2872
KAYE-SMITH, Sheila, 1887–1956 *see* SMITH, Sheila Kaye-, 1887–1956.
KEACH, Benjamin, 1640–1704. 4835b
KEAN, Charles John, 1811?–68. 7229
KEAN, Edmund, 1787–1833–Libr. 2:1480
KEANE, Augustus Henry, 1833–1912–Bibs. 4:**3901–2**
KEARNEY, William, Dublin, fl.1571–97. **4949**
KEARSLEY, George, fl.1758–97.
— *Beauties of Johnson.* 11438
KEATE, George, 1729–97–Bibs. 1:**3903**
KEATING, Geoffrey, 1570?–1644?
— Bibs. 1:**3903m**
— *Foundation of knowledge on Ireland.* 1756 1765
— *History of Ireland*–Bibs. 1:**3903m**
KEATING, George T., 1892– –Libr. 1:2868; 9656
KEATING SOCIETY, fl.1863? 6442
KEATS, John, 1795–1821. 2322 7243 **11648–98** 13005
— *La belle dame.* 11669 11672
— Bibs. 1:54–5 672 **3902a–10**
— Bksllng. 11658
— Collns. 3039 3045 11662
— *Endymion.* 11696
— *Eve of St. Agnes.* 11689 11697
— *Eve of St. Mark.* 11648–9
— *Fill for me a brimming bowl.* 11688
— Handwr. 516 11693
— *Hyperion.* 11671 11673 11680
— *In a drear-nighted December.* 11655 11667 11686
— *I stood tip-toe.* 11681 11695
— *Lamia.* 11690
— Letters. 3045 7338 11663 11677
— Libr. 11650–1 11659 11666 11674 11694
— *Lines on the Mermaid tavern.* 11648–9

— Mss. 780 11648–9 11652 11654 11656 11660 11669 11671 11673 11679 11681 11683 11685–6 11688 11692 11695
— — Bibs. 1:3911
— *O come dearest Emma.* 11688
— *Ode on a Grecian urn.* 11684 11692
— *Ode to a nightingale.* 11687
— *O solitude.* 11688
— *Poems.* 2342 11668
— *Pot of basil.* 11648–9
— Publ. 5226 5822 11676 11684
— Sonnets. 11682
— *Teignmouth.* 11664
— Text. 11655 11664 11667 11671 11673 11675 11680 11687 11692 11697
KEATS MUSEUM, Hampstead. 13008
KEATS-SHELLEY MEMORIAL HOUSE, Rome. LIBRARY–Collns. 1:676 2020–1
KEBLE, John 1792–1866. **11699–701**
— Bibs. 1:**3915**
— *Christian year.* 11699–701
— Mss. 11699
KEDERMINSTER, sir John, 1586–1631. 2611
KEELE HALL, Staffordshire–Libr. *see* SNEYD, Walter, 1809–88–Libr.
KEELING, William, d.1620. **11702–4**
KEENE, Charles Samuel, 1823–91. 3496 7420a
— Bibs. 1:**3916**
KEEPSAKE PRESS, Richmond, Surrey, est. 1951. **4950–1**
— Bibs. 1:**3347r**
KEEPSAKES. 7246 7879
KEGAN PAUL, TRENCH, TRÜBNER, fl.1883–1941. 5564a
KEITH, sir Arthur, 1866–1955–Bibs. 1:**3916m–n**
KELE, Richard, fl.1546–52. **4952** 6056
— *Christmas carols.* 4952
KELLETT, Edward, fl.1608–41–Bibs. 1:**3917**
KELLEY AND SONS, fl.1770–1911. **4953–4**
KELLY, Thomas, 1772–1855. 1294
KELLY, Thomas Hughes, 1865–1933–Libr. 2940
KELMSCOTT MANOR, Lechlade. 4993
KELMSCOTT PRESS, Hammersmith, 1891–8. 752 760 **4955–5005** 5527 6057 6083 6086 6088 6099 6103 6114 6142 6319 6323 6475–6 6488 6490 6492 6502 12525 12533
— Bibs. 1:401 1245f **1347x–55** 4298 4301
— *Chaucer's Works.* 4974 4978 4990 4995 6610
— Mss. 4989
— *Rossetti's Hand and soul.* 4992
— Type. 4970 4982 4994 6098 6610 6637

KELSO, Roxb. **1741**
— Librs. 1633 1741
— Ptg. 3887
KEMBLE, Frances Anne (mrs. Pierce Butler), 1809–93. 5250
KEMBLE, John Mitchell, 1807–57–Bibs. 1:**3918**
KEMPE, Adrian van Boukhout, Antwerp, fl.1536–7. 834
KEMPE, William, fl.1580–93–Bibs. 1:**3919**
KEMPIS, Thomas à see THOMAS À KEMPIS, 1380–1471.
KENDAL, Westm.
—Bksllng. see ASHBURNER, Anthony, fl.1763–8.
— GRAMMAR SCHOOL. LIBRARY. 2590
KENDALL, George, 1610–63–Bibs. 1:**3920**
KENDALL, John, fl.1476. 6971
KENDALL, William, 1768–1832. **11705**
— Poems. 11705
KENDRICK, Matthew, fl.1675–Libr. 14215
KENEALY, Edward Vaughan, 1819–80–Bibs. 1:**3920m**
KENNALL VALE, Cornw.–Paper. 1083b
KENNEDY, James, fl.1663. **11706**
— Æneas Britannicus. 11706
KENNEDY, James, fl.1758. **11707**
— New description of the pictures. 11707
KENNEDY, James, fl.1920?–Bibs. 1:**3921**
KENNEDY, Walter, 1460?–1508?–Bibs. 1:**3922**
KENNETT, bp. White, 1660–1728–Libr. 2724 3266
KENNY, Courtney Stanhope, 1847–1930–Bibs. 1:**3923**
KENRICK, William, 1725?–79. **11708**
KENSINGTON, London see LONDON. KENSINGTON.
KENT. **1151–61b**
— Bibs. 1:**900–1**
— Maps. 7498 7515
— Newspapers. 1152
— Paper see also DICKINSON, George, Charlton, fl.1834; HARRIS, Richard, fl.1738; HOLLINGWORTH'S, fl.1830; JOYNSON, William, St. Mary Cray, fl.1839–60; NASH FAMILY, St. Mary Cray, fl.1765–1949; WHATMAN, James, 1702–59; WHATMAN, James, 1741–98. 1155–6 1158 1158g 1161–a 3737 3772 3778 3891 3975 5256 5972 5975
KENT, William, 1684?–1748. **5006–7**
KENTISH MASTER PAPER MAKERS, 1803. 3891
KENTISH POST. 1152 1159
KENTISH TOWN see LONDON. KENTISH TOWN.

KENT STATE UNIVERSITY, Ohio. LIBRARY–Collns. 10936
KENTUCKY. UNIVERSITY. LIBRARY–Collns. 1:1543
KENYON, sir Frederick George, 1863–1952–Bibs. 1:**3923d**
KEPIER SCHOOL, Houghton-le-Spring. LIBRARY. 2638
— — Collns. 566
KER, John, 3d duke of Roxburgh, 1740–1804–Libr. 2314 2354 4131
KER, William Paton, 1855–1923–Bibs. 1:**3923h**
KERN, Jerome David, 1885–1945–Libr. 1:400; 2354 2863 2867 3649 10051
KERR, Lowell, fl.1965–Libr. 1:**4858**
KERR, Philip Henry, 11th marquess of Lothian, 1882–1940–Libr. 2898–9 2906–7
KERRY–Bibs. 1:**1087d–9**
KESSLER, Harry Klemens Ulrich, graf von, 1868–1937. 6645
KETTNER'S BOOK OF THE TABLE, 1877. 9790
KEW. ROYAL BOTANIC GARDENS see ROYAL BOTANIC GARDENS, Kew.
KEW, James, fl.1834–93. 5008
KEW GARDENS see ROYAL BOTANIC GARDENS, Kew.
KEYMER, John, fl.1584–1622.
— Observations touching trade. 12944
KEYNES, sir Geoffrey Langdon, 1887– . 68 3352a 7566
— Bibs. 1:**3923m–n**
— Libr. 1:369; 3348
KEYNES, John Maynard, 1st baron Keynes, 1883–1946.
— Bibs. 1:**3923q**
— Libr. 3068 12584
KEYNOTE SERIES. 5038a
— Bibs. 1:1722
KHULL, Edward, Glasgow, 1767–1844. 4746
KICKHAM, Charles Joseph, 1826–82. **11709**
KILBURN, William, 1745–1818. 6958a
KILDARE–Bibs. 1:1090
— Paper. 3756
KILDARE PLACE SOCIETY, Dublin, est. 1811. **5009**
KILHAM, Hannah (Spurr), 1774–1832. **11710**
KILKENNY. **1950–3**
— Bibs. 1:**1091–3** 1128
— Ptg. 1950–4 5685
— — Bibs. 1:**1091–3** 1128
KILLARNEY, co. Kerry–Bibs. 1:**1087d**
KILLIGREW, Thomas, 1612–83. 3499 **11711**
— Bibs. 1:**3924**
— Comedies and tragedies. 11711

KILLIGREW, sir William, 1606–95. **11712**
— *Siege of Urbin.* 11712
KILLILEA, John, Waterford, fl.1839–79. **5010**
KILLINEY, co. Dublin. FRANCISCAN LIBRARY–Collns. 1:2064
KILMARNOCK, Ayr. **1670**
— Librs. 1633
— Ptg. *see* WILSON, John, fl.1759–1821.
— MACKIE BURNSIANA LIBRARY *see* MACKIE BURNSIANA LIBRARY, Kilmarnock.
KILMARNOCK MIRROR AND LITERARY GLEANER. 1670
KILRUSH, co. Clare–Bibs. 1:**1046**
— Ptg.–Bibs. 1:1046
KILTIPPER, co. Dublin. **1945**
— Paper. 1945
KIMBER, Edward, 1719–69. **11713**
— *Relation of a late expedition.* 11713
KIMBER, Isaac, 1692–1755. 11713
KINCAID, Alexander, Edinburgh, 1711–77. 8557
KINCARDINESHIRE–Bibs. 1:981
— Librs. *see* FETTERCAIRN HOUSE.
— Newspapers. 5926
KINCARDINESHIRE ALMANAC. 5926
KINDER, Martin, fl.1913. 5931
KING, Alexander Hyatt, fl.1945–55. 7617
KING, George, Aberdeen, 1797–1872. 1639
— Libr. 1:1961
KING, bp. Henry, 1592–1669. **11714–15**
— Bibs. 1:**3924s**
— Mss. 10265 11714–15
KING, Henry Samuel, 1817–78. 5680
KING, Jonathan, fl.1948–Libr. 7041
KING, Josiah, fl.1648–98–Bibs. 1:**3925**
KING, Nicholas, Dublin, fl.1715. 5403
KING, Peter, 1st baron King of Ockham, 1669–1734–Libr. 12016a 12024–5 12027 12032
KING, Peter, 7th baron King of Ockham, 1776–1833–Bibs. 1:4069b
— Mss.–Bibs. 1:4069b
KING, Robert, fl.1926–9. 4864 4866
KING, William, 1624–80.
— *Poems of mr. Cowley composed.* 9694
KING, William, 1663–1712. **11716–17**
— *Fairy feast.* 11716
— *Miscellanies in prose and verse.* 11717
KING, William, 1685–1763–Bibs. 1:**3926**
KINGDOM'S INTELLIGENCER. 7658
KING EDWARD VI SCHOOL, Bury St. Edmunds *see* BURY ST. EDMUNDS. KING EDWARD VI SCHOOL.
KING LEIR. 2:396 1200 1428
KINGSALE, Gerald, 24th baron Kingsale, d.1762–Libr. 2213

KING'S CABINET OPENED, 1645. 7948
KINGS CLIFFE, Northants.–Librs. 2856
KINGSLAND, William G., d.1933. 14451
KINGSLEY, Charles, 1819–75. 784 **11718–23**
— *American notes.* 11722
— Bibs. 1:**3927–30**
— Bndg. 2014a
— Collns. 11720–3
— *Glaucus.* 11719
— Libr. 11718
— Mss. 11721 11723
— *Water babies.* 2014a
KINGSLEY, Darwin P., fl.1942–Libr. 2:295
KINGSLEY, Henry, 1830–76. **11724–5**
— Bibs. 1:**3931–2**
— *Geoffrey Hamlyn.* 11724
— *Mademoiselle Mathilde.* 11725
— *Meerschaum.* 7294
KING'S NORTON, Worcs.–Libs. 2464 2512
KING'S PRESS, Ireland. 1816
—, Perth. 1733
—, Shrewsbury. 1385 1387 3892
KING'S PRINTERS *see also individual printers, e.g.* BARKER, Christopher, fl.1640–80; BILL, John, 1576–1630; STRAHAN, William, 1715–85; WATSON, James, Edinburgh, 1664?–1722. 6082 6110 6144
KING'S PRINTING HOUSE. **5011–15**
KING'S SCHOOL, Canterbury *see* CANTERBURY. KING'S SCHOOL.
KING'S STATIONERS IN IRELAND. 1820 5403
KINGSTON, Ont. QUEEN'S UNIVERSITY. DOUGLAS LIBRARY–Collns. 1:2600
KINGSTON, Felix, 1597–1651. 8735
KINGSTON, William Henry Giles, 1814–80.
— Bibs. 1:**3933**
— Collns. 7322a
KINNEAR, Samuel, Edinburgh, fl.1816–1902. **5016**
KINROSS-SHIRE–Bibs. 1:996x-y
KINSELLA, Thomas, fl.1954–Bibs. 1:**3933d**
KIPLING, John Lockwood, 1837–1911. **5017–18**
KIPLING, Rudyard, 1865–1936. 474 766 786 **11726–90** 14387
— *Actions and reactions.* 477
— Bibs. 1:652 662 684 3586 **3934–62**
— Bndg. 11759
— *Book of the forty-five mornings.* 11766
— *City of dreadful night.* 11730
— Collns. 11728 11748 11759 11762 11764–5 11768 11772 11774–9 11782–4 11786 11789–90 13982
— *Departmental ditties.* 11771
— *Echoes.* 11780
— *Five nations.* 762
— Illus. 11749

KUNHOLT, Gabriel, fl.1677. **5028**
KUNZ, Siegried, fl.1863–89. 9419a
KYD, *pseud., see* CLARKE, Joseph Clayton, fl.1888–1912.
KYD, Thomas, 1557?–95? *see also MURDER OF JOHN BREWEN, 1592.* **11797–803**
— Bibs. 1:1597 **3968z–9a**
— *First part of Jeronimo.* 11799
— Handwr. 2:1892; 11800
— Ptg. 11803
— *Shakespeare's Hamlet.* 2:1180
— *Solyman and Perseda.* 7117 11802
— *Spanish tragedy.* 2:1200; 11797 11801 11803
— — Bibs. 1:3982
— Text. 11798–9
KYNASTON, sir Francis, 1587–1642.
— Mss. 9417
— *Troilus and Cressida.* 9417
KYNGSTON, Felix, fl.1597–1651 *see* KINGSTON, Felix, fl.1597–1651.

LABELS, BOOK *see also* BOOKPLATES. 2370 2375 3193 6310 9730
—, BOOKBINDERS'. 2097 2125
—, BOOKSELLERS'. 1099 4607 4899
—, LIBRARY–Bibs. 1:1189a
—, TITLE. 6295 6307 11158
LABOUR. 1165 3453 3758–9 3761a 3765 3768 5131 5333 5614 6145
LABOUR UNIONS *see* TRADE UNIONS.
LA CAVA. 798
LACE–Bibs. 1:1979m
LACKINGTON, James, 1746–1815. 3620 3639a 3659 **5029–34a** 6523
LA CROSE, Jean Cornand de, fl.1681–93. 4606
LADIES MERCURY. 7673
LADY MILL, Mounton. 1298a
LADY'S MAGAZINE. 7744 9739
— Bibs. 1:4259
LAFONTAINE, Jean de, 1621–95. 904
LAHEE (printer), fl.1823. 8598
LAID PAPER *see* PAPER, LAID.
LAING, David, 1793–1878. 23 11325 **11804**
— Bibs. 1:**3970**
— *Scott's Poems.* 11804
LAIR, Johann, Cambridge, fl.1521–2 *see* SIBERCH, John (Johann Lair), Cambridge, fl.1521–2.
LAMARTINE, Alphonse de, 1790–1869–Bibs. 1:**812**
LAMB, lady Caroline, 1785–1828. 5250
LAMB, Charles, 1775–1834. 474 477 4885 5091 7000a **11805–59** 13545
— *Album verses.* 11830
— *Beauty and the beast.* 7016

— Bibs. 1:661 **3971–85**
— *Book of the ranks* see *BOOK OF THE RANKS ... OF BRITISH SOCIETY, 1805.*
— Collns. 2386 3039 11825 11834–5 11838–9 11847–9 11856
— *Companionship.* 11838
— *Confessions of a drunkard.* 11807
— *Essays of Elia.* 471 2342 11806 11818 11832 11842
— Illus. 11828 11859
— *In the album of Orkney.* 11827
— *John Woodvil.* 11805
— *King and queen of hearts.* 11813 11823 11828
— *Last essays of Elia.* 11817 11831 11842
— *Letters.* 11841 11845
— Libr. 1:**3974**; 11808–9 11816 11818–19 11834 11837 11840 11848
— *Mrs. Leicester's school.* 11846
— Mss. 780 11807 11826 11832 11838 11843 11847 11852
— — Bibs. 1:3980d 3981 3982g 3984
— *Poetical pieces.* 11849
— *Poetry for children.* 11810
— Ptg. 11831
— Publ. 5226 5315 11829–30 11850
— *Quaker's meeting.* 11844
— *Specimens of English dramatic writers.* 11829 11858
— *Tales from Shakespeare.* 1:**3985**; 11850 11855
— — Bibs. 1:3985
— Text. 11811 11845 11858
— *To a young lady.* 11814
— *Witches and other night fears.* 11843
— *Works.* 11836
LAMB, John, d.1822.
— *Letter to Windham.* 11809
LAMB, Mary Ann, 1764–1847. 4752 7000a
— Publ. 5226
LAMBARDE, William, 1536–1601. **11860**
— *Archaionomia.* 2:1038–42 1044 1046
— *Archeion.* 11860
— Libr. 2924 7152a
— Mss. 11860
LAMBE, sir John, 1566?–1647–Libr. 3396a
LAMBERT, Aylmer Bourke, 1761–1842.
— *Description of the genus pinus.* 6948
LAMBERT, mrs. Gerard B. 8624
LAMBERT, Richard Stanton, 1894– *see* STANTON PRESS, Wembley Hill, 1921–4.
LAMBERT, Samuel Waldron, 1859–1942–Libr. 14222
LAMBERT, William Harrison, 1842–1912–Libr. 1:4915
LAMBETH, London. *see* LONDON. LAMBETH.
LAMB HOUSE, Rye, Sussex–Libr. 11348

Vol. **1** = *Bibliographies*   **2** = *Shakespeare*   **4** = 1–8221   **5** = 8222–14616

LAMBOURN, Peter Spendelowe, 1722–74–Bibs. 1:**3990**
LAMBTON, John Frederick, 5th earl of Durham, 1884–1970–Libr. see LAMBTON CASTLE, Durham.
LAMBTON CASTLE, Durham–Libr. 2905
LAMPORT HALL, Northants.–Libr. 2536 3086 3386
LAMPSON, Frederick Locker-, 1821–95. 2741 **11861–6**
— Bibs. 1:**3991**
— Collns. 11865
— Libr. 1:493–4; 2354 2615 2741
— *Lyra elegantiarum.* 11863–4 11866
— Paper. 11864
LANARKSHIRE. **1685–94a**
— Bibs. 1:**1002–4**
— Paper see CRAIG, Robert, Airdrie, est. 1820.
LANCASHIRE. **1162–83**
— Bibs. 1:**902–11**
— Directories–Bibs. 1:903a
— Librs. see also CARTMEL PRIORY. 1162
— Maps. 7486 7495 7530
— — Bibs. 1:**1791–3**
— Newspapers. 1163 5856
— — Bibs. 1:1854 1862
— Paper. 1164–5 3734a
— Ptg.–Bibs. 1:903
LANCASHIRE INDEPENDENT COLLEGE. LIBRARY. 3072
LANCASHIRE JOURNAL. 5856
LANCASTER, Lancs.
— Bksllng. see HOPKINS, Christopher, d.1742.
— Maps. 7492
LANCASTER, Joseph, 1778–1838. **11867**
LANDEY, William, fl.1681. **5035**
LANDOR, Robert Eyres, 1781–1869. 809
— *Dun cow.* 11883
— *Guy's porridge pot.* 809 11870 11883
LANDOR, Walter Savage, 1775–1864. 10586 **11868–95** 13941
— Bibs. 1:**3992–7**
— Collns. 11884 11894
— *Diana de Poictiers.* 11893
— *Gebir.* 11891
— *Heroic idylls.* 11877
— *Imaginary conversations.* 11889 11895
— *Letters by Calvus.* 11869
— Libr. 11890
— Mss. 11878–9
— — Bibs. 1:3995
— *Offerings to Buonaparte.* 11888
— *Poet's dream.* 11878
— Publ. 11874 11877 11880 11887 11889 11895
— *Remarks on a suit.* 11879

— *Sponsalia Polyxenae.* 11881
— Text. 11868 11871 11876
— *Warwickshire talents.* 11892
LANDSEER, sir Edwin Henry, 1802–73. 9983
LANE, John, 1854–1925 see also BODLEY HEAD PRESS, est. 1887. **5036–8a** 5163
— Bibs. 1:1722
— Libr. 5036
LANE, JOHN AND CO., NEW YORK. 11229
LANE, William, 1738–1814 see also MINERVA PRESS, 1790–1820. 5196–7 5199
LANE, sir William Arbuthnot, 1856–1943–Bibs. 1:**4000–1**
LANG, Andrew, 1844–1912. 2:58; **11896–902**
— Bibs. 1:**4002–6**
— Collns. 11901
— *Fairy book stories.* 11896
— *He.* 11899
— *Lines on the Shelley society.* 11902
LANGBAINE, Gerard, 1656–92. **11903**
— *New catalogue.* 2:1369
— Publ. 11903
LANGHAM, William, fl.1597.
— *Garden of health.* 7367
LANGLEY FAMILY, Shrop.–Libr. 3043
LANGLEY MARISH, Bucks.–Librs. 2611
LANGSTROTH, Charles, fl.1960–Libr. 1:3098c
LANGTON, Robert, 1493–1524. **11904**
— *Pilgrimage.* 11904
LANGUAGE see also CONCORDANCES; DICTIONARIES; GRAMMARS; RHETORIC; SHORTHAND; SPELLING-BOOKS; STYLE. 14264
— Bibs. 1:2201–4
LANSDOWNE, George Granville, baron, 1666–1735 see GRANVILLE, George, baron Lansdowne, 1666–1735.
LANSDOWNE, sir William Petty, 1st marquis of, 1737–1805 see PETTY, sir William, 1st marquis of Lansdowne, 1737–1805.
LANSTON, Tolbert, 1844–1913. 6123
LANSTON MONOTYPE CORPORATION, est. 1897. 5217
LANT, Richard, fl.1537–58. 6056
LANTEGLOS BY FOWEY, Cornw.–Paper. 1083b
LARDNER, Dionysius, 1793–1859–Bibs. 1:1530
— *Cabinet cyclopaedia.* 7245
LARGE PAPER COPIES. 6231 6234–5 6239 10326 10328 11024
LARKING, Bartholomew, Youghal, fl.1638. **5039**

LARK MILL, Mounton. 1298a
LARNER, William, fl.1641–59. 6067
— Bibs. 1:595a
LA ROCHEFOUCAULD, François, duc de, 1613–80. 9854a
LARPENT, John, 1741–1824. 3499 7219–20a 11987
— Libr. 1:1633d–f 1635c
LARRISON, Earl, fl.1967–Libr. 1:4614
LASCELLES, Rowley, 1770–1841. 11905
LASKI, Harold Joseph, 1893–1950–Bibs. 1:4006d
LASLEY, Thomas, Hereford, fl.1687. 5040
LASSELS, Richard, 1603?–68–Bibs. 4006g
— Voyage of Italy–Bibs. 1:4006g
LASSO, Orlando di, d.1594. 5899
LASSWADE, Midloth.
— Bksllng. 1716
— Paper. 1712
LAST SPEECH OF GERALD BYRNE, 1780–1. 1987
LATHBURY, John, fl.1350. 1371
LATIMER, bp. Hugh, 1485?–1555. 11906
— Seven sermons. 11906
LATIMER, William Thomas, d.1919–Bibs. 1:4006t
LATIN GRAMMARS see GRAMMARS, LATIN.
LATIN LITERATURE see ANGLO-LATIN LITERATURE; FOREIGN BOOKS PUBLISHED IN BRITAIN–Classical-Latin; PRINTING IN LATIN.
LATIN, PLACENAMES IN see PLACE-NAMES IN LATIN.
LAUD, archbp. William, 1573–1645. 3433 3502 3574 4660 11907–11
— Bibs. 1:1514 4007
— Libr. 2266 11910
— Summary of devotions. 11908
LAUDER, sir Thomas Dick, 1784–1848–Bibs. 1:4008
LAUDER, William, d.1771. 5574 7333 7338
— Delectus auctorum sacrorum Miltono. 3550
LAUDERDALE, John Maitland, 2d earl and 1st duke of, 1616–82 see MAITLAND, John, 2d earl and 1st duke of Lauderdale, 1616–82.
LAUDERDALE, Richard Maitland, 4th earl of, 1653–95 see MAITLAND, Richard, 4th earl of Lauderdale, 1653–95.
LAURENCE, John, 1668–1732–Bibs. 1:4008a
LAURENTIUS GULIELMUS, 1414?–1503 see GULIELMUS, Laurentius, 1414?–1503.
LAURISTON CASTLE, Edinburgh–Collns. 1:1546
LAUSANNE, Switz. 8480 8481a–2 8488
LAUXIUS, David, fl.1496 see LOWIS, David, fl.1496. 1555

LAVATER, Johann Caspar, 1741–1801–Bibs. 1:845a
LAVEROCK PRESS, fl.1960. 6495
LAVERSTOKE, Hants.
— Paper see also PORTAL, Henri, 1690–1747; PORTAL, John, 1764–1848; PORTAL, Joseph, 1720–93. 1132a
LAVIN, Mary (mrs. W. Walsh, afterward mrs. M. M. Scott), 1912– –Bibs. 1:4008q
LAVIS, Henry James Johnston-, 1856–1914–Bibs. 1:4009
LAW see also BOOK TRADE, LISTS–Law patentees; BRIEFS; STATUTES. 709 1069 1596 7079 7471–9
— Bibs. 1:1265 2209–14d
— Collns. 3194 3343
— Ptg. 1275 5541 7471
LAW AND BIBLIOGRAPHY. 206
LAW, sir Alfred Joseph, 1860–1939–Libr. 2809 8777 8802 9030
LAW, archbp. James, 1560?–1632–Libr. 3297
LAW, John, 1671–1729. 11912–13
LAW, Matthew, fl.1595–1629.
— Shakespeare's Richard 2. 2:1654
LAW, William, 1686–1761. 2856 11914
— Bibs. 1:4009a
— Collns. 11914
LAW AND SHAKESPEARE–Bibs. 2:115
LAWES, Henry, 1596–1662. 2:1974; 11915–16 12341–2
— Airs and dialogues. 11916
— Bibs. 1:4010
LAWES, William, d.1645. 11917–18
— Mss. 11917–18
LAWLER, John, fl.1898–1906–Libr. 3311
LAWLESS, Matthew James, 1837–64. 7420a
LAWRENCE, Kans. STATE UNIVERSITY see KANSAS. STATE UNIVERSITY, Lawrence.
LAWRENCE, David Herbert, 1885–1930. 11919–42
— Bibs. 1:684 1597 4011–24
— Collns. 11922 11924–5 11928–30
— Complete poems. 11937
— Death of a porcupine. 11920
— Kangaroo. 11935 11937
— Lady Chatterley's lover. 11923 11931
— Last poems. 11940
— Letters. 11939
— — Bibs. 1:4023
— Mss. 11922 11924 11926–7 11929–30
— — Bibs. 1:4016e 4016g 4017d 4019 4020c–d 4021
— Odour of chrysanthemums. 11941
— Publ. 4649 11920–1
— The rainbow. 11936 11942
— Text. 11931 11934–5 11937 11940–1
— White peacock. 11921
— Women in love. 11927 11934

LAWRENCE, sir Edwin Durning-, bart., 1837–1914–Libr. 2911 8360
LAWRENCE, George Alfred, 1827–76. 11943
— Bibs. 1:4025
— Collns. 7322a
— Songs of feast. 11943
LAWRENCE, James Henry, 1773–1840. 11944
— Empire of the Nairs. 11944
LAWRENCE, Peter, Dublin, d.1709. 5041
LAWRENCE, Thomas Edward, afterwards Shaw, 1888–1935. 11945–9
— Bibs. 1:4026–8c
— Collns. 11783 11949
— Letters–Bibs. 1:4028
— Mss. 828 11947
— Ptg. 11946
— Revolt in the desert. 11945
— Seven pillars of wisdom. 828 11945–8
LAWRENCE, William John, 1862–1940–Bibs. 1:4028n
LAWS, POOR see POOR LAWS.
LAWSHALL, Suff.–Librs. 1400
LAWSON, Adam Mansfeldt Cardonnel-, d.1820 see De CARDONNEL, Adam Mansfeldt, afterwards Cardonnel-Lawson, d.1820.
LAWSON, Cecil Gordon, 1851–82. 7420a
LAWSON, Francis Wilfred, 1842–1935. 7420a
LAWSON, John, d.1712. 11950
— Bibs. 1:4028a
— Voyage to Carolina. 11950
LAWSON, John, 1723–79.
— Simson's Treatise concerning porisms. 7547
LAWSON, John, fl.1865–1902. 7420a
LAXEY MILL, I.O.M. 1296a
LAY SUBSIDY ROLLS. 3626
LAYTON, Thomas, 1819–1911–Libr. 2771
LAZARUS, George L., fl.1960–Libr. 1:4020; 3195
LEA AND BLANCHARD, Philadelphia, fl.1792–1890. 10187
LEACH, Dryden, fl.1759–63. 5042
LEADENHALL PRESS, 1868–91. 5043
LEADHILLS, Lanark.–Librs. 1633 2459
LEAF, John, fl.1861. 9278
LEAKE, William, fl.1584–1633.
— Shakespeare's Venus and Adonis. 2:1942
LEAKE FAMILY, fl.1660–1764. 5044
LEAMINGTON. PUBLIC LIBRARY–Collns. 2:130
LEAP FROG BIBLE see BIBLE–Versions– 'Leap frog'.
LEAR, Edward, 1812–88. 11951–5
— Bibs. 1:4029–c
— Book of nonsense. 11951–2 11954–5

LEATHER BINDINGS see BOOK-BINDINGS, LEATHER.
LEAVES, BLANK see BLANK LEAVES.
LEAVIS, Frank Raymond, 1895–1978–Bibs. 1:4030
LE BLOND, Abraham, 1819–94. 3963 5045-b 6194
— Bibs. 1:1356–7
LE BLOND, Jacques Christophe, 1670–1740. 6192
LE BLOND AND COMPANY, 1840?–94. 5045 6202
LECHLADE, Glos. KELMSCOTT MANOR see KELMSCOTT MANOR, Lechlade.
LECLERC, Georges Louis, comte de, 1707–88. 908
LECONFIELD, Charles Henry Wyndham, 3d baron, 1872–1952. 2854
LEDBURY, Herefs. 5867
— Maps. 5867
LEDELH, Jacobus, fl.1481–95–Bibs. 1:4030d
LEDESTON PRESS, Mullingar, 1820–53 see LYONS, John Charles, Mullingar, 1792–1874.
LEDGERS, PAPERMAKERS' see PAPER-MAKERS' LEDGERS.
—, PRINTERS' see PRINTERS' LEDGERS.
LEDIARD, Thomas, 1684–1743–Bibs. 1:4030t
LEDWIDGE, Francis, 1891–1917–Bibs. 1:4031–2
LEE, Francis, 1661–1719. 11089
LEE, John, 1779–1859. 11956
— Libr. 3050
— Memorials. 11956
LEE, Nathaniel, 1653?–92. 11957–62
— Bibs. 1:1597 4033–4
— Constantine the great. 11957
— Mithridates. 11960 11962
— Princess of Cleve. 11958
— Publ. 11959
— Text. 11958
LEE, Samuel, Dublin, fl.1677–94. 1907
LEE, Samuel Adams, 1829– . 11275
LEE, sir Sidney, 1859–1926. 2:32 1001
LEE, Vernon, pseud. of Violet Paget, 1856–1935–Bibs. 1:4036
LEECH, John, fl.1623.
— Musæ priores. 9353
LEECH, John, 1817–64. 2297 5046 6192 9983
— Bibs. 1:4037–9
— Dickens' Pickwick papers. 9982
LEEDS, Yorks. 1441
— Bksllng. 1441
— Librs. 1441 3031
— Maps–Bibs. 1:1812

Vol. 1 = Bibliographies   2 = Shakespeare   4 = 1–8221   5 = 8222–14616

LEMPERLEY, Paul, 1858–1939–Libr. 789 2308 2341

LENDING LIBRARIES see LIBRARIES, CIRCULATING.

LENGLET DU FRESNOY, Nicolas, 1674–1755. 4474
— Chronological tables. 11426

LE NEVE, sir William, 1600?–61–Libr. 2971

LENNOX, Charlotte (Ramsay), 1720–1804–Bibs. 1:4045

LENNOX, ld. William Pitt, 1799–1881. 11972
— The tuft-hunter. 11972

LENTON, Francis, fl.1630–40–Bibs. 1:4045d
— Mss.–Bibs. 1:4045d

LENOX, James, 1819–80. 5485

LEON, sir Herbert Samuel, 1850–1926–Libr. 2975

LEOPOLD SHAKESPEARE. 2:711

LEPIDOPTERA see BUTTERFLIES AND MOTHS.

LE ROY, Louise, 1510?–77. 6359

LE SAGE, Alain René, 1668–1747. 13490 13503

LE SAGE, sir John Merry, 1837–1926. 7860

LESLIE, Charles, 1650–1722. 11973–4
— New association. 11974
— Short and easy method. 11973

LESLIE, George, c.1590–1637–Bibs. 1:4046

LE SQUYER, Scipio, 1579–1659–Libr. 3040

LESSING, Gotthold Ephraim, 1729–81–Bibs. 1:822g

LESSON, Henry. 7th earl of Milltown, 1837–91–Libr. 1889

LESTER, Thomas, fl.1816–18. 1207
— Illustrations of London. 1207

L'ESTRANGE, sir Roger, 1616–1704. 7666 11975–6
— Bibs. 1:4047–d
— Dissenter's sayings. 11976
— Josephus' Works. 11975

L'ESTRANGE, Thomas, 1822–1910–Bibs. 1:4047f

LETCHWORTH, Herts.–Ptg. see TEMPLE PRESS, est. 1906.

LETHABY, William Richard, 1857–1931.
— Ernest Gimson. 5634

LETI, Gregorio, 1630–1701. 949

LETTER ... CONCERNING LITERARY PROPERTY, 1769. 3526

LETTER-CUTTERS see TYPEFOUNDERS AND LETTER-CUTTERS.

LETTER PAPER see PAPER, LETTER.

LETTERS see also TEXTUAL CRITICISM AND EDITING–Letters, and under names of particular authors. 492 778–9 847a
— Bibs. 1:363f 363h 374p; 8276 8293 8306 8308 8693 8730 9220 9224 9491 11435

11445 11513 11607 11939 12249 13443 13967 11435 11487
— — Arnold. 2336b 2338a 2343–4
— — Berkeley. 1:2451c
— — Boyle. 1:2517c
— — Browning, E. B. 1:2572
— — Browning. 1:2589d
— — Burke. 1:2621d
— — Byron. 1:2692 2694
— — Carlyle. 1:2711b
— — Chettle. 1:2787d
— — Cobbett. 1:2821b
— — Cowper. 1:2895p
— — Crashawe. 1:2916
— — Curle. 1:2941c
— — Dickens. 1:3066b 3091e 3098c
— — Eliot, T. S. 1:3262
— — Gardiner. 1:3395g
— — Gosse. 1:3479e
— — Hardy. 1:3588b 3604
— — Housman. 1:3718b 3727a
— — Hunt. 1:3765
— — James. 1:3806
— — Johnson. 1:3841 3842b 3844 3850f
— — Lawrence. 1:4023
— — Lawrence, T. E. 1:4028
— — Macaulay. 1:4089a
— — Meredith. 1:4203
— — Minto. 1:4250b
— — Moore, G. A. 1:4270g
— — Nelson. 1:4328
— — Pearson. 1:4404b
— — Rutherford. 1:4561
— — Sayers. 1:4586
— — Scott. 1:4609
— — Scott, J. 1:4589x
— — Shelley. 1:4653
— — Sidney. 1:4689d
— — Southey. 1:4743
— — Tennyson, F. 1:4904
— — Thoresby. 1:4965
— — Watkins. 1:5030e
— — Waugh. 1:5042b–d 5043
— — Wise. 1:5147
— — Woodger. 1:514s
— — Wordsworth, C. 1:5159m
— Collns. 540–1 3055 3227 8032
— Text. 396 8713 9001 9293

LETTERS FROM ELIZA TO YORICK, 1775. 13632

LETTERS OF AN ITALIAN NUN, 1781. 7289

LETTER TO CLARINDA. 9025

LETTER-WRITERS–Bibs. 1:1760–a

LETTOU, John, fl.1480. 5058 6055 6081

LEVELLER BOOKS. 3502

LEVENTHORPE, Thomas, d.1498–Libr. 2879

LEVER, Charles James, 1806–72. 747 831a
11977
— Bibs. 1:**4048**
— *Our mess.* 11977
LEVINGE, Godfrey, Mullingar, fl.1839. 5059
LEVINS, Peter, fl.1587.
— *Manipulus vocabulorum.* 7087
LEVYTT, John, fl.1599.
— *Machiavelli's Discourses.* 948
LEWES, Sussex–Paper. 1412
LEWES, George Henry, 1817–78–Collns. 10429
LEWIN, sir Justinian, 1613–73–Libr. 3396a
LEWIS, Alun, 1915–44–Bibs. 1:**4048b**
LEWIS, Benjamin, d. 1749. **11978**
LEWIS, Benjamin Roland, 1884–1959. 2:1032
LEWIS, Charles, 1786–1836. **5060–1**
LEWIS, Charles George, 1808–80. **5062**
LEWIS, Cecil Day-, 1904–72–Bibs. 1:**4048d**
LEWIS, Clive Staples, 1898–1963. **11979**
— Bibs. 1:**4049–50**
— Mss. 11979
LEWIS, Ellis, fl.1661. **11980**
— *Winterton's Drexel.* 11980
LEWIS, Henry King, 1822–99. **5063–4**
LEWIS, Howell Elvet, 1860–1953–Bibs. 1:**4050g**
LEWIS, John, fl.1740–5. **5065–9**
LEWIS, John Frederick, 1805–76. 6202
LEWIS, Mary G., fl.1823–5.
— *Zelinda.* 11983
LEWIS, Matthew Gregory, 1775–1818. **11981–94**
— Bibs. 1:**4051–2**
— *The monk.* 11982 11984–5 11988 11990–1 11993–4
— — Bibs. 1:**4052–a**
— Mss. 11993–4
— Publ. 11988 11990
— *Tales of terror.* 3884 11981 11986
— *Tales of wonder.* 11986 11992
LEWIS, bp. Owen, 1532–94–Libr. 3346
LEWIS, Percy Wyndham, 1884–1957–Bibs. 1:**4052n–s**
LEWIS, Roy, fl.1957 *see also* KEEPSAKE PRESS, Richmond, Sy., est. 1957. 4950–1
LEWIS, Samuel, d.1862.
— *History of Islington.* 1245
LEWIS, Samuel, d.1865.
— *Topographical dictionary of Wales.* 1531
LEWIS, Stephen, fl.1653–62. 5070–1
LEWIS, Thomas, fl.1653–62. 5070
LEWIS, Walter, Cambridge, 1878–1960. 5215a
— Bibs. 1:879
LEWIS, William, Cardiff, 1833–1920. **5072**
LEWIS, William Luther, 1884–1952–Libr.

2:249 314; 3338
LEWIS, Wilmarth Sheldon, 1895– –Libr. 2374 14184 14195
LEWKENOR, sir Lewis, d.1626. 601
LEWYNGTON, Thomas, fl.1503. **11995**
— *Art of good living.* 11995
LEY, William, fl.1656. 7207
LEYBOURN, Thomas, 1795–1835.
— *Mathematical repository.* 7542
LEYBOURN, William, 1626–1716? **11996**
LEYCESTER, John, fl.1622–39.
— *Enchiridion.* 8073
LEYDEN, John, 1775–1811.
— Bibs. 1:**4053**
— Collns. 3050
— Mss.–Bibs. 1:4053
LEYTON. PUBLIC LIBRARIES–Collns. 1:890
LIBBIS, G. Hilder, fl.1950?–Libr. 11309
LIBERAL, THE. 7817a
LIBRARIANS AS BOOKCOLLECTORS. 2280 2305–6 2371 2383
LIBRARIANSHIP AND BIBLIOGRAPHY. 183 220 237
LIBRARIES. 2281 2352 **2398–3404** 3426
— 1475–1500. 3436
— 1475–1640. 2445
— 1475–1700. 2445 2449
— 1641–1700. 1375 2429 2593 3396a
— 1701–1800. 1361 1375 2431 2435 2437 2450 5199
— 1801–1900. 1546 2443 2454
—, CATHEDRAL *see also* LIBRARIES, DIOCESAN *and individual cathedral libraries, e.g.* BANGOR; CANTERBURY; CARLISLE; CASHEL; CHELMSFORD; DUNDEE; DURHAM; EDINBURGH; EXETER; GLOUCESTER; HEREFORD; LICHFIELD; LINCOLN; LONDON. ST. PAUL'S CATHEDRAL; LONDON. WESTMINSTER ABBEY; NORWICH; RIPON; ROCHESTER; SALISBURY; WATERFORD; WELLS; WINCHESTER; WORCESTER; YORK. 2436 2455 2459 3390a
— Bibs. 1:1760g
— Wales. 2436
—, CATALOGUES *see* CATALOGUES, LIBRARY.
—, CATHOLIC *see* CATHOLICS–Librs.
—, CHAINED. 1097 2021 2399–402 2404–5 2415–16 2419–20 2422–3 2425 2429 2438 2493 2504 2895 2901
— Bibs. 1:560
—, CHURCH *see also* LIBRARIES, PARISH. 1180a 1541 1639 1669 2429 2488 2643 2665 2687 2848 2858 3069 3286 3320 3327 3375 3399

LIBRARIES, CIRCULATING *see also*
LIBRARIES, PROPRIETARY;
LIBRARIES, SUBSCRIPTION; MUDIE,
Charles Edward, 1818–90. 2406–7 2421
2427–8 2431 2435 2442 2456 3444 6039
7279
— Aberdeen. 1633
— Banff. 1633
— Belfast. 2450
— Bibs. 1:1139m
— Blandford. 5661
— Cowbridge. 2450
— Dublin. 2450
— Dundee. 1633
— Edinburgh. 1633 1695
— Glasgow. 1633
— Halifax. 1440
— Inverness. 1683
— Ireland. 1813 2450
— Kelso. 1741
— King's Cliffe. 2856
— Leeds. 3031
— Leith. 1633
— Liverpool. 1166 1169
— London. 1203–4 1251 1280 5064 5199
— Oxford. 2792
— Paisley. 1633
— Peebles. 1633
— Perth. 1633
— Scotland. 1657 9078
— Wales. 2450
—, DIOCESAN *see also* LIBRARIES,
CATHEDRAL, *and individual libraries, e.g.*
ABERDEEN; BANGOR; BRECON;
CARDIFF; CASHEL; DUNBLANE;
LLANDAFF; LONDON. LAMBETH
PALACE. LIBRARY; ST. ASAPH; ST.
DAVID'S; WATERFORD.
— Ireland. 1834
— Wales. 1507 1510
—, FACTORY. 1685
—, INDIVIDUAL. **2460–3404**
—, LENDING *see* LIBRARIES,
CIRCULATING.
—, LISTS OF. 1546 1675 2411 2446 2452
2455 3444
—, NATIONAL *see also* BRITISH MUSEUM;
IRELAND. NATIONAL LIBRARY,
Dublin; SCOTLAND. NATIONAL
LIBRARY, Edinburgh; WALES.
NATIONAL LIBRARY, Aberystwyth. 2455
—, PARISH *see also* LIBRARIES, CHURCH.
1400 1541 2411 2426 2429 2439 2446
2450–1 2456 2459 2464 2842 3155 2609
2611 3390
—, PERSONAL *see also* EX LIBRIS BOOKS
and –Libr. *after names of individuals.* 1628
2454

— Catalogues *see also* BOOKLISTS. 2051a
2441 2509 2513 2571 2636 2642 2662 2720
2728 2817 2881 2903a 2999 3008 3040
3076 3096 3100 3107 3114 3125 3131 3174
3191 3194 3213 3235a 3280 3282 3284
3302 3319 3322 3343–4 3364 3379 3383
3395b 3396a 3398b 3493 4170 8115 8428a
8923 9133 9633 9713 10078 10593 10670
10847 11319 11595 11837 12024 12028
12032 12574 12710–11 12756 12957 13124
13471 13478–9 13618 13722 13732 14113
14203
—, PRISON. 2416
—, PRIVATE *see* LIBRARIES, PERSONAL.
—, PROPRIETARY. 2437 3376b 3394a 3396
12775
—, PROVINCIAL.
— Aberdeenshire *see also* MAR LODGE;
SKENE HOUSE.
— — Aberdeen *see also* BELMONT
CONGREGATIONAL CHURCH;
COMMON LIBRARY OF NEW
ABERDEEN. 1633 1639 1652 1657 1664
— — Peterhead. 1633
— Forfarshire *see also* INSHEWAN.
— Angus. 1633
— — Arbroath. 1633
— — Dundee. 1571 1633 1668–9
— — Forfar *see* FORFAR LIBRARY.
— — Montrose. 1633
— Antrim. 1845
— — Belfast *see also* BELFAST LIBRARY
AND SOCIETY FOR PROMOTING
KNOWLEDGE. 1850 2450
— Argyllshire.
— — Campbeltown. 1633
— Ayrshire. Ayr *see* AYR LIBRARY
SOCIETY.
— — Kilmarnock *see also* MACKIE
BURNSIANA LIBRARY. 1633
— Banffshire.
— — Banff. 1633
— Bedfordshire.
— — Bedford. 2952
— Berwickshire.
— — Duns *see* DUNS SUBSCRIPTION
LIBRARY.
— Brecknockshire.
— — Brecon. 1510 1518
— — Trevecca *see* TREVECCA LIBRARY.
— Buckinghamshire *see* BIRCH HALL;
BRITWELL COURT; HARTWELL
HOUSE; WADDESDON MANOR.
— — Eton *see* ETON COLLEGE. LIBRARY.
— — Great Brickhill *see* BROOMHILL
HOUSE.
— — Langley Marish. 2611
— Cambridgeshire.

LIBRARIES, PROVINCIAL–Cambridgeshire–Cambridge *see also* CAMBRIDGE. UNIVERSITY *and* COLLEGE *libraries.* 1054 1071 2441 2445
— — Ely *see* ELY PAMPHLET CLUB.
— Cardiganshire. 3110
— — Aberystwyth. 1527
— Carmarthenshire. 1532
— — Carmarthen. 1535–6
— — Llandeilo *see* ST. MARY'S COLLEGE, Llandeilo.
— — Llandovery. 1540
— Carnarvonshire.
— — Bangor. 1510 1540f
— Channel Islands. 2754
— Cheshire. 1162
— — Knutsford *see* TOFT HALL.
— — Northwich *see* DELAMERE HOUSE.
— — Pott Shrigley *see* POTT SHRIGLEY. CHAPEL LIBRARY.
— Cornwall.
— — Penzance *see* PENZANCE LIBRARY.
— Denbighshire *see also* WYNNSTAY.
— — Llanarmon. 3029
— — Llangollen. 1541
—Derbyshire *see* CHATSWORTH HALL; SUDBURY HALL.
— Derry, Derry *see* ST. COLUMB'S COLLEGE. LIBRARY.
—Devonshire. 1097
— — Exeter. 1102b
— — Plymouth *see* PLYMOUTH PROPRIETARY LIBRARY
— — Totnes *see* TOTNES. CHURCH. LIBRARY.
— Dorsetshire.
— — Blandford. 5661
— — Wimborne Minster *see* WIMBORNE MINSTER. LIBRARY.
— Dublin *see also* DUBLIN. ROTUNDA HOSPITAL. LIBRARY; DUBLIN. UNIVERSITY. MARSH'S LIBRARY; DUBLIN. UNIVERSITY. TRINITY COLLEGE. LIBRARY; DUBLIN LIBRARY SOCIETY; MALAHIDE CASTLE; ROYAL DUBLIN SOCIETY. LIBRARY; ROYAL IRISH ACADEMY. LIBRARY. 1873 1901 2450
— — Killiney *see* KILLINEY. FRANCISCAN LIBRARY.
— Dumfriesshire. 1672
— — Dumfries. 1633
— — Wanlockhead. 1633
— — Westerkirk. 1633
— Durham *see* LAMBTON CASTLE; RAVENSWORTH CASTLE.
— — Houghton-le-Spring *see* KEPIER SCHOOL. LIBRARY.

— — Sunderland. 1110
— East Lothian.
— — Haddington. 1633 2488
— Essex *see also* OTES HOUSE. 2452
— — Barking *see* BARKING. ABBEY. LIBRARY.
— — Chelmsford *see* CHELMSFORD. CATHEDRAL. LIBRARY.
— Fifeshire.
— — Fife. 1675
— — Logie. 1633
— — St. Andrews *see also* ST. ANDREWS. UNIVERSITY. LIBRARY; ST. SALVATOR'S COLLEGE. LIBRARY. 1677–81
— Flintshire *see also* GWYSANEY (SEAT); MOSTYN HALL.
— — Hawarden *see* ST. DEINIOL'S THEOLOGICAL AND GENERAL LIBRARY.
— — St. Asaph. 1510 3326
— Glamorganshire.
— — Cardiff. 1544
— — Cowbridge *see* COWBRIDGE BOOK SOCIETY.
— — Llandaff. 1510
— — Swansea. 1546
— Gloucestershire. 2452
— — Bristol *see also* BRISTOL. BAPTIST COLLEGE. LIBRARY; BRISTOL LIBRARY. 1124 2459
— — Gloucester *see also* GLOUCESTER. CATHEDRAL. LIBRARY; GLOUCESTER. SOUTHGATE CHAPEL. LIBRARY. 2848
— Hampshire.
— — Winchester *see* WINCHESTER. CATHEDRAL. LIBRARY; WINCHESTER COLLEGE. LIBRARY.
— — Whitchurch. 2842
— Herefordshire.
— — Hereford *see also* HEREFORD. ALL SAINT'S CHURCH. LIBRARY; HEREFORD. CATHEDRAL. LIBRARY.
— Hertfordshire *see also* ASHRIDGE PARK; HATFIELD HOUSE.
— — Bishop's Stortford. 2593
— — Watford *see* CASSIOBURY PARK.
— Huntingdonshire.
— — Huntingdon *see* HUNTINGDON BOOK CLUB SOCIETY.
— Inverness-shire.
— — Inverness. 1683
— — Skye *see* STAFFORD HOUSE, Staffin.
— Ireland *see also* IRELAND. CHURCH OF IRELAND–Librs.; NATIONAL GALLERY, Dublin. LIBRARY; NATIONAL LIBRARY, Dublin. 1801 1813 1834 2281 2418 2450 2459

LIBRARIES, Kent.
— — Canterbury *see also* CANTERBURY. CATHEDRAL. LIBRARY. 1160–a
— Kincardineshire *see* FETTERCAIRN HOUSE.
— — Blairs *see* ST. MARY'S COLLEGE, Blairs.
— Lanarkshire.
— — Blantyre. 1685
— — Cambusnethan. 1633
— — Glasgow. 1633 1694–a
— Lancashire *see also* CARTMEL PRIORY CHURCH; KNOWSLEY HALL; LANCASHIRE INDEPENDENT COLLEGE. 1162
— — Leadhills. 1633 2459
— — Liverpool. 1166 1169 1171
— — Manchester *see also* CHETHAM HOSPITAL AND LIBRARY, Manchester; JOHN RYLANDS LIBRARY, Manchester; MANCHESTER PORTICO LIBRARY; MANCHESTER. PUBLIC LIBRARIES; UNITARIAN COLLEGE. MCLACHLAN LIBRARY. 1174 2459
— — Stonyhurst *see* STONYHURST COLLEGE.
— — Warrington. 1183
— — Wigan *see* HAIGH HALL.
— Leicestershire.
— — Church Langton. 3397
— — Leicester. 1184 2641
— Lincolnshire. 1185
— — Grantham. 2493 2504
— — Lindsey *see* GIRSBY MANOR.
— London *see also* FRENCH PROTESTANT HOSPITAL. LIBRARY; LONDON–BARBICAN. LIBRARY; –GUILDHALL. LIBRARY; –IRONMONGERS' COMPANY. LIBRARY; –LAMBETH. PALACE. LIBRARY; –ST. PAUL'S CATHEDRAL. LIBRARY –WESTMINSTER ABBEY. LIBRARY; –WESTMINSTER LIBRARY; ROYAL SOCIETY OF LONDON. LIBRARY; SION COLLEGE. LIBRARY. 1203–4 1208 1219 1251 1280 1295
— — Camberwell *see* DULWICH COLLEGE. LIBRARY.
— — Hampstead *see also* HAMPSTEAD LIBRARY; LONDON. HAMPSTEAD. PUBLIC LIBRARY. 2543a
— Midlothian *see* HATTON HALL; NEWBATTLE ABBEY; ROSSLYN CASTLE.
— — Dalkeith *see* DALKEITH SUBSCRIPTION LIBRARY.
— — Edinburgh *see also* BARNBOUGLE CASTLE; EDINBURGH SUBSCRIPTION LIBRARY; LAURISTON CASTLE. 1633 1695 1701 1724–30
— — Leith. 1633
— — Penicuik. 1633
— Monmouthshire *see* TREDEGAR PARK.
— — Llanarth. 8088
— Montgomeryshire *see* POWYS CASTLE.
— Norfolk *see also* BLICKLING HALL; HOLKHAM HALL; NARFORD HALL; NORFOLK AND NORWICH INCORPORATED LAW SOCIETY. LIBRARY; NORFOLK AND NORWICH LITERARY INSTITUTION. 1302–3
— — Norwich *see also* NORWICH. CATHEDRAL. LIBRARY; NORWICH. PUBLIC LIBRARY; NORWICH MEDICO-CHIRURGICAL SOCIETY. LIBRARY. 1306a–8
— Northamptonshire *see* ECTON HALL; LAMPORT HALL.
— — Kings Cliffe. 2856
— Northumberland *see* BAMBURGH CASTLE; WALLINGTON HALL.
— — Newcastle-upon-Tyne *see also* NEWCASTLE-UPON-TYNE. HANOVER SQUARE UNITARIAN CHAPELS. VESTRY LIBRARY. 1321
— Nottinghamshire *see* NEWSTEAD ABBEY; WOLLATON HALL.
— — Newark *see* NEWARK BOOK SOCIETY.
— — Worksop *see* CLUMBER PARK.
— Orkney.
— — Kirkwall. 1633
— Oxfordshire.
— — Chipping Norton *see* HEYTHROP COLLEGE. LIBRARY.
— — Oxford *see also* OXFORD. UNIVERSITY *and* COLLEGE *libraries.* 1360–1 1375 2445
— — Steeple Aston *see* ROUSHAM.
— Peebleshire *see* CASTLECRAIG.
— — Peebles. 1633
— Pembrokeshire.
— — St. David's. 1510
— Perthshire.
— — Creiff. 1731
— — Dunblane. 2525a
— — Innerpeffray. 1633 1731–2 2459 2846
— — Perth *see also* DRUMMOND CASTLE. 1633
— Renfrewshire.
— — Greenock. 1633
— — Paisley. 1633

LIBRARIES, Roxburghshire.
— — Kelso. 1633 1741
— Scotland. 1586 1628 1632–3 1635 2281 2418 2459 3330
— Selkirkshire.
— — Galashiels. 1633
— Shropshire *see* BROGYNTN CASTLE; LANGLEY FAMILY–Libr.
— — Ludlow *see* LUDLOW READING SOCIETY.
— — More. 2643
— — Shrewsbury *see* LONGNER HALL; SHREWSBURY. SCHOOL. LIBRARY.
— — Tong. 2858
— Somerset.
— — Wells *see* WELLS. CATHEDRAL. LIBRARY.
— Staffordshire *see* BETLEY HALL.
— Suffolk *see also* HELMINGHAM HALL. 1400
— — Assington. 1400
— — Beccles. 1400
— — Botesdale *see* BOTESDALE BOOK CLUB.
— — Brent Eleigh. 1400
— — Bury St. Edmunds *see also* BURY ST. EDMUNDS. KING EDWARD VI SCHOOL. LIBRARY. 1400 2663
— — Coddenham. 1400
— — Ipswich *see also* IPSWICH OLD TOWN LIBRARY. 1400 1402 2607
— — Lawshall. 1400
— — Milden. 1400
— — Nayland. 1400
— — Poslingford. 1400
— — Stokeby Nayland. 1400
— — Sudbury. 1400
— — Woodbridge. 1400
— — Yaxley. 1400
— Surrey.
— — Epsom *see* DURDANS.
— — Richmond *see* HAM HOUSE.
— Sussex *see also* ARUNDEL CASTLE; CUCKFIELD PARK; PARHAM HOUSE; PETWORTH HOUSE. 1411
— — Rye *see* LAMB HOUSE.
— Tipperary.
— — Cashel *see* CASHEL. CATHEDRAL. LIBRARY.
— Tyrone *see* CALEDON HOUSE.
— Wales. 1507 1510 1515 2450 2459
— Warwickshire *see also* STONELEIGH ABBEY.
— — Birmingham *see also* BIRMINGHAM BOOK CLUB; BIRMINGHAM LIBRARY. 1415 2452
— — Oscott *see* ST. MARY'S COLLEGE, Oscott. LIBRARY.

— — Stratford-upon-Avon *see also* SHAKESPEARE MEMORIAL LIBRARY; SHAKESPEARE'S BIRTHPLACE TRUST. LIBRARY. 1421 2646
— — Warwick *see* WARWICK. ST. MARY'S CHURCH. LIBRARY; WARWICK CASTLE.
— Waterford.
— — Waterford *see* WATERFORD. CATHEDRAL. LIBRARY.
— Westmorland *see* LOWTHER CASTLE.
— — Appleby *see* APPLEBY. GRAMMAR SCHOOL. LIBRARY.
— — Kendal *see* KENDAL GRAMMAR SCHOOL. LIBRARY.
— Wiltshire *see* ZEALS HOUSE.
— — Marlborough *see* MARLBOROUGH. COLLEGE. LIBRARY; MARLBOROUGH. ST. MARY'S CHURCH. VICAR'S LIBRARY.
— — Salisbury *see* SALISBURY. CATHEDRAL. LIBRARY.
— Worcestershire.
— — Broadway *see* MIDDLE HILL.
— — King's Norton. 2464 2512
— — Worcester *see* WORCESTER. CATHEDRAL. LIBRARY.
— Yorkshire *see* CASTLE HOWARD; HORNBY CASTLE.
— — Bradford *see* BRADFORD LIBRARY AND LITERACY SOCIETY; BRADFORD MECHANICS' INSTITUTE. LIBRARY.
— — Halifax. 1440
— — Hull *see also* HULL LYCEUM. LIBRARY. 2455 2595
— — Leeds *see also* LEEDS LIBRARY. 1441 3031
— — Skipton *see* SKIPTON. PUBLIC LIBRARY. PETYT LIBRARY.
— — York *see* YORK. MINSTER. LIBRARY.
—, PUBLIC. 2281 2283 2398 2418 2430 2455–6 2465 3466
— Bedford. 2952
— Bibs. 1:1139m
— Brentford. 2771
— Church Langton. 3397
— Colchester. 3359
— Dundee. 1633 1669
— Haddington. 1633
— Innerpeffray. 1633
— Ipswich. 1400 2607
— Kirkwall. 1633
— Leicester. 2641
— Llanarth. 8088
— Logie. 1633
— London. 2731 2774
— Perth. 1633

LIBRARIES, ROYAL see ALBERT FRANCIS CHARLES AUGUSTUS EMMANUEL, prince-consort of England, 1819–61; BRITISH MUSEUM. KING'S LIBRARY; CATHERINE OF ARRAGON, queen, 1485–1536; CATHERINE PARR, queen, 1512–48; CHARLES I, king of Great Britain & Ireland, 1600–49; EDWARD VI, king of England, 1537–53; ELIZABETH I, queen of England & Ireland, 1533–1603; FREDERICK LOUIS, prince of Wales, 1707–51; GEORGE III, king of Great Britain and Ireland, 1738–1820; HENRY VIII; king of England, 1491–1547; HENRY BENEDICT MARIA CLEMENT, card. York, 1725–1807; HENRY FREDERICK, prince of Wales, 1594–1612; JAMES I, king of England, 1566–1625; JAMES II, king of England, 1633–1701; MARY STUART, queen of Scots, 1542–87; RUPERT, prince, duke of Cumberland, 1619–82; WILLIAM IV, king of Great Britain and Ireland, 1765–1837; WILLIAM FREDERICK, duke of Gloucester, 1776–1834; WINDSOR CASTLE. ROYAL LIBRARY.
—, SCHOOL. 2429 2449 2457
— Aberystwyth. 1527
— Appleby. 2999
— Bury St. Edmunds. 2663
— Canterbury. 3331
— Carmarthen. 1536
— Chipping Norton. 3224
— Derry. 1864
— Dulwich. 2506 3182 9589
— Dundee. 1668
— Eton. 2494 3197–8 3332
— Guildford. 2402
— Houghton-le-Spring. 2638
— Kendal. 2590
— Lancashire. 3072
— Llandeilo. 1539
— Llandovery. 1540
— London. 2949
— Oscott. 3362
— St. Andrews. 1677
— Shrewsbury. 2459 2852 2946 3051 3275 3389
— Stortford. 2593
— Winchester. 3176 3312 3382b 9617
—, SCIENTIFIC. 8123 8127 8139 8144 8153
—, SUBSCRIPTION see also BOOK CLUBS; LIBRARIES, CIRCULATING; LIBRARIES, PROPRIETARY. 2455–6 3367 3617
— Arbroath. 1633
— Ayr. 1633

— Belfast. 1850 2450
— Cambusnethan. 1633
— Campbeltown. 1633
— Dalkieth. 1633
— Dublin. 1901 2450
— Dumfries. 1633
— Dundee. 1633
— Duns. 1633
— Edinburgh. 1633
— Forfar. 1633
— Galashiels. 1633
— Glasgow. 1633
— Greenock. 1633
— Hampstead. 2543
— Inshewan. 1633
— Ireland. 1813 2450
— Kelso. 1633
— Kilmarnock. 1633
— Leadhills. 1633
— London see also LONDON. WESTMINSTER LIBRARY; LONDON LIBRARY. 1204 1219 2443
— Montrose. 1633
— Newark. 3395a
— Norfolk. 1306a 3385
— Penicuik. 1633
— Penzance. 3396
— Perth. 1633
— Peterhead. 1633
— Scotland. 1633 9007
— Sunderland. 1110
— Wales. 1515
— Wanlockhead. 1633
— Westerkirk. 1633
—, TRAVELLING. 2432 2444 2507–8
—, TYPOGRAPHICAL see OXFORD. UNIVERSITY. BODLEIAN LIBRARY. JOHN JOHNSON COLLECTION; OXFORD UNIVERSITY PRESS. JOHN JOHNSON COLLECTION; ST. BRIDE FOUNDATION INSTITUTE. TECHNICAL REFERENCE LIBRARY.
—, UNIVERSITY see also individual university libraries, e.g. ABERDEEN; CAMBRIDGE; DUBLIN; DURHAM; EDINBURGH; GLASGOW; LEEDS; LONDON; MANCHESTER; OXFORD; ST. ANDREWS. 2455
LIBRARY, THE. 1:87–8; 318 320 324 331
LIBRARY ASSOCIATION, London. 1:89
— LIBRARY–Collns. 1:106
LIBRARY BINDINGS see BOOKBINDINGS, LIBRARY.
LIBRARY CATALOGUES see CATALOGUES, LIBRARY.
LIBRARY COMPANY OF PHILADELPHIA–Collns. 1:612; 2:793; 13799 14150
LIBRARY LABELS see LABELS, LIBRARY.

LIBRARY OF IRELAND–Bibs. 1:1075m
LIBRETTOS *see* OPERAS.
LIBRI (Guglielmus Brutus Icilius Timoleon, count Libri-Carucci dalla Somaja), 1803–69. 2314 3391 3400
LICENSING *see also* BOOK TRADE–Regulation; DRAMA–Regulation; PRINTING–Regulation; PRIVILEGES, PUBLISHING. 603 1281 3552–a 3556 3559 3562–3 3565 3566–7 3572–6 10231 11015 12470 13057
LICHFIELD, Staffs.
— Bksllng. *see* JOHNSON, Michael, 1657–1732.
—CATHEDRAL. LIBRARY–Collns. 2008
—JOHNSON HOUSE–Collns. 1:3841bb
LICHFIELD, Leonard, Oxford, 1604–57. 13876
LIDDEL, DUNCAN, 1561–1613. 11997
— Bibs. 1:4054–6
LIDDON, Henry Parry, 1829–90–Bibs. 1:4057
LIDYAT, John, fl.1670. 9756
LIEBERT, Herman Wardwell, 1911– –Libr. 1:3854
LIFE–Bibs. 1:3810
LIFE AND ADVENTURES OF LADY ANNE, 1823. 7004
LIGATURED TYPE *see* TYPE, LIGATURED.
LIGHT, William, 1784–1838. 11998
LIGHTBODY, John, fl.1798. 2:793
LIGHTFOOT, John, 1735–88.
— *Flora Scotica.* 6968
LILAC TREE PRESS, est. 1965. 5073
— Bibs. 1:1358
LILBURNE, John, 1614?–57–Bibs. 1:4058–a
LILLIPUTIAN LIBRARY, 1782. 7011
LILLO, George, 1693–1739. 11999
— Bibs. 1:4059
— *London merchant*–Bibs. 1:4059
LILLY, Josiah Kirby, 1861–1948 *see* INDIANA. UNIVERSITY. J. K. LILLY LIBRARY.
LILLY, William, 1602–81. 12000
— *Catastrophe mundi.* 12000
LILY, William, 1468?–1522. 7355
— *De octo orationis partum constructione.* 7349
— *Grammatices rudimenta.* 7357–8
LIMAVADY, co. Derry.
— Bibs. 1:1055f
— Ptg.–Bibs. 1:1055f
LIMERICK *see also* BOOK TRADE, LISTS–Limerick. 1954–7
— Bibs. 1:1095–100
— Newspapers. 1956
— Paper *see* SEXTON, Joseph, d.1782.
— Ptg. 1954–5 1957 6466 13733
— — Bibs. 1:1095–100

— PUBLIC LIBRARY–Collns. 1:1100
— SOCIETY OF GENTLEMEN *see* SOCIETY OF GENTLEMEN, Limerick, 18th cent.
LIMERICK NEWSLETTER. 1956
LIMITED EDITIONS *see* EDITIONS, LIMITED.
LIMITED EDITIONS CLUB, 1929–54–Bibs. 1:1359
LIMITED EDITIONS CLUB SHAKESPEARE. 2:754
LINACRE, Thomas, 1460?–1524. 2479 8661 12001
— *Galen de temperamentis.* 5645–6
— Handwr. 12001
— *Three parts of medicine.* 7554
LINCOLN, Lincs. 1186
— Ptg. 1186
— CATHEDRAL. LIBRARY. 2500 2532a 2823
— — — Collns. 1:456; 659 2903a–b 6973a
— CITY LIBRARIES–Collns. 1:913 4900
LINCOLN NOSEGAY BOOKS. 1:542
LINCOLN SCHOOL OF ART PRESS, fl.1960. 6495
LINCOLNSHIRE. 1185–7a
— Bibs. 1:913
— Librs. 1185
LINCOLN'S INN *see* LONDON. LINCOLN'S INN.
LINDER, Leslie Charles, fl.1966–Libr. 1:4450a
LINDFIELD, Sussex–Paper. 1412
LINDLEY, John, 1799–1865.
— Bibs. 1:4060
— *Vegetation of the Swan river colony.* 6959
LINDSAY, Alexander William, 25th earl of Crawford, 1812–80 *see* BIBLIOTHECA LINDESIANA.
Lindsay, sir David, 1490–1555. 12002–4
— Bibs. 1:4061–3
— *Convert's cordial.* 12002
— *Satire of the three estates.* 12004
— *Squire Meldrum*–Bibs. 1:4061
LINDSAY, Jack, 1900– *see* FANFROLICO PRESS, est. 1926.
LINDSAY, James Ludovic, 26th earl of Crawford, 1847–1913 *see* BIBLIOTHECA LINDESIANA.
LINDSAY, John, 1789–1870–Bibs. 1:4063h
LINDSAY, Robert James Loyd-, baron Wantage, 1832–1901–Libr. 2:556
LINDSEY, Lincs.–Librs. *see* GIRSBY MANOR.
LINE DRAWINGS *see* DRAWINGS, LINE.
LINEN HALL LIBRARY *see* BELFAST LIBRARY AND SOCIETY FOR PROMOTING KNOWLEDGE.

Vol. 1 = *Bibliographies*   2 = *Shakespeare*   4 = 1–8221   5 = 8222–14616

LINES BROTHERS, ltd., 1914–33. 7035
LING, Nicholas, fl.1570–1607. **5074–5a**
— *Passionate shepherd's song.* 2:1487
— *Wit's commonwealth.* 5075a
LINGARD, John, 1771–1851–Bibs. 1:**4064**
LINGUISTICS AND BIBLIOGRAPHY. 236
LINING PAPERS *see* BOOKBIND-INGS–Linings.
LINNELL, John, 1792–1882. 8598 8600
LINNET MILL, Mounton. 1298a
LINOTYPING. 6123 6161
LINTON, sir James Dromgole, 1840–1916. 7420a
LINTON, William James, 1812–97. 1165a 3842
LINTOT, Barnaby Bernard, 1675–1736. 3453a 3475 3616 3622 3639a **5076–7** 5868
— Bibs. 1:**1360**
— *Miscellaneous poems.* 12839
LINTOT, Henry, 1709–58. 3475 3639a 5076
LION AND UNICORN PRESS, est. 1955. **5078** 6495
— Bibs. 1:**1360d**
LISBON. INSTITUTO BRITÁNICO EM PORTUGAL *see* INSTITUTO BRITÂNICO EM PORTUGAL, Lisbon.
LISBURN, co. Antrim–Ptg. 1772
L'ISLE, William, 1569?–1637.
— Publ. 6536
— *Saxon treatise.* 6536
LISTER, Joseph, 1st baron Lister, 1827–1912–Bibs. 1:**4065–6**
LISTER, Martin, 1638?–1712.
— *De cochleis.* 8152
— *Historia conchyliorum.* 8152
LIST OF COVENT GARDEN LADIES. 7705 7758 7760
LISTS *see* —, LISTS OF *for* BOOK-BINDINGS; BOOK COLLECTORS; BOOK DONORS; BOOK TRADE; ENGRAVERS; ENGRAVINGS; ERRATA; LIBRARIES; OWNERS; PLAYS; PRESSES (AS MACHINES); SALES; WATER-MARKS.
—, SUBSCRIPTION *see* SUBSCRIPTION LISTS.
LITCHFIELD, Hubert L., fl.1952–Libr. 3141
LITERACY. 2450 3458 3466 3479
LITERARY AGENTS *see* AGENTS, LITERARY.
LITERARY ALMANACS *see* ALMANACS, LITERARY.
LITERARY COMPANION. 7844
LITERARY COURIER OF GRUB STREET–Bibs. 1:1900h
LITERARY CRITICISM *see* CRITICISM, LITERARY.
LITERARY EXAMINER. 7885

LITERARY MAGAZINE–Bibs. 1:3845f
LITERARY NEWSPAPERS AND PERIODICALS *see* NEWSPAPERS AND PERIODICALS, LITERARY.
LITERATURE *see* ENGLISH LITERATURE; ANGLO-IRISH LITERATURE; ANGLO-INDIAN LITERATURE; CHILDREN'S LITERATURE; SCOTTISH LITERATURE.
LITERATURE AND BIBLIOGRAPHY. 189 229–30 268 398
LITHOGRAPHIC PRESSES *see* PRESSES, LITHOGRAPHIC.
LITHOGRAPHS. 6219a 7416
— Bibs. 1:1754b
— Ptg. 6227
LITHOGRAPHY *see also* CHROMO-LITHOGRAPHY; LITHOTINTING; PHOTOLITHOGRAPHY. 1686a 4780 6123 6186–8 6200 6202 6210 6229 6259 6385 7608
—Ireland. 6206
LITHOTINTING. 6202 6222
LITHUANIAN LITERATURE *see* BIBLE, LITHUANIAN; FOREIGN BOOKS PUBLISHED IN BRITAIN–Lithuania.
LITTLE BARRINGTON, Glos.–Paper. 1120a
LITTLE GIDDING BINDERY, Huntingdonshire, 1625–7. **5079–87**
—Bndngs. 5079a 5081–3 9762
— *Concordance.* 5084–5
— *Harmonies.* 5080
LITTLE IVY MILL, Kent. 1161a
LITTLE MILL, Shirenewton. 1298a
LITTLE ORME'S HEAD, Llandudno, Carns. 1540g
LITTLE RED RIDING HOOD–Bibs. 1:1557
LITTLETON, Henry, 1823–88. 5314
LITTLETON, R. H., fl.1850.
— *History of Islington.* 1218
LITTLE TREATISE OF DIVERS MIRACLES ... IN HAYLES. 5475
LITURGIES *see also* BOOK OF COMMON PRAYER; BOOK OF COMMON ORDER; PRAYERBOOKS; PRIMERS. 1789
LIVERPOOL, Lancs. *see also* BOOK TRADE, LISTS–Liverpool. **1166–73**
— Bibs. 1:**905x–9**
— Bksllng. 1173 4158
— Directories. 1170 1173
— — Bibs. 1:905x
— Librs. 1166 1169 1171
— Newspapers. 1167
— — Bibs. 1:907
— Ptg. 1168 1172–3
— — Bibs. 1:907–9
— Publ. *see* CAXTON PRESS, fl.1814–21; GORE, John, fl.1712–72.

Vol. **1** = *Bibliographies*   **2** = *Shakespeare*   **4** = 1–8221   **5** = 8222–14616

LIVERPOOL. CATHEDRAL. RADCLIFFE LIBRARY–Collns. 1:372
— MEDICAL INSTITUTION. LIBRARY–Collns. 1:2230h
— PUBLIC LIBRARIES–Collns. 1:907
— UNIVERSITY. LIBRARY–Collns. 1:468–9 499 1226
LIVINGSTON, Flora Virginia (Milner), 1862– –Libr. 11776
LIVINGSTONE, David, 1813–73–Bibs. 1:4067
LIVINGSTONE, Edward, Edinburgh, 1832–1905. 5088
LIVINGSTONE, sir Richard Winn, 1880–1960–Bibs. 1:4067k
LIVY (Titus Livius), 59 B.C.–17 A.D. 894 11121
LLANARMON, Denbigh.–Librs. 3029
LLANARTH, Mons. PUBLIC LIBRARY. 8088
LLANDAFF, Glam.–Librs. 1510
LLANDEILO, Carms. 1539
— Librs. 1539
— ST. MARY'S COLLEGE see ST. MARY'S COLLEGE, Llandeilo.
LLANDOVERY, Carms. 1540
— Librs. 1540
LLANDOVERY COLLEGE–Libr. 1540
LLANDUDNO, Carns. 1521
— Bibs. 1:962t
— Ptg. 1540g
LLANELLY, Carms.–Ptg. see WILLIAMS, David, 1814–84.
LLANGOLLEN, Denbigh. 1541
—Librs. 1541
LLANRYDDOL. ST. FRANCIS XAVIER COLLEGE see ST. FRANCIS XAVIER COLLEGE, Llanryddol.
LLANRWST, Denbigh.–Ptg. see JONES, John, 1786–1865.
LLOYD, David, 1635–92. 12005
LLOYD, Edward, Dublin, fl.1714. 5089
LLOYD, Edward, 1815–90. 5090 7040
— Bibs. 1:1361
— Penny Pickwick. 10050
LLOYD, Evan, fl.1582.
— Almanac. 6749
LLOYD, John, 1750–1815–Libr. 3234
LLOYD, Owen, fl.1660. 708
LLOYD, Robert, Birmingham, 1778–1811. 5091
LLOYD, Thomas, fl.1718. 12006
— Siccrwydd Neu hyspysrwydd. 12006
LLOYD-SMITH, Wilton, 1894–1940 see SMITH, Wilton Lloyd-, 1894–1940.
LLWYD, Humphrey, 1527–68. 1517
LOADED PAPER see PAPER, LOADED.
L'OBEL, Matthias, 1538–1616.

— Adversaria. 6545
LOBO, Jeronymo, 1596–1678. 11468
LOCK, George, 1832–91 see also WARD, LOCK, est. 1854. 5941
LOCKE, John, 1632–1704. 2291 3140 12007–32
— Bibs. 1:4068–9d
— Collns. 12008 12011
— Essay concerning human understanding. 12012 12015 12019 12026
— Handwr. 12022
— Libr. 12010 12023–5 12028–30 12032
— Mss. 12007 12009 12015 12016a 12019 12024–5 12027
— — Bibs. 1:4069b
— Publ. 12012
— Some thoughts concerning education. 12013–14
— Two treatises of government. 12016 12018
— — Bibs. 1:4069c–ca
LOCKE, William John, 1863–1930–Bibs. 1:4070
LOCKER-LAMPSON, Frederick, 1821–95 see LAMPSON, Frederick Locker-, 1821–95.
LOCKHART, George, fl.1516–24–Bibs. 1:4112k
LOCKHART, John Gibson, 1794–1854. 3886 5250 12033–9 13217 13227 14552
— Ancient Spanish ballads. 12037
— Bibs. 1:1921–22 4071
— Bridal of Triermain. 12035
— Harold the dauntless. 12035
— Life of Scott. 12034 12039 13213
— Peter's letters. 12038
— Text. 12036 12039
LOCK HOSPITAL AND RESCUE HOME, London see LONDON. LOCK HOSPITAL.
LOCKMAN, John, 1698–1771.
— Ptg. 6154
— Travels of the Jesuits. 6154
LOCRINE. 8918 9580
LODGE, sir Oliver Joseph, 1851–1940–Bibs. 1:4072
LODGE, Thomas, 1558?–1625. 12040–3
— Bibs. 1:4073–4d
— Defence of poetry. 12042
— Flowers of Lodowicke. 12041
— Looking glass for London. 12043
— Rosalind. 12040
LOEWENSTEIN, Fritz Erwin, 1901– –Libr. 13269
LOFFT, Capel, 1751–1824. 12044
— Mss. 12044
LOGIE, Fife–Librs. 1633
LOGOGRAPHIC PRESS, 1794–1813 see WALTER, John, 1723–1812.
LOGOGRAPHIC PRINTING see PRINTING, LOGOGRAPHIC.

LONDON. DULWICH COLLEGE *see* DULWICH COLLEGE, Camberwell.
— EALING *see* EALING, Middlesex.
— ELIOT'S COURT *see* ELIOT'S COURT PRESS, 1584–1674.
— FANN STREET *see* FANN STREET FOUNDRY.
— FINSBURY. 1019
— FLEET STREET. 1200 1234 1284 1289 3821 3957 3974 4721 4834 5822 5872 5929 5941b 6016 6033
— FRENCH PROTESTANT HOSPITAL *see* FRENCH PROTESTANT HOSPITAL, London.
— GAELIC SOCIETY *see* GAELIC SOCIETY, London.
— GREYFRIARS. 4781 4783
— GREENWICH. 1025
— GRESHAM COLLEGE–Collns. 12924
— GREYSTOKE PLACE. 5521
— GUILDHALL. 2657
— — LIBRARY. 2:620; 2466 2478 2532 2598 2645 2657 2682 3151
— — — Collns. 1:477 590–1 916–b 1429 1839a 1878–9 2145 2178 2281f 3053 4279 4621a 4647 5108 5144 5146; 7693 7970 12493–4
— — — GRESHAM MUSIC LIBRARY–Collns. 1:1839a
— GUY'S HOSPITAL–Bibs. 1:**918**
— — WILLS' LIBRARY–Collns. 1:918
— HAMMERSMITH.
— — Bndng. *see* DOVES PRESS, 1900–16–Bndng.
— — Ptg. *see* DOVES PRESS, 1900–16; KELMSCOTT PRESS, 1891–8.
— — PUBLIC LIBRARIES–Collns. 1:1572
— HAMPSTEAD. 1018 1211a 1252 2543a
— — Bndng. *see* HAMPSTEAD BINDERY, 1898–1904.
— — KEATS MUSEUM *see* KEATS MUSEUM, Hampstead.
— — PUBLIC LIBRARY. 2774
— HAYMARKET. 3879
— HIGHGATE. 3879
— HOLBORN. 1200 1282 3953 6001
— — Publ. *see* BATSFORD, Bradley Thomas, 1821–1904.
— HOLYWELL STREET. 1206 4683
— HORNIMAN MUSEUM *see* HORNIMAN MUSEUM AND LIBRARY, London.
— HOSPITALS. 1244
— HUNSDON HOUSE. 6110
— INNS OF COURT–Bibs. 1:1594 1598 **2197f**
— INSTITUTE OF CONTEMPORARY ARTS *see* INSTITUTE OF CONTEMPORARY ARTS, London.

— INSTITUTE OF SHORTHAND WRITERS *see* INSTITUTE OF SHORTHAND WRITERS, London.
— IRONMONGERS' COMPANY. LIBRARY. 2612
— ISLINGTON. 1218 1233 1245 1250
— KENSINGTON.
— — HOLLAND HOUSE *see* HOLLAND HOUSE, Kensington.
— KENTISH TOWN. 1246 4048
— KING STREET. 1200
— KIPLING SOCIETY *see* KIPLING SOCIETY, London.
— LAMBETH. 1018
— — PALACE. LIBRARY. 2468 3189 3420 3271 3366
— — — — Collns. 550 4320 6888
— LIBRARY ASSOCIATION *see* LIBRARY ASSOCIATION, London.
— LINCOLN'S INN. LIBRARY.
— — — Collns. 1:1970; 3227 8039
— LITTLE BRITAIN. 1249 3475 3616
— LOCK HOSPITAL. 7378
— LONDON BRIDGE. 1210 1224 3616 5410
— MEDICI SOCIETY *see* MEDICI SOCIETY, est. 1908.
— MERCERS' COMPANY *see* WORSHIPFUL COMPANY OF MERCERS, London.
— MERCHANT TAYLORS' SCHOOL *see* MERCHANT TAYLORS' SCHOOL, London.
— MIDDLE TEMPLE INN. 10257
— MINORIES. 7023
— MUSEUM *see* LONDON MUSEUM.
— NATIONAL BOOK LEAGUE *see* NATIONAL BOOK LEAGUE, London.
— NATIONAL LIBERAL CLUB *see* NATIONAL LIBERAL CLUB. London.
— NATIONAL MARITIME MUSEUM *see* NATIONAL MARITIME MUSEUM, Greenwich.
— NEW BOND STREET. 4622–3
— NEW DUDLEY GALLERY *see* NEW DUDLEY GALLERY, Piccadilly, London.
— NEW SYDENHAM SOCIETY *see* NEW SYDENHAM SOCIETY, London, 1866–1905.
— ORATORY *see* ORATORY OF ST. PHILIP NERI, London.
— OXFORD STREET. 1251
— PALL MALL. 1200 5289
— PATERNOSTER ROW. 1191a 1200 1294 4897hh
— PECKHAM RYE. 4897hh
— PICCADILLY. 4846–7 5640 5708 5778
— POULTRY. 1199

Vol. 1 = *Bibliographies*   2 = *Shakespeare*   4 = 1–8221   5 = 8222–14616

LONDON.WESTMINSTER. 1215 4218a 4240 4245 4261 4272–3 4324 5890 6014 6055
— — CITY LIBRARIES–Collns. 1:2483–4 2489
— WESTMINSTER ABBEY. 2:954
— — LIBRARY. 2463 2532a
— WESTMINSTER HALL. 1213
— WESTMINSTER LIBRARY. 3376
— WILLIAM MORRIS SOCIETY *see* WILLIAM MORRIS SOCIETY, London.
— WIMBLEDON.
— — Ptg. *see* ART SOCIETY PRESS, est. 1953.
— WOOLWICH–Bibs. 1:**922m**
LONDON, George, 1833–58.
— *Penny cyclopædia.* 7238 7242
LONDON, Jack, 1876–1916–Bibs. 1:**848g**
LONDON, William, fl.1658. 3485
LONDON BOOKSELLERS' ASSOCIATION. 1290
LONDON BOOKSELLERS' COMMITTEE. 1290
LONDON CATALOGUE OF BOOKS. 1294 3486
LONDON CHRONICLE. 1268 7716
LONDON COMMITTEE OF SEQUESTRATION. 3396a
LONDONDERRY *see* DERRY.
LONDON GAZETTE. 4840 7666 7691–2
LONDON JOURNAL. 3561 4739
— Bibs. 1:3428a
LONDON JOURNEYMEN BOOKBINDERS. 1270
LONDON LIBRARY. 2443 2459 2546 2649 2659 2768 3016 3033 3289 3370 3385a 9279
— Collns. 3288
LONDON MAGAZINE. 1258 1278 8442 11713
— Bibs. 1:5005r
LONDON MAGAZINE AND MONTHLY CHRONOLOGER. 7590
LONDON MAGAZINE, CHARIVARI, AND COURRIER DES DAMES. 7873–4
LONDON MERCURY. 1196
— Bibs. 1:4760f
LONDON MUSEUM–Collns. 7041
LONDON NEWSBOOK. 7691
LONDON ORATORY *see* ORATORY OF ST. PHILIP NERI, London.
LONDON POLYTECHNIC SCHOOL OF ART *see* PRINNY PRESS, fl.1960.
LONDON REFLECTOR. 1266
LONDON SOCIETY. 7389
LONDON SOCIETY OF BOOKBINDERS, est. 1780 *see* SOCIETY OF LONDON BOOKBINDERS, est. 1780.

LONDON SOCIETY OF COMPOSITORS, est. 1845. 1275 **5092**
LONDON SOCIETY OF MASTER LETTER-FOUNDERS, 1793–1820. **5093**
LONDON TALES, 1858. 7304
LONDON UNION OF COMPOSITORS, est. 1834. 1275 5092
LONDON UNION SOCIETY, fl.1801. 5092
LONG, Gabrielle Margaret Vere (Campbell), 1888–1952 *see* BOWEN, Marjorie, *psued.*
LONG, Thomas, c.1621–1707–Bibs. 1:**4075**
LONG CRENDON, Bucks.
— Ptg. *see* SEVEN ACRES PRESS, 1926–33.
LONGE, Francis, 1748–1812–Libr. 2:538
LONGFELLOW, Henry Wadsworth, 1807–82. 994
— Bibs. 1:**849**
— *Courtship of Miles Standish.* 979 981
LONGFORD.
— Bibs. 1:**1101**
— Ptg.–Bibs. 1:1101
LONGHOPE, Glos.–Paper. 1120a
LONGLAND, bp. John, 1473–1547. **12045**
— *Sermon.* 12045
LONG LOST FOUND, 1847. 803
LONGMAN, Charles James, 1852–1934. 5099
LONGMAN, HURST, REES, ORME, BROWN AND GREEN, fl.1815. 3509 13242
LONGMAN, Thomas Norton, 1770–1842. 1294 3639a **5094–101** 5909 8099
— Libr. 14492
LONGMAN, Thomas Norton, fl.1897–Libr. 1:5166t
LONGMANS, GREEN AND COMPANY, fl.1889– . 5094–b 5095 14547
LONGNER HALL, Shrewsbury–Libr. 2:276 418 1941
LONGUEVILLE, Peter, fl.1727. **12046**
— *English hermit.* 12046
LONSDALE, earls of–Libr. *see* LOWTHER CASTLE, Westmorland.
LONSDALE, Hugh Cecil Lowther, 5th earl of, 1857–1944 *see* LOWTHER, Hugh Cecil, 5th earl of Lonsdale, 1857–1944.
LOOSE MILL, Kent. 1161a 5975
LOS ANGELES. PUBLIC LIBRARY–Collns. 11922
LOSELEY PARK, Guildford, Surrey. 9763
LOST BOOKS *see* BOOKS, LOST.
LOTHIAN, EAST *see* EAST LOTHIAN.
LOTHIAN, Philip Henry Kerr, 11th marquess of, 1882–1940 *see* KERR, Philip Henry, 11th marquess of Lothian, 1882–1940.

LOTHROP, Thorton Kirkland, 1830–1913–Libr. 1:2019
LOTTERIES, BOOK. 3663
'LOTTERY'. 7050
LOUDWATER, Herts.–Paper. 1139
LOUGH FEA, Carrickmacross–Libr. see SHIRLEY, Evelyn Philip, 1812–82–Libr.
LOUGHREA, co. Galway. **1946–8**
— Bibs. 1:**1086–7**
— Newspapers. 1948
— Ptg. 1946–7
— — Bibs. 1:1086–7
LOUGHREA JOURNAL. 1948
LOUSLEY, Job, 1790–1855–Libr. 3335
LOUTH. **1958–9**
— Bibs. 1:**1102–5**
— Bksllng. 1958b
— Ptg. *see also* JACKSON, John, fl.1797; SHEARDOWN, Robert, fl.1789. 1958–b
LOUVAIN IRISH PRESS, France, fl.1614. 6422 6427–8 6431 6438
LOVE, James, *pseud. of* James Dance, 1722–74. 10680
LOVE, John, Weymouth, 1752–93. **5102**
LOVELACE, Ralph Gordon Noel King Milbanke, 2d earl of, 1839–1906 *see* MILBANKE, Ralph Gordon Noel King, 2d earl of Lovelace, 1839–1906.
LOVELACE, Richard, 1618–58. **12047–50**
— Bibs. 1:**4076**
— *Mock song.* 12048
— Mss. 12048–9
— *The rose.* 12049
— Text. 12050
— *To Lucasta.* 12050
— *When I by thy fair shape.* 12047
LOVELACE COLLECTION, Bodleian library, Oxford *see* KING, Peter, 1st baron King of Ockham, 1669–1734–Libr.
LOVE LETTERS OF MRS. PIOZZI, 1843. 12787
LOVER AND THE READER–Bibs. 1:**4774**
LOW, Sampson, 1797–1886. **5103**
LOWELL. James Russell, 1819–91.
— *On democracy.* 1004
LOW COUNTRIES *see* NETHERLANDS.
LOWER, Richard, 1631–91.
— Bibs. 1:**4077**
— *De catarrhis.* 7570a
— *Tractatus de corde.* 7570a
LOWER BARFORD MILL, Hants. 1132a
LOWES, sir Patrick, Edinburgh, fl.1494. **5104–5**
LOWIS, David, fl.1496. 1555 **5106–7**
LOWNDES, William Thomas, 1798?–1843. **12051–6**
— *Bibliographer's manual.* 12051–3 12055

LOWRY, Clarence Malcolm, 1909–57–Bibs. 1:**4077c–d**
—Mss.–Bibs. 1:4077c
LOWTHER, Hugh Cecil, 5th earl of Lonsdale, 1857–1944–Libr. 2970
LOWTHER CASTLE, Westmorland.–Libr. 2970
— — Collns. 1:1853a
LOYAL LONDON MERCURY. 7687–8
LOYAL OBSERVATOR REVIV'D–Bibs. 1:3416a
LOYAL POST. 7788
LOYD-LINDSAY, Robert James, baron Wantage, 1832–1901 *see* LINDSAY, Robert James Loyd-, baron Wantage, 1832–1901.
LUBBOCK, sir John, baron Avebury, 1834–1913–Bibs. 1:**4078**
LUBBOCK, William, Newcastle-upon-Tyne, fl.1808–22. **51108**
LUCAS, Charles, 1713–73. 13752
LUCAS, Edward Verrall, 1868–1938.
—*Lamb's Letters.* 11841
— Libr. 3004
— Publ. 5527–8
LUCAS, Henry, fl.1740–79.
— *Poems.* 11462
LUCAS, Henry, fl.1795.
— *Earl of Somerset.* 1:3845
LUCIAN, c.115–200. 12224
LUCK, Robert, c.1674–1747–Bibs. 1:**4079**
LUCKOMBE, Philip, d.1803.
— *Concise history of the origin ... of printing.* 3609
LUCRETIUS (Titus Lucretius Carus), c.99–55 B.C.–Bibs. 1:**779–800a**
LUDLOW, Shrop.–Ptg. 5373
LUDLOW READING SOCIETY. 2452
LUDOLF, Heinrich Wilhelm, 1655–1710.
— *Grammatica Russica.* 5356
LUFT, Hans, *pseud. of* Johannes Hoochstraten, fl.1523–72 *see also* BALE PRESS, Marburg, fl.1528–46. 837 840
LUKE, John, Denny, fl.1800. **5108f**
LUMLEY, John, 1st baron Lumley, 1534?–1609–Libr. 3205
LUPSET, Thomas, 1495?–1530–Bibs. 1:**4080**
LURGAN, co. Armagh. **1851**
— Bibs. 1:**1036–7**
— Newspapers. 1851
— Ptg.–Bibs. 1:1036–7
LURGAN PAROCHIAL MAGAZINE. 1851
LUSK, Robert Baillie, Inverness, fl.1823. 1683
LUSTLEIGH, Devon–Ptg. *see* DAVY, William, 1743–1826.
LUTHER, Martin, 1483–1546. 8067
— *Touching the liberty of a Christian.* 871
LUTHERAN BOOKS. **8100**

LUTTRELL, Narcissus, 1657–1732–Libr.
2830 2832 2957 3204 3231
LYDGATE, John, 1370?–1451? **12057–63**
— *Assembly of gods* see *ASSEMBLY OF GODS,*
1498.
— *Churl and the bird.* 4292
— *Falls of princes.* 12060
— *Governance of kings.* 12057
— *Horse, sheep, and goose.* 12059 12061
— *Life of our lady.* 4278 4284 12062
— Mss. 12058 12062
— *Pilgrimage of the soul.* 4272 4306
— Ptg. 4272 4278 4284 4292 4306 12059–61
— *Serpent of division.* 12063
— *Verses on the kings.* 12058
LYDNEY, Glos.–Paper. 1120a
LYDON, Alexander Francis, 1836–1917. 6202
LYELL, James Patrick Ronaldson,
1871–1949–Libr. 2363 3109
LYELL LECTURES, Oxford university see
OXFORD. UNIVERSITY. LYELL
LECTURES.
LYLY, John, 1554?–1606. **12064–5**
— *The bee.* 12065
— Bibs. 1:1597 **4081–2a**
— *Euphues.* 12064
LYNAM, William F., d.1894–Bibs. 1:**4082j**
LYNCH, Joseph, fl.1935–Libr. 2955
LYNCH, Patrick, 1754–1818–Bibs. 1:**4083**
LYNDESAY, David, 1583–1667.
— *Convert's cordial.* 1646
LYNDSAY, sir David, 1490–1555 see
LINDSAY, sir David, 1490–1555.
LYNN, Mass. PUBLIC LIBRARY–Collns.
2:46
LYONS, John Charles, Mullingar,
1792–1874. **5109–10**
LYSONS, Daniel, 1762–1834. 7230
LYSONS, Samuel, 1763–1819. 1117a
LYTE, Henry, 1529?–1607.
— *New herbal or history of plants.* 6945
LYTE, Henry Francis, 1793–1847–Libr.
2941–2
LYTTLETON, George, 1st baron Lyttleton,
1709–73. **12066–8**
— Bibs. 1:**4084**
— *Court secret.* 12067
— — Bibs. 1:4084
— *Dialogues of the dead.* 12068
— Ptg. 12068
— *To the memory of a lady.* 12066
LYTTON, Edward George Earle Lytton
Bulwer-, 1st baron Lytton, 1803–73. 9078
12069–70
— Bibs. 1:**4084f**
— Collns. 7322a
— *Coming race.* 12069

— *Marah.* 12069
— Ptg. 12069
— Publ. 12070
LYTTON, Edward Robert Bulwer, 1st earl of
Lytton, 1831–91. 487 831a **12071–3**
— Bibs. 1:**4085–7**
— Collns. 12072
— Publ. 12071
LYTTON, Rosina (Wheeler) Bulwer-, lady
Lytton, 1802–82–Collns. 7322a

M, G. B., fl.1894. 8827
M., J.
— *Sports and pastimes.* 7483
MABBE, James, 1572–1642? 2:951; **12074**
MABBOT, George, d.1689.
— *Tables for leases.* 12591
MCADOO, Francis Huger, 1889– – Libr. 799
MACALISTER, sir John Young Walker,
1856–1925. 35
MCALPIN, David Hunter, 1816–1901–Libr.
1:2251
MACARTHY, Denis Florence, 1817–82–Libr.
2908
MACARTNEY, George, 1st earl Macartney,
1737–1806. **12075–8**
— Bibs. 1:**4088**
— Collns. 12075
— Mss. 12075–8
MACAULAY, Thomas Babington, 1st baron
Macaulay, 1800–59. 831a **12079–81**
— Bibs. 1:**4089–a**
— *History of England.* 12079
— Letters–Bibs. 1:4089a
— Libr. 1:373; 12081
— Publ. 6523
— *View of the history of France.* 12080
MACBEAN, William Munro, 1852–
1924–Libr. 1:712
MCCARTHY, Denis Florence, 1817–82–Bibs.
1:**4089**
MCCARTHY, Justin, 1830–1912–Bibs.
1:**4089m**
MACCARTHY–REAGH, Justin, comte de,
1744–1811 see REAGH, Justin MacCarthy,
comte de, 1744–1811.
MACCONROY, archbp. Florence,
1560–1629. 6422
MCCORMICK, Cyrus Hall, 1890–1936–Libr.
529
MCCOSH, James, 1811–94–Bibs. 1:**4090q**
MCCREERY, John, Liverpool, 1768–1832.
5111
— Bibs. 1:**1362**
MCCUTCHEON, George Barr, 1866–
1928–Libr. 1:3074 3586; 10038

MACDIARMID, Hugh, *pseud. of* Christopher Murray Grieve, 1892–1978–Bibs. 1:**4091–2c**

MACDONALD, George, 1824–1905. **12082–3**
— Bibs. 1:**4093–4a**
— Collns. 7322a 12082–3

MACDONALD, James Ramsay, 1866–1937–Bibs. 1:**4094d**
— Mss.–Bibs. 1:**4094d**

MCDOUGALL, William, 1871–1938–Bibs. 1:**4094e–f**

MACDURNAN GOSPELS BINDER, fl.1570. **5112**

MCFALL, Frances Elizabeth (Clarke), 1862–1943 *see* GRAND, Sarah, *pseud.*

MCFEE, William Morley Punshon, 1881–1961–Bibs. 1:**4094g**

MCGEE, Thomas D'Arcy, 1825–68–Bibs. 1:**4095**

MACGEOGHEGAN, James, 1702–63. 1812

MACGEORGE, Bernard Buchanan, 1845?–1924–Libr. 1:632; 2:511–12; 786 2802 8570–1 10835 11740

MCGILL UNIVERSITY, Montreal.
— FACULTY OF MEDICINE. LIBRARY–Collns. 1:**2215**
— LIBRARY–Collns. 1:1960; 10281

MCGLASHAN, James, Dublin, fl.1846–58. **5113**

MCGOWAN, John, fl.1825–45. **5114**

MACHEN, Arthur Llewelyn Jones, 1863–1947. 481 **12084–7**
— Bibs. 1:684 **4096–8c**
— Collns. 12087
— *Tobacco talk.* 12086

MACHIAVELLI, Niccolò, 1469–1527. 948 953
— Bibs. 1:**826d**
— *Discourses.* 948
— *Florentine history.* 6354
— Ptg. 6354

'MACHINE-PRINTING.' 3598

MACHINES–Bibs. 1:1745n
—, COLLATING *see* TEXTUAL CRITICISM AND EDITING–Collating machines.
—, COMPOSING *see* COMPOSING MACHINES.
—, PAPERMAKING *see* PAPERMAKING MACHINES.
—, PERFECTING *see* PERFECTING MACHINES.
—, TYPECASTING *see* TYPECASTING MACHINES.

MACHLINIA, William de, fl.1482–90. **5115–18** 6055 6081
— *Primer.* 5115–16
— *Speculum Christiani.* 5118
— *Yearbook.* 5117

MACHYNLLETH, Montgomeryshire.
— Bibs. 1:963h
— Ptg.–Bibs. 1:963h

MACKAY, mrs. Alexander, fl.1921–Libr. 1:**2473**

MACKAY, Mary, 1855–1924 *see* CORELLI, Marie, *pseud.*

MCKEE, Thomas Jefferson, 1840–99–Libr. 2566 2572 2576–7 2582 2588

MACKENZIE, Alexander, formerly Slidell, 1803–48 *see* SLIDELL, Alexander, afterwards MacKenzie, 1803–48.

MCKENZIE, Donald Francis, fl.1932– . 240

MACKENZIE, sir Edward Montague Compton, 1883–1972–Bibs. 1:**4099–100**

MACKENZIE, sir George, 1636–91. 1:**4101**

MACKENZIE, Henry, 1745–1831. **12088–9**
— Bibs. 1:1942 **4101d**
— *Man of feeling.* 12089

MCKERROW, Ronald Brunlees, 1872–1940. 2:887 915; 46–9 300a 324
— Bibs. 1:**4101m**
— *Shakespeare's Works.* 2:756 885

MACKIE, Alexander, 1825–94. **5119–20a**

MACKIE BURNSIANA LIBRARY, Kilmarnock–Collns. 1:**2634**

MACKINLAY, John, c.1737–1821. **5120k**

MACKLIN, Charles, 1697?–1797. **12090–2**
— *Love à-la-mode.* 12090 12092
— *Man of the world.* 12091

MACKY, John, d.1726. **12093–4**
— *Court characters.* 12093
— *Memoirs.* 12094

MACLACHLAN, Ewen, 1775–1822–Bibs. 1:**4102–4**

MCLACHLAN, Herbert, 1876–1958. 3074

MCLACHLAN LIBRARY, UNITARIAN COLLEGE, Manchester *see* UNITARIAN COLLEGE, Manchester. MCLACHLAN COLLEGE.

MACLAREN, Archibald, fl.1857–74. **12095**
— *Fairy family.* 12095

MCLEAN, Frank, 1837–1904–Libr. 1:**444**

MACLEAN, Murdoch, fl.1916–19–Bibs. 1:**4105**

MACLEHOSE, Agnes (Craig), 1759–1841. 9029

MACLEHOSE, James, Glasgow, 1811–85. **5121**
— Bibs. 1:**1362q**

MACLEHOSE, Robert, Glasgow, 1820–1910. 4746

MACLISE, Daniel, 1806–70. 9983

MCMANUS, Charlotte Elizabeth, d.1944 *see* MCMANUS, L., *pseud.*

MCMANUS, L., *pseud. of* Charlotte Elizabeth McManus, d.1944–Bibs. 1:**4106**

MACMATH, William, 1844–1922. 13235

MACMILLAN, Alexander, 1818–96 *see also*
CRANFORD SERIES (MACMILLANS);
MACMILLANS ILLUSTRATED STANDARD
NOVELS; MACMILLAN'S MAGAZINE.
3974 **5122–6** 7295
— Letters. 5123–4
MACMILLAN, Daniel, Cambridge, 1813–57.
3974 **5127**
MACMILLAN, sir Frederick Orridge,
1851–1936. 5122a
MACMILLAN AND COMPANY, est.
1843–Bibs. 1:**1863** 3952a
MACMILLAN'S ILLUSTRATED STANDARD
NOVELS. 7426
— Bibs. 1:1746
MACMILLAN'S MAGAZINE. 7851
— Bibs. 1:1716k 1927 3508
MCMURRY COLLEGE, Abilene, Texas. 9661
MCNAMARA, John, 1764?–1822–Libr. 2917
MACNEICE, Frederick Louis, 1907–63.
12096
— Collns. 12096
MACNEVIN, Thomas, fl.1845. **12097**
— Bibs. 1:**4106t**
MACOCKE, John, fl.1645–92.
— *Current intelligence.* 7659
MACPHERSON, James, 1736–96. 7338
12098–100 13371
— Bibs. 1:**4107–8d**
— *Fingal.* 12100
— *Original collection of Ossian.* 12098
— — Bibs. 1:4107–8d
— *Temora.* 12100
MACRAY, William Dunn, 1826–1916.
— *Parnassus plays.* 7162
MACREADY, William, 1832–71. 8909
MACREADY, William Charles, 1793–1873.
12441
— Libr. 2:1147
MACRONE, John, fl.1834–40? 9991 10054
10068–9 10091 10106
MACRORY, Adam J., Belfast, fl.1850–77. **5128**
MACSELF, Albert James, 1879–1952.
— *Plant portraits.* 6967
— Publ. 6967
MACSWINEY, Terence Joseph, d.1920–Bibs.
1:**4109**
MACY, George, fl.1939–48–Bibs. 1:**1359**
MADAN, Falconer, 1851–1935. 25 28 41
— Bibs. 1:**4109b**
— Libr. 1:935a
MADAN, Judith (Cowper), 1702–81–Bibs.
1:**4109d**
MADAN, Martin, 1725–90–Bibs. 1:**4109f**
MADDEN, Dodgson Hamilton,
1840–1928–Libr. 7373
MADDEN, sir Frederic, 1801–73. 86 2897
3358 3391

MADDEN, Richard Robert, 1798–1886–Libr.
2733
MADERTIE, David Drummond, 3d lord,
1611?–94 *see* DRUMMOND, David, 3d
lord Maderty, 1611?–94.
MADERTY, David Drummond, 3d lord,
1611?–94 *see* DRUMMOND, David, 3d
lord Madderty, 1611?–94.
MADE-UP EDITIONS *see* EDITIONS,
MADE-UP.
MADRID. BIBLIOTECA MUNICIPAL–
Collns. 2:365
MAGA see BLACKWOOD'S EDINBURGH
MAGAZINE.
MAGAZINE OF ART. 7835
MAGAZINE OF BOTANY. 6961
MAGEE, David Bickersteth, 1905–78–Libr.
14473
MAGGIN, Daniel, 1898– –Libr. 2:443
MAGGS BROTHERS, est. 1860. **5129–30**
MAGIC *see also* CONJURING. **7480–3**
— Bibs. 1:**2241–4**
— Collns. **7480–2**
MAGINN, William, 1793–1842. **12101**
— Bibs. 1:**4110–11**
MAHON, ld. Charles, 1753–1816 *see*
STANHOPE, Charles, 3d earl Stanhope,
1753–1816.
MAHON, Susan, fl.1960 *see* MERRION
PRESS, fl.1960.
MAHON, viscount, 1816–55 *see*
STANHOPE, Philip Henry, 5th earl
Stanhope, 1805–75.
MAHONEY, James, fl.1866–1910. 7420a
MAIDENS OF THE UNITED KINGDOM.
2252
MAIDMENT, James, 1795?–1879–Libr. 2977
MAIDSTONE, Kent. **1161a–b**
— Paper *see also* HARRIS, Richard, fl.1738;
HOLLINGWORTH'S, fl.1830;
WHATMAN, James, 1702–59;
WHATMAN, James, 1741–98. 1161a–b
3772 3891 5975
MAIDSTONE COLLEGE OF ART PRESS,
fl.1960. 6495
MAITLAND, Frederick William,
1850–1906–Bibs. 1:**4112–h**
MAITLAND, John, 2d earl and 1st duke of
Lauderdale, 1616–82 *see also* HAM
HOUSE, London–Libr. 2604
MAITLAND, Richard, 4th earl of Lauder-
dale, 1653–95. **12102–4**
— *Virgil's Georgics.* 12102 12104
MAITLAND CLUB, Glasgow, fl.1827–
47–Bibs. 1:3783d
MAJOR, John, 1469–1550. **12105**
— Bibs. 1:**4112k**
— *History of Greater Britain.* 12105

MALAHIDE CASTLE, co. Dublin. 8693 8698 8704
— Collns. 1:2508a 2508d
MALBY, sir Nicholas, 1530?–84.
— *Plain and easy way to remedy a horse.* 7372
— *Remedies for the diseases in horses.* 7372
MALCOLM, sir John, 1769–1833. 5250
MALCOLME, David, d.1748. **12106**
— *Letters illustrating the antiquities.* 12106
MALINES, Netherlands. 856
MALINOWSKI, Bronislaw Kaspar, 1884–1942–Bibs. 1:**4112q**
MALKIN, Benjamin Heath, 1769–1842. 13490
— Libr. 3334
MALLET, David, 1705?–65. **12107**
— *William and Margaret.* 12107
MALLET, John Gregory, 1604–81.
— *Brief method.* 969
MALLOCH, George Reston, d.1953–Bibs. 1:**4113**
MALLOCK, William Hurrell, 1849–1923–Bibs. 1:**4114**
MALMESBURY, James Edward Harris, 5th earl of, 1872–1950 *see* HARRIS, James Edward, 5th earl of Malmesbury, 1872–1950.
MALONE, Edmond, 1741–1812. 2:768 791 1936; 9786 11307 **12108–17**
— *Baratriana.* 12113
— *Critical works of Dryden.* 12111
— *Inquiry.* 12109
— Letters. 12112
— Libr. 2:530
— Ptg. 12111
MALONE SOCIETY REPRINTS. 7116 7122–3 7145 9385–6 14374
MALORY, sir Thomas, d.1471. **12118–21**
— Illus. 8434 12121
— *Morte d'Arthur.* 4284 8433–4 12118–21
— Ptg. 4284 12119–20
— Text. 12118
MALTHUS, Thomas, fl.1682–6. 8948
— Bibs. 1:**4114q–r**
MALVERN, Worcs. **1430**
— Newspapers. 1430
MALVERN MERCURY. 1430
MAN, ISLE OF *see also* PRINTING IN MANX. **1296–a**
— Bibs. 1:**922y–3**
— Maps–Bibs. 1:**1796**
— Newspapers–Bibs. 1:1862
— Paper. 1296–a
— Ptg.–Bibs. 1:923
MANASSEH BEN ISRAEL, 1604–57.
— *Hope of Israel.* 724
MANATON, Devon–Ptg. *see* BOAR'S HEAD PRESS, est. 1931.

MANCHESTER, Lancs. **1174–80**
— Bibs. 1:**910–a**
— Ballads. 1177
— Bndng. *see* FALKNER, George, fl.1891; FRYE, Bartholomew, fl.1818.
— Bksllng. 1174 1179
— Directories. 1176
— Librs. 1174 2459
— Maps–Bibs. 1:**1793**
— Newspapers. 1175–6 1178 1180 5131
— Ptg. 1176 5153
— — Bibs. 1:910
— Publ. *see* BRADSHAW, George, 1801–53.
— CHETHAM HOSPITAL AND LIBRARY *see* CHETHAM HOSPITAL AND LIBRARY, Manchester.
— HARTLEY VICTORIA COLLEGE. LIBRARY. 3081
— JOHN RYLANDS LIBRARY *see* JOHN RYLANDS LIBRARY, Manchester.
— PORTICO LIBRARY. 2624
— PUBLIC LIBRARIES. 3270
— — Collns. 1:661 5145; 2:193; 1177 2215 2381 4138 5814 9547 9954 10641
— — MOSS SIDE BRANCH–Collns. 1:2536 3018 3407
— — REFERENCE LIBRARY–Collns. 1:1139w 1161 1233–4 1276 1768 2279h 3367
— SPENSER SOCIETY *see* SPENSER SOCIETY, Manchester.
— STATISTICAL SOCIETY *see* MANCHESTER STATISTICAL SOCIETY.
— UNITARIAN COLLEGE *see* UNITARIAN COLLEGE, Manchester.
— UNIVERSITY.
— — ASHBURNE HALL. LIBRARY. 3117
— ZION'S TEMPLE *see* ZION'S TEMPLE, Manchester.
MANCHESTER CO-OPERATIVE NEWS. 5131
MANCHESTER CO-OPERATIVE PRINTING SOCIETY, est. 1869. **5131**
MANCHESTER GUARDIAN–Bibs. 1:4161
MANCHESTER STATISTICAL SOCIETY. 2455
MANCHESTER WEEKLY JOURNAL. 1175–6
MANDERSTON, William, fl.1515–40–Bibs. 1:**4112k**
MANDEVILLE, Bernard, 1670?–1733. **12122**
— Bibs. 1:**4115–16**
— *Fable of the bees.* 12122
MANDEVILLE, sir John, d.1372. **12123–6**
— Bibs. 1:**4116a–c**
— Illus. 12124–5
— Mss. 12123
— Ptg. 12124 12126
— *Travels.* 12124–6

Vol. **1** = *Bibliographies*   **2** = *Shakespeare*   **4** = 1–8221   **5** = 8222–14616

MANGAN, James Clarence, 1803–49–Bibs. 1:**4117–a**
MANGNALL, Richmal, 1769–1820. **12127**
— *Historical and miscellaneous questions.* 12127
MANLEY, Mary (De la Rivière), 1663–1724. 10528 **12128**
— *Secret memoirs.* 12128
MANN, sir Horace, 1st baronet, 1701–86. 14176
MANN, James, d.1927–Libr. 2862
MANN, Thomas, 1875–1955–Bibs. 1:**822m–n**
MANNING, Anne, 1807–79–Collns. 7322a
MANNING, card. Henry Edward, 1808–92–Bibs. 1:**4118**
MANNINGHAM, John, d.1622. 9600 **12129–31**
MANŒUVRES OF DON PEDRO ANTOS, 1803. 6992
MANSELL, Joseph, 1803–74. 6202
MANSFIELD, Katherine, *pseud. of* Kathleen (Beauchamp) Murry, 1888–1923. **12132–5**
— Bibs. 1:684 **4118a–e**
— Collns. 12135
— Mss. 12135
MANSION, Collard, Brussels, fl.1484. 4312
MANTON, Thomas, 1620–77. 708
MANUALS *see* BIBLIOGRAPHY–Manuals; BOOK COLLECTING–Manuals.
MANUCHE, Cosmo, fl.1652–Mss. 1:1606b
MANUSCRIPT NEWSPAPERS *see* NEWSPAPERS, MANUSCRIPT.
MANUSCRIPTS *see also* LETTERS, *and* –Mss. *after names of individuals.* 490 508 513 516 554 2375 2446 3043 3463 3793
— Alchemy. 6738
— Astrology. 6779
— Ballads. 1560 1635 6781 6783 6792
— — Bibs. 1:1468
— Baptists–Bibs. 1:2253x
— Bibliogr. descr. 134 3358 12704
MANUSCRIPTS–Bibs. 1:332 346k 348k 359 359e 363 371d 372b 403 427 534 600c 634 676 689c 1280n 1401e 1760m; (*see* Intro., p. xii). 527 538 540–1 544–5 797 800 1635 2897 7621a 8430 8513 8693 8697–8 8781 8792 8802 9223–4 9234 9250 9276–7 9666a 9722 9867 10067 10525 10744 11002 11290 11297 11417 11522 11607 11679 11838 11922 11924 11929 12024 12549 12711 12863 13088 13117 13344 13612 13775 13794 13832 13933 13968 14112 14324 14366 14492
— — Æ, *pseud.* 1:2311
— — Anstey. 1:2326d
— — Arnold. 1:2336f
— — Baxter. 1:2405b

— — Bennett. 1:2440x 2442
— — Bentham. 1:2448c
— — Berkeley. 1:2452
— — Boswell. 1:2508a–d
— — Brontë. 1:2532b 2541d
— — Brooke. 1:2550
— — Buchanan. 1:2604
— — Burns. 1:2636h
— — Byron. 1:2963–4b
— — Calverley. 1:2697b
— — Cambridge, R. O. 1:2697m
— — Carlyle. 1:2706r–s
— — Cary. 1:2744
— — Clare. 1:2807 2809a
— — Coleridge. 1:2824m 5166t
— — Combe. 1:2855h
— — Conrad. 1:2866g–i 2874
— — Cowper. 1:2896d
— — Crabbe. 1:2903
— — Crowley. 1:2923p
— — Cruikshank. 1:2935g
— — Davidson. 1:2961p
— — Defoe. 1:2987
— — De La Mare. 1:3008
— — Denham. 1:3011
— — Dickens. 1:3050h 3058 3066c 3068p 3095d 3100
— — Douglas. 1:3168k
— — Doyle. 1:3181r 3181w
— — Drury. 1:3194a
— — Dryden. 1:3200
— — Eliot. 1:3248f
— — Eliot, T. S. 1:3258
— — Elliott. 1:3265
— — Evans, T. 1:3273r
— — Fielding. 1:3307
— — Firbank. 1:3315
— — Fisher. 1:3318c
— — Ford, F. M. 1:3340–1
— — Fox. 1:3356k
— — Gardiner. 1:3395g
— — Garrick. 1:3399
— — Gibbon. 1:3421
— — Gill. 1:3437
— — Godwin. 1:4654d
— — Goldsmith. 1:3464d
— — Gore. 1:3477d
— — Guiney. 1:3537
— — Handel. 1:3571b
— — Hardy. 1:3587
— — Harvey. 1:3619f
— — Hodson. 1:3671h
— — Hogg. 1:3681b
— — Hopkins. 1:3703b 3703p
— — Hume. 1:3757
— — Huxley, A. L. 1:3778e
— — Huxley, T. H. 1:3779b 3779d
— — Jenner. 1:3822

MANUSCRIPTS–Bibs.–Johnson. 1:2508c
3837 3841b–c 3847–8 3851–2
— — Joyce. 1:3885 3890
— — Keats. 1:3911
— — King. 1:4069b
— — Kipling. 1:3952 3954
— — Lamb. 1:3980d 3981 3982g 3984
— — Landor. 1:3995
— — Lawrence. 1:4016e 4016g 4017d 4019
4020c–d 4021
— — Lenton. 1:4045d
— — Leyden. 1:4053
— — Locke. 1:4069b
— — Lowry. 1:4077c
— — Macdonald. 1:4094d
— — Meynell. 1:4212–13
— — Monro. 1:4261r
— — Moore. 1:4263m
— — Murdoch. 1:4317p
— — Patmore. 1:4400
— — Peele. 1:4406a
— — Percy. 1:4415q
— — Peter. 1:4416k
— — Pielou. 1:4424d
— — Piozzi. 1:3841b
— — Pope. 1:4443f
— — Powys, L. 1:4454d
— — Priestley. 1:4458c
— — Reid. 1:4503 4505
— — Reynolds. 1:4511f
— — Richard de Bury. 1:4513l
— — Richardson, H. H. 1:4516h
— — Ritson. 1:4523
— — Roscoe. 1:4537
— — Rosenberg. 1:4538
— — Rossetti. 1:4544k
— — Ruskin. 1:4556e
— — Sarolea. 1:4581m
— — Savile. 1:4585f
— — Scott, J. 1:4592
— — Scott, W. 1:4611
— — Shaw. 1:4634
— — Shelley. 1:4647 4652 4654 4654d
4657
— — Sheppard. 1:4460a
— — Shiel. 1:4676
— — Skelton. 1:4696a
— — Sorley. 1:4734h
— — Southcott. 1:4735n
— — Southwell. 1:4747
— — Stephen. 1:4776f
— — Stephens. 1:4784c–e
— — Sterne. 1:4790–2
— — Stevenson. 1:4799
— — Swift. 1:4836 4842d
— — Swinburne. 1:4849e 4856 4857g 4858
— — Taylor, T. 1:4882q
— — Tennyson. 1:4897–b

— — Tennyson, F. 1:4904b
— — Thackeray. 1:4922
— — Thompson. 1:4946 4949
— — Thomson. 1:4962 4963
— — Trollope. 1:4988
— — Victoria. 1:5000q
— — White, G. 1:5081
— — White, H. K. 1:5085
— — Wilde. 1:5103–4f
— — Wilson. 1:5127b
— — Wise. 1:5145
— — Woolf. 1:5159
— — Wordsworth. 1:5166t 5173 5176
— — Yeats. 1:5205 5207d 5208
— Botany–Bibs. 1:2129
— Collns. (Institutional). 507 527 538 543–5
2811 2852 2874 2902 2907 2984 3027 3037
3074 3081 3102 3109 3117 3134 3142–3
3154 3257 3298–9 3336 4066 4073 6442
12711
— Collns. (Personal). 2544 2683 2732 2767
2781 2851 2874 2885 2896–7 2909 2916–17
2953 2958 2966 2984 3022 3024 3026–7
3037 3088 3093 3102 3109 3125 3150 3208
3211 3241 3257 3261 3298 3347 3354 3358
3363 3379 3380a 3394 8159 9867 9869
13124 14206
— Drama. 7095 7115 7131–2 7136 7154 7158
7162 7185 7190 7196 7205 7210 7218–20
7226 7934
— — Bibs. 1:1606b–c 1607 1611b 1615
1633d–f 1635c 1650c
— Hunting–Bibs. 1:2197d
— Ireland. 3376a
— Maps. 7486 7518
— Methodists–Bibs. 1:2270d
— Music. 7621a
— — Bibs. 1:1839a
— Novels. 7272 7319
— Poetry. 7974 7975 7978 7980–1 7984 8000
8007 8009 8027
— — Bibs. 1:1986p 2033k
— Psalms. 6904
— Science. 8121–3 8148 8159
— — Bibs. 1:2279e–f
— Scotland. 1560 1635
— — Bibs. 1:1468
— Songs–Bibs. 1:1841m
— Tobacco–Bibs. 1:2288
— 1475–1500. 562 3569
— 1475–1640. 2:300; 637–8 657 7136
— 1801–1900. 797 800 808
— 1901– . 491
MANWAYRING, sir Henry, 1587–1653.
— Seaman's dictionary. 7072
MANX see PRINTING IN MANX.
MAPLISDEN, Peter, Newcastle-upon-Tyne,
fl.1710. 5503

MARKHAM, mrs., *pseud. of* Elizabeth (Cartwright) Penrose, 1780–1837. 5250
MARKIEVICZ, Constance Georgine (Gore-Booth), 1868–1927–Bibs. 1:**4120**
MARKINCH, Fife.–Ptg. *see* TULLIS, R. AND COMPANY, est. 1809; TULLIS AND RUSSELL; TULLIS RUSSELL, est. 1809.
MARKS, Harry F., fl.1923–36–Libr. 10032
MARKS, Henry Stacy, 1829–98. 7420a
MARKS OF OWNERSHIP *see* OWNERSHIP, MARKS OF.
MARLBOROUGH, Wilts.
— COLLEGE. LIBRARY. 3401a
— ST. MARY'S CHURCH. VICAR'S LIBRARY. 2687 3063–4 3401a
MARLER, Anthony, fl.1541. **5132**
MAR LODGE, Aber.–Libr. 1:325b; 2555
MARLOW, John, fl.1662–85. **12137**
— *Letters to a sick friend.* 12137
MARLOWE, Christopher, 1564–93. 2:428 1200; 7181 **12138–64**
— Bibs. 1:1597 **4120x–6**
— *Dido queen of Carthage.* 12145
— *Doctor Faustus.* 7160 12139 12143 12147 12152 12155–7 12160
— *Edward II.* 12140 12163
— *Hero and Leander.* 12153
— *Jew of Malta.* 12141 12158 12161
— *Massacre at Paris.* 12148–50 12154 12164
— *Ovid's Elegies.* 12159 12162
— Ptg. 12163
— Publ. 12159
— *Tamburlaine.* 12146 12151
— Text. 12139 12141–3 12147 12156–8 12160
MARMION, Edmund, fl.1653.
— *Quarles' Argalus.* 12934
MARMION, Shackerley, 1603–39. **12165**
— *Holland's leaguer.* 12165
MARIONETTES–Bibs. 1:**2214m**
MARPRELATE, Martin, *pseud.*, fl.1588–90 *see* MARTIN MARPRELATE PRESS, 1588–90.
MARRANO BOOKS. 7469
— Bibs. 1:2199b
MARRIED MAN'S FEAST, 1671. 707
MARRIOT, John, fl.1616–57.
— *Randolph's Aristippus.* 12977
MARRYAT, Frederick, 1792–1848. 783 **12166–71**
— Bibs. 1:**4130**
— *Children of the new forest.* 12171
— Collns. 7322a
— *Peter Simple.* 12166
— *Valerie.* 12170
MARSH, sir Edward Howard, 1872–54. 3173

MARSH, archbp. Francis, 1627–93 *see* DUBLIN UNIVERSITY. MARSH'S LIBRARY.
MARSHALL, Alfred, 1842–1924–Bibs. 1:**4131**
MARSHALL, Archibald, 1866–1934–Bibs. 1:**4132**
MARSHALL, Francis Albert, 1840–89–Libr. 1:380
MARSHALL, John, d.1607–Libr. 2646
MARSHALL, John, fl.1782–1815. **5133–7** 7051
— Bibs. 1:1564 1565a–b
MARSHALL, William, fl.1533–7. **5138** 8067
— Bibs. 1:**1364**
MARSHALL, William, fl.1630–50. **5139**
MARSHAM, Robert, 1708–97–Libr. 2386
MARSHE, Thomas, fl.1554–87. 6365
MARSH'S LIBRARY, Dublin *see* DUBLIN. UNIVERSITY. MARSH'S LIBRARY.
MARSTON, Edward, 1825–1914. **5140–2**
MARSTON, John, 1575?–1634. 9600 **12172–80**
— *Antonio's revenge.* 6350
— Bibs. 1:1597 **4133–7**
— *The fawn.* 12173 12176–7 12179
— Handwr. 12180
— *Insatiate countess.* 12173 12178
— *The malcontent.* 5660 11550 12173
— — Bibs. 1:4133
— Ptg. 5660 6350
— Publ. 5971
— *Scourge of villany.* 12174–5
— Text. 12172 12175 12179
MARTIAL (M. Valerius Martialis), fl.40–100. 3871
MARTIN, Douglas, fl.1958–61 *see* ORPHEUS PRESS, Leicester, 1958–61.
MARTIN, Henry Bradley, 1906– – Libr. 3341 6919
MARTIN, Jonathan, 1782–1838–Bibs. 1:**4138**
MARTIN, John, 1789–1854. **5143–5**
— Bibs. 1:**4138–b**
— Libr. 5145
— *Highland fortress.* 5144
MARTIN, Jonathan, 1782–1838. 5143
MARTIN, Matthew, fl.1771. 5975
MARTIN, Richard, fl.1808–32. 5143
— Bibs. 1:4138
MARTIN, Robert, fl.1757–96. 3912
— Bibs. 1:1256
MARTIN, Sarah Catherine, 1768–1826. **12181**
— *Old mother Hubbard.* 12181
MARTIN, Thomas, 1697–1771–Libr. 2518 2602

MARTIN, Violet Florence, 1865–1915—*for
works written under pseud. of* Martin Ross *in
collaboration with* E. A. Œ. Somerville *see*
SOMERVILLE, Edith Anna Œnone,
1858–1949.
MARTIN, William, fl.1786–1815. 4132 6572
6613
MARTIN, William, 1772–1851. 5143
— Bibs. 1:**4139**
MARTINDELL, Ernest Walter, fl.1921–Libr.
1:3944; 11764 11774 11777
MARTINEAU, Harriet, 1802–76–Bibs.
1:**4140–1**
MARTIN MARPRELATE PRESS, 1588–90.
1018 1311 **5146–55**
— Bibs. 1:**1364b–c**
— *Penry's Exhortation.* 5147 5154
— *Th'appellation.* 5146
MARTIN MAR-PRIEST PRESS, 1645–6.
6067
— Bibs. 1:**595a**
MARTYN, Edward, 1859–1923. **12182**
MARTYN, John, c.1619–80. 3471 **5156–7**
MARTYN, John, 1699–1768–Bibs. 1:**4142**
MARTYN, Thomas, 1735–1825. **12183–4**
— Bibs. 1:**4143–a**
— *Psyche*–Bibs. 1:4143
— *Universal conchologist.* 12184
MARVELL, Andrew, 1621–78. **12185–9**
— Bibs. 1:**4144–7j**
— *Miscellaneous poems.* 12185 12187 12189
— Text. 12188–9
— *Thyrsis and Dorinda.* 12186
— *To his noble friend.* 12188
MARY I, queen of England and Ireland,
1516–58. 3569
MARYLEBONE *see* LONDON. ST.
MARYLEBONE.
MARY STUART, queen of Scots, 1542–87. 1601
— Bibs. 1:712e **4148–51**
— Collns. 3258
— Libr. 2051–2 2516 2739
MASCARENHAS, bp. Ferdinand Martins,
d.1628–Libr. 2782
MASEFIELD, John Edward, 1878–1967.
12190–4
— Bibs. 1:**4152–62**
— Collns. 1:4162; 12192
— *Poem and two plays.* 12191
— Ptg. 12191
— *Salt-water ballads*–Bibs. 1:4160
— *Tragedy of Nan.* 12194
— *Young man's fancy.* 12190
MASHAM, sir Francis, 3d baronet,
d.1722/3–Libr. 3140
MASK, THE. 7887
MASON, Alfred Edward Woodley,
1865–1948–Bibs. 1:**4164**

MASON, John Henry, 1875–1951. **5158–
61**
— Bibs. 1:**1364f**
MASON William, 1724–97. 10832 **12195–6**
— Bibs. 1:**4165–7**
— Collns. 10838
— *Gray's Life and letters.* 10839
— Mss. 10838
— *Musaeus.* 12196
— Ptg. 12196
MASON, William Monck, 1775–1895–Libr.
2715
MASONIC CATECHISMS *see* CATE-
CHISMS, MASONIC.
MASQUE OF THE FOUR SEASONS, 1634.
9592–3
MASQUE OF THE TWELVE MONTHS, 1611.
9593
MASQUES–Bibs. 1:1603 1605–6 1615
MASSIE, Joseph, d.1784–Bibs. 1:**4168**
MASSACHUSETTS. GENERAL HOSPITAL.
LIBRARY–Collns. 2:471
MASSINGER, Philip, 1583–1640. 7181
12197–207
— *Believe as you list.* 12197 12200a
— Bibs. 1:**4169–b**
— *The bondman.* 6412
— *City madam.* 7995 12201 12204–5
— *Duke of Milan.* 12198
— Mss. 7995 12197 12200a
— Ptg. 6412 12205
— Text. 8464 8466–7 8471 12198–200
12205–7
MASSON, David, 1822–1907. 708
— Bibs. 1:**4170**
MASTER BINDERS' ASSOCIATION.
5591
MASTER OF THE REVELS *see* REVELS,
MASTER OF THE.
MASTER PAPER MAKERS, est. 1790s *see*
COMMITTEE OF MASTER PAPER
MAKERS, est. 1790s.
MASTERS, James E., fl.1924 *see* HIGH
HOUSE PRESS, Shaftesbury, est. 1924.
MASTERS, Mary, d.1771. 11490
MASTERS OF THE STAPLE *see* STAPLE,
MASTERS OF THE.
MATHEMATICAL REPOSITORY. 7542
MATHEMATICAL TRANSACTIONS. 7546
MATHEMATICS *see also* ARITHMETIC.
7541–53
— Bibs. 1:**2214s–t**
— Newspapers. 7542 7545–6
— — Bibs. 1:1900i
MATHER, Percival, fl.1857–92. 5966
MATHEW, John *see* LUKE, John, Denny,
fl.1800.
MATHEWS, Elkin, fl.1887–94. **5162–3**

MATHIAS, Thomas James, 1754?–
1835–Bibs. 1:**4170d**
— *Pursuits of literature*–Bibs. 1:4170d
MATRICES, TYPE *see* TYPE–Matrices.
MATTHEW, John, *pseud. of* John Rogers,
1500?–55.
— *Bible.* 6868–a
— — Bibs. 1:1485i
MATTHEWES, Augustine, fl.1619–53.
— *Middleton's Fair quarrel.* 12273
— *Shakespeare's Troublesome reign.* 2:1417;
12273
MATURIN, Charles Robert, 1780–1824.
— Bibs. 1:**4171**
— Mss. 13182
— Publ. 5250
MATZ, Bertram Waldrom, 1865–1925–
Bibs. 1:**4171e**
— Libr. 10037
MAUCHLINE BURNS CLUB. 9103
MAUGHAM, William Somerset, 1874–1965.
12208–20
— Bibs. 1:1597 **4172–9**
— Collns. 3331 12218
— *Cosmopolitains.* 12211
— *Liza of Lambeth.* 5888 12209
— *Moon and sixpence.* 12219
— *Mrs. Craddock.* 12220
— Mss. 12216–17
— *Of human bondage.* 12212
— *On a Chinese screen.* 12217
— *Painted veil.* 12210
— Publ. 5888 12210–11
— Text. 12209 12212
— *Theatre.* 12216
MAUND, Benjamin, 1790–1863.
— *Botanist.* 6947
MAUNSEL AND COMPANY, Dublin, est.
1904. **5164**
MAUNSELL, Andrew, d.1595. 3482 3485
MAURICE, Henry, 1648–91. 1517
MAURICE, Hugh, 1775?–1825. **12221**
MAVOR, Osborne Henry, 1888–1951 *see*
BRIDIE, James, *pseud.*
MAVOUR, William Fordyce, 1758–1837.
11416
MAXWELL, Caroline Elizabeth Sarah
(Sheridan) Stirling-, formerly mrs. Norton,
1808–77 *see* NORTON, Caroline Elizabeth
Sarah (Sheridan), afterwards lady Stirling-
Maxwell, 1808–77.
MAXWELL, George T., fl.1895–Libr. 2526
MAXWELL, James, fl.1502–Libr. 3381
MAXWELL, Mary Elizabeth (Braddon),
1837–1915 *see* BRADDON, Mary Elizabeth
(mrs. Maxwell), 1837–1915.
MAXWELL, sir William Stirling-,
1818–78–Libr. 3259

MAY, Edward, fl.1633–Bibs. 1:**4183**
MAY, Thomas, 1595–1650–Mss. 1:1606b
MAYBOLE, Ayr.–Ptg. 5583
MAYER, Charles, fl.1894. **12222**
— *Shadows of life.* 12222
MAYES, William, 1856–1935–Libr. 2959
MAYFLOWER BIBLE, 1597 *see*
BIBLE–Versions–'Mayflower'.
MAYLER, John, fl.1539–45. 6056 8067
MAYNARD, Robert Ashwin, fl.1925–31 *see*
RAVEN PRESS, Harrow Weald, est. 1931.
MAYNE, Jasper, 1604–72. **12223–4**
— Bibs. 1:**4185**
— *Part of Lucian.* 12224
— Ptg. 12223–4
MAYNARD, Theodore, 1890–1956–Bibs.
1:**4184**
MAYO. **1960**
— Bibs. 1:1055q **1106**
MAYOW, John, 1643–79–Bibs. 1:**4186**
MEAD, Richard, 1673–1734.
— Bibs. 1:**4187**
— Libr. 277 2525
MEADES, Anna, fl.1737?–71.
— *History of Harrington.* 13028 13032
MEADOWS, Joseph Kenny, 1790–1874.
— *Heads of the people.* 5909
— *Illustrated Shakespeare.* 5909
— *Pickwick characters.* 9982
MEARNE, Charles, fl.1685. **5165**
MEARNE, Samuel, fl.1669–81. 2205 2248
2677 **5166–74** 5385
MEARNS, James, 1855–1922–Libr. 1:1733
MEASURES, PRINTERS' *see* COMPOSING
STICKS.
MEASUREMENTS–Bibliogr. deser. 152 172
MEATH–Bibs. 1:**1107**
MECHANICAL PRINTING *see* PRINTING,
MECHANICAL.
MECHANICS' INSTITUTIONS. 2443 3466
MEDAL ENGRAVING *see* ENGRAVING,
MEDAL.
MEDALLION BINDER, fl.1545. **5175–6**
MEDICAL DIRECTORIES *see* DIRECT-
ORIES, MEDICAL.
MEDICAL MEN AS AUTHORS–Bibs.
1:368a 635
MEDICINE *see also* DISPENSATORIES;
PHARMACOPŒIAS. 258 481 1244 1596
1754 **7554–71**
— Bibs. 1:586 **2215–30i**
— Collns. 7563 7565 7569 7571
— Newspapers–Bibs. 1:2218
— Publ. 7565 7571
MEDICINE AND SHAKESPEARE–Bibs.
2:101
MEDICI SOCIETY, London, est. 1908. 4091
MEDLAND, Thomas, fl.1777–1822. **5177**

MEDLEY, THE. 7796
MEDWALL, Henry, fl.1486. **12225**
—*Fulgens and Lucrece.* 12225
— Text. 12225
MEDWAY MILLS, Kent–Paper. 1161a
MEDWIN, Thomas, 1788–1869.
— Bibs. 1:**4188**
— *Shelley papers.* 13364
MEEHAN, John Francis, Bath, d.1913
  5178
MEIRS, Richard Waln, 1866– –Libr. 4444
MELBANCKE, Brian, fl.1583. **12226**
—*Philotimus.* 12226
MELBOURNE. UNIVERSITY. QUEEN'S
  COLLEGE. LIBRARY–Collns. 1:5068
MELLON, Paul, 1907– –Libr. 1:486 2100d;
  573 6223
MELLOR, Oscar Buckley, 1921– –Bibs.
  1:1322g
MELMOTH, William, 1710–99. 13594
MELVILL, Andro, d.1640–Libr. 1625
MELVILLE, George John Whyte-, 1821–78.
— Bibs. 1:**4189–90**
— Publ. 5372
MELVILLE, Herman, 1819–91.
— *Mardi.* 4004
— *Moby Dick.* 987 12986
— *Story of Toby.* 996
— *Typee.* 991
MELVILLE MILL, Lasswade. 1712
MEMOIRS. 1863
MEMOIRS OF THE COURT OF LILLIPUT,
  1727. 13741
MEMOIRS OF THE LORD VISCOUNT
  DUNDEE, 1714. 734
MEMORIAL RECONSTRUCTIONS. 11076
MENDENHALL, John Cooper, 1886– –Libr.
  1:1665; 7288
MENDIP, Som.–Paper. 1390
MENNEN, William Gerhard, 1884–
  1968–Libr. 2:474 476
MENNES, sir John, 1599–1671. **12227**
— *Musarum deliciæ.* 12227
MENNONS, John, Glasgow, 1747–1818.
  12228
— Bibs. 1:**1365**
MENZIES, John, Edinburgh, 1808–79. **5179**
  9280
MERBURY, FRANCIS, fl.1579. **12229–33**
— *Marriage of Wit and Wisdom.* 12229–32
— *Moral play of Wit and Science.* 12233
MERCERS *see* WORSHIPFUL COMPANY
  OF MERCERS, London.
MERCHANT TAYLORS' SCHOOL, Lon-
  don. LIBRARY. 2949
MERCURIUS AULICUS. 1358
— Bibs. 1:1871–2 1881
MERCURIUS BELLICUS. 7679

MERCURIUS BRITANNICUS. 7691
MERCURIUS CIVICUS. 7657
MERCURIUS DOMESTICUS. 7665 7671
MERCURIUS POETICUS. 7683
MERCURIUS POLITICUS. 7680 7696
MERCURIUS ROMANUS. 7731
MEREDITH, George, 1828–1909. 465
  12234–56 13081
— Bibs. 1:**4191–203**
— *Amazing marriage.* 12256
— Bndng. 12239–40 12243 12251
— *Cleopatra.* 12250
— *Collected poems.* 12240
— *Evan Harrington.* 12246
— Collns. 2849 3045 12235–6 12244 12248–9
  12253
— *The egoist.* 12239
— *Jump to glory Jane.* 11902
— Letters. 12249 12253
— — Bibs. 1:4203
— *Modern love.* 12255
— Mss. 12234 12248 12255
— *One of our conquerors.* 12241
— *Poems.* 12238 12254
— *Poems and lyrics.* 12237
— Ptg. 12252 12256
— Publ. 4359 12237 12245 12247
— *Reading of life.* 12242
— *Rhoda Fleming.* 12247
— *Sharing of Shagpat.* 12243 12251
— Text. 12252
— *Tragic comedians.* 12252
MEREDITH, Owen, *pseud., see* LYTTON,
  Edward Robert Bulwer, 1st earl of Lytton,
  1831–91.
MERES, Francis, 1565–1647. **12257–8**
— *Palladis tamia.* 12257–8
MERGENTHALER, Ottmar, 1854–99. 6123
MERRITT, Edward Percival, 1860–1932–
  Libr. 14189
MERIONETHSHIRE. **1547**
— Maps–Bibs. 1:**1813b**
MERRETT, Christopher, 1614–95. **12259**
— *Pinax rerum.* 12259
MERRICK, James, 1720–69. **12260**
— *Benedicite paraphrased.* 12260
MERRICK, Leonard, 1864–1939–Bibs.
  1:**4205–6**
MERRION PRESS, fl.1960. 6495
MERRY AND PLEASANT PROGNOSTI-
  CATION, 1577. 6760
MERRY DEVIL OF EDMONTON, 1612. 7104
  7163
MERRY MUSES OF CALEDONIA, 189–?
  9112–13
MESSIAS, Joseph, fl.1721. 7468
METAL BINDINGS *see* BOOKBINDINGS,
  METAL.

METAL RELIEF PRINTING see PRINTING, METAL RELIEF.
METAMORPHOSES. 7018
METAPHYSICAL POETRY see POETRY, METAPHYSICAL.
METAXAS, Nikodemos, fl.1585–1646. 5180–2
— Bibs. 1:1365b–c
METHODIST BOOKS see also ANTIMETHODIST BOOKS. 5183 8101
— Bibs. 1:2270c–p
— Bksllng. 8101
— Collns. 8101a
— Mss.–Bibs. 1:2270d
— Newspapers–Bibs. 1:2207p
— Wales–Bibs. 1:2270c
METHODIST PUBLISHING HOUSE, est. 1739. 5183
METHUEN AND CO., est. 1889. 11942
METHUEN FACSIMILES. 2:620 1406 1825
METRE. 6181
— Bibs. 1:1999
MEXICO. 10550
MEYERSTEIN, Edward Harry William, 1889–1952.
— Bibs. 1:227a 4207–a
— Libr. 9406
— Mss. 3163
MEYLER, William, Bath, 1792–1821. 11880
MEYNELL, Alice Christiana Gertrude, 1847–1922. 12261–4
— Bibs. 1:4208–13
— Bndng. 12263
— Hearts of controversy. 12263
— Mss.–Bibs. 1:4212–13
— Other poems. 1145
— Preludes. 12262
— Ptg. 12261
— Ten poems. 12261
MEYNELL, Everard, 1882–1926. 3682
MEYNELL, sir Francis Meredith Wilfrid, 1891–1975 see also PELICAN PRESS, 1916–23. 5301 5303 5306 6098 12261
MEYRICK, Edmund, d.1713–Libr. 1535 2631
MEYRICK, sir William, d.1668–Libr. 3396a
MEZZOTINT ENGRAVING see ENGRAVING, MEZZOTINT.
MEZZOTINTS. 4140 6191 6550
MICHELL, Roger, fl.1627–31. 10240
MICHIGAN. UNIVERSITY. LIBRARY– Collns. 1:2707 2823a 3491a
— — WILLIAM L. CLEMENTS LIBRARY– Collns. 10796 11246
MICKIEWICZ, Adam, 1798–1855–Bibs. 1:834–6
MICKLE, William Julius, 1734–88–Bibs. 1:4213h
MICROFILMS. 7177

MIDDLE HILL, Broadway–Libr. see PHILLIPPS, sir Thomas, 1792–1872–Libr.
MIDDLE TEMPLE INN, London see LONDON. MIDDLE TEMPLE INN.
MIDDLETON, Christopher, 1560?–1628.
— Short introduction to swim. 10191
MIDDLETON, George, Aberdeen, 1828–95. 1655 5184
MIDDLETON, Godfrey Ernest Percival Willoughby, 10th baron, 1847–1924–Libr. see WOLLATON HALL, Notts.
MIDDLETON, Richard Barham, 1882–1911–Bibs. 1:4214–15d
MIDDLETON, Thomas, 1570?–1627. 12265–84
— Ant and the nightingale. 12270–1
— Bibs. 1:1597 4216–a
— The changeling. 12278 12280–1
— Fair quarrel. 12272–3
— Father Hubburd's tales. 12270
— Game at chess. 2:1688; 7146 12265–6 12269 12277
— Ghost of Lucrece. 2:276 418
— Mad world. 12274
— Michaelmas term. 12276 12283
— Mss. 12265–6 12268–9 12275 12277 12279
— Old law. 12275
— The phoenix. 12282
— Ptg. 12272–4 12276 12282–3
— Revenger's tragedy see REVENGER'S TRAGEDY.
— Roaring girl. 12279
— Spanish gypsy. 12280
— Text. 8468 12278
— Trick to catch. 12284
— Wit at several weapons. 8468
— The witch. 2:953; 9748 12268
— Women beware women. 12267
— Your five gallants. 7165 12276
MIDDLETON, William, fl.1541–7. 5185 6056
— Borde's Introduction to knowledge. 8659
MIDGLEY, James, 1786–1852–Libr. 8096
MIDLOTHIAN. 1695–730
— Librs. see HATTON HALL; NEWBATTLE ABBEY; ROSSLYN CASTLE.
— Paper see also WATKINS, Richard, Edinburgh, d.1747. 1710 1712
MIDWINTER, Daniel, d.1757. 5186
MIEJSKIEJ LIBRARY, Warsaw. 2:1249
MIERDMAN, Stephen, Antwerp, c.1510–46. 868 5186a–b
— Bibs. 1:1366
MILBANKE, Ralph Gordon Noel King, 2d earl of Lovelace, 1839–1906. 9238
MILBOURNE, William, fl.1638. 12285
— Sapientia clamitans. 12285
MILDEN, Suff.–Librs. 1400

MILITARY BOOKS. **7572-5**
— Bibs. 1:**2231-40a**
— Collns. 7574
— Newspapers–Bibs. 1:2237
MILITARY DICTIONARIES *see* DICTIONARIES, MILITARY.
MILITARY DISCIPLINE, 1623. 7573
MILL, John, 1645–1707. 8521
— Bibs. 1:**4216t**
MILL, John Stuart, 1806–73. **12286-95**
— Bibs. 1:**4217-c**
— *Autobiography.* 12290-2
— Letters. 12287-8
— Mss. 12286 12294
— *Principles of political economy.* 12289
— Publ. 6523
— *System of logic.* 12286
— Text. 12290 12292 12294
MILLAIS, sir John Everett, 1829–96. 7420a 13898
MILLAR, Andrew, 1707–68. 1241 3622 3639a **5187-9** 10488
— *Hume's History.* 11252
MILLARD, Alice (Parsons), 1873–1938–Libr. 6098a
MILLARD, Christopher Sclater, 1872–1927. 3862
— Libr. 1:5103
MILL END, Herts.–Paper. 1139
MILLENIAL STAR. 7847
MILLER, Alexander, Glasgow, fl.1724–45? 4746
MILLER, George, Dunfermline, 1771–1835. **5190-1**
MILLER, James, 16th cent.–Libr. 3193
MILLER, James, 1706–44. **12296**
— *Seasonable reproof.* 12296
MILLER, James, Dunfermline, 1791–1865. 5190-1
MILLER, John, 1783–1809. **5192**
MILLER, Sydney Richardson Christie-, 1874–1931–Libr. *see* BRITWELL COURT.
MILLER, Thomas, 1807–74. **12297**
— Bibs. 1:**4217d**
MILLER, William, 1769–1844. 6510a
MILLER, William, Edinburgh, fl.1807–43. 6613
MILLER, William, 1869–1909–Libr. 1:3033a 3094b; 7609 10112
MILLER, William Henry, 1789–1848–Libr. *see also* BRITWELL COURT, Bucks. 1:347; 2314
MILLER FAMILY, Dunfermline, 1771–1865–Bibs. 1:**1367**
MILLES, Thomas, d.1627. **12298**
MILLHALL, Kent–Paper. 1161a
MILLIET DE CHALES, Claude François, 1621–78. 884

MILLINGTON, Edward, fl.1660–1703. 3670 3684
MILLINGTON, Thomas, fl.1593–1603. 5193
MILLS, PAPER *see* PAPER MILLS.
—, PARCHMENT *see* PARCHMENT MILLS.
MILLTOWN, Henry Lesson, 7th earl of, 1837–91 *see* LESSON, Henry, 7th earl of Milltown, 1837–91.
MILLTOWN PARK COLLEGE, Dublin. LIBRARY–Collns. 1:459
MILMAN, Henry Hart, 1791–1868. 5250
MILMAN, William Henry, 1825–1908. 2694
MILNE, Alan Alexander, 1882–1956–Bibs. 1:684 1597 **4217m**
MILNER, bp. John, 1752–1826–Bibs. 1:**4218**
MILNER, William, Halifax, 1803–50. **5193a**
MILNER-GIBSON, Thomas, 1806–84 *see* GIBSON, Thomas, 1806–84.
MILNES, Richard Monckton, 1st baron Houghton, 1809–85. **12299**
— Libr. 8561
MILTON, Elizabeth Minshull, fl. 1638–80–Libr. 6885 6887b
MILTON, John, 1608–74. 6877 9400 10387 **12300-457**
— *Ad patrem.* 12431
— *Animadversions upon Smectymnuus.* 12364-5
— — Bibs. 1:**4235**
— *Arcades.* 12432
— *Areopagitica.* 3559 3573 12343 14028
— *Artis logicæ.* 12359
— Bibs. 1:1981e **4218a-49b**
— Collns. 1:4249; 2661 3039 12319 12330 12336 12355 12437 12457
— *Comus.* 11915 12338-9 12341-2 12352 12371 12387 12437 12441 12449
— — Bibs. 1:**4230d** 4235
— *De doctrina Christiana.* 12454
— *Defensio secunda.* 12385 12395 12422 12439
— — Bibs. 1:**4230** 4245
— *Eikonoklastes.* 12412 12418
— *Epitaphium Damonis.* 12349 12444 12452
— Handwr. 12327-9 12333 12350 12356 12361 12372 12409-10 12414
— *History of Britain.* 12324 12368
— *Hobson poems.* 12370 12392 12455
— *Hymn on Christ's nativity.* 12313
— Illus. 12399 12405 12449
— *Il penseroso*–Bibs. 1:1981e
— *Justa Edovardo King.* 12442
— *L'Allegro*–Bibs. 1:1981e
— Libr. 12308 12323 12340 12347 12354 12367 12372 12376 12379-80 12401 12403 12406-7 12414 12426 12446 12450
— *Literae pseudo-senatus Anglicani.* 12423 12435
— — Bibs. 1:**4242a**

MILTON, John, 1608–74. *Lycidas.* 12318
12334 12346 12373 12394 12447
— Mss. 12314 12322 12326 12328 12330
12341–2 12344 12352 12372 12392 12397
12419 12427 12432 12437–8 12455
— *Of education.* 12396
— *Of prelatical episcopacy*–Bibs. 1:4235
— *Of reformation*–Bibs. 1:4235
— *Paradise lost.* 2342 5574 5869–70 7338
8520 10340 12300 12302–4 12307
12314–17 12320 12344 12348 12375 12381
12386 12391 12399–400 12404–5 12408
12413 12417 12420–1 12428
— — Bibs. 1:1981e 4221 4237 4239–40
— *Paradise regained.* 12301 12305 12362
— *Poems.* 3929 12438 12445
— *Pro populo anglicano defensio.* 12331 12374
12388 12393 12395 12402
— — Bibs. 1:4236 4238 4242
— *Proposals of certain expedients.* 12377
— *Prose works.* 12306 12345 12434
— Ptg. 12320 12325 12364–5 12383 12386
12400 12421 12442
— Publ. 5869–70 12300–1 12317 12378
12390
— *Ready and easy way.* 12309
— *Samson agonistes.* 12312 12440 12456
— — Bibs. 1:4218aa–b
— *Tenure of kings.* 12453
— — Bibs. 1:4227
— Text. 9512 12304–5 12312 12318 12334–6
12338 12343 12345 12348 12370–1 12383
12387 12391–2 12394 12417–19 12424
12428 12434 12440 12447–8 12456
MINERS' READING SOCIETIES. 1633
MINERVA PRESS, 1790–1820. 3442
5194–202
— Bibs. 1:**1368–a**
MINET PUBLIC LIBRARY, Camber-
well–Collns. 1:944h–i
MINIATURE BOOKS. 4941 6745 7010–11
7576–82 10541 14274
— Bibs. 1:381 **1819**
— Collns. 7582
MINIATURE CLASSICAL LIBRARY. 6941
MINIATURE PRESS, Richmond, Surrey, est.
1935. 6495
MINNESOTA. UNIVERSITY. LIBRARY–
Collns. 1:599
MINSHEU, John, fl.1617.
— Bibs. 1:**4250**
— *Guide into the tongues.* 6562
— Publ. 6562
MINSHULL, John, Chester, d.1712. **5203**
MINTO, William, 1845–93–Bibs. 1:**4250b**
— Letters–Bibs. 1:4250b
MINTON, Francis John, 1917–57. **5204**
— Bibs. 1:**1368q**

MIRK, John, fl.1403? **12458–9**
— Bibs. 1:**4251**
— *Liber festivalis.* 12458–9
— *Quattuor sermones.* 12458–9
MIRROR FOR MAGISTRATES. 587 602–3
616 619 622 626 628 635 641 13136
— Bibs. 1:530a
MIRROR FOR SHORTHAND WRITERS.
8173
MISCELLANEA MATHEMATICA. 7545
MISCELLANIES, *see also* ANTHOLOGIES.
5871a 5874–6 7982–a 7990 7992–3 7995
7997–9 8001 8005–7 8008 8012 8014–15
8017–18 8020 8022–4 8030 12829
— Bibs. 1:1307 1309–11 1407 1623a 1991
1994 1997 2002 2006 2007a 4378–9 4443a
—, RIBALD. 7722
— — Bibs. 1:2000
MISOGONUS, 1570. 7144 7151
MISPRINTS. 275 400 2238c 8965 10015
10042 10349 10822 11194 11199 11217
11225 11331 11582 11589 11600 11606
11664 11724 11871 12165 12212 12338
13080 13644 13981 14070 14498 14582
14587
MISSALS. 8038 8043–4 9751
MIST, Nathaniel, d.1737 *see WEEKLY
JOURNAL.*
MR. TASTE'S TOUR, c.1732. 12831
MITCHEL, John, 1815–75–Libr. 2697
— Bibs. 1:**4252–3**
MITCHEL, William, 1670?–1739–Bibs.
1:**4254–6**
MITCHELL, James Leslie, 1901–35 *see*
GIBBON, Lewis Grassic, *pseud.*
MITCHELL LIBRARY *see* NEW SOUTH
WALES. PUBLIC LIBRARY, Sydney.
MITCHELL LIBRARY.
MITCHELL LIBRARY, Glasgow–Collns.
1:553 1002a 2639; 9053
MITFORD, John, 1781–1859.
— *Tottel's Miscellany.* 5876
MITFORD, Mary Russell, 1787–1855.
12460–3
— *Belford Regis.* 12463
— Bibs. **4257–60**
— *Our village.* 12461
— Ptg. 6137
MITTERER, Herman Joseph, 1764–1829.
6227
MOCATTA LIBRARY *see* JEWISH
HISTORICAL SOCIETY OF ENGLAND.
MOCATTA LIBRARY.
MODELLED BINDINGS *see* BOOK-
BINDINGS, MODELLED.
MOGG, William Rees-, 1928– –Libr. 3308
MOHILL, co. Leitrim–Bibs. 1:1094
— Ptg.–Bibs. 1:1094

Vol. **1** = *Bibliographies*   **2** = *Shakespeare*   **4** = 1–8221   **5** = 8222–14616

MOIRA. BROOKFIELD AGRICULTURAL SCHOOL *see* BROOKFIELD AGRICULTURAL SCHOOL, Moira.
MOLESWORTH, Mary Louisa (Stewart), 1839–1921. **12464**
— Bibs. 1:**4260a**
MOLESWORTH, sir William, 1810–55.
— *Hobbes' English works.* 11092
MOLIÈRE (Jean Baptiste Poquelin), 1622–73. 914
— Bibs. 1:**813**
MOLLE, John, d.1638? 2414
MOLLINEUX, Emeric, fl.1590–1600. 7507
MOLLOY, Arthur, Dublin, fl.1870–4. **5205**
MOLYNEUX, William, 1656–98. 1838
— Bibs. 1:**4261**
— *Case of Ireland's being bound*–Bibs. 1:4261
MONAGHAN. 1961–3
— Bibs. 1:**1108–11**
— Newspapers. 1962–3
— Ptg.–Bibs. 1:1108–11
MONKTON COMBE, Som. **1395a**
— Paper. 1395a
MONKLAND FRIENDLY SOCIETY. 1633
MONMOUTH, Mons.
— Ptg. *see* HEATH, Charles, 1761–1831.
MONMOUTH, Charles Mordaunt, 1st earl of, 1658–1735 *see* MORDAUNT, Charles, 3d earl of Peterborough and 1st earl of Monmouth, 1658–1735.
MONMOUTHSHIRE *see also* BOOK TRADE, LISTS–Monmouthshire. **1297–301** 1509
— Bibs. 1:**3365**
— Librs. *see* TREDEGAR PARK.
— Newspapers. 1509
— — Bibs. 1:1917; 1477
— Paper. 1298a
— Ptg. 1300 1477
MONOGRAMS *see* BOOKBINDINGS–Monograms.
MONOPOLIES *see also* PATENTS; STATIONERS' COMPANY–Monopolies. 1599
MONOTYPE CORPORATION *see* LANSTON MONOTYPE CORPORATION, est. 1897.
MONOTYPING. 6123
MONRO, Harold, 1879–1932–Bibs. 1:**4261r**
— Collns. 1:4261r
—Mss.–Bibs. 1:4261r
MONRO, Thomas Kirkpatrick, 1865–1952–Libr. 8851
MONTAGU, Basil, 1770–1851. **12465**
— Mss. 12465
MONTAGU, lady Mary Wortley (Pierrepont), 1689–1762 *see also* NONSENSE OF COMMON SENSE. **12466–9** 12803

— Libr. 7097 12466 12469
MONTAGU, Richard, fl.1743–58. **5206**
MONTAGU, Walter, 1603–77. **12470–1**
— *Miscellanea spiritualia.* 12470
— Publ. 12470
MONTAGUE, Charles Edward, 1867–1928–Bibs. 1:**4262**
MONTAIGNE, Michel Eyquem de, 1533–92. 900a
— *Essays.* 2:1000a 1012 1016 1022 1027
MONTEAGLE, Thomas Spring Rice, 1st baron, 1790–1866 *see* RICE, Thomas Spring, 1st baron Monteagle of Brandon, 1790–1866.
MONTGOMERIE, Alexander, 1556?–1610?–Bibs. 1:**4263**
MONTGOMERY, Henry Riddell, 1818–1904. **12472**
— Bibs. 1:**4263b**
MONTGOMERY, James, 1771–1854. **12473**
MONTGOMERY, John, fl.1570–Mss. 8166
— *Navy of England.* 8166
MONTGOMERY, Lall G., fl.1953–Libr. 9323
MONTGOMERYSHIRE.
— Bibs. 1:**963h**
— Librs. *see* POWYS CASTLE.
MONTH, THE–Bibs. 1:1926
MONTHLY CATALOGUE. 3487 5077
MONTHLY MAGAZINE–Bibs. 1:**4259**
MONTHLY MERCURY. 5525
MONTHLY MISCELLANY. 7740
MONTHLY PRECEPTOR. 6999
MONTHLY REVIEW. 7716 7755 7795 7889
— Bibs. 1:1901–2 3621d
MONTREAL. MCGILL UNIVERSITY *see* McGILL UNIVERSITY, Montreal.
MONTROSE, Angus.
— Librs. 1633
— Newspapers–Bibs. 1:1930g
— Publ. *see* WALKER, George, 1831–89.
MOODY, G. C., fl.1889. 14458
MOOR, James, 1712–79. **12474**
— *De analogia.* 12474
MOORE, Albert Joseph, 1841–93. 7420a
MOORE, Dugald, Glasgow, 1805–41. **5207**
— Bibs. 1:**4263d**
— Mss. 5207
MOORE, Ed., Cambridge, fl.1740–60. **5208**
MOORE, Edward, 1712–57–Bibs. 1:**4263m**
— Mss.–Bibs. 1:4263m
MOORE, Francis, fl.1656–81–Bibs. 1:**4264**
MOORE, Frederic, 1830–1907.
— *Lepidoptera of Ceylon.* 6981
MOORE, George Augustus, 1852–1933. 762 **12475–82**
— Bibs. 1:684 **4265–70g**

MOORE, George Augustus, 1852–1933.
— *Cloches de Corneville.* 762
— *Confessions.* 12480
— *Ephemera critica.* 12478
— *Esther Waters.* 5527–8 12481
— *Flowers of passion.* 12482
— *The lake.* 12481
— Letters–Bibs. 1:4270g
— *Modern painting.* 12477
— *Peronnik the fool.* 4897e
— Ptg. 6098 8754 12475
— Publ. 12477 12479
— *Talking pine.* 4897e
— Text. 12476 12481
— *Untilled field.* 12479
— *Wild goose.* 12481
MOORE, George Edward, 1873–1958–Bibs.
1:4270m–p
MOORE, Julian, fl.1936–Libr. 2128
MOORE, Thomas, 1779–1852. **12483–7**
— Bibs. 1:**4271–3**
— *Epistles, odes and other poems.* 12487
— *Irish melodies.* 12484 12486
— *Life of Byron.* 5250
— Mss. 12483
— Paper. 12486
— *Suppressed letters.* 12485
MOORE, Thomas Sturge, 1870–1944–Bibs.
1:**4274–a**
MORALITY see CENSORSHIP, MORAL.
MORALITY PLAYS–Bibs. 1:1601a
MORAN, C., fl.1760–70. **5209**
MORAN, card. Patrick Francis, 1830–
1911–Bibs. 1:**4274b**
MORANT, Philip, 1700–70.
— *History of Essex.* 1112
MORAY, James Stewart, earl of, 1531?–70
see STEWART, ld. James, earl of Mar, and
of Moray, 1531?–70.
MORDAUNT, Charles, 3d earl of Peter-
borough, and 1st earl of Monmouth,
1658–1735. 4835b
MORDEN, Robert, fl.1668–1703. 6550 7486
7490
MORE, Shrop.–Librs. 2643
MORE, Cresacre, 1572–1649.
— *Life of More.* 12511
MORE, Hannah, 1745–1833 see also *CHEAP
REPOSITORY TRACTS.* 7000a **12488–90**
14196
— Bibs. 1:**4274d**
— Publ. 12489
— *Search after happiness.* 12489
MORE, Henry, 1614–87.
— Bibs. 1:**4275–a**
— *Opera theologica.* 6521
— Publ. 6521
MORE, John, fl.1508–92. 871a

MORE, sir Thomas, 1478–1535. **12491–512**
— Bibs. 1:**4276–84**
— Collns. 12493–4 12500–2 12505
— *Dialogue of comfort.* 12492
— Libr. 12491 12508 12512
— *Life of Johan Picus.* 12506
— Ptg. 12492 12494 12506
— *Utopia.* 3035 12499 12503–4
— — Bibs. 1:4278 4280–1
— *Works.* 2537
MORE, William, 1472–1559? 2681
MORE HINTS ON ETIQUETTE. 13977
MORENARDO PRESS, Birmingham, est.
1960? 6499
MORES, Edward Rowe, 1731–78. 3475
— Bibs. 1:**4290**
— *Dissertation upon English typographical
founders.* 6573 6627
— Libr. 6627
MORGAN, A. J., fl.1900–Libr. 2586
MORGAN, Abel, 1673–1722.
— *Cyd-gordiad Egwaddorawl*–Bibs. 1:706
MORGAN, Charles Langbridge,
1894–1958–Bibs. 1:**4291**
MORGAN, Frederick Charles John, 6th
baron Tredegar, 1908–62–Libr. 3112
MORGAN, John, fl.1744. 14341
MORGAN, John Pierpont, 1837–1913–Libr.
see also PIERPONT MORGAN LIBRARY,
N.Y. 1:427; 3059
MORGAN, Joseph, fl. 1739. **12513–14**
— *Phœnix Britannicus.* 12513–14
MORGAN, Matthew Somerville, 1839–90.
7872
MORGAN, Richard Cope, 1827–1908.
5209a–c
MORGAN, William Frend de, 1839–1917 see
DE MORGAN, William Frend, 1839–1917.
MORGANWG, Iolo, *pseud., see* WILLIAMS,
Edward, 1746–1826.
MORICE, James, fl.1509–53–Libr. 3293
MORICE, John, fl.1844. 7393
MORICE, sir William, 1602–76. 7666
MORIER, James Justinian, 1780?–1849.
— *Hajji Baba.* 5250
MORISON, James, 1770–1840. **12515**
— Bibs. 1:**4291g**
MORISON, sir Richard, d.1556. **12516**
— *Lamentation of rebellion.* 12516
— *Remedy for sedition.* 12516
MORISON, Stanley Arthur, 1889–1967. 2374
5211–18a 6490 6622
— Bibs. 1:**4291n–r**
MORISON FAMILY, Perth, est. 1774? **5210**
MORLAND, George, 1763–1804. 5778 **12517**
— Publ. 12517
MORLAND, sir Samuel, d.1695. **12518**
MORLEY, Henry, 1822–94–Bibs. 1:**4292**

Vol. **1** = *Bibliographies*   **2** = *Shakespeare*   **4** = 1–8221   **5** = 8222–14616

MORLEY, John, viscount Morley of Blackburn, 1838–1923.
— Bibs. 1:**4293**
— Collns. 3117
— Libr. 3117
MORLEY, Thomas, 1557–1604? **12519–20**
— Bibs. 1:**4294**
— *First book of airs.* 2:1107 1109
— *Madrigals to four voices.* 12520
— Mss. 2:1109
— *Plain introduction.* 12519
— — Bibs. 1:4294
MORNING CHRONICLE. 7770 7865
MORNING POST. 3977 7723 7894
— Bibs. 1:5179
MORNING STAR. 7839
MOROCCO BINDER, fl.1563. **5219**
MORRELL, W. J. AND J., fl.1890. 5220
MORRELL, W. T., d.1881. **5220**
MORRIS, Claver, fl.1686–1726–Libr. 2900
MORRIS, Francis Orpen, 1810–93.
— *Country seats.* 4650
MORRIS, Lewis, 1700–65–Libr. 2987
MORRIS, William, 1834–96 *see also* KELMSCOTT PRESS, Hammersmith, 1891–8. 486 752 4334 **12521–33** 24387 14436
— Bibs. 1:652 **4295–304**
— Bndng. 2023 2025a
— Collns. 12525–6 12531–2
— *Defence of Guenevere.* 12521
— Handwr. 12530
— Letters. 12532
— Libr. 1:427; 12523
— Mss. 12528
— *Tale of king Florus.* 2023 2025a
— *Willow and the red cliff.* 12529
MORRISON, Alfred, 1821–97–Libr. 2544
MORRISON, Lois Goddard, fl.1898–1953–Libr. 746
MORTEN, Thomas, 1836–66. 7420a
MORTIMER'S CROSS, Herefs.–Paper. 1138
MORTON, bp. Thomas, 1564–1659.
— *Apologia catholica.* 647
MOSAIC BINDINGS *see* BOOKBINDINGS, MOSAIC.
MOSELEY, Humphrey, d.1661. **5221–2**
— Bibs. 1:**1369–70**
— *Milton's Poems.* 12445
MOSELEY, Walter Acton, d.1793. 1433
MOSHER, Thomas Bird, Portland, Maine, 1852–1923. 4820 5527 7342 8766 11226
— *Swinburne's Love's cross currents.* 13813
MOSS, William Edward, fl.1934–52–Libr. 1:2477; 2199 2973 5625
MOST WONDERFUL EXAMPLE ... OF A CERTAIN MOUNTAIN, c.1585. 665

MOSTYN, Joseph Cecil Mary, 1891–1971–Libr. 9603
MOSTYN, Roger, d.1678–Libr. 3396a
MOSTYN HALL, Flintshire–Libr. 7126
MOTE HOLE, Kent–Paper. 1161a
MOTHE-FÉNELON, François de Salignac de la, 1651–1715 *see* FÉNELON, François da Salignac de la Mothe-, 1651–1715.
MOTHER GOOSE. 7000a
MOTHER GOOSE'S MELODY. 7047
MOTHERWELL, William, 1797–1835.
— Bibs. 1:**4310**
— *Minstrelsy.* 6787
MOTHS *see* BUTTERFLIES AND MOTHS.
MOTTE, Benjamin, d.1738. 13708 13744
— *Swift's Gulliver's travels.* 13719
— *Swift's Miscellanies.* 13769
MOTTEUX, Peter Anthony, 1663–1718. **12534**
— Bibs. 1:**4311–12**
— *Love's a jest.* 12534
— Ptg. 12534
MOTTOES. 2378 2382 2390 6661
—, BOOKSELLERS'. 4524
—, PRINTERS'. 258 6693
MOTTRAM, Ralph Hale, 1883–1971–Bibs. 1:**4313**
MOUFET, Thomas, 1553–1604–Libr. 3294
MOULD MAKERS *see* PAPERMOULD MAKERS.
MOULDS, TYPE *see* TYPE–Moulds.
MOUNTAGUE, Richard, fl.1716–28. **5223**
MOUNTCASHELL, Margaret Jane (Kingsborough), countess of Mountcashell, 1773–1835. **12535**
— *Romantic letters.* 12535
MOUNTFORT, William, 1664?–92. 7159
MOUNT HENNETH, 1782. 745
MOUNTON, Mons.–Paper. 1298a
MOUNT TRENCHARD PRESS, co. Limerick, fl.1863. 6466
MOURNING MUSE OF ALEXIS, 1695. 1905
MOXON, Edward, 1801–58. **5225–6a** 7420a
— Bndng. 5226a
MOXON, Joseph, 1627–1700. **5227–33**
— Bibs. 1:**1371–4**
— *Mechanic exercises.* 5227 5229 5231–2 6345 6364 6371 6375 12725
— Type. 6442 6613
MOYES, James, 1779–1838. **5234**
— *Tennyson's Poetical works.* 13906
MOZLEY, Thomas, 1806–93–Bibs. 1:1925a
MUBASHSHIR IBN-FĀTIK *see* CAXTON, William, 1422?–91. *Dictes or sayings of the philosophers.*
MUCEDORUS. 7179
— Ptg. 7107

MUDDIMAN, Henry, fl.1629–65. 7666 7692
— Bibs. 1:1873bb
MUDFORD, William, 1782–1848. 10889–90
MUDGE, John, Dock, fl.1814. 5235
MUDIE, Charles Edward, 1818–90. 3450
3436–8 6522 6524
MUFFET, Thomas, 1553–1604 see MOUFET, Thomas, 1553–1604.
MUGGINS, William, fl.1603.
— London's mourning garment. 629
MUGGLETON, Lodowicke, 1609–98. 12536
MUIR, Edwin, 1887–1959–Bibs. 1:4314–16
MUIR, Willa (Anderson), 1890–1948–Bibs.
1:4316
MUIRHEAD, Arnold Meadowcroft, 1900–
–Libr. 3012 8516
MUIRHEAD, James Patrick, 1813–98–Libr.
3025
MUIRHEAD, Lionel Boulton Campell
Lockhart, fl.1940–Libr. 3025
MULGRAVE, John Sheffield, 3d earl of,
1648–1721 see SHEFFIELD, John, 3d earl
of Mulgrave, 1648–1721.
MULLER, Rowland Burdon-, fl.1939–Libr.
8481
MULLINGAR, co. Westmeath–Bibs.
1:1135
— Ptg.–Bibs. 1:1135
MULOCK, Dinah Maria (mrs. Craik),
1826–87.
— Bndng. 2124
— John Halifax, gentleman. 2124
MULVANEY, Charles Pelham, 1835–85. 7869
MUM–Bibs. 1:2008
MUNBY, Alan Nöel Latimer, 1913–74. 2384
MUNDAY, Anthony, 1553–1633. 12537–47
— Bibs. 1:4317–b; 2:1871 1876
— Death of Huntington. 12544
— Defence of contraries. 12543
— Downfall of Huntington. 12544
— Handwr. 2:1892 1909
— John a Kent. 2:943
— Mss. 2:943; 12537–8
— Sir Thomas More see SIR THOMAS MORE.
— Text. 12541 12544
MUNDELL, Alexander, fl.1790–1846. 1680
MUNDELL, James, Glasgow, fl.1795–9. 4746
MUNRO, Hector Hugh, 1870–1916 see
SAKI, pseud.
MURDER OF JOHN BREWEN, 1592. 9585
MURDOCH, Jean Iris (mrs. J. O. Bayley),
1919– . 12548–9
— Bibs. 1:4317m–p
— Mss. 12549
— — Bibs. 1:4317p
— Text. 12548
— Under the net. 12548
MURDOCK, Harold, 1862–1934–Libr. 2944

MURISON, John, 1852–1921–Libr. 1:2637;
9087 9093–4
MURPHY, Arthur, 1727–1805. 12550–1
— Englishman from Paris. 12551
— Mss. 12551
— Works of Sallust. 12550
MURPHY, Jeremiah, fl.1840–1915.
— Bibs. 1:4317t
MURPHY, bp. John, 1772–1847–Libr. 2699
MURRAY, Charles Fairfax, 1849–1919. 3120
— Letters. 3314a 12532
— Libr. 3120
MURRAY, David, 1842–1928–Bibs. 1:4318
MURRAY, Eustace Clare Grenville, 1824–81.
12073
MURRAY, George Gilbert Aimé,
1866–1957–Bibs. 1:4319–a
MURRAY, John, 1745–93. 3475 3639a
5239–45 5250 6510a
MURRAY, John, 1778–1843. 5246–51a 5909
6510a 8332 9199 9736 13242
— Handbooks. 5250 5252b
— Letters. 5250 5251a
MURRAY, John, c.1786–1851.
— Observations and experiments on ... paper.
3782
MURRAY, John, 1808–92. 5252–4 6938a
11880
— Letters. 5252b
MURRAY, sir John, 1851–1928. 5255–a
MURRELL, John, fl.1630.
— Murrell's two books of cookery and carving. 7063
MURREY, Thomas Jefferson, fl.1880–
95–Libr. 1:2141b
MURRY, John Middleton, 1889–1957–Bibs.
1:4320
MURRY, Kathleen (Beauchamp), 1888–1923
see MANSFIELD, Katherine, pseud.
MUSAEUS, fl.500–Bibs. 1:801a
MUSEUM, THE. 7751 7762 7923
— Bibs. 1:4259
MUSGRAVE, James, d.1778–Libr. 12574
MUSGRAVE, sir William, 1735–1800. 9786–7
12552–3
— Mss. 12552–3
MUSIC see also BOOK TRADE,
LISTS–Music; HYMNS; OPERAS;
SONGBOOKS; TUTORS, INSTRU-
MENTAL; and individual musicians, e.g.
BEETHOVEN, Ludwig van, 1770–1827;
Dowland, John, 1563?–1626? FIELD,
John, 1782–1837; HANDEL, George
Frideric, 1685–1759; HAYDN, Franz Josef,
1732–1809; LAWES, Henry, 1596–1662;
MORLEY, Thomas, 1557–1604?;
PLAYFORD, John, 1623–86; PURCELL,
Henry, 1659?–95; WILLIAMS, Ralph
Vaughan, 1872–1958. 7583–625

MUSIC–Bibliogr. descr. 128
— Bibs. 1:1621 1623a 1624f **1825–42** 2087
— Bksllng. *see* MUSIC SELLING.
— Catalogues. 7610 7618 7622
— Collns. 779 1625 1810 2784 3054 3347
5430 7593 7603 7605 7609 7612 7622
7624
— Ireland. 1784 1810 1874 1890 1897 1908
1925
— — Bibs. 1:1828
— Mss. 7621a
— Ptg. *see* MUSIC PRINTING.
— Publ. *see* BOOK TRADE, LISTS–Music
publishers, etc.; MUSIC PUBLISHING.
— Scotland. 1621 1625
— — Bibs. 1:1827k
— Wales. 1494
— — Bibs. 1:1732k

— 1475–1640. 7583 7585 7587–9 7592
8861
— 1475–1700. 7413 7621a
— 1701–1800. 7413 7590 7601 7603
— 1801–1900. 8902
MUSICAL DICTIONARIES *see* DICT-
IONARIES, MUSICAL.
MUSICAL TIMES. 3546
MUSIC AND BIBLIOGRAPHY. 7615a
7617a–b 9166
MUSIC AND SHAKESPEARE–Bibs. 2:120
123
MUSIC PAPER *see* PAPER, MUSIC.
MUSIC PRINTING *see also* TYPE-
FACES–Music. 3437 3452 5262 5314
7584 7588–9 7594 7596 7598–9 7607–8
7620 7624
— Bibs. 1:1149f 1154 1831–2 1834 1841b
— Ireland. 1874 1890 1897 1908
MUSIC PROGRAMMES *see* PRO-
GRAMMES, MUSIC.
MUSIC PUBLISHING. 7584 7586
— 1475–1700. 7614 7625
— 1641–1700. 5429
— 1701–1800. 4116 5932–4 7604 7614
7625
— 1801–1900. 7614 7625
MUSIC SELLING. 1908 1925 7614 7625
MUSIC WRAPPERS *see* WRAPPERS, MUSIC.
MUTINY ON THE 'BOUNTY' *see*
'BOUNTY', MUTINY ON THE.
MYCHELL, John, Canterbury, fl.1533–60.
4180 **5255b**
MYERS AND COMPANY, fl.1838–58. 6202
MYLLAR, Andrew, Edinburgh, fl.1503–8.
4369 4372 **5255c**
MYSTERIOUS MOTHER, 1791. 14190
MYTHOLOGICAL POETRY *see* POETRY,
MYTHOLOGICAL.

MYTHOLOGY–Bibs. 1:1981f 1993 2018

NAAS, co. Kildare–Ptg. 1770
NAILSWORTH, Glos.–Paper. 1120a
Naish, Arthur John, 1816–89. 8097
NAMIER, sir Lewis Bernstein,
1888–1960–Bibs. 1:**4320p**
NANGLE, Edward, Achill, fl.1827–66–Bibs.
1:1240
NAPIER, John, 1550–1617.
— Bibs. 1:**4321**
— Libr. 2672
NAPIER, William, fl.1794. **12554**
— *Selection of Scots songs.* 12554
NAPIER, sir William Francis Patrick,
1785–1860.
— *History of the Peninsular war.* 5250
NAPIER PLATEN PRESS. 6312
NAPLES. CARTHUSIAN CHURCH.
LIBRARY. 3346
NAPOLEONIC LITERATURE *see*
BONAPARTE, Napoleon, 1769–1821–
Collns.
NARCISSUS PLAYS. 7108
NARFORD HALL, Norf.–Libr. 2587 11031
NARRATIVE POETRY *see* POETRY,
NARRATIVE.
NASH, Joseph, 1809–78. 6202
NASH, Paul, 1889–1946–Bibs. 1:**4322**
NASH, Thomas, St.Paul's Cray, 1801–45.
5256
NASH, Thomas Henry, St.Paul's Cray,
1866–1949. 5256
NASH, William, St.Paul's Cray, 1765–1824.
1139 **5256–7**
NASH, William, St.Paul's Cray, 1836–79.
5256
NASH, William Gardiner, St.Paul's Cray,
1864–1914. 5256
NASHE, Thomas, 1567–1601. 684 **12555–9**
— Bibs. 1:**4323–5a**
— *Choice of valentines.* 12559
— *Christ's tears.* 12558
— *Have with you.* 12557
— Illus. 12557
— *Pierce Penniless.* 12556
— *Publ.* 12556 12558
— *Return of Pasquill.* 12555
— *Terrors of the night.* 12558
— *Unfortunate traveller.* 12558
NASH MILLS, Hemel Hempstead. 4544–5a
NATAL. UNIVERSITY. LIBRARY–Collns.
1:583
NATHAN, Alfred, 1866–1933–Libr. 526
NATION, THE. 12097 13611
— Bibs. 1:4106t 4784

NEWRY, co. Down. **1868**
— Bibs. 1:1062–6
— Ptg. 1770 1868
— — Bibs. 1:1062–6
NEWSAGENTS PUBLISHING COMPANY, 19th cent. **5286**
NEW SESSION OF THE POETS. 13705
NEWSBOOKS *see* NEWSPAPERS AND PERIODICALS.
NEWS FROM ABROAD, 1722. 1178 1180
NEW SHAKSPERE SOCIETY. 2:55
NEWSLETTERS *see* NEWSPAPERS AND PERIODICALS–1601–1700.
NEW SOUTH WALES. PUBLIC LIBRARY, Sydney. MITCHELL LIBRARY.
— — — Collns. 1:2876; 2:245d
NEWSPAPER LITERATURE SYNDICATE, 19th cent. 5856
NEWSPAPER PRESS DIRECTORY. 7836
NEWSPAPER STAMP ABOLITION COMMITTEE. 3546
NEWSPAPER STAMPS. 3546 4855 5984 7701 7801 7894
NEWSPAPERS AND PERIODICALS *see also* ANNUALS; BOOKS IN PARTS; BOOK TRADE, LISTS–Newspapers; COR-ANTOS. 1214 1238 **7631–936**
— Bibs. *see also titles of individual newspapers and periodicals, e.g.* Albemarle; All the year round; Anglo-Saxon review; Annals of agriculture; Annual review; Athenæum; Ayscough's weekly courant; Bentley's miscellany; Bentley's quarterly review; Blackwood's Edinburgh magazine; Bradford antiquary; Bradford scientific journal; British and foreign review; British critic; British quarterly review; Butterfly; Chitchat; Contemporary review; Cornhill magazine; Courier; Court and city register; Court magazine; Critical review; Daily news; Done; Dublin review; Dublin university magazine; Edinburgh mirror; Edinburgh review; Englishman; European magazine; Evergreen; Examiner; Fortnightly review; Frasers' magazine; Fun; Gentleman's magazine; Grub street journal; Home and foreign review; Household words; Irish review; Lady's magazine; Life; Literary courier of Grub street; Literary magazine; London journal; London magazine; London mercury; Lover and the reader; Loyal observer reviv'd; Macmillan's magazine; Manchester guardian; Mercurius Aulicus; Month, The; Monthly magazine; Monthly review; Morning post; Museum; Nation; National Review; New monthly magazine; Nineteenth century; North British review;

Pageant; Pall Mall gazette; Prospective Review; Punch; Quarterly magazine; Quarterly review; Quarto; Rambler; Round table; Saturday review; Savoy; Shamrock; Sinn Fein; Spectator; Spy; Times literary supplement; Town-talk; Train; True crime; Venture; Welsh review; Westminster review; Yellow book. 1:1693 **1845–954**
— Censorship. 3503–5 3556 3559 7691
— Circulation. 7761 7765 7793 7800 7813–15 7904 7910 7919
— Collns. 7649–51 7693 7696 7777 7916
— Editions. 7631 7635 7638
— Ptg. 1285 6676 7644
— — 1601–1700. 6121b 7688 7691
— — 1701–1800. 6121b 7691 7757 7764 7778 7783–4 7790 7794–9 7804–6 7813
— — 1801–1900. 1275 5092 6123a 6348 7903 7907
— Regulation. 1827 1844 3542 3546 3551 3556 3558–9 3561 3566 7666 7681–2 7691–2 7800–1 7894 7910
— Type. 6637 6676
— **1601– –**Bibs. 1:1833 **1845–62** 2096 2218
— — Bristol–Bibs. 1:896p 1855
— — Bromley–Bibs. 1:901
— — Ireland *see* NEWSPAPERS, PROVIN-CIAL–Ireland.
— — Oxfordshire–Bibs. 1:933–4
— — Scotland *see* NEWSPAPERS, PROVINCIAL–Scotland.
— — Wales *see* NEWSPAPERS, PROVINCIAL–Wales.
— **1601–1700** *see also titles of individual newspapers and periodicals, e.g.* Athenian gazette; Certain (weekly) news; Commonwealth mercury; Corant out of Italy; Current intelligence; Dawks's news-letter; English mercury; Gazette des Londres; Index intelligencer; Jones's evening newsletter; Kingdom's intelligencer; Ladies mercury; London gazette; London newsbook; Loyal London mercury, Mercurius aulicus; Mercurius bellicus; Mercurius Britannicus; Mercurius civicus; Mercurius domesticus; Mercurius poeticus; Mercurius politicus; Nouvelles ordinaires de Londres; Paisley annual miscellany; Philosophical transactions; Post boy; Sum of intelligence; True diurnal; Weekly memorials; Weekly news; Weekly review (Defoe's); Works of the learned. 673 852 1019 3503–5 3551 3556 3559 3566 7644 **7654–96**
— — Bibs. 1:**1870–81** 1965–6 1972 2237
— **1601–1800—**Bibs. 1:931 1837a **1885–94**

NEWSPAPERS AND PERIODICALS, 1701–1800 *see also titles of individual newspapers and periodicals, e.g.* Aberdeen journal; Account of the progress of the gospel; The adventurer; The ambulator; Annual register; The anti-Jacobin; Applebee's weekly journal; Ayscough's weekly courant; Beauties of magazines; The bee; Bell's weekly messenger; Berrow's Worcester journal; Botanical magazine; British Apollo; Budgell's Bee; Caledonian mercury; The champion; Cheltenham journal; Chester weekly journal; Christian magazine; Cirencester flying-post; Cotes's weekly courant; The craftsman; Critical review; The critics; Daily advertiser; Daily journal; Daily universal register; Domestic intelligence; Dublin weekly oracle; Dumfries mercury; Edinburgh advertizer; English freeholder; Eurgrawn Cymraeg; Evening post; The examiner; The flapper; Free Briton; Freeman's journal; The gazetteer; Gentleman's magazine; Gloucester journal; Grand magazine; Gloucester journal; Grand magazine of magazines; Grand magazine of universal intelligence; The guardian; The harp; The intelligencer; Inverness journal; Jackson's Oxford journal; Journal politique et littéraire d'angleterre; Kentish post; Lady's magazine; Limerick newsletter; List of Covent garden ladies; London chronicle; London journal; London magazine and monthly chronologer; London mercury; Loyal post; Malvern mercury; Manchester weekly journal; Mathematical transactions; The medley; Mercurius Romanus; Miscellanea mathematica; Monthly mercury; Monthly miscellany; Monthly review; Morning chronicle; Morning post; The museum; National journal; New annual register; Newcastle chronicle; New copper plate magazine; News from abroad; Nonsense of common sense; Noon gazette; Northampton mercury; North Britain; Norwich cabinet; Norwich post; Observer; Old England; The oracle; Owen's weekly chronicle; Preston journal; The rambler; Reading mercury; The remembrancer; St. Ives mercury; St. James's chronicle; Salisbury and Winchester journal; Shropshire journal; The spectator; Stamford mercury; The star; Strabane magazine; Stratford, Shipston and Aulcester journal; The tatler; The telegraph; Thespian telegraph; The times; Le traiteur; The tribune; Universal chronicle; Universal spectator; Universal

visitor; Walshingham's free Briton; The watchman; Weekly history; Weekly journal; Western miscellany; The whig; Whimsical depository; Worcester post-man; The world; York courant. 1040 1163 1294 1320 1345 1822 1844 1878 1884 1896 1900 3462 3561 3566 5271 5541 7287 7644 **7697–816** 8155 9791

—— Bibs. 1:821 1657 1698 **1900–12** 2005g 4699

— 1801–1900 *see also titles of individual newspapers and periodicals, e.g.* The academy; All the year round; Alnwick mercury; Annals of the fine arts; Annual anthology; The annuals; The artist; The athenæum; The atlas; Ballyhullan register; Banter; Bath magazine; Bentley's miscellany; Bijou almanac; Blackwood's Edinburgh magazine; Bolton evening news; The bookseller; Boys of England; Boy's own paper; British and foreign review; British critic; British star; The champion; Churchman's family magazine; Church times; City press; College magazine; The comet; Comet almanack; Comic news; Constable's miscellany; Cope's tobacco plant; Cork freeholder; Cork magazine; Cornhill magazine; Daily chronicle; Daily news; Daily telegraph; The dome; Dramatic inspector; Dublin and London magazine; Dublin penny journal; Dublin Saturday magazine; Dublin university magazine; Dunfermline news; The echo; Eclectic review; Edinburgh literary journal; Edinburgh monthly magazine; Edinburgh philosophical journal; Edinburgh review; The field; Florist's magazine; Foreign review; Fortnightly review; Fraser's magazine; The friend; The germ; German review; The globe; Good words; The gorgon; The harlequin; Hood's comic annual; Household words; Illustrated London news; The inquisitor; Inverness courier; Irish penny journal; Irish metropolitan magazine; Irish penny magazine; Islington gazette; Janus, or The Edinburgh literary almanack; John Bull; Journal of auctions and sales; Juvenile library; The kaleidoscope; Kilmarnock mirror and literary gleaner; Kincardineshire almanac; Lancashire journal; Leeds mercury; Leigh Hunt's London journal; Leisure hour; The liberal; Literary companion; Literary examiner; London gazette; London journal; London magazine; London magazine, charivari, and courrier des dames; London reflector; London society; Loughrea journal; Mac-

NEWSPAPERS AND PERIODICALS, 1801–1900 cont.

millan's magazine; Magazine of art; Magazine of botany; Manchester co-operative news; The mask; Mathematical repository; The messenger; Millenial star; Monthly preceptor; Monthly review; Morning chronicle; Morning star; The museum; Musical times; The nation; National instructor; Naval chronicle; Newspaper press directory; Notes and queries; Old British spy; The omnium; Once a week; Oxford and Cambridge magazine; Paisley repository; Pall Mall gazette; Pan; Panoramic miscellany; Paris illustré; Parley's penny library; The parthenon; The pen; Penny post; Pictorial times; Plain Englishman; Poor man's guardian; Potteries free press; Printers' athenæum; Psalter of Cashel; Punch; Quarterly review; The quiver; The rambler (Catholic); The reflector; The representative; The retaliater; Retrospective review; St. James's gazette; Saturday review; Scots magazine; Smith street gazette; The spectator; Speculum academicum; Spirit lamp; The spy; The standard; Suffolk literary chronicle; The summary; Temple bar; Theatric tourist; Theological inquirer; Thistle magazine; The times; The tomahawk; The tomtit; The town; True Briton; Union jack; Vanity fair; Waterford chronicle; Waterford freeman; Weekly journal (Edinburgh); Weekly medico-chirugical and philosophical magazine; Weekly selector; Western vindicator; Westminster journal; Westminster review; Wheble's lady's magazine; Whittington gazette; Woman's world; Westmorland gazette; Wood's typographic advertiser; Women's world; The world; Yellow book; Yr Ymofynydd; Young folks; Young gentleman's magazine. 792 866 1040 1167 1221 1279 1420 1829 3442 3465 5909 6548 6778a 7003 7038 7040 7045 7389 7407 7430 7644 **7817–936** 10033
—— Bibs. 1:760 821 1166 1560 1698 1716k 1906 **1915–27c** 2249c 4699 4899
— 1901– *see also titles of individual newspapers and periodicals, e.g.* Banba; Branar; Cymru; Harp of Erin; Irish review; John O'London's weekly; Red hand; Rounde table; Sioladóir.
—— Bibs. 1:14
—, AGRICULTURAL–Bibs. 1:2096
—, ARCHITECTURAL. 6778a
—, BAPTIST. 8080

—, BIBLIOGRAPHICAL *see* Book collector; Bookseller; British printer; The Fleuron; Imprint; The Library; Printer's athenæum; Signature; Wood's typographic advertiser. 1:**111–200**
—— Bibs. 1:1156
—, BOOKBINDING–Bibs. 1:1139s
—, BOOKCOLLECTING–Bibs. 1:1156
—, BOOKTRADE–Bibs. 1:1186b
—, BOTANICAL. 7327 7914
—, CATHOLIC–Bibs. 1:1853
—, CHILDREN'S. 5518 6999 7002–3 7005 7009 7024 7037–8 7040 7045
—— Bibs. 1:1560 1857
—, CYCLING–Bibs. 1:2157p
—, DRAMATIC. 7102 7713 7745 7803 7930 7934–5
—— Bibs. 1:1586 1860 1920
—, EVENING. 7633 7640 7644 7880
—, FICTITIOUS. 7641–2 7842 7871
—, FORGED *see* FORGERIES, NEWS-PAPER.
—, FRENCH. 1195 1198 7743 7776 7858
—, FRIENDS'. 1930
—, GREEK. 1228
—, HUMOROUS–Bibs. 1:1954
—, ILLUSTRATED. 7389 7407 7430 7732 7753 7858
—, JEWISH–Bibs. 1:1861
—, LITERARY. 1776 7690 7761 7824 7844 7885
—, MANUSCRIPT. 1647
—, MATHEMATICAL. 7542 7545–6
—— Bibs. 1:1900i
—, MEDICAL–Bibs. 1:2218
—, METHODIST–Bibs. 1:2207p
—, MILITARY–Bibs. 1:2237
—, PRESBYTERIAN–Bibs. 1:1946
—, PRINTING–Bibs. 1:1139m 1156–7 1162
—, PROVINCIAL. 1019 3462 7639 7653 7800 7810 7813 7894
—— Bibs. 1:1904–5 1907 1911–12
— Aberdeenshire.
—— Aberdeen. 1644 1647 1653 1656
—— Bibs. 1:1931e–g
— Angus.
—— Dundee. 1665–a
——— Bibs. 1:1930 1931a
—— Montrose
——— Bibs. 1:1930g
— Antrim.
—— Belfast.
——— Bibs. 1:1026–8
— Armagh.
—— Lurgan. 1851
— Berkshire. 1039–40
—— Reading. 1042

SUBJECTS

NEWSPAPERS, PROVINCIAL–Caithness-shire.
— — Caithness. 1671
— Cambridgeshire.
— — Cambridge. 1049 1064
— Cheshire–Bibs. 1:1862
— — Chester. 1076 1078
— Cork. 1856 1859
— Cornwall. 1084
— Cumberland–Bibs. 1:1854
— Derbyshire.
— — Derby. 1093
— Dublin. 1763 1870 1878 1884–6 1888 1896 1900 1917 1920 1922 1930
— — Bibs. 1:1950 1952 1954
— Essex.
— — Witham. 1116
— Galway.
— — Loughrea. 1948
— Gloucestershire. 1118 1120–1
— — Bristol–Bibs. 1:1855
— — Cheltenham. 13760
— — Cirencester. 1129
— Hampshire. 1133 7768
— Huntingdonshire. 1144
— — St. Ives. 1148
— Hertfordshire–Bibs. 1:1856
— Inverness-shire–Bibs. 1:1931
— — Inverness. 1684
— Ireland. 1753 1763 1766 1776 1779 1799 1803 1814 1819 1822 1827 1829 1844 7736 7869 7910 13609
— — 1601– –Bibs. 1:1946–7
— — 1601–1700–Bibs. 1:1950–1
— — 1701–1800–Bibs. 1:1952–b
— — 1801–1900–Bibs. 1:1953–4
— Kent. 1152
— — Bromley–Bibs. 1:901
— — Canterbury. 1152 1159
— Kerry.
— — Tralee–Bibs. 1:1952b
— Kincardineshire. 5926
— Lanarkshire.
— — Glasgow. 1690–1 1693
— — — Bibs. 1:1934x
— Lancashire. 1163 5856
— — Bibs. 1:1854 1862
— — Bolton. 5856–7
— — Liverpool. 1167
— — — Bibs. 1:907
— — Manchester. 1175–6 1178 1180 5131
— — Preston. 1181
— Limerick. 1956
— Lincolnshire.
— — Stamford. 1187
— Man, Isle of–Bibs. 1:1862
— Midlothian.
— — Edinburgh. 1600 1704 3886

— — — Bibs. 1:1932–3
— Monaghan. 1962–3
— Monmouthshire. 1509
— — Bibs. 1:1917; 1477
— Norfolk.
— — Norwich. 1306 7749
— Northamptonshire. 1311
— — Northampton. 1311–12
— Northumberland.
— — Alnwick. 1316
— — Newcastle-upon-Tyne. 1320 1323 5668
— Nottinghamshire.
— — Nottingham. 1343–5
— — — Bibs. 1:931 1903a
— Oxfordshire–Bibs. 1:933–4
— — Oxford. 1358 1376 7771 7890 11195
— Roxburghshire.
— — Hawick. 1739
— Scotland. 1557 1570 1595 1598
— — 1601– –Bibs. 1:1930–4
— — — Aberdeen–Bibs. 1:1931e–g
— — — Dundee–Bibs. 1:1930 1931a
— — — Montrose–Bibs. 1:1930g
— — 1601–1700. 1656
— — 1701–1800. 1600 1690 1693 3462
— — — Bibs. 1:1934x–5a
— — — Glasgow–Bibs. 1:1934x
— — 1801–1900–Bibs. 1:1936–44
— Shropshire. 1384–5
— Sligo. 1964–5
— Somerset.
— — Bath. 1395
— — Bibs. 1:1851
— Surrey–Bibs. 1:1859
— Tipperary.
— — Cashel. 1968
— Tyrone.
— — Strabane. 1973–5
— Wales. 1497 1543
— — 1601– –Bibs. 1:1928
— — — Bibs. 1477
— — 1701–1800. 1509
— — 1801–1900. 1479
— — 1801–1900–Bibs. 1:1928u–9
— Warwickshire.
— — Birmingham. 1418 1420
— — — Bibs. 1:1923
— — Stratford-upon-Avon. 1423
— Waterford. 1976–7 1979 1982–4
— Westmorland. 9955
— — Bibs. 1:1854
— Wiltshire. 1426–7
— Worcestershire.
— — Malvern. 1430
— — Worcester. 1431–2
— Yorkshire–Bibs. 1:1858
— — Bradford. 1437–8
— — — Bibs. 1:949

Vol. **1** = *Bibliographies*   **2** = *Shakespeare*   **4** = 1–8221   **5** = 8222–14616

NIETZSCHE, Friedrich Wilhelm, 1844–1900. 928

NIGHTINGALE, Florence, 1820–1910. **12592**
— Bibs. 1:**4347–9**
— *Notes on nursing.* 12592

NIMMO, John Cumming, d.1907. **5298**

NINETEENTH CENTURY–Bibs. 1:1716k 1916

NIVEN, Anna Jane (Vardill), 1781–1852–Bibs. 1:**4350**

NIXON, Anthony, fl.1602–16. **12593**
— *Footpost of Dover.* 12593

NIXON, Howard Millar, 1909– . 2249 3476a

NOBLE, Mark, 1754–1827.
— *Life of John Donne.* 10275

NOBLE, Theophilus Charles, fl.1860–89.
— *Caxton memorial.* 4248

NOBLE, William, 1838–1912–Libr. 1:1226

NOBODY AND SOMEBODY, 1606. 7183

NOCTES AMBROSIANÆ–Bibs. 1:1940a

NOEL, Judith, baroness Wentworth, lady, d.1822–Bibs. 1:2694

NOEL, Nathaniel, fl.1681–1753. **5299**

NOEL, sir Ralph Milbanke, d.1825. 9224
— Bibs. 1:2694

NOLLEKENS, Joseph, 1737–1823–Libr. 2621 2759

NONCONFORMIST BOOKS–Bibs. 1:**2271–2a**

'NON EST MORTALE QUOD OPTO'. 2378 2382 2390
— Bibs. 1:581c

NONESUCH PRESS, est. 1923. 778 **5300–6** 6099 6490
— Bibs. 1:**1375–7**
— *Congreve's Complete Works.* 6703
— *Dickens' Works.* 10089 10095 10178
— *Donne's Poems.* 10248
— *Shakespeare's Works.* 2:773a

NONSENSE OF COMMON SENSE. 12467–8

NOONAN, Robert, 1870–1911 *see* TRESSELL, Robert, *pseud.*

NOON GAZETTE. 7712

NOORTHOUK, John, d.1816. 5791

NOOT, Jan Baptista van der, 1539/40–90 935

NORDEN, Frederick Lewis, 1708–42.
— *Travels in Egypt.* 5976

NORDEN, John, 1548–1625? 7502 **12594–8**
— Bibs. 1:**4351–2**
— *Pathway to penitence.* 12597
— *Speculum Britanniæ.* 12594

NORFOLK. **1301–9**
— Bibs. 1:**924**
— Bksllng. 1304
— Librs. 1302–3
— Maps–Bibs. 1:**1798**
— Paper *see also* BACON, Richard McKenzie, d.1844. 1302

— Ptg. 1302

NORFOLK, DUKE OF (PRESS). **5307**

NORFOLK AND NORWICH INCORPORATED LAW SOCIETY. LIBRARY. 1306a

NORFOLK AND NORWICH LITERARY INSTITUTION. 1306a 3385

NORLIE, OLAF MORGAN, 1876–1962–Libr. 1:1488

NORMAN, sir Henry, 1858–1939–Libr. 2520

NORMAN, Hubert, fl.1939– –Libr. 3002

NORNAVILLE, John, 1754–1837. 4623

NORRIS, Herbert Ellis, 1859–1931–Libr. 1:**898**

NORRIS, John, 1657–1711–Bibs. 1:**4352h**

NORRIS, William Edward, 1847–1925–Collns. 7322a

NORTH, Christopher, *pseud. of* John Wilson, 1785–1854. 12038
— Bibs. 1:**4353–b**
— Illus. 1:**4353b**
— *Penny plain, twopence coloured*–Bibs. 1:4353b
— *Recreations*–Bibs. 1:4353a

NORTH, John, Dublin, fl.1679–97. **5308–9**

NORTH, John William, 1841–1924. 7420a

NORTH, Roger, 2d baron North, 1530–1600. 4209

NORTH, Roger, 1653–1734. **12599–600**
— *Arguments for a register.* 12600
— Mss. 12599

NORTH, sir Thomas, 1535?–1601? **12601–2**
— *Plutarch's Lives.* 12601–2
— Text. 12601–2

NORTHAMPTON, Northants. **1312**
— Bndng. *see* BIRDSALL AND SON, fl.1890.
— Newspapers. 1311–12
— Ptg. *see* DICEY, William, fl.1713–54.
— PUBLIC LIBRARY–Collns. 1:2809a

NORTHAMPTON, James Compton, 3d earl of, 1622–81 *see* COMPTON, James, 3d earl of Northampton, 1622–81.

NORTHAMPTON JOURNAL. 1311

NORTHAMPTON MERCURY. 1312

NORTHAMPTON MISCELLANY. 1311

NORTHAMPTONSHIRE. **1310–12**
— Bksllng. 1310–11
— Librs. *see* ECTON HALL; LAMPORT HALL.
— Maps–Bibs. 1:**1799**
— Newspapers. 1311
— Ptg. 1310–11

NORTHAMPTONSHIRE JOURNAL. 1311

NORTH BRITISH REVIEW–Bibs. 1:1716k 1927

NORTH BRITON. 7699 7733 7746 7757 7759 14185

NORTH BRITON EXTRAORDINARY, 1765. 7950

NORTHCLIFFE, Alfred Charles William Harmsworth, viscount, 1865–1922 *see* HARMSWORTH, Alfred Charles William, viscount Northcliffe, 1865–1922.

NORTHERN ENGLAND *see* ENGLAND, NORTHERN.

NORTHERN TYPOGRAPHICAL UNION, 1830–44. 5884

NORTH LITTLETON, Worcs.–Paper. 1429a

NORTH LONSDALE, Lancs. **1180a**

NORTH SHIELDS, Nthmb.
— Ptg. *see* PRIORY PRESS, fl.1926–9.

NORTH TEXAS STATE UNIVERSITY. LIBRARY–Collns. 2244

NORTHUMBERLAND. **1313–27**
— Bibs. 1:**925–7**
— Bndng. 1313
— Book trade–Bibs. 1:926k
— Librs. *see* BAMBURGH CASTLE; WALLINGTON HALL.
— Librs. *see also* NATURAL HISTORY SOCIETY OF NORTHUMBERLAND. LIBRARY.
— Maps–Bibs. 1:**1800**

NORTHUMBERLAND, Henry Percy, 9th earl of, 1564–1632 *see* PERCY, Henry, 9th earl of Northumberland, 1564–1632.

NORTHUMBERLAND MANUSCRIPT. 2:1021 1023

NORTHUMBRIA–Book collecting. 2266
— Booktrade. 1031–2

NORTH WALES PAPER COMPANY, Oakenholt. 1542

NORTHWEST ENGLAND *see* ENGLAND, NORTHWEST.

NORTHWICH, Ches.–Librs. *see* DELAMERE HOUSE.

Norton, Alice (Law), fl.1641–2. 5310

NORTON, Caroline Elizabeth Sarah (Sheridan), afterwards lady Stirling-Maxwell, 1808–77. 5250

NORTON, John, fl.1612–43–Libr. 3396a

NORTON, John, fl.1628–36. 6683

NORTON, Thomas, 1532–84. **12603**
— Bibs. 1:1597
— *Gorboduc.* 12603

NORTON FACSIMILE. 2:623–4

NORWEGIAN LITERATURE *see* FOREIGN BOOKS PUBLISHED IN BRITAIN; SHAKESPEARE, William, 1564–1616–WORKS IN NORWAY.

NORWICH, Norf. **1305–8**
— Librs. 1306a–8
— Newspapers. 1306 7749
— Paper *see* BACON, Richard McKenzie, d.1844.
— Ptg. 1018–19 1306

— CATHEDRAL. LIBRARY. 1306a 2698b 3182a
— PUBLIC LIBRARY. 1306a
— — — Collns. 1:1148 2492 2565 4327 4566; 2:51; 3350 6036

NORWICH CABINET. 7749

NORWICH MEDICO-CHIRURGICAL SOCIETY. LIBRARY. 1306a

NORWICH POST. 1306

NOSEGAY BOOKS. 659
— Bibs. 1:542

NOTARY, Julian, fl.1498–1520. **5311–12** 6055–6 6081

NOTEBOOKS. 3739

NOTES AND QUERIES. 7819 7878 7922

NOTT, John, 1751–1865.
— *Dekker's Gull's hornbook.* 6397
— Ptg. 6397

NOTTINGHAM, Notts. *see also* BOOK TRADE, LISTS–Nottingham. **1341–5**
— Bibs. 1:**930**
— Bksllng. 1342 1344
— Bndng. 1342 1344
— Librs. *see* WOLLATON HALL.
— Newspapers. 1343–5
— — Bibs. 1:931 1903a
— Ptg. 1342 1344 8099
— — Bibs. 1:930
— PUBLIC LIBRARIES–Collns. 1:928–9 4024 5085
— UNIVERSITY. LIBRARY–Collns. 1:4024

NOTTINGHAMSHIRE *see also* BOOK TRADE, LISTS–Nottinghamshire. **1328**
— Bibs. 1:**928–32** 5023–4
— Chapbooks–Bibs. 1:1538
— Directories–Bibs. 1:928
— Librs. *see* NEWSTEAD ABBEY.
— Maps. 7503
— — Bibs. 1:**1800n**
— Ptg. 1328
— — Bibs. 1:1538

NOTTINGHAMSHIRE. COUNTY LIBRARY–Collns. 1:4024

NOURSE, John, fl.1730–80. 923

NOUVELLES ORDINAIRES DE LONDRES. 1198

NOVELLO, Joseph Alfred, 1810–96. 5313–14

NOVELLO, Vincent, 1781–1861. **5313–15**
— Collns. 5313

NOVELS *see also* FICTION; YELLOW-BACKS. 7264 7267
— Bndng. 2119
— Collns. 7262 7272 7284–5 7288 7292 7303 7307–9 7311–13 7315–17 7319 7321 7322a
— Illus. 6229 7260 7286 7297 7435
— Mss. 7272 7319
— Ptg. 7263

NOVELS–1601–1700. 7275–6
— 1701–1800. 7279 7281–8 7292
— 1801–1900. 464 792 2119 4003 5090 5197 5199 6229 6524 6772 7296 7303 7307–19 7324 7426
—, BURLESQUE–Bibs. 1:1710
—, EPISTOLARY *see* EPISTOLARY FICTION.
—, GYPSY. 7360
—, REGIONAL–Bibs. 1:1716
—, RELIGIOUS–Bibs. 1:1717d
—, SEQUENCE–Bibs. 1:1662 1666 1670 1694y
—, THREE-VOLUME. 7314 7323
—, UNFINISHED–Bibs. 1:2077
—, UNIVERSITY–Bibs. 1:1667–8
—, WELSH. 7261
NOWELL, Alexander, 1507?–1602. 1501
NOWELL, Laurence, d.1576–Libr. 2924
NOWELL-SMITH, Simon Harcourt, 1909– *see* Smith, Simon Harcourt Nowell-, 1909–
NOYES, Alfred, 1880–1958–Bibs. 1:4354–b
NUGENT, Thomas, 1700?–72.
— *Cellini.* 943
NUGENT'S CORRECT AND GENUINE MOORE'S ALMANAC, 1861. 1800
NUMBERING OF EDITIONS *see* EDITIONS, NUMBERING OF.
NUNN FAMILY (papermakers?). 1817
NYCHOLSON, James, Southwark, fl.1535–8 *see* NICHOLSON, James, Southwark, fl.1535–8.

OAKENHOLT, Flintshire–Paper. 1542
OAKES, Edward, fl.1664–72. 6683
O'BRIEN, Michael Fitz-James, 1828–62–Bibs. 1:4355
O'BRIEN, William, 1832–89–Libr. 1:459
OBSCENITY *see* CENSORSHIP, MORAL.
OBSERVER, THE. 7724 9023
ÓCASAIDE, Séamus, 1878–1943. 54
O'CASEY, Sean, 1880–1964. 12604–5
—Bibs. 1:1597 4355y–6a
— Mss. 12605
— *Story of the Irish citizen army.* 12604
OCCASIONAL BOOKS. 511 519 522
OCCULT SCIENCES *see also* MAGIC; WITCHCRAFT.
— Bibs. 1:2241–4
O'CONNELL, Daniel, 1775–1847. 523
O'CONNOR, Daniel, 1880–
— *Luck of the bean rows.* 4708
— Illus. 4708
O'CONNOR, Dermo'd, fl.1823. 1765
O'CONNOR, Frank, *pseud.* of Michael O'Donovan, 1903–66–Bibs. 1:4356c–d

O'CONWAY, Matthew James, 1716–1842. 7077
OCTAVIAN THE EMPEROR, 1504–6. 6031
OCTAVO FORMAT *see* FORMAT–Octavo.
OCTODECIMO FORMAT *see* FORMAT–Octodecimo.
O'CURRY, Eugene, 1794–1862–Bibs. 1:4357
O'DALY, John, d.1878. 12606
ODE FOR MUSIC ON THE LATITUDE, 1727. 10654
ODES–Bibs. 1:2005e
O'DONOGHUE, David James, 1866–1917–Libr. 1777
O'DONOVAN, John, 1809–61. 12607–8
— *Annals of Ireland.* 12607–8
— Bibs. 1:4358
— Publ. 12607
O'DONOVAN, Michael, 1903–66 *see* O'CONNOR, Frank, *pseud.*
O'DUFFY, Eimar, 1893–1935. 12609
OFFALY–Bibs. 1:1112
— Ptg.–Bibs. 1:1112
OFFOR, George, 1787–1864–Libr. 2557 2560 6856
'OFF-PRINT'. 3604
OFF-PRINTS. 6533
OFFSETS *see* SET-OFF.
O'FLAHERTY, Liam, 1897– –Bibs. 1:4359–a
OGBORNE, John, 1755–1837. 5316
OGILBY, John, 1600–76. 5317–21
— *Æsop's Fables.* 5321
— — Bibs. 1:4360b
— Bibs. 1:4360–b
— *Britannia.* 5317a
— *Entertainment.* 5319
OGILVIE, James Dean, 1861–1949–Libr. 1:717–19
OGILVY, Henri Gabriel, fl.1856. 901
O'GRADY, Standish James, 1846–1928. 8235
— Bibs. 1:4361–2
O'HANRAHAN, Michael, fl.1914–Bibs. 1:4363
O'HEGARTY, Patrick Sarsfield, 1879–1955. 74 12610–11
— Collns. 12610–11
— Libr. 1:5206; 2:653; 7969 12611
O'HIGGINS, Kevin Christopher, 1892–1927–Bibs. 1:4364
OHIO. STATE UNIVERSITY, Columbus. LIBRARY–Collns. 1:1636
OHIO. UNIVERSITY. LIBRARY–Collns. 1:1636
O'KELLY, Patrick, 1773?–1858–Bibs. 1:4364h
O'KELLY, Seumas, 1881–1918–Bibs. 1:4365
OKES, John, d.1643. 6683
OKES, Nicholas, fl.1608–36. 5322 6683
— *Shakespeare's King Lear.* 2:1450

OKEY, John, d.1662. 708
OLD BRITISH SPY. 7896
OLDCASTLE, Hugh, fl.1543.
— *Profitable treatise.* 6725
OLD ENGLAND. 14188
OLDFIELD, Claude Houghton, 1889–1961 *see* HOUGHTON, Claude, *pseud.*
OLDHAM, John, 1653–83–Bibs. 1:4366
OLD LONDON 1229
OLDMEADOW, Ernest James, 1867–1940. 7921 7932
OLDMIXON, John, 1673–1742. 12612–13
— Bibs. 1:4366d
— *Britannia liberata.* 12612
— *Histories.* 12613
— *History of England*–Bibs. 1:4366d
— Ptg. 12613
OLD-SPELLING EDITIONS *see* EDITIONS, OLD-SPELLING.
OLD TENURES, 1594. 5469
OLD TESTAMENT *see* BIBLE. O.T.
OLDYS, William, 1696–1761. 12614
— *Critical and historical account of libraries.* 3698a
O'LEARY, Peter, 1839–1900–Bibs. 1:4366f–g
OLIPHANT, Margaret Oliphant (Wilson), 1828–97. 12615
— Bibs. 1:4366h
OLIVER, George, 1781–1861. 12616
— *History of the Catholic religion.* 12616
— Text. 12616
OLIVER, George, 1873–1961 *see* ONIONS,
OLIVER, Reginald, Ipswich, fl.1534. 5323
OLLIVANT, Alfred, 1874–1927. 12617
— *Owd Bob.* 12617
OLNEY, Bucks. COWPER AND NEWTON MUSEUM *see* COWPER AND NEWTON MUSEUM, Olney, Bucks.
OMAGH–Ptg. 1770–1
O'MAHONY, Con., 1594–1650/6? 12618
— *Disputatio apologetica.* 12618
OMAN, sir Charles William Chadwick, 1860–1946–Bibs. 1:4366m
OMNIUM, THE. 7883
O'MOLLOY, Francis, d.1677? 12619–20
— *Grammatica Latino-Hibernica.* 12620
— *Lucerna fidelium.* 12619
ONCE A WEEK. 3496 7389 7849 10400 12989 13081 14166
O'NEILL, Francis, 1760–1848–Libr. 3054
ONIONS, Charles Talbut, 1873–1965–Bibs. 1:4367
ONIONS, Oliver, *pseud* of George Oliver, 1873–1961–Bibs. 1:4368
ONWHYN, Thomas, d.1886.
— *Dickens' Pickwick papers.* 9982
OPENINGS PRESS–Bibs. 1:1239

OPERAS. 7218 7601 7608
OPERAS–Bibs. 1:1624f 1833r 1837c 3416b 4044s
OPERATIVE PRINTERS' ASSISTANTS SOCIETY *see* NATIONAL SOCIETY OF OPERATIVE PRINTERS AND ASSISTANTS, est. 1889.
OPHTHALMOLOGY. 7560–1 7564
OPIE, Amelia (Alderson), 1769–1853. 12621
— Bibs. 1:4369
OPPENHEIM, David, d.1736–Libr. 2956
OPPENHEIM, Edward Phillips, 1866–1946–Bibs. 1:4369d
ORACLE, THE. 3977
O'RAHILLY, Michael Joseph, 1875–1916–Bibs. 1:4369m
ORANGE SOCIETY–Bibs. 1:2244e
ORATORY OF ST. PHILIP NERI, London–Collns. 1:538g
ORCHARDSON, sir William Quiller, 1832–1910. 7420a
ORD, Craven, 1756–1832. 7168
ORDERS AND ORDINANCES OF THE HOSPITALS, 1532. 7558
ORDERS OF HIS HIGHNESS THE LORD PROTECTOR FOR REGULATING PRINTING, 1655. 3559
ORDINANCES. 709
ORDINARIES (BINDINGS) *see* BOOKBINDINGS–Ordinaries.
OREGON. UNIVERSITY. LIBRARY–Collns. 1:4724
O'REILLY, Edward, d.1829.
— *Irish-English dictionary.* 7074
— Libr. 1810
ORFORD, Horace Walpole, 4th earl of, 1717–97 *see* WALPOLE, Horace, 4th earl of Orford, 1717–97.
ORFORD, Robert Walpole, 1st earl, 1676–1745 *see* WALPOLE, sir Robert, 1st earl of Orford, 1676–1745.
ORFORD, Robert Horace Walpole, 10th earl, 1854–1931 *see* WALPOLE, Robert Horace, 10th earl of Orford, 1854–1931
ORIENTAL TALES–Bibs. 1:1691
ORKNEY ISLANDS–Bibs. 1:1005
ORME, Cosmo, fl.1814. 1294
ORME, Edward, 1774–1848.
— *British field sports.* 8192
ORMSBY-GORE, William George Arthur, 4th baron Harlech, 1885–1964 *see* GORE, William George Arthur Ormsby-, 4th baron Harlech, 1885–1964.
ORNAMENT *see* ILLUSTRATIONS.
ORNAMENTS, TYPE *see* TYPE–Ornaments.
ORNITHOLOGY *see* BIRDS.

ORNSBY, Robert, 1820–89.
— *The changed mother.* 12569
ORPHEUS PRESS, Leicester, 1958–61.
5324–5
ORRERY, John Boyle, 5th earl of, 1707–62
see BOYLE, John, 5th earl of Cork, and
Orrery, 1707–62.
ORRERY, Roger Boyle, 1st earl of, 1621–79
see BOYLE, Roger, 1st earl of Orrery,
1621–79.
ORTHOGRAPHY *see also* CAPITAL-
IZATION; GRAMMAR; METRE;
PARENTHESES; PUNCTUATION;
SPELLING. 6177–8 6184 9745
ORTON, Charles William Previté-,
1877–1947–Bibs. 1:4369t
ORWELL, George, *pseud. of* Eric Blair,
1903–50–Bibs. 1:**4370–3**
OSBORN, James Marshall, 1906–76 *see also*
YALE. UNIVERSITY. LIBRARY.
OSBORN COLLECTION. 3279
— Libr. 1:2744
OSBORN, John, fl.1733–45.
— *Richardson's Pamela.* 13024 13038
OSBORN, William, fl.1720–1. 7468
OSBORNE, Charles Glidden, fl.1949–Libr.
1:4811; 13663
OSBORNE, Dorothy (lady Temple), 1627–95.
12622–3
— Letters. 12622–3
— Text. 12622–3
OSBORNE, Edgar, 1890– –Libr. *see*
TORONTO. PUBLIC LIBRARIES.
OSBORNE COLLECTION.
OSBORNE, Francis, 1593–1659–Bibs. 1:**4375**
OSBORNE, George Godolphin, 10th duke
of Leeds, 1862–1927–Libr. *see* HORNBY
CASTLE, Yorks.
OSBORNE, John James, 1929– –Bibs.
1:1597 **4376–a**
OSBORNE, Thomas, d.1767. 3475 3622
5326–8
OSCOTT, Warws.
— Librs. *see* ST. MARY'S COLLEGE,
Oscott. LIBRARY.
OSGOOD, Charles Grosvenor, 1871–
1964–Libr. 13578
O'SHAUGHNESSY, Arthur William Edgar,
1844–81. **12624–5**
— *Epic of women.* 12624
— Letters. 12625
OSLER, sir William, bart., 1849–1919. 26–7
7566
— Libr. 1:2215
OSSIAN, *pseud., see* MACPHERSON, James,
1736–96.
O'SULLIVAN, Richard, d.1880 *see*
SULLIVAN, Richard, d.1880.

O'SULLIVAN, Seumas, *pseud. of* James
Sullivan Starkey, 1879–1958–Bibs.
1:**4377–a**
O'SULLIVAN, Timothy, fl.1795. **12626**
— Bibs. 1:**4378–9**
— *Pious miscellany.* 12626
— — Bibs. 1:**4378–9**
O'SULLIVAN, Vincent, 1872–1940–Bibs.
1:**4380**
OSWEN, John, Ipswich, fl.1548–53 *see*
OWEN, John, Ipswich, fl.1548–53.
OTAGO UNIVERSITY, Dunedin, N.Z.
LIBRARY–Collns. 1:2009
OTES HOUSE, Essex–Libr. 3140
OTHAM, Kent–Paper. 1161a
OTTLEY, Charles, LANDON AND
COMPANY, fictitious publishers. 14420–1
OTWAY, Thomas, 1652–85. 11957 **12627–8**
— *Caius Marius.* 12628
OUGHTRED, William, 1575–1660. **12629–31**
— *Circles of proportion.* 12630
— *Mathematical recreations.* 12631
— *Trigonometries.* 12630
OUIDA, *pseud. of* Marie Louise de la
Ramée, 1839–1908. 12632
OUSELEY, sir Frederick Arthur Gore,
1825–89–Bibs. 1:**4381**
'OUT OF PRINT'. 3580 3582 3607
OVERBURY, Worcs.–Paper. 1429a
OVERBURY, sir Thomas, 1581–1613. **12633**
— Bibs. 1:**4382**
— *Characters.* 10221 12633
OVERLAYING *see* PRINTING–Presswork.
OVERTON, Hants.–Paper. 1132a
OVERTON, John, 1640–1713. **5329** 6550
OVERTON, Richard, fl.1642–63 **12634–5**
— Bibs. 1:**4383–4**
— *Man's mortality.* 12635
OVID (Publius Ovidius Naso), 43 B.C.–18
A.D. 876 890a 4233 4344 12159 12162
12332–3 13147–8 13150–3
— *Metamorphoses.* 2:1011–13
OWEN, C. T., fl.1909–21–Libr. 7010
OWEN, George, 1552–1613. **12636–7**
— *Description of Pembrokeshire.* 12637
— Mss. 12636–7
OWEN, Goronwy, 1723–69–Libr. 3398b
OWEN, John, Ipswich, fl.1548–53. 1401 **5330**
— Bibs. 1:947
OWEN, John, 1560?–1622.
— Bibs. 1:**4384k**
— *Epigrammata.* 12638–9
— — Bibs. 1:**4384k**
OWEN, John, 1741–1823–Libr. 3291
OWEN, Lewis, 1532–94 *see* LEWIS, bp.
Owen, 1532–94.
OWEN, Nicholas, 1752–1811. 1517
OWEN, Robert, 1771–1858–Bibs. 1:**4385–9**

OXFORD, Edward De Vere, 17th earl of,
1550–1604 see DE VERE, Edward, 17th
earl of Oxford, 1550–1604.
OXFORD, Edward Harley, 2d earl of,
1689–1741 see HARLEY, Edward, 2d earl
of Oxford, 1689–1741.
OXFORD, Robert Harley, 1st earl,
1661–1724 see HARLEY, Robert, 1st earl
of, 1661–1724.
OXFORD AND CAMBRIDGE MAGAZINE.
7933
OXFORD INTER-COLLEGATE CAT-
ALOGUE. 618 623 625 631 634 655
OXFORD JOURNAL see *JACKSON'S
OXFORD JOURNAL.*
OXFORD MOVEMENT. 7927 **8102–4**
— Bibs. 1:**2273–b**
— Collns. 8103–4
*OXFORD OLD-SPELLING SHAKE-
SPEARE.* 2:756 885
OXFORDSHIRE. **1346–83**
— Bibs. 1:**933–7a**
— Newspapers–Bibs. 1:933–4
OXFORD UNIVERSITY PRESS, est. 1584 see
also WOLVERCOTE MILL, Oxford and
names of persons connected with the Press, e.g.
BARNES, Joseph, fl.1584–1618; BASKETT,
Mark, fl.1742–7; BENSLEY, Thomas, d.
1833; BLACKSTONE, sir William,
1723–80; CANNAN, Charles, 1858–1919;
COMBE, Thomas, 1797–1872; FELL, bp.
John, 1625–86; GUY, Thomas, 1644–1724;
HART, Horace, 1840–1916; JOHNSON,
John DeMonins, 1881–1956; LICHFIELD,
Leonard, 1604–57; RICHARDSON,
Samuel, 1689–1761; STANHOPE, Charles,
3d earl, 1753–1816. 3912 4656 4658 4660–1
4826 **5331–66** 5720 5723 8763
— Bibs. 1:1201a 1256 3283b
— Bndng. 5333–4
— Collns. 5348
— Correctors. 6405
— *Hickes' Thesaurus.* 11087
— Libr. 11145
— Paper. 5333 5335 5359
— Type. 5332–3 5335 5342 5366 6572 6613
6637 6648–9
— BIBLE PRESS. 5333 5357 5359 5362
— CLARENDON PRESS. 11294
— CONSTANCE MEADE COLLECTION
see JOHN JOHNSON COLLECTION.
— DELEGACY. 3929 5341 5355 5359
— JOHN JOHNSON COLLECTION.
5349–54 5361 5364–5 6098 6722
— — Collns. 1:623 1195–6
— RECORD ROOM. 5349–53
— 1475–1640. 5347 5355
— 1641–1700. 5341 5343–5 5355–6 6405

— 1701–1800. 5332 5360 5362–3 5366 6405
— 1801–1900. 5333 5334a 5357 5362 5366

PADSOLE, Kent–Paper. 1161a
PADUA. UNIVERSITA. BIBLIOTECA
–Collns. 2:541a 573 870
PAGE, James Rathwell, 1884–1962–Libr.
1:1522
PAGE, William, 1590–1663.
— *Treatise of bowing.* 647
PAGEANT–Bibs. 1:1721
PAGEANT OF POPES. 2:1033
PAGEANTS–Bibs. 1:1603
PAGET, Henry Marriott, 1856–1936.
— *Dickens' Pickwick papers.* 9982
PAGET, sir James, 1814–99–Bibs. 1:**4391**
PAGET, Violet, 1856–1935 see LEE, Vernon,
pseud.
PAGINATION. 6268 6289
— Bibliogr. descr. 97 143 254
PAGITT, Ephraim, 1575?–1647. 7527
PAILTHORPE, Frederick W., fl.1870–86.
— *Dickens' Pickwick papers.* 9982
PAINE, Thomas, 1737–1809.
— *Age of reason.* 4182a
PAINTINGS, OIL.
— Ptg. 6202
PAISLEY, Renfrew. **1737–8**
— Librs. 1633
PAISLEY ANNUAL MISCELLANY. 1737
PAISLEY REPOSITORY. 1738
PALÆOGRAPHY see also HANDWRITING.
6637
PALGRAVE, Francis Turner, 1824–97.
12645–9
— Bibs. 1:**4392**
— *Golden treasury.* 12645–9
— — Bibs. 1:4392
— Mss. 12647
— Publ. 12646 12649
PALGRAVE PRESS, fl.1842. **5367**
PALL MALL GAZETTE. 7908 8290 8296
10643 14283
— Bibs. 1:**2338**
PALMER, George Herbert, 1842–1933–Libr.
1:1990
PALMER, Herbert Edward, 1880–1961–Bibs.
1:**4393**
PALMER, Samuel, d.1732. 3475 3819
PALMER, Samuel, 1805–81. 9983 9997a
PALMER, Thomas, fl.1553–64. **12650–3**
— *Emblems.* 12650–3
— Mss. 12650–3
PALMERIN OF ENGLAND. 11694
PALSGRAVE, John, d.1554.
— *Acolastus.* 891

PALTOCK, Robert, d.1767. **12654**
— *Peter Wilkins.* 12654
PAMPHLETS *see also* BROADSIDES;
   PROCLAMATIONS; SERMONS. 3475
   7937–51
— Bibs. 1:**1960–79j**
— Collns. 2489 2592a 3295
— Excise. 7949
— Ireland. 1783 1805 1858 2713
— — Collns. 2713
— Scotland. 3258
— Wales–1801–1900. 1457 4507
— 1475– –Bibs. 1:**1960–1**
— 1475–1640–Bibs. 1:**1965–6**
— 1475–1700. **7938–48**
— — Bibs. 1:634 **1970–1t**
— 1641–1700 *see also* THOMASON, George,
   d.1666. 6368 7938–42 7945 7948
— — Bibs. 1:899 **1972–3**
— 1701–1800. 6770 **7949–51** 8013
— — Bibs. 1:**1975–8i** 2172 2621d   4443g
   4447
— 1801–1900–Bibs. 1:**1978x–9** 2172
PAMPLIN, William, 1806–99. **5368**
PAN. 7857
PANDORA PRESS, Leicester, est. 1960.
   5369–70
— Bibs. 1:**1378–a**
PANDY MILLS, Chepstow. 1298a
PANELLED BINDINGS *see* BOOK-
   BINDINGS, PANELLED.
PANIZZI, sir Anthony, 1797–1879. 2443
PANORAMIC MISCELLANY. 14001
PANTER, George William, d.1928–Libr.
   1795
PAPER. 257 259 263 269 2278 2347 2375
   3699–809
— Bibliogr. descr. 97 128 160–1
— Bibs. 1:1139c 1139 m **1139z–zd** 1150
— Chainlines *see also* FORMAT–Turned
   chainlines. 6253
— — Bibliogr. descr. 155
— Dendritic markings. 3712
— Excise. 1514 1837 3546 3707 3717 3746
   3765 3767–a 3769 4545 5359 5909 5935
   5975
— Forgeries. 3732 3798 3801 7256–a
— Inventories. 3725 5359
— Ireland. 1840 3717
— Prices. 3690 3765 5799
— Scotland. 3717
— Sizes *see also* LARGE PAPER COPIES.
   3740 3747 3891 5799 6231 6234–5
— Storage. 3736 3738
— Terms and concepts. 3737 3752–3
— Wales. 1502 3765
— Watermarks *see* WATERMARKS.
— 1475–1500. 3690 3728

— 1475–1640. 3701 3731
— 1475–1700. 3453 3780 3777
— 1641–1700. 3725 3734 3736
— 1701–1800. 278 3453 3707 3720 3734
   3743 3745 3763–a 3765 3771 5799
— 1801–1900. 3453 3702 3763a 3771 3782
   6291
—, BANK NOTE *see* BANK NOTES.
—, BLOTTING. 3723
—, BROWN. 3784a
—, CHEQUE. 3714
—, COLOURED. 3700
—, DECORATED. 6291
—, DOUBLE ATLAS. 5975
—, GLAZED. 3939
—, GILT. 3744 6291
—, HANDMADE. 3709 3714 3717–18 3755
   3770 3772 3780 3783a 3891
—, IMPORTATION OF. 3717 3728 3731
   3765 3777 3784–a 3797
—, INDIA. 3719 3726 5333 9337
—, LAID. 3714
—, LETTER. 6275
—, LOADED. 3708
—, MARBLED. 3701 3722 3742 6291 12832
— Bibs. 1:1139zb
—, MUSIC. 3762a
—, POST. 3792 3797
—, TRANSPARENT. 1165 3778
—, UNCUT. 3721
—, WHITE *see also* COMPANY OF WHITE
   PAPER MAKERS OF ENGLAND,
   1686–96; SCOTS WHITE PAPER
   MANUFACTORY, 1695. 4144
—, WOVE. 3757 3939 3714 6253
—, WRITING. 1101 3929
PAPER-COVERS *see also* WRAPPERS,
   BOOK. 2029 2070
PAPERMAKERS *see also* BACON, Richard
   McKenzie, Norwich, d.1844; BALSTON,
   William, 1759–1849; BURNABY, Eustace,
   fl.1677–98; CALLENDER'S PAPER
   COMPANY, Celbridge; COMPANY OF
   WHITE PAPER MAKERS OF ENGLAND,
   1686–96; CRAIG, Robert, Airdrie, est.
   1820; DICKINSON, George, Charlton,
   fl.1834; DICKINSON, John, 1782–1869;
   DIDOT, Pierre François, 1732–95;
   DIDOT-SAINT-LEGER, Pierre François,
   1767–1829; DONKIN, Bryan, 1768–1855;
   DUXBURY, Yates, Bury, 1818–91;
   FOURDRINIER, Henry, 1766–1854;
   FOURDRINIER, Sealy, d.1847; GAMBLE,
   John, fl.1801; GREAVES, Thomas, fl.1787;
   GREEN, Frank, 1835–1902; HALL, John,
   1764–1869; HARRIS, Richard, Maidstone,
   fl.1738; HOLLINGWORTH'S, Maidstone,
   fl.1830; HUTTON, Robert, Sunderland,

PAPERMAKING–Sussex. 1412
— Wales. 1502 1506 1514 3717 3767 3785a
— Warwickshire *see also* HUTTON, William, Birmingham, 1723–1815. 1419
— Worcestershire. 1429a
— Yorkshire. 1442
— 1475–1640. 3709–10 3764 3779
— 1475–1700. 3716 3724 3729 3733 3735 3762 3764–5a 5256
— 1641–1700. 3710–11 3714 3773 3797
— 1701–1800. 3430 3706 3711 3713 3724 3735 3754 3758 3762a 3764–5a 3769 3797 5256
— 1801–1900. 1083a 3700 3717 3748 3750–1 3757–60 3761a 3762a 3765 3768 3774 3785 6348
PAPERMAKING MACHINES. 1046 1165 3715 3717 3757 3760 3765 3776 3785 4545a
PAPERMAKING PATENTS *see* PATENTS, PAPERMAKING.
PAPER MERCHANTS. 4789
PAPER-MILLS *see also* PAPERMAKING. 3741 3749 3766–8 3776 3783
PAPERMOULD-MAKERS. 3775
PAPERS, END *see* BOOKBINDINGS–Endpapers.
—, LINING *see* BOOKBINDINGS–Linings.
PAPER WINDOWS *see* WINDOWS, PAPER.
PAPYRUS. 259 269
PAR, Alfonso, fl.1930–Libr. 2:64
PARACELSUS (Theophrastus Bombastus von Hohenheim), 1493–1541. 2:156
'PARCHMENT'. 3602
PARCHMENT. 269 1132 3690
PARCHMENT MILLS. 1945
PARADISE OF DAINTY DEVICES. 7979
PARDOE, Frank Ernest, Birmingham, est. 1957. 6495
PARENTHESES. 9746
PARGA, A POEM, 1819. 8031
PARHAM HOUSE, Sussex–Libr. 2:1016
PARIS. 844 866 5334 7228 8043 8057 10498 12499
— ACADÉMIE ROYALE DE SCIENCES *see* FRANCE. ACADÉMIE ROYALE DE SCIENCES. IMPRIMERIE ROYALE *see* ROYAL PRINTING OFFICE, Paris.
PARISER, Maurice Philip, 1906–68–Libr. 1:5145; 14446–7
PARISH LIBRARIES *see* LIBRARIES, PARISH.
PARISH REGISTERS. 6457
PARIS ILLUSTRÉ. 7858
PARIS SCIENTIFIC TYPE, 1702. 6637
PARK, Arthur, d.1863. 5371
PARK, Julian, 1888–1965–Libr. 1:673

PARKE, sir James, baron Wensleydale, 1782–1868. 3546
PARKER, Henry, d.1470.
— *Dives et pauper.* 5466–7 5471
PARKER, Henry, fl.1717–21–Bibs. 1:1379
PARKER, John William. 1792–1870. 5372
PARKER, archbp. Matthew, 1504–75. 12655–9
— *De antiquitate Britannicæ ecclesiæ.* 10237
— *Flores historiarum.* 12659
— Letters. 12657
— Libr. 2211 12655–8
PARKER, Peter, fl.1665–1703. 4822
PARKER, Stephen, Dublin, fl.1765–90. 6440
PARKHURST, sir William, fl.1643–Libr. 3396a
PARKINSON, Richard, 1748–1815.
— *Tour in America.* 8217
PARK MILL, Kent. 1161a
PARKS, William, Reading, fl.1719–50. 5373–4
— Bibs. 1:1379c
PARKYN, Robert, d.1570. 12660
— Mss. 12660
PARLEY'S PENNY LIBRARY. 7822
PARLIAMENT *see* GT. BRIT. PARLIAMENT.
PARLIAMENTARY BINDINGS *see* BOOKBINDINGS, PARLIAMENTARY.
PARLIAMENTARY PRINTING *see* PRINTING, PARLIAMENTARY.
PARLOUR LIBRARY. 1848
— Bibs. 1:1715
PARNASSUS PLAYS. 7120 7138 7162 7186
PARNELL, Thomas, 1679–1718. 12661–2
— Mss. 12662
— *Ode on the longitude.* 12661
— *Poems.* 4135
PARODIES *see also* IMITATIONS. 876 10820 13169
PARR, Katherine, 1512–48 *see* CATHERINE PARR, queen, 1512–48.
PARR, Samuel, 1747–1825. 12663–4
— Bibs. 1:4394–5c
— Libr. 12663
— *Notes on Rapin's Dissertation.* 12664
— — Bibs. 1:4395
PARRISH, Morris Longstreth, 1867–1944. 7305 7310 13995
— Libr. 1:1707 2722–3 2850 3929 4921 4985–6; 2113 7303 7307–10 7312–13 7315 7319 9328 10130 10962 11720 12072 14108 14111 14114
PARROTT, Thomas Marc, 1866–1960. 9380
PARRY, John, 1835–97–Libr. 3029
PARRY, Richard, fl.1544–1624. 1505
PARSONS, Charles, fl.1940. 7326
PARSONS, Edwin, fl.1836–1906. 5375

PEACOCK, Thomas Love, 1785–1866. *Nightmare abbey.* 12677
— *Sir Hornbook.* 12675
PEAKE, Mervyn Laurence, 1911–68–Bibs. 1:**4403**
PEAKE FAMILY, fl.1612–67. 6550
PEARCH, George, fl.1768–71.
— *Collection of poems.* 8018
PEARSE, Padraic Henry, 1879–1916–Bibs. 1:**4404**
PEARSON, John, fl.1873. 13381
PEARSON, Karl, 1857–1936–Bibs. 1:**4404b**
— Letters–Bibs. 1:4404b
PEARSON, William, fl.1699–1735. 5431
PEAR TREE PRESS, Bognor Regis, 1899–1952. **5396–400**
— Bibs. 1:**1380**
PEASE, John William, d.1901–Libr. 1:2458
PEAT. 3756
PECHAM, John, fl.1279–92–Bibs. 1:**4402p**
PECHEY, John, 1655–1716–Bibs. 1:**4404a**
PECK, Francis, 1692–1743.
— *New memoirs.* 12348
PECK, Roger, fl.1890. **5401**
PECKHAM RYE *see* LONDON. PECKHAM RYE.
PECKOVER, Alexander, baron Peckover of Wisbech, 1830–1919–Libr. 6859
PEDDIE, Robert Alexander, 1869–1951. 583
PEEBLES, Peebleshire–Librs. 1633
PEEBLESSHIRE–Bibs. 1:1007
— Librs. *see* CASTLECRAIG.
PEEL, sir Robert, 1788–1850. 5250
— Libr. 2567
PEELE, George, 1558?–97? **12679–88**
— *Battle of Alcazar.* 7125
— Bibs. 1:**4405–6b**
— *David and Bethsabe.* 12683
— *Edward I.* 12686–7
— Handwr. 2:1899
— *Hunting of Cupid.* 12688
— Mss. 9572
— — Bibs. 1:4406a
— *Old wives tale.* 12684–5
— Ptg. 12687
— *Tale of Troy.* 12681
— Text. 12679–80 12683 12686
PEET, William Henry, 1849–1916. 24
PEIRCE, sir Edmond, fl.1642–60. **12689**
PELGRIM, Joyce, fl.1506–14. 1197
— Bibs. 1:920a
PELHAM–HOLLES, sir Thomas, 5th baronet Pelham, 1st duke of Newcastle, 1693–1768 *see* HOLLES, sir Thomas Pelham-, 5th baronet Pelham, 1st duke of Newcastle, 1693–1768.
PELICAN BINDINGS *see* BOOKBINDINGS, PELICAN.

PELICAN PRESS, 1916–23. **5402**
PELICAN SHAKESPEARE. 2:811
PELL, Duncan C., fl.1963–Libr. 12792
PEMBROKE, Mary (Sidney) Herbert countess of, 1561–1621 *see* HERBERT, Mary (Sidney), countess of Pembroke, 1561–1621.
PEMBROKE, William Herbert, 3d earl of, 1580–1630 *see* HERBERT, William, 3d earl of Pembroke, 1580–1630.
PEMBROKESHIRE. **1548**
— Bibs. 1:**964**
— Paper. 1551
— Ptg. 1548
PEMBROKE SOCIETY, fl.1741–91. 1515
PEN, THE. 7824
PENA, Pierre, fl.1535–1605. 6545
PEN-AND-INK CORRECTIONS *see* CORRECTIONS, PEN-AND-INK.
PENDRED, John, 1742?–93. 3462
PENGUIN SHAKESPEARE. 2:807–8
PENICUIK, Midloth.–Librs. 1633
PENINGTON, sir John, 1568?–1651–Libr. 3396a
PENINGTON, John, 1655–1710.
— *People called quakers.* 6242
— Ptg. 6242
PENKETHMAN, John, fl.1623–38. **12690**
PENN, William, 1644–1718. **12691–2**
— Bibs. 1:**4406x–7**
— *Great case of liberty.* 12692
— — Bibs. 1:**4407**
— Ptg. 12691
PENNANT, Thomas, 1726–98. **12693–8**
— Bibs. 1:**4408–a**
— Libr. 12697
— *North American birds.* 12696
— *Tours in Scotland.* 12694–5
— *Tours in Wales.* 12693 12695
PENNECUIK, Alexander, 1652–1722–Bibs. 1:**4409**
PENNECUIK, Alexander, d.1730. **12699**
— Mss. 12699
PENNELL, Elizabeth (Robins), 1855–1936–Libr. 1:2141d
PENNELL, Joseph, 1857–1926. 4974
PENNINES–Paper. 3734a
PENNINGTON, John, 1655–1710 *see* PENINGTON, John, 1655–1710.
PENNINGTON FAMILY–Libr. 3044
PENNSYLVANIA. STATE TEACHERS' COLLEGE, West Chester. LIBRARY–Collns. 2:473
— UNIVERSITY. LIBRARY–Collns. 1:603 1490 1665 2796 3671; 643 693 6860 6878 7284 7288 7603 9244 9247 11762 12075 13029 13444 13782

PENNSYLVANIA. UNIVERSITY.
LIBRARY–Collns. HORACE HOWARD
FURNESS MEMORIAL. 2:287 343
— — — — Collns. 2:288
PENNY, Anne Bulkeley (Hughes),
b.1728–Bibs. 1:**4411**
PENNY CYCLOPÆDIA. 7238 7242
PENNY POST. 7877
PENRITH, Cumb.
— Chapbooks. 6988
— Ptg. 6988
PENROSE, Boies, 1902– –Libr. 8209 8216
PENROSE, Elizabeth (Cartwright),
1780–1837 *see* MARKHAM, mrs., *pseud.*
PENRY, John, 1559–93. 5154–5
— *Exhortation.* 5148 5154
PENRYN, Cornw.–Paper. 1083b
PENTATEUCH *see* BIBLE. O.T.
PENTATEUCH.
PENZANCE LIBRARY. 3396
PEOPLE'S CHARTER UNION, fl.1832.
3546
PEPLER, Harry (Hilary) Douglas Clarke,
1878–1951 *see also* ST. DOMINIC'S
PRESS, Ditchling, est. 1916. 5579a
PEPWELL, Henry, d.1540. 1197 6081
PEPYAT, Jeremiah, Dublin, fl.1711–15.
5403
PEPYS, Samuel, 1633–1703. **12700–31**
— Bibs. 1:**4412–13**
— *Diary.* 2309 12713 12721
— Libr. *see also* CAMBRIDGE.
UNIVERSITY. MAGDALENE COLLEGE.
PEPYSIAN LIBRARY. 1:2280; 12700–12
12714 12716 12719–20 12722–5 12727–31
— Mss. 12717
— Text. 12713 12718
PEPYS-COCKERELL, John, fl.1931 *see*
COCKERELL, John Pepys-, fl.1931.
PERCEVAL, Arthur Philip, 1799–1850.
12732
PERCIVAL AND COMPANY, 1889–93.
5555
PERCY, Henry, 9th earl of Northumberland,
1564–1632 *see also* PETWORTH HOUSE,
Sussex. 4209
— Libr. 3219–20 3282
PERCY, bp. Thomas, 1729–1811. **12733–56**
— *Ancient English and Scottish poems.* 12747
— Ballads. 1635
— Bibs. 1:**4415**
— *Hau Kiou Choaan.* 12734 12740
— Libr. 1635 6796 10994 12733 12738 12742
12750 12755–6
— *Memoir of Goldsmith.* 12744
— Mss. 12740–1 12747 12749 12753–4
— Ptg. 12745 12751
— Publ. 12743

— *Reliques of ancient English poetry.* 6787 8612
12735–7 12745 12748–9 12751–4 13374
— *Surrey's Poems.* 11232
PERCY, William, 1575–1648. 9587 **12757**
— Bibs. 1:**4415q**
— Mss. 12757
— — Bibs. 1:4415q
PERCY FAMILY–Libr. *see* PETWORTH
HOUSE, Sussex.
PERCY SOCIETY, est. 1840. 9599
PEREZ, Antonio, d.1611.
— *Relations.* 4665
PERFECTING *see* PRINTING–Perfecting.
PERFECTING MACHINES. 6312
PERIODICALS *see* ANNUALS; NEWS-
PAPERS AND PERIODICALS.
PERIODICAL WRAPPERS *see* WRAPPERS,
PERIODICAL.
PERIODS. *For subject headings divided by
periods, see* BOOKS AND SUBJECTS.
PERKINS, Frederick Beecher, 1828–99–Libr.
2:269
PERKINS, Walter Frank, 1865–1946–Libr.
1:2094 2098
PERKINS, William, 1558–1602. 11124 **12758**
— *Four great liars.* 12758
PERKINS SCHOOL OF THEOLOGY,
Dallas. BRIDWELL LIBRARY *see*
DALLAS. SOUTHERN METHODIST
UNIVERSITY. PERKINS SCHOOL OF
THEOLOGY. BRIDWELL LIBRARY.
PERRINS, Charles William Dyson,
1864–1958–Libr. 3022 3073 3241 3253
3262 3265
PERRY, Henry, 1560?–1617? 1517
PERRY, James, 1756–1821–Libr. 2883
PERRY, Marsden Jasiel, 1850–1935–Libr.
1:401 1351; 2:176 197 413 1004
PERRY, William, fl.1774–1808–Bibs. 1:**4416**
PERSHORE, Worcs.–Paper. 1429a
PERSONAL LIBRARIES *see* LIBRARIES,
PERSONAL.
PERTH, Perthshire. *see also* BOOK TRADE,
LISTS–Perth. **1733–6**
— Bibs. 1:**1005b–6**
— Bndng. 1735–6
— Bksllng. 1735–6
— Librs. 1633
— Ptg. 1733–4 1736
— — Bibs. 1:1005d
— Publ. 1736
— WRIGHT INCORPORATION *see*
WRIGHT INCORPORATION, Perth.
PERTHSHIRE. **1731–5**
— Bibs. 1:**1005b–6**
PETER, John ('Ioan Pedr'), 1833–77–Bibs.
1:**4416k**
— Mss.–Bibs. 1:4416k

Vol. **1** = *Bibliographies*   **2** = *Shakespeare*   **4** = 1–8221   **5** = 8222–14616

PETERBOROUGH NATURAL HISTORY, SCIENTIFIC, AND ARCHÆOLOGICAL SOCIETY–Collns. 1:2807
PETERHEAD, Aber.
— Librs. 1633
— Ptg. *see* BUCHON, Peter, 1790–1854.
PETER MARTYR *see* VERMIGLI, Pietro Martire, 1500–62.
PETERS, Alfred Vout, fl.1934–Libr. 2930
PETERS, Hugh, 1598–1660. 708 **12759**
PETER WILKINS see PALTOCK, Robert, d.1767.
PETHER, William, 1738?–1821. **5405**
PETHERICK, Edward Augustus, 1847–1917. 70 92
PETRARCH (Francesco Petrarca), 1304–74–Bibs. 1:**833–a**
PETRE, Edwin Alfred Robert Rumball-, 1881–1954–Libr. 6881
PETRIE, George, 1789–1866. 6430 6432 6442
PETRIE, James A., fl.1900–51–Libr. 3071
PETRONIUS ARBITER, d.66. 886 **895–6**
PETRUS GRUYPHUS, fl.1509 *see* GRYPHUS, Petrus, fl.1509.
PETTER AND GALPIN, 1878–83. 4207
PETTIE, John, 1839–93. 7420a
PETTY, John William, Leeds, 1820–1900. **5405**
PETTY, sir William, 1623–87. **12760**
—Bibs. 1:**4417–a**
PETTY, sir William, 1st marquis of Lansdowne, 1737–1805–Libr. 11632
PETWORTH HOUSE, Sussex–Libr. 2845 2853–4
PETYT, Silvester, 1640–1719–Libr. *see* SKIPTON. PUBLIC LIBRARY. PETYT LIBRARY.
PETYT LIBRARY, Skipton *see* SKIPTON. PUBLIC LIBRARY. PETYT LIBRARY.
PEVSNER, sir Nikolaus Bernhard Leon, 1902– –Bibs. 1:**4417q**
PFORZHEIMER, Carl Howard, 1879–1957–Libr. 1:577
PHARMACOPŒIAS. 1744 1891
PHELPS, William, d.1906–Libr. 2:511
PHILADELPHIA.
— Ptg. 9010 14489
— FREE LIBRARY–Collns. 1:417g 3467 4481; 3236 5493a 10176 11315
— LIBRARY COMPANY *see* LIBRARY COMPANY OF PHILADELPHIA.
PHILIPOTT, John, 1589–1645.
— *Villare Cantianum.* 1153
PHILIPPS, Fabian, 1601–90.
— *King Charles the first.* 3975
PHILIPPS, John Henry, 1808–76 *see* SCOURFIELD, sir John Henry, 1808–76.

PHILIPS, Ambrose, 1674–1749. **12761–7**
— *Armigero.* 12767
— Bibs. 1:**4418–19**
— *Collection of old ballads.* 12761 12763
— *Persian tales.* 12764
PHILIPS, John, 1676–1709. 11456 **12768**
— Bibs. 1:**4419w–20**
— *Cider.* 12768
— — Bibs. 1:4420
— *Poems.* 11456
PHILIPS, Katherine (Fowler), 1631–64. **12769**
— Mss. 12769
PHILIPS, William Pyle, 1882–1950–Libr. 1:541; 2:473 475
PHILLIMORE, John, fl.1920–42–Libr. 8087
PHILLIP, John, fl.1560–90. **12770**
— Bibs. 1:**4420a**
PHILLIPPS, James Orchard Halliwell-, 1820–89. 2:592 1229a; 3144 3391 **12771–6**
— Libr. 2:171 270 321 366 530 569 1285 1570; 2314 7162 8159 10922 12771 12773–4 12776
— *Shakespeare's Works.* 2:778
PHILLIPPS, sir Thomas, 1792–1872. 2780 3121 3144 3157 3337 3376a 3391 3394b 3841
— Bibs. 1:**4421**
— Libr. 2:1229a; 2314 2613 2732 2758 2953 3125 3148 3175 3207–9 3251 3292 3324 3361
PHILLIPS, Dorothy Una McGrigor (Ratcliffe), 1891– – Libr. 1:2191
PHILLIPS, Edward, 1630–96?
— *Theatrum poetarum.* 12425
PHILLIPS, James, fl.1775–6. 8099
PHILLIPS, John, d.1640. **12777**
— *Perfect path to paradise.* 12777
PHILLIPS, John, 1631–1706. **12778–80**
— Bibs. 1:**4422**
— *Responsio.* 12395 12780
— — Bibs. 1:4422
— *Satyr against hypocrites.* 12778
PHILLIPS, Joseph, 1824–1902–Libr. 1187a
PHILLIPS, Judith, fl.1595–Bibs. 1:**4422g**
PHILLIPS, sir Richard, 1767–1840. 5406–7 6510a 13257
PHILLIPS, Stephen, 1864–1915–Bibs. 1:**4423**
PHILLPOTTS, Eden, 1862–1960. **12781–2**
— Bibs. 1:**4424**
— *Three brothers.* 12781
PHILOBIBLON SOCIETY, 1853–84. **5408**
PHILOSOPHICAL TRANSACTIONS. 7694
PHILOSOPHY–Bibs. 1:**3758**
PHIZ, *pseud., see* BROWNE, Hablôt Knight, 1815–82.
PHOENIX PRESS, est. 1935? 5860

PHOTOGRAPHIC COMPOSITION *see* COMPOSITION, PHOTOGRAPHIC.
PHOTOGRAPHIC ETCHING *see* ETCHING, PHOTOGRAPHIC.
PHOTOGRAPHIC FACSIMILES *see* FACSIMILES, PHOTOGRAPHIC.
PHOTOGRAPHS. 1631 6211 6218 7459
— Bibs. 1:1754 1754k
PHOTOGRAVURE. 6186
— Ireland. 1808
PHOTOLITHOGRAPHY. 6186 6204
— Ireland. 6206
PHYSICAL BIBLIOGRAPHY *see* BIBLIOGRAPHY, PHYSICAL.
PICCOLOMINI, Æneas Silvius (pope Pius II), 1405–64 *see* ÆNEAS SILVIUS PICCOLOMINI (pope Pius II), 1405–64.
PICK, Robert Freeman, fl.1907–Libr. 1:3940; 11728
'PICKED COPIES'. 3596
PICKERING, Charles, fl.1828–54. **5409** 6229
PICKERING, sir William, 1516–75–Libr. 3212
PICKERING, William, fl.1557–71. **5410**
— Bibs. 1:**1381**
PICKERING, William, 1796–1854. 2136 **5411–16** 6123b 6476
— Bibs. 1:**1382**
PICKERSGILL, Frederick Richard, 1820–1900. 7420a
PICKFORD, Herts.–Paper. 1139
PICNIC PAPERS, 1841. 10060
PICTORIAL RECORDS OF LONDON, 1862. 1240
PICTORIAL TIMES. 5909
PIECEWORK *see* PRINTING–Piecework.
PIELOU, Pierce Leslie, 1870–1962—Bibs. 1:**4424d**
— Mss.–Bibs. 1:4424d
PIENNE, Peter de, Waterford, fl.1647–55. **5417**
— Bibs. 1:**1383**
— *Colgan's Lives of saint David.* 5417
PIERCE, sir Edmund, d.1667–Libr. 3396a
PIERPONT MORGAN LIBRARY, New York. 507
— Collns. 1:1491 1562 1565c 3848 4605 4890; 672 797 2123a 5118 5597a 6933 7048 7053 8910 10067 10684 11786 13775
PIERREPONT, Henry, 1st marquis of Dorchester, 1606–80–Libr. 2609
PIGOTT, Harriett, fl.1814–46. 14022
PIGOT'S DIRECTORY, 1820. 1794
PIKE, W. T., Brighton, fl.1898–1911. 1:1511c
PILGRIM PRESS–Bibs. 1:**1384**
PILLANS, James, Edinburgh, 1745–1831. **5418**
— Bibs. 1:**1384g**

PILLS TO PURGE MELANCHOLY *see* WIT AND MIRTH, 1698–1720.
PINDAR, 522–442 B.C. 12450
PINDAR, sir Paul, 1565?–1650. 9946
PINDAR, Peter, *pseud. of* John Wolcot, 1738–1819. **12783–4**
— Mss. 12784
PINE, John, 1690–1756. **5419–20** 7521
— *Horace.* 5419–20
— Type. 5420
— *Virgil.* 5420
PINERO, sir Arthur Wing, 1855–1934. 7234
— Bibs. 1:1597 **4425k**
PINES, THE, Putney *see* DUNTON, Walter Theodore Watts–, 1832–1914.
PINHORN, Malcolm, fl.1960–Libr. 1:5104g; 14328
PINKER, James Brand, 1863–1922. 3477 11341
— Libr. 477
PINNER, Middlesex–Ptg. *see* CUCKOO HILL PRESS, est. 1950.
PINTER, Harold, 1930– –Bibs. 1:1597 **4424n**
PINWELL, George John, 1842–75. 7420a
PIOCHE DE LA VERGUE, Marie-Madeleine, countesse de Fayette, 1634–92–Bibs. 1:**811**
PIONEER, THE (Allahabad). 11757
PIOZZI, Hester Lynch (Salusbury), formerly mrs. Thrale, 1741–1821. **12785–92**
— *Anecdotes of dr. Johnson.* 12789
— Bibs. 1:3841b **4425–a**
— Collns. 3380a 11417 12791
— *Journey through France.* 12792
— Letters. 12790
— Mss. 11417 12788
— — Bibs. 1:3841b
— Ptg. 12789
PIRACIES *see* BOOKS, PIRATED.
PIRATES. **7958–63**
— Bibs. 1:**2245d**
— Collns. 7960 7962–3 8209
PIRIE, Robert S., fl.1963–Libr. 1:552
PISAN, Christine de, fl.1363–1431 *see* CHRISTINE DE PISAN, fl.1363–1431.
PISSARRO, Lucien, 1863–1944. 4628 4631–2
— Letters. 4631–2
PITCAIRNE, Archibald, 1652–1713. **12793**
— *Archimedis epistola.* 12793
PITHOU, Pierre, 1539–96. 10230
PITMAN sir Isaac, 1813–97. **5421–4**
— Bibs. 1:**4425i**
PITSLIGO PRESS, Burntisland, 1852–83. **5424d**
— Bibs. 1:**1385–a**
PITT PRESS, Cambridge, est. 1833. 4167 6463

Vol. 1 = *Bibliographies*   2 = *Shakespeare*   4 = 1–8221   5 = 8222–14616

PITT-RIVERS, Augustus Henry Lane Fox, 1827–1900 *see* RIVERS, Augustus Henry Lane Fox Pitt-, 1827–1900.
PITTS, John, 1765–1844. **5425–6**
— Bibs. 1:**1385g**
— Collns. 5426
PIUS II, pope *see* ÆNEAS SILVIUS PICCOLOMINI (pope Pius II), 1405–64.
PIX, Mary (Griffith), 1666–1720? **12794**
— Ptg. 12794
— *Spanish wives.* 12794
PLACE, Francis, 1771–1854. 3546
— Libr. 11638
PLACE, Pierre Simon, marquis De la, 1749–1827 *see* DE LA PLACE, Pierre Simon, marquis, 1749–1827.
PLACENAMES IN LATIN. 254 257–8
PLAGIARISM. 8212 8964 9268 9982 11230 11972 13104
PLAGUE. **7694** 12690
— Bibs. 1:916a; 2:156
PLAIN ENGLISHMAN. 7821
PLAISTOW, Essex–Ptg. *see* CURWEN PRESS, est. 1918.
PLANCIUS, Petrus, 1552–1622. 7506
PLANOGRAPHY. 6187
PLANS *see* MAPS.
PLANTIN, Christopher, 1514–89. 6124
PLANTIN-MORETUS MUSEUM, Antwerp *see* ANTWERP. MUSÉE PLANTIN-MORETUS.
PLAT, sir Hugh, 1552?–1611?–Bibs. 1:**4425ˣ–9**
PLATEN PRESSES *see* PRESSES, PLATEN.
PLATO, 427–348 B.C. 13293 13329 13332
— Bibs. 1:**777**
PLAYBILLS. 1398 **7965–73**
— Bibs. 1:944 **1979p–80**
— Collns. 7965 7967 7969–72
— Edinburgh. 7232
— Ireland. 1865–6 7969
— 1641–1700. 7968
— 1701–1800. 7967
— 1801–1900. 7971 7973
PLAYERS, THE, New York. WALTER HAMDEN MEMORIAL LIBRARY. 2:335
PLAYERS' SHAKESPEARE. 2:723b
PLAYFORD, Eleanor, fl.1685. **5427**
PLAYFORD, John, 1623–86. **5428–32** 7413
— *Apollo's banquet.* 5431a
— Bibs. 1:**4430**
— *Dancing master*–Bibs. 1:4430
PLAYING CARDS *see* CARDS, PLAYING.
PLAYS *see* DRAMA.
—, LISTS OF. 7199 7206–8 7219–20
PLIMPTON, George Arthur, 1855–1936–Libr. 4269 6026

PLOMER, Henry Robert, 1856–1928–Bibs. 1:**4430d**
PLOT, Robert, 1640–96.
— *Natural history of Oxfordshire.* 8128
PLUME, Thomas, 1630–1704–Libr. 1:362
PLUMPTRE, James, 1770–1832. 2:785; 3509 7224
PLUNKETT, Edward John Moreton Drax, 18th baron Dunsany, 1878–1957. **12795–6**
— Bibs. 1:684 **4430a–2**
— Collns. 12796
— *Night at an inn.* 12795
PLUNKETT, Joseph Mary, 1887–1916. 4399
— Bibs. 1:**4432b**
PLUTARCH. 12601–2
— *Lives.* 2:1030
PLYMOUTH, Devon.
— Ptg. *see* MUDGE, John, Dock, fl.1814.
— PUBLIC LIBRARY–Collns. 1:886b
PLYMOUTH MEDICAL SOCIETY. LIBRARY–Collns. 1:886b
PLYMOUTH PROPRIETARY LIBRARY. 12775
POCOCK, sir George, 1706–92–Libr. 4833
POCOCK, Nicholas, 1741?–1821. 7888
POCOCK, Robert, Gravesend, 1760–1830. **5433**
POCOCKE, Edward, 1604–91. 6453
POE, Edgar Allan, 1809–49. 7265–6
— Bibs. 1:**850**
— *Valdemar's case.* 995
POEL, William, 1852–1934. **12797**
— Collns. 12797
POEMS OF AFFAIRS OF STATE. 8020 8024
POEMS ON SEVERAL OCCASIONS. 8008 12822
POEMS SELECTED BY A SMALL PARTY OF ENGLISH, 1792? 858
POETICAL MISCELLANY, 1630. 7995
POETRY *see also* BALLADS; SONGBOOKS. 519 522 524 **7974–8032**
— Bibs. 1:**1981–2035**
— Collns. 7976 7978 8023–4
— Ireland. 8011
— — Bibs. 1:**2035**
— Mss. 7974–5 7978 7980–1 7984 8000 8007 8009 8027
— — Bibs. 1:1986p 2033k
— Scotland. 1608 1637
— Text. 373 7994
— Wales. 7359a
— — Bibs. 1:327–8 1573db–dc **1981–6p**
— 1475–1500–Bibs. 1:**1987**
— 1475–1700. 1637 7359a **7979–8007**
— — Bibs. 1:1623a **1988–98a 2034**
— 1701–1800. 858 1608 7807a 7992 7994 **8008–24**
— — Bibs. 1:1693 1994 **1999–2009**

PRANCE, Claude Annett, fl.1962–Libr. 2386
11856 14016

PRANCERIANA. 13397

PRATLING STREET, Kent–Paper. 1161a

PRAYER BOOKS *see also* BREVIARIES;
MISSALS; PRIMERS, *and titles of individual
prayer books, e.g.* BOOK OF COMMON
PRAYER; BOOK OF COMMON ORDER.
1825 1895 2516 4514 5171 **8033–54** 10444
11031 12512

— Collns. 2909 2918 8049 8052

— Scotland. 1554 1584

— Wales. 1471 1517 3873 8054

PREEDY, George R., *pseud., see* LONG,
Gabrielle Margaret Vere (Campbell),
1888–1952.

PREFACES. 5660 6267 10077 13037

PREMIER BOX COMPANY, Bolton. 5856

PRENDERGAST, John Patrick, 1808–93.
12891

PRESBYTERIAN BOOKS–Bibs. 1:1946

— Newspapers–Bibs. 1:1946

PRESCOT, Bartholomew, fl.1822–9. 1168

PRESENTATION BINDINGS *see*
BOOKBINDINGS, PRESENTATION.

PRESENTATION BOOKS *see also*
DEDICATIONS; PRESENTATION
COPIES. **8055** 12586 13545

— Bibs. 1:325 **2035a–7d**

— Collns. 3117

PRESENTATION COPIES *see also*
ASSOCIATION COPIES; GIFT BOOKS.
784 3596 6239 8972 9122 9239a 9535 9696
9756 10010 10035 10128 10193 10253
10366 10469 10476 10744 10948 11192
11216 11324 11498 11628 12201 12204
12254 12404 12588 13046 13825–6 13938
13958 13986 13994 14067 14212 14215

— Bibs. 1:3841a–b

PRESS, Charles A. Manning, fl.1890–1908.
1:1511c

PRESS AND PUBLIC SERVICE, 1857. 12073

PRESS CLUB, London. 7649 13142

— LIBRARY–Collns. 1:1852 1888

PRESS CORRECTIONS *see* CORRECTIONS
AT PRESS.

PRESS CORRECTORS *see* CORRECTORS
OF THE PRESS.

PRESSES (AS MACHINES) *see also*
PRINTING MACHINES. 6057 **6312–33**

— Illus. 6313–14 6317 6329 10610 12105

— 1475–1500. 128 257 10610

— 1801–1900. 4129a 5982

—, ALBION. 4410 6319 6332

—, COLUMBIAN. 6326 6332–3

—, COMMON. 6318 6321–2 6324

— Bibs. 6321

—, CYLINDER. 6227 6312 6392

—, GOUDY. 5002

—, HAND *see* PRESSES, COMMON.

—, INSTRUCTIONAL *see also* BODLEIAN
LIBRARY PRESS; WATER LANE PRESS,
Cambridge, est. 1952. 252 6353

—, LISTS OF. 6324 6326 6333

—, LITHOGRAPHIC. 6227

—, PLATEN. 6312

—, POLE. 6227

—, PORTABLE. 1866 6227

—, PRINTING *see* PRESSES (AS MACH-
INES).

—, ROTARY. 5264a 6227 6312 7903

—, SCRAPER. 6227

—, STANHOPE. 5723 6326 6332

—, STAR-WHEEL. 6227

—, STEAM. 7764

—, WOODEN *see* PRESSES, COMMON.

PRESSES (AS PUBLISHERS)–Bibs. 1:1139m
1219–423

—, PRIVATE *see* PRINTING, PRIVATE.

—, PROVINCIAL–Bibs. 1:866–8

—, SECRET *see* PRINTING, SECRET.

—, UNIVERSITY *see also under names of in-
dividual presses, e.g.* ABERDEEN U.P.;
CAMBRIDGE U.P.; DUBLIN U.P.;
GLASGOW U.P.; OXFORD U.P.; ST.
ANDREWS U.P. 6075 6119

PRESS-FIGURES *see* PRINTING–Press-
figures.

PRESSICK, George, fl.1656–63. **12892**

PRESSMEN–Wages. 1275

PRESSWORK *see* PRINTING–Presswork.

PRESTEIGNE, Herefs.–Paper. 1138

PRESTON, Lancs. **1181**

— Newspapers. 1181

— Paper. 3734a

— HARRIS PUBLIC LIBRARY *see* HARRIS
PUBLIC LIBRARY, Preston.

PRESTON, Kerrison, fl.1944–53–Libr.
1:2483–4 2489

PRESTON JOURNAL. 1181

PREVITÉ-ORTON, Charles William,
1877–1947 *see* ORTON, Charles William
Previté-, 1877–1947.

PRICE, John, 1803–87–Libr. 2838

PRICES OF BINDING. 1053 2021 2158
2169a 3690 5381 5392

PRICES OF BOOKS *see also* BOOKS,
CHEAP; RESALE PRICE MAIN-
TENANCE. 97 128 2279 2352 2427
3686–98a 5225 6532

— Armstrong. 3697

— Barrie. 758

— Baxter, G. 3963–4 3964bc

— Beerbohm, M. 471

— Bible. 3692–3

— Borrow. 755

PRINTING, LOGOGRAPHIC *see also* WALTER, John, 1723–1812. 5936–8

—, MECHANICAL *see also* PRINTING MACHINES. 6348 6375a 6389a

—, METAL RELIEF. 6228

—, MUSIC *see* MUSIC PRINTING.

—, NATURE *see* NATURE-PRINTING.

—, NEWSPAPER *see* NEWSPAPERS AND PERIODICALS–Ptg.

—, PARLIAMENTARY. 1294 1306 4830 7952 7955–6

—, PIRATE *see* BOOKS, PIRATED–Ptg.

—, PRIVATE. 264 4997–8 6328 6353 6370 **6458–502** 7461

— Bibs. 1:1139m; 6463

— Collns. 6496–7 6501

— Type. 6610 6615 6643

— Aberdeenshire.

— — Fintray *see* CUMMING, John, 1820–1900.

— Antrim. Belfast *see* MACRORY, Adam J., fl.1850–77.

— Berkshire.

— — Reading *see* WILLIAMS, Thomas Edmunds, 1781–1849.

— — Waltham St.Lawrence *see* GOLDEN COCKEREL PRESS. est. 1921.

— Buckinghamshire.

— — Long Crendon *see* SEVEN ACRES PRESS, 1926–33.

— Cambridgeshire.

— — Cambridge *see* RAMPANT LION PRESS, est. 1934; WATER LANE PRESS, est. 1952.

— — Grantchester *see* WIDNALL, Samuel Page, 1825–94.

— Cardiganshire *see* JOHNES, Thomas, 1748–1816.

— Carnarvonshire.

— — Llandudno. 1540g

— Cornwall. 1084

— Devonshire.

— — Lustleigh *see* DAVY, William, 1743–1826.

— — Manaton *see* BOAR'S HEAD PRESS, est. 1931.

— — Totnes *see* ARK PRESS, 20th cent.

— — Wirksworth *see* BROOKS PRESS, fl.1904–21.

— Dorsetshire.

— — Shaftesbury *see* HIGH HOUSE PRESS, est. 1924.

— Dublin *see* COLUMBA PRESS, 1912–16; DOLMEN PRESS, est. 1951; DUN EMER PRESS, 1903–7; MOLLOY, Arthur, fl.1870–4; SYNGE, John, 1788–1845.

— — Dundrum *see* CUALA PRESS, est. 1903.

— Dumfriesshire.

— — Dumfries *see* RAE, Peter, 1671–1748.

— Essex.

— — Colchester *see* GEMINI PRESS, 1934–6.

— — Great Totham *see* GREAT TOTHAM PRESS, 1830–62.

— — Plaistow *see* CURWEN PRESS, est. 1918.

— Fifeshire.

— — Burntisland *see* PITSLIGO PRESS, 1852–83.

— Gloucester.

— — Chipping Camden *see* ALCUIN PRESS, est. 1928; ESSEX HOUSE PRESS, 1898–1909.

— Huntingdonshire.

— — Hemingford Grey *see* VINE PRESS, est. 1956.

— Ireland. 1842 6466

— Isle of Wight.

— — Ryde *see* BELDORNIE PRESS, 1840–3.

— Kent *see* LEE PRIORY PRESS, 1813–22.

— — Canterbury *see* CANTERBURY COLLEGE OF ART PRESS, fl.1960.

— — Maidstone *see* MAIDSTONE COLLEGE OF ART PRESS, fl.1960.

— — Stansted *see also* WAY, Lewis, d.1840. 1408

— Lanarkshire.

— — Dunsyre *see* WILD HAWTHORN PRESS, fl.1962.

— Lancashire.

— — Coniston *see* YELLOWSANDS PRESS, est. 1919.

— — Heaton Mersey *see* CLOISTER PRESS, est. 1921.

— — Wigan *see* BIRCHLEY HALL PRESS, 1604–55.

— Leicestershire.

— — Coalville *see* MOUNT ST. BERNARD ABBEY PRESS, est. 1952?

— — Leicester *see* LEICESTER COLLEGE OF ART PRESS, est. 1902; ORPHEUS PRESS, 1958–61; PANDORA PRESS, est. 1960.

— — Wymondham *see* BREWHOUSE PRESS, est. 1962.

— Limerick *see* MOUNT TRENCHARD PRESS, fl.1863.

— London.

— — Chelsea *see* ASHENDENE PRESS, 1894–1923.

— — Hammersmith *see* DOVES PRESS, 1900–16; KELMSCOTT PRESS, 1891–8.

PRINTING, PRIVATE–London. Chiswick *see* CARADOC PRESS, 1900–9; CHISWICK PRESS, 1844–1962.
— — Stratford *see* GOGMAGOG PRESS, est. 1957.
— — Twickenham *see* STRAWBERRY HILL PRESS, 1757–97.
— — Wimbledon *see* ART SOCIETY PRESS, est. 1953.
— Louth.
— — Drogheda *see* JOHNSTON, C. L. or L. C., fl.1830.
— Middlesex.
— — Harrow Weald *see* RAVEN PRESS, est. 1931.
— — Pinner *see* CUCKOO HILL PRESS, est. 1950.
— — Wembley Hill *see* STANTON PRESS, 1921–4.
— Midlothian.
— — Edinburgh *see* HOLYROOD PRESS, 1686–8.
— Monmouthshire.
— — Brockweir *see* TINTERN PRESS, 1934–6.
— Montgomeryshire.
— — Newtown *see* GREGYNOG PRESS, est. 1922.
— Norfolk.
— — Norwich *see* WALPOLE PRESS, est. 1913.
— Northamptonshire. 1311
— Northumberland.
— — North Shields *see* PRIORY PRESS, fl.1926–9.
— — Wylam *see* ALLENHOLME PRESS, est. 1956.
— — Oxford *see also* DANIEL, Charles Henry Olive, 1836–1919; DIXEY, Harold Giles, est. 1922; FANTASY PRESS, est. 1951. 4090
— Renfrewshire.
— — Greenock *see* SIGNET PRESS, est. 1956.
— Shropshire.
— — Ludlow *see* NICHOLSON, George, 1760–1825.
— Surrey.
— — Richmond *see* KEEPSAKE PRESS, est. 1951; MINIATURE PRESS, est. 1935; RYDER, John Stanley, fl.1960.
— Sussex. 1408
— — Bognor Regis *see* PEAR TREE PRESS, 1899–1952.
— — Chichester *see* COCK ROBIN PRESS, est. 1932.
— — Ditchling *see* ST. DOMINIC'S PRESS, est. 1916.

— — Easebourne. 1408
— — Eastbourne. 1408
— — Haywards Heath. 1408
— Wales. 1490 1492
— Warwickshire.
— — Birmingham *see* BIRMINGHAM. CENTRAL SCHOOL OF ARTS AND CRAFTS. SCHOOL OF PRINTING; MORENARDO PRESS, est. 1960?; PARDOE, Frank Ernest, est. 1957.
— Waterford.
— — Bonmahon *see* DOUDNEY, David Alfred, 1811–94.
— Westmeath.
— — Mullingar *see* LYONS, John Charles, 1792–1874.
— Worcestershire.
— — Callow End *see* STANBROOK ABBEY PRESS, est. 1876.
— Yorkshire.
— — Leeds *see* DAMASINE PRESS, fl.1960.
—, PROVINCIAL. 264 1017–21 1025 1028–30 5884 6081 6142 6994 8099
— Aberdeenshire. 1524
— — Aberdeen *see also* CHALMERS, James, 1764–1810; DOUGLAS, Francis, 1719–86; RABAN, Edward, d.1658. 1596 1640–3 1645 1648–51 5491–2a 8439
— — Peterhead *see* BUCHAN, Peter, 1790–1854.
— Anglesey. 1517
— — Bodedern. 1517
— Angus.
— — Dundee. 1665 1666
— Antrim.
— — Belfast *see also* ALLEN, David, est. 1857; BLOW, James, d.1759; MACRORY, Adam J., fl.1850–77. 1849
— — — Bibs. 1:1026–30 1030f
— — Greenisland. 1770
— — Lisburn. 1772
— Argyllshire.
— — Campbeltown. 9256
— Armagh–Bibs. 1:1031–5
— — Lurgan–Bibs. 1:1036–7
— — Portadown–Bibs. 1:1038
— — Tandragee–Bibs. 1:1039
— Ayrshire.
— — Kilmarnock *see* WILSON, John, fl.1759–1821.
— — Maybole. 5583
— Berkshire.
— — Abingdon. 1017 1025
— — Newbury *see* HALL AND MARSH, fl.1839.
— — Reading *see* PARKS, William, fl.1719–50; WILLIAMS, Thomas Edmunds, 1781–1849.

PRINTING, PROVINCIAL–Berkshire–
Reading–Bibs. 1:874
— Berwickshire–Bibs. 1:986
— — Speenhamland. 4827
— Brecknockshire.
— — Trevecca *see also* HARRIS, Howell,
1714–73. 1519
— Buckinghamshire.
— — Eton *see also* POTE, Joseph, 1704–87.
1019
– Caithness-shire–Bibs. 1:990
— — Caithness. 1671
— Cambridgeshire.
— — Cambridge *see also* CAMBRIDGE
UNIVERSITY PRESS, est. 1521 (*and in-
dividuals associated with the Press listed there*).
FENNER, William, fl.1725–35;
MACMILLAN, Daniel, 1813–57;
RAMPANT LION PRESS, est. 1934;
WATER LANE PRESS, est. 1952. 1017–18
1025 1048 1051–3 1055–8 1061 1070
— — — Bibs. 1:877 879 881m
— — Sawston *see* CRAMPTON, John,
1833–1910.
— Cardiganshire *see also* JOHNES, Thomas,
1748–1816. 1523
— — Aberystwyth–Bibs. 1:962
— — Adpar–Bibs. 1:1280
— — Carlow. 1770 1852
— — Bibs. 1:1039–40 1129
— Carmarthenshire.
— — Carmarthen *see also* CARTER, Isaac,
fl.1718–41; DANIEL, John, 1784–1823;
ROSS, John, fl.1764–1811. 1533–4 1537–8
— — — Bibs. 1:962q 1280
— — Llandudno. 1540g
— — Llanelly *see* WILLIAMS, David,
1814–84.
— Cavan. 1853
— — Bibs. 1:1041–4a
— — Cootehill–Bibs. 1:1044
— Channel Islands. 1992
— Cheshire.
— — Chester *see also* FLETCHER, John,
fl.1784–1831. 1019 1075 1081
— — — Bibs. 1:883d
— Clare.
— — Ennis. 1854 1955
— — — Bibs. 1:1045
— — Kilrush–Bibs. 1:1046
— Connaught. 1788
— Cork *see also* BAGNELLS AND
KNIGHTS, est. 1762. 1771 1857–8 1860
— — — Bibs. 1:1047–50
— — Fermoy–Bibs. 1:1051
— — Youghal–Bibs. 1:1052
— Cornwall. 1084 1099
— Cumberland.

— — Carlisle. 6988
— — Penrith. 6988
— — Whitehaven. 6988 8117
— Denbighshire.
— — Denbigh *see* JONES, Thomas,
1756–1820.
— — Llanrwst *see* JONES, John, 1786–1865.
— — Wrexham *see* HUGHES AND SON,
est. 1823.
— Derbyshire. 1089–91
— — Bibs. 1:884x–5
— — Derby *see also* BEMROSE, sir Henry
Howe, fl.1827–93; BEMROSE, William,
1792–1880. 1091–2 1094
— Derry. 1861
— — Bibs. 1:1053–4
— — Coleraine. 1865–6
— — — Bibs. 1:1055
— — Limavady–Bibs. 1:1055f
— Devonshire. 1099–100
— — Exeter. 1019 1025 1102b 1102e
— — Plymouth *see* MUDGE, John, Dock,
fl.1814.
— — Tavistock. 1017 1025 1103
— Donegal.
— — Ballyshannon–Bibs. 1:1056
— Dorsetshire.
— — Corfe Mullen. 4826
— Down.
— — Banbridge–Bibs. 1:1058
— — Brookfield. 1867
— — Donaghdee. 1771
— Dorsetshire.
— — Weymouth *see* LOVE, John, 1752–93.
— Down.
— — Downpatrick–Bibs. 1:1057
— — Hillsborough–Bibs. 1:1057
— — Newry. 1770 1868
— — — Bibs. 1:1062–6
— — Newtownards–Bibs. 1:1067
— Dublin (*county and city*) *see also*
BRAWDERS, William, 1815–62; BROCAS,
John, fl.1696–1707; BROWNE, Thomas,
fl.1730–50; CAREY, Mathew, 1760–1839;
CARTER, Cornelius, fl.1696–1727;
CHAMBERS, John, 1754–1837;
COLUMBA PRESS, 1912–16; CONZATTI,
Zachary, fl.1686; COONEY, Peter, fl.1789;
CROOKE, John, d.1669; DICKSON,
Francis, d.1713; DOLMEN PRESS, est.
1951; DUN EMER PRESS, 1903–7;
FRANCKTON, John, fl.1600–18;
FULLER, Samuel, fl.1720–36;
GRIERSON, George, 1709–53;
HELSHAM, Samuel, fl.1681–9; HUGHES,
Robert, fl.1648–51; JONES, Edward,
fl.1690–1706; KEARNEY, William,
fl.1571–97; LLOYD, Edward, fl.1714;

PRINTING, PROVINCIAL–Hunting-donshire–Gravesend see POCOCK, Robert, 1760–1830.

— Kerry.

— — Tralee–Bibs. 1:1088–9

— Kildare.

— — Athy–Bibs. 1:1090

— — Naas see also CAROGH ORPHANAGE PRESS. 1770

— — Kilkenny see also BUTLER, Michael, d.1779; FINN, Edward, d.1777. 1950–4 5685

— — — Bibs. 1:1091–3 1128

— Lanarkshire.

— — Glasgow see also ANDERSON, Agnes (Campbell), 1637?–1716; ANDERSON, Andrew, d.1676; ANDERSON, George, d.1647; BROOKMAN, George, fl.1827–37; BROWN, Hugh, fl.1714; CARMICHAEL, Alexander, fl.1724–36; COLLINS, William, 1789–1853; DUNCAN, Andrew, d.1840; FOULIS, Andrew, 1712–75; FOULIS, Andrew, d.1829; FOULIS, Robert, 1707–76; FREEBAIRN, Robert, fl.1701–47; GOVAN, Donald, fl.1714–19; HARVIE, Thomas, fl.1704–56; HUTCHISON, Robert, fl.1827–38; KHULL, Edward, 1767–1844; MCCREERY, John, 1768–1832; MACLEHOSE, James, 1811–85; MACLEHOSE, Robert, 1820–1910; MENNONS, John, 1747–1818; MILLER, Alexander, fl.1724–45?; MUNDELL, James, fl.1795–9; RICHARDSON, George, d.1872; SANDERS, Robert, 1630?–94; SANDERS, Robert, d.1730; SCRYMGEOUR, James, fl.1803–4; SCRYMGEOUR, John, fl.1803–9; URIE, Robert, 1711?–71. 1596 1686–9 1692 4691 6066

— — — Bibs. 1:1002–a 1726

— Lancashire.

— — Bibs. 1:903

— — Blackley. 1164a

— — Bolton see TILLOTSON, John, fl.1834–1915; TILLOTSON, William Frederick, 1844–99.

— — Coniston see also BEEVER, John, 1793–1857; YELLOWSANDS PRESS, est. 1919. 1165a 1180a

— — Liverpool see also WILLIAMSON, Robert, fl.1752–63. 1168 1172–3

— — — Bibs. 1:907–9

— — Manchester see also HEYWOOD, Abel, est. 1832; ADAMS, Orion, 1717–97; ADAMS, Roger, 1661?–1741; ANDERTON, Thomas, fl.1762; HODGKINS, John, fl.1588–9. 1176 5153

— — — Bibs. 1:910

— — — Stockport see CLARKE, Joseph, fl.1790–1808.

— — — Ulverston see SOULBY, John, 1771?–1817; SOULBY, John, fl.1796–1842.

— Leicestershire. 6501

— — Coalville see MOUNT ST. BERNARD ABBEY PRESS, est. 1952?

— — Leicester see LEICESTER COLLEGE OF ART PRESS, est. 1902; ORPHEUS PRESS, 1958–61; PANDORA PRESS, est. 1960; SPENCER, John, 1828–92.

— Leitrim–Bibs. 1:1094

— — Ballinamore–Bibs. 1:1094

— — Carrick-on-Shannon–Bibs. 1:1094

— — Mohill–Bibs. 1:1094

— Limerick see also MOUNT TRENCHARD PRESS, fl.1863. 1954–5 1957 13733

— — Bibs. 1:1095–100

— Lincolnshire.

— — Lincoln. 1186

— London. 1205 1206a 1230 1235–6 1254 1267 1288 1294

— — Bibs. 1:827ac 915

— — 1475–1500. 1215

— — 1475–1640. 1189 1199 1215 1222 1255 1257 1284 1287 1289 1291

— — 1475–1700. 1209 1243 5092

— — 1641–1700. 1259

— — 1701–1800. 1256 1271 1275 1384 5092 8099

— — 1801–1900. 1212 1256 1269 1271 1275 1286a 1293 8099

— — BANK OF ENGLAND. 7256

— — Finsbury. 1019

— — Greenwich. 1025

— — Lambeth. 1018

— — Soho. 951

— — Southwark see NICHOLSON, James, fl.1535–8.

— — Stepney see VENGE, Edward, fl.1578–1605.

— — Wandsworth. 1018

— Longford–Bibs. 1:1101

— Louth. 1958–b

— — Drogheda see also JOHNSTON, C. L. or L. C. fl.1830. 1959

— — — Bibs. 1:1102–3

— — Dundalk–Bibs. 1:1104–5

— — Louth see JACKSON, John, fl.1797; SHEARDOWN, Robert, fl.1789.

— Man, Isle of–Bibs. 1:923

— Mayo.

— — Achill. 1960

— — — Bibs. 1:1106 1240

— — Ballinrobe–Bibs. 1:1106a

— — Castlebar–Bibs. 1:1106b

— Meath.

PRINTING, PROVINCIAL–Meath.
— — Trim–Bibs. 1:1107
— — Bala *see* JONES AND COMPANY, 1803–4.
— Midlothian.
— — Edinburgh *see also* ARBUTHNET, Alexander, fl.1576–85; BALLANTYNE, Alexander, 1774–1847; BALLANTYNE, James, 1772–1833; BASSANDYNE, Thomas, fl.1568–77; BLAIKIE, Walter Biggar, 1847–1928; CHAMBERS, Robert, 1802–71; CHAMBERS, W. & R., fl.1860–90; CHAMBERS, William, 1800–83; CHARTERIS, Henry, fl.1544–99; CHARTERIS, Robert, fl.1596–1610; CHEPMAN, Walter, 1473?–1538?; CLARK, R. & R., est. 1846; CONSTABLE, T. & A., est. 1760; DAVIDSON, Thomas, fl.1541; DONALDSON, Alexander, fl.1750–94; FINLASON, Thomas, fl.1604–27; GED, William, 1690–1749; HART, Andrew, d.1621; HOLYROOD PRESS, 1686–8; JOHNSTON, Alexander Keith, 1804–71; KINCAID, Alexander, 1711–77; KINNEAR, Samuel, fl.1816–1902; LEKPREVIK, Robert, fl.1561–88; MYLLAR, Andrew, fl.1503–8; NEILL, Patrick, 1725–89; NEILL, Patrick, 1776–1851; PILLANS, James, 1745–1831; RABAN, Edward, d.1658; ROSS, John, fl.1574–80; RUDDIMAN, Thomas, 1674–1757; RUTHVEN, John, fl.1813; SCOT, John, fl.1552–71; SMYTH, Robert, fl.1564–1602; STORY, John, fl.1520; WALDEGRAVE, Robert, 1554?–1604; WATSON, James, 1664?–1722; WILLIAMSON, Peter, 1730–99; WREITTOUN, John, fl.1624–39. 1255 1596 1696–7 1703 1708 1721–2 5418 9896 13423 13585
— Monaghan–Bibs. 1:1108–11
— Monmouthshire. 1300 1477
— — Monmouth *see* HEATH, Charles, 1761–1831.
— — Pontypool. 1301
— Montgomeryshire.
— — Machynlleth *see also* EVANS, Adam, 1819–96; EVANS, Timothy, fl.1789–96; JONES, Richard, 1786–1855; PUGH, David, 1806–31.
— — — Bibs. 1:963h
— Norfolk. 1302
— — Norwich *see also* BACON, Richard McKenzie, d.1844; BURGES, Francis, d.1706; SOLEMNE, Anthony de, fl.1565–80; WALPOLE PRESS, est. 1913. 1018–19 1306
— — Yarmouth. 1309

— Northamptonshire. 1310–11
— — Northampton *see* DICEY, William, fl.1713–54.
— Northumberland.
— — Alnwick *see also* DAVISON, William, 1781–1858. 1314–16 4210
— — — Bibs. 1:926m
— — Berwick-upon-Tweed. 1317 4210
— — Gateshead. 1019
— — Newcastle-upon-Tyne *see also* ANGUS, George, fl.1783–1829; ANGUS, William, fl.1789; BEILBY, Ralph, 1744–1817; BEILBY AND BEWICK, 1777–97; BEWICK, John, 1760–95; BEWICK, Thomas, 1753–1828; REID, Andrew, 1823–96; SLACK, Thomas, 1723–84; WHITE, John, fl.1711–61. 1019 1320–2 1324–7 4210 5131
— — — Bibs. 1:926–7a
— Nottinghamshire. 1328
— — Bibs. 1:1538
— — Newark. 1329–30
— — Nottingham *see also* DERRY AND SONS, est. 1867. 1342 1344 8099
— — — Bibs. 1:930
— Offaly.
— — Birr–Bibs. 1:1112
— Omagh. 1770–1
— Oxfordshire.
— — Banbury *see also* CHENEY, John, 1732–1808. 6985
— — — Bibs. 1:1286
— — Oxford *see also* OXFORD UNIVERSITY PRESS, est. 1584 *and individual printers listed at that heading; and* DANIEL, Charles Henry Olive, 1836–1919; DIXEY, Harold Giles, est. 1922; FANTASY PRESS, est. 1951. 883 1017–18 1025 1347–52 1355–9 1362 1364–7 1370 1372–3 2156 3719 6055 6421 6447
— — — Bibs. 1:935–7 1300–2 1871–2 2653
— — Stonor. 1018
— Pembrokeshire. 1548
— — Haverfordwest *see also* BULMER, John, 1784–1857. 1549–50
— — — Bibs. 1:964
— Perthshire.
— — Perth *see also* KING'S PRESS, Perth. 1733–4 1736
— — — Bibs. 1:1005d
— Roscommon.
— — Boyle–Bibs. 1:1113
— Roxburghshire.
— — Jedburgh. 1740
— — Kelso. 3887
— Scotland *see also* PRINTING IN GAELIC. 264 1567 1585 1589 1603 1610 1701 4746

Vol. 1 = *Bibliographies*   2 = *Shakespeare*   4 = 1–8221   5 = 8222–14616

PRUDEN, Russell G., fl.1938–Libr. 796

PRUJEAN, sir Francis, 1593–1666–Libr. 3396a

PRY, Paul, *pseud. of* William Heath, 1795–1840. 7046 **12918**

— *Dickens' Pickwick papers.* 9982

PRYCE, Anna Maria, lady, fl.1720–Libr. 2515

PRYNNE, William, 1600–69. **12919**

— Bibs. 1:**4466–7**

— Mss. 12919

— *Newes from Ipswich.* 5583

PRYS, John Pritchard, fl.1721. 1517

PSALMANAZAR, George, 1679?–1763. 7333 7338

PSALTER OF CASHEL. 1968

PSALTERS *see* BIBLE. O.T. PSALMS.

PSEUDONYMA *see* ANONYMA AND PSEUDONYMA.

PSEUDO-XENOPHON. 885

PTOLOMY (Ptolemaeus Claudius), fl.139–61. 896a 2051–2

PUBLIC *see* MARKET FOR BOOKS.

PUBLIC LIBRARIES *see* LIBRARIES, PUBLIC.

PUBLIC LIBRARIES ACT. 2455

PUBLIC RECORD OFFICE *see* GT. BRIT. PUBLIC RECORD OFFICE.

'PUBLISHER'. 3595

PUBLISHERS *see also* BOOK TRADE, LISTS–Publishers; PRESSES (AS PUBLISHERS). 3430

—, FRIENDS AS. 8093–4 8099

PUBLISHERS' AGREEMENTS. 4003 6503 6521 7798 10076 10079 10088 10361 10757

PUBLISHERS' BINDINGS *see* BOOK-BINDINGS, PUBLISHERS'.

PUBLISHERS' CATALOGUES *see* CATALOGUES, PUBLISHERS'.

PUBLISHERS' DEVICES *see* DEVICES, PUBLISHERS'.

PUBLISHERS' LEDGERS *see also* BOOKSELLERS' DAYBOOKS. 4037 4155 5789 5793–4 5797–9 5865 5869

PUBLISHERS' PROPOSALS *see* PROPOSALS.

PUBLISHERS' READERS. 4003 5791 6534 12245

PUBLISHERS' SIGNS *see* SIGNS, PUBLISHERS'.

PUBLISHERS' TRAVELLERS. 5264a

PUBLISHING *see also* BOOKLISTS–Bibs.; PRESSES (AS PUBLISHERS); SIZE OF ISSUE. 257 259 269 2375 3443 3449 3455 3460 3464 3480 **6503–50**

— Bibs. 1:107 1139m 1161 **1184–6f**

— Newspapers–Bibs. 1:1139m 1166

— 1475–1640. 3476 6512 6535 6545–6 6562

— 1475–1700. 6121b 6509 6550

— 1641–1700. 3453a 6513 6517 6519 6536 6557 10361

— 1701–1800. 3453a 3459 3720 6121b 6504 6515 6549 6554 7798 8093 10672 10757 11443

— 1801–1900. 3477 5226 6503 6507 6510a–11 6523–4 6530–1 6534 6539 6548 6556 7894 10076 10079 10088

— 1901– . 2458 3480

—, COMMISSION. 6503

—, PROVINCIAL.

— Aberdeenshire. Aberdeen *see* SMITH, ELDER AND COMPANY, 1816–1917; THOMSON, John, 1840–1911.

— Anglesey. 5697

— Angus.

— — Montrose *see* WALKER, George, 1831–89.

— Cambridgeshire. Cambridge *see* CAMBRIDGE UNIVERSITY PRESS, est. 1521 *and individuals associated with the Press listed there.*

— Cheshire. Chester *see* CODDINGTON, William, 1770?–1804.

— Derbyshire. 1091

— — Derby. 1091

— Dublin *see also* BENT, John. 18th cent.; DUFFY, James, d.1871; FAULKNER, George, 1699?–1775; GILL, Michael Henry, fl.1856–72; KILDARE PLACE SOCIETY, est. 1811; MCGLASHAN, James, fl.1846–58; MAUNSEL AND COMPANY, est. 1904. 1914–15 1929 9886 9888 9894 12698 13026 13382 14190

— East Lothian. 5191

— Fifeshire.

— — Dunfermline *see* MILLER FAMILY, 1771–1865.

— Gloucestershire.

— — Cirencester *see* RUDDER, Samuel, 1726–1801.

— — Gloucester *see* CHANCE FAMILY, 1872–1922; RAIKES, Robert, 1690–1757; RAIKES FAMILY, fl.1722–1802; WALKER FAMILY, fl.1802–71.

— Ireland. 1818 10418

— Lanarkshire.

— — Glasgow *see also* BLACKIE, John, 1782–1874; BLACKIE, Walter Graham, 1816–1906. 1687

— Lancashire.

— — Liverpool *see* CAXTON PRESS, fl.1814–21; GORE, John, fl.1712–72.

— — Manchester *see* BRADSHAW, George, 1801–53.

— London. 1264 1294

— — 1475–1640. 1281

PUBLISHING, PROVINCIAL–London–1701–1800. 1261–3 8099

— — 1801–1900. 1200 1286a 8099

— — Holborn see BATSFORD, Bradley Thomas, 1821–1904.

— Midlothian. Edinburgh see also BALLANTYNE, John, 1774–1821; BLACKWOOD, Alexander, 1806–45; BLACKWOOD, George William, 1876–1942; BLACKWOOD, James Hugh, 1878–1951; BLACKWOOD, John, 1818–79; BLACKWOOD, Robert, 1808–52; BLACKWOOD, William, 1776–1834; BLACKWOOD, William, 1836–1912; BLACKWOOD AND SONS; CADELL, Robert, 1788–1849; CONSTABLE, Archibald, 1774–1827; CONSTABLE, T. & A., est. 1760; CREECH, William, 1745–1815; DONALDSON, James, 1751–1830; JOHNSON, James, d.1811; NELSON, Thomas, 1780–1861; NELSON, William, 1816–87. 1711

— Northumberland.

— — Newcastle-upon-Tyne see AKENHEAD, Robert, fl.1722–71; BELL, John, 1783–1864; BRYSON, Martin, fl.1722–59; GOODING, John, fl.1713–51.

— Oxfordshire.

— — Oxford see also OXFORD UNIVERSITY PRESS, est. 1584 and individual publishers listed there; SLATTER AND MUNDAY, fl.1810; TALBOYS, David A., fl.1840. 1355 1368

— Perthshire.

— — Perth see also MORISON FAMILY, est. 1774? 1736

— Scotland. 1604 1617 1630 5361b

— Somerset.

— — Bath see HAZARD, Samuel, fl.1772–1806; MEYLER, William, 1792–1821.

— Suffolk.

— — Ipswich see also OLIVER, Reginald, fl.1534. 1403

— Sussex.

— — Brighton see PIKE, W. T., fl.1898–1911.

— Wales. 1449 1451 1476a 1478 1496a 1511–12 5696 10455

— Warwickshire.

— — Stratford-upon-Avon. 1422

— Worcestershire.

— — Worcester see BRYAN, Stephen, d.1748.

—, SERIAL see BOOKS IN PARTS; BOOKS IN SERIES; NEWSPAPERS AND PERIODICALS.

—, SUBSCRIPTION see SUBSCRIPTION PUBLISHING.

PUBLISHING OF BIBLES see also OXFORD UNIVERSITY PRESS, est. 1584. BIBLE PRESS. 3540 6891

PUBLISHING OF BIBLIOGRAPHY. 6604

PUBLISHING OF CHARTS. 7517 7630

PUBLISHING OF CHILDREN'S LITERATURE. 5279 5283 6229 6995 7012 7047 9720 13030 13509

PUBLISHING OF ENGRAVINGS. 6550

PUBLISHING OF FICTION. 7290

PUBLISHING OF JUVENILE DRAMA. 7021 7023 7030–1 7033–5 7042

PUBLISHING OF MAPS. 6550–1 7517

PUBLISHING OF MEDICAL BOOKS. 7565 7571

PUBLISHING OF MUSIC see MUSIC PUBLISHING.

PUBLISHING OF PLAYS. 2:434 844 855; 7127 7133 7172 7184 7745

PUBLISHING OF SCIENCE. 8144 8153

PUBLISHING OF SERMONS. 10227

PUBLISHING OF SONGBOOKS. 8186–7

PUBLISHING PRIVILEGES see PRIVILEGES, PUBLISHING.

PUBLISHING SOCIETIES. 283 285 6505 6514 6544

PUCKLE, James, 1667?–1724–Bibs. 1:**4468**

PUE, Richard, Dublin, fl.1712. 1906

PUGH, David, Machynlleth, 1806–31–Bibs. 1:963h

PUGH, Ellis, 1656–1718.

— Annerch i'r Cymru–Bibs. 1:706

PUGHE, William Owen, formerly Owen, 1759–1835. **12920–3**

— Libr. 12921

— Publ. 12920

— Welsh and English dictionary. 12920

PUNCH. 3450 3496 7848 7856 7862 7866 7894 7909 13972

— Bibs. 1:1428 4901 4924

PUNCHES, TYPE see TYPE–Punches.

PUNCTUATION. 97 627 6176 10225 12420 14497 14513

— Ptg. 6710

PURCELL, Henry, 1659?–95. **12924–5**

— Bibs. 1:**4469**

— Collns. 12925

— Mss. 12924

— Vocal music of the prophetess. 10358

PURCELL, Richard, fl.1750–66 see CORBUTT, C., pseud.

PURCHAS, Samuel, 1575?–1626. **12926**

— Pilgrims. 10785 12926

PURKESS, George, fl.1836–62. **5457**

PURKESS, George, fl.1857–90. 5457

PURNEY, Thomas, 1695–c.1727–Bibs. 1:**4470**
PUSEY, Edward Bouverie, 1800–82–Bibs. 1:**4471**
PUTTENHAM, George, d.1590.
— Bibs. 1:**4472**
— *Art of English poesy*–Bibs. 1:**4472**
PUTTICK AND SIMPSON, fl.1847–1934. **5458**
PUZZLEWITS. 522
PYE-SMITH, Philip Henry, 1839–1914 *see* SMITH, Philip Henry Pye-, 1839–1914.
PYNSON, Richard, d.1530. 1215 **5459–77** 6055–6 6076 6081
— *Assembly of gods.* 5472
— Bibs. 1:**1385m** 4251
— *Friends of North Newington.* 5474
— *Gilbertus' Tractatus.* 5473
— Indulgences. 5462 5468
— *Little treatise of divers miracles . . . Hayles.* 5475
— *Old tenures.* 5469
— *Mandeville's Travels.* 12126
— *Mirk's Liber festivalis.* 12458–9
— *Mirk's Quattuor sermones.* 12458–9
— *Parker's Dives et pauper.* 5466–7 5471
— *Robin Hood.* 5470 5477
— Type. 6572
— *Virtue.* 5472
PYRAMUS AND THISBE BINDING. 2236

Q., *pseud.* of sir Arthur Thomas Quiller-Couch, 1863–1944–Bibs. 1:**4473–6**
QUADRUPLE IMPOSITION *see* IMPOSITION, QUADRUPLE.
QUAKERS *see* FRIENDS, SOCIETY OF.
QUAKERS' BOOKS *see* FRIENDS BOOKS.
QUARITCH, Bernard, 1819–99. 2314 3391 **5478–86** 7974 9120 13116 13961
— Collns. 555
QUARITCH, Bernard Alfred, 1871–1913. **5483**
QUARLES, Francis, 1592–1644. **12927–35**
— *Argalus and Parthenia.* 12932 12934
— Bibs. 1:**4478**
— *Emblems.* 12928–9
— *Enchiridion.* 12927 12935
— Illus. 12934
— Publ. 12928
— *Solomon's recantation.* 12930
QUARTERLY MAGAZINE–Bibs. 1:4086
QUARTERLY REVIEW. 5250 5251 7893
— Bibs. 1:1716k 1921–2 1924 1927 2920 3346
QUARTO–Bibs. 1:1721
QUARTO FORMAT *see* FORMAT–Quarto; FORMAT–Quarto, folio form.

QUARTOS–Bibs. 1:1624
—, BAD. 7125 7166–7 7170 7178 7197 8180 12155
QUARTOS AS PROMPTBOOKS. 8461 10376
QUEEN MARY BINDER, fl.1550? 2187 **5487–8**
QUEEN'S BINDERS, fl.1670. **5489–90**
QUEEN'S UNIVERSITY, Kingston, Ont. *see* KINGSTON, Ont. QUEEN'S UNIVERSITY.
QUENINGTON, Glos.–Paper. 1121a
QUEVEDO Y VILLEGAS, Francisco Gómez de, 1580–1645. 973a 6992
QUICK, John, 1636–1706–Bibs. 1:**4479**
QUICK, Robert Hebert, 1831–91.
— *Essays on educational reformers.* 8116
QUILLER-COUCH, sir Arthur Thomas, 1863–1944 *see* Q., *pseud.*
QUIN, Henry George, 1760–1805. 3353a
QUINN, John, 1869–1924–Libr. 1:665; 468 2801 9641 9643 9664 10437
QUIVER, THE. 4207

RABAN, Edward, Edinburgh, d.1658. **5491–2a**
— Bibs. 1:**1386**
— Type. 5492a
RABINOWITZ, Louis Mayer, 1887–1957–Libr. 1:363g 577f
RACE PROGRAMMES *see* PROGRAMMES, RACE.
RACKHAM, Arthur, 1867–1939. **5493–a** 7408
— Bibs. 1:**4480–3b**
— Collns. 5493–a
RADCLIFFE, Lancs.–Paper. 1165
RADCLIFFE, Ann (Ward), 1764–1823. **12936**
— *Poems.* 12936
RADCLIFFE-BROWN, Alfred Reginald, 1881–1955 *see* BROWN, Alfred Reginald Radcliffe-, 1881–1955.
RADCLIFFE LIBRARY, Liverpool *see* LIVERPOOL. CATHEDRAL. RADCLIFFE LIBRARY.
RADICAL LITERATURE. 1294 1829
RADNORSHIRE–Paper. 1138
RAE, Peter, Dumfries, 1671–1748. **5494**
— Bibs. 1:**1387–8**
RAE, Thomas, 1928– . 5654–6
RAFFALD, Elizabeth (Whitaker), 1733–81.
— *Experienced English housekeeper.* 8712
RAIKES, Robert, Gloucester, 1690–1757. 3475 **5495** 7000a
— Bibs. 1:**1388b**
RAIKES FAMILY, Gloucester, fl.1722–1802. 1120

RAYNALDE, Thomas, fl.1541–55 *see* REYNOLD, Thomas, fl.1541–55.
RAY SOCIETY, est. 1844. **5515**
— Bibs. 1:**919**
READ, Alexander, 1586–1641.
— Libr. 2888
— *Manual of anatomy.* 7567
READ, sir Herbert Edward, 1893–1968.
— Bibs. 1:**4491i–j**
— *Parliament of women.* 5907
READ, Newbury Frost, fl.1923–31–Libr. 10039
READ, Thomas, d.1624 *see* REID, Thomas, d.1624.
READ, sir William, d.1715.
— *Treatise of the eyes.* 7561
READ, William Augustus, 1858–1916–Libr. 1:401d
READE, Charles, 1814–84. 831a 3997 **12983–92**
— Bibs. 1:**4492–7**
— *Cloister and the hearth.* 12984 12988
— Collns. 12990–1
— *Dora.* 12985
— *Good fight.* 12989
— Libr. 12986
— Mss. 12983 12991
— *Nance Oldfield.* 12987
— Publ. 5680 10158
READE, William Winwood, d.1875–Bibs. 1:**4500**
READERS *see* MARKET FOR BOOKS; NEWSPAPERS–Circulation; WOMEN AS READERS.
READERS OF THE PRESS *see* CORRECTORS OF THE PRESS.
READERS, PUBLISHERS' *see* PUBLISHERS' READERS.
READING, Berks. **1041–2**
— Bibs. 1:**873x–4**
— Newspapers. 1042
— Ptg. *see* PARKS, William, fl.1719–50.
— — Bibs. 1:874
— PUBLIC LIBRARIES–Collns. 1:873
— UNIVERSITY. LIBRARY–Collns. 1:874 1912
READING, William, 1674–1744. 2694
READING MERCURY. 1042
READING SOCIETIES *see also* MINERS' READING SOCIETIES. 2450 2452
REAGH, Justin MacCarthy-, comte de, 1744–1811. 5986
RECONSTRUCTIONS, MEMORIAL *see* MEMORIAL RECONSTRUCTIONS.
RECORD, Robert, 1510–58. 884
RECUSANT BOOKS *see also* RELIGION–CATHOLIC BOOKS. 4050–1
REDBOURNE, Herts.–Paper. 1139

RED CROSS SALES *see* SALES, RED CROSS.
REDFORD, John, fl.1535. **12993–4**
— *Wit and science.* 12993–4
RED HAND. 1799
REDMAN, Robert, d.1540. **5516–17** 6081 7479
— *Brumfels' Prayers of the Bible.* 5516–17 8067
RED-SHANKS SERMON, 1642. 1602
REDWAY, George, fl.1880. 14420
REED, mrs. David A.–Libr. 535
REED, Henry Hope, 1808–54. 14515
REED, Isaac, 1742–1807. 12685 **12995**
— *Baker's Biographia dramatica.* 8381–2
— Libr. 12995
— *Pearch's Collection of poems.* 8018
REED, Talbot Baines, 1852–93. **5518** 6637
— Bibs. 1:**4501**
— Libr. 4079
— *Old English letter foundries.* 6613 6616
REES, Owen, fl.1814–37. 1294
REES, Thomas, 1777–1864. 1200.
REES, Thomas Ifor, fl.1933–54. 10550
REES-MOGG, William, 1928– *see* MOGG, William Rees-, 1928– .
REEVES, bp. William, 1815–92–Bibs. 1:**4502**
REFERENCE BIBLIOGRAPHY *see* BIBLIOGRAPHY, REFERENCE.
REFLECTOR, THE. 7886
REFUSAL OF THE HAND. 8009
REGENSBURGER, Reinhold, 1891–1972–Libr. 3260
REGIONAL BIBLIOGRAPHY *see* name of country or place.
REGIONAL NOVELS *see* NOVELS, REGIONAL.
REGISTER–Bibliogr. descr. 128
REGISTER OF BOOKS. 3493a
REGISTERS, PARISH *see* PARISH REGISTERS.
REGISTRATIONS, PRINTERS' *see* PRINTERS' REGISTRATIONS.
REGISTRIES. 1743
REGNAULT, François, Paris, 1501–40. 6874
REGULATION *see* BOOKTRADE–Regulation; DRAMA–Regulation; NEWSPAPERS–Regulation; PRINTING–Regulation.
REID, Andrew, Newcastle-upon-Tyne, 1823–96. **5518g–j**
REID, Forrest, 1875–1947.
— Bibs. 1:**4503–5**
— Mss.–Bibs. 1:**4503** 4505
REID, Hugh R., fl.1894–Libr. 2:462p
REID, Thomas, d.1624. **12996**

REID, Thomas Mayne, 1818–83. **12997**
— Bibs. 1:**4506**
— Collns. 7322a
— Letters. 12997
REID, William, Glasgow, 1764–1831.
4107
— Bibs. 1:2022
REINOLDS, John, d.1614. **12998**
— *Prima chilias.* 12998
RELIGIO CLERICI, 1821. 793
RELIGION *see also* BAPTIST BOOKS;
BIBLE; BOOK OF COMMON ORDER;
BOOK OF COMMON PRAYER;
CATHOLIC BOOKS; CENSORSHIP,
RELIGIOUS; FRIENDS, SOCIETY OF;
HYMNS; LUTHERAN BOOKS;
METHODIST BOOKS; OXFORD
MOVEMENT; PRAYER BOOKS;
PRIMERS; SERMONS. 1596 4611
8079–104
— Bibs. 1:**2250–73a**
— Wales. 1497 5697
RELIGION AND SHAKESPEARE–Bibs.
2:102
RELIGIOUS NOVELS *see* NOVELS,
RELIGIOUS.
RELIGIOUS POETRY *see* POETRY,
RELIGIOUS.
RELIGIOUS TRACT SOCIETY, fl.1810–99.
5519
'REMAINDER'. 3591 3593 13130
REMAINDER BINDINGS *see* BOOK-
BINDINGS, REMAINDER.
REMAINDERING. 1294 3655–6 6503 6527
6536 6545–6
REMEDY FOR SEDITION, 1536. 599
REMEMBRANCER, THE. 14188
REMINGTON AND COMPANY, fl.1889–95.
5520
REMORSE OF CONSCIENCE, 1510? 6032
— Bibs. 1:1420a
RENFREWSHIRE. **1737–8**
REPAIRS, BOOK *see* BOOK REPAIRS.
REPORTING, PARLIAMENTARY. 3566
7954
REPRESENTATIVE, THE. 5250
REPRINTS. 512 675 804 6175 6507 6940
6962 7290 7326a 7641 7783 7806 8061
8070 8563 8660 8787 11698 12487
— Bibliogr. descr. 128
REPRODUCTION OF WATERMARKS *see*
WATERMARKS–Reproduction.
REPTON, Humphry, 1752–1818. 6193
— Bibs. 1:**4507**
RERESBY, sir John, 1634–89. **12999**
— Mss. 12999
RESALE PRICE MAINTENANCE. 3623a
6511 6523

RESOLUTIONER–PROTESTER CONTRO-
VERSY–Bibs. 1:717
RESPUBLICA see UDALL, Nicholas, 1505–56.
RESTALRIG MILL, Edinburgh. 1712
RETALIATER, THE. 1962–3
RETROSPECTIVE REVIEW. 7929
REVEIRS, George Philip, 1874–1911. **5521–2**
REVELS, MASTER OF THE. 1281
REVELS MSS. 9574–5 9578 9779–89 12553
REVENGER'S TRAGEDY. 4563 14074–6
REVIEWING AND REVIEWS. 4603 6533
8971 11135 11274 11849 11519
REVISED VERSION (BIBLE), 1881–5 *see*
BIBLE–Versions–Revised.
REVISION *see* –Text *after authors' names.*
REVOLTER, 1687. 7209
REVOLUTIONARY LITERATURE–Collns.
2632
REWARD BOOKS. 7025
REYMES, Bullen, 1614–72–Libr. 2810
REYNES, John, fl.1521–44. **5523**
REYNOLD, Thomas, fl.1541–55. 6056
— *Roesslin's Birth of mankind.* 7557 7559
REYNOLDS, bp. Edward. 1599–1676. **13000**
— *Three treatises.* 13000
REYNOLDS, George William Macarthur,
1814–79. **13001–4**
REYNOLDS, John Hamilton, 1796–1852.
13005–9
— Bibs. 1:**4508–11f**
— Collns. 13008
— Letters. 13007
— Mss.–Bibs. 1:**4511f**
— *To F- B-.* 13005
REYNOLDS, sir Joshua, 1723–92. **13010–11**
— Bibs. 1:3841 **4512**
— *Discourses.* 13011
— Libr. 13010
RHEIMS AND DOUAI BIBLE, 1582 *see*
BIBLE–Versions–Rheims and Douai;
BIBLE. N.T.–Versions–Rheims and Douai.
*RHEOL O GYFARWYDDYD IW HARFER
WRTH YMWELED AR CLAF, 1629.* 1470
RHETORIC–Bibs. 1:**2275–6a**
RHIWLEDYN PRESS, Llandudno. 1540g
RHODES, Cecil John, 1853–1902–Bibs.
1:**4513**
RHODES, Henry, fl.1680–1720. **5524–5**
RHYDDERCH, John, Shrewsbury,
fl.1708–35. 1465 6754
RHYS, Ioan Dafydd, 1534–1609. 1517
RIBALD MISCELLANIES *see* MISCEL-
LANIES, RIBALD.
RIBNER, Irving, 1921–72.
— *Kittredge's Shakespeare.* 2:803
RICARDO, David, 1772–1823–Bibs. 1:**4513d**
RICE, James, 1843–82.
— Collns. 7322a

RICE, Thomas Spring, 1st baron Monteagle of Brandon, 1790–1866 *see* MOUNT TRENCHARD PRESS, co. Limerick, fl.1863.
RICHARD II (WOODSTOCK). 2:943; 7¹⁰⁵
— Mss. 2:943; 7¹⁰⁵
RICHARD, DUKE OF YORK see SHAKESPEARE, William, 1564–1616. *3 HENRY 6.*
RICH, Jeremiah, d.1660? 8177
RICHARD DE BURY (Richard Aungerville), bp., 1287–1342? **13012–19**
— Bibs. 1:**4513h–l**
— Libr. 13012–13 13015 13019
— Mss.–Bibs. 1:4513l
— *Philobiblon.* 13014 13016–18
— — Bibs. 1:4513h–l
RICHARDS, Godfrey, fl.1655. 6550
RICHARDS, Ivor Armstrong, 1893– –Bibs. 1:**4513n**
RICHARDS, Thomas, fl.1897–1961–Bibs. 1:**4513s**
RICHARDS, Thomas Franklin Grant, 1872–1948. **5526–9** 9838 11165
— Letters. 5529
— Libr. 11174
RICHARDS, William, 1643–1705. **13020**
— *Christmas ordinary.* 13020
RICHARDS, William, 1749–1818–Bibs. 1:**4513u**
RICHARDSON, Dorothy Miller (mrs. Alan Odle), 1882–1957–Bibs. 1:**4514–16**
RICHARDSON, Francis, fl.1897–Libr. 13170
RICHARDSON, George, Glasgow, d.1872. 4746 **5530**
RICHARDSON, Henry Handel, *pseud.* of Henrietta Ethel Florence Lindesay Richardson (mrs. John G. Robertson), 1870–1946. 1:**4516h**
— Mss.–Bibs. 1:4516h
RICHARDSON, James Mallcott, c.1771–1854. **5531**
RICHARDSON, John, 1664–1747.
— *True interest of the Irish nation.* 1811
RICHARDSON, sir John, 1787–1865–Bibs. 1:**4516m**
RICHARDSON, Jonathan, 1665–1745. **12348**
RICHARDSON, Jonathan, 1694–1771. **12348**
RICHARDSON, Joseph, d.1763. **5532**
RICHARDSON, Nelson Moore, 1855–1925–Libr. 6823
RICHARDSON, Peter Bolton, Loughrea, fl.1821–34. **5533**
RICHARDSON, Samuel, 1689–1761. **13021–39** 14613
— *Apprentice's vade mecum.* 13036
RICHARDSON, Samuel, 1689–1761.
— Bibs. 1:**1389 4517–20**

— *Clarissa Harlowe.* 13021 13031 13033–4 13037
— *History of Pamela.* 4035 4038 13022 13024–5 13027 13034–5 13038–9
— Illus. 13023 13034
— Letters. 5540
— Publ. 6510a 13024–6 13038
— *Sir Charles Grandison.* 6510a 13026 13029 13034
— Text. 13037 13039
—AS PRINTER. 3475 3620 3639a 5360 **5534–47**
RICHARDSON, William, 1698–1775. 6935
RICHARDSON, William, 1743–1814. **13040**
— *Essays on Shakespeare.* 13040
RICHMOND, Surrey. **1406**
— Bksllng. 1406
— Librs. *see* HAM HOUSE.
— Ptg. 1406
— PUBLIC LIBRARY–Collns. 1:4994
RICHMOND, Yorks. **1442**
— Paper. 1442
RICHMOND, Va. STATE LIBRARY *see* VIRGINIA. STATE LIBRARY, Virginia.
RICHMOND, Margaret Beaufort, countess of, 1443–1509 *see* BEAUFORT, Margaret, countess of Richmond and Derby, 1443–1509.
RICKETTS, Charles de Sousy, 1866–1931. 5891 5893
— Bibs. 1:**4520d**
RID, Samuel, fl.1610–12.
— *Art of juggling.* 7483
RIDDELL, Charlotte Elizabeth Lawson (Cowan), 1832–1906–Bibs. 1:**4521**
RIDDELL, Maria, fl.1792. **13041–2**
— *Metrical miscellany.* 13041
— *Sketch of Burns.* 13042
— Text. 13042
RIDDELL, Robert, 1755–94–Libr. 1635 9028 9033 9071
RIDER'S BRITISH MERLIN, c.1732. 6751
RIDER, John, 1562–1632. 3538
RIDER, William, 1723–85.
— *Candidus or The optimist.* 903
RIDING, Laura (mrs. S. B. Jackson), 1901– . 4897e 5617
RIDPATH, George, 1717?–72. **1633**
RIGHT INSTITUTION OF BAPTISM, 1549. 687
RILKE, Rainer Maria, 1875–1926–Bibs. 1:**822s**
RIMBAULT, Edward Francis, 1816–76. 7605
RIPON. CATHEDRAL. LIBRARY. 2698a
— — — Collns. 4313a 4314 4329
RIPPON, John, 1751–1836.
— *Tunebook.* 8183

Vol. **1** = *Bibliographies*   **2** = *Shakespeare*   **4** = 1–8221   **5** = 8222–14616

RITCHIE, Anne Isabella (Thackeray), lady, 1837–1919. 5680
RITSON, Joseph, 1752–1803. 2:718; 13043–5
— *Bibliographica Scotica.* 13044
— Bibs. 1:4522–3
— Libr. 6796
— Mss. 6783 13043–4
— — Bibs. 1:4523
— *Observations on English poetry.* 13045
RIVERS, Augustine, 1588–1650? see ABBOT, John, 1588–1650?
RIVERS, Augustus Henry Lane Fox Pitt-, 1827–1900–Bibs. 1:4524–c
RIVERS, John, 1588–1650? see ABBOTT, John, 1588–1650?
RIVIERE, Robert, 1809–82. 2322 5548–53
RIVINGTON, Charles, 1688–1742. 1294 5554–5
RIVINGTON, Charles, fl.1746–90. 13035
RIVINGTON, Charles, 1754–1831. 5554–5
RIVINGTON, Francis, 1745–1822. 5554–5
RIVINGTON, Francis, 1806–85. 5554–5
RIVINGTON, James, 1724–1803. 5555
RIVINGTON, John, 1720–92. 3639a 5555
RIVINGTON, John, d.1785. 5555
RIVINGTON, PERCIVAL AND COMPANY, 1893–7. 5555
RIVINGTON AND COMPANY, 1897. 5555
RIVINGTON FAMILY–Bibs. 1:1908
ROADBOOKS AND ITINERARIES. 1033–7 5317a
— Bibs. 1:870 1764 1768 4360 4397 4408
— England. 1034–7 5320
— Ireland. 1034–5
— — Bibs. 1:870 1025
— Scotland–Bibs. 1:975–7
— Wales. 1036
— — Bibs. 1:960
ROBERT, Nicolas Louis, 1761–1828. 3785 4571m
ROBERTS, Charles, 1846–1902–Libr. 1:2270
ROBERTS, Henry, fl.1585–1616.
— *Pheander.* 675
ROBERTS, Griffith, fl.1555–1611. 7359a
ROBERTS, James, fl.1564–1615. 2:918 1233
— *Shakespeare's Hamlet.* 2:1232–3
— *Shakespeare's Merchant of Venice.* 2:1233
— *Shakespeare's Titus Andronicus.* 2:1810
ROBERTS, James, fl.1706–54. 6402
ROBERTS, John, fl.1714 5556
ROBERTS, John, fl.1721–50. 2:1659
ROBERTS, Michael, fl.1630. 5557
ROBERTS, Michael, *pseud. of* William Edward Roberts, 1902–48. 1:4525c
ROBERTS, Morley Charles, 1857–1942–Bibs. 1:4525
ROBERTS, Robert, fl.1661–1700. 2:681

ROBERTS, Robert, d.1898–Libr. 2:519 592
ROBERTS, sir Sydney Castle, 1889–1966. 4169 4178
— Libr. 3160
ROBERTS, Thomas Francis, 1860–1919. 13046
— *Drych y prif oesoedd.* 13046
ROBERTS, William, 1767–1849.
— *Memoirs of Hannah More.* 12490
ROBERTS, William, 1828–72–Libr. 2783
ROBERTS, William, 1862–1940.
— Bibs. 1:4525k
— Libr. 3020 3028
ROBERTS, William Edward, 1902–48 see ROBERTS, Michael, *pseud.*
ROBERTSON, Andrew, fl.1589–91. 13047
ROBERTSON, Bartholomew, fl.1617–20. 13048
— *Adagia.* 8073 13048
— — Bibs. 1:4526
ROBERTSON, Bartholomew, fl.1617–20– Bibs. 1:4526
ROBERTSON, Duncan, d.1782? 2534
ROBERTSON, James, 1714–95. 13049
ROBERTSON, James 'Gallus,' d.1820. 8087
ROBERTSON, Joseph, 1810–66–Libr. 2912
ROBERTSON, Thomas William, 1829–71. 13050
— Bibs. 1:1597
ROBERTSON, Walford Graham, 1886– 1948–Libr. 1:2471m
ROBERTSON, William, 1721–93–Libr. 1635
ROBERT THE DEVIL, 1550?–Ms. 7988
ROBERTUS CASTELLENSIS, fl.1480–99. 6971
ROBIN HOOD. 5470 5477 13051–3
— Bibs. 1:928 4527–c
ROBINSON, Agnes Mary Frances, later Darmesteter, later Duclaux, 1857–1944 see DUCLAUX, Agnes Mary Frances (Robinson), formerly Darmesteter, 1857–1944.
ROBINSON, Bartholomew, fl.1617–20 see ROBERTSON, Bartholomew, fl.1617–20.
ROBINSON, Elisha Smith, Bristol, 1817–85. 5558
ROBINSON, George, 1737–1801. 1294
ROBINSON, Henry Crabb, 1775–1867. 13054
— Bibs. 1:4527p
ROBINSON, Hugh, 1584?–1655. 1517
— *Preces et grammaticalia.* 8110
ROBINSON, Humphrey, fl.1623–70. 5559
ROBINSON, Mary (Darby), 1758–1800–Bibs. 1:4527r
ROBINSON, Richard, fl.1576–1600. 13055–8
— Bibs. 1:4527t–u
— *Eupolemia.* 13055–7
— Mss. 13057

ROSENBERG, Isaac, 1890–1918. **13077**
— Bibs. 1:**4538**
— Libr. 1:4538
— Mss.–Bibs. 1:4538
ROSENWALD, Lessing Julius, 1891– –Libr. 1:2476
ROSICRUCIAN BOOKS. **8105**
— Bibs. 1:2241a
— Ptg. 8105
— Type. 6667
ROSLIN CASTLE, Midloth. *see* ROSSLYN CASTLE, Midloth.
ROSS, Alexander, 1699–1784. **13078**
— *Helenore*. 13078
ROSS, J. H. *see* LAWRENCE, Thomas Edward, afterwards Shaw, 1888–1935.
ROSS, John, Carmarthen, fl.1764–1811. 5562 8963
ROSS, John, Edinburgh, fl.1574–80. 1591
ROSS, Martin, *pseud. of* Violet Florence Martin, 1865–1915. *For works written in collaboration with* E. A. Œ. Somerville *see* SOMERVILLE, Edith Anna Œnone, 1858–1949.
ROSS, Robert Baldwin, 1869–1918–Libr. 1:5103
ROSS, sir Ronald, 1857–1932–Bibs. 1:**4539–40a**
ROSS, Thomas Edward, 1867– –Libr. 1:1490; 6878
ROSS, Thomas, fl.1828–51. 5563
ROSSETTI, Christina Georgina, 1830–94. **13079–80** 13082
— Bibs. 1:652 **4541–d**
— Bndng. 13079
— Handwr. 13094
— *A pageant*. 13079
— *Songs in a cornfield*. 13080
— Text. 13080
ROSSETTI, Dante Gabriel, 1828–82. 7420a **13081–97** 13898 14387 14436
— *Antwerp and Bruges*. 13097
— Bibs. 1:652 **4542–5**
— *Blessed damosel*. 12645 13089
— *The carillon*. 13097
— Collns. 3039 13088 13091
— *Early Italian poets*. 13095
— *Eden bower*. 13810
— *Hand and soul*. 4992
— Handwr. 13094
— *Jan van Hunks*. 13087
— Letters. 13085
— Mss. 13086 13088–9 13091–2 13810
— — Bibs. 1:4544k
— Publ. 13085
— *The ragiomenti*. 13084
— *Sordello*. 13093

— Text. 13097
— *White ship*. 13092
ROSSETTI, William Michael, 1829–1919. 13095 **13098–9**
— Bibs. 1:**4547**
— *Cor cordium*. 13098
— Letters. 13099
ROSSLYN CASTLE, Midloth.–Libr. 2543
ROTARY PRESSES *see* PRESSES, ROTARY.
ROTHAMSTED EXPERIMENTAL STATION, Harpenden. LIBRARY–Collns. 1:2091 2095
ROTHERAM. PUBLIC LIBRARIES–Collns. 1:3265
ROTHES MILL, Markinch. 5880
ROTHSCHILD, Nathaniel Mayer Victor, baron Rothschild, 1910– –Libr. 1:634 4836; 2374 2990 3186 5391
ROTHWELL, John, d.1661. 12378
ROUEN, France. 8067
ROUNDE TABLE. 11195 11211
— Bibs. 1:3780
ROUNDHAY HALL–Libr. *see* BROTHERTON, Edward Allen, 1st baron Brotherton of Wakefield, 1855–1930–Libr.
ROUNDWOOD, co. Wicklow. **1990–1**
— Ptg. 1990–1 4126
ROUS, John, 1411?–91. 2665 3185
ROUSHAM, Steeple Aston, Oxon.–Libr. 2799
ROUSSEAU, Jean-Jacques, 1712–78. 921 7000a 7011 7289
— Bibs. 1:**814–15**
ROUSSILLON, Gabriel, d.1729. 4473
ROUTH, Martin Joseph, 1755–1854–Libr. 3177 3192 3201
ROUTLEDGE, George, 1812–88. **5564–a** 12071
ROUTLEDGE, Thomas, 1819–87. 3745a 3784 **5564p–q**
ROWE, Bryan, d.1521–Libr. 3252 3296
ROWE, John, 1626–77–Bibs. 1:**4546**
ROWE, Nicholas, 1674–1718. **13100–1**
— Bibs. 1:**4550–1**
— Libr. 2:717; 13100
— Publ. 5868–70
— *Shakespeare's Works*. 1:4551; 2:708 729–30 734–6 743 748 752 759 1123m 1152; 5869–70 13101
— — Bibs. 1:4551
ROWFANT CLUB, Cleveland. 2741
ROWFANT LIBRARY *see* LAMPSON, Frederick Locker-, 1821–95–Libr.
ROWING–Bibs. 1:**2276f**
ROWLANDS, Richard, later Verstegan, fl.1565–1620 *see* VERSTEGAN, Richard, formerly Rowlands, fl.1565–1620.

ROWLANDS, Samuel, 1570?–1630? 7843 **13102–4**
— *Humor's antic faces.* 13102
— *Melancholy knight.* 13104
— *Theatre of delightful recreation.* 478
ROWLANDSON, Thomas, 1756–1827. 3816 **5565–6** 6192–3
— Bibs. 1:1738–9 **4552–3**
— Collns. 5566
ROWLEY, William, 1585?–1642?–Bibs. 1:1597
— Text. 8468
ROWLEY MILLS, Lydney. 1120a
ROWNTREE, Benjamin Seebohm, 1871–1954–Bibs. 1:**4553f**
ROXBURGH, John Ker, 3d duke of, 1740–1804 *see* KER, John, 3d duke of Roxburgh, 1740–1804.
ROXBURGHE CLUB, est. 1812. **5567–71** 11004
— Bibs. 1:1264 **1389d–f**
— Collns. 5570
— Mss. 5567
— *Roxburghe revels.* 5567
— LIBRARY. 5568
ROXBURGHSHIRE. **1739–41**
— Bibs. 1:**1007–9**
ROY, George Ross, 1924– –Libr. 1:2644
ROY, Louis Le, 1510?–77 *see* LE ROY, Louis, 1510?–77.
ROYAL ARMS. 6687
ROYAL BINDINGS *see* BOOKBINDINGS, ROYAL.
ROYAL BLACKBIRD. 6785
ROYAL BOOK COLLECTORS *see* BOOK COLLECTORS, ROYAL.
ROYAL BOTANIC GARDENS, Kew. LIBRARY. 6944
ROYAL COLLEGE OF ART, London *see* LONDON. ROYAL COLLEGE OF ART.
ROYAL COLLEGE OF PHYSICIANS, London. LIBRARY. 2860
LIBRARY. 2860
— Collns. 1:3619
ROYAL COLLEGE OF PHYSICIANS, Scotland. LIBRARY–Collns. 1:442
ROYAL COLLEGE OF SURGEONS OF ENGLAND. LIBRARY. 2470 3122
— Collns. 1:586 3770
ROYAL COLLEGE OF OBSTETRICIANS AND GYNÆCOLOGISTS, London. LIBRARY–Collns. 1:2225 2230i
ROYAL COLLEGE OF VETERINARY SURGEONS, London. LIBRARY–Collns. 1:2222–a
ROYAL COMMONWEALTH SOCIETY, London. 11790

ROYAL DUBLIN SOCIETY–Bibs. 1:**1074–5**
— LIBRARY. 1923
ROYAL GLASGOW INSTITUTE OF FINE ARTS. BURNS EXHIBITION, 1896 *see* BURNS EXHIBITION, Glasgow, 1896.
ROYAL HEADS BINDER, fl.1665. **5572**
ROYAL HISTORICAL SOCIETY–Bibs. 1:916f–g
ROYAL HORTICULTURAL SOCIETY. LINDLEY LIBRARY–Collns. 1:2187a
ROYAL IRISH ACADEMY, Dublin. LIBRARY–Collns. 1:444a 1975; 1762 1876 1887
ROYAL LIBRARIES *see* LIBRARIES, ROYAL.
ROYAL LIBRARY, WINDSOR CASTLE *see* WINDSOR CASTLE. ROYAL LIBRARY.
ROYAL MADRAS REGIMENT–Bibs. 1:2232–3
ROYAL OBSERVATORY, Edinburgh *see* EDINBURGH. ROYAL OBSERVATORY.
ROYAL PRINTERS *see* KING'S PRINTERS.
ROYAL PRINTING OFFICE, Paris. 3929 4161
ROYAL REMARKS. 2:700
ROYAL SHAKESPEARE. 2:711
ROYAL SHAKESPEARE THEATRE, Stratford-upon-Avon. 2:326
— LIBRARY–Collns. 2:234
ROYAL SOCIETY OF LONDON. 5156–7
— Bibs. 1:**917m**
— LIBRARY. 2497 2808 2815
— — Collns. 2:651
ROYALTIES, AUTHORS' *see also* AUTHORS–Payment. 3525 6503 10126
ROYAL WORKS. 6778
RUBAIYAT OF OMAR KHAYYAM see FITZGERALD, Edward, 1809–83.
RUBRICS–Bibliogr. descr. 97
RUDD, bp. Anthony, 1549?–1615. 7144
RUDDER, Samuel, Cirencester, 1726–1801. 1117a 5573
RUDDIMAN, Thomas, Edinburgh, 1674–1757. **5574**
— Bibs. 1:**1390**
— *Rudiments of Latin tongue.* 5574
RUE, Andreas, fl.1490–1517. 5312 **5575**
RUFF, William, 1905– –Libr. 1:4608
RUFFHEAD, Owen, 1723–69. 12817
— *Life of Pope.* 12827
RUFINUS, Tyrannius, Aquileiensis, fl.345–410. 1348 1363 1365
RULE, WORKING TO *see* WORKING TO RULE.
RULES, BOX. 8456 12400
—, BRASS. 5772a
—, CENTRE.
— Bibliogr. descr. 140

RULINGS. 6269

RUMANIA, BRITISH BOOKS PUBLISHED IN see BRITISH BOOKS PUBLISHED ABROAD–Rumania; SHAKESPEARE, William, 1564–1616–WORKS IN RUMANIA.

RUMBALL-PETRE, Edwin Alfred Robert, 1881–1954 see PETRE, Edwin Alfred Robert Rumball-, 1881–1954.

RUNDELL, Maria Eliza (Ketelby), 1745–1828.
— New system of domestic cookery. 5250

RUNNERS, BOOKSELLERS' see BOOKSELLERS' RUNNERS.

RUNNINGTITLES see also HEADLINES. 12534 14335
— Bibliogr. descr. 132 142–3 13150

RUPERT, prince, duke of Cumberland, 1619–82–Libr. 2636

RUSHWORTH, John, 1612?–90. 3508

RUSKIN, John, 1819–1900. 13105–28 14387 14406 14417 14436
— Bibs. 1:4553y–8 5147
— Bksllng. 13116
— Collns. 13111 13114 13118–19 13121
— Deucalion. 13117
— Early geology. 13117
— Essay on baptism. 13117
— Gold. 13105
— Handwr. 13106 13120
— Knight's faith. 13117
— Lectures on art. 13117
— Letters. 13116 13119 13121 13128
— Libr. 13112–13 13122 13124 13127
— Modern painters. 13126 14520
— Mss. 13105 13112–14 13117–19 13121
— — Bibs. 1:4556e
— Notes on Frederick William. 13117
— Notes on the Halcyon. 13117
— Our fathers have told us. 13117
— Poems. 13117 13123 13125
— — Bibs. 1:4557
— Proserpina. 6958a
— Ptg. 4852 6098 13125
— Publ. 3830a 5680 5704 13107–8 13125
— The queen's gardens. 13115
— St. Mark's rest. 13117
— Samuel Prout. 13117
— Storm cloud. 13117
— Supplement to the Report. 13110
— Text. 13126
— Valle crucis. 13117
— Verona and its rivers. 13117
— Works–Bibs. 1:4558

RUSKIN MUSEUM, Sheffield–Collns. 1:4553y

RUSSEL, William Augustus, fl.1777. 13129
— New history of England. 13129

RUSSELL, Bertrand Arthur William, 3d earl Russell, 1872–1970–Bibs. 1:4559g–h

RUSSELL, Edward, fl.1639–Libr. 2616

RUSSELL, Francis, 2d earl of Bedford, 1527?–85–Libr. 2881

RUSSELL, George, fl.1820.
— Abominations of the Jesuits exposed. 1463

RUSSELL, George William, 1867–1935 see Æ., pseud.

RUSSELL, John, 1711–1804. 1404

RUSSELL, Matthew, 1834–1912–Bibs. 1:4559p

RUSSELL, Thomas, 1748–1822.
— History of Guildford. 1404

RUSSELL, William Clark, 1844–1911–Collns. 7322a

RUSSELL-COTES ART GALLERY AND MUSEUM, Bournemouth. 11312

RUSSHE, John, fl.1479–98. 5463–4

RUSSIAN LITERATURE see BRITISH BOOKS PUBLISHED ABROAD; FOREIGN BOOKS PUBLISHED IN BRITAIN; SHAKESPEARE, William, 1564–1616–WORKS IN RUSSIA.

RUST, bp. George, d.1670–Bibs. 1:4560

RUTGERS UNIVERSITY. LIBRARY–Collns. 1:2821b; 2:677; 807 3090 8782 9491 9493 10405 10937 11696

RUTHERFORD, Mark, pseud. of William Hale White, 1831–1913. 13130–1
— Bibs. 1:4560a–2
— Bndng. 2146
— Catharine Furze. 2146 13130
— Letters–Bibs. 1:4561
— Mss. 13130

RUTHERFURD, Samuel, c.1600–61–Bibs. 1:4563

RUTHERSTON, Albert Daniel, 1881–1953. 4480 5576
— Bibs. 1:4563i–j

RUTHLIN, Mons.–Paper. 1298a

RUTHVEN, John, Edingburgh, fl.1813. 6332

RYDE, I.O.W.–Ptg. see BELDORNIE PRESS, 1840–3.

RYDER, John Stanley, Richmond, Surrey, fl.1960. 6495

RYE, Sussex–Librs. see LAMB HOUSE.

RYE, Walter, 1843–1929–Bibs. 1:4564–6

RYE HOUSE PLOT, 1683. 706

RYLANCE, R., fl.1815. 6742

RYLANDS, John, 1801–88–Libr. see also JOHN RYLANDS LIBRARY, Manchester. 2:470g

RYLANDS, Thomas Glazebrook, 1818–1900–Libr. 1:468 499

RYLE, bp. John Charles, 1816–1900–Bibs. 1:4567

RYMER, James Malcolm, fl.1842–56–Bibs.
1:**4567m**
RYMER, Thomas, 1641–1713–Bibs. 1:**4567q**
RYVES, Bruno, 1596–1677–Libr. 3396a

S., T. *see* SHERMAN, Thomas, fl.1671–84.
SABINE, Henry, fl.1763–1800. 7733
SACHEVERELL, Henry, 1674?–1784. 11974
13132–3
— Bibs. 1:**4567x**
SACKVILLE, Charles, 6th earl of Dorset,
1638–1706. **13134–5**
— Bibs. 1:**4568**
— Mss. 13135
SACKVILLE, Thomas, 1st earl of Dorset,
1536–1608. 2730 **13136**
— Mss. 13136
SACKVILLE-WEST, Victoria Mary, lady
Nicolson, 1892–1962 *see* WEST, Victoria
Mary Sackville-, lady Nicolson, 1892–1962.
SACRED HEART UNIVERSITY, Bridgeport,
Conn. LIBRARY–Collns. 1:**3968b**
SADLEIR, Michael Thomas Harvey,
1888–1957. 64 76–7 210 790 7320
— Bibs. 1:**4568p**
— Libr. 1:**4986**; 2374 2992 3196 7306 7311
SADLER, Ralph, Dublin, d.1703. **5577**
SAGE, Alain René le, 1668–1747 *see* LE
SAGE, Alain René, 1668–1747.
SAGE, sir John Merry le, 1837–1926 *see* LE
SAGE, sir John Merry, 1837–1926.
SAINLIENS, Claude de, fl.1568–97 *see* DE
SAINLIENS, Claude, fl.1568–97.
SAINSBURY, John, fl.1836–65–Libr. 2650
ST. ALBANS, Herts.–Ptg. 1017 1025
ST. ALBANS, Francis Bacon, baron Verulam
and viscount, 1561–1626 *see* BACON,
Francis, baron Verulam and viscount St.
Albans, 1561–1626.
ST. ANDREWS, Fife. **1676–81**
— Bibs. 1:**998–1000**
— Bndng. 1676
— Bksllng. 1676
— Librs. 1677–81
— Ptg. 1596 5491 5492a
— — Bibs. 1:**999**
— Type *see* WILSON, Alexander, 1714–86.
— HAMMERMEN *see* HAMMERMEN OF
ST. ANDREWS.
— ST. SALVATOR'S COLLEGE *see* ST.
SALVATOR'S COLLEGE, St. Andrews.
— UNIVERSITY–Bibs. 1:**1000**
— — LIBRARY. 1677a–81 3065
— — — Collns. 1:475; 2:477–8; 8923
ST. ANDREWS UNIVERSITY PRESS. 5879
ST. ANN'S STEAM BINDING WORKS,
London. 4673

ST. ASAPH, Flintshire–Librs. 1510 3326
ST. BONAVENTURE UNIVERSITY, St.
Bonaventure, N.Y. FRIEDSAM
LIBRARY–Collns. 1:**4933**
ST. BOTOLPH'S CHURCH, Boston,
Lincs. *see* BOSTON, Lincs. St. Botolph's
church.
ST. BRIAVELS, Glos.–Paper. 1120a
ST. BRIDE FOUNDATION INSTITUTE,
London. 6321
— TECHNICAL REFERENCE LIBRARY.
6568–9 6574 6619
— — Collns. 1:424 1015 1141–3 1146 1157
1203 1250 1266q 1556; 4079 4081
ST. BRIDE PRINTING LIBRARY *see* ST.
BRIDE FOUNDATION INSTITUTE, Lon-
don. TECHNICAL REFERENCE
LIBRARY.
ST. COLUMB'S COLLEGE, Derry.
LIBRARY. 1864
ST. CUTHBERT'S COLLEGE, Ushaw.
LIBRARY–Collns. 2210
ST. DAVID'S, Pembrokeshire–Librs. 1510
ST. DEINIOL'S THEOLOGICAL AND
GENERAL LIBRARY, Hawarden. 2514.
ST. DOMINIC'S PRESS, Ditchling, est. 1916.
5578–80
— Bibs. 1:**1391–d**
ST. EDMUND'S COLLEGE, Ware. OLD
HALL LIBRARY–Collns. 1:502
SAINT-ÉVREMOND, Charles de Marguetel
de Saint-Denis de, 1616–1703. 10347
ST. FRANCIS XAVIER COLLEGE, Llanryd-
dol. LIBRARY. 3313 3355
ST. GEORGE'S CHURCH, Doncaster *see*
DONCASTER. ST. GEORGE'S CHURCH.
ST. GERMAN, Christopher, 1460?–1540.
13137–8
— Bibs. 1:**4568a**
— *Doctor and student.* 13137
— Libr. 13138
ST. IVES, Hunts. **1147–8**
— Bksllng. 1147
— Newspapers. 1148
— Ptg. 1147
ST. GILES WITHOUT CRIPPLEGATE *see*
LONDON. ST. GILES CRIPPLEGATE.
ST. IVES MERCURY. 1148
ST. JAMES'S CHRONICLE. 7709
ST. JAMES'S GAZETTE. 9317
ST. JOHN, Cynthia (Morgan), 1852–
1919–Libr. 1:5170 5172 5176
ST.JOHN, Henry, 1st viscount Bolingbroke,
1678–1751. **13139–40**
— Bibs. 1:**4569–71**
— *Letters on history.* 13140
— *Letters on patriotism.* 13139
— Ptg. 13139

Vol. **1** = *Bibliographies*   **2** = *Shakespeare*   **4** = 1–8221   **5** = 8222–14616

ST.JOHN., Percy Bolingbroke, 1821–89.
13141
— Collns. 13141
ST. LOUIS. PUBLIC LIBRARY–Collns. 2:52
— WASHINGTON UNIVERSITY *see* WASHINGTON UNIVERSITY.
ST. LUKE'S PRINTING WORKS. 7256
ST. MAGNUS CHURCH, London *see* LONDON. ST. MAGNUS CHURCH.
ST. MARTIN'S-IN-THE-FIELDS *see* LONDON. ST. MARTIN'S-IN-THE-FIELDS.
ST. MARY CRAY, Kent–Paper *see* JOYNSON, William, fl.1839–60; NASH, Thomas, 1801–45; NASH, Thomas Henry, 1866–1949; NASH, William, 1765–1824; NASH, William, 1836–79; NASH, William Gardiner, 1864–1914.
ST. MARYLEBONE *see* LONDON. ST. MARYLEBONE.
ST. MARY'S CATHEDRAL LIBRARY *see* EDINBURGH. CATHEDRAL. LIBRARY.
ST. MARY'S CHURCH, Dundee *see* DUNDEE. ST. MARY'S CHURCH.
ST. MARY'S CHURCH, Marlborough. VICAR'S LIBRARY *see* MARLBOROUGH. ST. MARY'S CHURCH. VICAR'S LIBRARY.
ST. MARY'S CHURCH, Warwick *see* WARWICK. ST. MARY'S CHURCH.
ST. MARY'S COLLEGE, Blairs. LIBRARY–Collns. 2162
ST. MARY'S COLLEGE, Llandeilo. LIBRARY. 1539
ST. MARY'S COLLEGE, Oscott. LIBRARY. 3362
— — Collns. 1:2263
ST. MARY'S MILL, Chalford. 1120a
ST. MAUR, Raymond de, *pseud. of* Nicolas François Dupré de Saint-Maur, 1695–1774.
— *Milton's Paradise lost.* 12348
ST. NEOTS, Hunts. **1149–50**
— Bksllng. 1150
— Ptg. 1149–50
ST. OMER, France. ENGLISH COLLEGE. 841
ST. OMERS' COLLEGE PRESS, 1608–42 *see also* BIRCHLEY HALL PRESS, Wigan, 1604–36; HEIGHAM, John, fl.1568–1632.
— Bibs. 1:**1392–3**
ST. OSWALD'S CHURCH, Durham *see* DURHAM. ST. OSWALD'S CHURCH.
ST. PANCRAS *see* LONDON. ST. PANCRAS.
ST. PATRICK'S PURGATORY. 13738
ST. PAUL'S CATHEDRAL *see* LONDON. ST. PAUL'S CATHEDRAL.

ST. PAUL'S CRAY, Kent.
— Paper *see* NASH, Thomas, 1801–45; NASH, Thomas Henry, 1866–1949; NASH, William, 1765–1824; NASH, William Gardiner, 1864–1914.
ST. PAUL'S CRAY MILLS, Kent. 5256
ST. SALVATOR'S COLLEGE, St. Andrews. LIBRARY. 1677
SAINTSBURY, George Edward Bateman, 1845–1933.
— Bibs. 1:**4575–6c**
— *Caroline poets.* 7996
ST. WEONARDS, Herefs.–Paper. 1138
SAKI, *pseud. of* Hector Hugh Munro, 1870–1916–Bibs. 1:**4571**
SALA, George Augustus, 1828–96. **13142**
— Bibs. 1:**4578**
— Collns. 3013 7322a 13142
SALE CATALOGUES *see also* AUCTION AND SALE CATALOGUES. 3234 3334 3493 3636 3660 3673 4131 4139 7618 9245 9922 11010 11374 13731 13734 14025 14033–4 14037 14177 14192 14204
— Bibs. 1:340 1189a 1276h 1443a–58
— Collns. 3059 3311
— Ireland. 1821
SALES. 2269 **3660–85**
— 1475–1700. 279 2265 2596 2971 3660 3666 3668–72 3674–5 3688
— 1701–1800. 1320 3203 3662 3665 3680–1 3684 3688
— 1801–1900. 2720 2961 3661 3664–5 3667 3673 3676 3688 4639
— 1901– . **424–94** 2505 2526 2531 2539–40 2557 2572 2582–3 2588 2724 2727 2742–4
—, AUCTION. 1320 2265 2269 2272 2278 2352 2354 2357–8 3203 3661 3665–74 3688 3991 4639 5706 7593
— Ireland. 3671
—, LISTS OF. 2275 3991 5706
—, RED CROSS. 492–3
—, REMAINDER *see* REMAINDERING.
—, TRADE. 1294 3426 3625a 3662 3664 3681 3685
SALESBURY, William, 1520?–1600? *see* SALISBURY, William, 1520–1600?
SALFORD–Maps–Bibs. 1:1793
SALISBURY, Wilts.
— Bksllng. *see* COLLINS, Benjamin, fl.1729–85.
— CATHEDRAL. LIBRARY. 2806a
— — — Collns. 2164 14213
SALISBURY, Enoch Robert Gibbon, 1819–90–Libr. 2972
SALISBURY, Robert Arthur James Gascoyne-Cecil, 5th marquis of, 1893– *see* CECIL, Robert Arthur James Gascoyne-, 5th marquis of Salisbury, 1893– .

SALISBURY, Thomas, 1567?–1620?–Bibs. 1:**1393**v

SALISBURY, William, 1520?–1600? **13143**
— Bibs. 1:**4578**h
— *Dictionary in English and Welsh.* 3547

SALISBURY AND WINCHESTER JOURNAL. 7768

SALLUST (Gaius Sallustius Crispus), 86–34 B.C. 3991 4728 12550

SALLUSTE DU BARTAS, Guillame de, 1544–90 *see* DU BARTAS, Guillame de Saluste, 1544–90.

SALMON, David, fl.1882–1912–Libr. 8111

SALMON, Thomas, 1648–1706.
— *Essay to the advancement of music.* 7602

SALMON, William, fl.1736–45.
— *Builder's guide.* 6777

SALOMONS, sir David Lionel Goldsmid-Stern, 1851–1925–Libr. 1:1745; 7422

SALTER, James, c.1648–1718–Bibs. 1:**4579**

SALTER, James, c.1695–1767–Bibs. 1:**4580**

SALTER, John William, 1820–69.
— *Palæontology of niti in the northern Himalayas.* 8132

SAMBOURNE, Edwin Linley, 1844–1910. 7420a

SAMPSON, John, fl.1559–75 *see* AWDELEY, John, fl.1559–75.

SAMUEL, William, fl.1551–69. **13144**
— *Practice practiced.* 13144
— *Warning for London.* 13144

SAMUELS, S., fl.1963–Libr. 1:3437

SAN ANTONIO COLLEGE, Texas. LIBRARY–Collns. 746

SANDARS, Harry, formerly William John Stannard, d.1880.
— *Art exemplar.* 6228

SANDARS LECTURES IN BIBLIOGRAPHY *see* CAMBRIDGE. UNIVERSITY. SANDARS LECTURES.

SANDBY, Paul, 1725–1809. 6193

SANDBY, William, 1717–99. **5581**

SANDERS, Robert, Glasgow, 1630?–94. 1692 4746 **5582–3**
— Bibs. 1:**1394**

SANDERS, Robert, Glasgow, d.1730. 4746

SANDERS, Robert, 1727–83.
— *Complete English traveller.* 8201
— *Universal family Bible.* 6853

SANDERSON, Richard Cobden-, fl.1920. 4583

SANDERSON, Thomas James Cobden-, 1840–1922 *see also* DOVES PRESS, Hammersmith, 1900–16. 2028 4584 4588a 4589a 4995 **5584–98** 6088
— Bibs. 1:1314g
— Collns. 5597a

SANDERSON, sir William, 1586?–1676. 2208

SANDFORD, Christopher, 1902– *see* BOAR'S HEAD PRESS, Manaton, est. 1931.

SANDLING, Kent–Paper. 1161a

SANDYS, Anthony Frederick Augustus, 1829–1904. 3496 7420a

SANDYS, sir Edwin, 1561–1629. **13145**
— *Relation of religion.* 13145

SANDYS, George, 1578–1644. 12332 **13146–56**
— Bibs. 1:**4581**
— *Christ's passion.* 13150
— Libr. 13155
— Mss. 13149 13154 13156
— *Ovid's Metamorphoses.* 13147–8 13150–3
— *Paraphrase upon the divine poems.* 13146
— *Paraphrase upon the Song of Solomon.* 13154 13156
— Publ. 13148 13151

SANDYS, William, 1792–1874. 8026

SAN GARDE, William Edmonds, 1837–1914–Libr. 3403

SANGORSKI, Francis Longinus, 1875–1912. **5599–602**
— *Omar Khâyyâm.* 5599–600 5602 5778

SANGORSKI AND SUTCLIFFE. 2322 5601

SANSBURY, John, d.1609. 2191

SARE, Richard, d.1723. **5603**

SARGEANT, Waldo, fl.1900. 1229

SAROLEA, Charles, 1870–1953. **13157**
— Bibs. 1:**4581**m
— Mss. 13157
— — Bibs. 1:**4581**m

SARPI, Paolo, 1552–1623. 11501 11506

SARRATT, Herts.–Paper. 1139

SARTORIUS, Francis, 1734–1804. 5611

SARUM BOOKS *see* PRIMERS.

SASSOON, Siegfried Lorraine, 1886–1967–Bibs. 1:**4581**y–2b

SATIN BINDINGS *see* BOOKBINDINGS, SATIN.

SATIRES–Bibs. 1:1999d 2007

SATIRICAL POETRY *see* POETRY, SATIRICAL.

SATURDAY REVIEW. 7838 7894 14282
— Bibs. 1:1716k 3508 5058

SAUMAISE, Claude de, 1588–1653.
— *Defensio regia.* 12331 12395

SAVAGE, Ernest Albert, 1877– . 89

SAVAGE, Richard, d.1743–Bibs. 1:**4583**–b

SAVAGE, William, 1770–1843. 6192 6194

SAVILE, George, 1st marquis of Halifax, 1633–95. **13158–60**
— Bibs. 1:**4584–5**
— *Character of a trimmer.* 13158–9
— Mss. 13158–9

SAVILE, sir Henry, 1549–1622. 1019 13161
— Bibs. 1:4585f
— Libr. 13161
— Mss.–Bibs. 1:4585f
SAVILE, Henry, 1568–1617–Libr. 2635 2642 2886 3354
SAVONAROLA, Girolámo, 1452–98. 952
— Bibs. 1:845
SAVOY–Bibs. 1:1721
SAWSTON, Cambs.–Ptg. see CRAMPTON, John, 1833–1910.
SAWYER, Charles James, 1876–1931. 5604
— Libr. 1:3084; 10067
SAXTON, Christopher, fl.1570–96. 7486 7495 7499 7504
— Bibs. 1:1763
SAYER, Robert, fl.1751–94. 1:1558
SAYERS, Dorothy Leigh (mrs. Fleming), 1893–1947.
— Bibs. 1:4586
— Bndng. 2127
— Documents in the case. 2127
— Letters–Bibs. 1:4586
SAYLE, Charles Edward, 1864–1924. 33
— Bibs. 1:4586a
SCANDANAVIA. 12527
SCARLETT, James Richard, 8th baron Abinger, 1914– –Libr. 1:4654d; 13344
SCARRON, Paul, 1610–60. 9854b
SCATTERGOOD, Antony, 1611–87. 6816 6826
SCHEVEZ, archbp. William, d.1497–Libr. 3284
SCHIFF, Mortimer Leo, 1877–1931–Libr. 2121
SCHIFF, Sydney, 1869?–1944 see HUDSON, Stephen, pseud.
SCHILDERS, Richard, d.1634. 836
— Bibs. 1:1347d 1395
SCHILLER, Benjamin, fl.1695. 3640
SCHILLER, Johann Christoph Friedrich von, 1759–1854. 927 931
— Bibs. 1:823
SCHLOSSER, Leonard Benjamin, 1924– –Libr. 1:4248
SCHOLARTIS PRESS, est. 1926. 5605
— Bibs. 1:1396
SCHOLDERER, Julius Victor, 1880–1971. 67 72
— Bibs. 1:4586g–h
— Type. 6445
SCHOOLBOOKS see also A.B.C. BOOKS; EDUCATION. 3426 8106–17
— Bibs. 1:2277–9
— Collns. 8111 8114
— Ireland–Bibs. 1:2278
— Wales. 8111

— 1475–1700. 8106–7 8109–11 8113 8115
— 1701–1800. 8108 8112 8117
— 1801–1900. 8114 8117
SCHOOL LIBRARIES see LIBRARIES, SCHOOL.
SCHOOLMASTER PRINTER, St. Albans, fl.1479–86. 5606–7 6055
— Berners' Book of St. Albans. 5607
SCHOOL PRESS, 1832. 5608–9
SCHOOLS see EDUCATION.
SCHOPENHAUER, Arthur, 1788–1860. 10972
SCHWERDT, Charles Francis George Richard, 1862–1939–Libr. 8193–4
SCIENCE see also ALCHEMY; ASTROLOGY; BOTANY; GEOLOGY; MEDICINE; NATURAL HISTORY. 8118–60
— Bibliographers. 8144 8153
— Bibs. 1:1947 2217 2279d–f
— Bksllng. 8144–5 8153
— Collns. 2812 3015 3023 3235 8123 8127 8139
— Mss. 8121–2 8148 8159
— — Bibs. 1:2279e–f
— Newspapers. 1776 1779 7694 8118 8144 8153 8155
— — Bibs. 1:1849 1947 2938
— Publ. 8144 8153
SCIENCE AND BIBLIOGRAPHY see also BIBLIOGRAPHY AS SCIENCE. 221 8144 8153 8159
SCIENCE FICTION. 792
— Bibs. 1:1669 1711 1723m
SCIENTIFIC LIBRARIES see LIBRARIES, SCIENTIFIC.
SCIENTIFIC SOCIETIES. 8144
'SCILENS'. 2:1018k
SCILLY ISLES–Maps–Bibs. 1:1818p–q
SCLATER, William, fl.1626–60–Bibs. 1:4587
SCOGAN, John, fl.1565–Bibs. 1:4587m
SCORPION PRESS, 20th cent. 5610
SCOT, John, Edinburgh, fl.1552–71. 1591
SCOTLAND see also BOOK TRADE, LISTS–Scotland; PRINTING IN GAELIC. For Scottish books arranged by period see BOOKS–Scotland. 1552–741
— Agriculture. 6735
— Almanacs. 1568 1642 1654 1699
— Ballads. 1560 1635 12737 12739
— — Bibs. 1:1460b 1468
— Bible. 1565 1572 1703
— — Ptg. 1698
— — O.T. PSALMS. 1569 1651
— — — — Bibs. 1:1513
— — N.T. 8087
— Bibs. 1:965–1009 2290
— Bndng. see also BOOKBINDINGS, SCOTTISH. 1:712e 725

SCOTLAND–Bndng. 1564 1581–2 1590 1592 1606 1609 1615 1620 1636
— Book collecting. 2267
— Bksllng. 1556 1604 1624 1627 1629 4605
— Broadsides. 1588 1638
— Censorship. 1570
— Chapbooks. 6991
— — Bibs. 1:1540a 1545
— Conjuring–Bibs. 1:2139
— Copyright. 1552 1599 1680
— Drama–Bibs. 1:1586 1652g
— Engraving. 1593 1611
— Heraldry. 7361–2
— History–Bibs. 1:965–6
— Hymns. 1575
— Illustrated books. 1631
— — Bibs. 1:1754k
— Librs. 1586 1628 1632–3 1635 2281 2418 2459 3330
— Library catalogues–Bibs. 1:1760f 1760j 1760p
— Maps. 1607
— — Bibs. 1:968 1813d–17
— Mss. 1560 1635
— — Bibs. 1:1468
— Music. 1621 1625
— — Bibs. 1:1827k
— Newspapers. 1557 1570 1595 1598
— — 1601– –Bibs. 1:1930–4
— — 1601–1700. 1656
— — 1701–1800. 1600 1690 1693 3462
— — — Bibs. 1:1934x–5a
— — 1801–1900.
— — — Bibs. 1:1936–44
— Pamphlets.
— — Collns. 3258
— Paper. 1616 1626 1710 3717 3776
— Poetry. 1608 1637
— — 1475–1700–Bibs. 1:2034
— Prayer books. 1554 1584
— Ptg. 1567 1585 1589 1603 1610 1701 4746
— — Bibs. 1:968 970
— — 1475–1500. 1555
— — 1475–1640. 264 1561–3 1591 1619 1624 1627 1629 6063 6081 6124
— — 1701–1800. 1574 1624 1627 1629 6121a 8099
— — 1801–1900. 5614 8099
— Publ. 1604 1617 1630 5361b
— Roadbooks and itineraries–Bibs. 1:975–7
— Sermons. 1602
— Statutes. 11321
— Topography–Bibs. 1:968
— Type. 1605 6575 6583 6637 6661 6670 6677
— Type specimens. 6687
— Watermarks. 3714 3732

— Witchcraft–Bibs. 1:2290
— CHURCH OF SCOTLAND. 1:1514
— — Book of canons, 1636. 1594
— — Book of common order see BOOK OF COMMON ORDER.
— — GENERAL ASSEMBLY. 1579
— — — The protestation–Bibs. 1:714f
— — LIBRARY–Collns. 1:442
— GENERAL TYPOGRAPHICAL ASSOCIATION see GENERAL TYPO-GRAPHICAL ASSOCIATION OF SCOTLAND.
— INSTITUTE OF CHARTERED ACCOUNTANTS see INSTITUTE OF CHARTERED ACCOUNTANTS OF SCOTLAND, Edinburgh.
— NATIONAL LIBRARY, Edinburgh. 1725–30
— — Collns. 1:367 442 466–7 488 712e 719a 1266m–n 1506 1512–13 1546 1612 1733 1942a 3567; 2:247 1109; 1632 1728 1730 2841 2995 3050 4066 4073 7097 7099 7188 8718 9033 9103 11101
— — ADVOCATES' LIBRARY. 1726–7 5574 8718 11250
— ROYAL COLLEGE OF PHYSICIANS see ROYAL COLLEGE OF PHYSICIANS, Scotland.
— SIGNET LIBRARY see SOCIETY OF WRITERS TO H.M. SIGNET, Edinburgh. LIBRARY.
— UNITED FREE CHURCH. COLLEGE. LIBRARY–Collns. 1:442
SCOTS BOOKS PUBLISHED ABROAD see also BRITISH BOOKS PUBLISHED ABROAD. 1562 1596
SCOTS BRIDGE, Herts.–Paper. 1139
SCOTS MAGAZINE. 4059–60
SCOTS WHITE PAPER MANUFACTORY, 1695. 1710 1712
SCOTT, Alexander, 1525?–84? 11804
— Bibs. 1:4588–9
SCOTT, Alexander John, 1768–1840. 3974
SCOTT, John, 1710–82.
— Bibs. 1:4589x–90
— Elegy. 13162
— Letters–Bibs. 1:4589x
SCOTT, John, 1st earl of Eldon, 1751–1838. 9233
SCOTT, John, 1774–1827. 5611
SCOTT, John, 1784–1821. 800
— Bibs. 1:4592
— Mss.–Bibs. 1:4592
SCOTT, John, 1830–1903–Libr. 1:4149; 2618
SCOTT, Michael, 1175?–1234? 13163
— Bibs. 1:4595
— Physionomia. 13163

SCOTT, sir Michael, fl.1609.
— *Philosopher's banquet.* 670
SCOTT, Michael, 1789–1835. **13164**
— Letters. 13164
SCOTT, Robert, fl.1633–1706. 3471 **5612**
SCOTT, Sarah (Robinson), 1723–95. **13165**
— Bibs. 1:**4595k**
— *History of Mecklenburg.* 6151
— *Millenium hall.* 13165
— Ptg. 6151
SCOTT, sir Walter, 1771–1832. 487 782 1633
  2322 3440 3886 5775 7243 9011 **13166–243**
— *Ancient and modern British drama.* 13167
— *Anne of Geierstein.* 13168
— *The antiquary.* 13221
— *Apology for tales of terror.* 3884–5 3888–9
  11981
— Ballads. 1635 13235
— *Battle of Sempach.* 13212
— Bibs. 1:672 **4595u–614b**
— *Black dwarf.* 13175
— *Border antiquities.* 13232
— *Border minstrelsy.* 3036 13166 13216 13220
— *Bride of Lammermoor.* 13179
— *Chronicles of the Canongate.* 13208
— Collns. 13194 13197 13203
— *Count Robert.* 13204
— *English minstrelsy.* 13177
— *Eothen.* 13191
— *Fortunes of Nigel.* 13205
— Illus. 13173 13176
— *Ivanhoe.* 13168
— *Journal.* 13207 13213
— *Kenilworth.* 13178
— *Lady of the lake.* 13211
— *Lay of the last minstrel.* 13198
— Letters. 12034 13190 13215 13229
— — Bibs. 1:4609
— *Letters on demonology.* 13199
— Libr. 1:1544b; 1635 13182 13234 13236
  13240 13732
— *Life of Napoleon*–Bibs. 1:4610
— *Marmion.* 5250 13169 13227
— Mss. 1635 13168 13170 13175 13179
  13181 13183–4 13193 13199 13212
  13218–19 13223–4 13230 13233 13235
— — Bibs. 1:4611
— *Old mortality.* 13202
— *Paul's letters.* 11009
— *Peveril of the Peak.* 13225
— *Pirate.* 13214 13230
— *Poetry contained in the novels.* 13189
— Ptg. 13186 13201 13208 13220 13243
— Publ. 4403 5250 13205 13210 13227
  13232 13242
— *Redgauntlet.* 13184 13186
— *Shakespeare's Works.* 2:706 802; 13237
— *Shepherd's tale.* 13200

— *Siege of Malta.* 13219
— *Swift's Works.* 13798
— *Tales of my landlord.* 13174
— Text. 13178 13191 13198 13200 13207
  13213 13228
— *Vision of don Roderick.* 13210 13238
— — Bibs. 1:4612
— *Waverley.* 2342 13168 13181 13195 13206
  13231
— *Waverley novels.* 464 3442 3886 13172–3
  13209 13224 13233 13239 13241
— — Bibs. 1:4603 4611 4613
— *Woodstock.* 13226
SCOTTISH EPISCOPAL CHURCH.
  THEOLOGICAL HALL. 1:442
— — FORBES LIBRARY–Collns. 1:442
SCOTTISH HISTORY–Bibs. 1:965–6
SCOTTISH LITERATURE–Bibs. 1:41
SCOTTISH TYPOGRAPHICAL ASSOCIA-
  TION, est. 1853. **5613–14**
SCOURFIELD, sir John Henry, 1808–
  76–Bibs. 1:**4615**
SCRAPER PRESSES *see* PRESSES,
  SCRAPER.
SCRIBAL TRANSCRIPTS *see* TRAN-
  SCRIPTS, SCRIBAL.
SCRIBES *see also* CRANE, Ralph,
  fl.1575–1632; KNIGHT, Edward,
  fl.1624–32; WOODHOUSE, Richard,
  1788–1834. 12433 12718 14540
SCRIBNER, Charles, 1854–1930–Libr.
  1:3982g 3983; 11838–9
SCRIBNER, publ., New York. 1:4805b
SCRIPTURE CATECHISM, 1801. 1952
SCROPE, William, 1772–1852. 5250
SCRYMGEOUR, James, Glasgow, fl.1803–4.
  4746
SCRYMGEOUR, John, Glasgow, fl.1803–9.
  4746
SCUNTHORPE. PUBLIC LIBRARIES–
  Collns. 2:137
SEA, PRINTING AT *see* PRINTING,
  SHIPBOARD.
SEAGAR, Francis, fl.1549–1611. **13244–5**
— *Album amicorum.* 13244
— *Certain psalms.* 13245
SEAGER, John, fl.1614–56–Bibs. 1:**4616**
SEAMAN, Lazarus, d.1675–Libr. 279 2265
  3660 3666 3671
SEARCH, Daniel, fl.1710. **5615**
SEBRIGHT, sir John, 1725–94. 8981
*SECOND BOOK OF THE RHYMER'S CLUB,
  1894.* 8030
'SECOND HAND'. 3607
SECOND MAIDEN'S TRAGEDY. 7118 7145
SECRET OF SECRETS, 1572. 649
SECRET PRINTING *see* PRINTING,
  SECRET.

Vol. **1** = *Bibliographies*   **2** = *Shakespeare*   **4** = 1–8221   **5** = 8222–14616

SECRETS. 8120
— Bibs. 1:2100
SEDGWICK, Adam, 1785–1873–Bibs.
  1:**4616f**
SEDGLEY, Richard, Oxford, 1647–1719.
  5616
SEDLEY, sir Charles, 1639?–1701.
— Bibs. 1:**4617**
— There was a little man. 5808
SEIZIN PRESS, 1927–39. **5617–18**
— Bibs. 1:**1396t**
SELBOURNE SOCIETY. LIBRARY–Collns.
  1:5081
SELDEN, John, 1584–1654. **13246–9**
— Libr. 2266 13247–8
— Mare clausum. 13249
— Mss. 13246
— Publ. 13249
— Table talk. 13246
SELKIRKSHIRE–Bibs. 1:1007
SELLER, John, fl.1667–1700. 6550
— Atlas Anglicanus. 6551
SELOUS, Edmund, fl.1905–31–Bibs. 1:**4618**
SEMPHILL, sir James, 1566–1625.
— Packman's paternoster. 13881
SENECA, Lucius Annaeus, d.65. 889 898
  11069
— De senectute see CAXTON, William,
  1422?–91. Tully of old age and friendship.
SENEFELDER, Johann Nepomuc Franz
  Aloys, 1771–1834. 6123 6188 6200 6202
  6227
SENTENTIAE. 654
SEPTUAGINT see BIBLE. O.T. SEPT-
  UAGINT.
SEQUELS–Bibs. 1:1662 1666 1670
SEQUEL TO DON JUAN. 9176
SEQUENCE NOVELS see NOVELS,
  SEQUENCE.
SERBIA see SHAKESPEARE, William,
  1564–1616–WORKS IN SERBIA.
SERES, William, d.1579? **5620** 8056
SERIAL FICTION see FICTION, SERIAL.
SERIALIZATION see BOOKS IN PARTS.
SERMON NECESSARY FOR THESE TIMES,
  1636. 683
SERMONS. **8161–5**
— Bibs. 1:920 **2060–4**
— Publ. 10227
— Scotland. 1602
SERVICE AND PATON'S ILLUSTRATED
  ENGLISH LIBRARY. 7426
— Bibs. 1:1746
SESSIONS, Mary, York, fl.1886–99. 5621
SESSIONS, William, York, 1843–86
  5621
'SET'. 3589
SET-OFF. 4289 4336

SETTE OF ODD VOLUMES, est. 1878. 462
  1768
— Bib. 1:**1396v–w**
SETTLE, Dionyse, fl.1577.
— True report of the last voyage by Frobisher.
  8208a 8209a
SETTLE, Elkanah, 1648–1724. 3475 5622–6
  13250–2
— Bibs. 1:**4619–21a**
— Bndng. 5622 5624–6
— Collns. 5622 5625
— Empress of Morocco. 13250
— Fairy queen. 13252
— — Bibs. 1:4621
SEVEN ACRES PRESS, Long Crendon,
  1926–33. 4825–6
— Bibs. 1:1339
SEVEN DEADLY SINS. 553
SEVEN SAGES OF ROME, 1798. 6990
SEVEN SOVEREIGN MEDICINES, 1603. 682
SEVEN VIRTUES. 565
SEVEN WISE MASTERS, 1717. 1649
SEWARD, Anna, 1747–1809. 1430 **13253**
— Letters. 13253
SEWELL, Anna, 1820–78. **13254–5**
— Black beauty. 13254–5
— Bndng. 13254
SEWELL, George, d.1726.
— Ovid's Metamorphoses. 890a
SEXTON, Joseph, Limerick, d.1782. 1842a
SEYMOUR, Robert, 1800?–36. **5628** 9983
— Dickens' Pickwick papers. 9982
SEYSSELL, archbp. Claude de, 1450–1520.
  6017a
SHACKLETON, Mary, 1758–1826. 8972
SHADRACH, Azariah, 1774–1844–Bibs.
  1:**4622**
SHADWELL, Thomas, 1642?–92. **13256**
— Enchanted island. 10368
— On the British princes. 13256
SHAFTESBURY, Dorset–Ptg. see HIGH
  HOUSE PRESS, est. 1924.
SHAFTESBURY, Anthony Ashley Cooper, 3d
  earl, 1671–1713 see COOPER, Anthony
  Ashley, 3d earl of Shaftesbury, 1671–1713.
SHAKESPEARE, William, 1564–1616. 2299
  2322 2343 3509 6791 7159
— ACT AND SCENE DIVISION. 2:582 614
  862 864–5 1211 1447
— ADAPTATIONS. 1563 4621
— — Bibs. 2:205–6 213 217
— ADAPTIONS FOR CHILDREN. 7026
— — Bibs. 2:232
— ALL'S WELL THAT ENDS WELL–Text.
  2:**1080–5**
— — — 2.1.110 (715). 2:1067
— — — 3.2.113 (1519). 2:1081
— — — 4.2.38 (2063). 2:1080–1 1083–5

Vol. 1 = Bibliographies   2 = Shakespeare   4 = 1–8221   5 = 8222–14616

SHAKESPEARE, William, 1564–1616.
HENRY V–Text. 2:3.17 (839). 2:937 1310
1321 1323–6
— — — 3.3.35 (1294). 2:1328
— HENRY VI. 2:428 1200 1340 1673 1877
— 1 HENRY VI. 2:765
— — Bibs. 2:1335
— — Text. 2:1340–2
— — — 1.5.29 (625). 2:1067
— 2 HENRY VI. 2:441
— — Ptg. 2:1295 1356
— — Proofsheet. 2:1355–6
— — Text. 2:909 1200 1241 1350–70
— — — 1.4.74–5 (700–1). 2:1370
— 3 HENRY VI. 2:441
— — Text. 2:909 1200 1354 1357 1360
1362–3 1366–7 1369 1380
— HENRY VIII. 2:876 943 1877
— — Text. 2:1385–6
— — — 1.1.72 (122–3). 2:1385
— ILLUSTRATIONS. 2:58 708 730 743 748;
5909
— ILLUSTRATORS see also ABBEY, E.A.;
BLAKE, W.; BOYS, alderman;
CRUIKSHANK, G.; DEWITT, J.;
PEACHAM, H. 2:710 716 782
— INDEXES. 2:15–24
— JOHN see KING JOHN.
— JULIUS CAESAR. 2:371 704 1880; 4873
— — Bibs. 2:1395
— — Text. 2:843b 1398–407
— — — 2.1.83 (708). 2:1399
— — — 2:186–228 (713–886). 2:1405
— — — 3.1.174 (1395). 2:1398 1400
— — — 4.3.129–66 (2114–60). 2:1405
— KING JOHN. 2:1200; 756 12273
— — Ptg. 2:1417
— — Text. 2:595 853 1415–17
— KING LEAR. 2:(147) 381 532
— — Bibs. 2:1425
— — Ptg. 2:1438 1442 1449–50 1457 1459
1462–3
— — Proofsheet. 2:585
— — Text. 2:588 843b 919 951 961 1200
1427–72 1680
— — — 1.1.173 (184). 2:1463
— — — 1.1.271 (293) 2:1432
— — — 1.2.21 (355). 2:1445
— — — 2.4.135 (1411). 2:1466
— — — 2.4.170 (1451). 2:1455
— — — 2.4.289 SD (1586). 2:1466
— — — 3.2.1–3 (1656–8). 2:1454
— — — 3.7.65 (2137). 2:1441
— — — 4.1.10 (2189). 2:1452
— — — 4.2.57. 2:1460
— — — 4.3.21. 2:1430
— — — 4.6.163 (2602–3). 2:1453
— — — 5.3.17 (2957). 2:1458

— — — 5.3.320–7 (3295–302). 2:1472
— LOVE'S LABOURS LOST. 2:563 680 1710
— — Copies–Kean. 2:1480
— — Text. 2:1069 1480–92
— — — 2.1.115–27 (610–22). 2:1482
— — — 2.1.195 (693). 2:1482
— — — 4.3.177 (1515). 2:1490
— — — 4.3.255 (1574). 2:1486 1490–1
— — — 5.2.67 (1957). 2:1484 1489
— — — 5.2.678 (2627). 2:1481
— Libr. 2:1005
— LUCRECE. 2:276 418 1942 1945
— — Bibs. 2:1930
— MACBETH. 2:226 371–2 535 573 769
— — Bibs. 2:1500
— — Text. 2:843b 953 1070 1200 1505–23
— — — 4.1.97 (1641). 2:1514
— — — 4.3.34 (1853). 2:1506
— — — 4.3.107 (1934). 2:1521
— — — 5.3.55 (2278). 2:1509–12
— MANUSCRIPTS. 1:1606b; 2:370–1 885a
901 936
— — Bibs. 2:185 212 223
— — Collns. 2:321
— MEASURE FOR MEASURE. 2:372 573
— — Text. 2:853 1530–5
— — — 1.2.135 (222). 2:1533
— — — 1.3.43 (335). 2:1534
— — — 2.1.39 (493). 2:1531 1533
— — — 3.1.94 (1309). 2:1530 1535
— — — 3.1.97 (1312). 2:1535
— MERCHANT OF VENICE. 2:381
— — Bibs. 2:1542
— — Ptg. 2:1233 1551–2
— — Text. 2:1547–52
— — — 2.1.35 (553). 2:1550
— — — 3.2.206 (1551). 2:1548
— — — 3.5.82 (1885). 2:1545
— MERRY WIVES OF WINDSOR. 2:381 411
1200; 5550
— — Text. 2:853 876 953 1069 1155 1351
1560–73
— — — 1.3.93 (375). 2:1563
— — — 1.3.111 (393). 2:1560
— — — 2.1.228 (749). 2:1562
— — — 2.2. 2:1585
— — — 5.5. 2:1566 1572
— MIDSUMMER NIGHT'S DREAM. 2:381
— — Ptg. 2:949 1587
— — Text. 2:1070 1580–7
— — — 2.1.77 (452). 2:1585
— — — 5.1.4–16 (1796–808). 2:1584
— — — 5.1.59 (1856). 2:1581–2
— MUCH ADO ABOUT NOTHING. 5658
5660
— — Ptg. 2:1295 1298 1598
— — Text. 2:859 1595–8
— — — 4.1.145–60 (1807–20). 2:1596

Vol. 1 = Bibliographies   2 = Shakespeare   4 = 1–8221   5 = 8222–14616

SHAKESPEARE, William, 1564–1616.
—SIGNATURES—Florio. 2:1000a 1012
1016 1022 1027 1031
— — Golding. 2:1018
— — Jewitt. 2:1030
— — Lambarde. 2:1038–42 1044 1046
— — Ovid. 2:1011–13
— — *Pageant of popes.* 2:1033
— — Plutarch. 2:1030
— — Stephens. 2:1028
— — Will. 2:1002 1020 1024–5 1027 1035–6
1043
— *SONNETS.* 2:1029–a 1942 **1960–81**; 5853
11584
— — Bibs. 2:1960–2
— SOURCES–Bibs. 2:77 205
— *TAMING OF THE SHREW.* 2:1877
— — Text. 2:**1750–7**
—*TEMPEST, THE.* 10368
— — Text. 2:843b 1070 **1765–78**
— — — 1.2.100 (197). 2:1773
— — — 1.2.175 (285). 2:1765
— — — 1.2.269 (396). 2:1766
— — — 3.1.15 (1250). 2:1767 1772 1774–5
1777–8
— TEXTUAL STUDIES *see also* Text *under
titles of individual texts.* 2:**830–964**
— — Collected emendations. 2:**1060–72**
— THESES *see* — DISSERTATIONS.
— *TIMON OF ATHENS.*
— — Text. 2:**1785–90**
— — — 3.2.70 (1044). 2:1790
— — — 3.4.112 (1247). 2:1785–6 1788–9
—*TITUS ANDRONICUS.* 2:1877; 6181
— — Ptg. 2:949 1805 1810
— — Text. 2:909 **1800–12**
— — — 1.1. 2:1804 1809
— — — 1.1.18 (25). 2:1804
— TRANSLATIONS *see* — WORKS IN—.
— *TROILUS AND CRESSIDA.* 2:943
— — Bibs. 2:1815
— — Ptg. 2:(147) 502 532 580 1787 1820
1827 1829
— — Text. 2:588 919 951 953 **1820–31**
— — — 2.2. 2:1826
— — — 3.3.3 (1852). 2:1821
— — — 5.7.11 (3480–1). 2:1826
— *TWELFTH NIGHT.* 2:371 563 1200
— — Text. 2:1064a **1840–3**
— — — 1.1.5 (9). 2:1840
— *TWO GENTLEMEN OF VERONA.* 2:563
— — Text. 2:853 876 **1850–1**
— *TWO NOBLE KINSMEN see* FLETCHER,
John, 1579–1625. *Two noble kinsmen.*
— *VENUS AND ADONIS.* 2:276 418 943
1936 1941–4
— — Bibs. 2:1932
— VERSIFICATION. 2:841

— WATERMARKS. 2:401–2 433 527
— *WINTER'S TALE.* 2:372 573; 9744 9749
— — Text. 2:853 876 **1860–3**
— WORKS *see also titles of individual works.*
2:**359–74**; 5869–70 11390 11399 11437
11444 11470 11480 11489 11503 13101
13237
— — Bibs. 2:**170–252**
— — Bndng. 5550
— — Prices. 2:281 360a 510 512 520
— — Printers. 2:360 1942
— WORKS, COLLECTED–Bibs. 1:**34a** 174
175a–b
— WORKS IN ARGENTINA–Bibs. 2:146
— WORKS IN AUSTRALASIA–Bibs. 2:39
— WORKS IN BRASIL–Bibs. 2:104 135 144
— WORKS IN CROATIA–Bibs. 2:125
— WORKS IN CZECHOSLOVAKIA–Bibs.
2:145 149 1586
— WORKS IN DENMARK–Bibs. 2:78
— WORKS IN FRANCE–Bibs. 2:62 109 138
— WORKS IN GERMANY–Bibs. 2:56a 78a
87a 134
— WORKS IN GREEK. 2:71
— — Bibs. 2:139
— WORKS IN HEBREW–Bibs. 2:94
— WORKS IN HUNGARY–Bibs. 2:56 117
— WORKS IN ICELAND–Bibs. 2:74
— WORKS IN INDIA–Bibs. 2:31 68 128a
— WORKS IN IRELAND. 2:366 704 758
— — Bibs. 2:204 218 231
— WORKS IN ISRAEL *see also* —WORKS
IN HEBREW. 2:148
— WORKS IN ITALY–Bibs. 2:76 133
— WORKS IN JAPAN–Bibs. 2:66 73 75
— WORKS IN LATIN. 2:71
— WORKS IN NORWAY–Bibs. 2:84 92
— WORKS IN POLAND–Bibs. 2:91 140–1
— WORKS IN PORTUGAL–Bibs. 2:129
— WORKS IN RUMANIA–Bibs. 2:124
— WORKS IN RUSSIA–Bibs. 2:131–a 143
149a
— WORKS IN SERBIA–Bibs. 2:63
— WORKS IN SPAIN–Bibs. 2:57 64 365
— WORKS IN SWEDEN–Bibs. 2:93
— WORKS IN SWITZERLAND–Bibs. 2:116
— WORKS IN TURKEY–Bibs. 2:119
— WORKS IN UNITED STATES. 2:707 719
749
— —Bibs. 2:132 134 170 222 280
— WORKS IN YIDDISH–Bibs. 2:95
SHAKESPEARE ASSOCIATION FACSIMILES.
2:436
SHAKESPEARE HEAD PRESS, Stratford-
upon-Avon, 1904–42. **5629–39** 6319 6490
6502
— Bibs. 1:**1397a**
— Type. 5634

Vol. **1** = *Bibliographies*   **2** = *Shakespeare*   **4** = 1–8221   **5** = 8222–14616

SHAKESPEARE MEMORIAL EXHIBI-
TION, Whitechapel art gallery, London.
2:1005
SHAKESPEARE MEMORIAL LIBRARY,
Stratford-upon-Avon. 2:322
— Collns. 2:31
SHAKESPEARE PRESS, 1819. 4128a 4132
5288 9967
SHAKESPEARE'S BIRTHPLACE TRUST,
Stratford-upon-Avon. 2:326
— LIBRARY–Collns. 1:544; 2:185 212 223
381
SHAKESPEARE TERCENTENARY–Bibs.
2:54
SHAKESPEARIAN SOCIETIES. 2:61
SHAMROCK, THE–Bibs. 1:4082j
SHARED PRINTING *see* PRINTING,
SHARED.
SHARP, Cecil James, 1859–1924–Libr. 3139
SHARP, sir Cuthbert, 1781–1849–Bibs.
1:4623
SHARP, Hugh Frederick Bower,
1897?–1937–Libr. 2995
SHARP, John, 1572?–1648?
— *Cursus theologicus.* 10597
SHARP, Thomas, 1770–1841.
— *Dissertation on the pageants.* 7225
SHARP, William, 1855–1905.
— *Sonnets of this century.* 8025
SHARPE, Charles Kirkpatrick,
1781?–1851–Libr. 6781
SHARPE, Henry, Warwick, fl.1830. 11880
SHARPE, John, 1777–1860. 5640
SHARPE, Lancelot, 1774–1851. 13257
SHARPE, Richard, fl.1502–15. 10536
SHARPHAM, Edward, fl.1607. 13258
SHARPS MILL, Sussex. 1412
SHARROCK, Robert, 1630–84.
— *History of the propagation of vegetables.* 6737
SHAW, Cuthbert, 1738–71. 13259–60
SHAW, George Bernard, 1856–1950. 778
7234 13261–81
— Bibs. 1:684 4625–45
— Bksllng. 13275
— Collns. 380a 13268–70
— *Four farthing candles.* 13259
— Handwr. 13281
— *The heretics.* 13261 13265
— — Bibs. 1:4628
— *John Bull's other island.* 13267
— Mss. 13270–1 13278
— — Bibs. 1:4634
— *Passion, poison.* 13263
— Ptg. 6098 6114 8754 13262 13272 13276
— Publ. 4858a 5527–8 5705
— *Socialism for millionaires.* 13266
— Text. 13289
— *War issues.* 13277

SHAW, Henry, 1800–73. 6229
SHAW, John Byam Lister, 1872–1919.
7408
SHAW, Thomas Edward, formerly Lawrence,
1888–1935 *see* LAWRENCE, Thomas
Edward, afterwards Shaw, 1888–1935.
SHAW, Vero Kemball, fl.1879–1913. 7089
SHAW, sir William Napier, 1854–1945–Bibs.
1:4636
SHAW AND SONS, est. 1750. 5641
SHAYLOR, Joseph, 1844–1923. 3636
SHEARDOWN, Robert, Louth, fl.1789.
1958b
SHEARES, William, fl.1623–62. 12173
SHEARING, Joseph, *pseud., see* LONG,
Gabrielle Margaret Vere (Campbell),
1888–1952.
'SHE' BIBLE, 1611 *see* BIBLE–Ver-
sions–'She'.
SHEEHAN, bp. Richard Alphonsus,
1845–1915–Libr. 2714
SHEEHY-SKEFFINGTON, Francis,
1878–1916 *see* SKEFFINGTON, Francis
Sheehy-, 1878–1916.
SHEFFARD, William, fl.1621–30–Bibs.
1:1873c
SHEFFIELD, Yorks. *see also* BOOK TRADE,
LISTS–Sheffield. 1442h
— Bibs. 1:950
— Ptg. *see* GARNET, John, fl.1736–53.
— Type *see* STEPHENSON, BLAKE AND
CO., est. 1819; STEPHENSON, sir Henry,
1826–1904.
— PUBLIC LIBRARIES–Collns. 1:1149 1487
2715 3265
— RUSKIN MUSEUM *see* RUSKIN
MUSEUM, Sheffield.
— UNIVERSITY. LIBRARY–Collns. 1:505
SHEFFIELD, Henry North Holroyd, 3d earl
of, 1832–1909 *see* HOLROYD, Henry
North, 3d earl of Sheffield, 1832–1909.
SHEFFIELD, John, 3d earl of Mulgrave,
1648–1721.
— *Tragedy of Julius Caesar.* 2:1404
SHELBURNE, sir William Petty, 2d earl of,
1737–1805 *see* PETTY, sir William, 1st
marquis of Lansdowne, 1757–1805.
SHELDON, Ralph, 1623–84.
— Libr. 2:506 533 1820
— Mss. 3014
SHELLEY, Harriet (Westbrook),
d.1816–Bibs. 1:4640
SHELLEY, Jane (Gibson), lady, d.1899.
— *Shelley and Mary.* 13360
SHELLEY, Mary Wollstonecraft (Godwin),
1797–1851 *see* GODWIN, Mary Woll-
stonecraft (mrs. P. B. Shelley), 1797–
1851.

SHELLEY, Percy Bysshe, 1792–1822. 2322
9170 **13282–370** 14406
— *Adonais.* 766 13304–5 13331
— — Bibs. 1:4652a
— Bibs. 1:54–5 672 **4641–58**
— Collns. 13282 13299
— *Dante's Convivio.* 13358
— *Endymion.* 13338
— *Ginevra.* 13345
— Handwr. 13342
— *Hellas.* 13303–5
— *History of a tour.* 13287
— Illus. 13331
— *Invocation to misery.* 13365
— Letters. 759 7333 7338 13294 13301 13324
13335 13339 13363
— — Bibs. 1:4653
— *Letter to Ellenborough.* 13286
— Libr. 13292 13319–20
— *Magnetic lady.* 13289
— Mss. 780 13288–9 13295 13307 13313
13323 13334 13340 13344 13346–8 13352
13357 13359 13365–7
— — Bibs. 1:4647 4652 4654 4654d 4657
— *Music, when soft voices die.* 13355
— *Necessity of atheism.* 13286
— *Ode to a nightingale.* 13348
— *Original poetry by Victor.* 13286
— *Ozymandias.* 13351
— *Philosophical view of reform.* 13298
— *Plato's Symposium.* 13293 13329 13332
— *Poems*–Bibs. 1:4655
— *Poetical works.* 13284 13367
— *Posthumous fragments.* 13286 13361
— *Posthumous poems.* 13306 13321 13349
13353
— *Prometheus unbound.* 13354
— *Proposals for an association.* 13314
— Publ. 5226 13294 13310 13328 13333
13351
— *Queen Mab.* 13285 13296–7 13327 13350
— *Recollection.* 13308
— *Revolt of Islam.* 13290 13315–16
— *Sadak the wanderer.* 13322
— *Stanzas written in dejection.* 13288 13318
— *Tasso.* 13356
— Text. 13285 13287 13293 13296 13298
13303 13308 13312 13315–17 13326 13329
13332 13334 13341 13353 13355–6 13362
13364–7 13369
— *To Constantia.* 13317 13370
— *True story.* 13309
— *Una favola.* 13366
— *Vindication of natural diet.* 13286
— *Wandering Jew.* 13333
SHELLEY-ROLLS, sir John Courton, bart.,
1871– *see* ROLLS, sir John Courton
Shelley-, bart., 1871–.

SHELLEY SOCIETY, 1886–92–Bibs. 1:4642a
SHELMERDINE, Thomas, 1698–1712. 5642
SHELTON, Thomas, fl.1612–20.
— *Don Quixote.* 966–8 970 3854 3857–8
SHELTON, Thomas, 1601–50?
— *Tachygraphy.* 8176
SHENSTONE, William, 1714–63. 3912
13371–9
— Bibs. 1:**4660**
— Letters. 13372
— Libr. 13371
— *Miscellany.* 13377–8
— Mss. 13377–9
— *Pastoral ballad.* 13379
SHEPHERD, Alfred, 1851–1940–Libr. 3056
SHEPHERD, Henry Savile, fl.1835.
— *Poetical remains.* 9246
— *The schoolmistress.* 13375–6
SHEPHERD, Joseph, fl.1858–92. 3969
SHEPHERD, Luke, fl.1548.
— *John Bon and mast Person.* 629
SHEPHERD, Richard Herne, 1842–95.
13380–1 13954 13961
— Bibs. 1:4901
SHEPPARD, John ('Jack'), 1702–24–Bibs.
1:**4660a**
— Mss.–Bibs. 1:4460a
SHERBORN, Charles William, 1831–1912.
5643
SHERBURNE, sir Edward, 1616–1702–Bibs.
1:**4661**
SHERIDAN, Frances (Chamberlaine),
1724–66. **13382**
— Bibs. 1:**4662**
— *History of Nourjahad.* 13382
SHERIDAN, Richard Brinsley, 1751–1816.
7279 **13383–412**
— *Authentic copy of a letter.* 13391
— Bibs. 1:1597 **4663–9**
— *The camp.* 13401
— *The critic.* 13383–4 13399 13401 13406
— *The duenna.* 13388 13400 13405 13407
— Mss. 2319 13404 13408–12
— *The rivals.* 13385 13395 13402
— *Robinson Crusoe.* 13403
— *St. Patrick's day.* 13387 13411
— *School for scandal.* 2319 13386 13388 13393
13396–8 13408 13410 13412
— — Bibs. 1:4669
— Text. 13385 13393 13395–6 13398 13401
SHERIDAN, Thomas, 1687–1738.
— *Inventory of dean swift's goods.* 13760–1
SHERIDAN, Thomas, 1719–88–Bibs. 1:**4673**
SHERLEY, sir Thomas, 1564–1628.
— *True discourse of the late voyage.* 7629
SHERLOCK, William, 1641?–1707.
— *Letter from a clergyman.* 13160
SHERMAN, Thomas, fl.1671–84. 8948

SIDNEY, sir Philip, 1554–86. **13423–43**
— *Alexander's Supplement to Arcadia.* 8246–7
— *Arcadia.* 11001 13423–5 13427–9 13434 13437 13439–40
— — Bibs. 1:4683 4687–9a
— *Astrophel and Stella.* 13435
— Bibs. 1:**4683–9d**
— Collns. 13431–2
— *Defence of Leicester.* 13426
— *Defence of poesy.* 13441
— Letters. 13443
— — Bibs. 1:4689d
— Libr. 13436 13438
— Mss. 13424–6 13428 13441–2
— *Paraphrase of psalms.* 13442
— Ptg. 13429 13424
— Text. 13427 13437
SIEGBURG. STADTISCHE BÜCHEREI. 5653
SIGNATURE. 1:99; 4487
SIGNATURES. 267 6248 6252 6261–2 6264 6270 13619
— Bibliogr. descr. 97 128 254
—, CANCEL. 6152
SIGNED BINDINGS see BOOKBINDINGS, SIGNED.
SIGNED EDITIONS see EDITIONS, SIGNED.
SIGNET LIBRARY, Edinburgh see SOCIETY OF WRITERS TO H.M. SIGNET, Edinburgh.
SIGNET PRESS, Greenock, est. 1956. **5654–6** 6495
— Bibs. 1:**1399y–400**
SIGN OF DR. HAY'S HEAD. 1929
SIGN OF MILTON'S HEAD. 4849
SIGN OF ST. JOHN THE EVANGELIST. 6042
SIGN OF THE BIBLE, CROWN AND CONSTITUTION. 3860
SIGN OF THE DIAL. 5891
SIGN OF THE RED PALE. 4253 4261 4330 5890
SIGN OF THE THREE CANDLESTICKS, Dublin. 4118–20.
SIGN OF THE WHITE HORSE. 6550
SIGN OF TULLY'S HEAD. 4559a–b
SIGNS. 3411 7248
—, BOOKSELLERS'. 1216–17 1234 3632–3 3860 5098
—, PRINTERS'. 6693
—, PUBLISHERS'. 7586
SILBERMANN, Gustave, Strasbourg, 1801–76. 6194
SILK BINDINGS see BOOKBINDINGS, SILK.
SILVER, Louis Henord, 1902–63–Libr. 1:1619

SIMMES, Valentine, fl.1585–1622. 2:1260; **5657–60**
— Bibs. 1:**1401**
— *Chapman's Gentleman usher.* 9379
— *Chapman's Humorous day's mirth.* 9384–5
— Paper. 5660
— *Shakespeare's 2 Henry 4.* 2:1286–7 1289 1295 1298
— *Shakespeare's 2 Henry 6.* 2:1295
—*Shakespeare's Much ado about nothing.* 2:1295
— *Shakespeare's Sonnets.* 2:1975
— Type. 5660
SIMMONDS, Samuel, Blandford, fl.1763–1828. **5661**
SIMMONS, Matthew, fl.1632–54. 12378
— *Milton's Paradise lost.* 12320
SIMMONS, William, fl.1609. 13685
SIMMS, Rupert, 1853–1937–Libr. 1:942
SIMMS, William Gilmore, 1806–70.
— *Shakespeare's Apocrypha.* 2:1908
SIMON, André Louis, 1877–1970–Libr. 3011 7065
SIMON, Oliver, 1895–1957. 4482–5 4487
SIMON, Richard, 1638–1712. 10189
SIMON AND SUSAN. 4917
SIMONIDES, Constantine, 1824–67. 3391
SIMONY, Arthur–Libr. 3239
SIMPLE SIMON–Bibs. 1:1557c
SIMPSON, George, fl.1824–92. **5662**
SIMPSON, Henry Winckworth, fl.1832–49.
— *Selected portions from the psalms.* 7374
SIMPSON, Percy, 1865–1962–Bibs. 1:**4690**
SIMPSON, William, 1823–99. 6202
SIMSON, Patrick, 1628–1715. 1689
— *Spiritual songs.* 1689
SIMSON, Robert, 1687–1768.
— *Treatise concerning porisms.* 7547
SIMULTANEOUS PRINTING see PRINTING, SHARED.
SIMWNT FYCHAN, 1530?–1606. 3871
SINCLAIR, bp. Henry, 1508–65–Libr. 3330
SINCLAIR, Mary (May) Amelia St.Clair, fl.1891–1931. **13444**
— Collns. 13444
SINCLAIR FAMILY–Libr. see ROSSLYN CASTLE–Libr.
SINGER, Charles Joseph, 1876–1960–Bibs. 1:4690b
SINGER, Godfrey Frank, 1905– –Libr. 1:1665; 7284 13029
SINGER, Patrick, Aberdeen, 1825–85. **5663**
SINGER, Samuel Weller, 1783–1858.
— *Text of Shakespeare vindicated.* 2:698
SINGLE-PAGE IMPOSITION see IMPOSITION, SINGLE-PAGE.

SINGLETON, Hugh, fl.1548–93. **5664–6**
— *Bale's Resurrection of the mass.* 8389 8391
— Bibs. 1:**1401d**
— *Orders for setting rogues to work.* 7340
— *Spenser's Shepherd's calender.* 5666
— *Stubbs' Discovery.* 5666
SINN FÉIN–Bibs. 1:4781
SIOLADÓIR, AN. 1799
SION COLLEGE, London. 2694
— LIBRARY. 2462 2485 2694 2707 2755
3026 3242 3356
— — Collns. 2795 3026
SIR JOHN OLDCASTLE. 2:433
SIRR, Joseph D'Arcy, 1794–1868–Bibs.
1:**4690k**
SIR THOMAS MORE. 2:(147) 924 943 1009
1026–7 1029a 1039 1179 1824 1877
1880–902 1904–7 1909–11 1913–14
1917–18; 7137 7139 7147 7165 12537
12539 12546
— Bibs. 2:1871
SISSON, Charles Jasper, 1885–1966. 94
— *Shakespeare's Works.* 2:776 780 1071
SITWELL, dame Edith, 1887–1964–Bibs.
1:**4691–2**
SITWELL FAMILY–Bibs. 1:**4693–4**
SIXTUS IV, pope, 1414–84.
— *Sex perelegantissime epistole.* 4222 4225
SIZES OF BOOKS *see also* FORMAT. 2300
6230 6252 6254 10423
— Bibliogr. descr. 97 112 124 128 254
SIZES OF IMPRESSIONS. 3819 6363 6368
6509 9929 12583 13827
SIZES OF ISSUES. 6506
SIZES OF PAPER *see* PAPER–Sizes.
SIZES OF TYPE *see* TYPE–Bodies;
TYPE–Sizes.
SKATING–Bibs. 1:**2282g**
SKEAT, Walter William, 1835–1912–Bibs.
1:**4694a–b**
— *Chaucer's Works.* 9419a
SKEFFINGTON, Francis Sheehy-,
1878–1916–Bibs. 1:**4695**
SKELETONS *see* PRINTING–Skeletons.
SKELT, Martin, fl.1835–50. **5667**
SKELTON, John, 1460?–1529. 7464
13445–51
— *Against a comely coystrown.* 13449
— Bibs. 1:**4696–b**
— *Certain worthy manuscript poems.* 13681
— *Colin Clout.* 13446
— Collns. 3039
— *Divers ballads.* 13449
— *Eleanor Rumming.* 13450
— *King Edward IIII.* 13451
— Mss. 13451
— — Bibs. 1:4696a
— *Pithy works.* 13681

— Ptg. 13449
— Text. 13445–6 13450
SKENE, James, 1775–1864–Libr. 6781
SKENE, sir John, ld. Curriehill, 1543?–1617.
— *De verborum significatione.* 7088
SKENE HOUSE, Aber.–Libr. 1:325b; 2555
*SKETCHES OF THE HUNGARIAN
STRUGGLE, 1848–51.* 6733
SKINNER, Cyriack, 1627–1700. 12779
SKIPPON, Philip, d.1660. **13452**
— *Pearl of price.* 13452
SKIPTON. PUBLIC LIBRARY. PETYT
LIBRARY. 3365
SKIRVING, William, d.1796.
— *Husbandman's assistant.* 6733
SKOT, John, fl.1521–37. 6056 6081
SKYPPE, George, d.1690–Libr. 3194
SLACK, Thomas, Newcastle-upon-Tyne,
1723–84. **5668–9** 8117
SLADE SCHOOL OF ART, London *see*
LONDON. UNIVERSITY. UNIVERSITY
COLLEGE. SLADE SCHOOL OF ART.
SLATER, John Herbert, 1854–1921. 74a 748
SLATER, Walter Brindley, fl.1909–Libr. 2660
SLATTER AND MUNDAY, Oxford, fl.1810.
11880
SLAVERY. **8181–2**
— Collns. 8181–2
SLEZER, John, d.1717–Bibs. 1:**4697**
— *Theatrum Scotiæ*–Bibs. 1:**4697**
SLIDELL, Alexander, afterwards MacKenzie,
1803–48.
— *Year in Spain.* 1010
SLIEGH, John, fl.1841–72. 2227
SLIGO. **1964–5**
— Bibs. 1:1055q **1114–15**
— Newspapers. 1964–5
— Ptg. 1771
— — Bibs. 1:1114–15
SLIPS, CANCEL *see* CANCEL SLIPS.
SLOANE, sir Hans, 1st baronet, 1660–1753.
13453
— Handwr. 13453
— Libr. 3034 3154 7525
SMALL, William, 1843–1929. 7420a
SMALL CARNATION BINDER, c.1680.
5670
*SMALL HANDFUL OF FRAGRANT
FLOWERS.* 7990
SMART, Christopher, 1722–71 *see also*
UNIVERSAL VISITOR. **13454–69**
— Bibs. 1:**4698–9**
— *Hymns for the amusement.* 13459 13463
— *Jubilate agno.* 13460 13464 13466
— Libr. 13468
— *Pope's Ode on St. Cecilia's day.* 13469
— *Song to David.* 13455–6
— Text. 13454–5 13461 13464–5

Vol. **1** = *Bibliographies*   **2** = *Shakespeare*   **4** = 1–8221   **5** = 8222–14616

SOCIETY OF WRITERS TO H.M. SIGNET, Edinburgh. LIBRARY. 1720d 9091
— — Collns. 1:428 442
SOCINIAN BOOKS. 960 3502
SOCRATES, 1822. 7228
SODOM–Ms. 7210
SOHO, London *see* LONDON. SOHO.
SOIRON, François, fl.1755–1813. **5702**
SOLDIERS' BIBLE *see* BIBLE–Versions–Soldiers'.
SOLEMNE, Anthony de, Norwich, fl.1565–80. **5703**
SOLEMN LEAGUE AND COVENANT, 1643. 1583 3502
SOLESBRIDGE, Herts.–Paper. 1139
SOLLY, George Edward, 1855–1930–Libr. 10628
SOLOMON, Simeon, 1840–1905. 7420a
SOLÓRZANO, Alonso de Castillo, 1584–1648 *see* CASTILLO SOLÓRZANO, Alonso de, 1584–1648.
SOMBRE BINDINGS *see* BOOKBINDINGS, SOMBRE.
SOME ACCOUNT OF KENTISH TOWN, 1821. 1246
SOMERSET *see also* BOOK TRADE, LISTS–Somerset. **1388–95a**
— Bibs. 1:**938–40a**
— Maps–Bibs. 1:**1802**
— Newspapers–Bibs. 1:1851
— Paper. 1388–90 1395a
— COUNTY LIBRARY, Street–Collns. 1:3734
SOMERVILLE, Edith Anna Œnone, 1858–1949. **13518–20**
— Bibs. 1:**4733–4**
— Bndng. 13519–20
— *In the vine country.* 13520
— *Slipper's ABC.* 13518
SOMERVILLE, Elizabeth, fl.1803–12. 7324a
SOMERVILLE, Mary (Fairfax), 1780–1872. 5250
SOMERVILLE, William, 1675–1742. **13521–2**
— *The chase.* 5611 13521–2
— Illus. 5611
— Ptg. 13522
SONGBOOKS *see also* BOOK TRADE, LISTS–Songbooks. 1621 1625 7621a 8002 **8183–9** 11059 11261
— Bibs. 1:1506 1827 2065–9 3206 4961
— Collns. 8189 12724 12726
— Ireland. 1762 1912 1959a
— — Bibs. 1:2065
— Publ. 8186–7
SONGS–Bibs. 1:**1621x** 16**23a** 16**24f** 1841m
— Mss.–Bibs. 1:1841m

SONNENSCHEIN, William Swan, later Stallybrass, 1855–1931. 4907 **5704–5**
SONNETS–Bibs. 1:1981e 2024
SONNETS FROM VARIOUS AUTHORS. 9566
SOOTHERAN, Henry, York, d.1813. 1448
SOPWELL, Herts.–Paper. 1139
SORLEY, Charles Hamilton, 1895–1915–Bibs. 1:**4734h**
— Mss.–Bibs. 1:4734h
SOTHEBY, James, 1656–1720–Libr. 2805
SOTHEBY, John, 1740–1807. **5706–a**
SOTHEBY, Samuel, 1771–1842. 280 3665 4538
SOTHEBY, Samuel Leigh, 1805–61.
— *Principia typographica.* 7386a
SOTHEBY, William, 1757–1833.
— *Schiller's Lied von der Glocke.* 931
SOTHEBY and co. ltd.–Bibs. 1:1443a
SOTHERAN, Henry, 1820–1905. **5707–8**
SOULBY, John, Ulverston, 1771?–1817. **5709**
— Bibs. 1:**1401a**
SOULBY, John, Ulverston, fl.1796–1842. 5709
— Bibs. 1:**1401a**
— Type. 5709
SOUTAR, William, 1898–1943. **13523**
— Bibs. 1:**4735**
SOUTHAMPTON.
— Ptg. *see* BAKER, Thomas, fl.1774–1805.
— PUBLIC LIBRARIES–Collns. 1:370
— UNIVERSITY. LIBRARY–Collns. 1:2094 2098
SOUTH AUSTRALIA. STATE LIBRARY, Adelaide–Collns. 1:623f
SOUTHCOTT, Joanna, 1750–1814.
— Bibs. 1:**4735m–n**
— Mss.–Bibs. 1:4735n
SOUTHERNE, Thomas, 1659–1746. **13523a–d**
— *The disappointment.* 13523a–d
— Ptg. 13523a 13523d
SOUTHEY, Robert, 1774–1843. 5250; **13524–46**
— Bibs. 1:1903a **4736–43a**
— Collns. 13541–2
— *An exposure.* 13540
— *Geographical history of Chili.* 13540
— Letters–Bibs. 1:4743
— Libr. 2196 13524 13528 13532 13543 13545–6
— *Life of Wesley.* 13538
— Mss. 13526 13535–6 13538 13541–2
— *Omnia.* 13525
— *Poems.* 13544
— *Robert Surtees, esq.* 13526
— *Specimens of poets.* 13537
— Text. 13538
— *Visions of judgement.* 13533

COMPANY, est. 1557.
—1475–1700. 1070 1468 1872 5760 5768 6073 6145
— 1641–1700. 3559 3991 5728 5736 5750 5763 12665
— 1701–1800. 3462 3819 4183a 5767–8 6145
— 1801–1900. 3512 3545 5726–7 5768
— COURT. 5744 5746 5750 5761
— LIBRARY. 5726 5731 5739 5750–1
STATIONERS' COMPANY OF CHESTER, est. 1534. 1077 1079–80
STATUTES see also LAW.
— Bibs. 1:903d 947 1265
— Ireland. 7953
— Ptg. 7953
— Scotland. 11321
— 1475–1640. 4006 7471 7475 7477 7479 7953
— 1641–1700. 7474
STC see SHORT-TITLE CATALOGUE.
STEAM PRESSES see PRESSES, STEAM.
STEBBING, Lizzie Susan, 1885–1943–Bibs. 1:4769d
STEDMAN, John, fl.1782. 13594
— Laelius and Hortensia. 13594
STEEL, Flora Annie (Webster), 1847–1929–Publ. 4858a
STEELE, sir Richard, 1672–1729 see also THE GUARDIAN; THE SPECTATOR; THE TATLER. 13595–604
— Bibs. 1:4770–4
— Christian hero. 13598
— — Bibs. 1:4771
— Conscious lovers. 13597 13599 13604
— Dramatic works. 10677
— Handwr. 13601
— Ladies library. 13595–6
— Lying lover. 13600
— Publ. 13597 13599–600
— Tender husband. 13602
STEEL ENGRAVING see ENGRAVING, STEEL; ENGRAVINGS, STEEL.
STEEPLE ASTON, Oxon.–Librs. see ROUSHAM.
STEEPLECHASING–Bibs. 1:2196f
STEEVENS, George, 1736–1800. 2:768; 3475 8381 13605
— Libr. 2:1123m; 11640
STEINGASS. Francis Joseph, 1825–1903–Bibs. 1:4775
STEMMATICS see TEXTUAL CRITICISM AND EDITING–Stemmatics.
STENOGRAPHY see SHORTHAND.
STENT, Peter, fl.1640–65. 6550
STEPHEN, sir James Fitzjames, 1829–94.
— Bibs. 1:4776–f
— Mss.–Bibs. 1:4776f
STEPHEN, sir Leslie, 1832–1904.

— Bibs. 1:4777
— Libr. 2649
STEPHENS, fl.1607.
— World of wonders. 2:1028
STEPHENS, Henry, fl.1693–1732. 13606
STEPHENS, James, 1882–1950. 770 13607–12
— Bibs. 1:684 4778–85
— Mss. 13610 13612
— — Bibs. 1:4784c–e
STEPHENS, Robert, fl.1643–97. 3471 5770–1
STEPHENS, William, 1692?–1731–Bibs. 1:4786
STEPHENSON, BLAKE AND COMPANY, Sheffield, est. 1819. 5772–a 6613
STEPHENSON, George, 1781–1848–Bibs. 1:4786m
STEPHENSON, sir Henry, Sheffield, 1826–1904. 5772a
STEPHENSON, J., fl.1816. 1526
STEPHENSON, John, Sheffield, d.1864. 5772
STEPNEY see LONDON. STEPNEY.
STEPNIAK-KRAVCHINSKY, Sergei Mikhailovich, 1852–95 see KRAVCHINSKY, Sergei Mikhailovich Stepniak-, 1852–95.
STEREOTYPING see also GED, William, Edinburgh, 1690–1749. 5721 5333 6348 6355 6360 6374 6377 6385
— Bibs. 1:1329
STERLING, John, 1806–44. 5250
STERLING, sir Louis Saul, d.1958–Libr. 1:359; 3017
STERN, Lewis, fl.1772.
— Woodhull's Poems. 13623
STERN, Gladys Bertha, 1890–1973. 13612q
— Tents of Israel. 13612q
STERNE, Laurence, 1713–68. 482 2459 13613–37
— Bibs. 1:4787–94
— Bndng. 13624
— Libr. 13618
— Collns. 13627 13630 13637
— Handwr. 13633
— Letters. 13620 13622 13627
— Letters from Yorick. 13632
— Mss. 13620
— — Bibs. 1:4790–2
— Political romance. 13617
— Ptg. 13617 13619
— Publ. 4559a 13636
— Sentimental journey. 3652 13625 13628–9 13631
— Tristram Shandy. 13613 13615–16 13619 13621 13624 13626 13635
— Works. 13614

STORTFORD see BISHOP'S STORTFORD, Herts.
STORY, John, Edinburgh, fl.1520. **5779**
STOTHARD, Thomas, 1755–1834. **5780**
— Burns' Poems. 9084
— Don Quixote. 5780
STOURTON PRESS, 1930–5–Bibs. 1:**1401g**
STOW, John, 1525?–1605. **13678–82**
— Annals of England. 13682
— Lydgate's Serpent of division. 12063
— Skelton's Certain manuscript poems. 13681
— Skelton's Pithy works. 13681
— Survey of London. 13678–80
STOWE, Harriet Elizabeth (Beecher), 1811–96.
— Bibs. 1:**851**
— Illus. 4454
— Uncles Tom's cabin. 983 988 1011 4454
STRABANE, co. Tyrone. **1973–5**
— Bibs. 1:**1123–7**
— Newspapers. 1973–5
— Ptg. 1772 1974
— — Bibs. 1:1123–7
STRABANE MAGAZINE. 1975
STRACHAN, Alexander, d.1866. 3974
STRACHEY, sir Arthur, 1858–1901–Bibs. 1:4818k
STRACHEY, Amy (Simpson), mrs. John St. Loe, b.1866–Bibs. 1:4818k
STRACHEY, sir Charles, 1862–1942–Bibs. 1:4818k
STRACHEY, sir Edward, 1812–1901–Bibs. 1:4818k
STRACHEY, Frances (mrs. W. H. C. Shaw), b.1874–Bibs. 1:4818k
STRACHEY, George, 1828–1912–Bibs. 1:4818k
STRACHEY, Giles Lytton, 1880–1932. **13683–4**
— Bibs. 1:**4817–18k**
— Books and characters. 13683
— Mss. 13684
— Text. 13683
STRACHEY, Henry, 1863–1940–Bibs. 1:4818k
STRACHEY, James, b.1887–Bibs. 1:4818k
STRACHEY, sir Richard, 1817–1908. 8132
STRACHEY, St. Loe, 1860–1927–Bibs. 1:4818k
STRACHEY, William, fl.1609–18. **13685**
— Text. 13685
STRACHEY FAMILY–Bibs. 1:**4818k**
STRADANUS, Johannes, 1523–1605 see STRAET, Jan van der, 1523–1605.
STRAET, Jan van der, 1523–1605. 6313
STRAHAN, Alexander, fl.1739–67.
— Virgil. 11380
STRAHAN, Andrew, fl.1785–1831. **5781** 5786

STRAHAN, William, 1715–85. 3475 3639a **5782–99** 7795
— Blackstone's Commentaries. 8554
— Ledgers. 5789 5793–4
— Letters. 5790
— Smollett's Works. 13493
STRANGE, sir Robert, 1721–92. **5800**
STRANGE AND WONDERFUL NEWS, 1688. 1299
STRASBOURG, France. 858
—UNIVERSITAIRE. BIBLIOTHEQUE. 5876
STRATFORD, London see LONDON. STRATFORD.
STRATFORD, SHIPSTON AND AULCESTER JOURNAL. 1423
STRATFORD-UPON-AVON, Warws. see also BOOK TRADE, LISTS–Stratford-upon-Avon. **1421–3**
— Bksllng. 1422
— Librs. 1421 2646
— Newspapers. 1423
— Ptg. 1422
— Publ. 1422
— ROYAL SHAKESPEARE THEATRE see ROYAL SHAKESPEARE THEATRE, Stratford-upon-Avon.
— SHAKESPEARE MEMORIAL LIBRARY see SHAKESPEARE MEMORIAL LIBRARY, Stratford-upon-Avon.
— SHAKESPEARE'S BIRTHPLACE TRUST see SHAKESPEARE'S BIRTHPLACE TRUST, Stratford-upon-Avon.
STRAUS, Ralph, 1882–1950.
— John Baskerville. 3938
— Libr. 3013
STRAWBERRY HILL PRESS, Twickenham, 1757–97. 277 **5801–9**
— Bibs. 1:**1402–6**
— Collns. 5803
— Garrick's To mr. Gray. 10629
— Gray's Odes. 10848
— Journal. 5807
— Sedley's There is a little man. 5808
STREATHAM see LONDON. STREATHAM.
STREET, Som. COUNTY LIBRARY see SOMERSET. COUNTY LIBRARY, Street.
STRETTELL, Amos, fl.1757–1820–Libr. 2666
STRODE, William, 1602–45. **13686**
— Bibs. 1:**4819**
— Mss. 13686
STRONG, Emilia Frances, 1840–1904 see DILKE, Emilia Frances (Strong), lady, 1840–1904.
STRONG, Leonard Alfred George, 1896–1958–Bibs. 1:**4820**
STROUD, Glos.–Ptg. 1119
STROUSE, Norman Hulbert, 1906– –Libr. 4589a

STROWAN *see* ROBERTSON, Duncan, d.1782–Libr.
STRUTT, Joseph, 1749–1802–Bibs. 1:**4820q**
STRYPE, John, 1643–1737–Bibs. 1:**4821**
STUART, Daniel, 1766–1846. **5810**
STUART, G. William, fl.1969–Libr. 12457
STUART, James, 1713–88. **5810k**
STUART, John Patrick Crichton, 3d marquis of Bute, 1847–1900–Libr. 1:1590e 2270b; 7188
STUART, Peter, fl.1788–1805. 5810
STUART, Vincent, fl.1934–6 *see* TINTERN PRESS, Brockweir, Mons., 1934–6.
STUBBES, Henry, 1632–76. **13687–9**
— *Indian nectar.* 13688
— *Legends no histories.* 13689
— Ptg. 13689
STUBBES, Philip, fl.1583–91. **13690–1**
— *Anatomy of abuses.* 13691
STUBBS, John, 1543?–91.
— *Discovery of a gaping gulf.* 5666
STUBBS, bp. William, 1825–1901–Bibs. 1:**4822–b**
STUKELEY, sir Lewis, d.1620. **13692**
— *Petition.* 13692
STURGIS, Howard Overing, fl.1891–1906. **13693**
— *Belchamber.* 13693
— Bndng. 13693
STURT, John, fl.1809–20. 503 **5811**
— Bibs. 1:**4823**
STUTTGART. WÜRTEMBERG STATE LIBRARY *see* WÜRTEMBERG. STATE LIBRARY, Stuttgart.
STYLE–Bibs. 1:1723C **2286c–e**
STYLE, HOUSE *see* PRINTING–House style.
SUBSCRIPTION LIBRARIES *see* LIBRARIES, SUBSCRIPTION.
SUBSCRIPTION LISTS. 6554–5
— Burns. 9019 9102
— Echard. 3991
— Gordon. 6556
— *Gradus.* 3991
— Hyde. 3991
— Pine. 5420
— Sallust. 3991
— Wales. 1463 1531 4942 6555 6561 12920
— Watson. 14249
SUBSCRIPTION PUBLISHING *see also* SUBSCRIPTION LISTS. 4760 5318 6553–62 10390 14038
SUBSCRIPTIONS. 3442
SUCKLING, sir John, 1609–41. **13694–8**
— Bibs. 1:**4824**
— *Copy of a letter.* 13695
— *Fragmenta aurea.* 13694
— Mss. 13697–8

— Ptg. 13695
— *Sessions of the poets.* 13697
SUDBURY, Suff.–Librs. 1400
SUDBURY, John, fl.1568–1618. 6551
SUDBURY HALL, Derbys.–Libr. 2:412
SUETONIUS, Tranquillus, Caius, fl.70–160. 11122
SUFFOLK. **1399–403** 4333 4340
— Bibs. 1:1971
— Librs. 1400
— Paper *see* DUXBURY, Yates, Bury, 1818–91.
SUFFOLK LITERARY CHRONICLE. 1399
SULLIVAN, Alexander Martin, d.1884–Bibs. 1:**4824m**
SULLIVAN, sir Arthur Seymour, 1842–1900. 1:**4823q**
SULLIVAN, Denis Baylor, d.1909–Bibs. 1:**4824m**
SULLIVAN, Edmund Joseph, 1869–1933. 7409
SULLIVAN, Richard, d.1880–Bibs. 1:**4824m**
SULLIVAN, Timothy Daniel, 1827–1914–Bibs. 1:**4824k–m**
SULLIVAN FAMILY–Bibs. 1:**4824m**
SULPITIUS, Joannes, Verulanus, 15th cent. 670 6021
SUMMARY, THE. 7820
SUMMERS, Alphonse Montague Joseph-Mary Augustus, 1880–1948. 10355 12627 **13699**
— Bibs. 1:**4825–a**
— Collns. 13699
SUM OF INTELLIGENCE, 1664. 1885
SUNDAY MAGAZINE. 7389
SUNDAY NEWSPAPERS *see* NEWSPAPERS, SUNDAY.
SUNDERLAND, Durham. **1108–10**
— Librs. 1110
— Paper *see also* HUTTON, Robert, 1799–1865. 1109
— Ptg. 1108
SUNDERLAND LIBRARY *see* SPENCER, Charles, 3d earl of Sunderland, 1674–1722–Libr.
SUNTER, Robert, York, 1795–1873. 1448
SUPERCHERIES LITTERAIRES–Bibs. 1:1691k
SUPERNATURAL AND SHAKES-PEARE–Bibs. 2:34
SUPERSTITION AND SHAKESPEARE–Bibs. 2:34 106
SUPPLY OF TYPE. 6590
SUPPRESSED BOOKS *see* BOOKS, SUPPRESSED.
SURREPTITIOUS PRINTING *see* PRINTING, SECRET.

SWIFT, Jonathan, 1667–1745. Text. 13723
13742 13750 13754 13760 13770 13779
13781 13786 13797–8
— Thersites. 14057
— To mr. Gay. 13776
— Verses on the death. 13730 13768 13778
13790
— Works. 13706 13737 13746 13795 13798
SWIMMING–Bibs. 1:2286j–k
SWINBURNE, Algernon Charles, 1837–1909.
462 13800–43 14383 14387 14406 14417
14433 14436
— Anactoria. 13803
— Atalanta in Calydon. 13808–9 13820
13824–7 13830 13834
— — Bibs. 1:4858
— Ave atque vale. 13817
— Ballad of Bulgary. 13841
— Ballads of the English border. 13835
— Bibs. 1:652 4844x–58
— Chronicle of Tebaldeo Tebaldei. 13814
— Cleopatra. 13810
— Collns. 2291 3090 13812 13823
— Dead love. 13843
— Devil's due. 14436
— Duriesdyke. 13829
— Handwr. 13833
— Heptalogia improved. 13842
— Hertha. 13805
— A leave-taking. 13828
— Lesbia Brandon. 13816 13818–19 13838
— Love's cross currents. 13813
— Mss. 10554 13803 13805–6 13808 13810
13814 13816–18 13821 13823 13828 13830
13832 13834–5 13837–40
— — Bibs. 1:4849e 4856 4857g 4858
— Off shore. 13837
— Ptg. 13804 13807 14420
— Publ. 13802 13804 13813 13815 13837
— The queen-mother. 13836
— Queen's pleasaunce. 13821
— Rosamond. 13836
— Sienna. 13811
— Text. 13829
— Triumph of time. 13828
— Under the microscope. 13807
— Word for the navy. 13831 14420
SWINDON. PUBLIC LIBRARIES–Collns.
1:3830
SWITZER, Stephen, 1682–1745.
— Compendious method for raising brocoli
6736
SWITZERLAND see also BRITISH BOOKS
PUBLISHED ABROAD–Switzerland;
FOREIGN BOOKS PUBLISHED IN
BRITAIN–Switzerland; SHAKESPEARE,
William, 1564–1616–WORKS IN
SWITZERLAND. 13757

SYDNEY. AUSTRALASIAN PIONEER
CLUB see AUSTRALASIAN PIONEER
CLUB, Sydney.
SYMINGTON, John Alexander,
fl.1927–38–Libr. 3090 8782 10405
SYMONDS, John Addington, 1840–93. 774
13844–6
— Bibs. 1:684 4858x–9
— Ptg. 13846
— Renaissance in Italy. 13845
SYMONS, Albert James Alroy, 1900–41.
3183
— Libr. 3049
SYMONS, Arthur William, 1865–1945. 13847
— Bibs. 1:4860–2
— Collns. 13847
— Massinger's Believe as you list. 12200a
SYMONSON, Philip, fl.1596. 7515
SYNAGOGUE, THE, 1640. 6044
SYNGE, John, Dublin, 1788–1845. 6466
SYNGE, John Millington, 1871–1909.
13848–58
— Aran islands. 13850
— Bibs. 1:1597 4863–70
— Collns. 13851–2
— Mss. 13848
— Text. 13849
SYRIAC see PRINTING IN SYRIAC.

TAKING OF THE ROYAL GALLEY, 1591.
615
TACITUS, Caius Cornelius, fl.55–117. 898a
TAILPIECES see TYPE–Ornaments.
TALBOT, Charles, fl.1844–80. 5815
TALBOT, William Henry Fox, 1800–77.
— Pencil of nature. 7459
TALBOYS, David A., Oxford, d.1840. 1368
TALE OF A TUB REVERSED, 1705. 728a
TALES FROM BLACKWOOD. 4065
TALFOURD, sir Thomas Noon, 1795–1854.
12462
— Bibs. 1:4875
— Publ. 5226
TALLIS, John and Frederick, fl.1820–48.
5816
TALLIS AND CO. SHAKESPEARE. 2:714
TALON, Nicholas, 1605–91. 13859
— Holy history. 13859
TAMAR MILL, Gunnislake. 1083b
TAMWORTH, Staffs. 4822
TANDRAGEE, co. Armagh–Bibs. 1:1039
— Ptg.–Bibs. 1:1039
TANNER, bp. Thomas, 1674–1735. 13860–2
— Bibliotheca Britannico-Hibernica. 13861–2
— Libr. 13860
— Publ. 13862
TAPLIN, N., fl.1803–4. 7089

TARGETT, James Henry, d.1913–Bibs.
1:4876
TARLTON, Richard, d.1588. 7464
TASSO, Torquato, 1544–95. 7419 9266–7
TATE. PUBLIC LIBRARY–Collns. 8360
TATE, John, d.1507. 3737a 5817–18
TATE, Nahum, 1652–1715. 13863–4
— Publ. 13864
TATIUS, Achilles, c.500 see ACHILLES
TATIUS, c.500.
TATLER, THE. 7738 7775a 7792 7804–5
13598
TAUCHNITZ, Christian Bernhard, Leipzig,
1816–95. 829 831a 846 847a 870 3543
10156
— Dickens' David Copperfield. 10157
— Dickens' Uncommercial traveller. 10023
— Dickens' Works. 10005
TAUCHNITZ AND CO., Leipzig–Bibs.
1:763–5
TAVERNER, Richard, 1505?–75.
— Bible. 6810 6815
— Erasmus. 939
TAVISTOCK, Devon.–Ptg. 1017 1025 1103
TAXES see EXCISE; NEWSPAPER STAMPS.
TAYLOR, miss, fl.1832. 13865
— Fatherless Fanny. 13865
TAYLOR, Alfred Edward, 1869–1945–Bibs.
1:4876c
TAYLOR, Ann (mrs. Gilbert), 1782–1866.
7000a
— City scenes. 8623
TAYLOR, Henry Calhoun, 1894–1971–Libr.
7628 10950
TAYLOR, Isaac, d.1788. 7493
TAYLOR, Isaac, 1730–1807. 5819–20
TAYLOR, James, 1813–92–Bibs. 1:4876n
TAYLOR, Jane, 1783–1824. 7000a
TAYLOR, bp. Jeremy, 1613–67. 13866–73
— Bibs. 1:4876x–8
— Christian consolations. 13871
— Mss. 13868 13872
TAYLOR, John, 1578–1653. 13874–81
— Bibs. 1:910a 4879–80
— Book of martyrs. 13877
— Great Britain all in black. 13878
— Mss. 13876
— Ptg. 13876
— Pedlar and a romish priest. 13881
— Publ. 13880–1
— Verbum sempiternæ. 6832 6854 13874 13879
TAYLOR, John, 1711–88.
— Letter to Johnson. 11396
TAYLOR, John, 1781–1864. 5821–3 9463
— Bibs. 1:1406g
TAYLOR, John, 1831–1901–Libr. 2573
TAYLOR, Kim see ARK PRESS, Totnes, 20th
cent.

TAYLOR, Richard, 1781–1858. 5824
TAYLOR, Robert, d.1672–Libr. 3076
TAYLOR, Robert H., fl.1957–Libr. 1:363f
363h; 540–1 3178
TAYLOR, Thomas, fl.1670–1721. 7513
TAYLOR, Thomas, 1758–1835. 13882
— Bibs. 1:4881–2
TAYLOR, Tom, 1817–80. 13883
— Bibs. 1:4882q
— Mss. 13883
— — Bibs. 1:4882q
TAYLOR, William, fl.1700–23.
— Defoe's Robinson Crusoe. 9886–7
TAYLOR, William Lawrence, 1829–1910
–Libr. 1:1505 1733; 2686 6898
TAYLOR FAMILY–Bibs. 1:4883–4
TEGG, Thomas, 1776–1845. 5825–7 13169
— Bibs. 1:1406p
TEGG, William, 1816–95. 5827
TEIXEIRA, Pedro, b.1570? 8204
TELEGRAPH, THE. 7704
TEMPLE, sir William, 1628–99. 13884–6
— Bibs. 1:4884a
— Lettre d'un marchand. 13885
— Libr. 13884
— Upon mrs. Catherine Philips. 13886
TEMPLE, archbp. William, 1881–1944–Bibs.
1:4884b
TEMPLE BAR. 7915
TEMPLE OF THE MUSES see LACKING-
TON, James, 1746–1815.
TEMPLE PRESS, Letchworth, Herts., est.
1906. 4534
TEMPLE PRINTING OFFICE, 1821. 5234
TEMPLE SHAKESPEARE. 2:703
TEMPLE UNIVERSITY. LIBRARY–Collns.
1:2871 3008
TENISON, archbp. Thomas, 1636–1715.
1464 3281
— Libr. 2465 3136
TENNANT, sir Charles, 1823–1906–Libr.
1:325ab
TENNANT, Frederick Robert, 1866–
1957–Bibs. 1:4884d
TENNIEL, sir John, 1820–1914. 2297 5828
7420a 9983
— Bibs. 1:4884f–g
TENNIS. 8196
— Bibs. 1:2286s–7
TENNYSON, Alfred, 1st baron Tennyson,
1809–92. 779 831a 7420a 13887–966 14387
14419 14436
— Ancient sage. 13905
— Becket. 13960
— Bibs. 1:652 672 674m 4885–902
— Bndng. 5226a
— Carmen saeculare. 13925
— Charge of the light brigade. 13952

Vol. 1 = Bibliographies   2 = Shakespeare   4 = 1–8221   5 = 8222–14616

THOMAS A KEMPIS, 1380–1471. 929 1517
— Bibs. 1:**824–5**
THOMASON, George, d.1666 *see also*
BRITISH MUSEUM. LIBRARY. DEPT.
OF PRINTED BOOKS–THOMASON
COLLECTION. **5837–47**
— Libr. 1:1873 1972; **5837**–9 5841–2 5845–7
6970
THOMASON ENGINEERING COLLEGE,
Roorkee. LIBRARY–Collns. 2:544a 549
THOMAS-STANFORD, sir Charles,
1858–1932 *see* STANFORD, sir Charles
Thomas-, 1858–1932.
THOMPSON, sir D'Arcy Wentworth,
1860–1948–Bibs. 1:**4944–b**
THOMPSON, Edward, 1738?–86. **14018**
THOMPSON, Francis Joseph, 1859–1907.
14019–20
— Bibs. 1:684 **4945–54b**
— Collns. 14019
— *Hound of heaven.* 14020
— — Bibs. 1:**4954b**
— Mss.–Bibs. 1:4946 4949
THOMPSON, George, 1804–78–Mss. 8182
THOMPSON, sir Henry, 1820–1904–Bibs.
1:**4955**
THOMPSON, Henry Yates, 1838–1928–Libr.
2749–50 2767 3042 3102 3382a
THOMPSON, Nathaniel, Dublin, 1648–87.
1907 3471 **5848–a**
THOMPSON, sir Peter, 1698–1720–Libr.
3172
THOMPSON, Roger, fl.1735–97. 7798
THOMPSON, Sylvanus Phillips, 1851–
1916–Libr. 1:2279d
THOMPSON, William, 1783?–1833–Bibs.
1:**4956c**
THOMS, William John, 1803–85. 12807
14021
— Libr. 2548
THOM'S DIRECTORY. 1808
THOMSON, mrs., fl.1787–1818. **14022**
THOMSON, Alexander, 1798–1868–Libr.
1:1961
THOMSON, George, 1757–1851. 9037
— Bibs. 1:2068–9
THOMSON, George Derwent, 1903– –Bibs.
1:**4956f**
THOMSON, Hugh, 1860–1920. **5849–50**
7408 10640 10642
— Bibs. 1:**4956**
— Collns. 5850
THOMSON, James, 1700–48. 12802
14023–53
— *Agamemnon.* 14040
— Bibs. 1:**4957–61**
— *Castle of indolence.* 14027 14043 14046
14048

— *Coriolanus.* 14047
— *Edward and Eleonora.* 14040
— *Elegy on Aikman.* 14030
— Illus. 7429
— Libr. 14025 14033–4 14037 14039
— *Milton's Areopagitica.* 14028
— Mss. 13036 14029–30 14044
— *On the death of his mother.* 14035
— *Original Scottish airs*–Bibs. 1:4961
— *Poem to mr. Congreve.* 14031
— Publ. 14038 14041
— *Rule Britannia.* 14024 14041
— *Scottish airs.* 14026
— *The seasons.* 7429 14023 14032 14036
14038 14045
— — Bibs. 1:**4960k**
— *Sophonisba.* 14052
— *Spring.* 14042
— — Bibs. 1:**4957**
— *Summer.* 14050
— *Tancred and Sigismunda.* 14053
— — Bibs. 1:**4958a–60**
— Text. 14024 14041 14047–8
— *To Amanda.* 14030
— *Works.* 14045 14049
THOMSON, James, 1834–82–Bibs. 1:684
4962–3
— Mss.–Bibs. 1:4962 4963
THOMSON, Joseph Charles, fl.1867–1908.
14443
THOMSON, John, Aberdeen, 1840–1911.
3810
THOMSON, sir St. Clair, 1859–1943–Bibs.
1:**4965**
THOMSON, William, fl.1733. **14054**
— *Orpheus Caledonius.* 14054
THORDARSON, Chester H., fl.1900–
29–Libr. 1:2279g; 2344 8123 8127 8139
THORESBY, Ralph, 1658–1725.
— Bibs. 1:**4965**
— Letters–Bibs. 1:4965
— Libr. 2469
THORN-DRURY, George, 1860–1931 *see*
DRURY, George Thorn-, 1860–1931.
THORNE, Robert, 1754–1820 *see also* FANN
STREET FOUNDRY, 1808–20. 6613 6716
THORNEY, Roger, 1499?–1515–Libr. 6018
THORNHILL, sir James, 1676–1734. **5851**
THORNTON, Robert, Dublin, fl.1682–93.
1907
THORNTON, Robert John, 1768?–1837.
6946 7327
— *Temple of flora.* 6058a 7330
THORP, Giles, fl.1604–22. 850 855
— Bibs. 1:755
THORPE, Thomas, 1570?–1635? 2:1978;
3471 **5853**
— *Shakespeare's Sonnets.* 2:1978

THORPE, Thomas, 1791–1851. 3391

THRALE, Hester Lynch (Salusbury), 1741–1821 see PIOZZI, Hester Lynch (Salusbury), formerly mrs. Thrale, 1741–1821.

THREE KINGS OF COLOGNE. 6023

THREE-VOLUME NOVELS see NOVELS, THREE-VOLUME.

THROPP, Richard, Chester, d.1668. 5854

THUMB BIBLE see TAYLOR, John, 1578–1653. *Verbum sempiternæ.*

THURSTON, John, 1774–1822. 2:710

THWAITES FAMILY–Libr. 3309

TICHBORNE, John, fl.1609.

— *Triple antidote.* 5322

TICKELL, Richard, 1751–93–Bibs. 1:4966

TICKELL, Thomas, 1686–1740. 7787 **14055–7**

— Bibs. 1:**4967–8**

— *Colin and Lucy.* 14056

— *Horn-book.* 14057

TICKETS, BOOKBINDERS' see BOOK-BINDERS–Tickets.

TICKNOR AND FIELDS, Boston, est. 1866. 8304 8872

TIDCOMBE, George, Watford, 1800–91. 1139 3785

TIGHE, mrs. George William, 1773–1835 see MOUNTCASHELL, Margaret Jane (Kingsborough) countess of Mountcashell, 1773–1835.

TIGHE, Mary (Blachford), 1772–1810. **14058–60**

— *Psyche.* 14058 14060

TILDE see TYPE–Individual sorts–Tilde.

TILLET, Titus, Cambridge, fl.1677. **5855**

TILLOTSON, archbp. John, 1630–94. 10389 **14061–2**

— *Protestant religion vindicated.* 14062

— Text. 14061

TILLOTSON, John, Bolton, fl.1834–1915. 5856

TILLOTSON, William Frederick, Bolton, 1844–89. 5856–7

TILNEY, Edmund, d.1610. **14063**

— *Duties in marriage.* 14063

— *Flower of friendship.* 14063

TIMBERLAKE, Henry, d.1626. **14064**

— *True discourse of the travels.* 14064

TIMES, THE. 7641 7742 7764 7784 7801 7842 7864 7871 7894 7903 9703 10922

— Bibs. 1:5042d

— Type. 6581

TIMES BOOK CLUB, est. 1905. 5680 6522

TIMES BOOK SHOP, London. 6496

TIMES LITERARY SUPPLEMENT–Bibs. 1:3005

TIMETABLES, RAILWAY. 8074

TINDAL, Matthew, 1657–1733.

— *Letter to a member of parliament* 3573

TINDALE, William, d.1536 see TYNDALE, William, d.1536.

TINDALL, John, fl.1562–83. 7477

TINKER, Chauncey Brewster, 1876–1963–Libr. 1:363; 10427

TINNELL, William, 1784–1845. 8117

TINSLEY, William, 1831–1902. 5858–9a

TINTERN PRESS, Brockweir, Mons., 1934–6. **5860**

TIPPERARY. **1966–72**

— Bibs. 1:**1118–21**

— Ptg.–Bibs. 1:1118

TITFORD, William Jowit, fl.1811.

— *Hortus botanicus americanus.* 6966

TITLE-LABELS see LABELS, TITLE.

TITLEPAGES. 976 1286 2278 2375 5416 6114 6260 6263 6269 6275 6283–5 6301 6309 6532 6597 6874 7201 7263 7613 10181 10602 10606 11089 11207 12408 12582 12677 13185 13420 13701

— Bibliogr. descr. 97 114 118 124 127–8 134 143 148 150 254

— Bibs. 1:330 1735y 1745f

— Collns. 2599 6266

— Type see TYPE–Borders.

—, CANCEL. 8728 11585 12191 12678

TITLES see also HALF-TITLES; HEAD-TITLES; RUNNINGTITLES. 6278 6508 11102 11327 13226

—, FORE-EDGE. 6308

TOBACCO. **8197–9**

— Bibs. 1:**2288–9**

— Collns. 8198–9

— Mss.–Bibs. 1:2288

TÓCHAR, co Wicklow see ROUNDWOOD, co. Wicklow.

TODD, George W., York, fl.1811–34. 1448

TODD, Henry John, 1763–1845.

— *Poetical works of Milton.* 12348

TODD, John, York, 1737?–1811. 1448

TODD, John, York, 1770–1837. 1448

TODD, William Burton, 1919– –Libr. 1:365

TODMORDEN. PUBLIC LIBRARY–Collns. 8198

TOFT, Mary, 1701–63. **14065**

TOFT HALL, Knutsford–Libr. 2:466

TOKENS see also BOOKSELLERS' TOKENS. 3429–30 3621

TOKYO. UNIVERSITY. FACULTY OF ECONOMICS. 13471 13478

— WASEDA UNIVERSITY see WASEDA UNIVERSITY, Tokyo.

TOLAND, John, 1670–1722.

— Bibs. 1:**4969–b**

— *Proposals for regulating the newspapers.* 3561

TOLKIEN, John Ronald Reuel, 1892–
1973–Bibs. 1:**4970–b**
TOLLEMACHE FAMILY–Libr. 2603 2985
3393a
TOLLETT, Elizabeth, 1694–1754–Libr. 754
TOMAHAWK, THE. 7872 7875
TOMKIS, Thomas, fl.1604–15. **14066–8**
— *Albumazar.* 167 14066–8
— Ptg. 14068
TOMLINS, Elizabeth Sophia, 1763–
1828–Bibs. 1:**4970j**
TOMLINSON, Henry Major, 1873–1958.
783 **14069–71**
— Bibs. 1:**4970p**
— *Bluebell at Thiepval.* 14071
— *Sea and the jungle.* 14069
— Text. 14070
TOM THUMB. 7020
TOMMY TRIP. 7008
TOMPSON, Richard, fl.1656–93. 6550
TOMTIT. 1116
TOMSON, Laurence, 1539–1608.
— *Bible.* 6867a 6887b
TONE, Theobald Wolfe, 1763–98. **14072–3**
— *Argument on behalf of the Catholics.* 14073
— *Belmont castle.* 14072
TONE, Theobald Wolfe, 1763–98–Bibs.
1:**4971**
TONG, Shrop.–Librs. 2858
TONGE, George, Warwick, fl.1682. **5861**
TONGUE COMBATANTS, 1684. 726
TONSON, Jacob, 1656?–1736. 2:419; 1241
3453a 3616 3620 3639a 3992 **5862–70** 6558
10189 10342
— Bibs. 1:**1406s**
— *Cæsar's Works.* 5866
— *Dryden's Miscellany poems.* 5870
— *Dryden's Virgil.* 10361–2 10390
— *Johnson's Shakespeare.* 2:709
— *Milton's Paradise lost.* 5869–70
— *Pope's Shakespeare.* 5869–70
— *Rowe's Shakespeare.* 5869–70
— *Wilmot's Poems.* 14363
TONSON FAMILY. 3639a 5869
TOOKE, John Horne, 1736–1812. 8978
TOOKER, Charles, 1598–1660–Libr. 3396a
TOOLS, BOOKBINDING *see* BOOK-
BINDING–Tools.
TOOVEY, James, fl.1894–Libr. 2521
TOPHAM, Francis William, 1808–77. 9983
9997a
*TOPOGRAPHICAL MEMORANDA OF THE
WARD OF FARRINGDON WITHOUT,*
19th cent. 1220
TOPOGRAPHICAL POETRY *see* POETRY,
TOPOGRAPHICAL.
TOPOGRAPHY *see also* GEOGRAPHY. 6193
— Bibs. 1:855–63

— Collns. 3057
— Scotland–Bibs. 1:968
TOPSELL, Edward, d.1625.
— *Fowls of heaven.* 6917
— Mss. 6917 6920
— *Two soliloquies.* 6920
TORONTO. PUBLIC LIBRARIES.
OSBORNE COLLECTION–Collns.
1:1567–8 1570
— UNIVERSITY. LIBRARY–Collns.
1:2697b; 2:233 241; 3394a 8913 9250
TORRINGTON, John Byng, 5th viscount,
1743–1813 *see* BYNG, John, 5th viscount
Torrington, 1743–1813.
TOTNES, Devon.
— Ptg. *see* ARK PRESS, 20th cent.
— CHURCH. LIBRARY. 3069
TOTNES, George Carew, earl of, 1555–1629
see CAREW, George, baron Clopton and
earl of Totnes, 1555–1629.
TOTTELL, Richard, fl.1530–94. 4150 **5871–6**
— Bibs. 1:**1407**
— *Miscellany.* 5871a 5873a–b 7998
— *More's Dialogue of comfort.* 12492
— Type. 6656
TOURNEISEN, Jean Jacques, Basle,
1754–1803. 865
— Bibs. 1:759 (1408)
TOURNEUR, Cyril, 1575?–1626. **14074–6**
— Bibs. 1:**4971a–b**
— *Revenger's tragedy see REVENGER'S
TRAGEDY.*
TOUT, Thomas Frederick, 1855–1929–Bibs.
1:**4971f–h**
TOVEY, sir Donald Francis, 1875–1940–Bibs.
1:**4971m**
TOVIL, Kent–Paper. 1161a
TOWN, THE. 7843
TOWNELEY PLAYS. 7135
TOWNS–Maps–Bibs. 1:1770h
TOWNSHEND, Aurelian, fl.1601–43. **14077**
— *Albion's triumph.* 14077
— Text. 14077
TOWNSHEND, George, 1st marquis,
1724–1807. **14078**
— *Miscellaneous poetry.* 14078
— Ptg. 14078
TOWNSHEND, Letitia Jane Dorothea
(Baker), fl.1892–1927–Bibs. 1:**4972**
TOWNSHEND, Richard Baxter, 1846–
1923–Bibs. 1:**4973**
TOWN-TALK–Bibs. 1:4774
TOY BOOKS *see* CHILDREN'S
LITERATURE.
TOY THEATRE *see* DRAMA, JUVENILE.
TOYNBEE, Arnold Joseph, 1889–1975–Bibs.
1:**4974–5c**
— *Study of history*–Bibs. 1:4975a

Vol. **1** = *Bibliographies*   **2** = *Shakespeare*   **4** = 1–8221   **5** = 8222–14616

TROLLOPE, Anthony, 1815–82. *Eustace diamonds*. 14092
— *Framley parsonage.* 14093 14104
— *History of the Post office.* 14102
— Illus. 14120
— *Is he Popenjoy.* 14107
— *La vendée.* 14126
— Letters. 4000 14108
— Libr. 14113 14115 14118 14125
— *Life of Cicero.* 14122
— *Macdermots of Ballycloran.* 14123
— *Miss Mackenzie.* 14117
— Mss. 14091 14095 14097 14100 14112 14116 14122 14124
— — Bibs. 1:4988
— *North America.* 14128
— *Orley farm.* 14119
— *Phineas Finn.* 14105
— *Phineas redux.* 14094 14099 14103
— Ptg. 14091 14093
— Publ. 14089 14107 14123 14127
— *Sir Harry Hotspur.* 14106
— Text. 14088 14094 14096–9 14101 14103–7 14109–10 14116–17 14119 14124
TROLLOPE, Frances (Milton), 1780–1863. **14129**
— Bibs. 1:**4989**
— Collns. 7322a
— *Domestic manners.* 14129
— Letters. 4000
— Mss. 14129
— Publ. 4000
TROLLOPE, Thomas Adolphus, 1810–92.
— Letters. 4000
— Publ. 4000 4359
TROTTER, John Bernard, 1775–1818–Bibs. 1:**4990**
TROTTER, Wilfred Batten Lewis, 1872–1939. **14130**
— Bibs. 1:**4990d**
— *Instincts of the herd.* 14130
TROUBLESOME REIGN see SHAKESPEARE, William, 1564–1616. *King John.*
TROWBRIDGE, Wilts.–Ptg. *see* DIPLOCK, John, fl.1828–40.
TRÜBNER, Nicholas, 1817–84. 3623
TRUCHY, J. F., Paris, fl.1837–45. 844
TRUE BRITON. 11051
TRUE CRIME–Bibs. 1:5005r
TRUE DIURNAL. 7669
TRUE ENCOUNTER, c.1510. 1613
TRUE RELATION OF THE FRENCH KING, 1592. 673
TRUE TRAGEDY see SHAKESPEARE, William, 1564–1616. *3 Henry VI.*
TRUMAN, T., fl.1746. **5878**
TRUSLER, John, 1735–1820.
— *Elements of modern gardening.* 7346

— Ptg. 7346
TRUSSELL, John, fl.1595–1642. **14131**
— Bibs. 1:**4990h**
— *Rape of fair Helen.* 14131
— — Bibs. 1:4990h
TRYON, Thomas, 1634–1703–Bibs. 1:**4990p**
TUAM, co. Galway. **1949**
— Bibs. 1:1087a
— Ptg. 1772 1949
— — Bibs. 1:1087a
TUCK, Raphael, 1821–1900. 5878d
TUER, Andrew White, 1838–1900. 5043
TULK, Charles Augustus, 1786–1849. 8602
TULLIS, George Smith, Cupar, 1805–48. 5879
— Bibs. 1:1408b–c
TULLIS, R. AND COMPANY, Markinch, est. 1809. 5879–80
TULLIS, Robert, Cupar, 1775–1831. **5879–80**
— Bibs. 1:**1408b–c**
TULLIS AND RUSSELL, Markinch. 5880
TULLIS RUSSELL, Markinch, est. 1809. 5880
TULLY *see* CICERO, Marcus Tullius, 106–43 B.C.
TUNSTALL, bp. Cuthbert, 1474–1559. 8065
— Libr. 3035
TUPPER, Martin Farquhar, 1810–89. 4846a
TURBERVILLE, George, 1540?–1610? **14132–4**
— *Book of falconry.* 14132–3
— *Noble art of venery.* 7089 14132
TURBERVILLE, Henry, d.1678.
— *Manual of controversies.* 1487
TURBUTT, G. M. R., fl.1905–Libr. 2:522–4 577
TURKEY *see also* SHAKESPEARE, William, 1564–1616–WORKS IN TURKEY.
— Paper. 3784
TURKEY MILL, Maidstone. 5975
TURNBULL, Alexander Horsburgh, 1868–1918–Libr. *see also* ALEXANDER TURNBULL LIBRARY, Wellington, N.Z. 8028
TURNER, Charles, 1774–1857. **5881**
TURNER, Dawson, 1775–1858–Bibs. 1:**4991**
TURNER, Dawson William, 1815–85–Libr. 8384
TURNER, John, Coventry, 1773–1863. **5882**
TURNER, Joseph Mallord William, 1775–1851. 3830a
TURNER, Robert Samuel, 1819–87–Libr. 1999 2476
TURNER, Tom, 1870–1949–Collns. 3159
TURNER, William, d.1568–Bibs. 1:**4992**
TURPIN, Richard, 1706–39. **14135**
TUTCHEIN, Robert, fl.1651. 5883
TUTORS, INSTRUMENTAL–Bibs. 1:1841d

TUTT, James William, 1858–1911.
— *British lepidoptera.* 6982
— *Natural history of British butterflies.* 6982
TWAIN, Mark, *pseud. of* Samuel Langhorne Clemens, 1835–1910. 4897cb
— *Innocents abroad.* 999
TWEEDSMUIR, John Buchan, 1st baron, 1875–1940 *see* BUCHAN, John, 1st baron Tweedsmuir, 1875–1940.
TWELVE BY EIGHT PAPERMILL, Leics., est. 1954. 3770 3775a 6495
TWENTYFOURS *see* FORMAT–Twentyfours.
TWICKENHAM *see* LONDON. TWICKENHAM.
TWINE, Laurence, fl.1564–76. 2:1641
TWISS, Horace, 1787–1849. 5250
TWISTLETON, Edward, 1809–74.
— *Letters of Junius.* 11641
TWO-PULL PRINTING *see* PRINTING, TWO-PULL.
TWO WATERS, Herts.–Paper. 1139
TWYCROSS, Edward, fl.1846–50.
— *Mansions of England and Wales.* 1082
TWYN, John, d.1660. 7666
TWYN BARLWM PRESS, 1931–2–Bibs. 1:1409
TWYNE, Brian, 1579?–1644–Libr. 3114
TYLDEN, William, fl.1660–Libr. 6761
TYLER, Royall, 1757–1826.
— *Algerine captive.* 1006.
TYMMS, William Robert, fl.1860. 6202
TYNDALE, William, d.1536. 829 837 **14136**
— Bibs. 1:**4993**
— *Bible.* 6857 6873
— — O.T. 6895
— — N.T. 6868 6905–6 6908–9
— *Parable of the wicked mammon.* 14136
TYPE *see also* TYPEFACES. 257 259 263 6077 **6563–722**
— Arabesques. 6661a
— Bibliogr. descr. 97 128 134 143 165 167 173 6605 6637
— Bibs. 1:1161 1245f; 6682
— Borders. 4008 4479 5982 6662–3 6670 6672 6674 6692 13429
— Classification. 6579a 6608 6637 6642 6652 6654
— Collns. 6610
— Compartments. 6661 6665–6 6670
— Devices *see* DEVICES.
— Factotums. 4703 5836 6003 6663
— Flowers. 4479 4658 6114 6667 6673 6680 6707
— Headpieces *see* Ornaments.
— Individual sorts. 257 **6696–713**
— — Ampersands. 6706
— — Brackets. 6712

— — Fist and index *see* Hands.
— — Hands. 6707 6711
— — I/J. 6699
— — Il. 6698
— — Numerals. 6707
— — S. 6697 6700–1 6704–5 6709–10 13393
— — Tilde. 6713
— — Trains. 6713a
— — U. 6696 6702
— — U/V. 6699
— Initials. 279 1248 4168 4479 4658 4660 4701 4703 5332 5836 5982 6003 6042 6657–9 6663 6669 6678 6692 6863
— — Bibliogr. descr. 128
— Ireland. 1808
— Matrices. 4660 5332 6716
— Moulds. 6716
— Ornaments. 1248 3827 3936 4008 4112 4168 4196 4479 4660 4700 4704 5284 5332 5541 5646 5660 5836 5982 6003 6006 6663 6667 6676 6679 6683 6686–8 6690 6692 6694 6695a
— Point system *see* Sizes.
— Presses, etc.
— — Allde. 3827
— — Ashendene press. 6610
— — Baskerville. 3912–13 3925 3930–1 3935–7 3939 3941 3945–6 3952 6572 6613 6637 6716
— — Bell, J. 3977–80 6637 6716
— — Berthelet. 4008
— — Brewster. 4112
— — Bulmer. 4132 4158
— — Cambridge university press. 4161 4167a 4168 4824 6610
— — Caslon. 4192–3 4196–8 4202–3 6572
— — Chiswick press. 6631
— — Cranach press. 6610 6645
— — Curwen press. 4479–80 4487
— — Daniel. 4499
— — Day. 6419 6613 6656
— — Doves press. 4588a
— — Eliot's court press. 1248
— — Elizabeth. 6436
— — Franckton. 4700–1 4703–4
— — Harrison. 6683
— — Judson. 6683
— — Kelmscott press. 4970 4982 4994 6098 6610 6637
— — Moxon. 6442
— — Norton. 6683
— — Okes. 6683
— — Oxford university press. 5332–3 5335 5342 5366 6613 6572 6637 6648–9
— — Pine. 5420
— — Porson. 6448
— — Proctor. 6447
— — Riccardi. 6463

TYPOGRAPHICAL SOCIETIES—*cont.*
THE BOOKBINDING AND PRINTING
TRADES; TYPOGRAPHICAL
ASSOCIATION, est. 1849; TYPO-
GRAPHICAL SOCIETY, Newcastle-upon-
Tyne.
— Mss. 1269
TYPOGRAPHICAL SOCIETY, Newcastle-
upon-Tyne–Bibs. 1:927a
TYPOGRAPHY. 263 269 5518 **6563–722**
— Bibs. 1:**1187–211;** 6628 6654
— Collns. 4079 4081 6564 6568 6609 6619
— Manuals–Bibs. 1:**1190–3**
— Newspapers. 6595
— Proposals *see* PROPOSALS.
— Specimens *see* TYPE SPECIMENS.
— Terms and concepts *see also* 'TYPO-
GRAPHER'. 3599 6615 6628 6654
— 1475–1640. 6589
— 1801–1900. 6229 6593 6607 6646
—, ECCLESIASTICAL. 6596
— AND BIBLIOGRAPHY. 6637 6650 6716
TYRANNIUS RUFINUS *see* RUFINUS,
Tyrannius, Aquileiensis, fl.345–410.
TYRIE, James, 1543–97. **14137**
TYRONE. **1973–5**
— Bibs. 1:**1121x–7**
— Librs. *see* CALEDON HOUSE.
— Ptg. 6466
TYRWHITT, Thomas, 1730–86. 9398
— *Chaucer's Canterbury tales.* 2:791; 9425
TYTLER, Alexander Fraser, ld. Wood-
houselee, 1747–1813–Libr. 1635
TYTLER, William, 1711–92.
— Libr. 1635
— Mss. 6783

UDALL, Nicholas, 1505–56. **14138–42**
— Bibs. 1:1597
— *Flowers of Terence.* 14140
— *Ralph Roister Doister.* 14139
— *Respublica.* 14141–2
— Text. 14141–2
ULRIC IN PERSONAS. 4370 4371a
ULSTER *see* IRELAND.
ULVERSTON, Lancs. 1180a
— Ptg. *see* SOULBY, John, 1771?–1817;
SOULBY, John, fl.1796–1842.
'UNCUT COPY'. 3611
UNCUT PAPER *see* PAPER, UNCUT.
UNDATED BOOKS *see* BOOKS, UNDATED.
UNDERWOOD, F. A., fl.1967–Libr. 11789
UNFINISHED BOOKS. 1773 **8218**
— Bibs. 1:**2074–7**
— Ireland–Bibs. 1:2076
UNFINISHED NOVELS *see* NOVELS,
UNFINISHED.

UNICORN BINDER, Cambridge, 15th cent.
5885
UNION JACK. 7037
UNION OF COMPOSITORS, London, est.
1834 *see* LONDON UNION OF
COMPOSITORS, est. 1834.
UNIONS, TRADE *see* TRADE UNIONS.
UNION THEOLOGICAL SEMINARY, New
York *see* NEW YORK. UNION THEO-
LOGICAL SEMINARY.
UNITARIAN CHAPELS, Newcastle-upon-
Tyne *see* NEWCASTLE-UPON-TYNE.
HANOVER SQUARE UNITARIAN
CHAPELS.
UNITARIAN COLLEGE, Manchester.
MCLACHLAN LIBRARY. 3074
UNITED FREE CHURCH COLLEGE
LIBRARY, Edinburgh *see* SCOTLAND.
UNITED FREE CHURCH. COLLEGE.
LIBRARY.
UNITED GRAND LODGE OF
ENGLAND–Collns. 2185
UNITED IRISHMEN. 4353–4
UNITED STATES OF AMERICA. 2288 2298
3977 5038 5795 6994 8615 8618 8781
9740–1 9822 10012 10030 10032 10056
10147 10656 10956 11524 11659 11663
12218 12367 12575 13155 13299
— Ptg. 6094 6111–12 6168 6463 6476
— Type. 6600 6637
— LIBRARY OF CONGRESS. 11186
UNITED STATES LITERATURE *see*
BRITISH BOOKS PUBLISHED
ABROAD; FOREIGN BOOKS PUB-
LISHED IN BRITAIN; SHAKE-
SPEARE, William, 1564–1616–WORKS IN
UNITED STATES.
UNITED WOMEN BOOKFOLDERS'
UNION, est. 1892. 6138
UNIVERSAL CHRONICLE. 5277
UNIVERSAL FAMILY BIBLE, 1773 *see*
BIBLE–Versions–Universal family.
UNIVERSAL SPECTATOR. 8384
UNIVERSAL SUFFRAGE, 1811. 13337
UNIVERSAL VISITOR. 13457 13462
UNIVERSITY LIBRARIES *see* LIBRARIES,
UNIVERSITY.
UNIVERSITY NEWSPAPERS *see*
NEWSPAPERS, UNIVERSITY.
UNIVERSITY NOVELS *see* NOVELS,
UNIVERSITY.
*UNIVERSITY OF PENNSYLVANIA LIBRARY
CHRONICLE.* 1:100–1
UNIVERSITY PRESSES *see* PRESSES,
UNIVERSITY.
UNIVERSITY PRESS SHAKESPEARE. 2:743a
'UNOPENED COPY'. 3611
UNWIN, George, fl.1826–77. **5886**

UNWIN, Jacob, fl.1823–60. **5887**
UNWIN, Matthew, Birmingham, d.1750. 5887
UNWIN, Thomas Fisher, 1848–1935. **5888–9**
UPCOTT, William, 1779–1845. 10465 **14143**
— *Borde's Introduction.* 8660
— Libr. 2563 2758
— Mss. 14143
UPDIKE, Daniel Berkeley, 1860–1941. 2374
UP MILL, West End, South Stoneham. 1132a
UPPER BARFORD MILL, Hants. 1132a
UPPER SPYLAW MILL, Midloth. 1712
URQUHART, sir Thomas, 1611–60. 12360
URIE, Robert, Glasgow, 1711?–71–Bibs. 1:**1410**
URRY, John, 1666–1715. 3475
URSWICK, sir Thomas, d.1479–Libr. 3113
USHAW COLLEGE, Durham *see* ST. CUTHBERT'S COLLEGE, Ushaw.
USSHER, archbp. James, 1581–1656–Libr. 2571 3211
UTOPIAS *see also* MORE, sir Thomas, 1478–1535–*Utopia.*
— Bibs. 1664b 1669–a 1686 1686d 1724
— Collns. 12500
UTTERSON, Edward Vernon, 1776?–1856. 3971
— Libr. 2666
UTTOXETER, Staffs.–Ptg. **1397**

VACHER, Thomas, fl.1751–1836. **5890**
VALENTINE, John, 1848–1925–Libr. 2655
VALENTINES. 6974 7249 7254
— Bibs. 1:1536k 1982a
VALE PRESS, 1896–1904. **5891–3** 6502
— Bibs. 1:**1411–12**
VALE PRESS SHAKESPEARE. 2:702
VALLADOLID. ENGLISH COLLEGE. LIBRARY–Collns. 2:652
VALLANCEY, Charles, 1721–1812. 7078 8981
VALLENGER, Stephen, d.1592–Libr. 2574 3322
VALPY, Abraham John, 1787–1854. 11880
VAN ANTWERP, William Clarkson, 1867–1938–Libr. 1:386 4605; 13203
VAN BOUKHOUT, Adrian Kempe, fl.1536–7 *see* KEMPE, Adrian van Boukhout, Antwerp, fl.1536–7.
VANBURGH, sir John, 1664–1726–Handwr. 14576
VANCOUVER, George, 1758–98–Bibs. 1:**4994**
VAN DEN KEERE, Pieter, fl.1599–1646. 7511
VANDERBANK, John, 1694–1739. **5894**
— Bibs. 1:**1412b**

VANDERBLUE, Homer Bews, 1888–1952–Libr. 1:4707
VAN DER ERVE, Egidius, fl.1555 *see* ERVE, Egidius van der, fl.1555.
VANDERPOEL, Halstead, fl.1968–78–Libr. 1:3103
VAN DER HAGEN, Godfried, fl.1534–5 *see* HAGEN, Godfried van der, fl.1534–5.
VAN DER GUCHT, Gerard, 1696–1776. 7451
VAN DER GUCHT, Michael, 1660–1725. 7451
VAN DOESBORCH, Jan, Antwerp, fl.1508–40? *see* DOESBORCH, Jan van, Antwerp, fl.1508–40?
VAN DUZER, Henry Sayre, 1853–1928–Libr. 1:4916
VAN DYKE, Henry, 1852–1933. 13942
— Libr. 1:4899
VAN HAGEN, Francis, Aberdeen, fl.1626–36. 1620 **5895**
VAN HAGEN, Francis, Aberdeen, fl.1659–69. **5896**
VAN HOVE, Frederick, fl.1671?
— *History of the Bible in cuts.* 6872
VANITY FAIR. 7428 7902
— Bibs. 1:1925
VARNISHES. 6259
VATCH MILL, Stroud. 1120a
VAUGHAN, Henry, 1622–95. **14144–51** 14518
— Bibs. 1:**4995–6a**
— *Chemist's key.* 14149
— Libr. 14150
— *Olor Iscanus.* 14146–8 14151
— Publ. 14145 14151
— *Silex scintillans.* 724
— Text. 14144
— *The world.* 14144
VAUGHAN, Rowland, fl.1629–58. **14152–3**
— *Bayley's Practice of priety.* 1487 14152
VAUGHAN, Thomas, 1622–66. **14154**
— Mss. 14154
VAUGHAN, William, 1577–1641.
— *Directions for health.* 592
VAUTROLLIER, Thomas, d.1587? 1591 4662 4662b **5897–902**
— Bibs. 1:**1412c**
— *Calvin's Institute.* 5898
— *Clement's Petty school.* 5902
— *Lasso's Recueil du mellange.* 5899
'VELLUM'. 3602
VELLUM *see also* BOOKBINDINGS, VELLUM; PRINTING ON VELLUM. 259 269 1913 2082 3690 4978
VELLUM BINDERS' SOCIETY, est. 1823. 2025

VELVET BINDINGS *see* BOOKBINDINGS, VELVET.
VENGE, Edward, Stepney, fl.1578–1605. 1211
VENGEROV, S. A. 2:131
VENNAR, Richard, d.1615? **14155**
— *Double PP.* 14155
VENNING, Ralph, 1620–73–Bibs. 1:4997
VENTURE–Bibs. 1:1721
VERDION, John de, d.1802. **5903**
VERDUN, France–Ptg. 6928
VERGILIUS, Polydorus, d.1555. **14156–8**
— *Adagia.* 14157
— Bibs. 1:**4998**
— *De inventoribus rerum.* 14157
— — Bibs. 1:**4998**
— *History of England.* 14156
— *Pleasant history of the first inventors.* 14158
VERMIGLI, Pietro Martire, 1500–62.
— *Decades.* 3118
VERMONT. UNIVERSITY. LIBRARY–Collns. 6721
VERNE, Jules, 1828–1905–Bibs. 1:**815a**
VERNON, Francis Lawrance William, 9th baron Vernon, 1889–1963–Libr. 2:412
VERNOR, HOOD AND SHARPE, fl.1806–12. 2:741; **5905**
VERSTEGAN, Richard, formerly Rowlands, c.1550–1641. 7236
— Bibs. 1:**4999–5000**
VERTOT, René Aubert de, 1655–1735. 4473
VERTUE, George, 1684–1756. 3475
VERULAM, Francis Bacon, baron and viscount St.Albans, 1561–1626 *see* BACON, Francis, baron Verulam and viscount St.Albans, 1561–1626.
VERWEIJ, Johannes, 1648–92?
— *Nova via docendi Graeca.* 3567
VETERINARY SCIENCE *see* MEDICINE.
VICARS' CHORAL LIBRARY, Hereford *see* HEREFORD. CATHEDRAL. LIBRARY. VICARS' CHORAL LIBRARY.
VICCARS, John, 1604–60.
— *Decapla in psalmos.* 6420
— Ptg. 6420
'VICES'–Bibs. 1:1601b
VICKERY, Willis, 1857–1932–Libr. 2:289
VICTORIA, Australia. PUBLIC LIBRARY, Melbourne. LIBRARY–Collns. 1:532 3089
VICTORIA, B.C. UNIVERSITY. MCPHERSON LIBRARY–Collns. 1:4491j
VICTORIA, queen of Great Britain and Ireland, 1819–1901–Bibs. 1:**5000q**
— Mss.–Bibs. 1:5000q
VICTORIA AND ALBERT MUSEUM, South Kensington, London–Collns. 1:3437b; 2:198–9 670 672 1174

— LIBRARY–Collns. 1:1575 2193m 2912eb 3050h 3059 5076c; 2012a 2043 2144 2168 2223 8438 10004 12266
— ART LIBRARY. 2619
— CLEMENTS COLLECTION. 2219 2222
— DYCE COLLECTION *see* DYCE, Alexander, 1798–1869–Libr.
— FORSTER COLLECTION *see* FOSTER, John, 1812–76–Libr.
VICTORIA UNIVERSITY OF WELLINGTON, N.Z. LIBRARY–Collns. 1:645
VIDA, bp. Marco Girolamo, d.1566. 964 10747 10754
VIENNA. NATIONALBIBLIOTHEK *see* AUSTRIA. NATIONALBIBLIOTHEK, Vienna.
VIGNETTES, TYPE *see* TYPE–Vignettes.
VILLADIEU, Alexandre, fl.1170–1250–Bibs. 1:807a
VINCENT, Augustine, 1584?–1626. 463 9126 **14159–60**
— *Discovery of errors.* 2:558; 14159–60
— Libr. 2:508 576
— Ptg. 14159–60
VINDEX ANGLICUS, 1644. 9268
VINE, Graham, fl.1935 *see* TINTERN PRESS, Chepstow, Mons., est. 1935.
'VINEGAR' BIBLE, 1716–17 *see* BIBLE–Versions–'Vinegar'.
VINE PRESS, Hemingford Grey, Huntingdonshire, est. 1956.
— Bibs. 1:**1413**
— *Read's Parliament of women.* 5907
VINER, Charles, 1679–1756–Bibs. 1:**5001**
— *General abridgement of law*–Bibs. 1:5001
VINEYARD OF DEVOTION, 1599. 624
VINOGRADOFF, sir Paul Gavrilovich, 1854–1925–Bibs. 1:**5001k**
VIRGIL (Publius Vergilius Maro), 70–19 B.C. 876 3927 5420 5574 8924 11380 12102 12104
— Bibs. 1:**8018**
VIRGIN AND CHILD BINDER, fl.1497. **5908**
VIRGINIA. STATE LIBRARY, Richmond–Collns. 1:1139d; 2:34a
— UNIVERSITY. LIBRARY–Collns. 1:536b 4898; 2:423; 6682
VIRTUE. 5472
VISITATIONS. 1474
VITRUVIUS POLLIO.
— *De architectura.* 11572
VIZETELLY, Henry Richard, 1820–94. **5909–11** 6192 6194 6202 6229
— *Extracts.* 5910–11
— *Four months among the goldfinders.* 5909a
VOITH, Johann Matthäus, b.1803. 3785

VOLTAIRE (François Marie Arouet), 1694–1778. 903 905 910 916–17 919 922–3 13496
— Bibs.1:**815y–18**
VOLUSENE, Florence, 1504?–47?–Bibs. 1:**5002**
VON HAYEK, Friedrich August, 1899– see HAYEK, Friedrich August von, 1899–
VOSSIUS, Isaac, 1618–89.
— *Catullus.* 893
— Libr. 2610
VOYAGES see TRAVEL BOOKS.
VOYAGES, IMAGINARY–Bibs. 1:1694
VRANKENBERGH, Henry, fl.1482 see FRANKENBERGK, Henry, fl.1482.
VULGAR ERRORS IN PRACTICE CENSURED, 1659. 705
VULGATE see BIBLE–Versions–Vulgate.
VYCHAN, Simwnt, 1530?–1606 see SIMWNT FYCHAN, 1530?–1606.

WADDESDON MANOR, Bucks.–Libr. 3269
WADE, Arthur Sarsfield, 1883–1959 see ROHMER, Sax, *pseud.*
WADE, Stephen Dallas Allan, 1881–1955–Libr. 1:**5207**
WAGES see also FEES.
— Compositors. 1275 5092
— Papermakers. 3717 3765
— Pressmen. 1275
WAGSTAFFE, William, 1685–1725. **14161**
— *Miscellaneous works.* 14161
WAITE, Arthur Edward, 1857–1942. 14154
WAKE, archbp. William, 1657–1737. 6770 **14162**
WALBANK, Felix Alan, 1913– –Libr. 7292
WALDEGRAVE, Robert, Edinburgh, 1554?–1604. 1591 3448 **5912–14**
WALE, Samuel, 1721?–86. **5915–16**
— Bibs. 1:**5003**
WALES see also BAPTIST ASSOCIATIONS OF WALES; BOOK TRADE, LISTS–Wales; PRINTING IN WELSH; WELSH BOOKS PRINTED ABROAD; WELSH HISTORY. 929 **1449–551**
— Almanacs. 1480 1493 6754
— Ballads. 1472 1503–4 1517
— — Bibs. 1:1461 1462a 1463h 1465h–i
— Bible see also BIBLE, WELSH. 1517
— — O.T.
— — — PSALMS. 1476
— Bibs. 1:**953–64** 2269
— Bndng. 1467
— Book trade. 1516
— Broadsides. 1484 3871
— Collns. 2997 3018 3099

— Copybooks. 1481
— Dedications. 1498
— Dictionaries see also DICTIONARIES, WELSH. 1534
— Directories–Bibs. 1:865
— Engraving. 1461a 1482
— Fiction–Bibs. 1:1717
— History–Bibs. 1:23–4
— Hymns. 4941 7376
— Illustrated books–Bibs. 1:1745d
— Librs. 1507 1510 1515 2450 2459
— Lost books. 827
— Maps. 7499 7513
— — Bibs. 1:1767g 1813
— Methodist books–Bibs. 1:2270c
— Music. 1494
— — Bibs. 1:1732k
— Newspapers. 1497 1543
— — 1601– –Bibs. 1:**1928**; 1477
— — 1701–1800. 1509
— — 1801–1900. 1479
— — — Bibs. 1:**1928u–9**
— Pamphlets.
— — 1801–1900. 1457 4507
— Paper. 1502 3765
— Papermaking. 1502 1506 1514 3785a
— Poetry–Bibs. 1:327–8 1573db–dc **1981–6p**
— — 1475–1640. 7359a
— Prayerbooks. 1471 1517 3873 8054
— Primers. 1475 1500–1
— Ptg. 1451 1477–8 1505a 1508 1513 5829 6435
— — Bibs. 1:1280
— Printing, Private. 1490 1492
— Proofs. 1489
— Proposals. 1449a 7363 10455
— Proverbs. 1466
— Publ. 1449 1451 1476a 1478 1496a 1511–12 5696 10455
— Religion. 1497 5967
— Roadbooks and itineraries. 1036
— — Bibs. 1:960
— Schoolbooks. 8111
— Subscription lists. 1463 1531 4942 6555 6561 12920
— Visitations. 1474
— BAPTIST ASSOCIATIONS see BAPTIST ASSOCIATIONS OF WALES.
— CHURCH IN WALES see CHURCH IN WALES.
— NATIONAL LIBRARY OF WALES, Aberystwyth. **1528–30**
— — Collns. 1:464–5 470 696 700 704 1813a–b 3273r; 2:200; 1493 3009 3018 3027 3037 3055 3082 3134 4796–8 7014 7971–2 8666 9853
— UNIVERSITY. UNIVERSITY COLLEGE, Aberystwyth. LIBRARY–Collns. 2:727

WALES. UNIVERSITY. UNIVERSITY COLLEGE, Bangor. LIBRARY–Collns. 1:366
WALES, BIBLIOGRAPHY IN. 1450 1455
WALEY, Arthur David, 1889–1966. **14163–5**
— Bibs. 1:**5003d–e**
— *Chinese poems.* 14163–4
— Mss. 14165
— Ptg. 14163
WALFORD, Edward, 1823–97. **14166**
WALKER, Anthony, 1726–65. **5917**
— Bibs. 1:**5004**
WALKER, sir Emery, 1851–1933. 5598 **5918–25** 6088 6637 6645
WALKER, Fountaine, fl.1892–Libr. 2505
WALKER, Frederick, 1840–75. 7420a
WALKER, George, Montrose, 1831–89. **5926**
WALKER, Henry, fl.1641–60. **14167**
WALKER, Herbert John Ouchterlony, 1843– –Libr. 1:2111
WALKER, John, fl.1750. 1294
WALKER, Richard, fl.1734–52. 5870
WALKER, Richard, 1679–1764.
— *Short account of the donation.* 12183
WALKER, Robert, fl.1744–55. **5927**
Walker, Robert, d.1758.
— *Shakespeare's Dramatic works.* 2:221
WALKER, William, 1729–93. **5928**
WALKER, William, 1840–1931–Bibs. 1:**5004k**
— Libr. 2:673a
WALKER FAMILY, Gloucester, fl.1802–71. 1120
WALKINGHAME, Francis, fl.1747–85. **14168**
— *Tutor's assistant.* 7551 14168
WALKLEY, Thomas, fl.1618–58.
— *Jonson's Works.* 11554 11561
— *Wither's Works.* 14462 14464
WALLACE, Alfred Russel, 1823–1913–Bibs. 1:**5005**
WALLACE, James, d.1688. **14169**
— *Account of Orkney.* 14169
WALLACE, Richard Horatio Edgar, 1875–1932. **14170**
— Bibs. 1:**5005r**
WALLACE, Walter Thomas, fl.1920–Libr. 1:395; 11825
WALLER, Edmund, 1606–87. 9952 **14171–2**
— Bibs. 1:**5006**
— Mss. 14171–2
— *Poems*–Bibs. 1:5006
— *Upon the present war.* 14171
WALLER, William, 1786–1869. **5929**
WALLINGTON HALL, Nthmb. LIBRARY –Collns. 1:373
WALLIS, Ralph, d.1669. 1117a
WALMESLEY, bp. Charles, 1722–97. **14173**
— *General history.* 14173
WALMESLEY, Gilbert, 1680–1951. 11506

WALPERGEN, Peter de, Oxford, 1646?–1703. **5930**
WALPOLE, Horace, 4th earl of Orford, 1717–97 *see also* STRAWBERRY HILL PRESS, Twickenham, 1757–97. 3475 3929 4187 5019 **14174–204**
— *Anedotes of painting.* 14181 14186 14201
— Bibs. 1:**5007**
— Collns. 14184 14187 14189 14195
— *DeGrammont's Memoirs.* 14182
— *Description of the villa.* 14178
— Handwr. 14197
— Illus. 14181
— Letters. 14176 14179 14191 14196
— Libr. 3681 12767 14174 14180 14185 14193–4 14199–200 14202–4
— Mss. 14198
— *On benefactions.* 14191
— Publ. 4559a 5250 14190
— Text. 14179 14196
— AS PRINTER *see* STRAWBERRY HILL PRESS, Twickenham, 1757–97.
WALPOLE, sir Hugh Seymour, 1884–1941. **14205–9**
— Bibs. 1:**5008–c**
— Bndng. 14205
— Collns. 3331
— *Dark forest.* 14205
— Libr. 14206–9
WALPOLE, sir Robert, 1st earl of Orford, 1676–1745–Libr. 2489
— Collns. 3021
WALPOLE, Robert Horace, 10th earl of Orford, 1854–1931–Libr. 2527
WALPOLE PRESS, Old Costessy, Norwich, est. 1913. **5931**
WALSH, John, d.1736. **5932–5**
— Bibs. 1:**1414–a** 3571
WALSH, John Henry, 1810–88. 7089
WALSH, Peter, 1618?–88.
— *History of the Irish remonstrance.* 1894
WALSH, Robert, 1772–1852.
— *History of Dublin.* 1931
WALSHINGHAM, sir Francis, 1530?–90. 2:1045
WALSHINGHAM'S FREE BRITON. 7763
WALSINGHAM, Edward, fl.1643–54.
— *Arcana aulica.* 6519
— Publ. 6519
WALTER, Arthur, 1847–1910. 7784
WALTER, John, 1723–1812. **5936–8** 7346 7764 7784
WALTER, John, 1776–1847. 7784
WALTER, John, 1818–94. 7784
WALTERS, Henry, Cowbridge, 1766–1829. **5939**
WALTERS, John, Cowbridge, 1721–97. **5940**

Vol. 1 = *Bibliographies*   2 = *Shakespeare*   4 = 1–8221   5 = 8222–14616

WELLINGTON, N.Z. PUBLIC LIBRARY –Collns. 1:584

WELLINGTON, Arthur Wellesley, 1st duke of, 1769–1852 see WELLESLEY, Arthur, 1st duke of Wellington, 1769–1852.

WELLS. CATHEDRAL. LIBRARY. 2402 2568a 2569 2630 3354b
— Collns. 1:544b

WELLS, Gabriel, 1862–1946. 3649

WELLS, Herbert George, 1866–1946. **14277–83**
— Bibs. 1:681 684 **5053v–60**
— Collns. 14280
— *In the days of the comet.* 14277
— *Love and mr. Lewisham.* 14278
— Mss. 14280
— *Outline of history*–Bibs. 1:5054a
— Publ. 4858a 14277–9 14281
— *Tales of space.* 14279
— *Time machine.* 14281
— *Tono-Bungay*–Bibs. 1:5053x

WELLS, John Edwin, 1875–1943–Libr. 14525

WELLS GARDNER, DARTON AND COMPANY, fl.1904. 4719a 7033

WELSH, PRINTING IN see PRINTING IN WELSH.

WELSH BIBLIOGRAPHICAL SOCIETY. 326

WELSH BOOKS PRINTED ABROAD. 1495–6

WELSH DICTIONARIES see DICTIONARIES, WELSH.

WELSH GRAMMARS see GRAMMARS, WELSH.

WELSH HISTORY–Bibs. 1:23–4

WELSH NOVELS see NOVELS, WELSH.

WELSH REVIEW–Bibs. 1:1929

WEMBLEY HILL, Middlesex–Ptg. see STANTON PRESS, 1921–4.

WENSLEYDALE, sir James Parke, baron, 1782–1868 see PARKE, sir James, baron Wensleydale, 1782–1868.

WESLEY, Charles, 1707–88–Bibs. 1:2270d 5065–9

WESLEY, John, 1703–91. 5183 **14284–93**
— Bibs. 1:2270d **5065–9**
— *Christian's pattern.* 14287
— Collns. 14293
— *Complete English dictionary.* 14291
— Libr. 14285 14288–9
— *Milton's Paradise lost.* 12413
— Mss. 14284–6
— *Primitive physic*–Bibs. 1:5069d

WESLEY, John, fl.1841–55. 1322 **5967**

WESLEY, Samuel, 1691–1739. **14294**
— *Poems on several occasions.* 14294

WESLEYAN METHODIST CONFERENCE, London. LIBRARY–Collns. 1:2270d

WESLYAN UNIVERSITY. OLIN LIBRARY –Collns. 1:5209a

WEST, dame Rebecca, *pseud. of* Cicily Isabel (Fairfield) Andrews, 1892–. **14295**
— Bibs. 1:**5070**
— *Return of the soldier.* 14295

WEST, Herbert Faulkner, 1898–1974–Libr. 1:3491

WEST, James, 1704?–72–Libr. 2239b 3098

WEST, Victoria Mary Sackville-, lady Nicolson, 1892–1962–Bibs. 1:5071–2

WEST, William, fl.1811–31. 5968–9
— Bibs. 1:**1417–18**

WEST, William, fl.1943–Libr. 1:4808

WEST AND JAMESON, 19th cent. 7418

WEST ASHLING, Sussex–Paper. 1412

WESTBOURNE, Sussex–Paper. 1412

WESTBURY, Richard Morland Tollemache Bethell, 4th baron, 1914–61–Libr. 7066

WEST CHESTER. STATE TEACHERS' COLLEGE see PENNSYLVANIA. STATE TEACHERS' COLLEGE, West Chester.

WEST COLTON, Lancs. 1180a

WEST END, South Stoneham–Paper. 1132a

WESTERKIRK, Dumf.–Librs. 1633

WESTERMAN, Percy Francis, 1876–1959–Bibs. 1:**5072f**

WESTERN MISCELLANY. 7727

WESTERN ONTARIO. UNIVERSITY. LIBRARY–Collns. 12457

WESTERN VINDICATOR. 7900

WEST HAM see LONDON. WEST HAM.

WESTMEATH. **1986**
— Bibs. 1:**1133–5**

WESTMINSTER see LONDON. WESTMINSTER.

WESTMINSTER, Matthew see *FLORES HISTORIARUM.*

WESTMINSTER ASSEMBLY OF DIVINES.
— Ptg. 8042
— *Westminster confession of faith.* 8042

WESTMINSTER JOURNAL. 7896

WESTMINSTER LIBRARY see LONDON. WESTMINSTER LIBRARY.

WESTMINSTER REVIEW. 7918

WESTMORLAND see also BOOK TRADE, LISTS–Westmorland. **1424**
— Librs. see LOWTHER CASTLE.
— Maps–Bibs. 1:**1809**
— Newspapers. 9955
— — Bibs. 1:1854

WESTMORLAND, Mildmay Fane, 2d earl of, d.1666 see FANE, Mildmay, 2d earl of Westmorland, d.1666.

WESTMORLAND GAZETTE. 9955

WEST SUSSEX. COUNTY RECORD OFFICE–Collns. 1:3437c

WILMERDING, Lucius, 1880–1949–Libr.
1:404
WILLS' LIBRARY, London see LONDON.
GUY'S HOSPITAL. WILLS' LIBRARY.
WILMERDING, Lucius, 1880–1949–Libr.
3128
WILMINGTON SOCIETY OF THE FINE
ARTS. 13091
WILMOT, John, 2d earl of Rochester,
1647–80. **14346–66**
— Artemisa to Cloe. 14356
— Bibs. 1:**5120–6**
— Directions for a minister of state. 14357a
— Mss. 14346 14357a 14362
— Poems on several occasions. 14350–3 14357
14359 14361 14363–4
— — Bibs. 1:5122–6
— Prosecutions of Sodom. 14364
— Ptg. 14363
— Publ. 14349 14351 14358
— Remains. 14346
— Satyr against mankind. 14355
— Text. 14359 14361–2
— To a lady in a letter. 14362
— Valentinian. 14358
WILSON, Alexander, St.Andrews, 1714–86.
4691 4696 **5993** 6572 6587 6613
WILSON, Angus Frank Johnstone, 1913– .
14365–6
— Bibs. 1:1724p **5127–b**
— Collns. 14365–6
— Mss. 14366
— — Bibs. 1:5127b
WILSON, Arthur, 1595–1652. **14367–8**
— Inconstant lady. 14368
— Mss. 14367–8
— — Bibs. 1:1606b
— The Swisser. 14367
WILSON, Carroll Attwood, 1886–1947–Libr.
2374
WILSON, Charles Henry, 1756?–1808.
— Select Irish poems. 8011
WILSON, Florence, 1504?–47? see VOL-
USENE, Florence, 1504?–47?
WILSON, Frank Percy, 1889–1963. 88 90
— Bibs. 1:**5128**
WILSON, James, Aberdeen, 1836–1916. **5994**
WILSON, James, Birmingham, 1850–1917.
5995
WILSON, James Farlow, 1829–1916. 5996
WILSON, James Holbert, fl.1853–62. 1240
WILSON, John, fl.1575–1645. 841
WILSON, John, 1595–1674. 9602 12049
14369
— Mss. 14369
WILSON, John, Kilmarnock, fl.1759–
1821–Bibs. 1:**1419b**
— Burns's Poems. 9051

WILSON, John, 1785–1854 see NORTH,
Christopher, pseud.
WILSON, John, 1799–1870. **14370**
— Mss. 14370
WILSON, John, fl.1827.
— Catalogue of ... books ... relating to
Shakespeare. 2:364
WILSON, John, d.1889. **5997**
WILSON, John Cook, 1849–1915–Bibs.
1:**5128p**
WILSON, John Dover, 1881–1969. 2:913 928
930 964 1733
— Bibs. 1:**5129–30**
— New Cambridge Shakespeare. 2:732 800
806 847 864 894 964 1198 1206 1274
1515 1517 1584 1733–4 1769 1841
1850–1
WILSON, John Forbes, fl.1866–96. **5998**
WILSON, Larry, fl.1958–Libr. 2:660
WILSON, Lea, fl.1845–Libr. 6835
WILSON, Robert, d.1600. 9941 **14371–6**
— Cobbler's prophesy. 14371 14373–4
— Ptg. 14371–2
— Text. 14374–6
— Three ladies of London. 14372 14375–6
WILSON, Robert, 1550?–1605?–Handwr.
2:1893
WILSON, Thomas, 1525?–81. **14377**
— Art of rhetoric. 14377
— Text. 14377
WILSON. Thomas, fl.1610–20.
— Christian dictionary. 2:521
WILSON, bp. Thomas, 1663–1755. 11447
WILSON, William, fl.1618–65. 6683
WILSON, William, fl.1851–71. 12615
WILTSHIRE. **1425–8**
— Collns. 8319
— Librs. see ZEALS HOUSE.
— Maps–Bibs. 1:**1809**
— Newspapers. 1426–7
WIMBLEDON see LONDON. WIMBLE-
DON.
WIMBORNE MINSTER. LIBRARY. **2423**
2475 2496 2623 3371–2
WINCHESTER, Hants. 1132 **1134–6**
— Bksllng. 1135–6
— Ptg. 1025 1134 1136
— CATHEDRAL. LIBRARY–Collns. 1:503
WINCHESTER COLLEGE. 1134 8110
— LIBRARY. 3176 3312 3382b 9617
— — Collns. 1:2845
WINCHCOMBE, Glos.–Paper. 1120a
WINCHILSEA, Anne Finch, countess of,
1661–1720 see FINCH, Anne, countess of
Winchilsea, 1661–1720.
WINDEBANK, sir Francis, 1582–1646–Libr.
3396a
WINDER, Roland, fl.1966–Libr. 1:2141a

WINDET, John, fl.1579–1611.
— *Sidney's Arcadia.* 13434
WINDHAM, William, 1717–61. **5999**
WINDHAM, William, 1750–1810–Libr. 11493
WINDOWS, PAPER. 6130
WINDSOR, Josiah, Dublin, fl.1667–81. 1907
WINDSOR CASTLE. ROYAL LIBRARY. 2266 2441 2494 2503 2503 2510 2578
— Collns. 2020 2187
— ST. GEORGE'S CHAPEL. 2902
— — CHAPTER LIBRARY–Collns. 1:1971t 2063c
WINE. 3011
'WING' see *SHORT-TITLE CATALOGUE, 1641–1700.*
WINGFIELD, Anthony, 1550?–1615?
— Ptg. 6148
— *True copy of a discourse.* 6148
WINGFIELD, Walter C., fl.1873–97.
— *The major's games of lawn tennis.* 8196
WINSLOW, Edward, 1599–1655. 6000
WINSTANLEY, Gerrard, fl.1648–52–Bibs. 1:**5130a–2**
WINTERTON, Ralph, 1600–36.
— *Drexelius' Considerationes.* 11980
WINSTON, James, 1773–1843–Mss. 7934
WIRE-STABBED BINDINGS see BOOK-BINDINGS, WIRE-STABBED
WIRKSWORTH, Derbys.–Ptg. see BROOKS PRESS, fl.1904–21.
WISBECH, Cambs. MUSEUM AND LITERARY INSTITUTE. 11993
WISCONSIN. UNIVERSITY. LIBRARY–Collns. 1:2230 2279g 5178; 8139
WISE, Thomas James, 1859–1937. 787 2374 3642 7337 9649 10790 **14378–458**
— Arnold. 8284 14387 14399
— Bibliogr. descr. 14445 14457
— Bibs. 1:3824 4901 **5133–49**
— Bksllng. 14387 14443
— Bndng. 14453
— Borrow. 14432
— Brontës. 8787
— Browning, E.B. 8867 8881 14387 14406 14417
— Browning, R. 14387 14406 14417 14436
— Byron. 14406 14417
— Collns. 14446–7
— Conrad. 9636 9659b 14417
— Cruikshank. 4451–2
— Dickens. 14387
— Eliot, G. 14387
— Kipling. 14387
— Letters. 14408–9 14418–19 14436 14454
— — Bibs. 1:5147
— Libr. *see also* BRITISH MUSEUM. ASHLEY LIBRARY. 1:332 342 2539 2589

2684 2686 2867 3200 3995 4442 4652 4680 4856 5171; 2374 8779 12821 14378 14380–2 14384 14400–1 14405 14435
— Morris. 14387 14436
— Mss.–Bibs. 1:5145
— Ptg. 14379 14448 14456
— Rossettis. 13095–6 13098 14387 14436
— Ruskin. 13128 14387 14406 14417 14436
— Shelley. 13307 13330 14406 14417
— Stevenson. 13662 14387
— Swinburne. 13819 13825 13831 13843 14383 14387 14406 14417 14420 14433 14436
— Tennyson. 13925 13948 13951 13954 13959 13961 14387 14409 14419 14436
— Thackeray. 14387
— *Verses.* 14428 14455
— — Bibs. 1:5149
— Watts-Dunton. 14406 14417
— Wordsworth. 14387 14406 14417
— Yates. 14387
WISEMAN, card. Nicholas Patrick Stephen, 1802–65–Bibs. 1:**5150**
WISHART, bp. George, 1599–1671. **14459–60**
— *De rebus Caroli.* 14459
— *Memoirs of Montrose.* 14460
WIT AND MIRTH, 1698–1720. 8014 8022
WITCHCRAFT *see also* WARBOYS, WITCHES OF. 481 **8219–21**
— Bibs. 1:899b **2290–1**
— Scotland–Bibs. 1:2290
WITCHCRAFT IN SHAKESPEARE–Bibs. 2:34
WITCHITA CITY. LIBRARY–Collns. 7963
WITHAM, Essex. **1116**
— Newspapers. 1116
WITHER, George, 1588–1667. **14461–72**
— *Abuses stripped and whipped.* 6093
— Bibs. 1:**5151–a**
— *A declaration.* 14468
— Mss. 14469 14471
— *Poems.* 14463
— *Psalms.* 14471
— Ptg. 6093
— Publ. 14461–2 14464 14470 14472
— *Scholar's purgatory.* 14470
— *Three private meditations.* 14467
— *Works.* 14461–2 14464
WITHERBY, Thomas, 1719–97. **6001**
WITHERING, William, 1741–99.
— *Botanical arrangement of all vegetables.* 6965
WITTGENSTEIN, Ludwig Josef Johann, 1889–1951–Bibs. 1:**5151p**
WODEHOUSE, sir Pelham Grenville, 1881–1975. **14473–4**
— Bibs. 1:**5152–3a**
— *Brinkmanship at Blandings.* 14474

WODEHOUSE, sir Pelham Grenville, 1881–1975. Collns. 14473
— Mss. 14474
WODHULL, Michael, 1740–1816.
— Illus. 13623
— Libr. 2188 3214
— *Poems.* 13623
WODROW, Robert, 1679–1734. 9890
— Bibs. 1:**5154**
WOGAN, Patrick, Dublin, fl.1773–1824. 1929
WOLCOT, John, 1738–1819 *see* PINDAR, Peter, *pseud.*
WOLF, Abraham, 1876–1948–Libr. 3015
WOLF, Morris, 1889– –Libr. 1:4328
WOLFE, Charles, 1791–1823. **14475**
— *Burial of sir John Moore.* 14475
WOLFE, James, 1727–59.
— Bibs. 1:**5154p**
— Libr. 2979
WOLFE, John, fl.1579–1601. 947 3448 **6002–4**
— Type. 6003
WOLFE, Reginald, fl.1530–73. **6005–6** 6056
— Type. 6006
WOLFF, M. A., fl.1954–Libr. 11780
WOLFF, Robert Lee, 1915– –Libr. 1:1719
WOLFRESTON, Frances (Middlemore), 1607–77–Libr. 3349
WOLLATON HALL, Notts.–Libr. 2:550f; 2819
WOLSEY, card. Thomas, 1475?–1530. 1934
WOLSON BRIDGE, Hants.–Paper. 1132a
WOLVERCOTE MILL, Oxford. 5333 5359 5362
WOLVERHAMPTON, Staffs. *see also* BOOK TRADE, LISTS–Wolverhampton. **1398**
— Bibs. 1:**943–4**
— Bksllng. 1398
— Ptg. 1398
— — Bibs. 1:944
WOMAN'S WORLD. 4207
WOMEN. 630
— Bibs. 1:537h
WOMEN AND SHAKESPEARE–Bibs. 2:108
WOMEN AS AUTHORS. 528
WOMEN AS BOOKBINDERS *see* GUILD OF WOMEN BOOKBINDERS, 1898–1904.
WOMEN AS BOOKCOLLECTORS. 2269 3461
WOMEN AS BOOKSELLERS. 3461
WOMEN AS PRINTERS. 3461 5614 6066 6096 6101 6138–9 6671
WOMEN AS READERS. 2459
WOMEN'S NEWSPAPERS *see* NEWSPAPERS, WOMEN'S.
WOMEN'S WORLD. 14326

WONDERFUL PROGNOSTICATION, 1591. 6747
WOOD, Anthony, 1632–95. 1380
WOOD, Arnold, 1872– –Libr. 1:4795 4810
WOOD, Ellen (Price), (mrs. Henry Wood), 1814–87. **14476**
— Bndng. 14476
— Collns. 7322a
WOOD, Harry, fl.1849–93. **6007**
WOOD, John, fl.1818–46. 7522
WOOD, John George, 1827–89. **14477**
WOOD, John Philip, d.1838.
— *Douglas' Peerage of Scotland.* 7361
WOOD, Michael, 16th cent. **6008**
WOOD, Robert, 1717?–71. **14478**
— *Essay on Homer.* 14478
WOOD, William, d.1788. **6009**
WOOD, William, 1774–1857.
— *Index entomologicus.* 8138
WOODBRIDGE, Suff.–Librs. 1400
WOODBURY, John P., fl.1922–Libr. 1:1744
WOODCROFT, Bennet, 1803–79. 6393
WOODCUTS *see also* ENGRAVING, WOOD. 279 3425 3496 5332 5982 6042 6189 6210 7390 7463 12124–5 12557
— Bibliogr. descr. 128
— Bibs. 1:1747–i
— Collns. 5518h–j
— Ptg. 4479 6189 6203
WOOD ENGRAVING *see* ENGRAVING, WOOD.
WOOD ENGRAVINGS *see* WOODCUTS.
WOODEN PRESSES *see* PRESSES, COMMON.
WOODES, Nathaniel, fl.1581. **14479**
— *Conflict of conscience.* 14479
WOODFALL, Henry Sampson, 1739–1805. 3475 5192
WOODFALL, William, 1746–1803. 3475
WOODFORD, Samuel, 1636–1700. 14212 **14480**
WOODGER, Joseph Henry, 1894– –Bibs. 1:**5154s**
— Letters–Bibs. 1:5154s
WOODHEAD, Abraham, 1609–78.
— Bibs. 1:**5155**
— *St. Teresa.* 975
WOODHOUSE, Richard, 1788–1834. 11685
WOODHOUSELEE, Alexander Fraser Tytler, lord, 1747–1813 *see* TYTLER, Alexander Fraser, lord Woodhouselee, 1747–1813.
WOODSTOCK see RICHARD II (WOODSTOCK).
WOOD'S TYPOGRAPHIC ADVERTISER. 7926
WOODWARD, Chester, 1876–1940–Libr. 2343

WYER, Robert, fl.1529-60. **6040-3** 6081
— Bibs. 1:**1423**
— *Heywood's Play of the weather.* 7141
— Types. 6042
WYE VALLEY, Bucks.–Paper. 1044
WYKES, Henry, fl.1557-69. 9669
WYKES, John *see* WYKES, Thomas, fl.1637-42.
WYKES, Thomas, fl.1637-42. **6044**
WYLAM, Nthmb.–Ptg. *see* ALLENHOLME PRESS, est. 1956.
WYLIE, Robert, d.1921–Libr. 1:**1003**
WYLLIE, David, Aberdeen, 1777-1844. **6045-6**
WYLSHMAN, Walter, 1572-1636–Bibs. 1:**5194**
WYMONDHAM, Leics.–Ptg. *see* BREW-HOUSE PRESS, est. 1962.
WYN, Watcyn, *pseud. of* Watkin H. Williams, 1844-1905–Bibs. 1:**5194f**
WYNN, Edward, 1618-69. 1517
WYNN FAMILY–Libr. *see* WYNNSTAY, Denbigh.
WYNNE, Ellis, 1671-1734–Bibs. 1:**5195**
— *Visions of the sleeping bard*–Bibs. 1:**5195**
WYNNE, Thomas, 1627-92. **14577**
WYNNE, William Watkin Edward, 1801-80. 6871
— Libr. 2723
WYNNSTAY, Denbigh.–Libr. 2:**555**; 3037
WYNTOUN, Andrew of, 1350?-1420?–Bibs. 1:**5196**
WYRE MILL, Pershore, Worcs. 1429a
WYSS, Escher, Zürich. 3785
WYSS, Johann David, 1743-1818. 10729
WYTHENSHAWE, Lancs.–Bibs. 1:**911**

XENOPHON, fl.444-354 B.C. 624
XYLOGRAPHIC BOOKS *see* BOOKS, XYLOGRAPHIC.
XYLOGRAPHY, CHROMO- *see* CHROMO-XYLOGRAPHY.

YALE FACSIMILE. 2:594-6
YALE SHAKESPEARE. 2:722 897
YALE UNIVERSITY. ELIZABETHAN CLUB. 7176
— LIBRARY. 6223 8529
— — Collns. 1:363g 541c 577f 935a 1253-4 1478 1750 2100d 2120 2289dc 2371 2417 2451c 2868-9 3100 3255 3468 3551 3587 3842 3885 4202 4513h 4813 5203; 543 674 699-700 796 806 1127 3099 4307 5850 6780 6931 7149 7174 7285 7326 7347 7650-1 8027 8104 8275 8281 8421 8424 8485 8490 8524 8527 8600 8606 8708 8710

8831 8890 8922 9531 9632 9691 9898-9 9906-7 9910 10427 10429 10431 10497 10501 10623 10652 10705-6 10750 10758 10950 11099 11433 11884 11928 12011 12192 12217 12236 12244 12287 12346 12355 12396 12499 12526 12897 12966 13111 13114 13118 13190 13194 13268 13404 13542 13668 13982 14222 14250 14821 14537 14553
— — OSBORN COLLECTION. 7095 9001
— — STERLING MEMORIAL LIBRARY–Collns. 1:363
— SCHOOL OF LAW. LIBRARY–Collns. 1:2467
YARDLEY, Harry John Desmond, 1905-72. **6046m**
YARDLEY, Richard, fl.1589-97. **6047**
YARMOUTH, Norf. **1309**
— Ptg. 1309
YATES, Edmund, 1831-94. 14387 **14578**
— *Mr. Thackeray.* 14578
YATES, William, 1738/40-1802. 7530
YAXLEY, Suff.–Librs. 1400
YEARBOOKS. 7222
YEATS, Elizabeth Corbet, 1868-1940 *see* CUALA PRESS, Dundrum, est. 1903.
YEATS, Jack Butler, 1871-1957–Bibs. 1:**5197**
YEATS, William Butler, 1865-1939. 811 **14579-604**
— Bibs. 1:684 1597 **5197s-209b**
— *Blake's Poems.* 14604
— *Byzantium.* 14583
— *Collected poems.* 14587 14591
— Collns. 14585 14588-9 14595
— *Countess Cathleen.* 14594
— *Easter 1916.* 14596
— Handwr. 14599
— Letters. 14597
— *Mosada.* 475
— Mss. 14594 14596 14603
— — Bibs. 1:**5205** 5207d 5208
— *Paragraphs from Samhain.* 14597
— Publ. 14592 14598
— *Red Hanrahan's song.* 14581
— *Shadowy waters.* 14603
— *Song of wandering Aengus.* 14581
— Text. 14582-3 14587 14590-4 14596 14601-3
— *Two trees.* 14600
— *Vision.* 14600
— *What then.* 14598
YELF, William, Newport, d.1832. **6048**
YELLOWBACKS. 2070 2119 2327 6229 6524 7292 7296 7299 7301-2 7318
YELLOW BOOK. 5038 7917 8432
— Bibs. 1:**1721**
YELLOWSANDS PRESS, Coniston, est. 1919. 1165a